Core Microeconomics

Gerald W. Stone
Metropolitan State College of Denver

Worth Publishers

To Josephine and Sheila

Senior Publisher: Craig Bleyer
Acquisitions Editor: Sarah Dorger
Development Editor: Bruce Kaplan
Development Editor, Media and Supplements: Marie McHale
Director of Market Development: Steven Rigolosi
Consulting Editor: Paul Shensa
Senior Marketing Manager: Scott Guile
Associate Managing Editor: Tracey Kuehn
Project Editors: Dana Kasowitz
Jennifer Carey, Matrix Publishing Services
Art Director: Babs Reingold
Senior Designer: Kevin Kall
Cover and Interior Designer: Karen Quigley
Illustrations: Matrix Publishing Services
Photo Editor: Cecilia Varas
Production Manager: Barbara Anne Seixas
Composition: Matrix Publishing Services
Printing and Binding: RR Donnelley

Library of Congress Control Number: 2007938459

ISBN-13: 978-1-4292-0620-4
ISBN-10: 1-4292-0620-9

First printing 2007

Worth Publishers
41 Madison Avenue
New York, NY 10010
www.worthpublishers.com

ABOUT THE AUTHOR

Gerald W. Stone is Emeritus Professor of Economics at Metropolitan State College of Denver. He has taught principles of economics to over 10,000 students throughout his career, and he has also taught courses in labor economics and law and economics. He has authored or coauthored over a half dozen books and numerous articles that have been published in economic journals such as the *Southern Economic Journal* and the *Journal of Economics and Sociology.* He earned his Bachelor's and Master's degrees in economics at Arizona State University, his Ph.D. in economics at Rice University, and a J.D. in law at the University of Denver.

PREFACE

Whoa. Not another principles of microeconomics book. How could it offer anything new? Hasn't everything been done by now? I hope you will answer *no* to both questions after you see what is available to you and your students with *CoreMicroeconomics*.

I sought to write a textbook that is interesting and usable for instructors. I also wanted to give students extra help to learn the material. My experience with my students at Metropolitan State College of Denver, who come from wide backgrounds in an urban setting, led me to produce a unique student supplement (*CourseTutor*) that is integrated with the text. Together, the textbook and unique supplement provide instructors and students something that no one else provides.

What Does *Core* Mean?

My students complained continually that their textbooks were too expensive, too long, and too encyclopedic, and as a result, one-third or more of the material in the text wasn't covered in the course. They often resented paying for this unused extra material.

CoreEconomics is not an encyclopedic offering. It does not cover every topic, but is partly based on a survey of economics professors to determine what they actually covered in their courses. Two important points emerged from this survey:

- **One chapter per week.** Instructors typically cover one chapter per week, or 15 chapters in a 15-week semester.
- **The majority of instructors teach roughly the same two-thirds of a standard economics textbook.** The overwhelming majority of instructors cover the same chapters in their course and then spend minimal time covering additional chapters. Over 90% of instructors cover roughly 15 chapters in their microeconomics text, which typically includes 19–22 chapters.

In this sense, *core* does not mean brief or abridged. Rather, it means that the textbook contains the chapters that most instructors need, and very few additional chapters or special-interest topics.

The Core Text

The organization is traditional and the coverage concise. Concepts are thoroughly explained and illustrated with contemporary examples and issues integrated seamlessly into the text with the aim of enhancing the reading–learning experience. A conscious effort has been made to resist putting too much information – more than students need and unnecessary detail – to keep students honed in on the most important concepts. The goal has been to give students what is needed and no more.

The text incorporates the historical development of economics so students see how ideas and theories evolve over time. A dozen historical figures are highlighted in biographies and, in addition, the biographies of particular Nobel Prize winners are included when their contributions are of particular importance to the material covered in the chapter.

The text is loaded with applications that I think instructors and students will find interesting. These applications are not boxed off – they appear seamlessly throughout. Here are a few of them:

- In Chapter 5, we look at Hubbert's Peak, the 1950s prediction by Marion King Hubbert that U.S. oil production would peak in the 1970s. This in fact happened. Hubbert's model predicts that *world* oil production will peak within the next decade. If true, what will happen? How will markets adjust?
- In Chapter 6, the curious case of tipping is discussed. Because we tip after we are served a meal in a restaurant, our tip cannot influence behavior, unless we are repeat customers. Why tip at all, or why tip anything other than the minimum amount? How does tipping fit with our model of rational consumer behavior?
- In the appendix to Chapter 6, for those instructors who cover indifference curve analysis, this analysis is applied to policies dealing with terrorism. How can we categorize the various policies, and which ones are likely to be most effective?
- In Chapter 13, we consider the economics of global warming. We look at the evidence to date and then consider various predictions and the assumptions that sit behind them. The goal is to provide an economic framework for thinking about global warming.

I have sought to make the end of chapter questions interesting by basing many of them on recent issues, quotes, and articles, extending the analysis in unique ways. These questions should make good lecture starters to get students involved in the chapter material. Sample answers are included in the Instructor's Manual.

The text is written with beginning students in mind. I set out to provide a text that reduced student anxiety and made the material more accessible and interesting.

What Is *CourseTutor*?

For many years I taught two classes that met only on Saturday for three hours each. It soon became clear that students needed more feedback than what a once-a-week meeting could provide. I gave short quizzes on Saturday, analyzed each student's responses on Sunday, and sent each student a personalized set of study suggestions and additional exercises on Monday. *CourseTutor* evolved from this approach and is intended to help students who need something more than just a traditional study guide.

CourseTutor is divided into two basic sections: tutorial and study guide. The tutorial section guides students through each section of each chapter, while the study guide provides traditional study guide material. Both sections are designed for interactivity.

Each section in *CourseTutor* begins with frequently ask questions (FAQs) with extensive answers. This helps students to see what is really important in this section. This is followed by a Quick Check (five to ten questions). Their results on the quiz are diagnosed and suggestions for additional study, if needed, are provided. These suggestions are backed up with solved problems, exercises, and an explanation of core graphs, equations, and formulas. Those students who traditionally become frustrated or have trouble with economics will find *CourseTutor* helpful and hopefully improve their attitude and interest in economics.

Following the tutorial section is a brief section called "Hints, Tips, and Reminders" that I have found helpful for students over my career. Also included for each chapter is a single-sheet exam preparation guide (ExamPrep) where the important concepts are boiled down to one sheet that students must complete. The ExamPrep sheets typically have enough space for students to add concise summaries of class notes. Also included for each chapter is a single-sheet homework assignment that you can require students to hand in, or students can complete online at the Worth online learning center and have their grades e-mailed directly to you.

Students learn by many different methods. *CourseTutor* addresses this by providing a buffet of learning choices. Students select those methods that best help them learn. Students having problems with specific material can turn to that particular section in *CourseTutor* for help. But, it is important to note that students are not expected to work through all of the material unless they absolutely need this level of additional help.

The remainder of each chapter in *CourseTutor* is standard study guide material including chapterwide matching, true-false, fill-in, multiple choice, essay questions, and problems for students to practice.

CourseTutor should save you time if students work through the tutorial before they come to see you; they should have fewer unfocused questions when they show up at your office for help. I believe you will find *CourseTutor* a worthwhile addition for your students.

Together, I think *CoreMicroeconomics* and *CourseTutor* provide something for you and your students that no one else in the market provides.

Outline of the Book

CoreMicroeconomics follows a traditional organizational sequence.

Students are introduced to microeconomics in the first five chapters that focus on the nature of economics, trade, markets, supply and demand. Chapters 1 and 2 provide a foundation for the study of economics along with a brief look at production and trade. Chapter 3 lays out supply, demand, and market equilibrium and details the efficiency of markets. Chapter 4 provides a balance to Chapter 3 by introducing the requirements for efficient markets, what happens when markets fail and how they tend to fail, and what government can do, in addition to a discussion of the impact of price ceilings and floors. These two chapters give students a good foundation in the benefits of markets along with some of the caveats. Chapter 5 introduces elasticity with its ramifications for total revenue and tax policy.

Chapters 6 and 7 provide students with an understanding of what is behind supply and demand curves. Chapter 6 on consumer decision making covers marginal utility analysis with an indifference curve appendix. Chapter 7 explores production and cost analysis for both the short run and long run.

The next three chapters (8–10) take students through market structure analysis plus a discussion of antitrust issues and an expanded coverage of game theory. The ability to discern behavior from market structure data is a fundamental aspect of microeconomics and these three chapters cover that material in detail.

Chapters 11 and 12 discuss the theory and issues surrounding input markets, especially labor markets. Chapter 11 uses market structure analysis to examine input markets and Chapter 12 goes into more detail on issues of human capital, economic discrimination, labor unions, and collective bargaining.

Market failures, public goods, and environmental economics are the issues discussed in Chapter 13, while poverty and income distribution are covered in Chapter 14. These two chapters provide the economic background for several of the most widely discussed topics in microeconomics today including poverty, growing income inequality, and global climate change.

The final chapter of the book is devoted to the international economy. Chapter 15 covers the classical issues of international trade including the gains from trade (the Ricardian perspective), the terms of trade, along with a discussion of the impacts of tariffs and quotas, and an expanded discussion and evaluation of the arguments against trade.

Supplements

A useful and seamless supplements package has been developed to accompany this textbook. The package was crafted to help instructors teach their principles course, with both the experienced and novice instructors in mind. Along with the accompanying *CourseTutor,* the additional ancillaries have been designed to help students work through the Core topics and to more readily grasp these key concepts. The entire package has been coordinated to guarantee uniformity and has been designed to work with the content, examples, and style of the Core text and *CourseTutor*.

For Instructors

Teaching Manual with Suggested Answers to Problems: The Teaching Manual prepared by Dr. Mary H. Lesser (Iona College) is an ideal resource for instructors trying to enliven their classroom lectures while teaching the Core concepts. The Teaching Manual focuses on highlighting varied ways to bring real-world examples into the classroom by expanding on examples and real-world problem material within the text. Portions of the Teaching Manual have been designed for use as student handouts.

Every chapter of the Teaching Manual includes:

- *Chapter Overview:* A brief summary of the main topics covered in each chapter is provided.
- *Ideas for Capturing Your Classroom Audience:* Written with both the experienced and novice instructor in mind, this section provides ideas for introducing the chapter material. The suggestions provided can be used in a number of ways; they can be in-class demonstrations or enrichment assignments, and can be used in on-site, distance-learning, or hybrid course formats.
- *Chapter Checkpoints:* Each chapter of the text has Chapter Checkpoint sections that provide both bulleted review points and questions designed to assess whether students have mastered the main points of the section material. The Teaching Manual provides the instructor with suggested answers to those questions, notations about points to emphasize, and suggestions about reinforcing the assessment of student learning.
- *Extended Examples in the Chapter:* The Teaching Manual reproduces the extended examples used in each chapter and provides a discussion of these examples. As with the Chapter Checkpoint material, teachers will find that these sections delineate points to emphasize and provide additional resources for spurring student interest.
- *Examples Used in the End-of-Chapter Questions:* A number of the End-of-Chapter Questions refer to specific articles in major newspapers or specific real-

world examples. The Teaching Manual provides the instructor with a succinct overview of those questions and cites additional resources that can be used to develop more in-depth analysis of the topics covered. Note that this is in addition to the sample answers that are also provided.

- *For Further Analysis:* Each Teaching Manual chapter contains an additional extended example that can be used in a variety of ways. Formatted as a one-page handout, it can be duplicated and distributed in class (or posted online), and is designed for use either as an in-class group exercise or as an individual assignment in both the on-site and online class format. Asking students to document research allows the instructor to use the example as a case study or group project as well. Learning objectives are specified and a one-page answer key is also available for reference or distribution.
- *Web-Based Exercise:* Each Teaching Manual chapter includes a Web-Based Exercise that requires students to obtain information from a web site and use it to answer a set of questions. This Web-Based Exercise can be used in a variety of ways as in-class group exercises or as individual assignments. Learning objectives are specified and suggested answers to questions are provided that can be used for reference or distribution.
- *Tips from a Colleague:* Each chapter of the Teaching Manual concludes with a "tips" section that shares ideas about classroom presentation, use of other resources, and insights about topics that students typically find difficult to master.

Test Bank: *Coordinator and Contributor:* Richard Croxdale (Austin Community College). *Test Bank Contributors:* Emil Berendt (Siena Heights University), Dennis Debrecht (Carroll College), Elizabeth J. Wark (Springfield College). The Test Bank contains nearly 2,250 carefully constructed questions to help you assess your students' comprehension, interpretation, analysis, and synthesis skills. Questions have been checked for continuity with the text content and reviewed extensively for accuracy.

The test bank features include the following:

- To aid instructors in building tests, each question has been categorized according to their general *degree of difficulty*. The three levels are: easy, moderate, or difficult. *Easy* questions require students to recognize concepts and definitions. These are questions that can be answered by direct reference to the textbook. *Moderate* questions require some analysis on the student's part. These questions may require a student to distinguish between two or more related concepts, to apply a concept to a particular situation, or to use an economic model to determine an answer. *Difficult* questions will usually require more detailed analysis by the students.
- To further aid instructors in building tests, each question is referenced by the page number and specific topic heading in the textbook. Questions are presented in the order in which concepts are presented in the text.
- Questions have been designed to correlate with the questions and problems within the text and *CourseTutor*. A beginning set of Objectives Questions are available in each chapter. These questions focus directly on the key concepts from the text that students should grasp after reading the chapter. These questions can be used easily for brief in-class quizzes.
- The test bank includes questions with tables that students must analyze to solve for numerical answers. It contains questions based on the graphs that appear in the book. These questions ask students to use the graphical models developed in the textbook and to interpret the information presented in the graph. Selected questions are paired with scenarios to reinforce comprehension.

Computerized Test Bank: Diploma was the first software for PCs that integrated a test-generation program with grade book software and an online testing system. Diploma is now in its fifth generation. The printed Test Banks for *CoreMicroeconomics* are available in CD-ROM format, powered by Brownstone, for both Windows and Macintosh users.

With Diploma, you can easily create and print tests and write and edit questions. You can add an unlimited number of questions, scramble questions, and include figures. Tests can be printed in a wide range of formats. The software's unique synthesis of flexible word processing and database features creates a program that is extremely intuitive and capable.

Instructor's Resource CD-ROM: Using the Instructor's Resource CD-ROM, instructors can easily build classroom presentations or enhance online courses. This CD-ROM contains all text figures (in JPEG and GIF formats), PowerPoint Lecture slides, and detailed solutions to all End-of-the-Chapter Questions. You can choose from the various resources, edit, and save for use in your classroom.

PowerPoint Lecture Presentation: PowerPoint slides provide graphs from the textbook, data tables, and bulleted lists of key concepts suitable for lecture presentation. Key figures from the text are replicated and animated to demonstrate how they build. The Checkpoints from the text have been included to facilitate a quick review of key concepts. These slides may be customized by instructors to suit individual needs. These files may be accessed on the instructor's side of the web site or on the Instructor's Resource CD-ROM.

For Instructors and Students

Companion Web Site: www.worthpublishers.com/stone: The Companion Web Site is a virtual study guide for students and an excellent resource for instructors. The tools on the site include:

Student Resources

- Self-Test Quizzes: This quizzing engine provides a set of quiz questions for each chapter with appropriate feedback and page references to the textbook. All student answers are saved in an online database that can be accessed by instructors.
- Key Term Flashcards: Students can test themselves on the key terms with these pop-up electronic flashcards.

Instructor Resources

- Quiz Gradebook: The site gives you the ability to track students' work by accessing an online gradebook. Instructors have the option to have student results emailed directly to them.
- PowerPoint Lecture Presentations: These PowerPoint slides are designed to assist instructors with lecture preparation and presentation by providing bulleted lecture outlines suitable for large lecture presentation. Instructors can customize these slides to suit their individual needs.
- Textbook Illustrations: A complete set of figures and tables from the textbook in JPEG and PowerPoint format is available.
- End-of-Chapter Problems: The text's End-of-Chapter Problems have been posted here in an electronic format for instructors to incorporate into assignments or in-class quizzes.

***CourseTutor* Online Study Center:** This dynamic site enables students to gauge their comprehension of concepts and provides a variety of resources to help boost their performance within the course. This Online Study Center provides an alternative to the pen and paper version of *CourseTutor*. Instead, students can work through *CourseTutor* content online. In this online format, students can follow their own pace and complete any or all steps of *CourseTutor*. All of this is possible with or without instructor involvement.

The Online Study Center contains an electronic version of the *CourseTutor* authored by Gerald W. Stone. Content is organized and accessible through the major headings within *CourseTutor*. The Quick Checks and Homework are available in an online quizzing engine for automatic grading. Answers to the Homework and End-of-Chapter Questions will be posted on the instructor side. Students will find the additional Interactive Resources where appropriate within the body of *CourseTutor*.

The interactive resources may also be accessed under the resources tab within the Online Study Center.

CourseTutor Online Study Center includes the following Interactive Resources:

- *Solved Problems*: Problems designed for this online environment using a graphing and assessment engine. Students may be asked to draw, interpret, or interact with a graph to provide an answer. Students will receive detailed feedback and guidance on where to go for further review.
- *Core Graphs:* Animated versions of these key graphs.
- *Audio Summaries*

STUDENTS: What can they do with the Online Study Center?

- Test mastery of important concepts from the text.
- Improve understanding of difficult topics by working with interactive tutorials and flashcards, along with an electronic version of your *CourseTutor*.
- Take notes on any of the resources and add them to a collection of favorites.
- Browse by chapter or search by topic if they need quick information about a specific concept.

INSTRUCTORS: What can you do with the Online Study Center?

- Interact with your students as little or as much as you like! You can assign the exercises as out-of-class activities, or encourage your students to work independently.
- If you so desire, monitor your students' progress within the Online Study Center using a sophisticated online gradebook.
- Export grades to your current Course Management System.
- Create customized web pages for your students.

Additional Online Offerings

Aplia—Integrated Textbook Solution: Aplia, founded by Paul Romer (Stanford University) is the first web-based company to integrate pedagogical features from a textbook with interactive media. Specifically designed for use with the Stone text, textbook resources have been combined with Aplia's interactive media to save time for professors and encourage students to exert more effort in their learning.

The integrated online version of the Aplia media and the Stone text will include:

- extra problem sets suitable for homework and keyed to specific topics from each chapter

- regularly updated news analyses
- real-time online simulations of market interactions
- interactive tutorials to assist with math
- graphs and statistics
- instant online reports that allow instructors to target student trouble areas more efficiently

With Aplia, you retain complete control and flexibility for your course. You choose the topics you want students to cover, and you decide how to organize it. You decide whether online activities are practice (ungraded or graded). You can even edit the Aplia content — making cuts or additions as you see fit for your course.

For a preview of Aplia materials and to learn more, visit http://www.aplia.com.

The Stone WebCT & Blackboard EPacks enable you to create a thorough, interactive, and pedagogically sound online course or course web site. The EPacks provide you with cutting-edge online materials that facilitate critical thinking and learning, including Test Bank content, preprogrammed quizzes, links, activities, animated graphs, and an array of other materials. Best of all, this material is preprogrammed and fully functional in the WebCT & Blackboard environment. Prebuilt materials eliminate hours of course-preparation work and offer significant support as you develop your online course. The result: an interactive, comprehensive online course that allows for effortless implementation, management, and use. The files can be easily downloaded from our Course Management System site directly onto your department server.

Package Options

i-clicker is a new two-way radio-frequency classroom response solution developed by educators for educators. University of Illinois physicists Tim Stelzer, Gary Gladding, Mats Selen, and Benny Brown created the i-clicker system after using competing classroom response solutions and discovering they were neither classroom appropriate nor student friendly. Each step of i-clicker's development has been informed by teaching and learning. i-clicker is superior to other systems from both a pedagogical and technical standpoint. To learn more about packaging i-clicker with this textbook, please contact your local sales rep or visit www.iclicker.com.

***Wall Street Journal* Edition**: For adopters of the Stone text, Worth Publishers and the *Wall Street Journal* are offering a 10-week subscription to students at a tremendous savings. Professors also receive their own free *Wall Street Journal* subscription plus additional instructor supplements created exclusively by the *Wall Street Journal*. Please contact your local sales rep for more information or go to the *Wall Street Journal* online at www.wsj.com.

***Financial Times* Edition**: For adopters of the Stone text, Worth Publishers and the *Financial Times* are offering a 15-week subscription to students at a tremendous savings. Professors also receive their own free *Financial Times* subscription for one year. Students and professors may access research and archived information at www.ft.com.

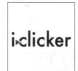

Acknowledgements

No project of this scope is accomplished alone. Many people have helped make this package a better resource for students, and I sincerely appreciate their efforts. These include reviewers of blocks of manuscript chapters, focus group participants, reviewers of single chapters and its accompanying *CourseTutor* chapter, accuracy reviewers, and the production and editorial staff of Worth Publishing.

First, I want to thank those reviewers who read through blocks of chapters in manuscript and offered many important suggestions that have been incorporated into this project. They include:

Dwight Adamson, South Dakota State University
Norman Aitken, University of Massachusetts, Amherst
Fatma Wahdan Antar, Manchester Community College
Anoop Bhargava, Finger Lakes Community College
Craig Blek, Imperial Valley College
Mike W. Cohick, Collin County Community College
Kathleen Davis, College of Lake County
Dennis Debrecht, Carroll College
Christopher Erickson, New Mexico State University
Shaikh M. Ghanzanfar, University of Idaho
Lowell Glenn, Utah Valley State College
Jack Hou, California State University, Long Beach
Charles Kroncke, College of Mount St. Joseph
Laura Maghoney, Solano Community College
Pete Mavrokordatos, Tarrant County College
Philip Mayer, Three Rivers Community College
John McCollough, Penn State University, Lehigh
Pat Mizak, Canisius College
Jay Morris, Champlain College
Jennifer Offenberg, Loyola Marymount University
Joan Osborne, Palo Alto College
Diana Petersdorf, University of Wisconsin, Stout
Oscar Plaza, South Texas Community College
Mary Pranzo, California State University, Fresno
Mike Ryan, Gainesville State College
Supriya Sarnikar, Westfield State College
Lee Van Scyoc, University of Wisconsin, Oshkosh
Paul Seidenstat, Temple University
Ismail Shariff, University of Wisconsin, Green Bay
Garvin Smith, Daytona Beach Community College
Gokce Soydemir, University of Texas, Pan America
Martha Stuffler, Irvine Valley College
Ngoc-Bich Tran, San Jacinto College
Alan Trethewey, Cuyahoga Community College
Chad Turner, Nicholls College
Va Nee L. Van Vleck, California State University, Fresno
Dale Warnke, College of Lake County

Second, I would like to take this opportunity to thank those focus group participants who devoted a lot of time and effort to discussing the elements of this project. Their thoughts and suggestions (and criticisms) contributed immensely to the development of this project. They include:

Emil Berendt, Friends University
Harmanna Bloemen, Houston Community College, Northeast
Mike Cohick, Collin County Community College
Rohini Divecha, San Jacinto College, South
Bob Francis, Shoreline Community College
John Kane, State University of New York, Oswego
Sukanya Kemp, University of Akron
Charlene Kinsey, Houston Community College, Northwest
Delores Linton, Tarrant Community College, Northwest
Fred May, Trident Tech
Saul Mekies, Kirkwood Community College
Diego Mendez-Carbajo, Illinois Wesleyan
Cyril Morong, San Antonio College
Oscar Plaza, South Texas Community College
Michael Polcen, Northern Virginia Community College
Jaishankar Raman, Valparaiso University
Belinda Roman, Palo Alto College
Ted Scheinman, Mt. Hood Community College
Marianna Sidoryanskaya, Austin Community College, Cypress
Lea Templer, College of the Canyons
Ngoc-Bich Tran, San Jacinto College, South
Don Weimer, Milwaukee Area Technical College, Downtown

Third, my thanks go out to those who took the time to review single chapters of the text and *CourseTutor* together, and to those who class-tested single chapters. Thanks for the reviews and the suggestions. These reviewers included:

Shawn Abbott, College of the Siskiyous
Roger Adkins, Marshall University
Richard Agesa, Marshall University
Ali Akarca, University of Illinois, Chicago
Frank Albritton, Seminole Community College
Anca Alecsandru, Louisiana State University
Innocentus Alhamis, Southern New Hampshire University
Basil Al-Hashimi, Mesa Community College
Samuel Andoh, Southern Connecticut State University
William Ashley, Florida Community College at Jacksonville
Rose-Marie Avin, University of Wisconsin, Eau Claire
Sukhwinder Bagi, Bloomsburg University
Dean Baim, Pepperdine University
Joanne Bangs, College of St. Catherine
Abby Barker, University of Missouri, St. Louis
Perry Barrett, Chattahoochee Technical College
David Bartram, East Georgia College
Robert Beekman, University of Tampa
Emil Berendt, Siena Heights University
Gerald Bialka, University of North Florida
Paul Biederman, New York University
Richard Bieker, Delaware State University
Tom Birch, University of New Hampshire, Manchester
John Bockino, Suffolk Community College
Orn Bodvarsson, St. Cloud State University
Antonio Bos, Tusculum College
Laurette Brady, Norwich University
Bill Burrows, Lane Community College
Rob Burrus, University of North Carolina, Wilmington
Tim Burson, Queens University of Charlotte
Dean Calamaras, Hudson Valley Community College
Charles Callahan, State University of New York, Brockport
Colleen Callahan, American University
Dave Cauble, Western Nebraska Community College
Henrique Cezar, Johnson State College
Matthew Chambers, Towson University
Lisa Citron, Cascadia Community College
Ray Cohn, Illinois State University
Kevin Coyne, Southern New Hampshire University
Tom Creahan, Morehead State University
Richard Croxdale, Austin Community College
Rosa Lea Danielson, College of DuPage
Amlan Datta, Cisco Junior College
Helen Davis, Jefferson Community & Technical College
Susan Davis, Buffalo State College
Dennis Debrecht, Carroll College
Robert Derrell, Manhattanville College
Julia Derrick, Brevard Community College
Jeffrey Dorfman, University of Georgia
Justin Dubas, St. Norbert College
Harold Elder, University of Alabama
G. Rod Erfani, Transylvania University
William Feipel, Illinois Central College
Rick Fenner, Utica College
James Ford, San Joaquin Delta College
Marc Fox, Brooklyn College
Lawrence Fu, Illinois College
Mark Funk, University of Arkansas, Little Rock
Mary Gade, Oklahoma State University
Khusrav Gaibulloev, University of Texas, Dallas
Gary Galles, Pepperdine University
Lara Gardner, Florida Atlantic University
Kelly George, Florida Community College at Jacksonville
Lisa George, Hunter College
JP Gilbert, Mira Costa College
Chris Gingrich, Eastern Mennonite University
James Giordano, Villanova University
Susan Glanz, St. John's University
Devra Golbe, Hunter College
Michael Goode, Central Piedmont Community College
Gene Gotwalt, Sweet Briar College
Glenn Graham, State University of New York, Oswego
David Gribbin, East Georgia College
Phil Grossman, St. Cloud State University
Marie Guest, North Florida Community College
J. Guo, Pace University
N.E. Hampton, St. Cloud State University
Deborah Hanson, University of Great Falls
Virden Harrison, Modesto Junior College
Fuad Hasanov, Oakland University
Scott Hegerty, University of Wisconsin, Milwaukee
Debra Hepler, Seton Hill College
Jim Henderson, Baylor University
Jeffrey Higgins, Sierra College
Jannett Highfill, Bradley University
Harold Hotelling, Lawrence Technological University
Wanda Hudson, Alabama Southern Community College
Terence Hunady, Bowling Green University
Mitchell Inman II, Savannah Technical College
Anisul Islam, University of Houston, Downtown

Eric Jamelske, University of Wisconsin, Eau Claire
Russell Janis, University of Massachusetts, Amherst
Andres Jauregui, Columbus State University
Jonathan Jelen, The City College of New York
George Jouganatos, California State University, Sacramento
David Kalist, Shippensburg University
Jonathan Kaplan, California State University, Sacramento
Nicholas Karatjas, Indiana University of Pennsylvania
Janis Kea, West Valley College
Deborah Kelly, Palomar College
Kathy Kemper, University of Texas, Arlington
Brian Kench, University of Tampa
Mariam Khawar, Elmira College
Young Jun Kim, Henderson State University
TC Kinnaman, Bucknell University
Paul Koch, Olivet Nazarene College
Andy Kohen, James Madison University
Lea Kosnik, University of Missouri, St. Louis
Charles Kroncke, College of Mount Saint Joseph
Craig Laker, Tri-State University
Carsten Lange, California Polytechnic State University, Pomona
Gary Langer, Roosevelt University
Leonard Lardaro, University of Rhode Island
Daniel Lawson, Drew University
Bill Lee, St. Mary's College
Mary Jane Lenon, Providence College
Mary Lesser, Iona College
Bozena Leven, The College of New Jersey
Ralph Lim, Sacred Heart University
Anthony Liuzzo, Wilkes University
Jennifer Logan, Southern Arkansas University
Dening Lohez, Pace University
Ellen Magenheim, Swarthmore College
Y. Lal Mahajan, Monmouth University
Mary Ellen Mallia, Siena College
Don Mathews, Coastal Georgia Community College
Phil Mayer, Three Rivers Community College
Norman Maynard, University of Oklahoma
Kimberly Mencken, Baylor University
John Messier, University of Maine, Farmington
Randy Methenitis, Richland College
Charles Meyer, Cerritos College
David Mitchell, Missouri State University
Ilir Miteza, University of Michigan, Dearborn
Jay Morris, Champlain College
Charles Myrick, Dyersburg State Community College
Natalie Nazarenko, State University of New York, Fredonia
Tim Nischan, Kentucky Christian University
Tom Odegaard, Baylor University
Jennifer Offenberg, Loyola Marymount University
Jack Peeples, Washtenaw Community College
Don Peppard, Connecticut College
Elizabeth Perry, Randolph-Macon Women's College
Dean Peterson, Seattle University
John Pharr, Cedar Valley College
Chris Phillips, Somerset Community College
Mary Pranzo, California State University, Fresno
Joseph Radding, Folsom Lake College
Jaishankar Raman, Valparaiso University
Donald Richards, Indiana State University
Bill Ridley, University of Oklahoma
William Rieber, Butler University
Dave Ring, State University of New York, Oneonta
Paul Robillard, Bristol Community College
Denise Robson, University of Wisconsin, Oshkosh
Rose Rubin, University of Memphis
Chris Ruebeck, Lafayette University
Randy Russell, Yavapai College
Marty Sabo, Community College of Denver
Hedayeh Samavati, Indiana University-Purdue University, Fort Wayne
Julia Sampson, Malone College
Paul Schoofs, Ripon College
Peter Schwarz, University of North Carolina, Charlotte
Paul Seidenstat, Temple University
T.M. Sell, Highline Community College
Chad Settle, University of Tulsa
Bill Seyfried, Rollins College
Maurice Shalishali, Columbus State
R. Calvin Shipley, Henderson State University
William Simeone, Providence College
Geok Simpson, University of Texas, Pan American
Noel Smith, Palm Beach Community College
Phil Smith, Georgia Perimeter College, Lawrenceville
Dennis Spector, Naugatuck Valley Community College
Todd Steen, Hope College
Richard Stratton, University of Akron
Stuart Strother, Azusa Pacific University
Martha Stuffler, Irvine Valley College
Boo Chun Su, Santa Monica Community College
Della Lee Sue, Marist College
Abdulhamid Sukar, Cameron University
Thomas Swanke, Chadron State College
Thomas Sweeney, Des Moines Area Community College
Michael Tansey, Rockhurst University

Henry Terrell, University of Maryland
Thomas Tiemann, Elon College
Dosse Toulaboe, Fort Hays State University
Christine Trees, State University of New York, Cobbleskill
Andrew Tucker, Tallahassee Community College
David Tufte, Southern Utah University
Jennifer VanGilder, Ursinus College
Yoav Wachsman, Coastal Carolina University
Craig Walker, Oklahoma Baptist University
Elizabeth Wark, Springfield College
Jonathan Warner, Dordt College
Roger White, Franklin & Marshall College
Jim Wollscheid, Texas A&M University, Kingsville
John Yarber, NE Mississippi Community College
Haichun Ye, University of Oklahoma
Anne York, Meredith College
Nazma Zaman, Providence College
Madeline Zavodny, Agnes Scott College

Fourth, I owe a special debt and want to give a special thanks to Eric Chiang of Florida Atlantic University, Garvin Smith of Daytona Beach Community College, and Ngoc-Bich Tran from San Jacinto College for their tireless effort at accuracy checking. Together, they caught errors that none of us want to see. Thanks again!

Fifth, a huge debt of gratitude is owed to Marie McHale and the supplements authors. Marie coordinated the development of the supplements and our on-line presence. She did a remarkable job and was able to get some great people to author the supplements. They include Mary H. Lesser from Iona College who authored the *Teaching Manual*. Among other things, she did a wonderful job of adding real-world examples designed for use as student handouts. My thanks to Richard Croxdale from Austin Community College who coordinated the development of the Test Bank along with creating questions. Emil Berendt of Siena Heights University, Dennis Debrecht of Carroll College, and Dr. Elizabeth J. Wark from Springfield College all contributed questions. Thanks to all of you for creating a Test Bank with nearly 2,250 questions.

Sixth, the production team at Worth is outstanding. My thanks to the entire team including Kevin Kall, Senior Designer, for a great set of interior and cover designs; Dana Kasowitz the Project Editor who kept the project on a strict timeline; Tracey Kuehn, the Associate Managing Editor; Babs Reingold, the Art Director; and Barbara Anne Seixas, the Project Manager—all who made sure each part of the production process went smoothly. A special thanks to both Jennifer Carey who worked tirelessly to see that we went smoothly from manuscript to book (one tough job) and Carol Gilbert at Matrix Publishing Services who flooded me with beautiful book pages. Thanks for a job well done.

I want to thank Charlie Van Wagner for signing this project and Sarah Dorger for smoothly picking it up and moving it along when he left. Thanks to Paul Shensa for his support and ideas on editorial changes and marketing; he is a valuable resource for any author. I really appreciate Craig Bleyer's many suggestions for the project, the way he kept the project moving along, and his faith in my vision for *CoreEconomics*. There is no way that I can thank Bruce Kaplan enough for what he has meant to this project and me. He has kept me focused and has suggested so many good ideas that I could fill several pages with his contributions. Thanks Bruce, you are the best!

You couldn't ask for a better marketing manager than Scott Guile. His enthusiasm is infectious and I appreciate the huge effort he has put into this project. Todd Elder's design for the marketing brochure was stunning. Steve Rigolosi created an extensive prelaunch marketing campaign that was second to none. Also I want to thank Tom Kling for helping sales reps see many of the benefits of this project. He is an incredible personality and I appreciate his efforts. Also, I want to thank Christine Ondreicka for handling the Fall, 2006 reviewing program.

I am also indebted to Andrew Carlson for his editing and suggested rewrites of the first draft of this project and to Michael McGrath for drafts of many of the historical and Nobel biographies. Finally, I am grateful to my wife, Sheila, for putting up with the forgone vacations given the demands a project like this requires. I hope it lives up to her expectations.

Gerald W. Stone

BRIEF CONTENTS

CONTENTS

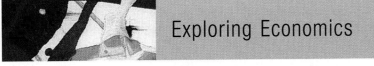

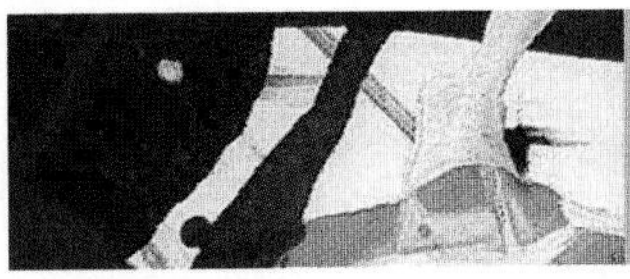

1 Exploring Economics

Production, Economic Growth, and Trade 2

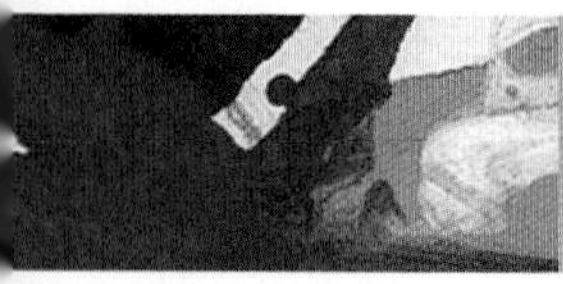

Supply and Demand 3

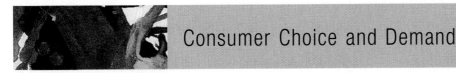

Production and Cost 7

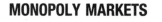

Public Goods, Common Resources, and Externalities 13

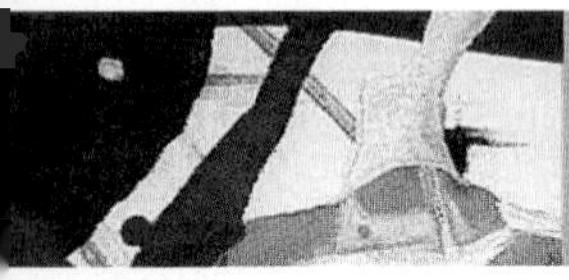

Poverty and Income Distribution 14

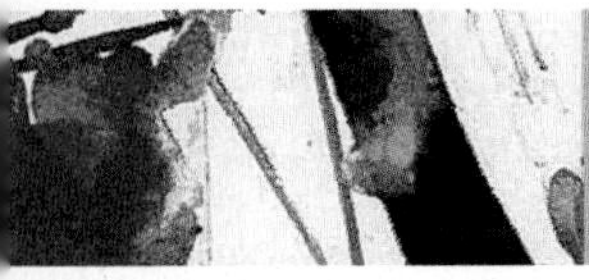

International Trade 15

1 Exploring Economics

> The ideas of economics and political philosophers, both when they are right and when they are wrong, are more powerful than is commonly understood. Indeed, the world is ruled by little else. I am sure that the power of vested interests is vastly exaggerated compared to the gradual encroachment of ideas.
>
> **John Maynard Keynes**

Ideas are important. They change civilizations. Most of the world in the last two decades has renewed its interest in economic ideas. The phrase "It's the economy, stupid" became the political mantra of the Clinton administration. Britain in the 1980s turned to markets to bring the economy out of the doldrums. Both the former Soviet Union and China have looked to economic incentives and markets to help spur their economies. China has had remarkable success. While the economy is improving in Russia, it is still a work in progress.

Why are governments so preoccupied with economic growth? Does it really matter that much? Answering the last question answers the first. Our level of economic growth today largely determines the standards of living for our children, and their children, and then their children.

How important is economic growth, really? To put this in perspective, let's conduct the following experiment. Today, our real gross domestic product (GDP; it represents all the goods and services produced annually, or you can think of it as our income) is roughly $12 trillion (that's a 12 with 12 zeros—a very big number). The United States has the largest economy in the world, with the European Union a close second. To see the importance of economic growth rates on our standard of living, let's assume that from 1930 to today our growth rate was just *1 percentage point* less every year. So, for example, if our economy grew at a 7% rate between 1953 and 1954, we will assume that it really only grew at a 6% rate.

What would be the impact of lowering our growth rate just 1 percentage point every year over the last 75 years? Simply subtracting 1 percentage point *would cut in half the size of our economy today.* Since we have removed the effects of inflation from our estimates, this small adjustment in economic growth rates each year would give us real (adjusted for inflation) aggregate income of less than $6 trillion today—not the $12 trillion we actually have.

While real GDP for the total economy is not a perfect measure of our standard of living, real GDP per capita, a better measure, would also roughly be cut in half. So, toss out half your stuff and move to an apartment half the size you are in today. Note that we have *ignored* a bunch of complementary impacts like reduced education, as well as reduced research and development, that are closely associated with lower incomes. These impacts probably would have reduced these numbers and our standard of living even further. If we were to conduct this little experiment going back to the beginning of the century rather than from 1930, we would likely have the standard of living of Mexico today.

This calculation shows that economic growth is crucial if we are to make this world a better place to live. This example leads to an obvious question: What causes economic growth? Why have some countries leaped ahead, while others have made little progress at all?

John Kay[1] examined 19 highly productive countries with the highest living standards in the world. He found that they were distinguished from the other countries in the world by numerous complex relationships. Highly productive countries have the following characteristics:

- Most are democracies.
- Most have high environmental standards.
- Most have cool climates.
- Most enjoy freedom of expression.
- Women's rights and freedoms are better protected.
- Most enjoy better health.
- Population is taller.
- Government is less corrupt.
- Income inequality is lower.
- Inflation is lower.
- Population is more literate.
- Most have fewer restrictions on trade (more open).
- Population growth is lower.
- Property rights are more secure.

John Kay noted that "correlation does not imply causation." Some of these characteristics follow from a nation being more productive and rich; some, like literacy and health, help promote productivity. These are clearly complex relationships. As Jared Diamond[2] has argued, development in Europe and the United States benefited from immense luck with the weather and the types of flora and fauna native to our regions. Without all three, he argued we would probably not have seen the high level of economic growth that has transpired.

That is why the structure of the society and the economy are so important, and why politicians and governments focus so much of their attention on economic issues. Economies do not develop overnight; it can take 50 years or more to produce modern living standards. For many countries of the world, even beginning today with the right economic programs and policies might mean it would not be until the end of this century before their living standards reach our standards of today. And by that time, much of the world will have moved on.

Today, some people are concerned about outsourcing, globalization, and international trade. Look at this from an undeveloped country's point of view. These things can help them rise from abject poverty to attain modern living standards.

---

[1]John Kay, *The Truth About Markets: Their Genius, Their Limits, Their Follies* (London: Allen Lane), 2003, pp. 27–31. The highly productive countries are United States, Singapore, Switzerland, Norway, Canada, Denmark, Belgium, Japan, Austria, France, Hong Kong, Netherlands, Germany, United Kingdom, Finland, Italy, Australia, Sweden, and Ireland.

[2]Jared Diamond, *Guns, Germs, and Steel: The Fates of Human Societies* (New York: WW Norton), 1999.

After all, the United States was once underdeveloped, and trade with richer nations like France and Britain helped us develop.

Modern technologies and improvements in computing, transportation, and communications all are accelerating the development process. For example, cellular phone infrastructure is so much cheaper to install than the landline technology of the past. This has meant that developing nations can now get a state-of-the-art communications network at a fraction of the price that the United States paid to lay and string cables over the last century. Future communications will undoubtedly be wireless, so many developing nations will be up to speed in a decade. We will see early in this book what countries can do to accelerate their economic growth.

This is the broad picture. Living standards are important, and economic growth improves living standards. Certain programs and policies can foster economic growth. So far, so good. But you are probably asking: What is in it for me? Why should I study economics if I am never going to be an economist? Probably the best reason is that you will spend roughly the next 40 years working in an economic environment. You will have a job; you will pay taxes; you will see the overall economy go from recession to a growth spurt and then maybe stagnate; you will have money to invest; and you will have to vote on economic issues affecting your locality, your region, and your country. It will benefit you to know how the economy works, what to expect in the future, and how to correct the economy's flaws.

But more than that—much more, in fact—economic analysis gives you a structure from which you can make decisions in a more rational manner. This course may well change the way you look at the world. It can open your eyes to how you make everyday decisions from what to buy to whom to marry. It may even make you reconsider your major.

Notice that we have just talked about economic analysis as a way of analyzing decisions that are not "economic" in the general sense of the term. That is the benefit of learning economic analysis. It can be applied all over the map. Sure, learning economic thinking may change your views on spending and saving, on how you feel about government deficits and public debt, and on your opinion of globalization and international trade. You may also reflect differently on environmental policies and what unions do. But you also may develop a different perspective on how much time to study each of your courses this term, or how much to eat at an all-you-can-eat buffet. Such is the broad scope of economic analysis.

In this introductory chapter, we will look at what economics is about. We take a brief look at a key method of economic analysis: model building. Economists use stylized facts and the technique of holding some variables constant to develop testable theories about how consumers, businesses, and government act. Second, we turn to a short discussion of some key principles of economics to give you a sense of the guiding concepts you will meet throughout this book.

The purpose of this introductory chapter is just that: introductory. It seeks to give you a sense of what economics is, what concepts it uses, and what it finds to be important. Do not go into this chapter thinking you have to memorize these concepts. You will be given many opportunities to understand and use these concepts throughout this course. Rather, use this chapter to get a sense of the broad scope of economics. Then return to this chapter at the end of the course and see if everything has now become crystal clear.

After studying this chapter you should be able to

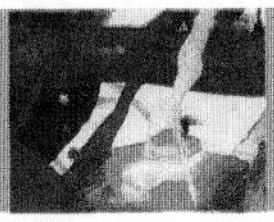

- Explain the scope of economics and economic analysis.
- Differentiate between microeconomics and macroeconomics.

- Describe how economists use models.
- Describe the *ceteris paribus* assumption.
- Discuss the difference between efficiency and equity.
- Describe the key ideas in economics.

What Is Economics About?

Economics is a very broad subject, and often it seems that economics has something important to say about almost everything.

For example, economics has some important things to say about crime and punishment. On first glance, you might think we are talking about the cost of a prison system when we apply economic analysis here. But if we categorize economics as a way of thinking about how people make rational decisions, we can broaden the discussion. Economics considers criminals and potential criminals as rational people who follow their incentives. Criminals are concerned with getting caught and being punished: That is their cost. Longer prison sentences potentially raise the cost of committing a crime. Possibly more important than longer prison sentences is the probability of being convicted for an offense: A long sentence is not an effective incentive if it is rarely used. This is why wounding or killing police officers is prosecuted aggressively and publicized: Potential criminals know they will pay a high cost if a police officer is harmed. Thus, economics looks at all of those factors that raise the cost of crime to criminals. Economics is a way of thinking about an issue, not just a discipline that has money as its chief focus.

Economists tend to put a rational spin (or analysis if you prefer) on nearly everything. Now all of this "analysis/speculation" may bring only limited insight in some cases, but it gives you some idea of how economists think. We look for rational responses to incentives. We begin most questions by considering how rational people would respond to the incentives that specific situations provide. Sometimes (maybe even often) this analysis leads us down an unexpected path. Be prepared to go down some unexpected avenues during your semester in this course.

Microeconomics Versus Macroeconomics

Microeconomics
Microeconomics focuses on decision making by individuals, businesses, industries, and government.

Economics is split into two broad categories: microeconomics and macroeconomics. **Microeconomics** deals with decision making by individuals, business firms, industries, and governments. It is concerned with issues such as which orange juice should you buy, which job to take, and where to go on vacation; which products a business should produce and what price it should charge; and whether a market should be left on its own or be regulated.

We will see that markets—from flea markets to real estate markets to international currency markets—are usually efficient and promote competition. This is good for society. The opposite of competitive markets—monopoly, where one firm controls the market—leads to high prices, and it is bad for society. There is also a vast middle between the extremes of competition and monopoly. Economists analyze the various forms that markets take when they look at market structure.

Microeconomics extends to such things as labor markets and environmental policy. Labor market analysis looks at both the supply (how much we as individuals are willing to work and at what wage) and demand (how much business is willing to hire and at what wage) of labor to determine market salaries. Designing policies to mitigate environmental damage uses the tools of microeconomics.

Adam Smith (1723–1790)

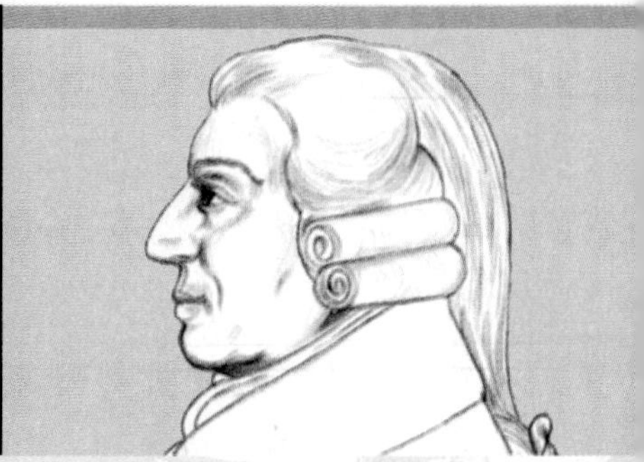

When Adam Smith was a 4-year-old boy, he was kidnapped by gypsies and held for ransom. Had the gypsies not taken fright and returned the boy unharmed, the history of economics might well have turned out differently.

Born in Kirkaldy, Scotland, in 1723, Smith graduated from the University of Glasgow at age 17. He then spent 6 years at Oxford—time he considered to be largely wasted, given the deplorable state of English education at the time. Returning to Scotland in 1751, Smith was named Professor of Moral Philosophy at the University of Glasgow.

After 12 years at Glasgow, Smith began tutoring the son of a wealthy Scottish nobleman. This job provided him with a lifelong income, as well as the opportunity to spend several years touring the European continent with his young charge. In Paris, Smith met some of the leading French economists of the day, which helped stoke his own interest in "political economy." The question that fundamentally guided Smith, as with all the other economists of his time, was, "How best to increase the wealth of the nation?"

Returning to Kirkaldy in 1766, Smith spent the next decade writing *The Wealth of Nations.* This seminal work of free market economic theory actually contained few new ideas. Smith's genius rather was in taking the disparate forms of economic analysis his contemporaries were then developing and putting them together in systematic fashion, thereby making sense of the national economy as a whole. Smith further demonstrated numerous ways in which individuals left free to pursue their own economic interests end up acting in ways that enhance the welfare of all. This is Smith's famous "invisible hand." In Smith's words: "By directing that industry in such a manner as its produce may be of the greatest value, he intends only his own gain, and he is in this, as in many other cases, led by an invisible hand to promote an end which was no part of his intention."

Macroeconomics, on the other hand, focuses on the broader issues we face as a nation. Most of us could care less whether you buy Nike or Merrell shoes. But whether prices of *all* goods and services rise is another matter. Inflation—a general increase in prices economy-wide—affects all of us. And as we have already seen, economic growth is a macroeconomic issue that affects everyone.

Macroeconomics
Macroeconomics is concerned about the broader issues in the economy such as inflation, unemployment, and national output of goods and services.

Macroeconomics uses microeconomic tools to answer some questions, but its main focus is on the broad aggregate variables of the economy. Macroeconomics has its own terms and topics: business cycle fluctuations such as recessions and depressions, unemployment rates, job creation rates, policies that increase economic growth rates, the impact of government spending and taxation, the effect of monetary policy on the economy, and inflation. Further, macroeconomics looks closely at theories of inflation, international trade, and international finance. All of these topics have broad impacts on our economy and our standard of living.

Although we break economics into microeconomics and macroeconomics, there is considerable overlap in the analysis. We use simple supply and demand analysis to understand both individual markets and the general economy as a whole. You will find yourself using concepts from microeconomics to understand fluctuations in the macroeconomy.

Economic Theories and Reality

If you are like me, the first thing you do when you buy a book is flip through the pages to see what's inside. If the number of charts and graphs in this book, along with the limited number of equations, started to freak you out, relax. All of the charts and graphs become relatively easy to understand since they all basically read the same way. The few equations in this book stem from fifth- or sixth-grade algebra. Once you get through one equation, the rest are similar.

Economics is a social science that uses many facts and figures to develop and express ideas. After all, economists try to explain the behavior of the economy and its participants. This inevitably involves facts and numbers. For macroeconomics, this means getting used to talking and thinking in huge numbers: billions (9 zeros) and trillions (12 zeros).

Graphs, charts, and equations are often the simplest and most efficient ways to express data and ideas. Simple equations are used to express relationships between two variables. Complex and wordy discussions can often be reduced to a simple graph or figure. These are efficient techniques for expressing economic ideas.

Model Building

As you study economics this semester or quarter, you will encounter stylized approaches to a number of issues. By *stylized,* we mean that economists boil down facts to their basic relevant elements and use assumptions to develop a stylized (simple) model to analyze the issue. While there are always situations that lie outside these models, they are the exception. Economists generalize about economic behavior and reach generally applicable results.

We begin with relatively simple models, then gradually build in more difficult issues. For example, in the next chapter we introduce one of the simplest models in economics, the production possibilities frontier that illustrates the limits of economic activity. This simple model has profound implications for the issue of economic growth. We can add in more dimensions and make the model more complex, but often this complexity does not provide any greater insight than the simple model.

Ceteris Paribus: All Else Held Constant

Ceteris paribus
Assumption used in economics (and other disciplines as well), where other relevant factors or variables are held constant.

To aid in our model building, economists use the ***ceteris paribus*** assumption: "Holding all other things equal" means we will hold some important variables constant. For example, to determine how many music CDs you might be willing to purchase in any given month, we would hold your monthly income constant. We then would change the prices of music CDs to see the impact on the number purchased (again holding your monthly income constant). Music labels use this information to set what they hope is an optimum price.

Though model building can lead to surprising insights into how economic actors and economies behave, it is not the end of the story. Economic insights lead to economic theories, but these theories must then be tested. We will see many instances where economic predictions turned out to be false. One of the major errors was the classical notion that economy-wide contractions would be of short duration. The Great Depression turned this notion on its head. New models were then developed to explain what had happened. So it may be best to think of model building as a *process* of understanding economic actors and the general economy: Models are created and then tested; if they fail to explain, new models are constructed. Some models have met the test of time. Others have had to be corrected or discarded. Progress, however, has been made.

Efficiency Versus Equity

Efficiency deals with how well resources are used and allocated. No one likes waste. Much of economic analysis is directed toward ensuring that the most efficient outcomes result from public policy. *Production efficiency* occurs when goods are produced at the lowest possible cost, and *allocative efficiency* occurs when individuals who desire a product the most (as measured by their willingness to pay) get those goods and services. It would not do for society to allocate to me a large amount of cranberry sauce—I would not eat the stuff. Efficient policies are generally good policies.

Efficiency
How well resources are used and allocated. Do people get the goods and services they want at the lowest possible resource cost? This is the chief focus of efficiency.

The other side of the coin is **equity** or fairness. Is it fair that the CEOs of large companies make hundreds of times more money than rank-and-file workers? Many think not. Is it fair that some have so much and others have so little? Again, many think not. There are many divergent views about fairness until we get to extreme cases. When just a few people earn nearly all of the income and control nearly all of a society's wealth, most people agree that this is unfair.

Equity
The fairness of various issues and policies.

Throughout this course you will see instances where efficiency and equity collide. You may agree that a specific policy is efficient, but think it is unfair to some group of people. This will be especially evident when you consider tax policy and its impact on income distribution. Fairness or equity is a subjective concept, and each of us has different ideas about what is just and fair. Economists generally stay out of discussions about fairness, leaving that issue to philosophers and politicians. When it comes to public policy issues, economics will help you see the tradeoffs between equity and efficiency, but you will ultimately have to make up your own mind about the wisdom of the policy given these tradeoffs.

In summary, the scope of economics is unusually broad, from decision making by individuals to businesses and large markets. In microeconomics, it looks at individual economic actors; in macroeconomics, it focuses on the economy at large. Economists use stylized models to understand economic activity and predict likely outcomes of various policies, but models are tested and refined or discarded as necessary. And economists tend to focus on matters of efficiency and avoid making sweeping judgments about equity, leaving each one of us to decide what is fair. Even so, the bottom line is that economics has much to say about many things.

Checkpoint
What Is Economics About?

REVIEW

- Economics is separated into two broad categories: microeconomics and macroeconomics.
- *Microeconomics* deals with individuals, firms, and industries and how they make decisions.
- *Macroeconomics* focuses on broader economic issues such as inflation, employment and unemployment, and economic growth.

- Economics uses a stylized approach, creating simple models holding all other relevant factors constant (*ceteris paribus*).
- Economists and policymakers often confront the tradeoff between efficiency and equity. Economists have much to say about efficiency.

QUESTIONS

In each of the following situations, determine whether it is a microeconomic or macroeconomic issue.

1. Hewlett-Packard announces that it is lowering the price of printers by 15%.
2. The president proposes a tax cut.
3. You decide to look for a new job.
4. The economy is in a recession, and the job market is bad.
5. Enron falsifies its accounting books and goes bankrupt.
6. The Federal Reserve announces that it is raising interest rates because it fears inflation.
7. You get a nice raise.
8. Average wages grew by 2% last year.

Answers to the Checkpoint questions can be found at the end of this chapter.

Key Ideas of Economics

Economics has a set of key principles that show up continually in economic analysis. Some are more restricted to specific issues, but most apply universally. As mentioned earlier, these principles should give you a sense of what you will learn in this course. Do not try to memorize these principles at this juncture. Rather, read through them now, and return to them later in the course to assess your progress. By the end of this course, these key principles should be crystal clear.

Choice and Scarcity Force Tradeoffs

Wouldn't it be grand if we all had the resources of Bill Gates or if nanotechnology developed to the point where any product could be made with sand and thus was virtually costless? But we don't, and it hasn't, so back to reality.

We all have limited resources. Some of us are more limited than others, but each of us has time limitations: There are only 24 hours in a day, and some of that must be spent in sleep. Our wants are always greater than our resources. Therefore, we face **scarcity**.

Scarcity
Our unlimited wants clash with limited resources, leading to scarcity. Everyone faces scarcity (rich and poor) because, at a minimum, our time is limited on earth. Economics focuses on the allocation of scarce resources to satisfy unlimited wants.

The fact that we have limited resources (scarcity) means that we must make tradeoffs in nearly everything we do. In fact, *economics is often defined as the study of the allocation of scarce resources to competing wants.* We have to decide between alternatives.

Such decisions as which car to buy, which school to attend (this may be constrained by factors other than money), and whether to study or party all involve tradeoffs. We cannot do everything we would like if for no other reason than our time on earth is limited.

Nobel Prize Paul A. Samuelson

In 1970, Paul Samuelson became the first American to win the Nobel Prize in Economics. One might say that Paul Samuelson literally wrote the book on economics. When he was a young professor at the Massachusetts Institute of Technology, the university asked him to write a standard text for the required junior year course in economics, no satisfactory alternative being available at the time. More than 4 million copies of his textbook, *Economics,* have been sold since it was first published in 1948. The book has been translated into 41 different languages.

Samuelson once described himself as one of the last "generalists" in economics. His interests are wide ranging, and his contributions include everything from the highly technical and mathematical to a popular column for *Newsweek* magazine, which ran from 1966 to 1981. As a scholar, he made original contributions in consumer theory, welfare economics, international trade, finance theory, capital theory, dynamics and general equilibrium, and macroeconomics.

Born in Gary, Indiana, in 1915, Samuelson attended the University of Chicago as an undergraduate. At graduate school at Harvard, where his thesis advisor was Joseph Schumpeter, he was considered something of a prodigy. When he was 21 and still working on his Ph.D., he published his first important contribution to economic theory, "A Note on the Measurement of Utility." In another article in 1938, he introduced the concept of "revealed preference," a breakthrough in the understanding of consumer choice involving the integration of empirical studies of observable behavior with theoretical constructs.

He began teaching at MIT in 1940 and was made a full professor after 6 years. In 1947, he published his magnum opus, the *Foundations of Economic Analysis,* a major contribution to the area of mathematical economics.

Samuelson introduced the concept of neoclassical synthesis, a synthesis of neoclassical microeconomics with Keynesian macroeconomics. Samuelson believed that government intervention through fiscal and monetary policy was sometimes necessary to achieve full employment. Once it reached that level, however, the market functioned well.

Samuelson was an advisor to President John F. Kennedy. In 1960, Samuelson warned of the danger of future inflation. He urged increased spending on defense, foreign aid, educational programs, welfare, unemployment programs, public works, and highway construction. A prolific writer, he averaged one technical paper each month during his active career.

Opportunity Costs Dominate Our Lives

Opportunity costs
The next best alternative; what you give up to do something or purchase something. For example, to watch a movie at a theater, there is not just the monetary cost of the tickets and refreshments, but the time involved in watching the movie. You could have been doing something else (knitting, golfing, hiking, or studying economics).

Economics is often categorized as the discipline that always weighs benefits against costs. This is straightforward enough. What makes this harder is that economists use a special concept: **opportunity costs**. If we undertake to do one activity, some other highly valued activity must be given up. For example, going to a movie requires buying a ticket and giving up our next highest valued activity that takes roughly two hours to perform. Economists refer to the *full costs* of attending the movie (ticket plus time) as *opportunity costs.*

We have limited resources. College students have limited budgets. Say we can purchase that new music CD we want or have ice cream for a week, but not both. Ice cream for a week is the opportunity cost of purchasing that music CD.

Every activity we do involves opportunity costs. Sleeping, eating, studying, partying, running, hiking, and so on, all require that we spend resources that could be used in another activity. This other activity represents the opportunity costs of the current activity chosen. Opportunity costs apply to us as individuals and to societies as a whole. The next chapter focuses on this issue in detail.

Rational Behavior Requires Thinking at the Margin

Have you ever noticed that when you eat at an all-you-can-eat buffet, you always go away fuller than when you order and eat at a normal restaurant? Is this phenomenon unique to you, or is there something more fundamental? Remember, economists look at facts to find incentives to economic behavior.

In this case, people are just rationally responding to the price of *additional* food. They are thinking at the margin. In a restaurant, dessert costs extra, and you make a decision as to whether the dessert is worth the extra cost. At the buffet, dessert is free. So now you don't have to ask yourself if dessert is worth the extra money since it costs nothing. Where you might be nearly full and decline dessert in a restaurant, you will often have dessert in the buffet even if you are stuffed afterwards.

Throughout this book, we will see examples of thinking at the margin. Businesses use marginal analysis to determine how much of their products they are willing to supply to the market. People use marginal analysis to determine how many hours to work. And governments use marginal analysis to determine how much pollution should be permitted.

People Follow Incentives

Tax policy rests on the idea that people follow their incentives. Do we want to encourage people to save for their retirement? Then let them deduct a certain amount that they can put in an individual retirement account (IRA), and let this money compound tax free. Do we want businesses to spend more to stimulate the economy? Then give them tax credits for new investment. Do we want people to go to college? Then give them tax advantages for setting up education savings accounts when children are young, and provide tuition tax credits.

Tax policy is an obvious example in which people follow incentives. But this principle can be seen in action wherever you look. Want to encourage people to use commuter trains during non-rush-hour times? Provide an off-peak discount. Want to spread out the dining time at restaurants? Give Early-Bird Special discounts for those willing to consider a 5:00 P.M. dinner time slot rather than a more popular 8:00 P.M. slot. Want to fill up airplanes during the slow days of Tuesday and Wednesday? Offer price discounts or additional frequent flyer miles for flying on those days.

Note that in saying that people follow incentives, economists do not claim that everyone follows each incentive at every time. You may not want to eat dinner at

4:30 P.M. But there might be a sufficient number of people who are willing to accept an earlier time slot in return for a cheaper meal.

Markets Are Efficient

Private markets and the incentives they provide are the best mechanisms known today for providing products and services. There is no government food board that makes sure that bread, cereal, coffee, and all the other food products you demand are on your plate in the evening. The vast majority of products we consume are privately provided, assuming, of course, that we have the money to pay for them.

Markets bring buyers and sellers together. Competition for the consumer dollar forces firms to provide products at the lowest possible price, or some other firm will undercut their high price. New products enter the market and old products die out. Such is the dynamic characteristic of markets. Starbucks has made latte drinkers of us all, whereas just a short time ago, few of us could even spell the word.

What drives and disciplines markets? Prices and profits are the keys. Profits drive entrepreneurs to provide new products (think of pharmaceutical firms or dot-coms) or existing products at lower prices (think of Wal-Mart). When prices and profits get too high in any market, new firms jump in with lower prices to grab away customers. This competition, or sometimes even the threat of competition, keeps markets from exploiting consumers.

Government Must Deal with Market Failure

As efficient as markets usually are, there are some products and services that markets fail to provide efficiently. Where consumers have no choice but to buy from one firm (local utility, telephone, or cable companies), the market will fail to provide the best solution, and government regulation is often used to protect consumers. Another example is pollution: Left on their own, companies will pollute the air and the water supplies—we will see why later in this book. Governments then intervene to deal with this market failure.

Information Is Important

Markets are efficient because people tend to make rational choices. To help make these choices, people rely on information. Each of us has to decide when we have enough information: Complete information may not be possible to obtain, and too much information can be debilitating. Some decisions require little information: What brand of table salt should you buy? Other decisions require more information: What type of automobile should you buy? Information is valuable.

As we will see before long, strange things happen to markets when one side of a transaction has a consistently superior information advantage. Martha Stewart was convicted of lying about selling stock based on insider information. The top officials of a business know much more quickly than anyone else if their company is developing business problems. These problems might lead to a fall in the price of the company's stock. If the officials act on this inside information while it is still secret, they can sell their stock before the price dips. This information gives them an unfair advantage over the other stockholders or people who may want to own the stock. That is why there are laws preventing insiders from taking undue advantage of their privileged position.

Markets work best when both sides of a transaction can weigh carefully the costs and benefits of goods and services. Superior information can provide significant advantages. We will see what markets can do to correct for information problems, and what government can do when the market cannot provide an acceptable solution.

Specialization and Trade Improve Our Lives

Trading with other countries leads to better products for consumers at lower prices. David Ricardo laid out the rationale for international trade almost two centuries ago, and it still holds true today. We will expand on this in the next chapter.

As you will learn, economies grow by producing those products where they have an advantage over other countries. This is why few of us grow our own food, sew our own clothes, make our own furniture, or write the books we read. We do those things we do best and let others do the same. In nearly all instances, they are able to do it cheaper than we can. The next time you come back from a shopping trip, look closely to discover where every product was made. More than likely, over half will have come from another country.

Productivity Determines Our Standard of Living

> **You can see the computer age everywhere but in the productivity statistics.**
>
> ***Robert Solow***

> **If you want jobs for jobs' sake, trade in bulldozers for shovels. If that doesn't create enough jobs, replace shovels with spoons. Heresy! But there will always be more work to do than people to work. So instead of counting jobs, we should make every job count.**
>
> ***Robert McTeer, Jr.***[3]

Imagine you need to hire someone in your own business (You've finished college and you are now an entrepreneur). You have narrowed the field down to two candidates who are equal in all respects except two. One person can do twice as much as the other (assume you can accurately measure these things), and this same person wants a salary that is 50% higher. Other than that they are equal. Whom should you hire?

The answer is obvious in this situation, because the more productive person is actually the best buy since she produces twice as much as the other candidate, but only wants half again as much pay. In this case, you would be willing to pay even more to get this person. Productivity and pay go together. Highly paid movie stars get high pay because they are worth it to the movie producer. The same is true of professional athletes, corporate executives, rocket scientists, and heart surgeons.

The same is true for nations. Those countries with the highest average per capita income are also the most productive. Their labor forces are highly skilled, and firms are willing to place huge amounts of capital with these workforces because this results in immense productivity. In turn, these workers earn high wages. So, high productivity growth results in solid economic growth, high wages and income, and large investments in education and research. All of this leads to higher standards of living.

Government Can Smooth the Fluctuations in the Overall Economy

All of us have heard of recessions and depressions. These terms refer to downturns in the general economy. The general movement of the economy from good times to bad and back again is called the business cycle.

Classical economic theory viewed the overall economy as a self-correcting mechanism that would quickly adjust to disturbances in the business cycle if only it was left to itself. Along came the Great Depression of the 1930s, which showed that the overall economy could get stuck in a downturn. The solution was government inter-

---

[3]Past president of the Federal Reserve Bank of Dallas.

vention. Just as government can intervene successfully in individual markets when market failure occurs, so too can government intervene successfully when the overall economy gets stuck in a downturn. You can observe this principle at work when you hear discussions of using a tax cut (or increased government spending) to pull an economy out of a recession.

The intricacies of what government can do to smooth out the business cycle are a major part of your study of macroeconomics. Remember that saying the government *can* successfully intervene does not mean it *always* successfully intervenes. The macroeconomy is not a simple machine. Successful policymaking is a tough task.

You will learn more about these important ideas as the semester progresses. For now, realize that economics rests on the foundation of a limited number of important concepts.

Checkpoint

Key Ideas of Economics

REVIEW

- Choice and scarcity force tradeoffs.
- Opportunity costs dominate our lives.
- Rational thinking requires thinking at the margin.
- People follow incentives.
- Markets are efficient.
- Government must deal with market failure.
- Information is important.
- Specialization and trade improve our lives.
- Productivity determines our standard of living.
- Government can smooth the fluctuations in the overall economy.

QUESTION

McDonald's has recently introduced a premium blend of coffee that sells for more than its standard coffee. How does this represent thinking at the margin?

Answers to the Checkpoint question can be found at the end of this chapter.

Key Concepts

Microeconomics, p. 4
Macroeconomics, p. 5
Ceteris paribus, p. 6
Efficiency, p. 7
Equity, p. 7
Scarcity, p. 8
Opportunity costs, p. 10

Chapter Summary

What Is Economics About?

Economics is about almost everything. Economic analysis can be usefully applied to topics as diverse as how businesses make decisions and how college students allocate their time between studying and relaxing, how individuals determine whether to "invest in themselves" by taking additional courses while on the job, and how government deals with electric utilities that pollute nearby rivers.

Economics is separated into two broad categories: microeconomics and macroeconomics. *Microeconomics* deals with individual, firm, industry, and public decision making. For example, microeconomics deals with issues such as whether you should go to the movies or study, and if you study, how you allocate your study time between all of your courses. Business firms consider issues such as how much output to produce and how many people to hire to sell the output.

Macroeconomics, on the other hand, focuses on the broader economic issues confronting the nation. Issues such as inflation (a general increase in prices economy-wide), employment and unemployment, and economic growth affect all of us.

Economics uses a *stylized* approach to a number of issues. Stylized models boil issues and facts down to their basic relevant elements. Then, using assumptions, stylized (simple) models are developed. Not all situations are covered by the models, because economists seek to generalize about economic behavior and reach generally applicable results.

To build models means that we make use of the *ceteris paribus* assumption and hold some important variables constant. This useful device often provides surprising insights about economic behavior.

Economists and policymakers often confront the tradeoff between efficiency and equity. Efficiency reflects how well resources are used and allocated; economic analysis often focuses on ensuring that efficient outcomes result from public policy. Sometimes the equity (or fairness) of the outcome is questioned. Because fairness is a subjective matter, there are differences of opinion about fairness except in extreme cases where people tend to come to a general agreement. For public policy issues, economics illuminates the tradeoffs between equity and efficiency. Economists have much to say about efficiency; they tend to keep quiet on the subjective issue of equity.

Key Ideas of Economics

Economics rests on some basic ideas. These are ideas that will be met again and again throughout this course.

Our economy has limited resources. Our wants are limitless. This means that we face scarcity and must make tradeoffs in nearly everything we do. Economics is often defined as the study of the allocation of scarce resources to competing wants.

Everything we do involves opportunity costs. All activities require that we spend resources (e.g., time and money) that could be used in another activity. This other activity represents the opportunity cost of the current activity chosen. Opportunity costs apply to us as individuals and to societies as a whole.

Rational thinking requires that you think and make decisions at the margin. Businesses use marginal analysis to determine how much output to produce. People use marginal analysis to determine which products to buy. And governments use marginal analysis to determine which tracts of land to allow oil leases on.

People follow their incentives. If society wants to discourage some behavior, it can tax it, punish it, or do a host of other things that increases its costs. Conversely, society can provide incentives such as tax benefits for behaviors it wishes to encourage.

Markets bring buyers and sellers together. Competition for the consumer's dollar forces firms to provide products at the lowest possible price, or some other firm will undercut the price. New products are introduced to the market and old products disappear. This dynamism makes markets efficient.

Though markets are usually efficient, there are recognized times when they are not. Pollution is an example of this. Government can provide a solution to problems of market failure.

Information is important. Superior information gives economic actors a decided advantage. Sometimes this is simply a fact of life. At other times, information advantages can result in dysfunctional markets.

Trading with other countries leads to better products for consumers at lower prices. Economies grow by producing those products where they have an advantage over other countries. This is why much of what we buy today comes from other countries. Specialization leads to tangible benefits.

Countries with the highest average per capita income are also the most productive. Their labor forces are highly skilled, and firms place huge amounts of capital with these workforces. This results in immense productivity and correspondingly high wages for the workers. High productivity growth results in high economic growth, which leads to high wages and high incomes, which stimulate large investments in education and research. All of this activity leads to higher standards of living.

The overall economy moves from growth spurts to recessions, then back to growth spurts. Economists have been unable to tame this business cycle, though government has been successful at smoothing the fluctuations in the overall economy.

Questions and Problems

1. *The Wall Street Journal* recently noted that bachelor's degrees in economics were up 40% between 1999 and 2004 and "There is a clear explosion in economics as a major," and "the number of students majoring in economics has been rising even faster at top colleges." What might be some reasons for this now? (Jessica E. Vascellaro, "The Hot Major for Undergrads is Economics," *Wall Street Journal,* July 5, 2005, p. A11.)

2. Gregg Easterbrook, in his book, *The Progress Paradox* (New York: Random House, 2003) noted that life in the United States is significantly better today than in the past and provided many statistical facts, including:
   a. Nearly a quarter of households (or 60+ million people) have incomes of at least $75,000 a year.
   b. Real (inflation adjusted) per capita income has more than doubled since 1960—people on average have twice the real purchasing power now as in 1960.
   c. In 1956, the typical American had to work 16 weeks for each 100 square feet of new housing. Today that number is 14 weeks, and new houses are considerably more luxurious.
   d. The United States accepts more legal immigrants than all other nations of the world combined.
   e. The quality of health care improved substantially over the last half century, and life spans have grown dramatically.

   This is just a sampling of the improvements in living standards Easterbrook catalogued. However, his book is subtitled *How Life Gets Better While People Feel Worse*, and this is a paradox he set out to explain. What reasons might explain why even though our lives have improved, people feel that life was better in an earlier time?

3. In 2001 Nobel Prize winner Robert Solow noted that "the computer age is seen everywhere except in productivity data." More recent studies suggest that it takes roughly seven years for investment in computers to have an impact on productivity. Why do you think this is the case?

4. The Black rhinoceros is extremely endangered. Its horn is considered a powerful aphrodisiac in many Asian countries, and a single horn fetches many

thousands of dollars on the black market, creating a great incentive for poachers. Unlike other stories of endangered species, this one might have a simple solution. Conservationists could simply capture as many rhinos as possible and remove their horns, reducing the incentive to poach. Do you think this will help reduce poaching? Why or why not?

5. In contrasting equity and efficiency, why do high-tech firms seem to treat their employees better (better wages, benefits, working environments, vacations, etc.) compared to how landscaping or fast-food franchises treat their employees? Is this fair? Is it efficient?

6. Does your going to college have anything to do with expanding choices or reducing scarcity? Explain.

7. With higher gasoline prices, the U.S. government wants people to buy more hybrid cars that use much less gasoline. Unfortunately, hybrids are approximately $4,000 to $5,000 more expensive to purchase than comparable cars. If people follow incentives, what can the government do to encourage the purchase of hybrids?

8. You normally stay at home on Wednesday nights and study. Next Wednesday night, the college is having a free concert on the main campus. What is the opportunity cost of going to the free concert?

9. People talk about a boom in the housing market. Who specifically is helped by this boom? Consider real-estate agents, current homeowners, home builders, banks or financing institutions, and newly married couples who want to buy a home. Now consider what happens if the economy is booming, but the housing market starts to stumble. What happens to the groups you discussed earlier? Assume the housing market is booming, but the economy starts to go into a recession. What groups would be hurt by this? What would this likely do to the housing market?

10. In 2006 the Nobel Peace Prize went to economist Muhammad Yunus and the Grameen Bank "for their efforts to create economic and social development from below." Yunus led the development of micro loans to poor people without financial security: loans of under $200 to people so poor they could not provide collateral, to use for purchasing basic tools or other basic implements of work. This helped to pull millions of people out of poverty. Discuss how economic prosperity and security for everyone can result in a more peaceful planet.

Answers to Checkpoint Questions

CHECKPOINT: WHAT IS ECONOMICS ABOUT?

(1) microeconomics, (2) macroeconomics, (3) microeconomics, (4) macroeconomics, (5) microeconomics, (6) macroeconomics, (7) microeconomics, (8) macroeconomics.

CHECKPOINT: KEY IDEAS OF ECONOMICS

McDonald's is adding one more product (premium coffee) to its line. Thinking at the margin entails thinking about how you can improve an operation (or increase profits) by adding to your existing product line or reducing costs.

Appendix: Working with Graphs and Formulas

You can't watch the news on television or read the newspaper without looking at a graph of some sort. If you have flipped through this book, you have seen a large number of graphs, charts, and tables, and a few simple equations. This is the language of economics. Economists deal with data for all types of issues. Just looking at data in tables often doesn't help you discern the trends or relationships in the data.

Economists develop theories and models to explain economic behavior and levels of economic activity. These theories or models are simplified representations of real-world activity. Models are designed to distill the most important relationships between variables, and then these relationships are used to predict future behavior of individuals, firms, and industries, or to predict the future course of the overall economy.

In this short section, we will explore the different types of graphs you are likely to see in this course (and in the media) and then turn to an examination of how graphs are used to develop and illustrate models. This second topic leads us into a discussion of modeling relationships between data and how to represent these relationships with graphs and simple equations.

After studying this appendix you should be able to

- Describe the four simple forms of data graphs.
- Make use of a straightforward approach to reading graphs.
- Read linear and nonlinear graphs and know how to compute their slopes.
- Use simple linear equations to describe a line and a shift in the line.
- Explain why correlation is not the same as causation.

Graphs and Data

The main forms of graphs of data are time series, scatter plots, pie charts, and bar charts. Time series, as the name suggests, plots data over time. Most of the figures you will encounter in publications are time series graphs.

Time Series

Time series graphs involve plotting time (minutes, hours, days, months, quarters, or years) on the horizontal axis and the value of some variable on the vertical axis. Figure APX-1 illustrates a time series plot for civilian employment of those 16 years and older. Notice that since the early 1990s, employment has grown by almost 20 million for this group. The vertical strips in the figure designate the last two recessions. Notice that in both cases when the recession hit, employment fell, then rebounded after the recession ended.

FIGURE APX-1

Civilian Employment, 16 Years and Older

This time series graph shows the number of civilians 16 years and older employed in the United States since 1990. Employment has grown steadily over this period, except in times of recessions, indicated by the vertical strips. Note that employment fell during the recessions, and then bounced back after each recession ended.

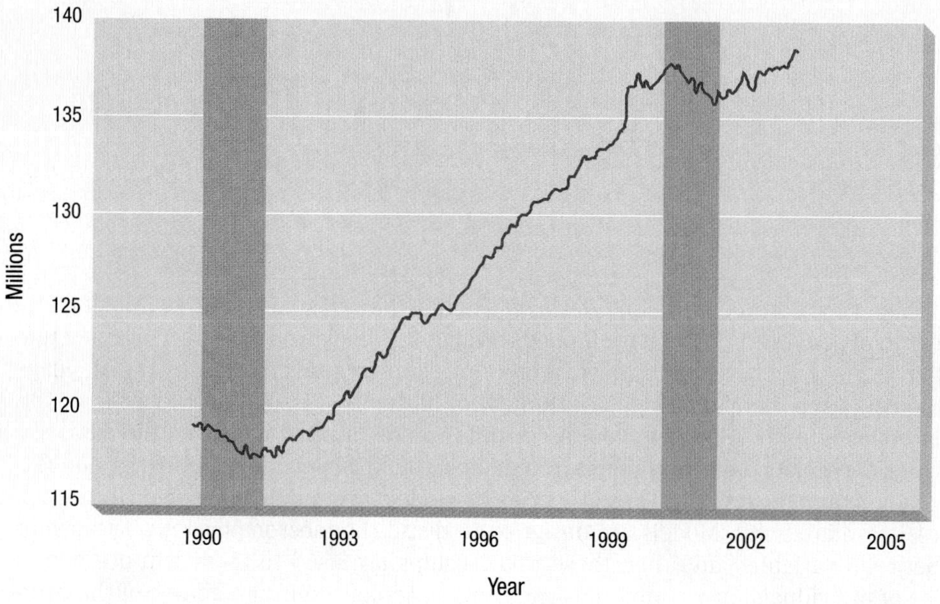

Scatter Plots

Scatter plots are graphs where two variables (neither variable is time) are plotted against each other. Scatter plots often give us a hint if the two variables are related to each other in some consistent way. Figure APX-2 plots one variable, the number of strikes, against another variable, union membership as a percent of total employment.

Two things can be seen in this figure. First, these two variables appear to be related to each other in a positive way. A rising union membership as a percent of employment leads to a greater number of strikes. It is not surprising that greater union membership and more strikes are related, because greater union membership means more employees are covered by collective bargaining agreements, and thus we would expect more strikes. Also, greater union membership means that unions would be more powerful, and strikes represent a use of this power. Second, given that the years for the data are listed next to the dots, we can see that union representation as a percent of total employment has fallen significantly over the last half century. From this simple scatter plot, we get a lot of information and ideas of how the two variables are related.

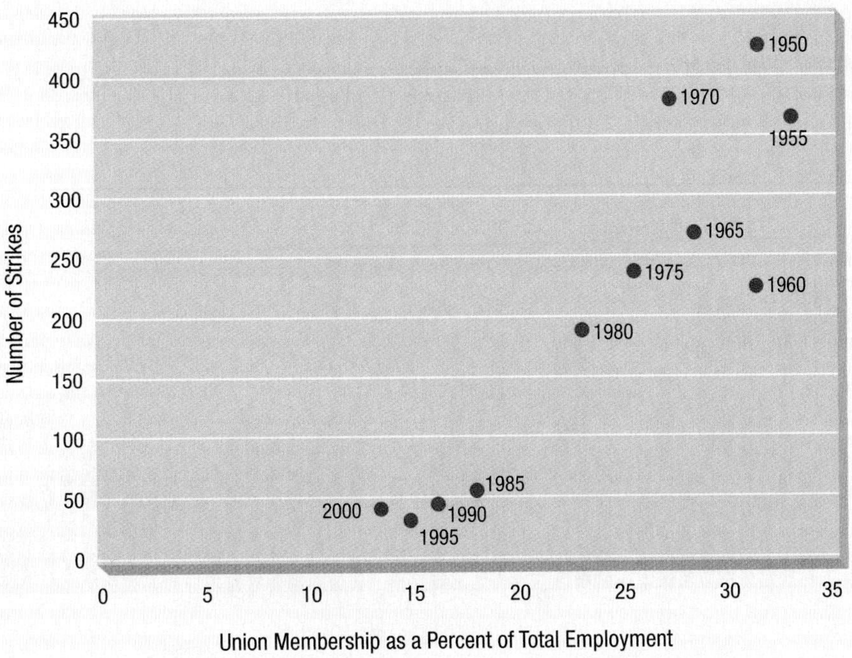

FIGURE APX-2

The Relationship between the Number of Strikes and Union Membership as a Percent of Total Employment

This scatter diagram plots the relationship between the number of strikes and union membership as a percentage of total employment. The number of strikes increased as union membership became a larger percentage of those employed. Note that union membership as a percentage of those employed has fallen in the last half century.

Pie Charts

Pie charts are simple graphs that show data that can be split into percentage parts that combined make up the whole. A simple pie chart for the relative importance of components in the consumer price index (CPI) is shown in Figure APX-3. It reveals how the typical urban household budget is allocated. By looking at each slice of the pie, we get a picture of how typical families spend their income.

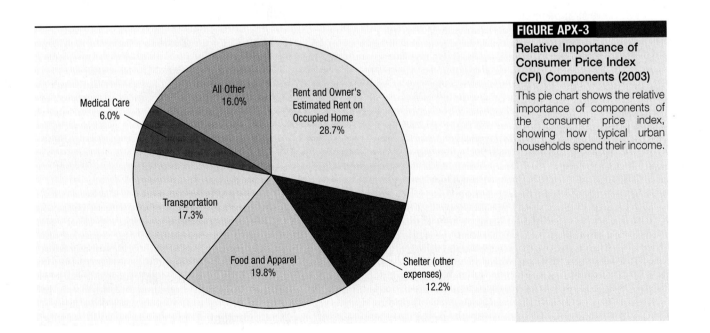

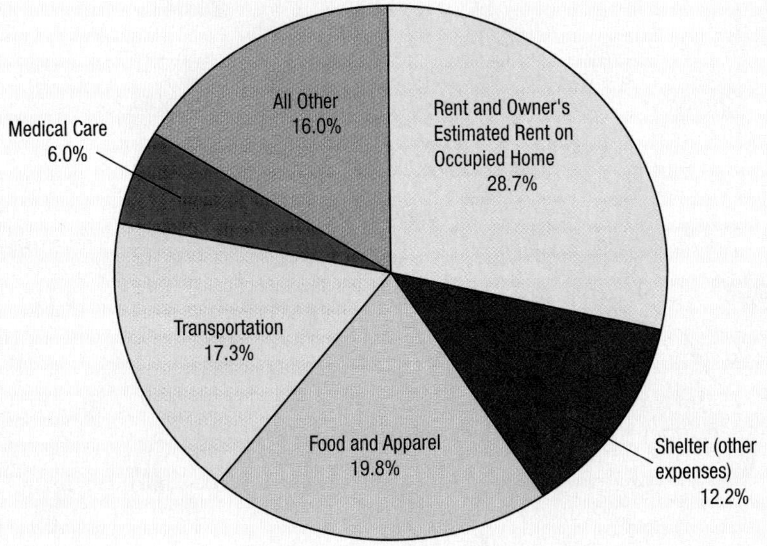

FIGURE APX-3

Relative Importance of Consumer Price Index (CPI) Components (2003)

This pie chart shows the relative importance of components of the consumer price index, showing how typical urban households spend their income.

Bar Charts

Bar charts use bars to show the value of specific data points. Figure APX-4 is a simple bar chart showing the annual changes in real (adjusted for inflation) gross domestic product (GDP). Notice that over the last 40+ years the United States has had only 5 years when GDP declined.

FIGURE APX-4

Percentage Change in Real (Inflation Adjusted) GDP

This bar chart shows the annual percentage change in real (adjusted for inflation) gross domestic product (GDP) over the last forty years. Over this time period, GDP has declined only five times.

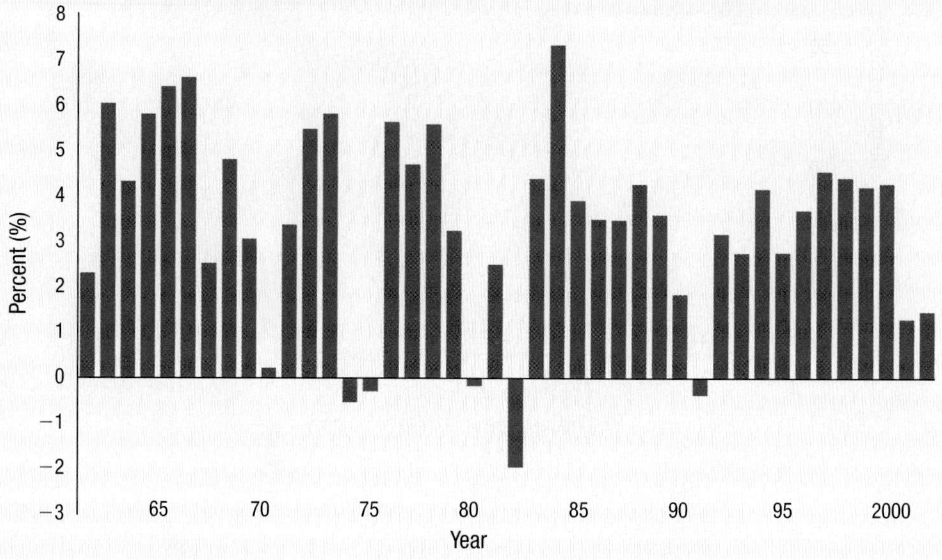

Simple Graphs Can Pack a Lot of Information

It is not unusual for graphs and figures to have several things going on at once. Look at Figure APX-5, illustrating the yield curve for government bonds. On the horizontal axis are years to maturity for the existing government bonds. At matu-

FIGURE APX-5

Yield Curve

This yield curve for government bonds shows that interest rates fell between the middle of 2002 and the middle of 2003, shown by each point on the August 2003 curve being below the corresponding point on the July 2002 curve. Also, this figure shows that the yield (rate of return) for each bond grew as the time to maturity grew. This is due to higher risk associated with longer term bonds.

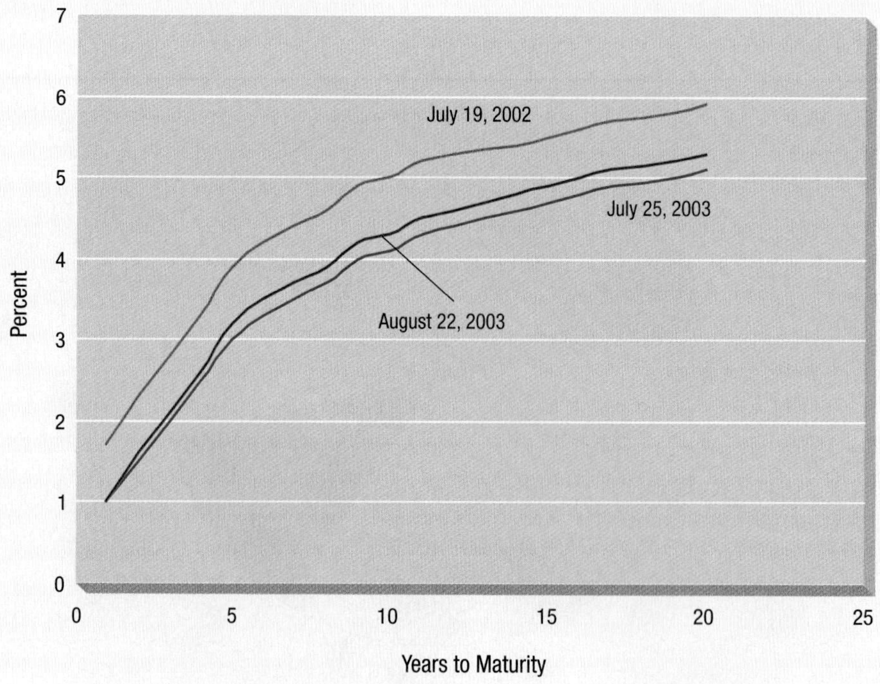

rity, the federal government must pay to the bond holders the principal amount of the bond (more about this in later chapters). On the vertical axis is the yield for each bond in percent. This is the monetary return to the bond expressed as a percent of the bond's price. Figure APX-5 shows three different yield curves for different periods. They include the most recent period shown (August 2003), a month previous (July 2003), and a year before (July 2002).

You should notice two things in this figure. First, at this time the yield curves sloped upward (they do not always do this). This meant that bonds that had a longer time to mature had higher yields; bonds with longer maturity periods are riskier and usually require a higher return. Second, interest rates fell over this period (July 2002 to August 2003) as shown by the position of the curves. Each point on the August 2003 curve is below the corresponding point on the July 2002 curve.

A Few Simple Rules for Reading Graphs

Looking at graphs of data is relatively easy if you follow a few simple rules. First, read the title of the figure to get a sense of what is being presented. Second, look at the label for the horizontal axis (x axis) to see how the data are being presented. Make sure you know how the data are being measured. Is it months or years, hours worked or hundreds of hours worked? Third, examine the label for the vertical axis (y axis). This is the value of the variable being plotted on that axis; make sure you know what it is. Fourth, look at the graph itself and see if it makes logical sense. Are the curves (bars, dots) going in the right direction?

Look the graph over and see if you notice something interesting going on. This is really the fun part of looking closely at figures both in this text and in other books, magazines, and newspapers. Often simple data graphs can reveal surprising relationships between variables. Keep this in mind as you examine graphs throughout this course.

One more thing. Graphs in this book are always accompanied by explanatory captions. Examine the graph first, making your preliminary assessment of what is going on. Then carefully read the caption, making sure it accurately reflects what is shown in the graph. If the caption refers to movement between points, follow this movement in the graph. If you think there is a discrepancy between the caption and the graph, reexamine the graph to make sure you have not missed something.

Graphs and Models

Let's now take a brief look at how economists use graphs and models, also looking at how they are constructed. Economists use what are called *stylized graphs* to represent relationships between variables. These graphs are a form of modeling to help us simplify our analysis and focus on those relationships that matter. Figure APX-6 is one such model.

Linear Relationships

Figure APX-6 on the next page shows a linear relationship between average study hours and your grade point average (GPA). The more you study, the higher your GPA (duh!). By a linear relationship, we mean that the "curve" is a straight line. In this case, if you don't study at all, we assume you are capable of making Ds and your GPA will equal 1.0, not enough to keep you in school for long. If you hit the books for an average of 10 hours a week, your GPA rises to 2.0, a C average. Studying for additional hours raises your GPA up to its maximum of 4.0.

The important point here is that the curve is linear; any hour of studying yields the same increase in your grade point. All hours of studying provide equal yields from beginning to end. This is what makes linear relationships unique.

FIGURE APX-6

Studying and Your GPA

This figure shows a hypothetical linear relationship between average study hours and grade point average. Without studying, a D average results, and with 10 hours of studying, a C average is obtained, and so on.

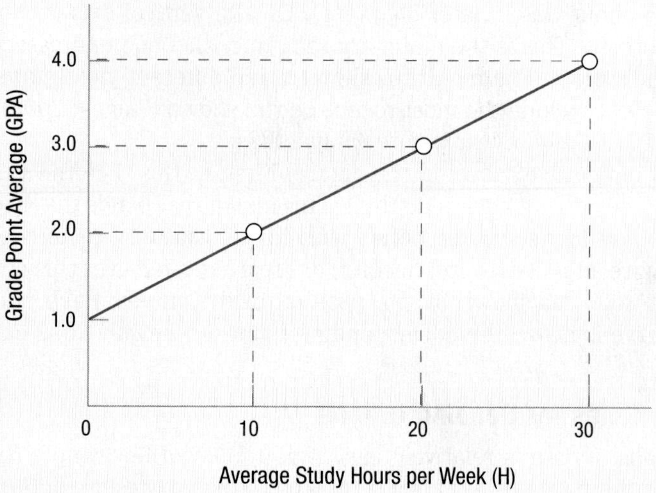

Computing the Slope of a Linear Line

Looking at the line in Figure APX-6, we can see two things: The line is straight, so the slope is constant, and the slope is positive. As average hours of studying increase, GPA increases. Computing the slope of the line tells us how much GPA increases for every hour that studying is increased. Computing the slope of a linear line is relatively easy and is shown in Figure APX-7.

FIGURE APX-7

Computing Slope for a Linear Line

Computing the slope is based on a simple rule: rise over run (rise divided by run). In the case of this straight line, the slope is equal to 0.1 because every 10 additional hours of studying yields a 1.0 increase in GPA.

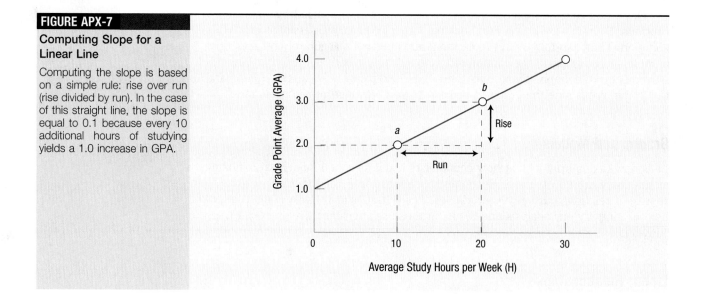

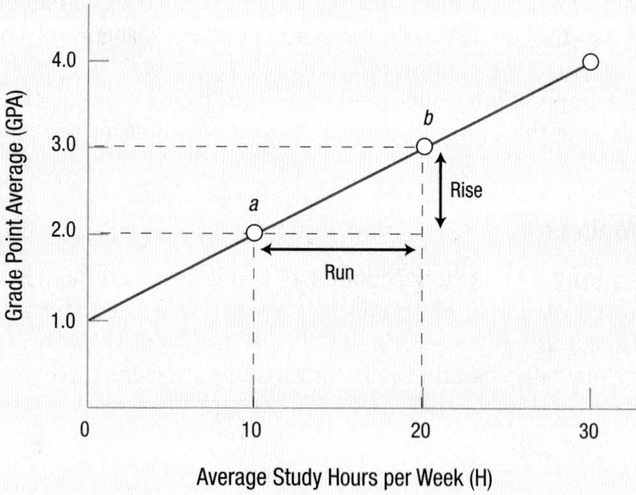

The simple rule for computing slope is: Slope is equal to rise over run (or rise ÷ run). Since the slope is constant along a linear line, we can select any two points and determine the slope for the entire curve. In Figure APX-7 we have selected points *a* and *b* where your GPA moves from 2.0 to 3.0 when studying increases from 10 to 20 hours per week.

Your GPA increases (rises) by 1.0 for an additional 10 hours of study. This means that the slope is equal to 0.1 ($1.0 \div 10 = 0.1$). So for every additional hour of studying you add each week, your GPA will rise by 0.1. Thus, if you would like to improve your grade point average from 3.0 to 3.5, you would have to study 5 more hours per week.

Computing slope for negative relations that are linear is done exactly the same way, except that when you compute the changes from one point to another, one of the values will be negative, making the relationship negative.

Nonlinear Relationships

It would be nice for model builders if all relationships were linear, but that is not the case. It is probably not really the case with the amount of studying and your GPA either. Figure APX-8 depicts a more realistic nonlinear and positive relationship between studying and GPA. Again, we assume that you can get a D average (1.0) without studying and reach a maximum of straight As (4.0) with 30 hours per week.

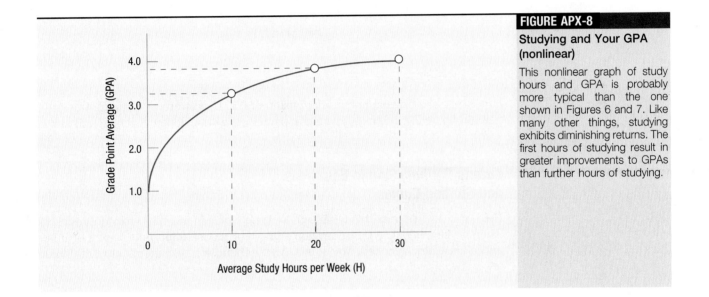

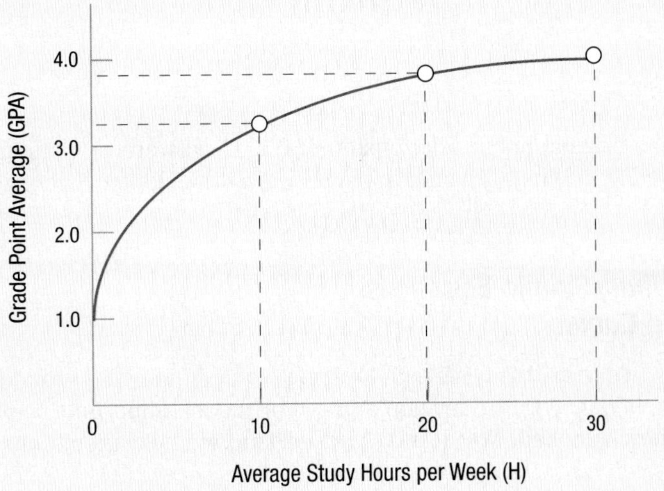

FIGURE APX-8

Studying and Your GPA (nonlinear)

This nonlinear graph of study hours and GPA is probably more typical than the one shown in Figures 6 and 7. Like many other things, studying exhibits diminishing returns. The first hours of studying result in greater improvements to GPAs than further hours of studying.

Figure APX-8 suggests that your first few hours of study per week are more important to raising your GPA than are the others. Your first 10 hours of studying yields more than the last 10 hours: You go from 1.0 to 3.3 (a gain of 2.3), as opposed to going only from 3.8 to 4.0 (a gain of only 0.2). This curve exhibits what economists call diminishing returns. Just as the first bite of pizza tastes better than the one-hundredth, so the first 5 hours of studying brings a bigger jump in GPA than the 25th to 30th hours.

Computing the Slope of a Nonlinear Curve

As you might suspect, computing the slope of a nonlinear curve is a little more complex than for a linear line. But it is not that much more difficult. In fact, we use essentially the same rise over run approach that is used for lines.

Looking at the curve in Figure APX-8, it should be clear that the slope varies for each point on the curve. It starts out very steep, then begins to level out above 20 hours of studying. Figure APX-9 on the next page shows how to compute the slope at any point on the curve.

Computing the slope at point a requires drawing a line tangent to that point, then computing the slope of that line. For point a, the slope of the line tangent to it is found by computing rise over run again. In this case, it is length $dc \div bc$ or $[(3.8 - 3.3) \div (10 - 7)] = .5 \div 3 = 0.167$. Notice that this slope is significantly

FIGURE APX-9

Computing Slope for a Nonlinear Curve

Computing the slope of a nonlinear curve requires that you compute the slope of each point on the curve. This is done by computing the slope of a tangent to each point.

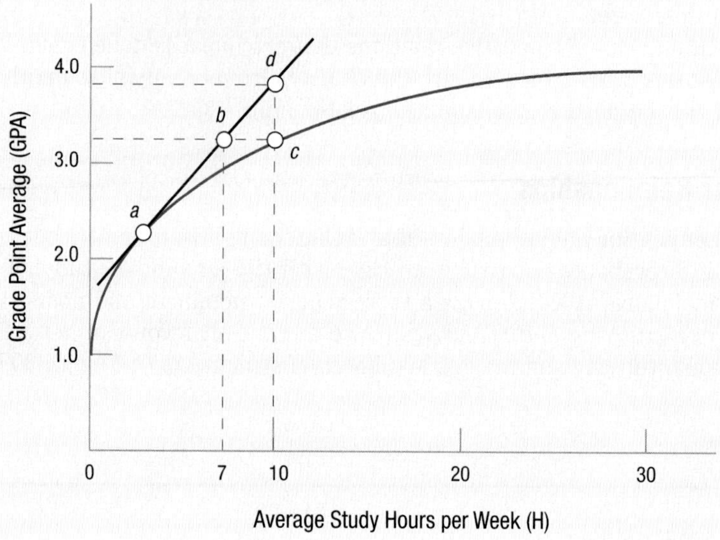

larger than the original linear relationship of 0.1. If we were to compute the slope near 30 hours of studying, it would approach zero (the slope of a horizontal line is zero).

Ceteris Paribus, Simple Equations, and Shifting Curves

Hold on while we beat this GPA and studying example into the ground. Inevitably when we simplify analysis to develop a graph or model, important factors or influences must be controlled. We do not ignore them, we hold them constant. These are known as *ceteris paribus* assumptions.

Ceteris Paribus: All Else Equal

By *ceteris paribus* we mean other things being equal or all other relevant factors, elements, or influences are held constant. When economists define your demand for a product, they want to know how much or how many units you will buy at different prices. For example, to determine how many DVDs you will buy at various prices (your demand for DVDs), we hold your income and the price of movie tickets constant. If your income suddenly jumped, you would be willing to buy more DVDs at all prices, but this is a whole new demand curve. *Ceteris paribus* assumptions are a way to simplify analysis; then the analysis can be extended to include those factors held constant, as we will see next.

Simple Linear Equations

Simple linear equations can be expressed as: $Y = a + bX$. This is read as, Y equals a plus b times X, where Y is the variable plotted on the y axis and a is a constant (unchanging), and b is a different constant that is multiplied by X, the value on the x axis. The formula for our studying and GPA example introduced in Figure 6 is shown in Figure APX-10.

The constant a is known as the vertical intercept because it is the value of your GPA when study hours (X) is zero, and therefore when it cuts (intercepts) the vertical axis and is equal to 1.0 (D average). Now each time you study another hour on average, your GPA rises by 0.1, so the constant b (the slope of the line) is equal to 0.1. Letting H represent hours of studying, the final equation is: GPA = 1.0 +

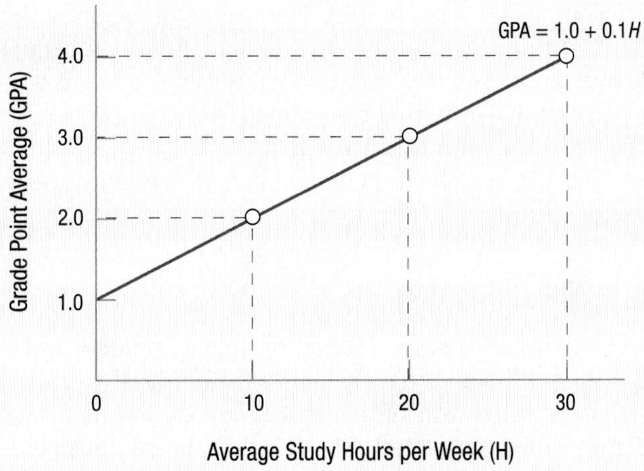

FIGURE APX-10

Studying and Your GPA: A Simple Equation

The formula for a linear relationship is $Y = a + bX$, where Y is the y axis variable, X is the x axis variable, and a and b are constants. For the original relationship between study hours and GPA, this equation is $Y = 1.0 + 0.1X$.

$0.1H$. You start with a D average without studying and as your hours of studying increase, your GPA goes up by 0.1 times the hours of studying. If we plug in 20 hours of studying into the equation, the answer is a GPA of 3.0 ($1.0 + (0.1 \times 20) = 1.0 + 2.0 = 3.0$).

Shifting Curves

Now let's introduce a couple of factors we have been holding constant (the *ceteris paribus* assumption). These two elements are tutoring and partying. So, our new equation now becomes GPA $= 1.0 + 0.1H + Z$, where Z is our variable indicating whether you have a tutor or whether you are excessively partying. When you have a tutor, $Z = 1$, and when you party too much, $Z = -1$. Tutoring adds to the productivity of your studying (hence $Z = 1$), while excessive late night partying reduces the effectiveness of studying; you are always tired (hence $Z = -1$). Figure APX-11 shows the impact of adding these factors to the original relationship.

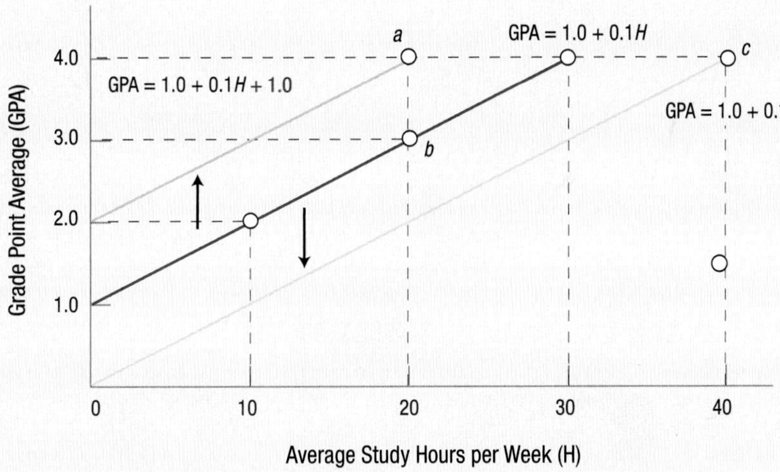

FIGURE APX-11

The Impact of Tutoring and Partying on Your GPA

The effect of tutoring and partying on our simple model of studying and GPA is shown. Partying harms your academic efforts and shifts the relationship to the right, making it harder to maintain your previous average (you now have to study more hours). Tutoring, on the other hand, improves the relationship (shifts the curve to the left).

With tutoring, your GPA-studying curve has moved upward and to the left. Now, because $Z = 1$, you begin with a C average (2.0), and with just 20 hours of studying (because of tutoring) you can reach a 4.0 GPA (point a). Alternatively, when you don't have tutoring and you party every night, your GPA-studying relationship has worsened (shifted downward and to the right). Now you must study 40 hours (point *c*) to accomplish a 4-point GPA. Note that you begin with failing grades.

The important point here is that we can simplify relationships between different variables and use a simple graph or equation to represent a model of behavior. In doing so, we often have to hold some things constant. When we allow those factors to change, the original relationship is now changed and often results in a shift in the curves. You will see this technique applied over and over as you study economics this semester.

Correlation Is Not Causation

Just because two variables seem related or appear related on a scatter plot does not mean that one causes another. Economists a hundred years ago correlated business cycles (the ups and downs of the entire economy) with sunspots. Because they appeared related, some suggested that sunspots caused business cycles. The only rational argument was that agriculture was the dominant industry and sunspots affected the weather; therefore, sunspots caused the economy to fluctuate.

Another example of erroneously assuming that correlation implies causality is the old Wall Street saw that related changes in the Dow Jones average to women's hem lines. Because two variables appear to be related does not mean that one causes the other to change.

Understanding graphs and using simple equations is a key part of learning economics. Practice helps.

2

Production, Economic Growth, and Trade

We live in a consumer world. Everywhere you look, people are purchasing and consuming things. Everything from plastic wrap to baseballs, from artichokes to cellular phones, gets produced, traded, and consumed. Whether an economy is a capitalistic market economy as in the United States, a capitalist marketplace with a strong touch of socialism as in many European countries, or a predominately communist economy as is true of many of China's markets, goods and services must change hands. Several centuries ago, individuals produced most of what they consumed. Today, most of us produce little of what we consume. Instead, we work at specialized jobs, then use our wages to purchase the goods we need. And purchase we do.

Though newspapers frequently report consumption excesses—and these excesses occur in rich *and* poor countries around the globe—we should not let these excesses obscure the fact that consumption is a great driver of economic growth. In many respects, consumption is simply a way for people to better themselves, to make their lives less of a drudgery, or to enrich their lives. Farmers in poor countries move from a precarious existence as subsistence farmers to producers of cash crops—keeping enough to live on but generating a surplus to sell—to obtain those consumption goods that better their lives.

Another great driver of economic growth is technological change. In 1950, only a small minority of households had television sets. Today, nearly every home has at least one color television set, and the average home has nearly three! In response to the resulting change in demand for programming, channels have multiplied; programming choices are almost limitless. But what brought about these changes in the first place? Technological advances from 1950 through the present day have led to cheaper, higher-performance television sets. This has allowed more families to afford not just one TV but also flat-screen HDTVs with huge screens and theater quality surround sound that are a fraction of the weight and size of older sets. New devices permit viewers to record and watch programs at their leisure.

Technological advances have similarly led to a telecommunications industry that simply was not dreamed of 50 years ago. In 1950, long distance phone calls were placed with the assistance of live operators, every minute costing the average consumer several hours' worth of pay. Today, fiber-optic cables allow thousands of calls to be made on one cable, thus drastically reducing the cost of telephone service. Cell phones, meanwhile, have become business necessities because of their convenience and productivity. The globe is shrinking as communications bring us closer together.

Another factor reducing the size of the world is airline travel. Fifty years ago, few people flew cross-country or overseas. Jets were nonexistent, tickets were expensive—the equivalent of a month's wages to fly coast to coast—and flights took forever. Today, because of technological change, jet aircraft can whisk us across the country or overseas at a price well within the budgets of most Americans.

A further driver of economic growth—trade—is less obvious. Yet its effect is clear. Nearly every country engages in commercial trade with other countries to expand the opportunities for consumption and production by its people. As products are consumed, new products must be produced, so increased consumption in one country can spur economic growth in another. Given the ability of global trade to open economic doors and raise incomes, it is vital for growth in developing nations.

In the previous chapter, we noted that a reduction in America's growth rate of only *1 percentage point* each year since 1930 would have significant consequences today. Figure 1 shows real (adjusted for inflation) gross domestic product (GDP) since 1930 and real GDP if the rate of growth was just 1 percentage point less. As the graph shows, real GDP would be roughly half today. One important point to get from the graph is that the 1 percentage point reduction had minimal impact for the first 20 years or so, but the impact widened as time marched forward. Policies that affect economic growth today will have their biggest impact several generations later.

This chapter will give you a framework for understanding economic growth. It provides a simple model for thinking about production, then applies this model to economies at large so you will know how to think about economic growth and its determinants. It then goes on to analyze international trade as a special case of economic growth. By the time you finish this chapter, you should understand the impor-

FIGURE 1

Real GDP Growth

This figure shows the impact of reducing the annual growth rate of real GDP by *1 percentage point.* Thus if the growth rate between 1953 and 1954 was 7%, we assume in the lower curve that the growth rate was actually 6%. As the figure illustrates, the impact of the reduction in growth had only a minor impact early on, but became more important over time.

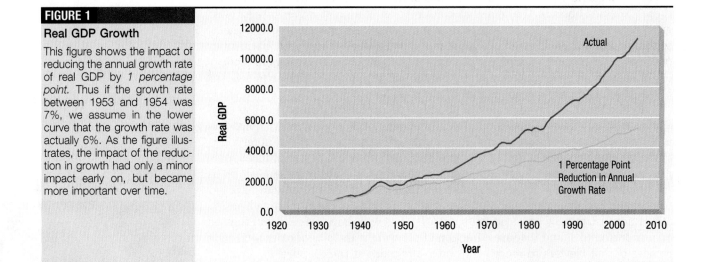

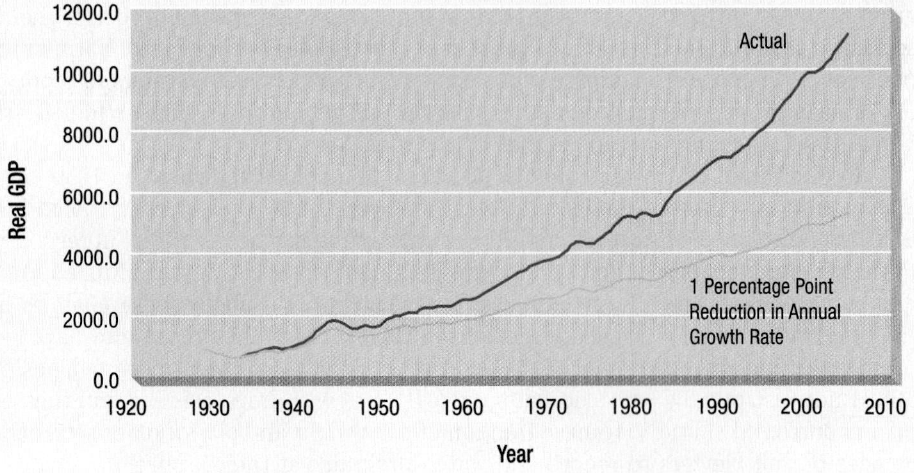

tance of economic growth and what drives it. To start, we turn to an examination of the three basic questions that every economy, no matter how it is organized, must solve.

After studying this chapter you should be able to

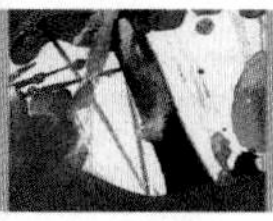

- Describe the three basic questions that must be answered for any economy.
- Describe production and the factors that go into producing various goods and services.
- Describe the opportunity cost an economy incurs to increase the production of one product.
- Use a production possibilities frontier (PPF) or curve to analyze the limits of production.
- Describe economic growth and the impacts of expanding resources through increasing human resources, capital accumulation, and technological improvements.
- Describe the concepts of absolute and comparative advantage and explain what they tell us about the gains from trade when countries specialize in certain products.
- Describe the practical constraints on free trade and how some industries might be affected.

Basic Economic Questions and Production

Regardless of the country, its circumstances, or its precise economic structure, every economy must answer three basic questions.

Basic Economic Questions

The three basic economic questions that each society must answer are:

- What goods and services are to be produced?
- How are these goods and services to be produced?
- Who will receive these goods and services?

The response an economy makes to the first question—What to produce?—depends on the goods and services a society wants. In a communist state, the government will decide what a society wants, but in a capitalist economy, consumers are allowed to signal what products they want by way of their demands for specific commodities. In the next chapter, we will investigate how the consumer demand for individual products is determined and how markets meet these demands. For now, we will assume that consumers, individually and as a society, are able to decide on the mix of goods and services they most want, and that producers supply these items at acceptable prices.

Once we know what goods a society wants, the next question its economic system must answer is how these goods and services are to be produced. In the end, this problem comes down to the simple question of how labor, capital, and land should be combined to produce the desired products. If a society demands a huge amount of corn, say, we can expect its utilization of land, labor, and

Friedrich von Hayek

Gunnar Myrdal

Nobel Prize Friedrich von Hayek and Gunnar Myrdal

All societies have to answer the three basic economic questions. The 1974 Nobel Prize winners Friedrich von Hayek and Gunnar Myrdal proposed very different answers.

Friedrich von Hayek was the foremost advocate of free markets and classical economics during the heyday of the Keynesian revolution. Born in 1899, von Hayek was the son of a botanist. After serving in World War I, he studied law and political science at the University of Vienna, later joining a group of young academics in a private seminar conducted by the eminent economist Ludwig von Mises. From 1932 until his death in 1992, von Hayek taught at several schools including the London School of Economics and the University of Chicago.

Von Hayek's early work was primarily concerned with business cycles. Von Hayek argued that economic booms could lead to financial conditions in which investment exceeded savings, resulting in a mismatch between consumption and output and, consequently, an economic contraction while a balance between the two was being achieved. Von Hayek viewed this "concertina effect" as the primary explanation for business cycles. He was one of the few economists of his era to predict the Great Depression.

After the mid-1930s, von Hayek focused on critiques of socialism and centralist economic planning. His impassioned defense of libertarian economics in the *Road to Serfdom* is, if anything, more widely read today than it was in 1940, the year of publication. Von Hayek attributed failures in socialism to an inefficient use of knowledge and information. Central planners, in his view, were no match for the pricing mechanism as a means of communicating information. The pricing system evolved spontaneously from the interplay of individuals with limited and particular information. A decentralized system with competition and price freedom, therefore, was the most efficient and socially beneficial way to organize an economy. He also saw markets as advancing human liberty and freedom.

In contrast to von Hayek, Swedish economist and sociologist Gunnar Myrdal argued for a different way to organize an economy. He advocated a more active role for government. Myrdal established his reputation with the 1944 publication of his book on race relations in the United States, *An American Dilemma.* Considered a classic of social scientific literature, the work has been compared to Alexis de Tocqueville's *Democracy in America.* Myrdal's criticisms of the doctrine of "separate but equal" had a major influence on the 1954 Supreme Court ruling in *Brown v. Board of Education,* which outlawed segregation in public schools.

Born in Sweden in 1898, Myrdal received his degree in law and economics in 1927 from Stockholm University. He later served in the Swedish senate and as Minister of Commerce after World War II. In 1957, he undertook a comprehensive study of economic trends and policies in Asia for the Twentieth Century Fund, which led to the book, *Asian Drama: An Inquiry into the Poverty of Nations and the Challenge of World Poverty,* where he advocated a major role for government in directing economies. Myrdal died in 1987.

capital will be different from a society that demands digital equipment. But even an economy devoted to corn production could be organized in different ways, perhaps relying on extensive use of human labor, or perhaps relying on automated capital equipment.

Once an economy has determined what goods and services to produce and how to produce them, it is faced with the distribution question: Who will get the resulting products? *Distribution* refers to the way an economy allocates the goods and services it produces to consumers. In a capitalist economy, most products are distributed through private markets. In a socialist economy, many goods are produced in state-owned facilities. Theoretically, governments in socialist economies use tax monies to subsidize producers, while governments in capitalist economies leave producers free to survive or perish based on their efficiency and the quality of their products.

Resources, Production, and Efficiency

Having answered the three basic economic questions, let's take a look at the production process. **Production** involves turning **resources** into products and services that people want. Let's begin our discussion of this process by examining the scarce resources used to produce goods and services.

Land

For economists, the term **land** includes both land in the usual sense, but it also includes all other natural resources that are used in production. Natural resources like mineral deposits, oil and natural gas, and water are all included by economists in the definition of land. Economists refer to the payment to land as *rents.*

Labor

Labor as a factor of production includes both the mental and physical talents of people. Few goods and services can be produced without labor resources. Improvement to labor capabilities from training, education, and apprenticeship programs, typically called human capital, all add to labor's productivity and ultimately to a higher standard of living. Labor is paid *wages.*

Capital

Capital includes all manufactured products that are used to produce other goods and services. This includes equipment such as drill presses, blast furnaces for making steel, and other tools used in the production process. It also includes trucks and automobiles used by business as well as office equipment such as copiers, computers, and telephones. Any manufactured product that is used to produce other products is included in the category of capital. Capital earns *interest.*

Production
The process of converting resources (factors of production)—land, labor, capital, and entrepreneurial ability—into goods and services.

Resources
Productive resources include land (land and natural resources), labor (mental and physical talents of people), capital (manufactured products used to produce other products), and entrepreneurial ability (the combining of the other factors to produce products and assume the risk of the business).

Land
Includes natural resources such as mineral deposits, oil, natural gas, water, and land in the usual sense of the word. The payment to land as a resource is called rents.

Labor
Includes the mental and physical talents of individuals that are used to produce products and services. Labor is paid wages.

Capital
Includes manufactured products such as welding machines, computers and cellular phones that are used to produce other goods and services. The payment to capital is referred to as interest.

Note that the term *capital* as used by economists refers to real capital—actual manufactured products used in the production process—not money or financial capital. Money and financial capital are important in that they are used to purchase the real capital that is used to produce products.

Entrepreneurial Ability

Entrepreneurs
Entrepreneurs combine land, labor, and capital to produce goods and services. They absorb the risk of being in business, including the risk of bankruptcy and other liabilities associated with doing business. Entrepreneurs receive profits for this effort.

Entrepreneurs *combine* land, labor, and capital to produce goods and services, and they assume the *risks* associated with running the business. Entrepreneurs combine and manage the inputs of production, and manage the day-to-day marketing, finance, and production decisions. Today, the risks of running a business are huge, as the many bankruptcies and failures testify to; and globalization has opened many opportunities as well as risks. For undertaking these activities and assuming the risks associated with business, entrepreneurs earn *profits.*

Production and Efficiency

Production turns *resources*—land, labor, capital, and entrepreneurial ability—into products and services. The necessary production factors will vary for different products. To produce corn, for instance, one needs arable land, seed, fertilizer, water, farm equipment, and the workers to operate that equipment. Farmers looking to produce corn would need to devote hundreds of acres of open land to this crop, plow the land, plant and nurture the corn, and finally harvest the crop. Producing digital equipment, in contrast, requires less land but more capital and highly skilled labor.

As we have seen, every country has to decide what to produce, how to produce it, and decide who receives the output. Countries desire to do the first two as efficiently as possible, but this leads to two different aspects of efficiency.

Production efficiency
Goods and services are produced at their lowest resource (opportunity) cost.

Production efficiency occurs when the mix of goods society decides to produce is produced at the lowest possible resource or opportunity cost. Alternatively, production efficiency occurs when as much output as possible is produced with a given amount of resources. Firms use the best technology available and combine the other resources to produce products at the lowest cost to society.

Allocative efficiency
The mix of goods and services produced are just what individuals in society desire.

Allocative efficiency occurs when the mix of goods and services produced are the most desired by society. In capitalist countries this is determined by consumers and businesses and their interaction through markets. The next chapter explores this interaction in some detail. Needless to say, it would be inefficient (a waste of resources) to be producing 45 rpm records in the age of the iPod, XM radio, and other digital music players. Allocative efficiency requires that the right mix of goods be produced at the lowest cost.

Every economy faces constraints or limitations. Land, labor, capital, and entrepreneurship are all limited. No country has an infinite supply of available workers or the space and machinery that would be needed to put them all to work efficiently; no country can break free of these natural restraints. Such limits are known as production possibilities frontiers (PPFs), and they are the focus of the next section.

Checkpoint

Basic Economic Questions and Production

REVIEW

- Every economy must decide what to produce, how to produce it, and who will get what is produced.

- Production is the process of converting factors of production (resources)—land, labor, capital, and entrepreneurial ability—into goods and services.
- Land includes land and natural resources. Labor includes the mental and physical resources of humans. Capital includes all manufactured products used to produce other goods and services. Entrepreneurs combine resources to produce products, and they assume the risk of doing business.
- Production efficiency requires that products be produced at the lowest cost. Allocative efficiency occurs when the mix of goods and services produced is just what society wants.

QUESTION

The one element that really seems to differentiate entrepreneurship from the other resources is the fact that entrepreneurs shoulder the *risk* of failure of the enterprise. Does this seem right? Explain.

Answers to the Checkpoint question can be found at the end of this chapter.

Production Possibilities and Economic Growth

As we discovered in the previous section, all countries, and all economies, face constraints on their production capabilities. Production can be limited by the quantity of the various factors of production in the country and its current technology. Technology includes such considerations as the country's infrastructure, its transportation and education systems, and the economic freedom it allows. Though perhaps going beyond the everyday meaning of the word *technology,* for simplicity, we will assume all of these factors help determine the state of a country's technology.

To further simplify matters, production possibilities analysis assumes that the quantity of resources available and the technology of the economy remain constant. Moreover, all economic agents—workers and managers—are assumed to be technically efficient, meaning that no waste will occur in production. Finally, we will examine an economy that produces only two products. While keeping our analysis simple, altering these assumptions will not fundamentally change our general conclusions.

Production Possibilities

Assume our sample economy produces leather jackets and microcomputers. Figure 2 with its accompanying table on the next page shows the production possibilities frontier for this economy. The table shows seven possible production levels (*a–g*). These seven possibilities, which range from 12,000 leather jackets and zero microcomputers to zero jackets and 6,000 microcomputers, are graphed in Figure 2.

When we connect the seven production possibilities, we delineate the **production possibilities frontier (PPF)** for this economy (some economists refer to this curve as the production possibilities curve). All points on the PPF curve are considered *attainable* by our economy. Everything to the left of the PPF curve is also attainable, but is an inefficient use of resources—the economy can always do better. Everything to the right of the curve is considered *unattainable.* Therefore, the PPF maps out the economy's limits; it is impossible for the economy to produce at levels beyond the PPF. What the PPF in Figure 2 shows is that, given an efficient use of limited resources and taking technology into account, this economy can produce any of the seven combinations of microcomputers and leather jackets listed. Also, the economy can produce any combination of the two products on or within the PPF, but not any combinations beyond it.

Production possibilities frontier (PPF)
Shows the combinations of two goods that are possible for a society to produce at full employment. Points on or inside the PPF are feasible, and those outside of the frontier are unattainable.

FIGURE 2

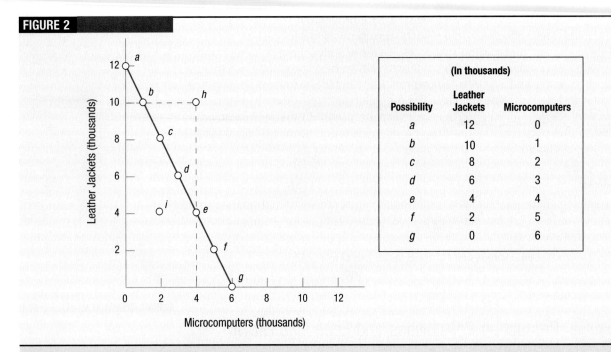

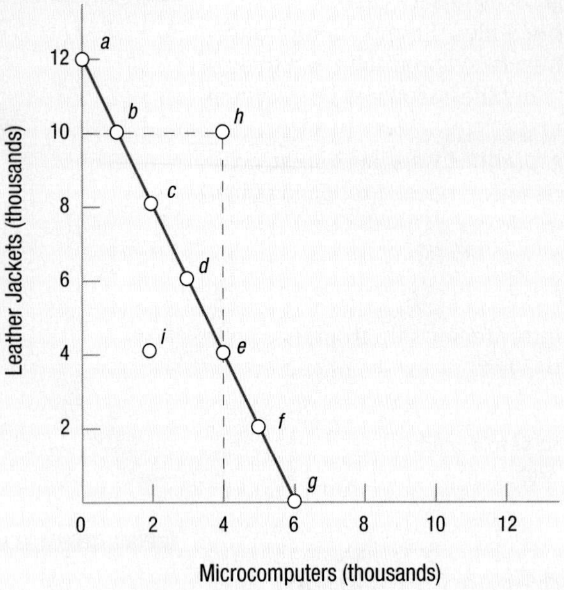

(In thousands)

Possibility	Leather Jackets	Microcomputers
a	12	0
b	10	1
c	8	2
d	6	3
e	4	4
f	2	5
g	0	6

Production Possibilities Frontier

Using all of its resources, this stylized economy can produce many different mixes of leather jackets and microcomputers. Production levels on, or to the left of, the resulting PPF are attainable for this economy. Production levels to the right of the PPF curve are unattainable.

Full Employment

As Figure 2 further suggests, all of the points along the PPF represent points of maximum output for our economy, that is, points at which all resources are being fully used. Therefore, if the society wants to produce 1,000 microcomputers, it will only be able to produce 10,000 leather jackets, as shown by point *b* on the PPF curve. Should the society decide Internet access is important, it might decide to produce 4,000 microcomputers, which would force it to cut leather jacket production down to 4,000, shown by point *e*.

Contrast points *c* and *e* with production at point *i*. At point *i* the economy is only producing 2,000 microcomputers and 4,000 jackets. Clearly some resources are not being used—unemployment exists. When fully employed, the economy's resources could produce more of both goods (point *d*).

Because the PPF represents a maximum output, the economy could not produce 4,000 microcomputers and still produce 10,000 leather jackets. This situation, shown by point *h*, lies to the right of the PPF and hence outside the realm of possibility. Anything to the right of the PPF is impossible for our economy to attain; all points along the curve represent full employment.

Opportunity Cost

Opportunity cost
The cost paid for one product in terms of the output (or consumption) of another product that must be foregone.

Whenever a country reallocates resources to change production patterns, it does so at a price. This price is called **opportunity cost**. Opportunity cost is the price an economy or an individual must pay, measured in units of one product, to increase its production (or consumption) of another product. In moving from point *b* to point *e* in Figure 2, microcomputer production increases by 3,000 units, from 1,000 units to 4,000 units. In contrast, our country must forego producing 6,000 leather jackets because production falls from 10,000 jackets to 4,000 jackets. Giving up 6,000 jackets for 3,000 more computers represents an opportunity cost of 6,000 jackets, or of two jackets for each microcomputer.

Opportunity cost thus represents the tradeoff required when an economy wants to increase its production of any single product. Governments must choose between guns and butter, or between military spending and social spending. Since there are limits to what taxpayers are willing to pay, spending choices are necessary. Think of opportunity costs as what you or the economy must give up to have more of a product or service.

Every day, everyone faces tradeoffs based on opportunity cost. A day has only 24 hours: You must decide how much time to spend eating, watching movies, going to class, sleeping, playing golf, partying, or studying—more time partying means less time for study. And if you set aside a certain amount of time for studying, more time studying biology means less time studying history. But time is not the only constraint we face. Money restricts our choices as well. Should you buy a new computer, move to a nicer apartment, or save up for next semester's tuition? Indeed, virtually every choice in life involves tradeoffs or opportunity costs.

Increasing Opportunity Costs

In most cases, land, labor, and capital cannot easily be shifted from producing one good or service to another. You cannot take a semitruck and use it to plow a farm field, even though the semi and a top-notch tractor cost about the same money. The fact is that some resources are suited to specific sorts of production, just as some people seem to be better suited to performing one activity over another. Some people have a talent for music or art, and they would be miserable—and inefficient—working as accountants or computer programmers. Some people find they are more comfortable working outside, while others require the amenities of an environmentally controlled, ergonomically correct office.

Thus, a more realistic production possibilities frontier is shown in Figure 3. This PPF curve is bowed out from the origin, since opportunity costs rise as more factors are used to produce increasing quantities of one product. Let us consider why this is so.

Let's begin at a point where the economy's resources are strictly devoted to leather jacket production (point *a*). Now assume that society decides to produce

FIGURE 3

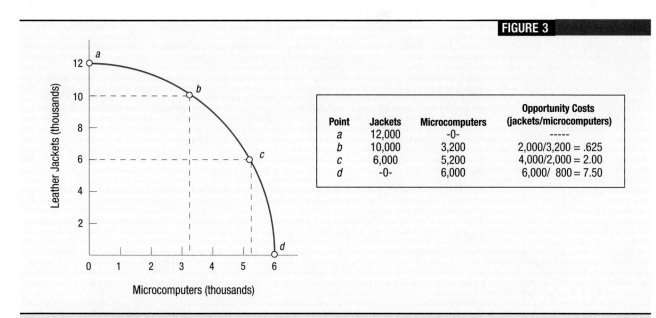

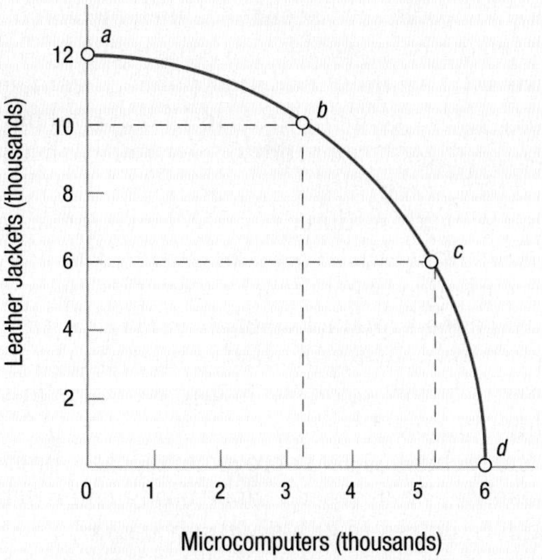

Point	Jackets	Microcomputers	Opportunity Costs (jackets/microcomputers)
a	12,000	-0-	-----
b	10,000	3,200	2,000/3,200 = .625
c	6,000	5,200	4,000/2,000 = 2.00
d	-0-	6,000	6,000/ 800 = 7.50

Production Possibilities Frontier (increasing opportunity costs)

This figure shows a more realistic production possibilities frontier for an economy. This PPF curve is bowed out from the origin since opportunity costs rise as more factors are used to produce increasing quantities of one product or the other.

3,200 microcomputers. This will require a move from point *a* to point *b*. As we can see, 2,000 leather jackets must be given up to get the added 3,200 microcomputers. This means the opportunity cost of 1 microcomputer will be 0.625 leather jackets (2,000 ÷ 3,200 = 0.625). This is a low opportunity cost, because those resources that are better suited to producing microcomputers will be the first ones shifted into this industry, resulting in rapidly increasing returns from specialization.

But what happens when this society decides to produce an additional 2,000 computers, or moves from point *b* to point *c* on the graph? As Figure 3 illustrates, each additional computer costs 2 leather jackets since producing 2,000 more computers requires the society to sacrifice 4,000 leather jackets. Thus, the opportunity cost of computers has more than tripled due to diminishing returns on the computer side, which arise from the unsuitability of these new resources as more resources are shifted to microcomputers.

To describe what has happened in plain terms, when the economy was producing 12,000 leather jackets, all its resources went into jacket production. Those members of the labor force who are engineers and electronic assemblers were probably not well suited to producing jackets. As the economy backed off jackets to start producing microcomputers, the opportunity cost of computers was low, since the resources first shifted, including workers, were likely to be the ones most suited to computer production and least suited to jacket manufacture. Eventually, however, as computers became the dominant product, manufacturing more computers required shifting leather workers to the computer industry. Employing these less suitable resources drives up the opportunity costs of computers.

You may be wondering which point along the PPF is the best for society. Economists have no grounds for stating unequivocally which mixture of goods and services would be ideal. The perfect mixture of goods depends on the tastes and preferences of the members of society. In a capitalist economy, resource allocation is determined largely by individual choices and the workings of private markets. We will consider these markets and their operations in the next chapter.

Economic Growth

We have seen that PPFs map out the maximum that an economy can produce: Points to the right of the PPF curve are unattainable. But what if that PPF curve can be shifted to the right? This shift would give economies new maximum frontiers. In fact, we will see that economic growth can be viewed as a shift in the PPF curve outward. In this section, we will use the production possibilities model to determine some of the major reasons for economic growth. Understanding these reasons for growth will enable us to suggest some broad economic policies that could lead to expanded growth.

The production possibilities model holds resources and technology constant to derive the PPF. These assumptions suggest that economic growth has two basic determinants: expanding resources and improving technologies. The expansion of resources allows producers to increase their production of all goods and services in an economy. Specific technological improvements, however, often affect only one industry directly. The development of a new color printing process, for instance, will directly affect only the printing industry.

Nevertheless, the ripples from technological improvements can spread out through an entire economy, just like ripples in a pond. Specifically, improvements in technology can lead to new products, improved goods and services, and increased productivity.

Sometimes, technological improvements in one industry allow other industries to increase their production with existing resources. This means producers can produce more output without using added labor or other resources. Alternately, they can get the same production levels as before while using fewer resources than before. This frees up resources in the economy for use in other industries.

When the electric lightbulb was invented, it not only created a new industry (someone had to produce lightbulbs), but it also revolutionized other industries. Factories could stay open longer since they no longer had to rely on the sun for light. Workers could see better, thus improving the quality of their work. The result was that resources operated more efficiently throughout the entire economy.

The modern day equivalent to the lightbulb might be the cellular phone. Widespread use of these devices enables people all across the world to produce goods and services more efficiently. Insurance agents can file claims instantly from disaster sites, deals can be closed while one is stuck in traffic, and communications have been revolutionized. Thus, this new technology has ultimately expanded time, the most finite of our resources. A similar argument could be made for the Internet. It has profoundly changed how many products are bought, sold, and delivered, and has expanded communications and the flow of information.

Expanding Resources

The PPF represents the constraints on an economy at a specific time. But economies are constantly changing, and so are PPFs. Capital and labor are the principal resources that can be changed through government action. Land and entrepreneurial talent are important factors of production, but neither is easy to change by government policies. The government can make owning a business easier or more profitable by reducing regulations, or by offering low-interest loans or favorable tax treatment to small businesses. However, it is difficult to turn people into risk takers through government policy.

Increasing Labor and Human Capital. A clear increase in population, the number of households, or the size of the labor force will shift the PPF outward, as shown in Figure 4. With added labor, the production possibilities available to the economy expand from PPF_0 to PPF_1. Such a labor increase can be caused by higher birthrates, increased immigration, or an increased willingness of people to enter the labor force. This last type of increase has occurred over the past several decades as more women have entered the labor force on a permanent basis. America's high immigration (legal and illegal) fuels our strong rate of economic growth.

Rather than simply increasing the number of people working, however, the labor factor can also be increased by improving workers' skills. Economists refer to this as *investment in human capital.* Activities such as education, on-the-job training, and other professional training fit into this category. Improving human capital

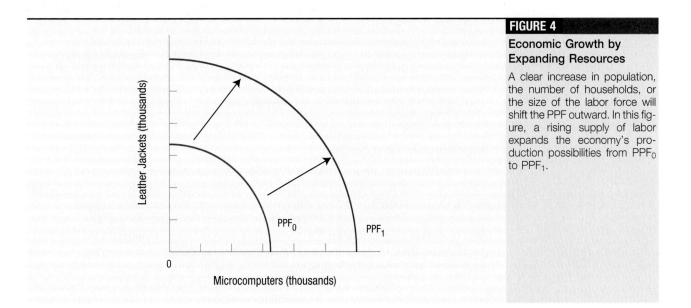

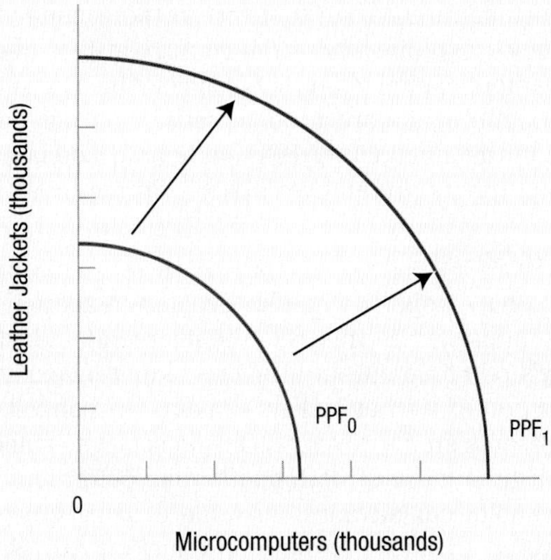

FIGURE 4

Economic Growth by Expanding Resources

A clear increase in population, the number of households, or the size of the labor force will shift the PPF outward. In this figure, a rising supply of labor expands the economy's production possibilities from PPF_0 to PPF_1.

FIGURE 5

Consumption and Capital Goods and the Expansion of the Production Possibilities Frontier

If a nation selects a product mix where the bulk of goods produced are consumption goods, it will initially produce at point *b*. The small investment made in capital goods has the effect of expanding the nation's productive capacity only to PPF_b over the following decade. If the country decides to produce at point *a*, however, devoting more resources to producing capital, its productive capacity will expand much more rapidly, pushing the PPF curve out to PPF_a over the following decade.

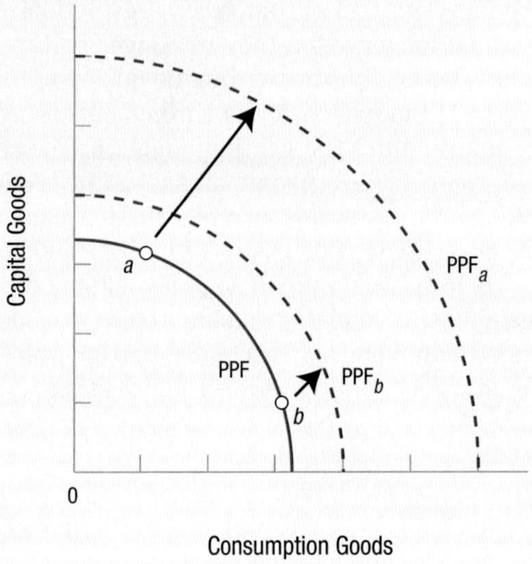

means people are more productive, resulting in higher wages, a higher standard of living, and an expanded PPF for society.

Capital Accumulation. Increasing the capital used throughout the economy, usually brought about by investment, would similarly shift the PPF outward, as shown in Figure 4. Additional capital makes each unit of labor more productive and thus results in higher possible production throughout the economy. Adding robotics and computer-controlled machines to production lines, for instance, means each unit of labor produces many more units of output.

The production possibilities model and the economic growth associated with capital accumulation suggest a tradeoff. Figure 5 illustrates the tradeoff all nations face between current consumption and capital accumulation.

Let's first assume a nation selects a product mix where the bulk of goods produced are consumption goods, that is, goods that are immediately consumable and have short life spans, such as food and entertainment. This product mix is represented by point *b* in Figure 5. Consuming most of what it produces, a decade later the economy will face PPF_b. Little growth has occurred, since the economy has done little to improve its productive capacity—the present generation has essentially decided to consume rather than to invest in the economy's future.

Contrast this decision to one where the country at first decides to produce at point *a*. In this case, more capital goods such as machinery and tools are produced, while fewer consumption goods are used to satisfy current needs. Selecting this product mix results in the much larger PPF curve a decade later (PPF_a), since the economy steadily built up its productive capacity during those 10 years.

Technological Change

Figure 6 illustrates what happens when an economy experiences a technological change in one of its industries, in this case the microchip industry. As the diagram shows, the economy's potential output of microcomputers expands greatly, though its maximum production of leather jackets remains unchanged. The area between the two curves represents an improvement in the society's standard of living. People produce and consume more of both goods than before: more microcomputers because of the technological advance, and more jackets because some of the resources once devoted to microcomputer production can be shifted to leather jacket production, even as the economy is turning out more computers than before.

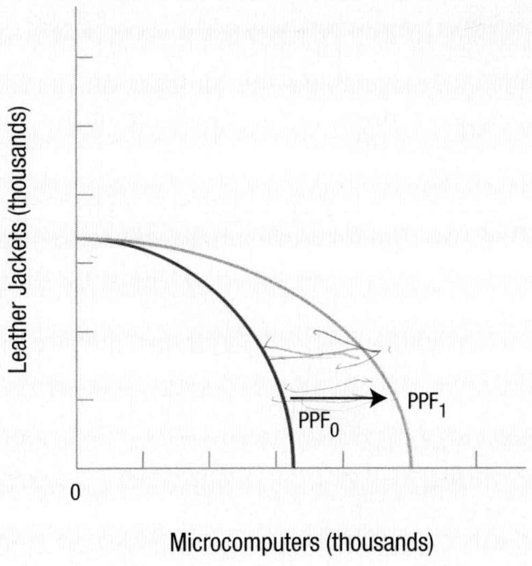

FIGURE 6

Technological Change and Expansion of the Production Possibilities Frontier

In this figure, an economy's potential output of microcomputers has expanded greatly, while its maximum production of leather jackets has remained unchanged. The area between the two curves represents an improvement in the society's standard of living, since more of both goods can be produced and consumed than before. Some of the resources once used for microcomputer production are diverted to leather jackets, even as the number of microcomputers increases.

This example reflects the United States today, where the computer industry is exploding with new technologies. Intel Corporation, the leading microprocessor manufacturer in the world, leads the way. Intel relentlessly develops newer, faster, and more powerful chips, setting a target time of 18 months for the development, testing, and release of each new generation of microprocessors. Consequently, consumers have seen home computers go from clunky conversation pieces to powerful, fast, indispensable machines. Today's microcomputers are more powerful than the mainframe supercomputers of just a few decades ago! The latest developments include PDAs and cell phones that surf the Web and download and play music, videos, and current TV programs.

Besides new products, technology has dramatically reduced the cost of microprocessor production. These cost reductions have permitted the United States to produce and consume more of other products as our consumption of high-tech items has soared. Our whole PPF has expanded outward.

But technological improvements result not only in smaller and cheaper microchips. An economy's technology also depends on how well its important trade centers are linked together. If a country has mostly dirt paths rather than paved highways, you can imagine how this deficiency will affect its economy: Distribution will be slow, and industries will be slow to react to changes in demand. In such a case, improving the roads might be the best way to stimulate economic growth.

As you can see, there are many ways to stimulate economic growth. A society can expand its output by using more resources, perhaps encouraging more people to enter the workforce or raising educational levels of workers. The government can encourage people to invest more, as opposed to devoting their earnings to immediate consumption. The public sector can spur technological advances by providing incentives to private firms to do research and development or underwrite research investments of its own.

Adrian Hillman

Estimating the Sources of Economic Growth

But just how important are each of these factors? A recent study by the Organisation for Economic Co-operation and Development (OECD)[1] focused on what has been driving economic growth in 21 nations over the last several decades. The study

[1] *The Sources of Economic Growth in the OECD Countries* (Paris: Organisation for Economic Co-operation and Development), 2003.

first looked at contribution to economic growth from the macroeconomic perspective of added resources and technological improvements as we have been discussing in this chapter. It then looked at some benefits from good government policies that stimulate growth and finally examined the industry and individual firm level for clues to the microeconomic sources of growth. Some of the findings include:

- A 1 percentage point increase in business investment as a percent of gross domestic product (GDP) leads to an increase in per capita GDP of 1.3%.
- An additional 1-year increase in average education levels increases per capita GDP by 4 to 7%.
- A 0.1 percentage point increase in research and development as a percent of GDP increases per capita GDP by 1.2%.
- Reducing both the level and variability of inflation by 1 percentage point leads to an increase in per capita GDP of 2.3%.
- A 1 percentage point decrease in the tax burden as a percent of GDP leads to a 0.3% increase in per capita GDP.
- An increase in trade exposure (a combined measure of imports and exports as a percent of GDP) of 10 percentage points increases per capita GDP by 4%.

In less numerical terms, greater investment by business (physical capital), higher levels of education (human capital), high levels of research and development, lower inflation rates, reduced tax burdens, and greater levels of international trade all result in higher standards of living (per capita GDP). One important point to take away from this discussion is that our simple stylized model of the economy using only two goods gives you a good first framework upon which to judge proposed policies for the economy. While not overly complex, this simple analysis is still quite powerful. Trying to discover why some countries grow and others do not is a complex undertaking and has occupied economists for several centuries. But as this study illustrates, a country can achieve greater economic growth and raise its standard of living by expanding trade with other countries. This is the subject of the next section.

Checkpoint

Production Possibilities and Economic Growth

REVIEW

- A production possibilities frontier (PPF) depicts the different combinations of goods that a fully employed economy can produce, given its available resources and current technology (both assumed fixed in the short run).
- Production levels inside and on the frontier are possible, but production mixes outside the curve are unattainable.
- Because production on the frontier represents the maximum output attainable when all resources are fully employed, reallocating production from one product to another involves *opportunity costs:* The output of one product must be reduced to get the added output of the other. The more of one product that is desired, the higher its opportunity costs because of diminishing returns and the unsuitability of some resources for producing some products.
- The PPF model suggests that economic growth can arise from an expansion in resources or improvements in technology. Economic growth is a shift out of the PPF curve.
- Economic growth can be enhanced by increasing the quantity or quality of labor.

QUESTION

Having abundant resources such as oil or diamonds would seem to be a benefit to an economy, yet some people have considered it a curse. Why would plentiful resources like these be a curse?

Answers to the Checkpoint question can be found at the end of this chapter.

Specialization, Comparative Advantage, and Trade

As we have seen, economics is all about voluntary production and exchange. People and nations do business with one another because all expect to gain from the transactions. Centuries ago, European merchants ventured to the Far East to ply the lucrative spice trades. These days, American consumers buy wines from Italy, cars from Japan, electronics from Korea, and millions of other products from countries around the world.

Many people assume that trade between nations is a zero-sum game—a game in which, for one party to gain, another party must lose. This is how poker games work. If one player walks away from the table a winner, someone else must have lost money. But this is not how voluntary trade works. Voluntary trade is a positive-sum game: Both parties to a transaction score positive gains. After all, who would voluntarily enter into an exchange if he or she did not believe there was some gain from it? To understand how all parties to an exchange (whether individuals or nations) can gain from it, we need to consider the concepts of absolute and comparative advantage developed by David Ricardo roughly 200 years ago.

David Ricardo (1772–1823)

David Ricardo's rigorous, dispassionate evaluation of economic principles influenced generations of theorists, including such vastly different thinkers as John Stuart Mill and Karl Marx. The son of Dutch-Jewish immigrants, Ricardo was born in London in 1772. As a teenager, he joined his father's business on the London Stock Exchange, but after marrying and converting to Christianity, Ricardo broke with his family and started his own business. Within 5 years, he amassed a small fortune as a stockbroker and devoted his energies to politics and writing. As a member of the British Parliament, Ricardo was an advocate of sound monetary policies and an outspoken critic of the Corn Laws, which placed high tariffs on imported grain to protect British landowners. His political views would figure prominently in his economic writings. In 1817, Ricardo published the *Principles of Political Economy and Taxation,* in which he made two of his most important contributions to economics, "the iron law of wages" and the "labor theory of value."

Ricardo believed that increasing wages would only lead to population increases among workers and, eventually, to falling wages. He linked the value of exchange goods to the labor needed to produce them. Protectionism for domestic agriculture, he reasoned, would lead to higher rents for landowners, higher prices for food, and higher subsistence wages for workers, which in turn would depress the rates of profit for capitalists and discourage economic development. Despite a pessimistic streak, Ricardo was an optimist when it came to free trade. His theory of "comparative advantage" suggested that countries would mutually benefit from trade by specializing in export goods they could produce at a lower opportunity cost than another country. His classic example was trade between Britain and Portugal. If Britain specialized in producing cloth, and Portugal in exporting wine, each country would gain from a free exchange of goods. Ricardo died in 1823, leaving an enduring legacy of classical economic analysis.

Absolute and Comparative Advantage

Absolute advantage
One country can produce more of a good than another country.

Figure 7 shows hypothetical production possibilities curves for the United States and Mexico. Both countries are assumed to produce only crude oil and microcomputer chips. Given the PPFs in Figure 7, the United States has an **absolute advantage** over Mexico in producing both products. An absolute advantage exists when one country can produce more of a good than another country. In this instance, the United States can produce 4 times more oil (40 million vs. 10 million barrels) and 10 times as many microcomputer chips (40 million vs. 4 million microchips) as Mexico.

At first glance you might wonder why the United States would even consider trading with Mexico. The United States has so much more productive capacity than Mexico, so why wouldn't it just produce all of its own crude oil and microcomputers? The answer lies in comparative advantage.

Comparative advantage
One country has a lower opportunity cost of producing a good than another country.

One country has a **comparative advantage** in producing a good if its opportunity cost to produce that good is lower than the other country's. In Figure 7, Mexico has a comparative advantage over the United States in producing oil. For the United States to produce an additional million barrels of crude oil, the *opportunity cost* is one million microcomputer chips. Each barrel of oil therefore costs the American economy one computer chip.

Contrast this with the situation in Mexico. For every microchip Mexican producers forgo, they are able to produce an additional 2.5 barrels of oil. This means one barrel of oil costs the Mexican economy only 0.4 computer chip. Therefore, Mexico has a comparative advantage in the production of crude oil, since a barrel of oil costs Mexico only 0.4 microchip, but to produce the same barrel of oil costs one microchip in the United States.

Conversely, the United States has a comparative advantage over Mexico in producing computer chips: Producing a microchip in the United States costs one barrel of oil, whereas the same chip in Mexico costs 2.5 barrels of oil. These relative costs suggest that the United States should pour its resources into producing computer chips, while Mexico specializes in crude oil. The two countries can then engage in trade to their mutual benefit.

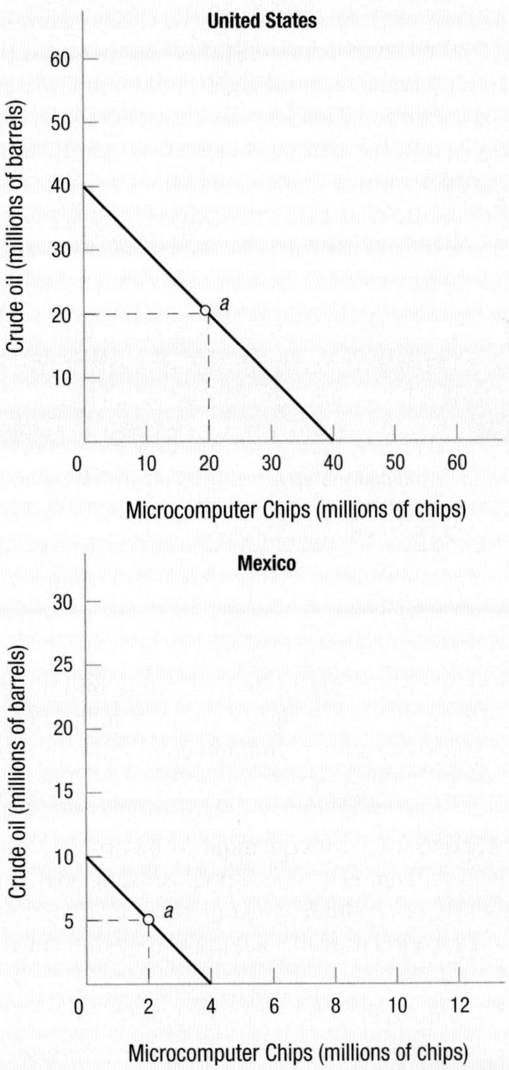

FIGURE 7

Production Possibilities for the United States and Mexico

One country has an absolute advantage if it can produce more of a good than the other country. In this case, the United States has an absolute advantage over Mexico in producing both microchips and crude oil—it can produce more of both goods than Mexico can. Even so, Mexico has a comparative advantage over the United States in producing oil, since it can increase its output of oil at a lower opportunity cost than can the United States. This comparative advantage leads to gains for both countries from specialization and trade.

The Gains from Trade

To see how specialization and trade can benefit both trading partners, even when one has the ability to produce more of both goods than the other, assume each country is at first (before trade) operating at point *a* in Figure 7. At this point, both countries are producing and consuming only their own output; the United States produces and consumes 20 million barrels of oil and 20 million computer chips; Mexico, 5 million barrels of oil and 2 million computer chips. Table 1 summarizes these initial conditions.

Table 1 **Initial Consumption-Production Pattern**

	United States	Mexico	Total
Oil	20	5	25
Chips	20	2	22

Now assume Mexico focuses on oil, producing the maximum it can: 10 million barrels. We will assume both countries want to continue consuming 25 million barrels of oil between them. So the United States only needs to produce 15 million barrels of oil since Mexico is now producing 10 million barrels. For the United States, this frees up some resources that can be diverted to producing computer chips. Since each barrel of oil in the United States costs one microchip, reducing oil output by 5 million barrels means that 5 million more microcomputer chips can be produced.

Table 2 shows each country's production after Mexico has begun specializing in oil production.

Table 2 Production after Mexico Specializes in Producing Crude Oil

	United States	Mexico	Total
Oil	15	10	25
Chips	25	0	25

Notice that the combined production of crude oil has remained constant, but the total output of computer chips has risen by 3 million chips. Assuming the two countries agree to share the added 3 million computer chips between them equally, Mexico will now ship 5 million barrels of oil to the United States in exchange for 3.5 million computer chips. From the 5 million additional computer chips the United States produces, Mexico will receive 2 million (its original production) plus 1.5 million for a total of 3.5 million, leaving 1.5 million additional chips for U.S. consumption. The resulting mix of products consumed in each country is shown in Table 3. Clearly, both countries are better off, having engaged in specialized production and trade.

Table 3 Final Consumption Patterns after Trade

	United States	Mexico	Total
Oil	20	5	25
Chips	21.5	3.5	25

The important point to remember here is that even when one country has an absolute advantage over another country, both countries will still benefit from trading with one another. In our example, the gains were small, but such gains can grow; as two economies become more equal in size, the benefits of their comparative advantages grow.

Ancient Humans and Trade

Neanderthals *(Homo neanderthalensis)* lived 200,000 years before *Homo sapiens* arrived on the scene. Both species then lived together in roughly the same ranges for another 10,000 years, at which time the Neanderthals died out. Modern evidence suggests that Neanderthals were roughly as intelligent, stronger, and also capable of speech. Until recently, the generally accepted reason for the Neanderthals' extinction was that *Homo sapiens* had more sophisticated tools, developed modern symbolic thinking, and created a more sophisticated language.

Digging in prehistoric *Homo sapiens'* caves has uncovered such items as paintings, spear points, stone tools made from materials not found in the same location, and seashell jewelry found in inland locations far from the ocean. These discoveries have produced a new theory of why *Homo sapiens* came to dominate the land: They were trading with other colonies of humans.[2] The theory is that trade led to specialization, whereby the best hunters hunted, and the others made weapons, clothes, and other necessities.

To test this theory, several anthropologists created a computer population simulation model that included such variables as rates of fertility and mortality, specialization and trade, hunting ability, and the same number of skilled hunters and craftsmen in each population. They gave *Homo sapiens* an edge in the ability to specialize and trade. As the model ran, *Homo sapiens* had superior hunting success, giving them more meat and driving up fertility and population. The model assumed the number of animals was fixed, so the available meat for the Neanderthals declined, and so did their population. Depending on the model's parameters, the time it took for Neanderthals to die out roughly coincided with that estimated by other anthropologists. Ancient humans may have known the benefits of trade long before David Ricardo developed his theory of absolute and comparative advantage.

Limits on Trade and Globalization

Before leaving the subject of international trade, we should take a moment to note some practical constraints on trade. First, every transaction involves costs, including transportation, communications, and the general costs of doing business. Even so, over the last several decades, transportation and communication costs have been declining all over the world, resulting in growing global trade.

Second, the production possibilities curves for nations are not linear, but rather governed by increasing costs and diminishing returns. Therefore, it is difficult for countries to specialize in producing one product. Complete specialization would be risky, moreover, since the market for a product can always decline, perhaps because the product becomes technologically obsolete. Alternately, changing weather patterns can wreak havoc on specialized agriculture products, adding further instability to incomes and exports in developing countries.

Finally, though two countries may benefit from trading with one another, expanding this trade may well hurt some industries and individuals within each country. Notably, industries finding themselves at a comparative disadvantage may be forced to scale back production and lay off workers. In such instances, the government may need to provide workers with retraining, relocation, and other help to ensure a smooth transition to the new production mix.

When the United States signed the North American Free Trade Agreement (NAFTA) with Canada and Mexico, many people experienced what we have just been discussing. Some American jobs went south to Mexico because of low production costs. By opening up more markets for American products, however, NAFTA did stimulate economic growth, such that retrained workers may end up with new and better jobs.

Before ending this chapter, let's take a moment to review what we have learned, then apply it briefly. We listed the three basic questions that any economy has to answer and discussed production. We used the production possibilities frontiers (PPF) model to understand what economic growth is. We then looked at the determinants of economic growth. Finally, we examined trade as a driver of economic growth. Now let's apply this growth framework.

[2]For a more detailed discussion of this issue, see "Human Evolution: Homo Economicus?" *The Economist,* April 9, 2005, pp. 67–68; and "Mrs. Adam Smith," *The Economist,* December 9, 2006, p. 85.

Economic growth in the United States has slowed over the second half of the 20th century, but our standard of living has nonetheless risen dramatically. Expansion of our resources and technological progress has driven this growth—just as our growth framework suggests. Women have entered the workforce in droves, immigration has expanded, and technology has advanced by leaps and bounds, thus spurring the production of more goods and services. Expanding global trade has opened up new markets for our products and increased imports from areas with lower production costs. These developments have contributed to America's economic growth and improved the economic welfare of its people.

Is There a Moral Dimension to Economic Growth?

> **Why do we care so much about economic growth? When we talk about microeconomic issues in economics, the conversation boils down to efficiency: How can we best organize economic activity—production, buying, selling, consuming—in order to keep the economy as close as possible to the frontier that represents the maximum possible production and satisfaction of the desires of all.**
>
> ***Benjamin M. Friedman***

Robin Jareaux/Getty Images

Clearly, economic growth expands the economy's production possibilities frontier and improves our standard of living, but does it improve the quality of life? Benjamin Friedman[3] made a compelling argument that we also care so much about growth because there are moral consequences to growth. This is the other side of the coin that is rarely discussed.

Looking back at two centuries of historical evidence of our country and others, he found that when the economy is growing and the general population feels they are getting ahead, they are more likely to protect and enhance their basic moral values. These, he argued, include providing greater opportunity for all; expanding tolerance for people of other races, ethnic groups, and religions; and improving our sense of fairness to those in need. As a result, we become more committed to our democratic institutions.

His analysis also brings a warning: When economic growth stagnates for an extended period, the evidence suggests that "predictable pathologies have flourished in American society in ways that we all regret." Friedman's analysis of the moral implications provides another dimension of economic growth to add to our toolbox.

How about around the globe? While poverty and starvation exist and are constant challenges to policymakers, there has been a clear trend of progress, spurred by international trade and technological advances. Cell phones are one simple example. Thirty years ago, policymakers focused on developing infrastructure such as roads and telephones to improve communication. These were not trivial tasks. To improve telephone usage, massive capital and labor outlays (think of putting up telephone poles and stringing the telephone wires) were needed. It was a huge, almost impossible, task. In this new century, countries have leaped beyond this because of technological breakthroughs in telecommunications: It is much less expensive to put up cell phone towers than put down the standard telephone pole infrastructure. Just as the United States has witnessed an explosion in cell phone usage, so have other places around the globe—with more dramatic results. Technology truly has improved communication almost overnight, and in its wake has come economic growth.

From this framework for understanding economic growth, especially trade, we turn to a discussion of the market system. The following chapter will look at how individual consumers and firms operate through markets to solve the three basic economic questions of what to produce, how to produce it, and who will ultimately consume the goods and services produced.

---

[3]Benjamin M. Friedman, *The Moral Consequences of Economic Growth* (New York: Knopf), 2005.

Checkpoint

Specialization, Comparative Advantage, and Trade

REVIEW

- An absolute advantage exists when one country can produce more of some good than another.
- A comparative advantage exists if one country has lower opportunity costs of producing a good than another country. Both countries gain from trade if each focuses on producing those goods at which it has a comparative advantage.
- Thus, voluntary trade is a positive-sum game, because both countries benefit from it.

QUESTION

Unlike most people, why do Hollywood stars (and many other rich people) have full-time personal assistants who manage their personal affairs?

Answers to the Checkpoint question can be found at the end of this chapter.

Key Concepts

Production, p. 31
Resources, p. 31
Land, p. 31
Labor, p. 31
Capital, p. 31
Entrepreneurs, p. 32
Production efficiency, p. 32
Allocative efficiency, p. 32
Production possibilities frontier (PPF), p. 33
Opportunity cost, p. 34
Absolute advantage, p. 42
Comparative advantage, p. 42

Chapter Summary

Basic Economic Questions and Production

Every economy must decide what to produce, how to produce it, and who will get the goods produced. How these questions are answered depends on how an economy is organized (capitalist, socialist, or communist), but in the end, all three questions must somehow be addressed.

Production is the process of converting factors of production—land, labor, capital, and entrepreneurial ability—into goods and services. Production processes can be labor- or capital-intensive depending on the available resources. Production efficiency occurs when goods and services are produced at the lowest possible resource cost. Allocative efficiency occurs when the mix of goods and services produced is that desired by society.

Production Possibilities and Economic Growth

The PPF curve shows the different combinations of goods that a fully employed economy can produce, given its available resources and current technology (both assumed to be fixed in the short run). Production levels inside and on the frontier are possible, but production mixes lying outside the curve are unattainable.

Production on the frontier represents the maximum output attainable by the economy when all resources are fully employed. At full employment, reallocating production from one product to another involves opportunity costs: The output of one product must be reduced to get the added output of the other. As an economy desires more of one product, the opportunity costs for this product will rise because of diminishing returns and the unsuitability of some specialized resources to be devoted to producing some products.

The production possibilities model suggests that economic growth can arise from an expansion in resources or from improvements in technology. Expansions in resources expand the production possibilities frontier for all commodities. Technological advances in one industry directly expand production only in that industry, but nonetheless allow more of all types of goods to be produced. The new technology allows previous output to be produced using fewer resources, thus leaving some resources available for use in other industries.

Economic growth can be enhanced by increasing the quantity or quality of labor available for production. Population growth, caused by higher birthrates or immigration, will increase the quantity of labor available. Investments in human capital will improve labor's quality. Greater capital accumulation will further improve labor's productivity and thus increase growth rates.

Specialization, Comparative Advantage, and Trade

An absolute advantage exists when one country can produce more of some good than another. A country has a comparative advantage if its opportunity costs to produce this good are lower than in the other country. Countries gain from voluntary trade if each focuses on producing those goods at which it enjoys a comparative advantage. Voluntary trade is thus a positive-sum game: Both countries stand to benefit from it.

Questions and Problems

1. When can an economy increase the production of one good without reducing the output of another?

2. The "Rule of 72" permits you to quickly determine how fast an economy can double by dividing 72 by the growth rate. For example, if the growth rate is 1%, an economy will double in size in 72 years; if the growth rate is 7%, it will double in roughly 10 years; and so on. In the table below assume that the economy starts with income of $100. When the growth rate equals 2%, income will double every two generations (consider a generation to be 18 years), as shown in the third column. In 36 years, income grows to $200, and 36 years later it is $400. Compute the doubling in the fourth column when growth rates rise to 4%. Are these different growth rates really so important? Who is most affected?

Generation	Years	2% Growth	4% Growth
1	18		______
2	36	200	______
3	54		______
4	72	400	______

3. Explain the important difference between a straight line PPF and the PPF that is concave (bowed out) to the origin.

4. The table on the next page shows the potential output combinations of oranges and jars of prickly pear jelly (from the flower of the prickly pear cactus) for Florida and Arizona.
   a. Compute the opportunity cost for Florida of oranges in terms of jars of prickly pear jelly. Do the same for prickly pear jelly in terms of oranges.

b. Compute the opportunity cost for Arizona of oranges in terms of jars of prickly pear jelly. Do the same for prickly pear jelly in terms of oranges.
c. Would it make sense for Florida to specialize in producing oranges and for Arizona to specialize in producing prickly pear jelly and then trade? Why or why not?

Florida		Arizona	
Oranges	**Prickly Pear Jelly**	**Oranges**	**Prickly Pear Jelly**
0	10	0	500
50	8	20	400
100	6	40	300
150	4	60	200
200	2	80	100
250	0	100	0

5. Complete the following based on the figure below where three different production possibilities curves are shown.

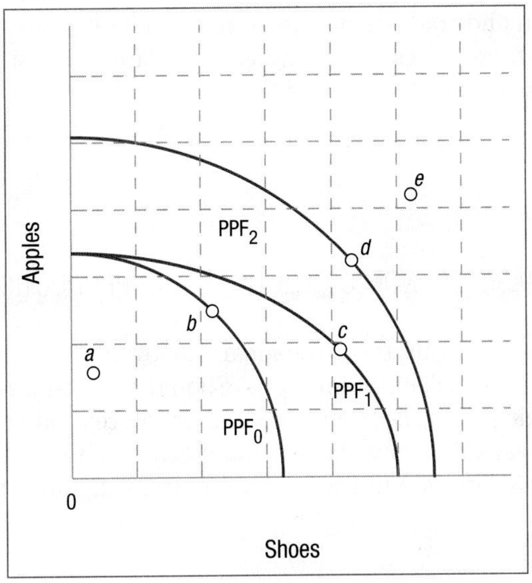

a. If the production possibilities frontier for this nation is PPF$_0$, then point a represents ____________________.
b. If the production possibilities frontier for this nation is PPF$_0$, then point e represents ____________________.
c. Production possibilities PPF$_1$ represents ____________________.
d. If the initial production possibilities frontier is PPF$_0$, then PPF$_2$ represents ____________________ and is caused by ____________________.

6. Describe how a country producing more capital goods rather than consumer goods ends up in the future with a PPF that is larger than a country that produces more consumer goods and fewer capital goods.

7. List the way an economy can grow given the discussion in this chapter.

8. Describe how opportunity cost is shown on a PPF.

9. The United States has an absolute advantage in making many goods, such as short-sleeve cotton golf shirts. Why do Costa Rica and Bangladesh make these shirts and export them to the United States?

10. In which of the three basic questions will technology play the greatest role?

11. As individuals, we all know what scarcity means: not enough time (even the rich face a scarcity of time); insufficient income so we are unable to buy that new car, vacation home, or water-ski boat we want. But for nations as a whole, what does it mean to face scarcity?

12. Why is it that America uses heavy street cleaning machines driven by one person to clean the streets, while China and India use many people with brooms to do the same job?

13. How would unemployment be shown on the PPF?

14. China has experienced levels of economic growth in the last decade that have been two to three times that of the United States (10% versus 3–4% per year in the U.S.). Has China's high growth rate eliminated scarcity in China?

15. If specialization and trade as discussed in this chapter lead to a win-win situation where both countries gain, why is there often opposition to trade agreements and globalization?

Answers to Checkpoint Questions

CHECKPOINT: BASIC ECONOMIC QUESTIONS AND PRODUCTION

Typically, entrepreneurs put their personal money into the business and often pledge private assets as collateral for loans. Should the business fail, they stand to lose more than their jobs, rent from the land, or interest on capital loaned to the firm. Workers can get other jobs, land owners can rent to others, and capital can be used in other enterprises. But the entrepreneur must suffer the loss of personal assets and move on.

CHECKPOINT: PRODUCTION POSSIBILITIES AND ECONOMIC GROWTH

Abundant resources like oil or diamonds can be a curse because the economy often depends only on these resources for income and develops little else in terms of commerce. Many of the countries in the Middle East and Africa face this situation. Because their major source of income is concentrated in one resource, corruption often results, harming development in other sectors of the economy.

CHECKPOINT: SPECIALIZATION, COMPARATIVE ADVANTAGE, AND TRADE

For Hollywood stars and other rich people, the opportunity cost of their time is high. As a result, they hire people at lower cost to do the mundane chores that each of us is accustomed to doing because our time is not as valuable.

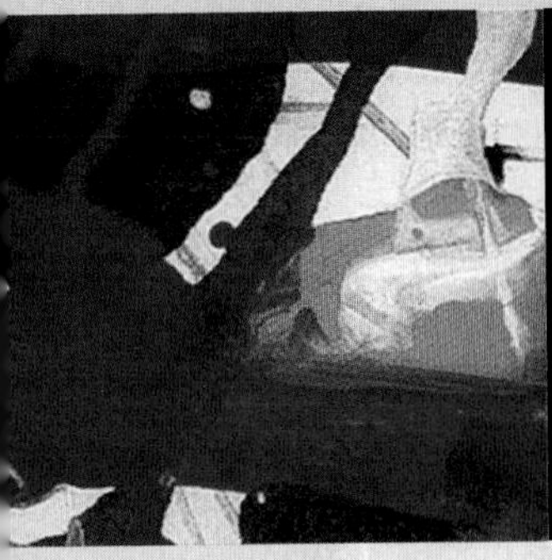

3 Supply and Demand

Imagine you are going to build a house. Your plans are drawn up, the land is purchased, and you are all set to begin construction. What is the first thing you do? Do you immediately start putting up walls or set the painters to work? Of course not! Before you can build any walls, much less start painting, you must lay a foundation. The same is true in economics: Before you can understand more complex economic concepts, you need a foundation. This chapter provides the basic foundation on which all other economic theory rests. This foundation—supply and demand analysis—explains how market economies operate. In the previous chapter on economic growth, we took markets for granted. Here we start examining markets in detail.

In our economy, most goods and services (including labor) are bought and sold through private markets. These products include everything from iPods to airline flights, from haircuts to new homes. Most markets offer consumers a wide variety of choices. The typical Wal-Mart, for instance, features over a half million different items, while even a small town has numerous competing choices of hair salons, movie theaters, and shoe stores.

In any given market, prices are determined by "what the market will bear." But which factors determine what the market will bear, and what happens when events that occur in the marketplace cause prices to change? For answers to these questions, economists turn to supply and demand analysis. The basic model of supply and demand presented in this chapter will allow you to determine why product sales rise and fall, what direction prices move in, and how many goods will be offered for sale when certain events happen in the marketplace. Later chapters will use this same model to explain complex phenomena such as how personal income is distributed.

This chapter introduces some of the basic economic concepts you will need to know to understand how the forces of supply and demand work. These concepts include markets, the law of demand, demand curves, the determinants of demand, the law of supply, supply curves, the determinants of supply, equilibrium, surpluses, and shortages.

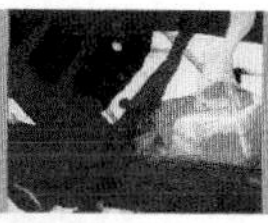

After studying this chapter you should be able to

- Describe the nature and purposes of markets.
- Describe the nature of demand, demand curves, and the law of demand.
- Describe the determinants of demand and be able to forecast how a change in one or more of these determinants will change demand.
- Describe the difference between a change in demand and a change in quantity demanded.
- Describe the nature of supply, supply curves, and the law of supply.
- Describe the determinants of supply and be able to forecast how a change in one or more of these determinants will change supply.
- Describe the difference between a change in supply and a change in quantity supplied.
- Determine market equilibrium price and output.
- Determine and predict how price and output will change given changes to supply and demand in the market.

Markets

Markets
Institutions that bring buyers and sellers together so they can interact and transact with each other.

A **market** is an institution that enables buyers and sellers to interact and transact with one another. A lemonade stand is a market because it allows people to exchange money for a product, in this case lemonade. Ticket scalping, though illegal in many states, similarly represents market activity since it leads to the exchange of money for tickets. As Chris Anderson pointed out in his recent book, *The Long Tail,*[1] the Internet, without a physical location, permits firms and individuals to sell a large number of low-volume niche products and still make money. This includes students who resell their textbooks on Amazon.com and Half.com.

Even though all markets have the same basic component—the transaction—they can differ in a number of ways. Some markets are quite limited because of their geographical location, or because they offer only a few different products for sale. Other markets, like the Wal-Mart superstore, feature literally thousands of items. The New York Stock Exchange serves as a market for just a single type of financial instrument, stocks, but it facilitates exchanges worth billions of dollars daily. Compare this to the neighborhood flea market, which is much smaller and may operate only on weekends, but offers everything from food and crafts to T-shirts and electronics. Cement manufacturers are typically restricted to local markets due to high transportation costs, whereas Internet firms can easily do business with customers around the world.

The Price System

When buyers and sellers exchange money for goods and services, accepting some offers and rejecting others, they are also doing something else: They are communi-

[1]Chris Anderson, *The Long Tail: Why the Future of Business is Selling Less of More* (New York: Hyperion), 2006.

cating their individual desires. Much of this communication is accomplished through the prices of items. If buyers sufficiently value a particular item, they will quickly pay its asking price. If they do not buy it, they are indicating they do not believe the item to be worth its asking price.

Prices also give buyers an easy means of comparing goods that can substitute for each other. If margarine falls to half the price of butter, this will suggest to many consumers that margarine is a better deal. Similarly, sellers can determine what goods to sell by comparing their prices. When prices rise for tennis rackets, this tells sporting goods stores that the public wants more tennis rackets, leading these stores to order more. Prices, therefore, contain a huge amount of useful information for both consumers and sellers. For this reason, economists often call our market economy the **price system**.

Price system
A name given to the market economy because prices provide considerable information to both buyers and sellers.

Checkpoint

Markets

REVIEW

- Markets are institutions that enable buyers and sellers to interact and transact business.
- Markets differ in geographical location, products offered, and size.
- Prices contain a wealth of information for both buyers and sellers.
- Through their purchases, consumers signal their willingness to exchange money for particular products at particular prices. These signals help businesses decide what to produce, and how much of it to produce.
- The market economy is also called the price system.

QUESTION

What are the important differences between the markets for financial securities such as the New York Stock Exchange and your local flea market?

Answers to the Checkpoint question can be found at the end of this chapter.

Demand

Whenever you purchase a product, you are voting with your money. You are selecting one product out of many and supporting one firm out of many, both of which signal to the business community what sorts of products will satisfy your wants as a consumer.

Economists, incidentally, typically focus on wants rather than needs because it is so difficult to determine what we truly need. Theoretically, you could survive on tofu and vitamin pills, living in a lean-to made of cardboard and buying all your clothes from thrift stores. Most people in our society, however, choose not to live in such austere fashion. Rather, they want something more, and in most cases they are willing and able to pay for more. These wants—the desires consumers have for particular goods and services, which they express through their purchases—are known as demands.

Demand
The maximum amount of a product that buyers are willing and able to purchase over some time period at various prices, holding all other relevant factors constant (the *ceteris paribus* condition).

The Relationship between Quantity Demanded and Price

Demand refers to the goods and services people are willing and able to buy during a certain period of time. Given the current popularity of television, most people would probably love to own a flat panel HDTV with surround sound and hook it to a digital satellite or cable system that features hundreds of channels. And, indeed, if the products needed for such a setup were priced low enough, virtually everyone owning a television would opt for this system.

As your television gets bigger, and as you upgrade from basic television to cable or digital satellite, the cost of your home entertainment system increases. Yet, as the price of these services increases, the quantity demanded will decrease, since fewer and fewer people will be willing to spend their money on such luxuries, if they even have the money.

Thus, in a survey of households with television sets, we would expect to find a few people with virtually no service, perhaps receiving only network broadcasts through rabbit-ear antennas. A few people would have digital satellite hookups giving them access to sports channels, movie channels, and every other channel imaginable. The vast majority of consumers, however, would fall between these two categories, receiving some, but not all, of the services and channels available, in accord with their tastes and means.

In a market economy, there is a negative relationship between price and quantity demanded. This relationship, in its most basic form, states that as price increases, the quantity demanded falls, and conversely, as prices fall, the quantity demanded increases.

The Law of Demand

Law of demand
Holding all other relevant factors constant, as price increases, quantity demanded falls, and as price decreases, quantity demanded rises.

This principle, that as price increases, quantity demanded falls, and as price decreases, quantity demanded rises—all other factors held constant—is known as the **law of demand**. The law of demand states that the lower a product's price, the more of that product consumers will purchase during a given time period. This straightforward, commonsense notion happens because, as a product's price drops, consumers will substitute the now-cheaper product for other, more expensive products. Conversely, if the product's price rises, consumers will find other, cheaper products to substitute for it.

To illustrate, when videocassette recorders first came on the market 30 years ago, they cost $3,000, and few homes had one. As VCRs became less and less expensive, however, more people bought them, and others found more uses for them. Today, DVD players and digital video recorders (DVRs) are everywhere, and VCRs are essentially consigned to museums. A similar battle is now brewing around the format for high-definition DVDs, and digital cameras have largely replaced 35mm film cameras.

Time is an important component in the demand for many products. Consuming many products—watching a movie, eating a pizza, playing tennis—takes some time. Thus, the price of these goods includes not only their money cost, but also the opportunity cost of the time needed to consume them. It follows that, all other things being equal, including the cost of a ticket, we would expect more consumers to attend a 2-hour movie than a 4-hour movie. The shorter movie simply requires less of a time investment.

The Demand Curve

Several decades ago, computers filling entire air-conditioned rooms laboriously churned out data. Now, inexpensive laptop computers, PDAs, and cellular phones can perform even more complex operations in a fraction of the time. This advance in computer technology has led to the widespread use of computers for both business and pleasure. Once offering only Pong, game companies now take millions of players a year into mythical adventures, space battles, military campaigns, and rounds of championship golf. Indeed, games on the three main platforms—Sony's

Playstation 3, Microsoft's XBox 360, and Nintendo's Wii—are a driving force behind the development of faster microprocessor technology because games are voracious users of speed.

The law of demand states that as price decreases, quantity demanded increases. When we translate demand information into a graph, we create a **demand curve**. This demand curve, which slopes down and to the right, graphically illustrates the law of demand.

Demand curve Demand schedule information translated to a graph.

For example, consider Betty and her demand for computer games. Figure 1 depicts her annual demand in both table (the demand schedule) and graphical (the demand curve) form. Looking at the table and reading down Betty's demand schedule, we can see that Betty is willing to buy more computer games as the price decreases, from zero games at a price of $100 to 20 games at a price of $20. It makes sense that Betty will buy more computer games as the price decreases.

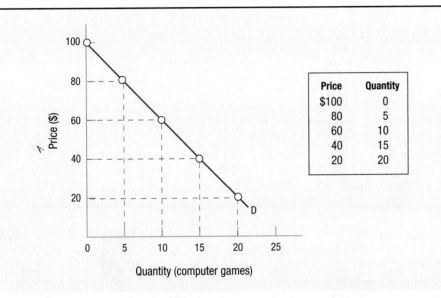

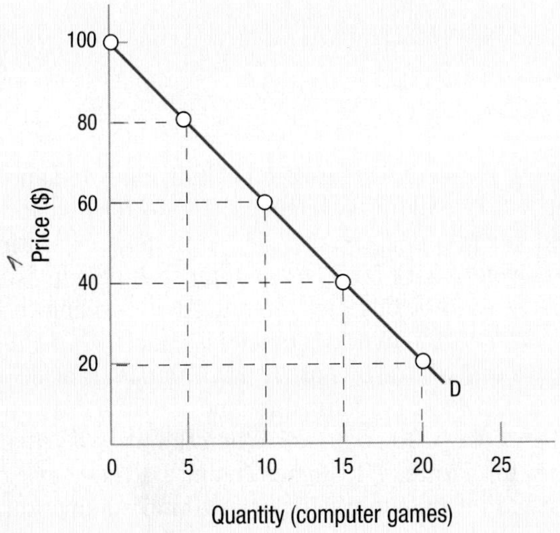

Price	Quantity
$100	0
80	5
60	10
40	15
20	20

FIGURE 1

Betty's Demand for Computer Games

This figure shows Betty's demand schedule (the table) and her demand curve (the graph) for computer games over a year. Betty will purchase 5 computer games when the price is $80, buy 10 when the price falls to $60, and buy more as prices continue to fall. The demand curve D is Betty's demand curve for computer games.

We can take the values from the demand schedule in the table and graph them in a figure, with price as the vertical axis and computer games as the horizontal axis, following the convention in economics of always placing price on the vertical axis and quantity demanded on the horizontal axis. This line is the demand curve. Comparing the table with the graph, we can see that they convey the same information. For instance, find the price of $60 on the vertical axis in the graph and look to the right to the point on the curve; then look down to locate the quantity of 10 computer games. This is the same information conveyed in the table: locating a price of $60 and looking to the right gives you the quantity of 10 computer games demanded.

Both the table and the graph portray the law of demand. As the price decreases, Betty demands more computer games. If the price of each game is $100, Betty will not purchase any games; they are just too expensive. Let the price drop to $40, however, and she will buy 15 games during the year.

Market Demand Curves

Though individual demand curves, like the one showing Betty's demand for computer games, are interesting, market demand curves are far more important to economists, as they can be used to predict changes in product price and quantity. Market demand is the sum of individual demands. To calculate market demand, economists simply add together how many units of a product all consumers will purchase at each price. This process is known as **horizontal summation**.

Horizontal summation Market demand and supply curves are found by adding together how many units of the product will be purchased or supplied at each price.

FIGURE 2

Market Demand: Horizontal Summation of Individual Demand Curves

Individual demand curves D_a and D_b are horizontally summed to get market demand, D_{Mkt}. Horizontal summation involves adding together the quantities demanded by each individual at each possible price.

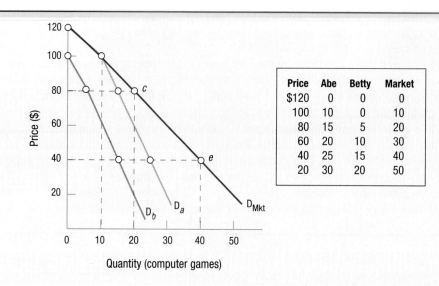

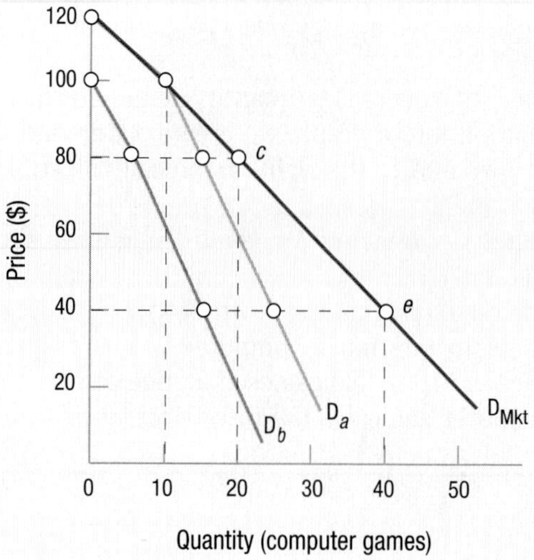

Price	Abe	Betty	Market
$120	0	0	0
100	10	0	10
80	15	5	20
60	20	10	30
40	25	15	40
20	30	20	50

Figure 2 shows an example of horizontal summation of individual demand curves to obtain a market demand curve. Two individual demand curves for Abe and Betty, D_a and D_b, are shown. For simplicity, let's assume they represent the entire market, but recognize this process would work for a larger number of people. Note that at a price of $100 a game, Betty will not buy any, though Abe is willing to buy 10 games at $100. Above $100, therefore, the market demand is equal to Abe's demand. At $100 and below, however, we add both Abe's and Betty's demands at each price to obtain market demand. Thus, at $80, individual demand is 15 for Abe and 5 for Betty, so the market demand is equal to 20 (point *c*). When the price is $40 a game, Abe buys 25 and Betty buys 15, for a total of 40 games (point *e*). The heavier curve, labeled D_{Mkt}, represents this market demand; it is a horizontal summation of the two individual demand curves.

This all sounds simple in theory, but in the real world estimating market demand curves is a tricky business, given that many markets contain millions of consumers. Marketing professionals use sophisticated statistical techniques to estimate the market demand for particular goods and services.

Determinants of demand Other nonprice factors that affect demand including tastes and preferences, income, prices of related goods, number of buyers, and expectations.

The market demand curve shows the maximum amount of a product consumers are willing and able to purchase during a given time period at various prices, all other relevant factors being held constant. Economists use the term **determinants of demand** to refer to these other, nonprice factors that get held constant. This is another example of the use of *ceteris paribus:* holding all other relevant factors constant.

Determinants of Demand

Up to this point, we have discussed only how price affects the quantity demanded, but several other factors also affect demand, including what people like, what their income is, and how much related products cost. More specifically, in addition to the price of the product, there are five determinants of demand: (1) tastes and preferences; (2) income; (3) prices of related goods; (4) the number of buyers; and (5) expectations regarding future prices, income, and product availability.

Tastes and Preferences

How many times have you heard the phrase, "It depends?" This phrase is often a shortened version of "It depends on whether I like it or not." We all have preferences for certain products instead of others, easily perceiving subtle differences in styling and quality. Automobiles, cellular phones, fashions, and music are just a few of the products that are subject to the whims of the consumer.

Businesses devote substantial resources to studying changes in consumer tastes and reacting to them, bringing out new products and casting away outdated items. They also spend considerable sums of money trying to influence consumer tastes and preferences through a barrage of media advertising. It is impossible to predict changes in tastes and preferences perfectly, but businesses use sophisticated market research techniques to try to gauge whether particular advertisements will increase or decrease the demand for their products.

Income

Income is another important factor influencing consumer demand. Generally speaking, as income rises, demands for most goods will likewise increase. Get a raise, and you are more likely to buy a nice car. Products for which demand is positively linked to income—when income rises, demand for the product also rises—are called **normal goods**.

Normal goods
A good where an increase in income results in rising demand.

But there are also some products for which demand declines as income rises. Economists call these products **inferior goods**. As your income grows, for instance, your consumption of public transportation will likely fall since you will probably own a car. Similarly, when you graduate from college and your income rises, your consumption of ramen noodles will fall as you begin dining in better restaurants.

Inferior goods
A good where an increase in income results in declining demand.

Prices of Related Goods

Though product price is the most important factor influencing quantity demanded, the prices of related commodities also affect consumer decisions. You may be an avid concert-goer, but with concert ticket prices often topping $50, if your local movie theater drops its ticket price to $5, you will probably end up seeing more movies than concerts. Movies, concerts, plays, and sporting events are good examples of **substitute goods**, since consumers can substitute one for another depending on their respective prices.

Substitute goods
Goods consumers will substitute for one another depending on their relative prices.

Movies and popcorn, on the other hand, are examples of **complementary goods**. These are goods that are generally consumed together, such that an increase or decrease in the consumption of one will similarly result in an increase or decrease in the consumption of the other—see fewer movies, and your consumption of popcorn will decline. Other complementary goods include cars and gasoline, hot dogs and mustard, and Windows Vista and DRAM (dynamic random access memory).

Complementary goods
Goods that are typically consumed together.

The Number of Buyers

Another factor influencing market demand for a product is the number of potential buyers in the market. Clearly, the more consumers there are who are likely to buy a particular product, the higher its market demand will be. As our average life span steadily rises, the demands for medical services, rest homes, and retirement communities will likewise increase.

Expectations about Future Prices, Incomes, and Product Availability

The final factor influencing demand involves consumer expectations. If consumers expect shortages of certain products or increases in their prices in the near future, they tend to rush out and buy these products immediately, thereby increasing the present demand for the products. During the Florida hurricane season, when a large storm forms and begins moving toward the coast, the demands for plywood, nails, water, and batteries quickly rise in Florida.

The expectation of a rise in income, meanwhile, can lead consumers to take advantage of credit to increase their present consumption. Department stores,

Goods

electronics shops, and furniture stores often run "no payments until next year" sales designed to attract consumers who want to "buy now, pay later." These consumers expect to have more money later, when they can pay, so they go ahead and buy what they want now, thereby increasing the present demand for the sale items.

To cite one more example, when mortgage interest rates hit rock bottom in late 2001 and 2002, many potential homeowners decided to buy before rates went back up, thus increasing the demand for new construction. This increase in home purchases has been credited with making the 2001–02 recession a relatively mild one. It also left many apartments vacant, resulting in great deals for new renters.

Changes in Demand Versus Changes in Quantity Demanded

When the price of a product rises, consumers simply buy fewer units of that product. This is a movement along an existing demand curve. However, when one or more of the determinants change, the entire demand curve is altered. Now, at any given price consumers are willing to purchase more or less depending on the nature of the change. This section focuses on this important distinction between a change in demand versus a change in quantity demanded.

Changes in Demand

Change in demand
Occurs when one or more of the determinants of demand changes, shown as a shift in the entire demand curve.

Changes in demand occur whenever one or more of the determinants of demand change and demand curves shift. When demand changes, the demand curve shifts either to the right or to the left. Let us look at each shift in turn.

Demand increases when the entire demand curve shifts to the right. At all prices, consumers are willing to purchase more of the product in question. We can see this with each of the determinants of demand. Changes in consumer preferences will change demand. Consumer preferences can be changed through advertising. Another way to increase demand is to tie a product in with another, more popular product. Walt Disney's animated feature films are often marketed along with stuffed animals, books, computer games, and CDs. These products sell well because young movie fans want to purchase everything associated with their favorite movies. Panel A of Figure 3 shows how demand increases for a computer game when it gets tied in with a movie; the demand curve shifts from D_0 to D_1. Notice that more of these "tied-in" computer games will be purchased at all prices along D_1 as compared to D_0.

FIGURE 3

Changes in Demand Versus Change in Quantity Demanded

A shift in the demand curve from D_0 to D_1 in Panel A indicates an *increase in demand* since consumers will buy more of the product at each price. A shift from D_0 to D_2 reflects a decrease in demand. A movement along D_0 from point *a* to point *c* in Panel B indicates an *increase in quantity demanded;* this type of movement can only be caused by a change in the price of the product.

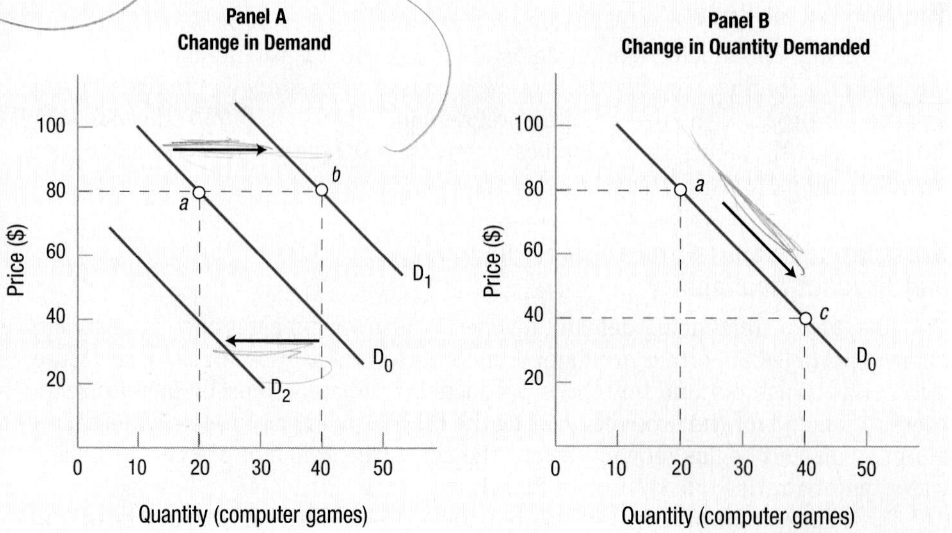

Another cause of an increase in demand is an increase in consumer income. For most products (at least for normal goods), people are inclined to buy more of them as their incomes rise. Thus, for these products, a rise in consumer income will cause an increase in demand. We also know that expectations of future price hikes cause demand to grow, shifting the demand curve to the right, and the presence of more buyers in the market will increase demand.

Now let us look at a decrease in demand, when the entire demand curve shifts to the left. At all prices, consumers are willing to purchase less of the product in question. A drop in consumer income will normally be associated with a decline in demand (the demand curve shifts to the left). This decrease in demand is shown in Panel A of Figure 3 as the demand curve shifting from D_0 to D_2. A decrease in demand can also arise from variations in the price or availability of related products. The advent of digital satellite television has made an amazingly broad range of programming available to homes. The demand for cable television will undoubtedly decline as many homes decide to shift to digital satellite systems. Current demand shrinks if prices are expected to fall in the near future, if the number of buyers falls, or if the price of a complementary product rises. All of these will shrink demand, resulting in a shift in the demand curve to the left.

Changes in Quantity Demanded

Whereas a change in demand can be brought about by many different factors, a **change in quantity demanded** can be caused by only one thing: *a change in product price.* This is shown in Panel B of Figure 3 as a reduction in price from $80 to $40, resulting in sales (quantity demanded) increasing from 20 to 40 games annually. This distinction between a change in demand and a change in quantity demanded is important. Reducing price to increase sales is different from spending a few million dollars on Super Bowl advertising to increase sales at all prices!

Change in quantity demanded
Occurs when the price of the product changes, and is shown as a movement along an existing demand curve.

These concepts are so important that a quick summary is in order. As Figure 3 illustrates, given the initial demand D_0, increasing sales from 20 to 40 games can occur in either of two ways. First, changing a determinant (say, increasing advertising) could shift the demand curve to D_1 in Panel A so that 40 games would be sold at $80 (point *b*). Alternatively, 40 games could be sold in Panel B by reducing price to $40 (point *c*). Selling more by increasing advertising causes an increase in demand, or a shift in the whole demand curve that brings about a movement from point *a* to point *b* in Panel A. Simply reducing the price, on the other hand, causes an increase in quantity demanded, or a movement along the existing demand curve, D_0, from point *a* to point *c* in Panel B.

Checkpoint

Demand

REVIEW

- Demand refers to the quantity of products people are willing and able to purchase at various prices during some specific time period, all other relevant factors being held constant.
- Price and quantity demanded have an inverse (negative) relation: As price rises, consumers buy fewer units; as price falls, consumers buy more units. This inverse relation is known as the law of demand. It is depicted as a downward-sloping (from left to right) demand curve.
- To find market demand curves, simply horizontally sum all of the individual demand curves.

- Demand curves shift when one or more of the determinants of demand change.
- The determinants of demand are consumer tastes and preferences, income, prices of substitutes and complements, the number of buyers in a market, and expectations about future prices, incomes, and product availability.
- A shift of a demand curve is a *change in demand.* An increase in demand is a shift to the right. A decrease in demand is a shift to the left.
- A *change in quantity demanded* occurs only when the price of a product changes, leading consumers to adjust their purchases along the existing demand curve.

QUESTIONS

Sales of hybrid cars are on the rise. The Toyota Prius, while priced above comparable gasoline-only cars, is selling well. Other manufacturers are adding hybrids to their lines as well. What has been the cause of the rising sales of hybrids? Is this an increase in demand or an increase in quantity demanded?

Answers to the Checkpoint questions can be found at the end of this chapter.

Supply

As mentioned earlier, the analysis of a market economy rests on two foundations: supply and demand. So far, we've covered the demand side of the market. The present section focuses on the decisions businesses make regarding production numbers and sales. These decisions cause variations in product supply.

The Relationship between Quantity Supplied and Price

Supply
The maximum amount of a product that sellers are willing and able to provide for sale over some time period at various prices, holding all other relevant factors constant (the *ceteris paribus* condition).

Supply is the maximum amount of a product that producers are willing and able to offer for sale at various prices, all other relevant factors being held constant. The quantity supplied will vary according to the price of the product.

What explains this relationship? As we saw in the previous chapter, businesses inevitably encounter rising opportunity costs as they attempt to produce more and more of a product. This is due in part to diminishing returns from available resources, and in part to the fact that, when producers increase production, they must either have existing workers put in overtime hours (at a higher hourly pay rate) or hire additional workers away from other industries (again at premium pay).

Producing more units, therefore, makes it more expensive for producers to produce each individual unit. These increasing costs give rise to the positive relationship between product price and quantity supplied to the market.

The Law of Supply

Law of supply
Holding all other relevant factors constant, as price increases, quantity supplied will rise, and as price declines, quantity supplied will fall.

Unfortunately for producers, they can rarely charge whatever they would like for their products; they must charge whatever the market will permit. But producers can decide how much of their product to produce and offer for sale. The **law of supply** states that higher prices will lead producers to offer more of their products for sale during a given period. Conversely, if prices fall, producers will offer fewer products to the market. The explanation is simple: The higher the price, the greater the potential for higher profits and thus the greater the incentive for businesses to produce and sell more products. Also, given the rising opportunity costs associated with increasing production, producers need to charge these higher prices to profitably increase the quantity supplied.

The Supply Curve

Just as demand curves graphically display the law of demand, **supply curves** provide a graphical representation of the law of supply. The supply curve shows the maximum amounts of a product a producer will furnish at various prices during a given period of time. While the demand curve slopes down and to the right, the supply curve slopes up and to the right.[2] This illustrates the positive relationship between price and quantity supplied: the higher the price, the greater the quantity supplied.

Supply curve
Supply schedule information translated to a graph.

Market Supply Curves

As with demand, economists are more interested in market supply than in the supplies offered by individual firms. To compute market supply, you use the same method used to calculate market demand, horizontally summing the supplies of individual producers. A hypothetical market supply curve for computer games is depicted in Figure 4.

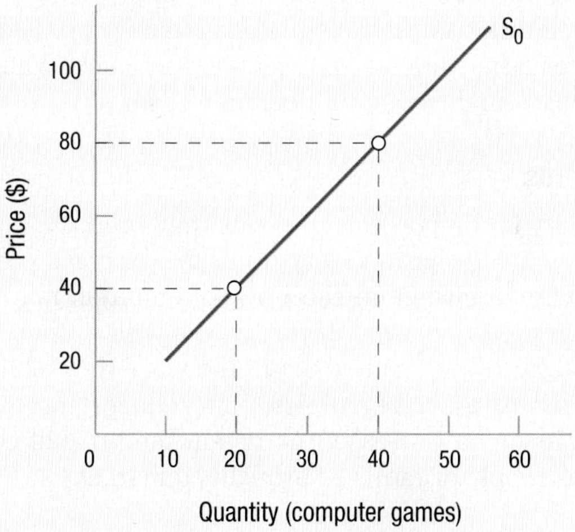

Price	Quantity
20	10
40	20
60	30
80	40
100	50

FIGURE 4

Supply of Computer Games

This supply curve graphs the supply schedule and shows the maximum quantity of computer games that producers will offer for sale over some defined stretch of time. The supply curve is positively sloped, reflecting the law of supply. In other words, as prices rise, quantity supplied increases; as prices fall, quantity supplied falls.

Determinants of Supply

Like demand, several factors other than price help to determine the quantity of a product supplied. Specifically, there are six **determinants of supply**: (1) production technology, (2) costs of resources, (3) prices of other commodities, (4) expectations, (5) the number of sellers (producers) in the market, and (6) taxes and subsidies.

Determinants of supply
Other nonprice factors that affect supply including production technology, costs of resources, prices of other commodities, expectations, number of sellers, and taxes and subsidies.

Production Technology

Technology determines how much output can be produced from given quantities of resources. If a factory's equipment is old and can turn out only 50 units of output per hour, then no matter how many other resources are employed, those 50 units are the most the factory can produce in an hour. If the factory is outfitted with newer, more advanced equipment, however, capable of turning out 100 units per hour, the firm can supply more of its product at the same price as before, or often even at a lower price.

Technology further determines the nature of products that can be supplied to the market. A hundred years ago, the supply of computers on the market was zero,

[2]There are some exceptions to positively sloping supply curves. But for our purposes, we will ignore them for now.

because computers did not yet exist. More recent advances in microprocessing and miniaturization brought a wide array of products not available just a few years ago to the market, including MP3 players, auto engines that go 100,000 miles between tune-ups, and constant monitoring insulin pumps that automatically keep a diabetic patient's glucose levels under control.

Costs of Resources

Resource costs clearly affect production costs and supply. If resources such as raw material or labor become more expensive, production costs will rise and supply will be reduced; the reverse is true if resource costs drop. The growing power of microchips along with their falling cost has resulted in cheap and plentiful electronics and microcomputers. Nanotechnology—manufacturing processes that fashion new products through the combination of individual atoms—may soon usher in a whole new generation of inexpensive products made from atoms of sand, an obviously cheap and plentiful resource. Some futurists even suggest that nanotechnology will one day end scarcity as we know it. (What would economists do then?)

On the other hand, if the cost of petroleum goes up, the cost of products using petroleum in their manufacture will go up, leading to the supply being reduced. If labor costs rise because immigration is restricted, this drives up production costs of California vegetables (fewer farm workers) and software in Silicon Valley (fewer software engineers from abroad) and leads to a decrease in supply.

Prices of Other Commodities

Most firms have some flexibility in the portfolio of goods they produce. A vegetable farmer, for example, might be able to grow celery, radishes, or some combination of the two. Given this flexibility, a change in the price of one item may influence the quantity of other items brought to market. If the price of celery should rise, for instance, most farmers will start growing more celery. And since they all have a limited amount of land on which to grow vegetables, this reduces the quantity of radishes they can produce. Hence, in this case, the rise in the price of celery may well cause a reduction in the supply of radishes brought to market.

Expectations

The effects of future expectations on market supplies can be complicated, and it is often difficult to generalize about how future supplies will be affected. When producers expect the prices of their goods to rise in the near future, they may react by increasing production immediately, causing current supply to increase. Yet, expectations of price cuts can also temporarily increase the supply of goods on the market as producers try to sell off their inventories before the price cuts hit. In this case, it is only over the long term that price reductions result in supply reductions, as we would expect.

Number of Sellers

Everything else being held constant, if the number of sellers in a particular market increases, the market supply of their product increases. It is no great mystery why: 10 shoemakers can produce more shoes in a given period than five shoemakers.

Taxes and Subsidies

To business, taxes and subsidies are costs. An increase in taxes (property, excise, or other fees) will reduce supply. Subsidies are the opposite of taxes. If the government subsidizes the production of a product, supply will rise. A luxury tax on power boats in the 1990s reduced supply (the tax was the equivalent of an increase in production costs), while today's subsidies to ethanol producers are expanding production.

Changes in Supply Versus Changes in Quantity Supplied

A **change in supply** results from a change in one or more of the determinants of supply; it causes the entire supply curve to shift. An increase in supply of a product, perhaps because advancing technology has made it cheaper to produce, means that more of the commodity will be offered for sale at every price. This causes the supply curve to shift to the right, as illustrated in Panel A of Figure 5 by the shift from S_0 to S_1. A decrease in supply, conversely, shifts the supply curve to the left, since fewer units of the product are offered at every price. Such a decrease in supply is here represented by the shift from S_0 to S_2.

Change in supply
Occurs when one or more of the determinants of supply change, shown as a shift in the entire supply curve.

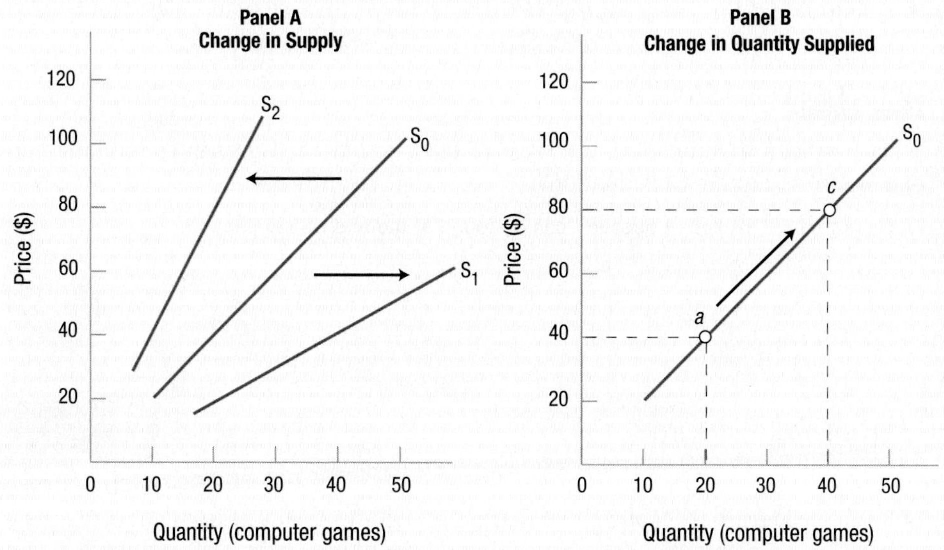

FIGURE 5

Changes in Supply Versus Changes in Quantity Supplied

A shift in the supply curve from S_0 to S_1 in Panel A indicates an *increase in supply* since businesses are willing to offer more of the product to consumers at every price. A shift from S_0 to S_2 reflects a decrease in supply. A movement along S_0 from point *a* to point *c* in Panel B represents an *increase in quantity supplied;* it results from an increase in the product's market price from \$40 to \$80.

A change in supply involves a shift of the entire supply curve. In contrast, the supply curve does not move when there is a **change in quantity supplied**. Only a change in the price of a product can cause a change in the quantity supplied; hence, it involves a movement along an existing supply curve rather than a shift to an entirely different curve. In Panel B of Figure 5, for instance, an increase in price from \$40 to \$80 results in an increase in quantity supplied from 20 to 40 games, represented by the movement from point *a* to point *c* along S_0.

Change in quantity supplied
Occurs when the price of the product changes, and is shown as a movement along an existing supply curve.

In summary, a change in supply is represented in Panel A by the shift from S_0 to S_1 or S_2, and this involves a shift in the entire supply curve. A change in quantity supplied is shown in Panel B and is a movement along an existing supply curve caused by a change in price of the product.

As on the demand side, this distinction between change in supply and change in quantity supplied is crucial. It means that when a product's price changes, only quantity supplied changes—the supply curve does not move.

Checkpoint

Supply

REVIEW

- Supply is the quantity of a product producers are willing and able to put on the market at various prices, all other relevant factors being held constant.

- The law of supply reflects the positive relationship between price and quantity supplied: the higher the market price, the more goods supplied, and the lower the market price, the fewer goods supplied.
- As with demand, market supply is arrived at by horizontally summing the individual supplies of all of the firms in the market.
- A change in supply occurs when one or more of the determinants of supply change.
- The determinants of supply are production technology, the cost of resources, prices of other commodities, expectations, the numbers of sellers or producers in the market, and taxes and subsidies.
- A *change in supply* is a shift in the supply curve. A shift to the right reflects an increase in supply, while a shift to the left represents a decrease in supply.
- A *change in quantity supplied* is only caused by a change in the price of the product; it results in a movement along the existing supply curve.

QUESTION

What has been the impact of the iPod, iTunes, and MP3 players in general on high-end stereo equipment production?

Answers to the Checkpoint question can be found at the end of this chapter.

Market Equilibrium

Before considering the concept of market equilibrium, let's take a quick look back at what we've covered so far. Demand and supply are both relationships between the price and quantity of some product over a given period of time, all other determinants being held constant. The quantity of a product supplied or demanded changes only when the product's price changes. Accordingly, changes in quantity supplied and quantity demanded cause movements along supply curves and demand curves, respectively. When one or more of the determinants of supply or demand changes, however, the curves themselves shift. This leads to more or less of the product being supplied or demanded at the current price. A summary of how the determinants impact both supply and demand is shown in Figure 6. You will find this a good reference when solving problems where supply and demand change.

Supply and demand together determine the prices and quantities of goods bought and sold. Neither factor alone is sufficient to determine price and quantity; it is through their interaction that supply and demand do their work, just as two blades of a scissors are required to cut paper.

Equilibrium
Market forces are in balance where the quantities demanded by consumers just equal quantities supplied by producers.

Equilibrium price
Market equilibrium price is the price that results when quantity demanded is just equal to quantity supplied.

Equilibrium quantity
Market equilibrium quantity is the output that results when quantity demanded is just equal to quantity supplied.

A market will determine the price at which the quantity of a product demanded is equal to the quantity supplied. At this price, the market is said to be cleared or to be in **equilibrium**, meaning the amount of the product that consumers are willing and able to purchase is matched exactly by the amount that producers are willing and able to sell. This is the **equilibrium price** and the **equilibrium quantity**. The equilibrium price is also called the market-clearing price.

Figure 7 puts together Figures 2 and 4, showing the market supply and demand for computer games. It illustrates how supply and demand interact to determine equilibrium price and quantity. Clearly, the quantities demanded and supplied equal one another only where the supply and demand curves cross, at point *e*. Alternatively, you can see this in the table that is part of the figure: Quantity demanded and quantity supplied are the same at only one particular point. At $60 a game, sellers are willing to provide exactly the same quantity as consumers would like to

FIGURE 6

Changes in Demand and Supply and Their Determinants

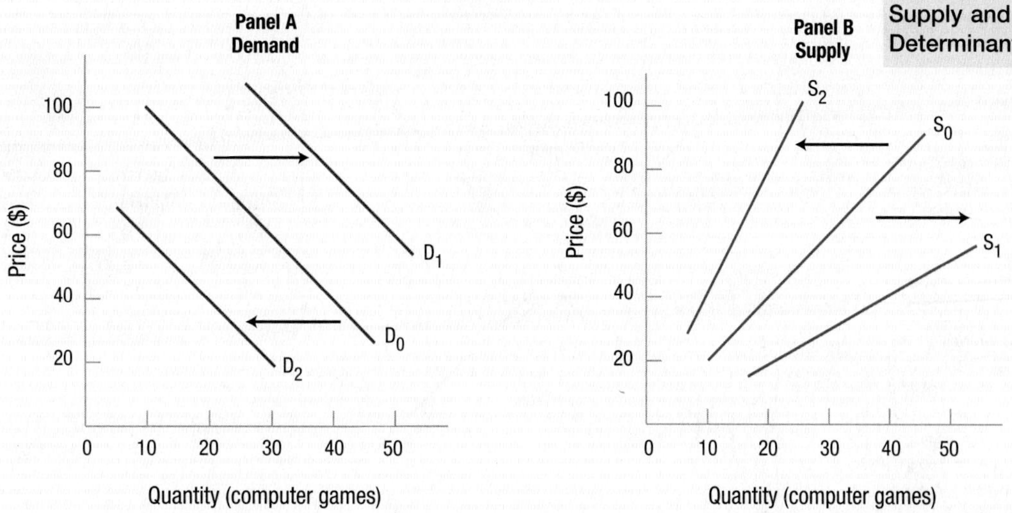

Determinants of Demand		Determinants of Supply	
Decrease in Demand	**Increase in Demand**	**Decrease in Supply**	**Increase in Supply**
Tastes and preferences decline (less advertising, out of fashion).	Tastes and preferences grow (more advertising, fad).	Technology harms productivity (unusual).	Technology improves productivity (production robots in factories increase productivity and supply).
Income falls (economy is in a recession).	Income rises (economy is booming).	Resource costs rise (tough collective bargaining by unions could lead to higher labor costs and reduce supply).	Resource costs fall (large discoveries of natural resources such as oil, natural gas, would reduce world prices, increasing supply of products using these resources).
Price of substitute falls (price of tea falls, coffee demand declines). Price of complement rises (price of gasoline rises, demand for big SUVs drops).	Price of substitute rises (chicken prices rise, demand for beef increases). Price of complement falls (price of DVD players falls, demand for DVD movies increases).	Price of a production substitute rises (cucumber prices rise, reducing the supply of radishes as more cucumbers are planted).	Price of a production substitute falls (price of apples falls, landowners plant grapes instead and eventually the supply of wine rises).
Number of buyers falls.	Number of buyers grows.	Expectation of a rise in future price of product (unsettled world conditions lead to expectations that gold will jump in price, which may lead to a withholding of gold from the market, reducing current supply).	Falling future price expectations for product (if beef prices are expected to fall, producers may sell more cattle now).
Expecting future glut; expected surplus in future leads to lower prices so consumers hold off buying now (some consumers wait for after Christmas sales of unsold—surplus—merchandise).	Expecting future shortages; leads to stocking up now to avoid higher prices in future (predicted gasoline shortages lead to filling of tanks now—an increase in current demand).	Decreasing number of sellers	Rising number of sellers
		Increase in taxes or reduction in subsidies (increasing taxes on cigarettes or reducing subsidies for ethanol will reduce supplies of both products).	Decrease in taxes or an increase in subsidies (reductions in excise taxes on luxury vehicles and increases in subsidies to education will increase the supply of both).

FIGURE 7

Equilibrium Price and Quantity of Computer Games

Market equilibrium is achieved when quantity demanded and quantity supplied are equal. In this graph, that equilibrium occurs at point *e*, at an equilibrium price of $60 and an equilibrium output of 30. If the market price is above equilibrium ($80), a surplus of 20 computer games will result (*b* – *a*), automatically driving the price back down to $60. When the market price is too low ($40), a shortage of 20 computer games will result (*d* – *c*), and businesses will raise their offering prices until equilibrium is again restored.

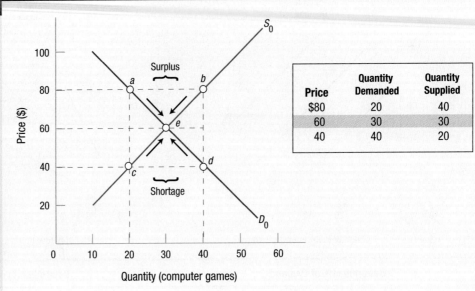

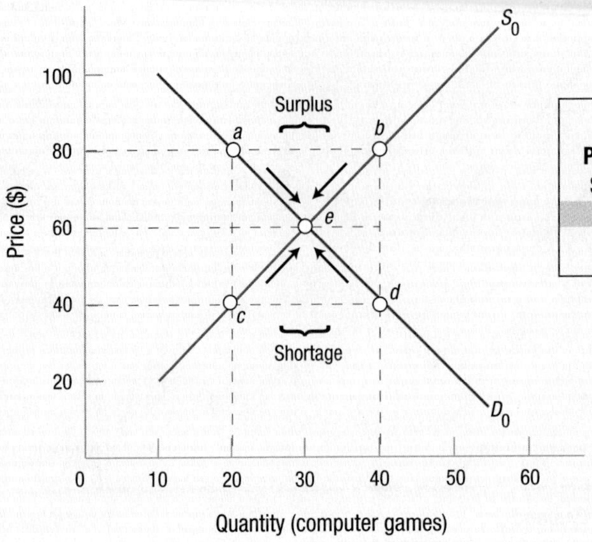

Price	Quantity Demanded	Quantity Supplied
$80	20	40
60	30	30
40	40	20

purchase. Hence, at this price, the market clears, since buyers and sellers both want to transact the same number of units.

The beauty of a market is that it automatically works to establish the equilibrium price and quantity, without any guidance from anyone. To see how this happens, let us assume that computer games are initially priced at $80, a price above their equilibrium price. As we can see by comparing points *a* and *b*, sellers are willing to supply more games at this price than consumers are willing to buy. Economists characterize such a situation as one of excess supply, or **surplus**. In this case, at $80, sellers supply 40 games to the market (point *b*), yet buyers want to purchase only 20 (point *a*). This leaves an excess of 20 games overhanging the market; these unsold games ultimately become surplus inventories.

Surplus
Occurs when the price is above market equilibrium, and quantity supplied exceeds quantity demanded.

Here is where the market kicks in to restore equilibrium. As inventories rise, most firms will cut production. Some firms, moreover, will start reducing their prices to increase sales. Other firms must then cut their own prices to remain competitive. This process will continue, with firms cutting their prices and production, until most firms have managed to exhaust their surplus inventories. This happens when prices reach $60 and quantity supplied equals 30, since consumers are once again willing to buy up the entire quantity supplied at this price, and the market is restored to equilibrium.

In general, therefore, when prices are set too high, surpluses result, which drive prices back down to their equilibrium levels. If, conversely, a price is initially set too low, say at $40, a **shortage** results. In this case, buyers want to purchase 40 games (point *d*), but sellers are only providing 20 (point *c*), creating a shortage of 20 games. Because consumers are willing to pay more than $40 to get hold of the few games available on the market, they will start bidding up the price of computer games. Sensing an opportunity to make some money, firms will start raising their prices and increasing production, once again until equilibrium is restored. Hence, in general, excess demand causes firms to raise prices and increase production.

Shortage
Occurs when the price is below market equilibrium, and quantity demanded exceeds quantity supplied.

When there is a shortage in a market, economists speak of a tight market or a seller's market. Under these conditions, producers have no difficulty selling off all their output. When a surplus of goods floods the market, this gives rise to a buyer's market, since buyers can buy all the goods they want at attractive prices.

We have now seen how changing prices naturally work to clear up shortages and surpluses, thereby returning markets to equilibrium. Some markets, once disturbed, will return to equilibrium quickly. Examples include the stock, bond, and money mar-

Alfred Marshall (1842–1924)

British economist Alfred Marshall is considered the father of the modern theory of supply and demand—price and output are determined by both supply and demand. He noted that the two go together like the blades of a scissors that cross at equilibrium.

He assumed that changes in quantity demanded were only affected by changes in price, and that all other factors remained constant. Marshall also is credited with developing the ideas of the laws of demand and supply, and the concepts of price elasticity of demand, consumer surplus, and producer surplus—concepts we will study in the next two chapters.

In 1890, he published *Principles of Economics* at age 48. In it he introduced many new ideas for the first time, but as Ray Canterbery noted, "without any suggestion that they are novel or remarkable."[3] During his lifetime, the book went through eight editions. In hopes of appealing to the general populace, Marshall buried his diagrams in footnotes. And, although he is credited with many economic theories, he would always clarify them with various exceptions and qualifications. He expected future economists to flesh out his ideas.

John Maynard Keynes, the most influential economist of the last century and Marshall's student, wrote a 70-page, 20,000-word memorial to Marshall published in the *Economic Journal,* 3 months after his death in 1924.[4]

Marshall was an enormous figure in economics, but a disappointment to his father, because he went to study mathematics and physics at St. John's College, Cambridge, instead of joining the clergy, as was expected. But after long walks through the poorest sections of several European cities and seeing their horrible conditions, he decided to focus his attention on political economy. More than anyone else, Marshall is given credit for establishing economics as a discipline of study.

kets, where trading is nearly instantaneous and extensive information abounds. Other markets react very slowly. Consider the labor market, for instance. For various psychological reasons, most people have an inflated idea of their worth to both current and future employers. It is only after an extended bout of unemployment, therefore,

[3]E. Ray Canterbery, *A Brief History of Economics: Artful Approaches to the Dismal Science* (New Jersey: World Scientific), 2001, p. 139.
[4]Robert Skidelsky, *John Maynard Keynes: Volume Two The Economist as Saviour 1920–1937* (New York: Penguin), 1992, p. 181.

that many people will face reality and accept a position at a salary lower than their previous job. Similarly, real estate markets can be slow to adjust since sellers will often refuse to accept a price below what they are asking for, until the lack of sales over time convinces sellers to adjust the price downward.

These automatic market adjustments can make some buyers and sellers feel uncomfortable: It seems as if prices and quantities are being set by forces beyond anyone's control. In fact, this phenomenon is precisely what makes market economies function so efficiently. Without anyone needing to be in control, prices and quantities will naturally gravitate toward equilibrium levels. Adam Smith was so impressed by the workings of the market that he suggested it is almost as if an "invisible hand" guides the market to equilibrium.

Given the self-correcting nature of the market, long-term shortages or surpluses are almost always the result of government intervention. We will discuss such instances in the next chapter. First, however, we turn to a discussion of how the market responds to changes in supply and demand, or to shifts of the supply and demand curves.

Moving to a New Equilibrium: Changes in Supply and Demand

Once a market is in equilibrium and the forces of supply and demand balance one another out, the market will remain there unless an external factor changes. But when the supply curve or demand curve shifts (some determinant changes), equilibrium also shifts, resulting in a new equilibrium price and/or output. The ability to predict new equilibrium points is one of the most useful aspects of supply and demand analysis.

Predicting the New Equilibrium When One Curve Shifts

When only supply or only demand changes, the change in equilibrium price and equilibrium output can be predicted. We begin with changes in supply.

Changes in Supply. Figure 8 shows what happens when supply changes. Equilibrium initially is at point *e*, with equilibrium price and quantity at P_0 and Q_0, respectively. But let us assume a rise in wages or the bankruptcy of a key business in the market (the number of sellers declines) causes a decrease in supply. When supply

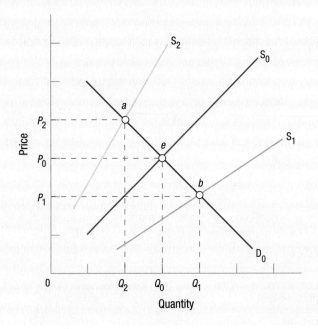

FIGURE 8

Equilibrium Price, Output, and Shifts in Supply

When supply alone shifts, the effects on both equilibrium price and output can be predicted. When supply grows (S_0 to S_1), equilibrium price will fall and output will rise. When supply declines (S_0 to S_2), the opposite will happen: Equilibrium price will rise and output will fall.

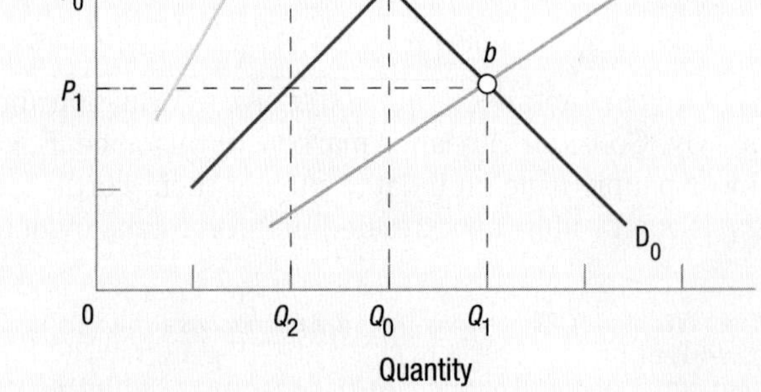

declines (the supply curve shifts from S_0 to S_2), equilibrium price rises to P_2, while equilibrium output falls to Q_2 (point *a*).

If, on the other hand, supply increases (the supply curve shifts from S_0 to S_1), equilibrium price falls to P_1, while equilibrium output rises to Q_1 (point *b*). This is what has happened in the electronics industry: Declining production costs have resulted in more electronic products being sold at lower prices.

Changes in Demand. The effects of demand changes are shown in Figure 9. Again, equilibrium is initially at point *e*, with equilibrium price and quantity at P_0 and Q_0, respectively. But let us assume the economy then enters a recession and incomes sink, or perhaps the price of some complementary good soars; in either case, demand falls. As demand declines (the demand curve shifts from D_0 to D_2), equilibrium price falls to P_2, while equilibrium output falls to Q_2 (point *a*).

During the same recession just described, the demand for inferior goods (beans and baloney) will rise, as declining incomes force people to switch to cheaper substitutes. For these products, as demand increases (shifting the demand curve from D_0 to D_1), equilibrium price rises to P_1, and equilibrium output grows to Q_1 (point *b*).

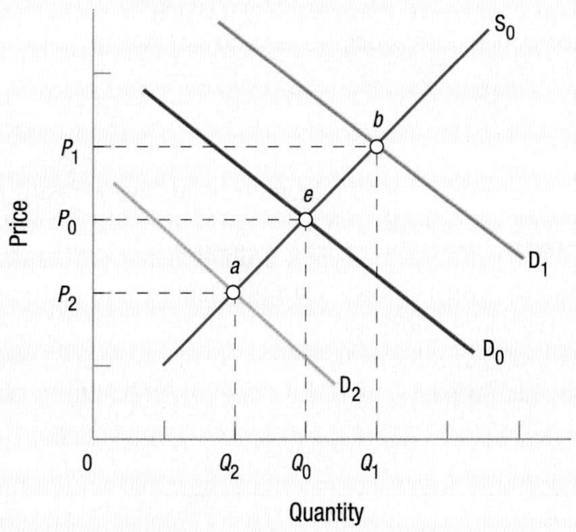

FIGURE 9

Equilibrium Price, Output, and Shifts in Demand

When demand alone changes, the effects on both equilibrium price and output can again be determined. When demand grows (D_0 to D_1), both price and output rise. Conversely, when demand falls (D_0 to D_2), both price and output fall.

Predicting the New Equilibrium When Both Curves Shift

When both supply and demand change, things get tricky. We can predict what will happen with price, in some cases, and output, in other cases, but not what will happen with both.

When Both Curves Shift in the Same Direction. Figure 10 on the next page portrays an increase in both demand and supply. Consider the market for corn. If government subsidizes the production of ethanol, demand for corn will increase. If bioengineering results in a new corn hybrid that uses less fertilizer and generates 50% higher yields, supply will increase. When demand increases from D_0 to D_1 and supply increases from S_0 to S_1, output clearly grows to Q_1. What happens to the price of corn, however, is not so clear. If demand grows relatively more than supply (Panel A), the new equilibrium price will be higher. Conversely, if demand grows relatively less than supply does (Panel C), the new equilibrium price will be lower.

In Figure 11 on the next page, supply and demand have declined to S_2 and D_2, respectively. If this is the cellular phone market, and cell phone use is shown to have serious detrimental health effects if used more than 10 minutes a day, the demand will decline. And if microchip production confronts the end of Moore's law

FIGURE 10

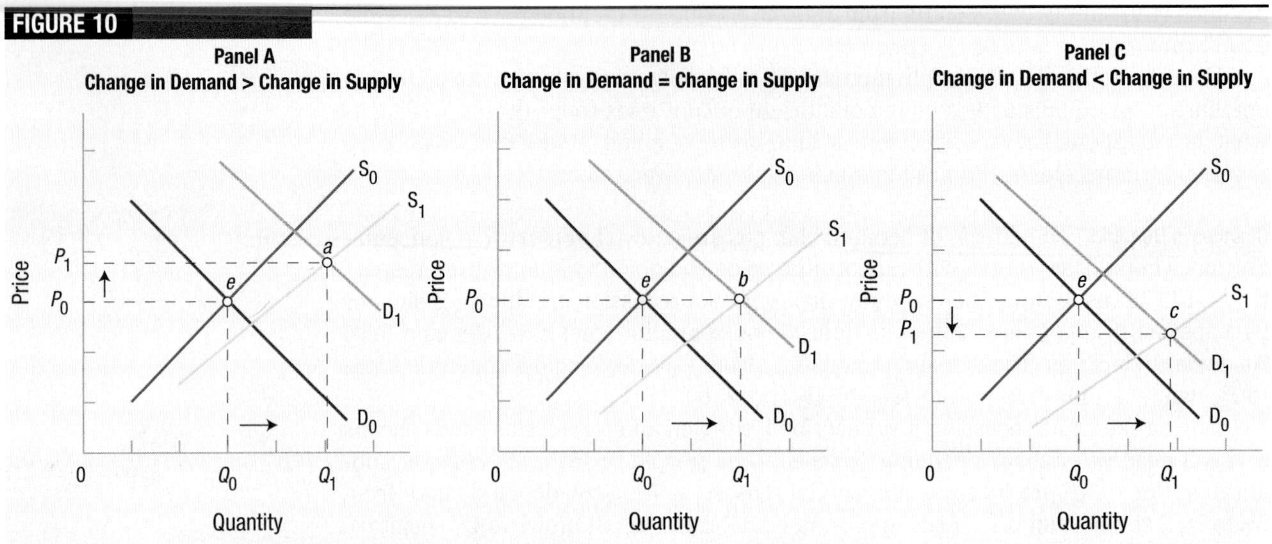

Increase in Supply, Increase in Demand, and Equilibrium

When both demand and supply increase, output will clearly rise. What will happen to the equilibrium price is uncertain, however. If demand grows relatively more than supply (Panel A), price will rise, but if supply grows relatively more than demand (Panel C), price will fall.

(speed of micro chips doubles every 18 months at lower costs) and costs rise substantially, supply will decline. In this case, we can see that output will fall to Q_2. Again, however, what happens to price is ambiguous. If demand declines more than supply, price will fall. Alternatively, if supply declines more than demand, the new equilibrium price will be higher.

Thus, when supply and demand decline or rise together, we can forecast what will happen to output. In such cases, however, the change in price cannot be pre-

FIGURE 11

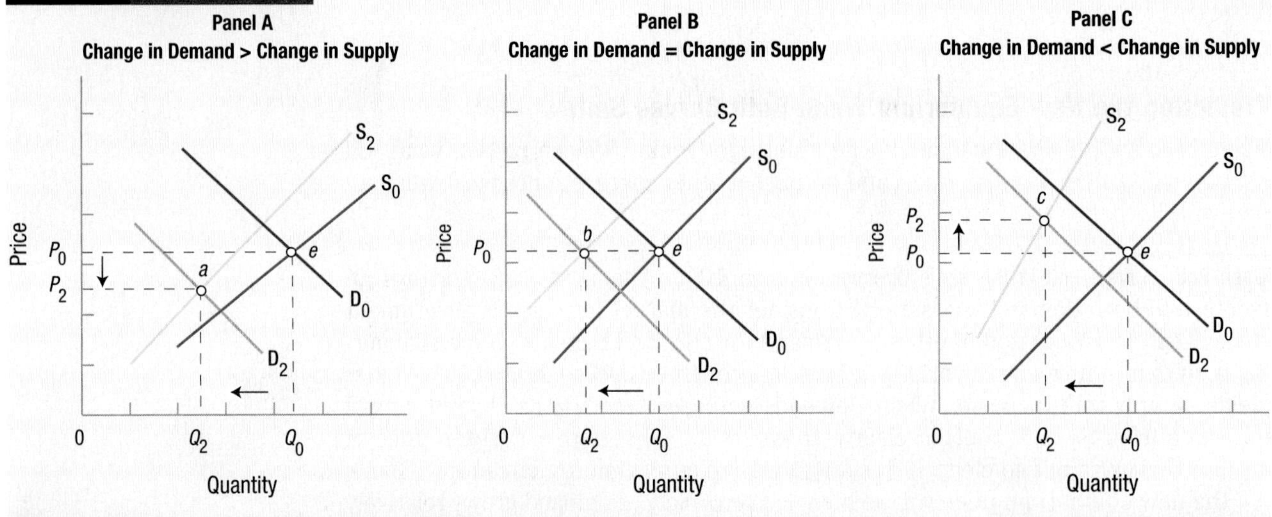

Decrease in Supply, Decrease in Demand, and Equilibrium

When both demand and supply decrease, output will clearly fall, but what happens to the new equilibrium price is again uncertain. If demand falls relatively more than supply, the new equilibrium price will fall, and vice versa.

dicted without further information regarding the relative magnitudes of the changes in supply and demand.

When the Curves Shift in Opposite Directions. Figure 12 illustrates the case of rising demand and decreasing supply. This might represent the market for General Motors' cars if China offers high prices and absorbs most of the world's steel output for its own development efforts, increasing the price of a major input into GM's cars. Not to be deterred, GM develops a plug-in hybrid that averages over 75 miles per gallon and demand rises substantially. Demand increases to D_1 and supply decreases to S_2, thus clearly raising price to P_2. Still, what happens to equilibrium sales is ambiguous. If demand grows more than supply declines (Panel A), the new equilibrium output will be higher than before. But if supply declines more than demand grows (Panel C), the new equilibrium output will be lower.

FIGURE 12

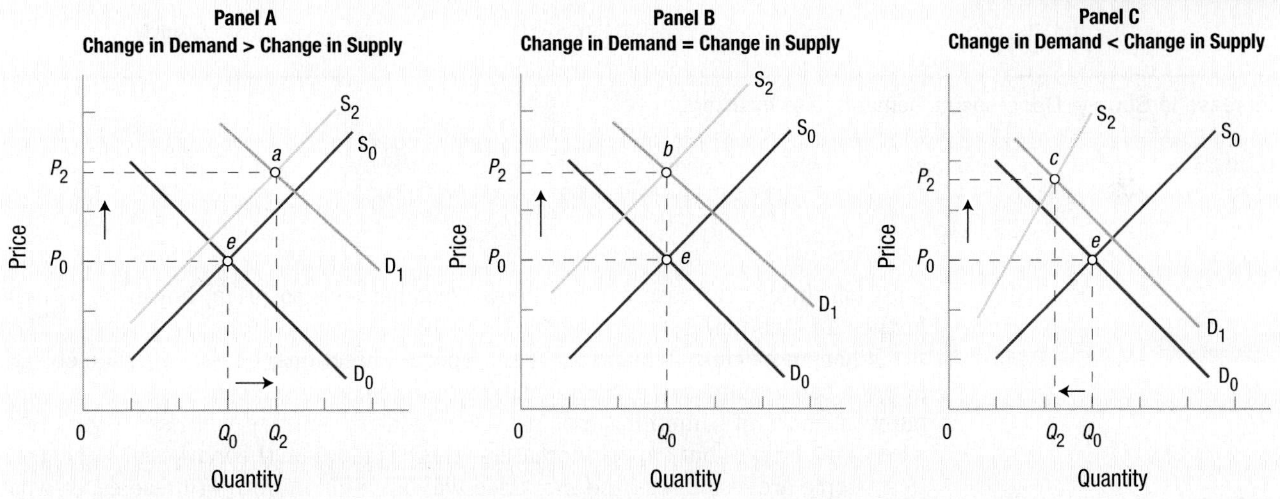

Decrease in Supply, Increase in Demand, and Equilibrium

If demand grows and supply falls, equilibrium price will clearly rise, but now what happens to equilibrium output is indeterminate. If supply declines relatively more than demand grows, output will fall. If supply declines less than demand grows, output will rise.

In Figure 13 on the next page, we have the opposite case, where demand declines to D_2 and supply rises to S_1. This might represent the market for tape players and recorders and their decline in demand in the digital age. However, costs to manufacture these players have fallen given changing production technology. In this case, we can see that price will fall to P_2, but again, what happens with output is uncertain. If demand declines more than supply grows (Panel A), output will fall. Conversely, if supply grows more than demand falls (Panel C), the new equilibrium output will rise.

Thus, when supply and demand move in opposite directions, the resulting change in price can be predicted. Forecasting the accompanying change in output is impossible, however, without additional information concerning the relative strength of the changes in supply and demand.

Summarizing Shifts and Equilibrium

With these results in hand, a summary of what happens when both curves shift is in order. When demand and supply both increase or both decrease together (whenever they move in the same direction), the change in sales or output can be predicted. Specifically, when both curves rise, sales rise, and when both curves fall,

FIGURE 13

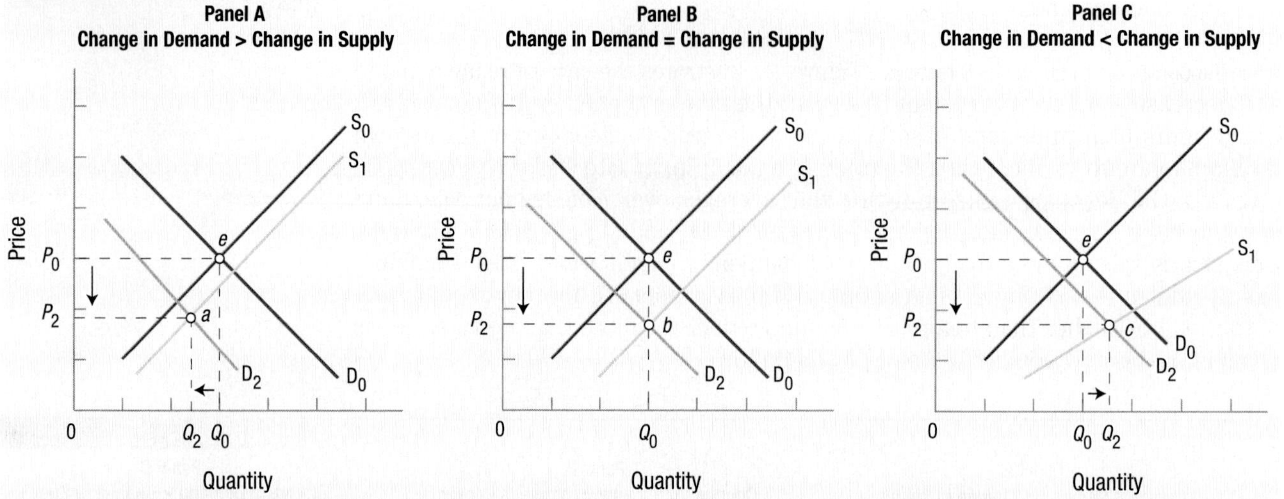

Increase in Supply, Decrease in Demand, and Equilibrium

When demand falls and supply grows, the new equilibrium price will clearly be lower than before, but the effect on output cannot be determined without further information. If supply grows relatively more than demand falls, output will rise. If supply grows relatively less than demand falls, output will fall.

sales fall. In neither case can we know what happens to price, however, without further information.

When supply and demand move in opposite directions, by contrast, the change in price can be forecasted. Specifically, when demand rises but supply falls—people want more of something that has become dearer—price will rise. Alternately, when demand falls but supply increases—there is more on the market of some good that people are less interested in—price will fall. Still, in both of these cases what happens to sales or output remains ambiguous without further information.

These results are summarized in Table 1. Where the table indicates that equilibrium price or quantity is indeterminate, it means that the change will depend on

Table 1 **The Effect of Changes in Demand or Supply on Equilibrium Prices and Quantities**

Change in Demand	Change in Supply	Change in Equilibrium Price	Change in Equilibrium Quantity	Figure Where Result is Shown
No change	Increase	Decrease	Increase	8
No change	Decrease	Increase	Decrease	8
Increase	No change	Increase	Increase	9
Decrease	No change	Decrease	Decrease	9
Increase	Increase	Indeterminate	Increase	10
Decrease	Decrease	Indeterminate	Decrease	11
Increase	Decrease	Increase	Indeterminate	12
Decrease	Increase	Decrease	Indeterminate	13

the relative magnitudes of the shifts in supply or demand, and price or quantity can rise, fall, or remain the same. The last column in the table shows the figure where this result is shown.

Checkpoint

Market Equilibrium

REVIEW

- Together, supply and demand determine market equilibrium.
- Equilibrium occurs when quantity supplied exactly equals quantity demanded.
- The equilibrium price is also called the market-clearing price.
- When supply and demand change, equilibrium price and output change.
- When only one curve shifts, the resulting changes in equilibrium price and quantity can be predicted.
- When both curves shift, we can predict the change in equilibrium price in some cases or the change in equilibrium quantity in others, but never both. We have to determine the relative magnitudes of the shifts before we can predict both equilibrium price and quantity.

QUESTIONS

As China and India (both with huge populations and rapidly growing economies) continue to develop, what do you think will happen to their demand for energy and specifically oil? What will suppliers of oil do in the face of this demand? Will this have an impact on world energy (oil) prices? What sort of policies or events could alter your forecast about the future price of oil?

Answers to the Checkpoint questions can be found at the end of this chapter.

Putting Supply and Demand to Work

Excess Grape Supply and Two-Buck Chuck

Let's apply these concepts to two short examples. The great California wines of the 1990s put California vineyards on the map. Demand, prices, and exports grew rapidly. Overplanting of new grape vines was a result. Driving along Interstate 5 or Highway 101 north of Los Angeles, grape vineyards extend as far as the eye can see, and most were planted in the mid to late 1990s. The 2001 recession reduced the demand for California wine, and a rising dollar made imported wine relatively cheaper. The result was a sharp drop in demand for California wine and a huge surplus of grapes.

Donald Gruener

Bronco Wine Company President Fred Franzia made an exclusive deal with Trader Joe's (an unusual supermarket that features exotic food and wine products), bought the excess grapes at distressed prices, and with his modern plant produced inexpensive wine under the Charles Shaw label. Selling for $1.99 a bottle, Two-Buck Chuck, as it is known, is available in chardonnay, merlot, cabernet sauvignon, shiraz, and sauvignon blanc. Consumers have flocked to Trader Joe's and literally haul cases of wine out by the carload. Today, Two-Buck Chuck sells well over a million cases a month. This is not rotgut: the 2002 shiraz beat out 2,300 other wines to win a double gold medal at the 28th Annual International Eastern Wine Competition in 2004.

Two-Buck Chuck was such a hit that other supermarkets were forced to offer their own discount wines. This good, low-priced wine has had the effect of opening up markets. As Figure 14 illustrates, people who previously avoided wine because of the cost have begun drinking more (demand curves do slope down and to the right). As *The Economist* has noted, the entire industry may benefit because "wine drinkers who start off drinking plonk often graduate to upmarket varieties."[5]

FIGURE 14

The Market for Wine

The glut of grapes and the subsequent reduction in grape prices caused the supply of wine to increase and the price to fall.

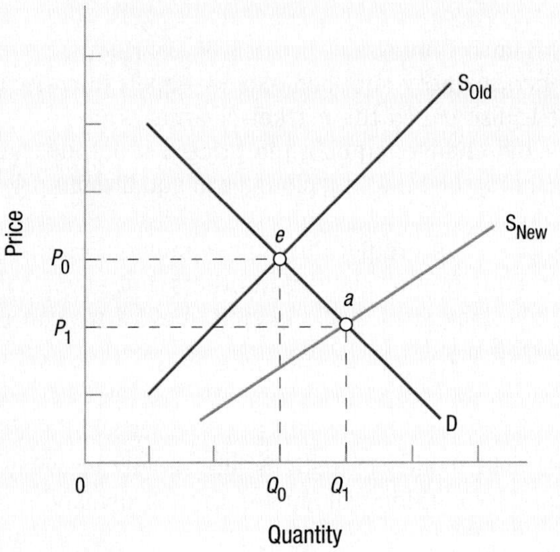

Trek Bicycles and Lance Armstrong

Hshen Lim

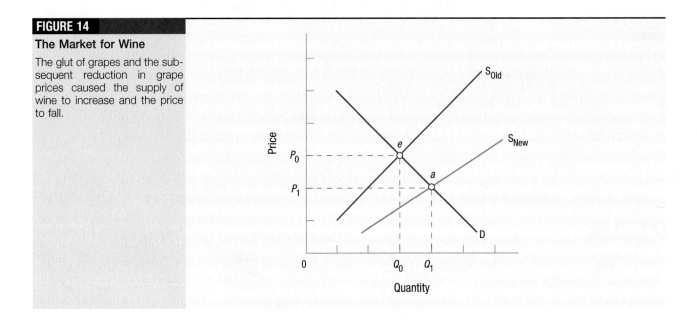

The second example deals with a growing demand but no change in supply. When Lance Armstrong won his seventh Tour de France cycling championship in July 2005, he rode a bicycle made by Trek of the United States.[6] So, on the demand side, we can expect demand for the victor's brand of bicycles to go up. This in fact happened, in both the United States and Europe. On the supply side, U.S. bicycle manufacturers such as Trek and Cannondale were willing to increase output, as shown in Figure 15 (note that the supply curve didn't change, only quantity supplied). This process worked well in the United States, but proved tougher in Europe, not so much in the actual production of the bicycles but in getting stores to stock them. Up until a few years ago, racing bicycles were almost exclusively made by European companies.

Using our supply and demand analysis, we see that demand increased. Since no determinant of supply changed, we know that output will increase, and prices for Trek bicycles will rise. Our supply and demand analysis gives us a useful framework for predicting how market participants will act, and what the resulting price and output might be.

You now have the fundamental tools of supply and demand analysis. In the next chapter, we will use these tools to analyze markets, policy choices, and government intervention.

[5]"California Drinking," *The Economist,* June 7, 2003, p. 56.

[6]See Ian Austen, "U.S. Bike Makers Seek Dominance in Europe," *New York Times,* December 30, 2003, p. W1.

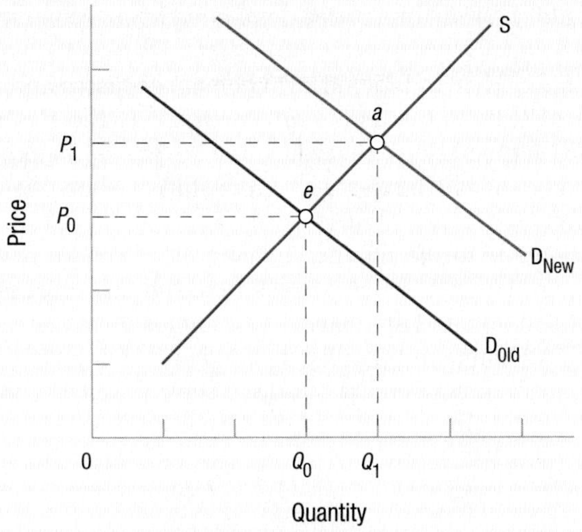

FIGURE 15

The Market for Bicycles

The demand for bicycles rose after Lance Armstrong won his seventh Tour de France, and as expected, prices of Trek bicycles rose.

Key Concepts

Markets, p. 52
Price system, p. 53
Demand, p. 53
Law of demand, p. 54
Demand curve, p. 55
Horizontal summation, p. 55
Determinants of demand, p. 56
Normal goods, p. 57
Inferior goods, p. 57
Substitute goods, p. 57
Complementary goods, p. 57
Change in demand, p. 58
Change in quantity demanded, p. 59
Supply, p. 60
Law of supply, p. 60
Supply curve, p. 61
Determinants of supply, p. 61
Change in supply, p. 63
Change in quantity supplied, p. 63
Equilibrium, p. 64
Equilibrium price, p. 64
Equilibrium quantity, p. 64
Surplus, p. 66
Shortage, p. 66

Chapter Summary

Markets

Markets are institutions that enable buyers and sellers to interact and transact business with one another. Markets differ in geographical location, products offered, and size. Prices contain an incredible amount of information for both buyers and sellers. Through their purchases, consumers signal their willingness to exchange money or other valuables for particular products at particular prices. These signals help businesses to decide what to produce and how much of it to produce. Consequently, the market economy is often called the price system.

Demand

Demand refers to the quantity of products people are willing and able to purchase during some specific time period, all other relevant factors being held constant. Price and quantity demanded stand in a negative (inverse) relationship: as price rises, consumers buy fewer units; and as price falls, consumers buy more units. This inverse relation is known as the law of demand. It is depicted in a downward-sloping demand curve.

Market demand curves are found by horizontally summing individual demand curves. We simply add the total quantities demanded by all consumers for each possible price.

The determinants of demand include (1) consumer tastes and preferences, (2) income, (3) prices of substitutes and complements, (4) the number of buyers in the market, and (5) expectations regarding future prices, incomes, and product availability. Demand changes (the demand curve shifts) when one or more of these determinants change.

A shift of the demand curve implies a change in demand. A shift to the right reflects an increase in demand, whereas a shift to the left represents a decline in demand. These shifts in demand are caused by changes in one or more of the determinants of demand. A change in quantity demanded occurs only when the price of a product changes, leading consumers to adjust their purchases along the existing demand curve.

Supply

Supply is the quantity of a product producers are willing and able to put on the market at various prices, all other relevant factors being held constant. The law of supply reflects the positive relationship between price and quantity supplied: The higher the market price, the more goods supplied; and the lower the market price, the fewer goods supplied. It is depicted in an upward-sloping supply curve. Market supply, as with market demand, is arrived at by horizontally summing the individual supplies of all of the firms in the market.

The six determinants of supply are (1) production technology, (2) the cost of resources, (3) prices of other commodities, (4) expectations, (5) the number of sellers or producers in the market, and (6) taxes and subsidies.

When one or more of the determinants of supply change, a change in supply results, causing a shift in the supply curve. A shift to the right reflects an increase in supply, whereas a shift to the left represents a decline in supply. A change in quantity supplied is only caused by a change in the price of the product; it results in a movement along the existing supply curve. A reduction in price results in a reduction of quantity supplied, whereas a price increase leads to an increase in quantity supplied.

Market Equilibrium

Supply and demand together determine market equilibrium. Equilibrium occurs when quantity demanded and quantity supplied are precisely equal. This means that producers are bringing precisely the quantity of some good to market that consumers wish to purchase, such that the market clears. The price at which equilibrium is reached is called the equilibrium price, or the market-clearing price.

If prices are set too high, surpluses result, which drive prices back down to equilibrium levels. If prices are set too low, a shortage results, which drives prices up until equilibrium is reached.

When supply and demand change (a shift in the curves), equilibrium price and output change. When only one curve shifts, then both resulting changes in equilibrium price and quantity can be predicted. For example, if demand increases, both equilibrium output and price will increase.

When the two curves both shift, the change in equilibrium price can be forecasted in some instances, and the change in equilibrium output in others, but never both. When both curves shift in the same direction, we can predict what will happen to output but not to price. When both curves shift in opposite directions, we can predict what will happen to price but not to output. We need more information on the relative magnitudes of the shifts in both curves before we can predict both equilibrium price and quantity.

Questions and Problems

1. Product prices give consumers and businesses a lot of information besides just the price. What are they?

2. Demand for tickets to sports events such as the Super Bowl has increased. Has supply increased? What does the answer to this tell you about the price of these tickets compared to a few years ago?

3. As the world population ages, the demand for cholesterol drugs will [increase/decrease/remain the same]? Assume there is a positive relationship between aging and cholesterol levels. Is this change a change in demand or a change in quantity demanded?

4. Describe some of the reasons why supply will change. Improved technology typically results in lower prices for most products. Why do you think this is true? Describe the difference between a change in supply and a change in quantity supplied.

5. In 2006 rental car companies often charged more to rent a compact car than an SUV or a luxury vehicle. Why do you think rental companies turned their normal pricing structure on its head?

6. Both individual and market demand curves have negative slopes and reflect the law of demand. What is the difference between the two curves?

7. Describe the determinants of demand. Why are they important?

8. 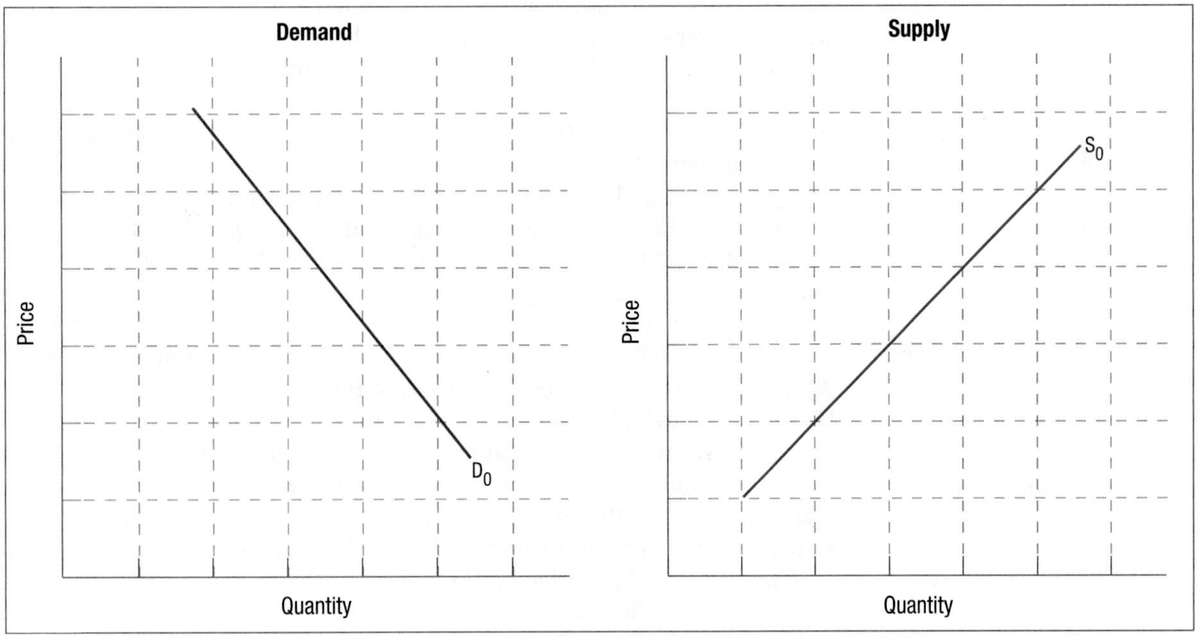

Using the figures above, answer the following questions:

a. On the Demand panel:
- Show an increase in demand and label it D_1.
- Show a decrease in demand and label it D_2.
- Show an increase in quantity demanded.
- Show a decrease in quantity demanded.
- What causes demand to change?
- What causes quantity demanded to change?

b. On the Supply panel:
- Show an increase in supply and label it S_1.
- Show a decrease in supply and label it S_2.
- Show an increase in quantity supplied.
- Show a decrease in quantity supplied.
- What causes supply to change?
- What causes quantity supplied to change?

9. Several medical studies have shown that red wine in moderation is good for the heart. How would such a study affect the public's demand for wine? Would it have an impact on the type of grapes planted in new vineyards?

10. Norrath is a place in the online game EverQuest II. It is a virtual world with roughly 350,000 players "arrayed over worlds that are tethered to dozens of servers." As Rob Walker noted, "EverQuest is filled with half-elves, castles, sword fights and such, and involves a fairly complex internal economy, whose currency is platinum pieces used to buy weapons, food and other goods." This virtual market, however, has led to a real-world market, with real dollars for virtual goods. Players sell weapons, complete characters, and other virtual items on EverQuest's internal market called Station Exchange and on eBay. Common items sell for $10 to $25, while extensive characters or weapons can fetch a thousand dollars or more. (Based on Rob Walker, "The Buying Game: A real market, overseen by a real corporation, selling things that don't really exist," *New York Times Magazine,* October 16, 2005, p. 28.)

    Why would someone buy virtual goods? Does supply and demand play any role in this real market for virtual goods? If there were virtual games similar to EverQuest II where everything is free, would any real markets exist for their virtual goods? How does paying for a virtual product differ from the situation where a buyer could purchase a nice watch for a reasonable price, but decides to buy a luxury brand for 10 to 20 times as much?

11. In December of 2005, the *Wall Street Journal* reported that Clark Foam, a major supplier of polyurethane cores (blanks) for hand-shaped surfboards, closed its plant and went out of business (Peter Sanders and Stephanie Kang, "Wipeout for Key Player in Surfboard Industry," *The Wall Street Journal,* December 8, 2005, p. B1). Clark Foam was the Microsoft of surfboard blank makers, and had been supplying foam blanks to surf shops for over 50 years. Polyurethane blanks, while light and sturdy, contain a toxic chemical, toluene diisocyanate (TDI). Over the last two decades the Environmental Protection Agency has increasingly been restricting the use of TDI. Clark Foam's owner Gordon "Grubby" Clark indicated in a letter to customers that he was tired of fighting environmental regulators, lawsuits over injury to employees, and fire regulations. Surf historian and author of *The Encyclopedia of Surfing,* Matt Warshaw said, "It's the equivalent of removing lumber for the housing industry."
    a. If you owned a retail surfboard shop and read this article in the *Wall Street Journal,* would you change the prices on the existing surfboards you have in the shop? Why or why not?
    b. If the demand for surfboards remains constant over the next few years, what would you expect to see happen on the supply side in this industry?

12. Polysilicon is used to produce computer chips and solar photovoltaics. Currently more polysilicon is used to produce computer chips, but the demand for ultra-pure polysilicon for solar panels is rising. According to a 2006 *Business Week* article (John Carey, "What's Raining on Solar's Parade," *Business Week,* February 6, 2006, p. 78), this has created a shortage, and prices have more than doubled between 2004 and 2006.

a. High oil and energy prices, along with subsidies from U.S. and European governments for solar power, has increased demand, but suppliers are reluctant to build new factories or expand existing facilities, because they fear governments can easily eliminate incentives and at this point they do not know if solar energy is just a fad as one executive suggested, "governments can take away incentives as easily as they put them in place," and asked "is the solar industry real or just a flash in the pan?" Are these legitimate concerns for business?

b. Given the uncertainty associated with building additional production capacity in the polysilicon industry, what might these manufacturers do to reduce the risk?

13. The table below represents the world supply and demand for natural vanilla in thousands of pounds. A large portion of natural vanilla is grown in Madagascar and comes from orchids that require a lot of time to cultivate. The sequence of events described below actually happened, but the numbers have been altered to make the calculations easier (See James Altucher, "Supply, Demand, and Edible Orchids," *Financial Times*, September 20, 2005, p.12). Assume the original supply and demand curves are represented in the table below.

Price ($/pound)	Quantity Demanded (thousands)	Quantity Supplied (thousands)
0	20	0
10	16	6
20	12	12
30	8	18
40	4	24
50	0	30

a. Graph both the supply (S_0) and demand (D_0) curves. What is the current equilibrium price? Label that point *a*.

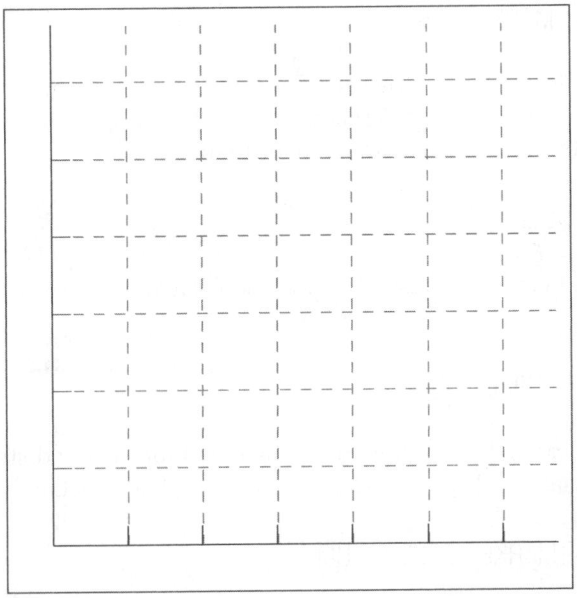

b. Assume that Madagascar is hit by a hurricane (actually occurred in 2000), and the world's supply of vanilla is reduced by 5/6, or 83%. Label the new supply curve (S_1). What will be the new equilibrium price in the market? Label that point *b*.

c. Now assume that Coca-Cola announces plans to introduce a new "Vanilla Coke," and this increases the demand for natural vanilla by 25%. Label the new demand curve (D_1). What will be the new equilibrium price? Label this new equilibrium point *c*. Remember that supply of natural vanilla was reduced by the hurricane earlier.

d. Growing the orchids that produce natural vanilla requires a climate with roughly 80% humidity, and the possible grower countries generally fall within 20° north or south of the equator. A doubling of prices encouraged several other countries (e.g., Uganda and Indonesia) to begin growing orchids or up their current production. Within several years, supply was back to normal (S_0), but by then, synthetic vanilla had replaced 80% of the original demand (D_0). Label this new demand curve (D_2). What is the new equilibrium price and output?

14. Assume initially that the demand and supply for premium coffees (one-pound bags) are in equilibrium. Now assume Starbucks introduces the world to premium blends, and so demand rises substantially. Describe what will happen in this market as it moves to a new equilibrium. If a hard freeze eliminates Brazil's premium coffee crop, what will happen to the price of premium coffee?

15. In late 2006 and early 2007, orange crops in Florida were smaller than expected, and the crop in California was put in a deep freeze by an Arctic cold front. As a result, the production of oranges was severely reduced. In addition, in early 2007, President George W. Bush called for the United States to reduce its gasoline consumption by 20% in the next decade. He proposed an increase in ethanol produced from corn and the stalks and leaves from corn and other grasses. What is the likely impact of these two events on food prices in the United States?

Answers to Checkpoint Questions

CHECKPOINT: MARKETS

The market for financial securities is a huge, well-organized, and regulated market compared to local flea markets. Trillions of dollars change hands each week in the financial markets, and products are standardized.

CHECKPOINT: DEMAND

Rising gasoline prices have caused the demand for hybrids to swell. This is a change in demand.

CHECKPOINT: SUPPLY

Since iPods and other MP3 players are substitutes for high-end stereo equipment, production and sales of high-end stereo equipment have declined.

CHECKPOINT: MARKET EQUILIBRIUM

Demand for both energy and oil will increase. Suppliers of oil will attempt to move up their supply curve and provide more to the market. Since all of the easy (cheap) oil has been found, costs to add to supplies will rise, and oil prices will gradually rise; in the longer term, alternatives will become more attractive, keeping oil prices from rising too rapidly.

4 Market Efficiency, Market Failure, and Government Intervention

Everywhere we look in the world there are markets, from the Tokyo fish markets, where every morning 20,000 flash-frozen tuna weighing 400–500 pounds each are auctioned off in a few hours; to Aalsmeer, Holland, where millions of fresh flowers are flown in from all over the world every day, auctioned off, then shipped to firms in other parts of the world; to Chicago, where billions of dollars of derivative securities and commodities are bought and sold on the futures market daily. Beyond these big markets, moreover, countless smaller markets dot our local landscapes, and many new virtual markets are springing up on the Internet.

Since the Soviet Union collapsed in 1989, markets and the market system have gained an even greater momentum as many countries have begun leaning more heavily on markets to allocate resources, products, and services. In earlier chapters, we saw that every economy faces tradeoffs in the use of its resources to produce various goods and services, as represented graphically by the production possibilities frontier (PPF). The last chapter considered how supply and demand work together to determine the quantities of various products sold and the equilibrium prices consumers must pay for them in a market economy. As we saw, Adam Smith's invisible hand works to ensure that, in a market society, consumers get what they want.

Thus far, the markets we have studied have been stylized versions of competitive markets: They have featured many buyers and sellers, a uniform product, consumers and sellers who have complete information about the market, and few barriers to market entry or exit.

In this chapter, we will consider some of the complexities inherent to most markets. The typical market does not meet all the criteria of a truly competitive market. That does not mean the supply and demand analysis you just learned will not be useful in analyzing economic events. Often, however, you will need to temper your analysis to fit the specific conditions of the markets you study. As we will find, some markets need constraints or rules to ensure that society gets the best results.

This chapter begins by considering the efficiency of the market system. We look at the conditions needed for a market to exist and be efficient. We also present a tool for determining economic efficiency. Efficient markets are rationing devices, ensuring that those who value a product the most are the ones who get it. Prices and profits help to carry out this rationing by serving as important market signals.

Markets rarely live up to our definition of the competitive market ideal. The second section of this chapter discusses markets in light of real-world experience, specifically focusing on market failures, or deviations from conditions of perfect competition. If a market is not competitive, this does not mean it collapses or is no longer a market. It just means that the market fails to contain the mechanisms for allocating resources in the best possible way, from the perspective of the larger society. In this section, we will also consider several of the common solutions to market failures. Some failures require just a minor fix, such as a new regulation or law, but others may require that the government take over and provide products.

In the final section of this chapter, we will consider what happens when markets work efficiently, but government intervenes by using price controls. The two most common examples of government price setting are rent controls (price ceilings) and minimum wage laws (price floors). You will see the price paid by society when government tampers with efficiently working markets.

After studying this chapter you should be able to

- Understand how markets allocate resources.
- Define the conditions needed for markets to be efficient.
- Understand how markets impose discipline on producers and consumers.
- Understand and be able to use the concepts of consumer and producer surplus.
- Understand what market failure is, and when it occurs.
- Describe the different types of market failure.
- Recognize why government may control prices.
- Understand the effects of price ceilings and price floors.
- Recognize that taxes lead to deadweight losses.

Markets and Efficiency

Markets are efficient mechanisms for allocating resources. Just think how much information a government bureaucrat would need to decide how many flat panel HDTVs should be produced, what companies should produce them, and who should get them. When you consider that our country has many millions of people who might want such televisions and several thousand possible suppliers, it becomes clear the likelihood of a lone bureaucrat or agency developing an efficient plan for HDTV production and distribution is extremely small. This was the problem the Soviet Union faced with virtually every good it produced, and it goes a long way toward explaining that nation's economic and political collapse.

The prices and profits characteristic of the market system provide incentives and signals that are nonexistent or seriously flawed in other systems of resource allocation. The old Soviet joke that "They pretend to pay us and we pretend to work" illustrates this problem. But efficient markets do not just spontaneously develop. They need reasonable laws and institutions to ensure their proper functioning.

Efficient Market Requirements

For markets to be efficient, they must have well-structured institutions. John McMillan[1] suggests five institutional requirements for workable markets: (1) Information is widely available, or in McMillan's words, "information flows smoothly"; (2) property rights are protected; (3) private contracts are enforced such that "people can be trusted to live up to their promises"; (4) spillovers from other actors are limited, or "side effects of third parties are curtailed"; and (5) competition prevails. Let's discuss each of these requirements in greater detail.

Accurate Information Is Widely Available

For markets to work efficiently, transactions costs must be kept low. One factor that reduces transactions costs is accurate and readily available information. Negotiations between the parties will be smoother if each party has adequate information about the product. Without good information, one party will not have the confidence needed to value the product so that party will be reluctant to enter into a transaction. Many products today are highly sophisticated, and consumers need high-quality information for good choices. As we will see, this is important for buyers and sellers.

When products are similar, such as oranges, coal, or blank CDs, informational requirements are easily satisfied. In other cases, where a product is extremely complex or conducive to fraud, governments often require that information be public. Securities markets, for instance, have statutory reporting requirements that help to ensure that investors have adequate and comparable information on which to base their investment decisions. This regulation creates the presumption of a fair market.

Property Rights Are Protected

"Imagine a country where nobody can identify who owns what, addresses cannot be easily verified, people cannot be made to pay their debts, resources cannot be conveniently turned into money, ownership cannot be divided into shares, descriptions of assets are not standardized and cannot be easily compared, and the rules that govern property vary from neighborhood to neighborhood or even from street to street."[2] These are the conditions Hernando de Soto found throughout most of the developing world.

Most of us are accustomed to elaborate title and insurance provisions that govern the transfer of automobiles, real estate, and corporate shares in this country. In many developing nations, however, no such provisions exist. When a government fails to establish and protect **property rights**, more informal economic mechanisms will evolve. But, as de Soto writes, these informal mechanisms often vary "from neighborhood to neighborhood or even from street to street." Thus, even though the poor in many developing countries often hold considerable assets, these assets are usually untitled, and this prevents them from being used as capital. You cannot borrow against your home, for instance, to purchase the sewing machine needed to

Property rights
The clear delineation of ownership of property backed by government enforcement.

[1]John McMillan, *Reinventing the Bazaar: A Natural History of Markets* (New York: WW Norton), 2002.
[2]Hernando de Soto, *The Mystery of Capital: Why Capitalism Triumphs in the West and Fails Everywhere Else* (New York: Basic Books), 2000, p. 15.

start a small tailoring business if your family's long-standing ownership of this home has never been legally documented. And this problem, according to de Soto, goes a long way toward explaining why much of the world is mired in poverty.

To see the importance of well-defined property rights, consider the following. Since the discovery of petroleum, whale oil has lost its economic importance, yet some countries and cultures still use whale products. But what if you were to gain ownership of all the whales in the world? How would you use your newly acquired resource? Would your ownership interest affect how whales are harvested? Of course it would. You would hire a marine biologist, for instance, to tell you the best harvest rate. You would not allow your valuable asset to be overharvested into extinction.

Property rights provide a powerful incentive for the optimal use of resources: With ownership comes the incentive not to waste. When property ownership is fuzzy or resources are owned in common by the whole society, the incentives to waste are much stronger. There will be more about this issue later in this chapter.

Contract Obligations Are Enforced

A well-functioning legal system makes doing business easier, and it is absolutely essential for large-scale business activity. Without the safeguards of a legal system, firms must rely on discussions with one another to determine whether customers are credit-worthy, or whether a customer's production order is trustworthy. The risk a seller can reasonably take on a given buyer depends on such information, yet getting information in this fashion is a costly process; it can prevent businesses from growing much larger.

Still, even when a legal system is operating well, markets require some informal rules to create the general presumption that bargains will be kept. Most civil court systems in developed nations take several years to hear and decide disputes. Lawsuits, moreover, are never cheap. You can only imagine the delays in some developing nations. For example, the average case in India may take a decade to litigate because too few resources are devoted to the courts. These problems mean informal arrangements develop, and this can mean that commercial development is severely restricted.

The more valuable the contract, the more a legal instrument is needed to ensure that it is honored. Business relationships involving small amounts can usually rely on simple honesty. But cheating on a large loan, contract, or shipment might be worth the sacrifice of one's reputation, so something more than a handshake is needed to ensure compliance. Large and complex markets need a well running legal system that enforces contracts and agreements.

There Are No External Costs or Benefits

When you drive your car on a crowded highway, you are inflicting *external costs* on other drivers and the larger society by adding to congestion and pollution. By attending a private college, conversely, you are conferring *external benefits* on the rest of us. You are more likely to become a better citizen, be less likely to commit a crime, and will probably pay a greater share of the tax bill. Thus, we all benefit from your education. These external costs and benefits are called *externalities.*

Markets operate most efficiently when externalities are minimized. As we will see later, markets tend to overproduce those commodities with external costs and underproduce those with external benefits. A product's market price reflects its value to consumers and its cost to producers most accurately when the product does not involve third-party costs or benefits.

Competitive Markets Prevail

When a market has many buyers and sellers, no one seller has the ability to raise its price above that of its competitors. To do so would mean losing most of its business. In competitive markets, products are close substitutes, so an increase in price by one firm would simply lead consumers to shift their purchases to other firms.

Competitive markets, moreover, tend to aggregate individual appraisals of value into market information. Without a market, values are determined in one-on-one encounters between buyer and seller. Competitive bargaining between many buyers and sellers gives rise to aggregate market prices and values much as prices are set in an auction.

To illustrate, the price for airing sports programming has skyrocketed in recent years, reflecting aggregate values and the power of competitive bidding. Early on, sports insiders knew that sports programming was valuable, but it took years before all the networks saw its real potential. When they finally did, market prices skyrocketed. Today, the National Football League's annual revenue from the sale of broadcast rights totals several billion dollars. In the beginning, only ABC, CBS, and NBC vied for the rights to broadcast games; today the three networks must compete with Fox, ESPN, pay-per-view, and several other cable channels. Competitive bidding has driven the price of carrying games through the roof.

Competitive markets must be open to entry and exit. If government regulations or private barriers restrict entry, higher prices will prevail. Restricted entry creates monopoly power in markets and leads to higher prices for consumers. If easy exit from a business is important for an efficient allocation of resources, the possibility of entry ensures that monopoly power cannot last for long. Restricted entry into the New York cab business, licenses for cornrow wrapping, and street vending permits do little but to protect existing firms, who lobby hard for such restrictions on the grounds of protecting consumers. The real reason for most regulations of this type is to protect incumbent firms.

Good information, protection of property rights, an efficient and fair legal system, the absence of externalities, and competition are all required if society is to get the best from its markets. These elements all work together to make markets efficient, as we will now see.

The Discipline of Markets

Markets impose discipline on consumers and producers. Sellers would like to get away with charging higher prices while producing shoddier goods, thereby earning greater profits. Few manufacturers or service providers turn out terrific goods and services simply to feel good. Rather, their economic survival depends on it. Markets can be brutal; just ask the former executives of Montgomery Ward and a whole host of dot-com firms.

As for us consumers, we all would like to drive better cars, wear nothing but designer clothes, drink the finest wines, and smoke Cuban cigars. (Well, some of us would like the cigars.) For the superrich, such consumption is not only possible but also commonplace. For the rest of us, however, the market rations us out of such goods, except on very special occasions. This is another function of the market: rationing. Given our limited resources, each of us must decide which products are most important to us, since we cannot have unlimited quantities. Everyone chooses based on their tastes, preferences, and limited incomes.

High prices in a market indicate that consumers value a product highly. Higher prices are usually accompanied by higher profits, and these higher profits will attract new firms into the market. These new firms will increase supply, and this reduces prices. The solution for high prices is high prices. As we will see later, however, if something keeps above-market prices from falling, surpluses will accrue. Conversely, if something keeps low prices from rising to their equilibrium level, shortages will result.

Markets can also be useful tools for the government, since markets allocate resources to those individuals or firms that are most efficient. For example, the government uses markets to allocate the radio and cellular spectrum, to supply the nation's electricity, and to reduce pollution. Central planning is difficult for governments, but private firms can use planning effectively, since a firm's management and stockholders have a vested interest in the firm's success. Product and financial markets, moreover, force a discipline on private firms that is absent when governments centrally plan. If a firm fails to innovate, or if it cooks its books as Enron, the British bank Barings, or the Italian firm Parmalat did, consumers will quit buying its products, financial markets will reduce or call in its loans, and stock markets will decimate its shares.

Consumer and Producer Surplus: A Tool for Measuring Economic Efficiency

Markets determine equilibrium prices and outputs. But both consumers and businesses get extra benefits economists call consumer and producer surplus.

Figure 1 illustrates both through a simple diagram. In both panels, the market determines equilibrium price to be $6 (point *e*), at which 6 units of output are sold when S_0 and D_0 are the original curves. Assume that each point on the demand curve represents an individual consumer. Some people value the product highly. For instance, the consumer at point *a* in Panel A thinks the product is worth $11. This consumer clearly gets a bargain, for although she would be willing to pay $11 for the product, the market determines that $6 will be the price everyone pays. Economists refer to this excess benefit that these consumers get ($11 − $6) as

FIGURE 1

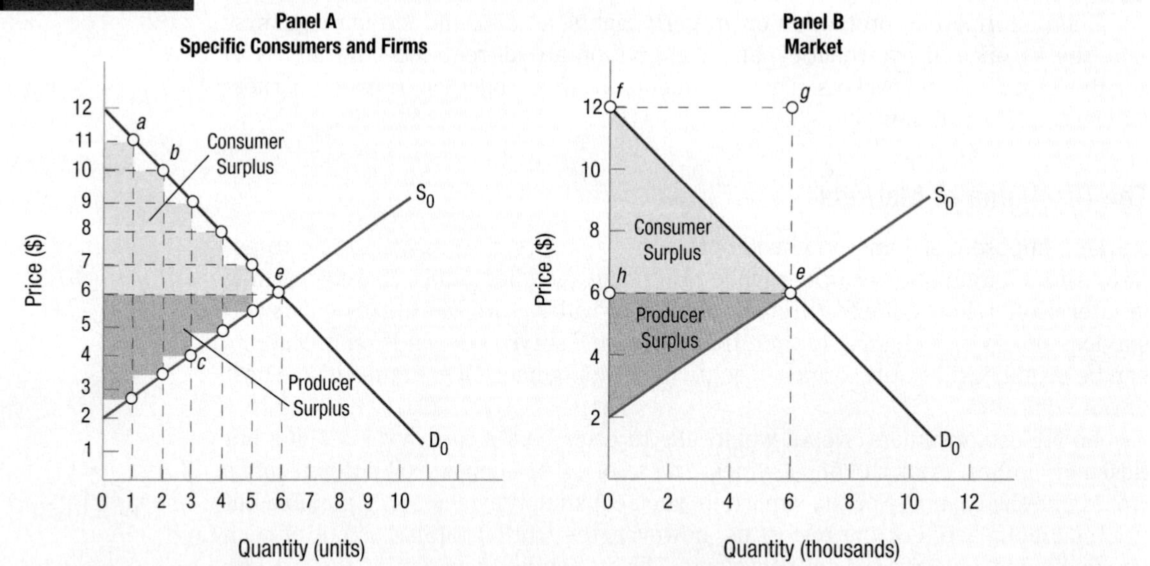

Consumer and Producer Surplus

Panel A shows a market with specific consumers and firms. This small market determines equilibrium price to be $6 (point *e*), at which 6 units of output are sold. Each point on the demand curve represents a specific consumer, and some people value the product highly. In Panel A, for instance, the consumer at point *a* thinks the product is worth $11. This consumer clearly gets a bargain, for although she would be willing to pay $11 for the product, she must pay only $6. This difference of $5 is *consumer surplus.* In Panel A, consumer surplus for this market is equal to the sum of individual surpluses. If each point on the supply curve represents a specific supplier, then for similar reasons, producer surplus is the sum of individual firms' producer surplus. Panel B shows how consumer surplus is computed when the market is huge. Consumer surplus is equal to the area under the demand curve but above the equilibrium price of $6. Thus, total market consumer surplus is equal to half of the rectangle *fgeh,* or [($12 − $6) × 6,000] ÷ 2 = ($6 × 6,000) ÷ 2 = $18,000. Producer surplus is the area under equilibrium price but above the supply curve and is computed in a similar fashion, and is equal to [($6 − $2) × 6,000] ÷ 2 = ($4 × 6,000) ÷ 2 = $12,000.

consumer surplus. So, for the consumer who purchases the first unit of output, consumer surplus is equal to \$5 (\$11 − \$6). For the consumer purchasing the second unit (point *b*), consumer surplus is a little less, \$4 (\$10 − \$6). And so on for buyers of the third though fifth units of output. Total consumer surplus for the consumers in Panel A is found by adding all of the individual consumer surpluses for each unit purchased. Total consumer surplus in Panel A is equal to \$5 + \$4 + \$3 + \$2 + \$1 = \$15.

Consumer surplus
The difference between market price and what consumers (as individuals or the market) would be willing to pay. It is equal to the area above market price and below the demand curve.

In a similar way, assume that each point on the supply curve represents a specific firm. Notice at point *c* that this supplier is willing to provide the third unit to the market at a price of \$4. Fortunately for them, equilibrium price is \$6, so they receive a **producer surplus** equal to \$6 − \$4 or \$2. Total producer surplus in Panel A is equal to the sum of each firm's producer surplus.

Producer surplus
The difference between market price and the price that firms would be willing to supply the product. It is equal to the area below market price and above the supply curve.

Panel B illustrates consumer and producer surplus for an entire market. For convenience we have simply assumed that the market is 1,000 times larger than that shown in Panel A so the *x* axis is output in thousands. Whereas in Panel A we had discrete individuals and firms, we now have a big market, so consumer surplus is equal to the area under the demand curve above equilibrium price or the area of the shaded triangle labeled "Consumer Surplus."

To put a number to the consumer surplus triangle in Panel B, we can compute the value of the rectangle *fgeh* and divide it in half. Thus total market consumer surplus in Panel B is [(\$12 − \$6) × 6,000] ÷ 2 = (\$6 × 6,000) ÷ 2 = \$18,000. The shaded area labeled "Producer Surplus" is found in the same way and is equal to [(\$6 − \$2) × 6,000] ÷ 2 = (\$4 × 6,000) ÷ 2 = \$12,000.

Markets are efficient from the standpoint that all consumers willing to pay \$6 or more got the product from those firms willing to supply it for \$6 or less. For demand and supply curves D_0 and S_0, total consumer and producer surplus is maximized. To see why, pick any price other than \$6, and you will see that total consumers' and producers' surplus is less.

These two concepts are important to help us understand the impacts of market shocks and policy changes on consumer and producer well-being. We will use consumer and producer surplus as a way to evaluate the efficiency of policies throughout the remainder of the book.

The vast bulk of economic analysis focuses on questions of efficiency. Economic analysis is good at telling us the costs and benefits associated with various possible courses of action. And this analysis can help us resolve policy disputes that hinge on considerations of equity (or fairness) versus efficiency. If a policy creates considerable unfairness, for instance, while spurring only a small gain in efficiency, some other policy might be better. Still, economists have no more to say about fairness than other people. One person's view of what is fair is just as good as anyone else's. In the end, fairness always comes down to a value judgment.

Checkpoint
Markets and Efficiency

- Markets are efficient mechanisms for allocating resources. Prices are signals of potential profit.
- For markets to be efficient, information must be widely available, property rights must be protected, private contracts must be enforced, spillovers should be minimal, and competition should prevail.
- Markets impose discipline on producers and consumers.
- Consumer surplus occurs when consumers would have been willing to pay more for a good or service than the going price. Producer surplus occurs when businesses would have been willing to provide products at prices lower than the going

price. Together, consumer and producer surplus can be used to understand the effects of public policies.

QUESTIONS

Business corporations are a basic form of entrepreneurship. When you think of a corporation, do you think of a big bureaucratic organization or a nimble company? Think of new and revolutionary products. For example, consider the Windows operating system produced by Microsoft: Was Microsoft a small or large company when this product was introduced? Do you consider Microsoft to be an entrepreneurial company now?

Answers to the Checkpoint questions can be found at the end of this chapter.

Market Failures

We have seen that for markets to be efficient, they must operate within robust institutional structures. These institutional requirements include accurate information for buyers and sellers, protection of property rights, a legal system that enforces private contracts, an absence of externalities or spillovers, and a fostering of competition. This is a tall order, and many markets do not meet these requirements. When one or more of these conditions are not met, the market is said to fail. Market failure does not mean a market totally collapses or stops existing as a market, but that it fails to provide the socially optimal amount of goods and services. As we will see later, there is one exception: when no goods whatsoever will be provided by private markets. In this section, we will examine market failures that arise from a failure to meet each of the requirements just listed, and suggest some possible solutions.

Accurate Information Is Not Widely Available: Asymmetric Information

One economist tells the story of a friend who for 10 years owned a house near a stream. Neighboring homes were plagued by rats and mice, but not the friend's house. When his neighbors complained about the infestation, the friend would profess never to having seen a rodent in his house. Then, as Todd Sandler tells it, "On the day before he was to sell his house, he was awakened in the middle of the night by a weird sound coming from the attic. Thinking that he would come face to face with his first rat, he went with a flashlight to inspect the attic. When he opened the trap door and stuck in his head, he let out a scream and dropped the light. The 10-year-old mystery had been solved—a large beady-eyed snake stared at him with a rat in its coils."[3]

Asymmetric information Occurs when one party to a transaction has significantly better information than another party.

This is a perfect example of **asymmetric information**, assuming the friend goes ahead and sells the house without mentioning anything about his rodent control secret. In this case, the seller knows more about the house than the buyer. To some, whether this information should properly be divulged in a real estate agreement is arguable. Some people would be unwilling to live in, or perhaps even purchase, a house in which they knew a snake was loose, while others would be happy know-

[3]Todd Sandler, *Economic Concepts for the Social Sciences* (Cambridge: Cambridge University Press), 2001, p. 110.

ing that the rodent problem was solved. For months my uncle would not visit our home because my son's boa was loose in the house.

It was suggested earlier that for markets to operate efficiently, accurate information must be widely available. But in many markets, one party to a transaction will almost always have better information than the other. Many buyers at garage sales have more information about the value of antiques being sold than their sellers. My brother-in-law earns a tidy living buying "junk" at weekend flea markets, then reselling it (at greatly increased prices) in his space in an antique mall.

More often, however, it is sellers who have the superior knowledge. Let us consider the used car market, which Nobel Prize winner George Akerlof studied many years ago.[4] Professor Akerlof wondered why the price of a new car drops so significantly once it is driven off the lot. Put five hundred miles on a car, then list it for sale, and the market price will be 10–20% less than the new-car price.

Let us first look at Figure 2, which assumes that all buyers and sellers have accurate information about used cars. We will divide the market into high-quality cars and low-quality cars, or lemons. For simplicity, we will also assume that sellers are willing to part with high-quality cars for $10,000 along supply curve S_{High}, and that sellers of lemons are willing to let them go for $5,000 along supply curve S_{Low}. Demand curve D_{UCars} shows the demand for used cars.

If we assume that the demand curve represents a ranking of consumers based on the prices they are willing to pay for cars, then length *ca* on the demand curve represents those people who are willing to pay $10,000 or more for a high-quality

FIGURE 2

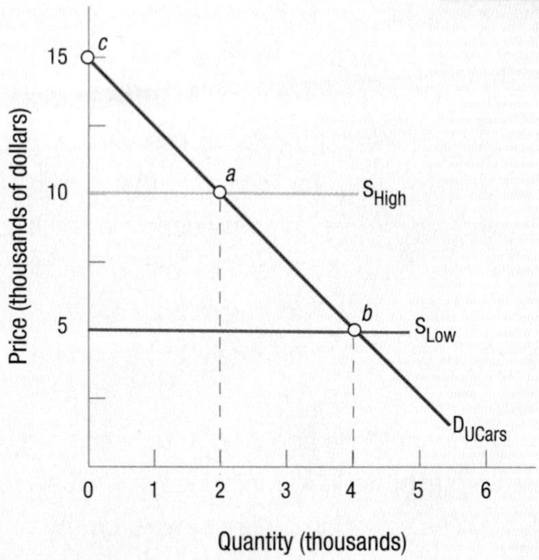

The Market for Used Cars

The market for used cars is divided into high- and low-quality cars (lemons). Sellers are willing to sell high quality cars for $10,000 along supply curve S_{High}, and others will sell lemons for $5,000 along supply curve S_{Low}. Demand curve D_{UCars} is the demand for used cars. If buyers and sellers have equal information, 2,000 high-quality cars are sold for $10,000 (point *a*), and 2,000 lemons are sold for $5,000 (point *b* minus point *a*). When sellers have better information than buyers, buyers cannot distinguish good from bad, so 4,000 lemons are sold at $5,000 each (point *b*), and high-quality cars go unsold in the market. To avoid this lemon problem, sellers of high-quality cars will give warranties and use other methods to signal to buyers that their cars are not lemons.

[4]George Akerlof, "The Market for Lemons: Quality, Uncertainty and the Market Mechanism," *Quarterly Journal of Economics,* 1970, pp. 488–500.

George Akerlof

A. Michael Spence

Joseph Stiglitz

Nobel Prize George Akerlof, A. Michael Spence, and Joseph Stiglitz

George Akerlof, Michael Spence, and Joseph Stiglitz won the Nobel Prize in Economic Sciences in 2001 for their ideas on the economics of information, providing important insights into everything from used car sales to insurance to sharecropping.

George Akerlof attended Yale University and earned his Ph.D. in economics from MIT. Shortly after joining the faculty at the University of California at Berkeley, he published "The Market for Lemons," which explored the impact of asymmetric information between buyers and sellers in the used car industry.

In his "Lemons" essay, Akerlof introduced the concept of "adverse selection," which suggested that inadequate information for a buyer might result in an industry-wide selling of low-quality products. Based on his experiences in India, Akerlof explored the impacts of information asymmetries in developing economies. He used the example of rural India, where lenders charged interest rates that were twice as high as those in urban areas. Akerlof laced his economic work with insights from sociology and anthropology, noting, for example, that social conventions like the caste system could have adverse impacts on economic efficiency.

Michael Spence did graduate work at Harvard University, where he studied mathematical economics and equilibrium theory from another Nobel laureate, Kenneth Arrow. In 1971, he began teaching analytic methods at Harvard's Kennedy School of Government.

Spence provided important ideas about how well-informed individuals in a market can "signal" their information to lesser informed individuals to prevent the problems associated with adverse selection. Spence explored the question of education as a signal for participants in the labor markets. He also examined the question of different "expectations-based" equilibria for education and wages.

Joseph Stiglitz attended Amherst College and earned his Ph.D. in economics from MIT in 1967. During the Clinton Administration, he served on the Council of Economic Advisors and was the World Bank's chief economist between 1997 and 2001, resigning after his pointed criticisms of the actions of the World Bank during the Asian economic crisis. In 2001, he joined the faculty of Columbia University.

Stiglitz coauthored a classic paper on how information problems can be resolved in the insurance industry when companies do not have adequate information on the risk situations of their clients. Stiglitz has suggested that economic models may be misleading if they disregard the asymmetry of information between the various actors.

In a paper with Andrew Weiss, Stiglitz argued that bankers might reduce losses from bad loans by limiting the number of loans rather than raising the lending rates. Stiglitz has made important contributions to the field of international development: One study focused on sharecropping as an optimal relationship in agriculture, given the asymmetric information between landowner and tenant about harvest conditions and the level of the labor effort.

used car. Given the supply, we can see that 2,000 high-quality cars will be sold. The remaining segment *ab* represents the demand by people who are willing to pay $5,000 or more for a lemon. These people would prefer to purchase high-quality used cars for this price, but that is impossible, given the limited supply. Assuming accurate information, 4,000 used cars will be sold, evenly split between high- and low-quality cars.

But what happens when sellers have better information than buyers? Now buyers cannot differentiate good cars from lemons. The sellers of high-quality automobiles will still not sell their cars for anything less than $10,000. But since buyers cannot tell lemons from good cars, they must assume that each car is a lemon. More specifically, if buyers offer anything less than $10,000 but more than $5,000, they know that only lemons will be offered, and thus they will end up overpaying by the difference between the sales price and $5,000. But if buyers offer $10,000 or more, many of the cars they purchase will still be lemons, even if they also get a few high-quality cars. Hence, paying anything more than $5,000 for a car turns out to be a crapshoot.

This analysis suggests that high-quality used cars will be driven from the market, and that 4,000 lemons will be sold. Before this happens, however, dealers will start offering warranties in an attempt to get higher prices for their used cars and to assure buyers that their cars are not lemons. Consumers can then be more confident of getting high-quality used cars from a dealer, since offering a warranty on lemons would be a losing proposition for dealers.

For private sellers of used cars, this means they must accept less for their cars, or at least do something to convince buyers they are not selling lemons. Some car owners keep scrupulous records of oil changes and repairs or else get their cars detailed so that they "show well." Buyers, trying to reduce their risk, may take used cars to mechanics for inspection before agreeing to purchase them. The lemons problem explains why many high-quality used cars are bought by the friends of the people who sell them: Sometimes only personal trust can overcome asymmetric information.

Adverse Selection

Adverse selection occurs when products of different qualities are sold at the same price because of asymmetric information. Adverse selection is most apparent in insurance markets. People who purchase health insurance or life insurance know far more about their lifestyles and general states of their health than can an insurance company, even if the insurance company requires a physical.

Adverse selection
Occurs when products of different qualities are sold at the same price because of asymmetric information. Insurance is a typical example because people know far more about their health and risk levels than the companies insuring them.

Insurance rates are determined using averages, but the market includes some people who are higher than average risks and some people who are below average. Who do you think is more likely to purchase insurance? Overwhelmingly, it is those people above the average risk level who will buy insurance, while those below the average risk level are more likely to self-insure. The insurance pool therefore tends to be filled with higher-risk individuals, which can lead to payouts exceeding projections and insurance companies losing money. In this case, then, adverse selection skews the insurance pool, giving it a risk level higher than the social average.

How can insurance underwriters deal with this problem? The answer is that they offer policies at different prices to different groups. Health insurance companies, for instance, use deductibles and copayments to attract low-risk individuals. A deductible means that you must pay the first, say, $1,000 in medical expenses, then the insurance company begins covering a part, or even all, of the remaining costs. Copayments are small cash payments paid for each visit to the doctor. These policies are attractive to low-risk clients since they have lower monthly premiums. For low-risk people, the likelihood of their needing to cover copayments or pay their full deductible is low.

Conversely, a high-deductible policy is not attractive to high-risk individuals, since they can project that the cost of the policy will be too high. They know they will probably have to pay all their monthly premiums, many copayments, and their full deductible. These people will tend to opt for policies with higher premiums but lower deductibles. Thus, people who are high risk will select policies that accurately reflect their true state of health and lifestyle.

As a thought experiment, ask yourself why private unemployment insurance is not offered on the market? Who would most want to buy such insurance? How would an insurance company deal with slackers? Recently Robert Shiller[5] has suggested "livelihood insurance," which would create a futures market with trading based on forecasts of average incomes in various professions. Many of us choose our profession based on its expected future income. Technology introduces considerable uncertainty into many professions—just ask those computer professionals who were getting high wages in telecommunications. This market would permit people to hedge against future displacements. To reduce shirking and adverse selection, Shiller suggests that people whose pay is below a profession's average would not be reimbursed.

Moral Hazard

Moral hazard
Asymmetric information problem that occurs when an insurance policy or some other arrangement changes the economic incentives and leads to a change in behavior.

Moral hazard occurs when an insurance policy or some other arrangement changes the economic incentives we face, thus leading us to change our behavior, usually in a way that is detrimental to the market. Think about what happens when you get comprehensive coverage, which includes theft insurance, on your car. Does this affect how scrupulously you lock your car doors? Of course it does. The moral hazard occurs because the insurance policy, which compensates you in case of loss, changes your behavior to make loss *more* (not *less*) likely.

Insurance companies place restrictions on individual behavior in some contracts. For example, insurance designed to protect the ability of professional athletes to honor multiyear contracts often prohibits dangerous activities such as skiing, inline skating, hang gliding, and mountain climbing. In this way they reduce the moral hazard aspects of the policy. Some rental car companies, knowing that you won't check the oil in a rental car, rarely rent cars for more than a month at a time. They want to get their cars back into the shop to ensure all is well.

When high-quality information is not equally available to buyers and sellers, markets must adapt. The less complex the product and the better the information, the more efficient the market will be.

Information Markets: The Wisdom of Crowds

> **Things sometimes work better than we had a right to expect from our abstract interpretations of theory.**
>
> ***Vernon Smith (2002 Nobel Prize winner)***

Will we land astronauts on Mars by 2015? Will Osama bin Laden be caught? Will an Asian flu pandemic reach the United States? The probabilities associated with

[5]Robert Shiller, *The New Financial Order: Risk in the 21st Century* (Princeton, NJ: Princeton University Press), 2003.

all of these questions are being forecasted every day by information (or prediction) markets. Some of these markets are small and just for fun, while others are large and have hundreds of millions of dollars at stake. Information markets have proved highly accurate with both real and virtual money.

Information markets began in 1988 at the University of Iowa. The Iowa Electronic Market, a real money market where participants are limited to an investment of $500, has done a better job of forecasting U.S. presidential election results than popular polls. Examples of other information markets include The Hollywood Stock Exchange (www.hsx.com), which focuses on the box office gross of newly released movies and the future success of stars, and TradeSports (www.tradesports.com), a site that has a huge set of sports, political, and entertainment futures contracts. The large-scale economic derivatives used to forecast the likely outcome of future economic data releases (www.economicderivatives.com) permit firms and financial institutions to hedge their portfolios against adverse macroeconomic data (e.g., consumer price index [CPI], gross domestic product [GDP], and employment) that are released on a regular basis. The release of disappointing economic numbers often plays havoc with large portfolios.

Before 9/11/2001, intelligence in the United States was decentralized among many agencies including the Defense Department, the CIA, the National Security Agency, and the FBI. As the 9/11 Commission discovered, many of these agencies were not sharing information with each other, some because of the law, and others because of interagency competition. This resulted in the knowledge gaps and a failure to "connect the dots." Information markets tend to aggregate this information in one spot. The Policy Analysis Market (PAM) program instituted by the Defense Advanced Research Projects Agency (DARPA) in 2003 was going to be a public market that would be used to predict terrorist activities and other important political events in the Middle East. Many critics suggested that it might suffer from foul play from terrorists driving up the market price of an event and profiting from an attack, or using the market to mislead intelligence authorities. This market was scrapped, yet the intelligence services now have internal markets that are used to aggregate information and aid their forecasts of world events. As James Surowiecki[6] noted,

> *PAM would have helped break down the institutional barriers that keep information from being aggregated in a single place. Since traders in a market have no incentive other than making the right prediction—that is, there are no bureaucratic or political factors influencing their decision—and since they have that incentive to be right, they are more likely to offer honest evaluations, rather than tailoring their opinions to fit the political climate or satisfy institutional demands.*

Information is important to the efficient functioning of markets and good public policy. Paradoxically, markets are good mechanisms to aggregate information for policymakers. Information markets can be used to reduce market failures due to incomplete information.

Problems with Property Rights

We saw earlier that property rights provide a powerful incentive to use resources wisely. We noted that incentives to waste are much stronger when property

[6]James Surowiecki, *The Wisdom of Crowds: Why the Many Are Smarter Than the Few and How Collective Wisdom Shapes Business, Economics, Societies, and Nations* (New York: Doubleday), 2004, pp. 91–92. For a more detailed discussion of these issues, see Robert Hahn and Paul Tetlock (eds.), *Information Markets: A New Way of Making Decisions* (Washington, DC: AEI-Brookings Joint Center for Regulatory Studies), 2006.

ownership is fuzzy or resources are owned in common. Here we want to look at these cases in detail, discussing two general instances of market failure caused by property right issues: public goods and common property resources.

Public Goods

Most of the goods we deal in are private goods: airline seats, meals at restaurants, songs on iTunes, bicycles, and the like. When we purchase such goods, we consume them, and no one else can benefit from them. To be sure, when you buy an airline ticket, other passengers will be on the same flight, but no one else can sit in your seat for that flight; only you can enjoy its benefits. Thus, private goods are those the buyer consumes, and this precludes anyone else from similarly enjoying them.

Public goods
Goods that, once provided, no one person can be excluded from consuming (nonexclusion), and one person's consumption does not diminish the benefit to others from consuming the good (nonrivalry).

Free rider
When a public good is provided, consumers cannot be excluded from enjoying the product, so some consume the product without paying.

Contrast private goods with **public goods**, goods that one person can consume without diminishing what is left for others. My watching PBS does not mean that there is less PBS for you to watch. Economists refer to such a situation as one of *nonrivalry*. Public goods are also *nonexclusive*, meaning that once such a good has been provided for one person, others cannot be excluded from enjoying it. Normally, public goods are both nonrival and nonexclusive, whereas private goods are rival and exclusive.

Public goods give rise to the **free rider** problem. Once a public good has been provided, other consumers cannot be excluded from it, so many people will choose to enjoy the benefit without paying; they will free ride. National Public Radio (NPR) and PBS are public goods. They exist because they receive donations from individuals, foundations, and governments, but their weeklong begging and guilt-transference sessions notwithstanding, most listeners and viewers (maybe as high as 90%) still choose to enjoy their services without pledging support.

Other public goods include weather forecasts, national defense, lighthouses, flood control projects, GPS satellites, World Court rulings, and mosquito eradication. Because these goods are nonrival and nonexclusive, they invariably end up being provided by governments.

Public goods are the one case where market failure typically leads to no goods at all being provided by private markets. Government must step in. Who would contribute—or contribute adequately—to the costs of providing accurate weather forecasts if your neighbors were free riders? Contributions would soon dry up, and the public good in question would not be provided at all.

Knowledge, too, can be a public good. As a result, markets need ways of protecting intellectual property if its development is not to be discouraged. These days, this protection is more crucial than ever with digital information technologies and the Internet. Digital files can fly around the world and be reproduced for nearly nothing. If work can be copied so quickly, what is the incentive to produce it in the first place? Protections and incentives are needed to ensure that individuals and companies continue to produce such products. Still, some compromise is needed between absolute protection and no protection to strike a balance between producer incentives and consumer interests. Patents, trademarks, and copyrights all convey some monopoly power, so their protections must have limits; otherwise, producers could take advantage of consumers.

Drug innovations take on public good aspects when intellectual property rights—in this case patents—are not enforced internationally. The Indian government does recognize patents with varying degrees for food and drugs, which helps explain why India has over 20,000 drug manufacturers. These companies can copy drugs patented in the United States and Europe, paying only their production costs, since their research and development costs are zero. As a result, Indian drugs cost only pennies on the dollar compared to prices in the United States and in Europe.

Similarly, Brazil encouraged drug manufacturers to copy American antiviral drugs for AIDS sufferers. The government then bought these drugs at greatly reduced prices and distributed them to patients. Brazilian AIDS sufferers could not afford the expensive drug cocktail American drug companies were offering, so the Brazilian government felt compelled to ignore the patents on these medicines.

Private research and development efforts by medical and drug companies in the United States and Europe, and the resulting drugs, often become public goods in much of the rest of the world. The developing world is free riding, with higher American insurance and prescription drug costs subsidizing the rest of the world.

To a lesser extent, European nations have engaged in similar free riding at the expense of American drug companies, but a recent study commissioned in Europe concluded that this may be costing Europe more than it helps. Keeping drug prices artificially low through price controls and government negotiations with drug companies has resulted in research and development funds, and scientists, flowing from Europe to the United States. Today, over 60% of all drug research and development in the world is done in the United States.

The other side of this issue is that few highly priced drugs would be sold in the developing world anyway. Poor people living on a dollar or two a day simply cannot afford to buy high-cost, high-tech drugs, so American and European pharmaceutical companies lose little revenue when these people are provided with cheap imitations of their products. Indeed, because the cost to pharmaceutical firms is so small and the benefits to developing countries and their people are so great, some drug companies have even begun selling their own products to developing nations at reduced rates.

As this drug example shows, public goods can lead to market failure if the free rider problem is present. If drug companies reap profits, they will continue to invest in research and development. If foreign nations free ride, they diminish the incentives that drug companies have to invest in product innovation. The more that drugs become like public goods, the less likely that new drugs will be developed.

Common Property Resources

Another market failure caused by problems with property rights occurs when a good is a **common property resource** or open-access resource. The market failure associated with commonly owned properties is often referred to as "the tragedy of the commons,"[7] where the tendency is for commonly held resources to be overused and overexploited. Because the resource is held in common, individuals have little incentive to use them in a sustainable fashion, so each person races to "get theirs" before others can do the same.

Common property resources Resources that are owned by the community at large (parks, ocean fish, and the atmosphere) and therefore tend to be overexploited because individuals have little incentive to use them in a sustainable fashion.

Ocean fisheries are a good example. Fish in the ocean were once in excess supply; there was no need for use of this resource to be restricted. Very often people fished one species until it was exhausted, then moved on to fish another. Since the ocean was so big and fish species so plentiful, no one noticed. As the global demand for fish has risen, improved fishing technologies and boats have made it possible for fishing boats to increase their hauls and to range around the world. Because many of the world's fisheries are still unregulated, one population after another has been fished out, so much so that nearly 90% of the ocean's predators are gone. The situation is clearly unsustainable, and indeed, as fish populations have shrunk, so have fishing fleets.

The most recent example of overfishing is the Patagonian toothfish (Chilean Sea Bass).[8] It is a big, ugly, black fish from deep cold waters weighing 40–80 pounds. Chefs discovered its meat to be very forgiving when cooking: It is difficult to overcook and has a nice oily texture that accepts nearly all spices. Because of these qualities, it became a huge hit in the United States, and the fish has been hunted to extinction. Scientists estimate that 40% of the preexploitation species (biomass)

[7]Hardin, Garrett, "The Tragedy of the Commons," *Science,* 162, pp. 1243–48, 1968.

[8]See Paul Greenberg, "The Catch," *New York Times Magazine,* October 23, 2005, and G. Bruce Knecht, *Hooked: Pirates, Poaching and the Perfect Fish* (Rodale Books), 2006.

is needed for sustainable fishing, and environmental groups and governments in the southern waters are concerned that this critical number may have been breached. They have recently begun to set limits on the catch. This has led to the problem of poaching. The Australian Coast Guard recently chased a poacher through Antarctic waters during a storm with a catch worth one million dollars. The trawlers today have 15-mile-long lines with 15,000 hooks. No species can withstand this type of predation. Common property resources need government regulation ultimately to protect these assets.

In summary, when property rights are clearly defined, people have an incentive to use resources efficiently. But property rights are not always clearly defined, and this leads to market failure and waste. In the case of public goods, the free rider problem means that these goods may not be provided at all if left to private devices—government needs to step in. With common property resources, there is an incentive for each individual to grab as much as he or she can. Government regulation can protect these resources.

Contract Enforcement Is Problematical

When an efficient legal system for the enforcement of contracts is lacking, contracts will inherently be small, given that large contracts with complex financial provisions are difficult to enforce informally. Only if the parties to a contract have long histories together and want to continue doing business will an informal system work. Just as the corporate structure was pivotal in Western economic development, enforcement mechanisms for contracts are essential for widespread business and commercial expansion.

When public officials are corrupt, businesses will invest less. Corrupt officials are like people who fish: They know any funds they fail to squeeze out of a firm will be appropriated by the next corrupt bureaucrat, so they try to extort as much as possible, just as people who fish are afraid of leaving fish behind for anyone else to catch. It is not surprising that higher corruption in a country is associated with lower economic growth.

There Are Significant External Costs or Benefits: Externalities

External cost
Occurs when a transaction between two parties has an impact on a third party not involved with the transaction. External costs are negative such as pollution or congestion. The market provides too much of the product with negative externalities at too low a cost.

External benefits
Positive externalities (also called spillovers) such as education and vaccinations. Private markets provide too little at too high a price of goods with external benefits.

Markets rarely produce the socially optimal output when external costs or benefits are present. The market tends to overproduce goods with external costs, providing them at too low a price. To see why, consider Figure 3, keeping in mind that an **external cost** is some socially undesirable effect of economic activity such as pollution, overfishing, or traffic congestion.

Demand curve D_P and supply curve S_P represent the private demand and supply for some product. Market equilibrium is at point *a*. Assume this good's production creates pollution—an external cost. If its producer were forced to clean up its production process, the firm's costs would rise, and the supply curve would decrease to $S_{P+\text{Cleanup Costs}}$. The result is a new equilibrium at point *b* with a higher price and lower output.

Output Q_1 is the socially desirable output for this product. But left on its own, this market will produce at Q_0 because consumers and producers of this product will not take this pollution (and cleanup costs) into consideration. The larger society bears the brunt of the pollution. Markets fail because they do not contain mechanisms forcing firms to eliminate external costs. Left unregulated, the firm in this example will produce more of its product than the society wants, pushing the increased costs of this production off onto the larger society as an undesirable externality.

In a similar way, markets tend to provide too little of products that have **external benefits**. Figure 4 depicts the market for college education with external ben-

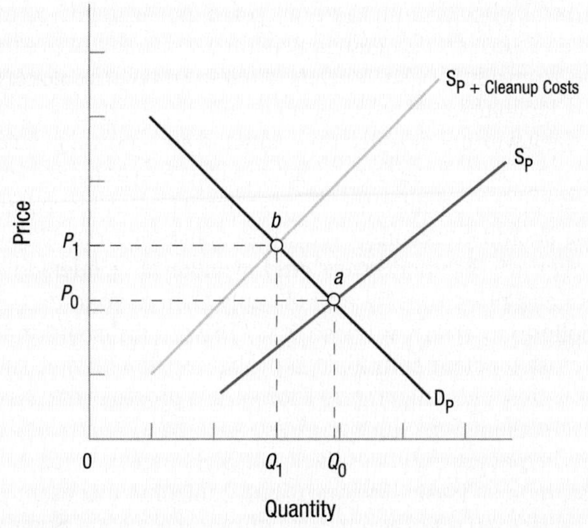

FIGURE 3

Markets with External Costs

Markets tend to overproduce goods with external costs. Demand curve D_P and supply curve S_P represent the private demand and supply. Market equilibrium is at point *a*. Assume this good's production creates pollution (an external cost). If the producer were forced to clean up the production process, the firm's costs would rise, and the supply curve would decrease to $S_{P+\text{Cleanup Costs}}$. The result is the socially optimal equilibrium at point *b* with a higher price and lower output. Now producers and consumers of this product are paying the full costs associated with the good's production. Markets do not inherently contain mechanisms that force firms to pay for external costs.

efits. Again, demand curve D_P and S_P represent private demand and supply, with equilibrium at point *a*.

Since education provides benefits not only to students but also to the society as a whole, the demand for college education is equal to the private demand plus external benefits, or $D_{P+\text{Social Benefits}}$. This moves the market equilibrium to point *b*, where more education, Q_1, is desired. The society can bring about this shift in equilibrium by subsidizing higher education to the tune of *bc.* (Perhaps the government pays part of students' tuition costs—does this sound familiar?) This lowers the price of higher education, which results in more people going to college, to the benefit of the larger society.

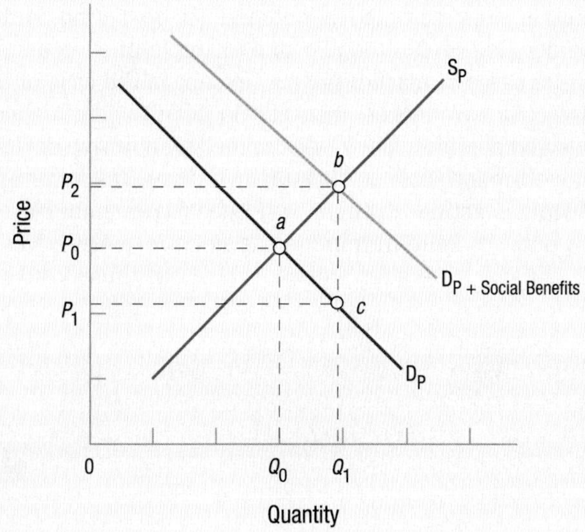

FIGURE 4

Markets with External Benefits

Private markets tend to provide too little of products that have external benefits (education). Curves D_P and S_P represent private demand and supply, with equilibrium at point *a*. Since education provides benefits not only to students but also to the society as a whole, the demand for college education is equal to the private demand plus external benefits, or $D_{P+\text{Social Benefits}}$. This moves the market equilibrium to point *b*, where more education, Q_1, is desired. By subsidizing higher education by an amount equal to *bc*, the price of higher education is lowered, resulting in more people going to college.

Externalities lead to market failure. To ensure that products are available at the socially desirable price and output, some government intervention may be required. Regulation or taxation can be used, for instance, to give markets the incentives they need to produce what society wants. Today, the government even uses the market as a mechanism to reduce pollution.

Originally, the government relied on command and control policies to reduce emissions from specific pollution sources. Using markets to achieve environmental goals seemed oxymoronic. Eventually the federal government began issuing marketable permits allowing limited emissions. Companies could then buy and sell these permits, thereby adjusting their pollution levels. And, wonder of wonders, it worked! Pollution levels were reduced more quickly and cheaply than anyone had thought possible.

Why did pollution permits work so well? Private firms and individuals are good at finding the most efficient solutions to problems. Sometimes, these solutions will produce externalities, but when market forces are properly harnessed, they can also be used to solve problems facing the entire society.

With the right regulatory incentives, markets can be used to reduce pollution at the least cost, remove trash efficiently, and confront such other problems as overfishing, road congestion, and the overuse of national parks. Some communities are looking at user fees for single passenger cars in underused HOV lanes. The revenue from these fares would expand highway funds and allocate scarce lane space to those who most value the resource.

When externalities are present, unregulated markets will fail to deliver socially optimal output. External costs, for example, are spread over the rest of society. Some form of governmental intervention is needed to ensure that markets provide what society wants. But market mechanisms can be used as part of a comprehensive plan to force markets to operate as desired.

Competitive Markets Do *Not* Prevail: Monopoly Power

In theory, a market left to itself should be competitive. In practice, however, the government must promote competition in the marketplace if it wants to see the most efficient outcomes. One problem is that some markets tend toward monopoly, and when a monopoly does control the market, prices go up. In the late 19th century, the monopolistic practices of the "robber barons" spurred passage of a series of antitrust laws that are still used today to promote competitive markets. The Department of Justice can block proposed mergers if they will harm competition in the marketplace. The Antitrust Division of the Department of Justice routinely files suit against companies deemed to be acting anticompetitively; the Microsoft case decided in 2000 is just one example of such a suit.

In all of these cases of market failure (except in the case of pure public goods), markets do not collapse. Rather, markets do not provide the most efficient distribution of goods and services. They need some ameliorative device, often something provided by government such as laws or incentives, but often provided by private firms and individuals acting on their own behalf (remember used car warranties). The important point to keep in mind is the need for correctives when market failure is present. We will have a lot more to say about these issues in a later chapter.

Checkpoint

Market Failures

REVIEW

- When markets fail, they typically do not totally collapse (with the exception of public goods)—they simply fail to provide the socially optimal amount of goods and services.

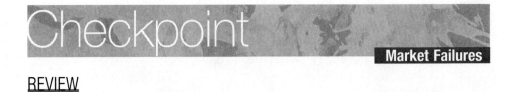

- Asymmetric information—when one party to a transaction has better information than another—can lead to market failure.
- Adverse selection occurs when products of different qualities are sold at one price. Moral hazard occurs when an insurance policy or other arrangement changes the economic incentives people face and so leads them to change their behaviors.
- Private goods can be consumed only by the person who purchases them: They are rival and exclusive. Public goods are nonrival and nonexclusive: My consumption does not diminish your consumption, and others cannot be excluded from enjoying it.
- Public goods give rise to the free rider problem.
- Common property resources are typically subject to overexploitation.
- Markets rarely produce the socially optimal output when external benefits or costs are present.
- Monopoly markets result in prices higher than what is socially optimal.

QUESTION

One professor (who will go unnamed), wanting to remove the "grade grubbing" pressure from the classroom, announced to the class that all students who regularly attended his class would get an A, and all others in the class would receive Bs. Would this announcement create any moral hazard problems? Explain.

Answers to the Checkpoint question can be found at the end of this chapter.

Government-Controlled Prices

When competitive markets are left to determine equilibrium price and output, they clear. Businesses provide consumers with the quantity of goods they want to purchase at the established prices; there are no shortages or surpluses. When market failure occurs, individual or government action can improve the situation, bringing markets back to efficiency.

Problems arise because this bias toward government action (used to mitigate market failure) sometimes leads to government action when markets are efficient and doing what they are supposed to do. Why would government try to regulate freely working markets? In one word: fairness. There are times when the equilibrium price may not be what many people consider to be a desired or fair price. For political or social reasons—not economic ones—governments will intervene in the market by setting limits on such things as wages, apartment rents, electricity, or agricultural commodities. Government uses price ceilings and price floors to keep prices below or above market equilibrium. What happens when government meddles with efficiently working markets?

Price Ceilings

When the government sets a **price ceiling**, it is legally mandating the maximum price that can be charged for a product or service. This is a legal maximum; regardless of market forces, price cannot exceed this level.

Price ceiling
A government-set maximum price that can be charged for a product or service. When the price ceiling is set below equilibrium, it leads to shortages. Rent control is an example.

Figure 5 on the next page shows an *effective* price ceiling, or one in which the ceiling price is set below the equilibrium price. In this case, equilibrium is at P_e, but the government has set a price ceiling at P_c. Quantity supplied at the ceiling price is Q_2, whereas consumers want Q_1, so the result is a shortage of $Q_1 - Q_2$ units of the product. Note that if the price ceiling is set above P_e, the market simply settles at P_e, and the price ceiling has no impact.

FIGURE 5

Price Ceiling Below Equilibrium Price Creates Shortages

A price ceiling is a maximum sales price for a product. When the government enacts a price ceiling below equilibrium, it will create shortages. Consumers will demand Q_1 output at a price of P_c, but business will supply only Q_2, creating a shortage equal to $Q_1 - Q_2$. The product's price cannot rise to restore equilibrium because of the legal price ceiling.

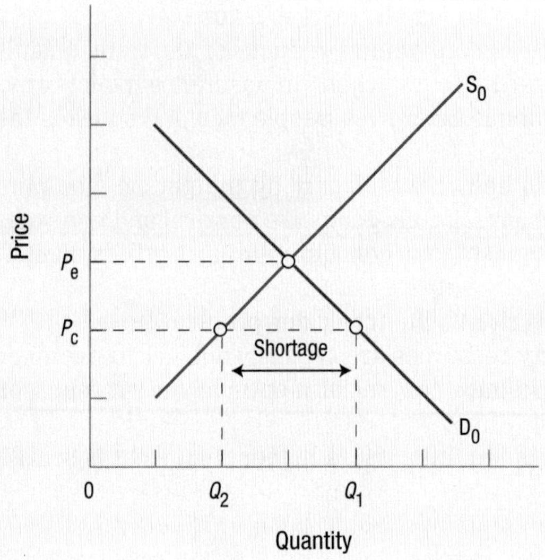

Rent controls are a classic example of price ceilings. Many local governments have decided affordable housing is a priority and that tenants need protection from high rental rates (presumably protection from greedy landlords). And in the short run, rent controls work. Landlords cannot easily convert apartment units to alternative uses, so they have little choice but to rent out these units at the lower rates. But as soon as they can, landlords will convert their real estate holdings to condominiums or offices. Other landlords, facing a ceiling on the rents they can charge, will not incur additional upkeep charges and so will let their properties deteriorate. Few landlords, meanwhile, will invest in more rental units. So the shortage we see in Figure 5 will come from a reduced number of rental units due to condo conversion and no new units, while current units are allowed to deteriorate.

Okay, you might say, there will be a shortage of rental units over time, but at least the rents charged will be "fairer." The question is, fairer to whom? The chief beneficiaries are the people already renting. Over time, their rents will be much lower than the equilibrium price. Sufferers include people moving to the area who cannot find a place to rent, or growing families that are trapped in small apartments. When these people do find a potential place, there is a huge incentive for landlords to ask for under-the-table payments, such as a $5,000 payment for keys to the apartment. In New York City, rent control instituted during Word War II is still in place: The beneficiary class is not the poor, but people lucky enough to be renters during the early phases of the rent control and who have passed on their apartments to their family. This has led to the gruesome habit of would-be renters reading obituaries to discover renters who died with no obvious heirs. This behavior is a far cry from the normal act of looking for an apartment when markets work freely.

More recently, the federal government has begun placing a form of price ceiling on the Medicare payments to doctors and hospitals. Doctors who accept Medicare patients are not allowed to charge patients more that what is allowed by Medicare for specific procedures. These maximum prices have been getting lower as the Medicare budget has been squeezed. As a result, some doctors no longer accept new Medicare patients, since the fees they can charge will no longer cover their costs. For some patients who are just retiring and joining Medicare, finding a doctor can be difficult. The price ceilings have created a shortage of doctors willing to treat Medicare patients.

Energy deregulation in California provides an example of how partial deregulation and price ceilings can go awry. In the early 1990s, California deregulated wholesale electricity prices, but not retail prices to end users. As a result, the market failed to function efficiently when it ran into a supply crisis. Wholesale electricity prices rose, but retail prices were prevented from rising to reduce the quantity demanded. Consumers thus continued to use as much electricity as before, resulting in rolling brownouts; not an efficient means of reducing usage, but one that worked. What the California energy market needed was flexible prices at the retail level to send signals to consumers to consume less, and profit signals to producers to produce more. Partial deregulation failed to provide this structure.

The key point to remember here is that price ceilings are intended to keep the price of a product below its market or equilibrium level. The ultimate effect of a price ceiling, however, is that the quantity of the product demanded exceeds the quantity supplied, thereby producing a shortage of the product in the market.

Price Floors

A **price floor** is a government-mandated minimum price that can be charged for a product or service. Regardless of market forces, product price cannot legally fall below this level.

Price floor
A government-set minimum price that can be charged for a product or service. If the price floor is set above equilibrium price it leads to surpluses. Minimum wage legislation is an example.

Figure 6 shows the economic impact of price floors. In this case, the price floor, P_f, is set above equilibrium, P_e, resulting in a surplus of $Q_2 - Q_1$ units. At price P_f, businesses want to supply more of the product (Q_2) than consumers are willing to buy (Q_1), thus generating a surplus. Again, note that if the price floor is set below equilibrium, it has no impact on the market.

For over a half century, agricultural price supports or price floors have been used to try to smooth out the income of farmers, which often fluctuates wildly due to wide annual variations in crop prices. Government acts as a buyer of last resort, and if surpluses result, the government purchases these commodities. Since these price supports typically are above market equilibrium prices, frequent surpluses have resulted. These surpluses have been stored and earmarked for use in the event of future shortages, but few such shortages have arisen due to improvements in farm technology and rising crop yields. Consumers pay more for agricultural commodities, and surpluses arise and often rot, all in the expectation that the income of farmers will be steady. Despite their questionable economic justification, political pressures have ensured that agricultural price supports and related programs still command a sizable share of the discretionary domestic federal budget.

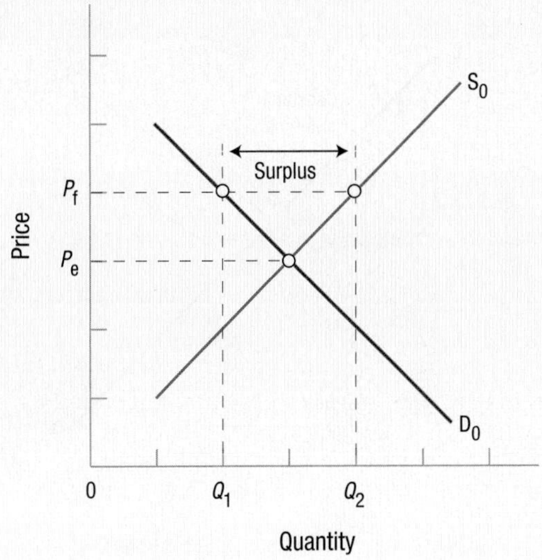

FIGURE 6

Price Floor Above Equilibrium Price Creates Surpluses

A price floor is the lowest price at which a product can be sold. When the government sets a floor above equilibrium, it creates surpluses. Businesses try to sell Q_2 at a price of P_f, but consumers are willing to purchase only Q_1 at that price. The result is a market surplus equal to $Q_2 - Q_1$. The price floor prevents the product's price from falling to equilibrium.

Another area in which price floors are used is the minimum wage. To the extent that the minimum wage is set above the equilibrium wage, unemployment—a surplus of labor—will result. The groups most affected by this unemployment tend to be low-skilled workers and teenagers, groups that already suffer high unemployment rates. Such people might have been able to find jobs had employers been allowed to pay them the equilibrium wage rate, but these jobs go uncreated when employers are forced to pay the higher minimum wage.

As these examples of price floors and price ceilings show, when government intervenes in functioning markets to promote fairness, problems occur. But we have also seen that government intervention can be useful in cases of market failure to promote economic efficiency. Markets require several institutions to ensure efficiency and socially desirable outcomes. These include good information, protection of property rights, contract enforcement, an absence of externalities, and commitment to competition. But many of these elements are not always present in markets, leading to market failure that often means government regulation of some aspects of production or distribution.

Some countries use extensive market regulation and public ownership to provide some goods and services. The United States has traditionally relied less on regulation, and increasingly uses market incentives to solve market failures.

Taxes and Deadweight Loss

As well as regulation and public ownership, government also affects economic efficiency through taxes. Governments need tax revenue to operate. Governments also use taxes to influence incentives. We have a large mix of taxes in the United States from income (both corporate and individual), excise (taxes on specific products such as cigarettes, alcohol, and luxury goods), to property and sales taxes. In this section we take a quick look at how taxes affect the market.

To keep our analysis simple, we will just consider the excise tax shown in Figure 7. The original supply and demand curves are D_0 and S_0, and the market is in equilibrium at \$6 with 6,000 units sold (point *e*). Now assume that the government levies a \$2 excise tax to be paid by suppliers. This in effect increases wholesale prices by \$2 and results in supply shifting leftward to $S_{Tax\ (\$2)}$. Equilibrium moves up to point *a* and the new price is \$7.25 and sales drop to 4,700 units. Several conclusions pop out from this analysis and Figure 7.

FIGURE 7

Taxes, Consumer and Producer Surplus, and Deadweight Loss

In this figure a \$2 excise tax is levied on the producer. The result is that supply shifts leftward by the tax, resulting in lower output sold at a higher price (point *a*). Taxes drive a wedge between what consumers pay and what producers receive. Also, consumer and producer surpluses decline. The deadweight loss (loss of consumer surplus and producer surplus that evaporate) shown in the figure is the inefficiency associated with this tax.

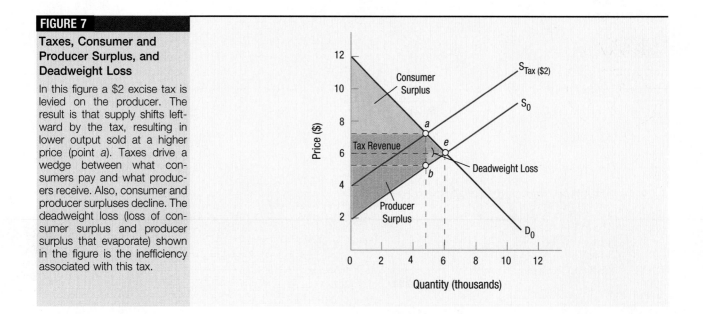

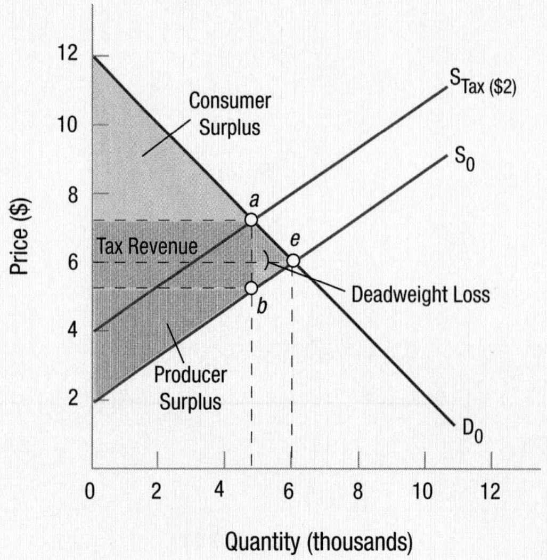

First, the excise tax has driven a \$2 wedge between what consumers pay and what producers receive. So, producers have to charge more (\$7.25 rather than \$6) but receive less (\$5.25 rather than \$6). Second, the government collects tax revenue (in this case revenue is equal to $\$2 \times 4{,}700 = \$9{,}400$). Third, both consumer and producer surplus have shrunk as shown in the figure.

And, fourth, and most interesting, there is an additional loss of consumer and producer surplus equal to the triangle labeled "Deadweight Loss" in the figure. Economists refer to this as a **deadweight loss** because it is the inefficiency costs of public policies (in this case, an excise tax) because the optimal level of price and output is disrupted. In this case, 1,300 units of this product ($6{,}000 - 4{,}700$) are not traded in the market. This loss is dead weight because it is lost to all of society: not captured by consumers, not by producers, and not by society in the form of tax revenues.

Deadweight loss The loss in consumer and producer surplus due to inefficiency because some transactions cannot be made and therefore their value to society is lost.

Throughout the remainder of your study of economics, you will find the supply and demand model a good first approach to analysis. In addition, we will use producer and consumer surplus, and deadweight loss to evaluate the efficiency of various public policies. Economic and public policy questions are often amenable to this analysis, tempered by the considerations discussed in this chapter.

Checkpoint
Government-Controlled Prices

REVIEW

- Competitive markets clear: Businesses provide consumers with the quantity of goods they want to purchase at the established price.
- People may ask government to intervene even when markets work because people may not think the equilibrium price is fair.
- Governments use price floors and price ceilings to intervene in markets.
- A price ceiling is a maximum legal price that can be charged for a product. Price ceilings set below equilibrium result in shortages.
- A price floor is the minimum legal price that can be charged for a product. Price floors set above market equilibrium result in surpluses.
- Deadweight losses often result from the inefficiencies inherent in public policies. But this has to be balanced against the benefits of the policies.

QUESTION

Rent controls are found in cities such as New York and Santa Monica, California, where land prices are at a premium and the city is relatively built-out (very little vacant land remains). Why is rent control not found in cities such as Phoenix, Arizona, or Denver, Colorado?

Answers to the Checkpoint question can be found at the end of this chapter.

Bruno Budrovic/Getty Images

Who Is Watching Your Money? Bank Regulation and Information Problems

Like most people, you probably have a bank account, maybe a checking and savings account. Who is watching your money? What do you know about your bank? Probably very little. The bank certainly knows much more about its business strength and viability than you do. Should you care about this information asymmetry? Probably not at this time, because of FDIC (Federal Deposit Insurance Corporation) insurance: Your account is insured by a federal agency up to $100,000. So this federal insurance encourages you to put your savings in a bank. In other words, the FDIC insurance deals with the information problem that you really can not know very much about who is handling your money.

FDIC insurance did not stem from the Founding Fathers. It is a more recent thing. Federal deposit insurance grew out of the bank panics of the Great Depression.[9] These bank panics started in October of 1930, ebbing and flowing until 1933.

Consider a time without deposit insurance. You put your money in a local bank. How much do you really know about its financial strength? Not much. Let's see where this information problem led.

Say a bank in another locality nearby fails, meaning it closes its doors. People who had their savings in this bank cannot get them out—they will lose everything. You start to wonder whether the same thing will happen to your bank, so you decide to withdraw your money, just to be on the safe side. The next morning, you go to your bank, only to find a long line of like-minded savers. You wait in line. Meanwhile, people who pass by see this line and start to think that maybe their banks are not safe, so they go to withdraw their savings.

One factor that makes this process more dangerous is the fact that your bank never sits there with all of your savings gathering dust in a lockbox just waiting for you to come in and withdraw some. Your bank takes your money, keeps a small portion for everyday bank transactions, and loans out the rest. This means that a run on the bank—when people line up to take out their entire savings—is apt to cause problems for even a well-run solvent bank: How can it quickly turn its loans into cash during a bank run? If it cannot and receives no help from other financial institutions, the bank will have to close its doors. And when this happens, people at other banks will consider withdrawing their money, too.

This is precisely what happened during the Great Depression. One bank run led to another, leading to regional bank panics. Economic activity collapsed when savings could not go to potential business borrowers. To deal with this problem of asymmetric information—you know so little about your bank that it may be prudent to withdraw your money at the slightest whiff of trouble—the FDIC was created on January 1, 1934. Now you do not have to worry about withdrawing your money: You will recover your savings even if the bank fails. Since the creation of the FDIC, there have been no bank panics in the United States. Even during the failure of several savings and loans in the 1980s, bank runs were limited to the affected banks, and even here the bank runs soon dissipated when it became clear that savings were safe.

However, federal deposit insurance has not been an unqualified success. Solving one information problem has brought about another: a moral hazard problem. Without the insurance, there were information asymmetry problems, though at least there was a virtue in you knowing something about your bank. You would not want to lose your money, so you had to keep an eye on your bank to some degree. If you became nervous about your bank's financial strength, you would withdraw your savings. If enough people did this, it would be a signal that something might be amiss. This market action would then discipline the bank. With deposit insurance, you do not have to watch your bank, so the deposit insurance takes away this market discipline. It causes moral hazard: Without this potential market discipline, banks can engage in riskier loans where the payoff may be higher but the chance of success lower.

It turns out that financial institutions attract high-risk-taking individuals. Think of it: All of that money to play with, and not a penny of it the bank officer's. This is a key reason that financial institutions are so heavily regulated.

---

[9]See Milton Friedman and Anna Jacobson Schwartz, *A Monetary History of the United States, 1867–1960* (Princeton, NJ: Princeton University Press), 1963.

If information asymmetries led to bank runs and bank panics, and deposit insurance solved that problem but brought with it the problem of moral hazard, how has the federal government dealt with the problem of moral hazard? First, the federal government has to monitor financial institutions very closely. It is harder to take on high risks when you are watched all the time. Second, the federal government mandates specific capital requirements, limiting forays into risky loans. Third, financial institutions are forced to diversify their holdings among various asset classes. You can get a sense of these various requirements by reading a bank's annual report.

Do these requirements solve the problem of moral hazard? "Solve" is too strong a word. They make the problem less likely to occur, but as long as other people's money is involved, financial buccaneers will be attracted to it.

What does this response to information problems in the banking industry suggest? The proper course of action is to recognize the efficiency of markets and do what we can to get them to work. This approach may require adjustments and further adjustments. Deposit insurance may solve one problem while bringing about another problem, though of lesser scope. And the solution to the new problem may be less than perfect. But economic analysis provides us with a powerful set of tools to use in dealing with information problems.

Key Concepts

Property rights, p. 83
Consumer surplus, p. 87
Producer surplus, p. 87
Asymmetric information, p. 88
Adverse selection, p. 91
Moral hazard, p. 92
Public goods, p. 94
Free rider, p. 94
Common property resources, p. 95
External cost, p. 96
External benefits, p. 96
Price ceiling, p. 99
Price floor, p. 101
Deadweight loss, p. 103

Chapter Summary

Markets and Efficiency

Markets are efficient mechanisms for allocating resources. The prices and profits characteristic of market systems provide incentives and signals that are nonexistent or seriously flawed in other systems of resource allocation.

For markets to be efficient, they must have well-structured institutions. These include (1) information is widely available; (2) property rights are protected; (3) private contracts are enforced; (4) spillovers are minimal; and (5) competition prevails.

Markets impose discipline on producers and consumers. Producers would like to charge higher prices and earn greater profits. But their economic survival depends on turning out quality goods at reasonable prices. As consumers, we would all like to engage in frequent extravagant purchases. But given our limited resources, each of us must decide which products are most important to us. As a result, markets are also rationing devices.

Because many consumers are willing to pay more than market equilibrium prices for many goods and services, they receive a consumer surplus. In a similar way, since many businesses would be willing to provide products at prices below equilibrium prices, they receive a producer surplus. The concepts of consumer and producer surplus are helpful when we wish to examine the impacts of public policy.

Market Failures

For markets to be efficient, they must meet the five institutional requirements identified earlier. When one or more of these conditions is not met, the market is said to fail. Market failure usually does not mean that a market totally collapses or fails to exist, but that it fails to provide the socially optimal amount of goods and services.

In some markets, one party to a transaction may almost always have better information than the other. In this case, the market is said to fail because of asymmetric information. Asymmetric information can result in the inability of sellers to find buyers for the products, but it usually just involves adjustments in contracting methods.

Adverse selection occurs when products of different qualities are sold at one price and involve asymmetric information. Insurance customers, for instance, know far more about their own health than do insurance companies. And because high-risk individuals are most likely to purchase insurance, adverse selection skews the insurance pool, giving it a risk level higher than average.

Moral hazard occurs when an insurance policy or some other arrangement changes the economic incentives people face, leading people to change their behavior, usually in a way detrimental to the market. Theft insurance for cars, for instance, tends to make people less scrupulous about locking their car doors.

Private goods are those goods that can be consumed only by the individuals who purchase them. Private goods are rival and exclusive. Public goods, in contrast, are nonrival and nonexclusive, meaning my consumption does not diminish your consumption and that once such a good has been provided for one person, others cannot be excluded from enjoying it.

Public goods give rise to the free rider problem. Once a public good has been provided, other consumers cannot be excluded from it, so many people will choose to enjoy the benefit without paying for it: They will free ride. And because of the possibility of free riding, the danger is that no one will pay for the public good, so it will no longer be provided by private markets, even though it is publicly desired. Pure public goods usually require public provision.

Common property resources are owned in common by the community and are subject to the "tragedy of the commons" and overexploitation.

When an efficient legal system for the enforcement of contracts is lacking, contracts will be small because large contracts with complex financial provisions are difficult to enforce informally.

Markets rarely produce the socially optimal output when external costs or benefits are present. The market overproduces goods with external costs, selling them at too low a price. Conversely, markets tend to provide too little of products that have external benefits.

Some markets tend toward monopoly, and when a monopoly does control the market, prices go up. In the late 19th century, the monopolistic practices of the "robber barons" spurred passage of a series of antitrust laws that are still used today to promote competitive markets.

Government-Controlled Prices

When competitive markets are left to determine equilibrium price and output, they clear; businesses provide consumers with the quantity of goods they want to purchase at the established prices. Nevertheless, the equilibrium price may not be what many people consider fair. The government may then use price ceilings or price floors to keep prices below or above the market equilibrium.

A price ceiling is the maximum legal price that can be charged for a product. Price ceilings set below equilibrium result in shortages. A price floor is the minimum legal price that can be charged for a product. Price floors set above market equilibrium result in surpluses.

Questions and Problems

1. Many observers consider it a market failure when the pharmaceutical industry refuses to do research and development on what are known as neglected diseases: cures for malaria and tuberculosis and vaccines for other diseases in developing countries where the profit potential is small. Further, many drug firms are unwilling to make vaccines for illnesses such as influenza and other biohazards such as anthrax and small pox. Vaccines are especially prone to large lawsuits because when they are administered, they are administered to millions of people in an emergency, and if there are serious unanticipated side effects, settlement costs can be huge. With anthrax vaccine, ethical considerations prevent exposing someone to anthrax and then injecting the medicine, so these types of vaccines often are used in emergencies without sufficient testing.
   a. One of the solutions currently used for neglected diseases is the public–private partnership (PPP). Grants by the Bill & Melinda Gates Foundation currently fund most of the PPPs that are conducted on a "no profit, no loss" basis. The firm's research and development costs are covered, but firms must sell the drugs at cost to developing countries. Why would pharmaceutical firms be willing to spend time on these types of projects?
   b. Since lawsuits are an important impediment to research and development of vaccines, what policies could the government institute to solve this problem?
   c. Besides the use of the PPP, what other policies might the government introduce to encourage drug firms to do research and development on neglected diseases and orphan diseases (diseases that affect only a few people and thus have extremely limited markets)?

2. "If millions of people are desperate to buy and millions more desperate to sell, the trades will happen, whether we like it or not." This quote by Martin Wolf[10] refers to trades in illicit goods like narcotics, knockoffs (counterfeit goods), slaves, organs, and other goods we generally refer to as "bads." He suggests that the only way to eliminate traffic in these illicit goods is to eliminate their profitability. Do you agree? Why or why not?

3. Academic studies suggest that the amount people tip at restaurants is only slightly related to the quality of service, and that tips are poor measures of how happy people are with the service. Is this another example of market failure? What might account for this situation?

4. The U.S. Department of Labor reports that of the roughly 145 million people employed, just over half (73.9 million) are paid hourly, but less than 3% earn the minimum wage or less; 97% of wage earners earn more. And of those earning the minimum wage or less, 25% are teenagers living at home. If so few people are affected by the minimum wage, why does it often seem to be such a contentious political issue?

5. Adam Smith, in his famous book *The Wealth of Nations,* noted, "Every individual . . . neither intends to promote the public interest, nor knows how much he is promoting it. By preferring the support of domestic to that of foreign industry he intends only his own security; and by directing that industry in such a manner as its produce may be of the greatest value, he intends only his own gain, and he is in this, as in many other cases, led by an invisible hand to promote an end which was no part of his intention." What was he describing and what did it do?

---

[10]Martin Wolf, "The Profit Motive May Be Universal but Virtue Is Not," *Financial Times,* November 16, 2005, p.13.

6. When professors get tenure, essentially guaranteeing them lifetime jobs, does this affect the effort they expend on teaching and research? What concept might be used to explain your answer?

7. Are buying brands (e.g., Coke, Sony, and Dell) a way consumers compensate for asymmetric information? Explain.

8. What is the purpose of a warranty given by a used-car dealer? Evaluate one used-car warranty that gives your money back if not satisfied in a certain time period, and one that does not give you back your money but lets you put this money toward the purchase of another used car. Which warranty would you prefer?

9. Farm price supports (price floors) have been a part of the economic landscape for the better part of a century as farming has evolved from a way of life to today where most agricultural products are produced on large corporate farms. Stable farm prices are the benefit of these policies. What are the costs?

10. In 2006 Medicare recipients were permitted to sign up for a federally subsidized drug benefit plan. The sign-up phase had a May 15th deadline, and those signing up after that date faced a premium penalty. Does this deadline have anything to do with adverse selection? Explain.

11. Nobel Prize winner Gary Becker and Judge Richard Posner[11] suggested that "unions strongly favor the minimum wage because it reduces competition from low-wage workers (who, partly because most of them work part time, tend not to be unionized) and thus enhances unions' bargaining power." They further argued that "although some workers benefit—those who were paid the old minimum wage but are worth the new higher one to the employers—others are pushed into unemployment, the underground economy or crime. The losers are therefore likely to lose more than the gainers gain; they are also likely to be poorer people." Are both of these statements consistent with the model of price floors discussed in this chapter? Why or why not?

12. Describe consumer surplus. Describe producer surplus. Using the graph below show both. Now assume that a new technology reduces the cost of production. What happens to consumer surplus? Show the impact of the change in the graph.

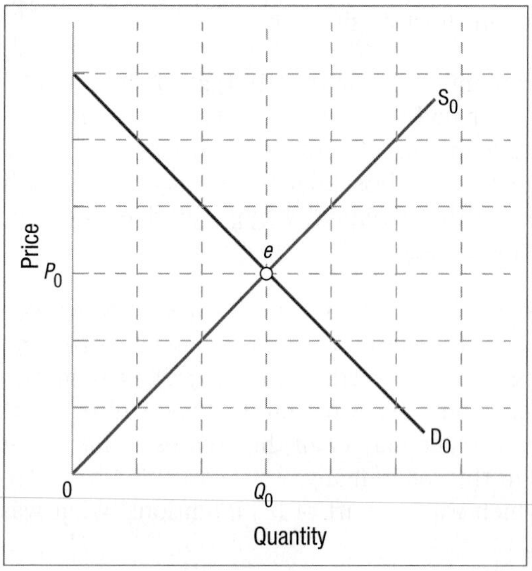

[11]Gary Becker and Richard Posner, "How to Make the Poor Poorer," *The Wall Street Journal,* January 26, 2007, p. A11.

13. Define public goods. What is the free rider problem? Give several examples of public goods.

14. Describe a price ceiling. What is the impact of an effective price ceiling? Show this on the figure below. Give an example. Describe a price floor. What is the impact of an effective price floor? Show this on the figure below. Give an example.

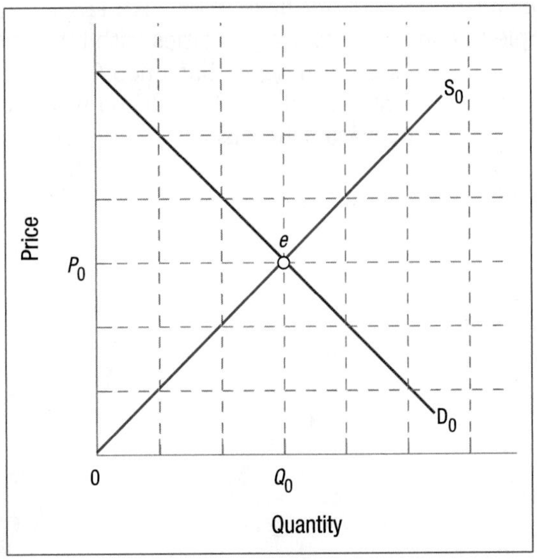

15. Describe the tragedy of the commons. Give some examples. How might this tragedy be avoided?

16. Professor Donald Boudreaux wrote (*Wall Street Journal*, 8/23/06, p. A11), that "There are heaps of bad arguments for raising the minimum wage. Perhaps the worst . . . is that a minimum wage increase is justified if a full-time worker earning the current minimum wage cannot afford to live in a city such as Chicago." He then asked "why settle for enabling workers to live only in the likes of Chicago? Why not raise the minimum wage so that everyone can afford to live in, say, Nantucket, Hyannis Port or Beverly Hills, within walking distance of Rodeo Drive?" Should the minimum wage be a "living wage," so a full-time worker can live comfortably in a given locale? What would be the impact if minimum wages were structured this way?

Answers to Checkpoint Questions

CHECKPOINT: MARKETS AND EFFICIENCY

Some large corporations are innovative and nimble (Google, Genentech, and Apple are examples), but most become bureaucratic and reactive to developments in their markets. Microsoft was a reasonably large firm when it produced Windows. Microsoft is less innovative today in that it spends so much time and effort defending its existing products. It is, however, spending huge sums on research and development.

CHECKPOINT: MARKET FAILURES

This approach to the class would and did alter student behavior. Once students understood that the professor intended to stand behind the offer (essentially made it a contract with students) attendance dropped off, and many settled for a grade of B. Even though he was a good professor, students, like many others, have commitments on their time and optimized by accepting a B instead of attending class and getting an A.

CHECKPOINT: GOVERNMENT-CONTROLLED PRICES

Cities with a lot of vacant land do not have rents high enough to support activists who try to get people to control rents. Only in cities with little vacant land and high population densities are rents high enough that enough people think it "unfair," resulting in rent controls. If rent controls are introduced where a lot of vacant land exists, the land simply remains vacant because development is stymied.

5 Elasticity

In 2003, gasoline prices—previously fairly stable—started to climb. Driven by problems in the Middle East and increased demand from China and India, gasoline prices kept climbing. By April 2006, gasoline had reached a price of over $3.00 per gallon, twice as high as two years previously.

If you drove a car during this period, what did you do? At first, you probably did nothing but bear with it and pay the higher price. What *could* you do? It is not as if gasoline is the same as chewing gum: A large rise in the price of chewing gum might cause you to give it up. Things are not so easy with gasoline. Maybe you drove a little less. Over time, however, you may have considered alternatives such as buying a smaller car or a hybrid that gets much better gas mileage. Or you may have considered car pooling or public transportation. The 15% drop in sales in 2007 of large gas-guzzling sport utility vehicles (SUVs) tells us that over time, people responded to the steady rise in gasoline prices by cutting their quantity of gasoline purchased.

Elasticity—the responsiveness of one variable to changes in another—is the term economists use to measure this change. In this gasoline example, we know that the price of gasoline is one variable and the quantity of gasoline demanded is the other variable. The amount of gasoline we buy does not change very much in the short run even though the price might rise. Over the long run, the rise in the price of gasoline has led to some attempts to cut back usage. We can speculate that there will be greater attempts to use less gasoline as prices rise. But how much does the price have to rise before quantity demanded falls significantly? The concept of elasticity lets us measure the relative change in quantity demanded for various changes in the price of gasoline.

Elasticity can be measured for many different items. If the price of cancer-preventing drugs rises, how much will demand for them fall? As well as price elasticity, we can look at another elasticity measure, income elasticity, which measures changes in consumer demand in response to changes in consumer income. In a slowing economy, with consumer incomes falling, will the public's demand for cars and trucks fall off? By how much? Automobile makers will want to know how much sales of trucks and cars will decline in response to a fall in consumer income.

Elasticity is a simple economic concept that nonetheless contains a tremendous amount of information about demand for specific products. In the last two chapters, we saw that, when prices rise, quantity demanded will fall. But how much will quantity demanded fall? If a firm raises its price by 50 cents, will it end up with more in revenue, or will the increase in price lead to a drop in quantity demanded that more than offsets the price increase? If gasoline goes up by 25 cents per gallon, will you still take a summer driving trip? What if the price increase is $1 per gallon?

Knowing a product's price elasticity allows economists to predict the amount by which quantity demanded will drop in response to a price increase, or grow in response to a price decline. Measures of elasticity have a further benefit: By putting changes in a relative (percentage) context, economists can compare the supply and demand curves for different products without worrying about their absolute magnitudes. In essence, the concept of elasticity helps you to put supply and demand concepts to work.

After studying this chapter you should be able to

- Understand the concept of elasticity and why percentages are used to measure it.
- Describe the difference between elastic and inelastic demand.
- Compute price elasticities of supply and demand.
- Use income elasticity of demand to define normal, inferior, and luxury goods.
- Describe cross elasticity of demand and use this concept to define substitutes and complements.
- Describe the relationship between total revenue and price elasticity of demand.
- Describe the determinants of elasticity of demand and supply.
- Use the concept of price elasticity of supply to measure the relationship between quantity supplied and changes in product price.
- Describe the time periods economists use to study elasticity, and describe the variables that companies can change during these periods.
- Describe the relationship between elasticity and the burden and incidence of taxes.

Elasticity of Demand

We know by the law of demand that as prices rise, quantity sold falls. But how much revenue, in dollar terms, will a business gain or lose if it raises the price of one of its products? If a small price increase results in a large reduction in quantity sold, then raising prices probably is not a good idea. However, if a large price increase will elicit only a small loss in quantity demanded, then raising prices will undoubtedly make sense.

Price elasticity of demand A measure of the responsiveness of quantity demanded to a change in price, equal to the percentage change in quantity demanded divided by the percentage change in price.

Price elasticity of demand (E_d) is a measure of how responsive quantity demanded is to a change in price and is defined as

$$E_d = \frac{\text{Percentage Change in Quantity Demanded}}{\text{Percentage Change in Price}}$$

For example, if prices of strawberries rise by 5% and sales fall by 10%, then the price elasticity of demand for strawberries is

$$E_d = -10 \div 5 = -2$$

Alternately, if a 5% reduction in strawberry prices results in a 10% gain in sales, the price elasticity of demand also is -2 ($E_d = 10 \div -5 = -2$).

Often we are not given percentage changes. Rather, we are given numerical values and have to convert them into percentage changes. For example, to compute a change in price, take the new price (P_{new}) and subtract the old price (P_{old}), then divide this result by the old price (P_{old}). Finally, to put this ratio in percentage terms, multiply by 100. In equation form:

$$\text{Percentage Change} = \frac{(P_{new} - P_{old})}{P_{old}}$$

For example, if the old price of gasoline (P_{old}) was \$2.00 a gallon and the new price goes up by \$1.00 to \$3.00, then the percentage change is

$$\text{Percentage Change} = \frac{\$3.00 - \$2.00}{\$2.00} = \frac{\$1.00}{\$2.00} = .50 \text{ or } 50\%$$

Just a reminder: .50 times 100 is 50%.

Elasticity as an Absolute Value

The price elasticity of demand is always a negative number. This reflects the fact that the demand curve's slope is negative: As prices increase, quantity demanded falls. Price and quantity demanded stand in an inverse relationship to one another, resulting in a negative value for price elasticity. Economists nevertheless frequently refer to price elasticity of demand in positive terms. They simply use the *absolute value* of the computed price elasticity of demand. Recalling our examples, where $E_d = -2$, we can take the absolute value of -2, written as $|-2|$ and simply refer to E_d as 2. For most comparisons, we can use the absolute value of elasticity and ignore the minus sign.

What does this elasticity value of 2 tell us? Quite simply, that for every 1% increase in price, quantity demanded will decline by 2%. Conversely, for every 1% decline in price, quantity demanded will increase by 2%.

Measuring Elasticity with Percentages

Measuring elasticity in percentage terms rather than specific units enables economists to compare the characteristics of various unrelated products. Comparing price and sales changes for jet airplanes, cars, and hamburgers in dollar amounts would be so complex as to be meaningless. Because a dollar increase in price for gasoline is different from a dollar increase in the price of a BMW, by using percentage change, we can compare the sensitivity of demand curves of different products. Percentages allow us to compare changes in prices and sales for any two products, no matter how dissimilar they are; a 100% increase is the same percentage change for any product.

We have seen how to compute the elasticity of demand, and we know why working with percentage changes is so important. Elasticity is a relative measure giving us a way to compare products with widely different prices and output measures.

FIGURE 1

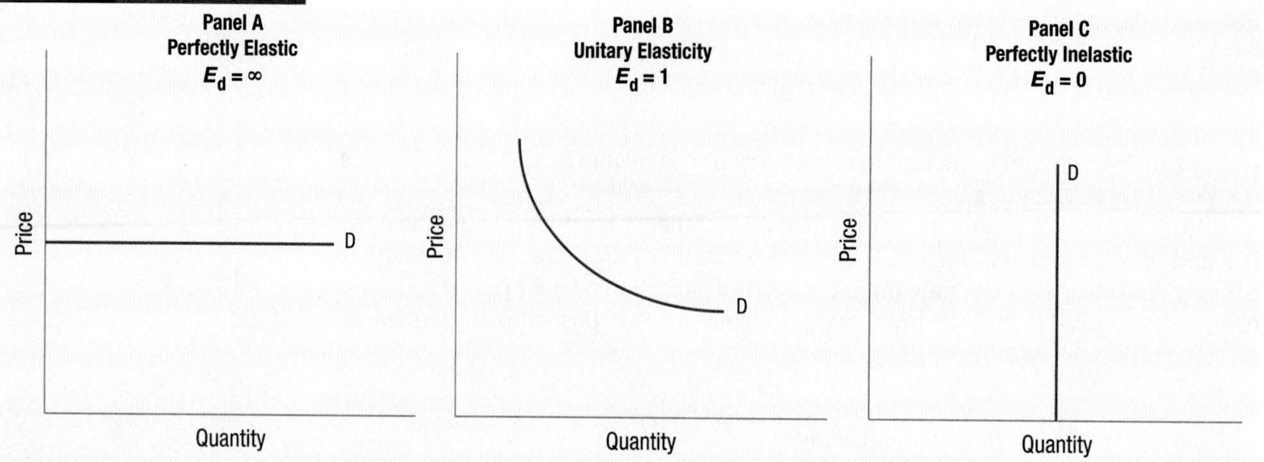

Perfectly Elastic, Unitary Elastic, and Perfectly Inelastic Demand Curves

The horizontal demand curve in Panel A represents a perfectly elastic demand in that when price increases, quantity demanded drops to zero. Panel C, on the other hand, illustrates a demand curve where quantity demanded is insensitive to changes in price. Panel B shows that if elasticity of demand is unitary, then a 1% increase in price will result in a 1% decrease in quantity demanded. Note that the unitary elastic demand curve is not a straight line.

Elastic and Inelastic Demand

All products have some price elasticity of demand. When prices go up, quantity demanded will fall. That is the basis of the negative slope of the demand curve. But people are more responsive to changes in the prices of some products than in others. Economists label goods as either *elastic, inelastic,* or *unitary elastic.*

Elastic

Elastic demand
The absolute value of the price elasticity of demand is greater than 1. Elastic demands are very responsive to changes in price. The percentage change in quantity demand is greater than the percentage change in price.

When the absolute value of the computed price elasticity of demand is greater than 1, economists refer to this as **elastic demand**. An elastic demand curve is one that is responsive to price changes. At the extreme is the *perfectly elastic* demand curve shown in Panel A of Figure 1. Notice that it is horizontal, showing that the slightest increase in price will result in zero output being sold.

In reality, no branded product—Coca-Cola, Apple iPod, or Toyota Prius—ever has a perfectly elastic demand curve. For many of us, no other products can perfectly substitute for these products. Still, products with many close substitutes face highly elastic demand curves. One recent study of several brands of bath tissue found the price elasticities of demand for Scott, Kleenex, Charmin, Northern, and other brands ranged from 2.0 to 4.5—highly elastic.[1] Raise the price of Charmin, and watch how quickly sales fall as people switch to Northern or Scott. Canned peaches, nuts and bolts, cereal, and bottled water are all examples of products facing highly elastic demands. If one bottled water company were to raise its price by much, many consumers would simply switch to other brands, since bottled water is nearly identical.

Inelastic

At the other extreme, what about products that see little change in sales even when prices change dramatically? The opposite of the perfectly elastic demand curve is

[1]Lawrence Wu, "Two Methods of Determining Elasticities of Demand and Their Use in Merger Simulation," in Lawrence Wu, *Economics of Antitrust: New Issues, Questions, and Insights* (New York: National Economic Research Associates), 2004, pp. 21–33.

the curve showing no response to changes in price. Economists call this a *perfectly inelastic* demand curve. An example appears in Panel C of Figure 1. This curve is vertical, not horizontal as in Panel A. For products with perfectly inelastic demands, quantity demanded does not change when price changes.

What products might be inelastically demanded? Consider products that are immensely important to our lives but have few substitutes, for example, drugs that ameliorate life-threatening illnesses such as heart disease or strokes, and insulin for diabetics. If people who need these products have the money, they will buy them, no matter how high their price. Some products that are relatively, though not perfectly, inelastic include gasoline, tobacco, and most spices. If gasoline prices rise too sharply, some consumers will curtail their driving. Still, it takes a fairly drastic rise in gasoline prices before most people curtail their driving significantly. A doubling of the price of cinnamon will probably not reduce our demand since it is such a small fraction of our overall food budget. Economists define **inelastic demand** as demand curves with elasticity coefficients that are less than 1.

Inelastic demand
The absolute value of the price elasticity of demand is less than 1. Inelastic demands are not very responsive to changes in price. The percentage change in quantity demand is less than the percentage change in price.

Note that the demand for gasoline is inelastic, but the elasticity for specific brands of gasoline is elastic. Brand preferences for homogeneous commodities such as gasoline are weak, and many different outlets exist for buying gas. If your Shell dealer raises gasoline prices by a significant amount, you probably will go to the Texaco dealer down the street. Giving up using gasoline altogether, on the other hand, is much harder. Over time, public transportation or electric (or hybrid) cars may be possible substitutes for gas-powered cars, but few people will be able to adopt these substitutes in the short run. On the contrary, many people are highly dependent on their gas-powered cars, so gas purchases do not drop substantially when prices rise, as we have seen in the run-up of gas prices described earlier. Thus, demand for a particular brand of gas (Exxon, Shell) will be elastic, while the demand for gasoline as a commodity will be inelastic.

Unitary Elasticity

Elastic demand curves have an elasticity coefficient that is greater than 1, while inelastic demand curves have coefficients less than 1. That leaves those products with an elasticity coefficient just equal to 1. This condition is called *unit* or **unitary elasticity of demand**. It means the percentage change in quantity demanded is precisely equal to the percentage change in price. Panel B of Figure 1 shows a demand curve where price elasticity = 1. Note that this demand curve is not a straight line. The reasons for this will become clear in our discussion later on in the chapter.

Unitary elasticity of demand
The absolute value of the price elasticity of demand is equal to 1. The percentage change in quantity demand is just equal to the percentage change in price.

Determinants of Elasticity

Price elasticity of demand measures how sensitive sales are to price changes. But what determines elasticity itself? The four basic determinants of a product's elasticity of demand are (1) the availability of substitute products, (2) the percentage of income or household budget spent on the product, (3) the time period being examined, and (4) the difference between luxuries and necessities.

Substitutability

The more close substitutes, or possible alternatives, a product has, the easier it is for consumers to switch to a competing product and the more elastic the demand. Beef and chicken are substitutes for many people, as are competing brands of cola such as Coke, Pepsi, and RC Cola. All have relatively elastic demands. Conversely, if a product has few close substitutes, such as insulin for diabetics or tobacco for heavy smokers, its elasticity of demand will tend to be lower.

Proportion of Income Spent on a Product

A second determinant of elasticity is the proportion (percentage) of household income spent on a product. In general, the smaller the percent of household income spent on a product, the lower the elasticity of demand. For example, you probably spend little of your income on salt, cinnamon, or other spices. As a result, a hefty increase in the price of salt, say, 25%, would not affect your salt consumption because the impact on your budget would be tiny. But if a product represents a significant part of household spending, elasticity of demand tends to be greater, or more elastic. A 10% increase in your rent, for example, would put a large dent in your budget, significantly reducing your purchasing power for many other products. Such a rent increase would likely lead you to look around earnestly for a cheaper apartment.

Time Period

The third determinant of elasticity is the time period under consideration. When consumers have some time to adjust their consumption patterns, the elasticity of demand becomes more elastic. When they have little time to adjust, the elasticity of demand tends to be more inelastic. Thus, as we saw earlier, when gasoline prices rise suddenly, most consumers cannot immediately change their transportation patterns, so gasoline sales do not drop significantly. However, as gas prices continue to remain high, we will see shifts in consumer behavior, to which automakers will respond by producing smaller, more fuel-efficient hybrid cars.

Luxuries Versus Necessities

Luxuries tend to have demands that are more elastic than do necessities. Necessities like food, electricity, health care, and tobacco for smokers are more important to everyday living, and quantity demanded will not change significantly when prices rise. Luxuries like trips to Hawaii, yachts, and Johnny Walker Blue label scotch, on the other hand, can be postponed or forgotten when prices rise. Table 1 provides a sampling of estimates of elasticities for specific products. Note that as we might expect, medical care and taxi service have relatively inelastic price elasticities of demand, while foreign travel and restaurant meals have relatively elastic price elasticities of demand.

Computing Price Elasticities

When elasticity is computed between two points, the calculated value will differ depending on whether price is increasing or decreasing. For example, in Figure 2, if the price *increases* from \$1.00 to \$2.00, elasticity is equal to

$$\begin{aligned} E_{\mathrm{d}} &= \frac{300 - 500}{500} \div \frac{2.00 - 1.00}{1.00} \\ &= \frac{-200}{500} \div \frac{1.00}{1.00} \\ &= -.4 \div 1.00 \\ &= |-.4| \\ &= .4 \end{aligned}$$

But, when price *decreases* from \$2.00 to \$1.00 elasticity is equal to

$$\begin{aligned} E_{\mathrm{d}} &= \frac{500 - 300}{300} \div \frac{1.00 - 2.00}{2.00} \\ &= \frac{200}{300} \div \frac{-1.00}{2.00} \\ &= .67 \div -0.5 \\ &= |-1.34| \\ &= 1.34 \end{aligned}$$

Table 1 Selected Estimates of Price Elasticities of Demand					
Inelastic		**Roughly Unitary Elastic**		**Elastic**	
Salt	.1	Movies	.9	Restaurant meals	2.3
Cigarettes	.24	Private education	1.1	Air travel	2.4
Medical care	.3	Shoes	.9	Foreign travel	4.0
Taxi service	.6	Automobiles	1.2	Furniture	1.5
Gasoline (short run)	.2	Tires	1.0	Fresh vegetables	2.5
Medical prescriptions	.3			Commuter rail service (long run)	1.6
Pesticides	.2–.5			Shrimp	1.25

Source: Compiled from numerous studies reporting estimates for price elasticity of demand.

Using Midpoints to Compute Elasticity

To avoid getting different results computing elasticity from different directions, economists compute price elasticity using the midpoints of price $[(P_1 + P_0)/2]$ and the midpoints of quantity demanded $[(Q_1 + Q_0)/2]$ as the base.

Therefore, the *price elasticity of demand* formula (assuming price falls from P_0 to P_1 and quantity demanded rises from Q_0 to Q_1) is

$$E_d = \frac{Q_1 - Q_0}{(Q_1 + Q_0)/2} \div \frac{P_1 - P_0}{(P_1 + P_0)/2}.$$

FIGURE 2

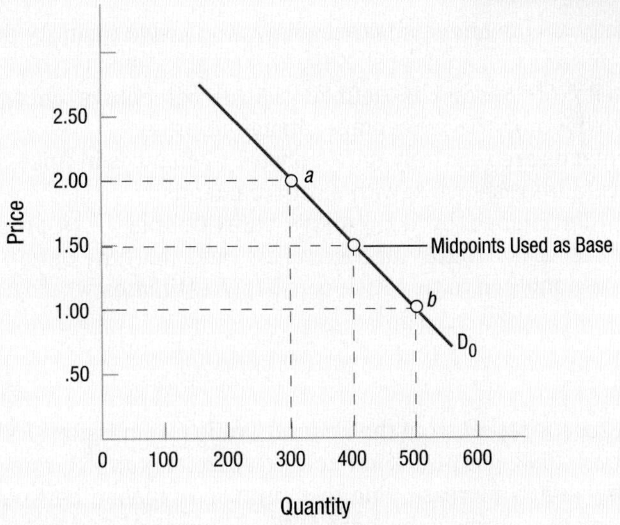

Computing Elasticity of Demand Using Midpoints

A problem can occur when calculating elasticity over a range of prices. The calculated value can vary depending on whether price is increasing or decreasing. To avoid getting different results when approaching the same analysis from different directions, economists use midpoint price and midpoint quantity. Compute the differences in quantities demanded over the sum of the two quantities divided by 2, divided by the differences in prices over the sum of the two prices divided by 2. The following formula can be used:

$$E_d = \frac{Q_1 - Q_0}{(Q_1 + Q_0)/2} \div \frac{P_1 - P_0}{(P_1 + P_0)/2}.$$

Using the midpoints of price and quantity to compute the relevant percentage changes essentially gives us the average elasticity between point *a* and point *b*. Price elasticity of demand is the difference in quantity over the sum of the two quantities divided by 2, divided by the difference in price over the sum of the two prices divided by 2. In Figure 2, the price elasticity of demand between points *a* and *b* would equal

$$
\begin{aligned}
E_d &= \frac{500 - 300}{(500 + 300)/2} \div \frac{1.00 - 2.00}{(1.00 + 2.00)/2} \\
&= \frac{200}{400} \div \frac{-1.00}{1.50} \\
&= .5 \div -.67 \\
&= |-.75| \\
&= .75
\end{aligned}
$$

Check for yourself to see that this elasticity formula yields the same results whether you compute elasticity for a price increase from $1.00 to $2.00 or for a price decrease from $2.00 to $1.00.

Now that we have seen what price elasticity of demand is and how to calculate it, let's put this to work by looking at how elasticity affects total revenue.

Checkpoint

Elasticity of Demand

REVIEW

- Elasticity summarizes how responsive one variable is to a change in another variable.
- Price elasticity of demand summarizes how responsive quantity demanded is to changes in price.
- Price elasticity of demand is defined as the percentage change in quantity demanded divided by the percentage change in price.
- Inelastic demands are relatively unresponsive to changes in price, while quantity demanded is more responsive with elastic demands.
- Elasticity is determined by a product's substitutability, its proportion of the budget, whether it is a luxury or a necessity, and the time period considered.
- Economists use midpoints to derive consistent estimates whether price rises or falls.

QUESTIONS

According to a recent report from the Federal Trade Commission (FTC), in the first 3 weeks of August 2003, gas prices in Phoenix, Arizona, jumped from $1.52 to $2.11 a gallon, roughly a 40% increase, due to a ruptured pipeline between Tucson and Phoenix. The pipeline normally brought 30% of Phoenix's fuel from a Texas refinery. During this period, Phoenix gas stations were able to buy gas from West Coast refineries at higher prices. By the end of the month, the rupture was repaired and prices returned to normal. During this 3-week period of supply disruption gasoline sales fell by 8%. What was the approximate price elasticity of demand for gasoline during this period? If the gas stations were unable to get additional gas from the West Coast, and supplies fell by the full 30%, how high might have prices risen during that 3-week period?

Answers to the Checkpoint questions can be found at the end of this chapter.

Elasticity and Total Revenue

Elasticity is important to firms because elasticity measures the responsiveness of quantity sold to changes in price, which has an impact on the total revenues of the firm. **Total revenue** TR is equal to the number of units sold Q times the price of each unit P, or

$$TR = P \times Q$$

The sensitivity of output to price changes greatly influences how much total revenue changes when price changes.

Total revenue
Price times quantity demanded (sold). If demand is elastic and price rises, quantity demanded falls off significantly and total revenue declines, and vice versa. If demand is inelastic and price rises, quantity demanded does not decline much and total revenue rises, and vice versa.

Inelastic Demand

When consumers are so loyal to a product, or so few substitutes exist, that consumers continue to buy the product even when its price goes up, the product is inelastically demanded. Panel A of Figure 3 shows the impact such a price increase has on total revenue when the demand for a product is inelastic. Price rises from \$2.00 to \$4.00, and sales decline from 600 to 500 units. In this case, total revenue *rises*. We know this because the revenue gained from the price hike [(4.00 − 2.00) × 500 = \$1,000], is greater than the revenue lost [(2.00 × (600 − 500) = \$200]. We can see this by looking at the area of the Revenue Lost box and comparing it to the Revenue Gained box in the figure. What has happened here? The price hike has driven off only a few customers (a small percent), but the firm's many remaining customers are paying a much higher price (a larger percent), thus driving up the firm's total revenue. This is to be expected: Demand for the firm's product is inelastic, so price increases will be accompanied by smaller declines in sales. The percentage change in quantity (20%) is smaller than the percentage change in price (100%).

This may suggest firms would always want the demand for their products to be inelastic. Unfortunately for them, inelastic demand has a flip side. Specifically, if supply increases (due to a technical advance, say), sales will rise only moderately,

FIGURE 3

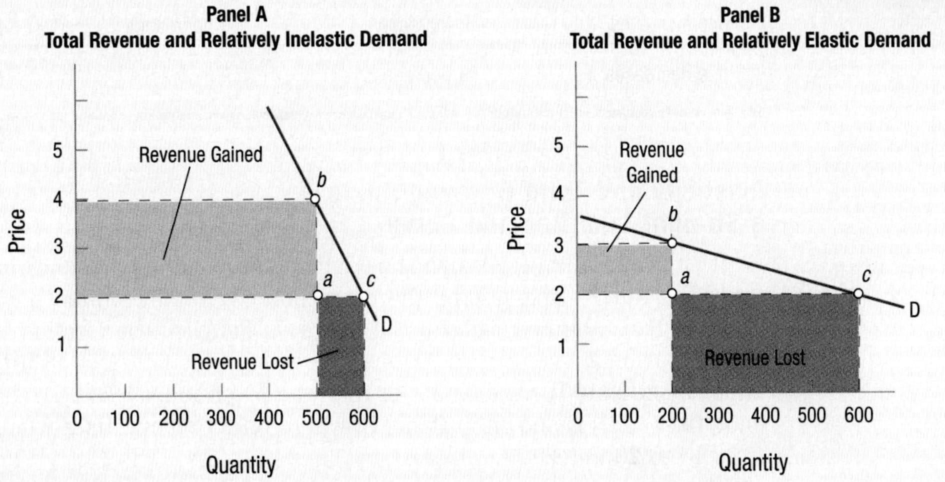

Total Revenue and Elasticity of Demand

Given inelastic demand in Panel A, when price rises from \$2 to \$4, revenue rises because the revenue gained from the price hike (\$1,000) is greater than the revenue lost (\$200). The price hike may have driven off a few customers, but the firm's many remaining customers are paying a much higher price, thus increasing the firm's revenue. When products have elastic demands as shown in Panel B, usually because many substitutes are available, firms feel a greater impact from changes in price. A small rise in price causes sales to fall off dramatically. Total revenue falls because the revenue lost greatly exceeds the revenue gained.

even as prices fall dramatically. This leads to a drop in total revenue: Consumers indeed buy more of the product at its new lower price, but not enough more to pay the firm for the decline in price.

Elastic Demand

Elastic demand is the opposite of inelastic demand. Firms with elastically demanded products will see their sales change dramatically in response to small price changes. Panel B of Figure 3 shows what happens to total revenue when a firm increases the price of a product with elastic demand. Although price does not increase much, sales fall significantly. Revenue lost greatly exceeds the revenue gained from the price increase, so total revenue falls.

The opposite occurs when prices fall and demand is elastic. The high elasticity of demand faced by restaurants helps explain why so many of them offer "buy one get one free" specials and other discounts. As prices fall to their discounted levels, sales have the potential to expand rapidly, thus increasing revenue.

Unitary Elasticity

We have looked at the impact of changing prices on revenue when demand is elastic and inelastic. When the elasticity of demand is unitary ($E_d = 1$), a 10% increase in price results in a 10% reduction in quantity demanded. As a result, total revenue is unaffected.

Table 2 summarizes the effects price changes have on total revenue for different price elasticities of demand.

Table 2 **Total Revenue, Price Changes, and Price Elasticity of Demand**

	Elasticity		
Price Change	**Inelastic**	**Elastic**	**Unitary**
Price increases	TR increases	TR decreases	No change in TR
Price decreases	TR decreases	TR increases	No change in TR

Elasticity and Total Revenue Along a Straight-Line Demand Curve

Elasticity varies along a straight-line demand curve. Figure 4 shows a linear demand curve in Panel A and graphs the corresponding total revenue points in Panel B. Table 3 shows the raw data for the figure. In Panel A, the elastic part of the curve is that portion above point *e*. Notice that when price falls from \$11 to \$10, the revenue gained (\$100) is much larger than the revenue lost (\$10), and thus total revenue rises. This is shown in Panel B, where total revenue rises when output grows from 10 to 20 units.

As we move down the demand curve, elasticity will eventually equal 1 (at point *e*) and elasticity will be unitary. Price was falling up to this point, while total revenue kept rising until the last price reduction just before \$6, where revenue did not change. Revenue is at its maximum at point *e* or a price of \$6 in both panels.

As price continues to fall below \$6, the demand curve moves into an inelastic range because the percentage change in quantity demanded is less than the percentage change in price. Therefore, when price falls from \$3 to \$2, revenue declines. The revenue gained (\$20) is less than revenue lost (\$90). This decline in revenue is shown in Panel B, as total revenue falls as output rises from 90 to 100 units sold.

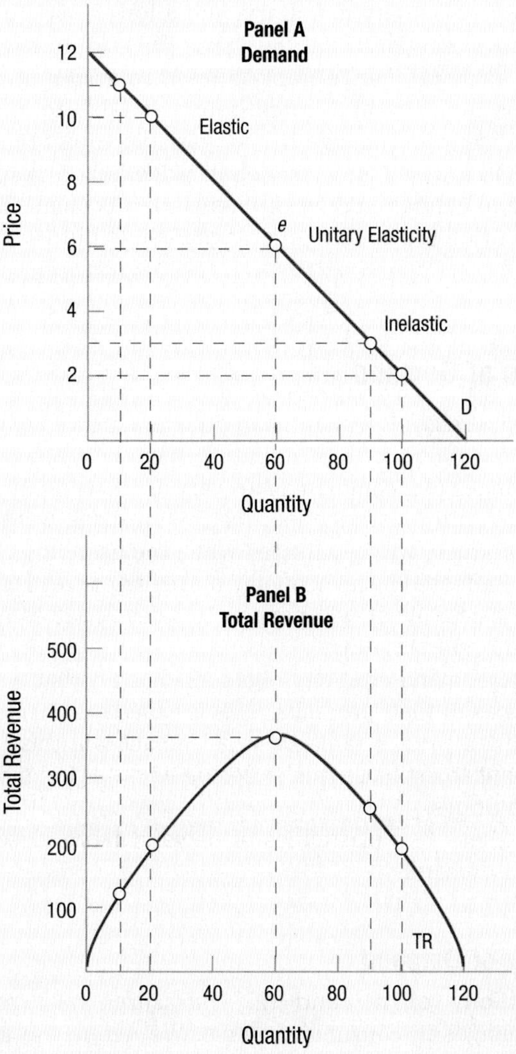

FIGURE 4

Price Elasticity and Total Revenue Along a Straight Line (Linear) Demand Curve

Price elasticity varies along a straight line demand curve. In Panel A, the elastic part of the curve lies above point *e*. Thus, when price falls from $11 to $10, revenue rises, as shown in Panel B. As we move down the demand curve, elasticity equals 1 (at point *e*) and elasticity is unitary. Revenue is maximized at this point. As price continues to fall below $6, demand moves into an inelastic range. When price falls from $3 to $2, revenue declines, as shown in Panel B.

Table 3 **Data for Demand, Elasticity, and Total Revenue for Figure 4**

Price	Quantity	Elasticity	Description	Total Revenue
12	0			0
11	10	23.00	Elastic	110
10	20	7.00	Elastic	200
9	30	3.80	Elastic	270
8	40	2.43	Elastic	320
7	50	1.67	Elastic	350
6	60	1.18	Unitary elastic	360
5	70	0.85	Inelastic	350
4	80	0.60	Inelastic	320
3	90	0.41	Inelastic	270
2	100	0.26	Inelastic	200
1	110	0.14	Inelastic	110
0	120	0.04	Inelastic	0

To summarize, all linear demand curves have an upper portion that is elastic, a midpoint where elasticity is unitary, and a lower part that is inelastic. The logic underlying this fact is straightforward. The slope is constant along the demand curve, so each $1 change in price leads to a 10-unit change in quantity demanded. Slope is the ratio of *change* in one variable to another. Elasticity is the ratio of the *percentage* change in one variable to another. Thus, when the price of a product is low, a 1-unit change in price is a large percentage change while the percentage change in quantity demanded is small, When price is high, a 1-unit change in price is a small percentage change but the percentage change in quantity is large.

Other Elasticities of Demand

Besides the price elasticity of demand, two other elasticities of demand are important. The first, *income elasticity of demand,* measures how responsive quantity demanded is to changes in income. Incomes vary as the economy expands and contracts. To plan their future production, many industries want to know how the demand for their products will be affected when the economy changes. How much will airline travel be affected if the economy moves into a recession? What will happen to automobile sales? What will happen to sales of lattes at Starbucks? Each business faces a different situation.

Another type of demand elasticity registers changes that occur when competitors change the prices of their products. This is called *cross elasticity of demand.* If Toyota is planning a price reduction, what impact will this have on the sale of Fords? Ford will want to estimate this to decide whether to ignore Toyota or lower its own automobile prices.

Let's consider these two elasticities of demand more closely, beginning with income elasticity of demand.

Income Elasticity of Demand

Income elasticity of demand
Measures how responsive quantity demanded is to changes in consumer income.

The **income elasticity of demand** (E_Y) measures how responsive quantity demanded is to changes in consumer income. We define the income elasticity of demand as

$$E_Y = \frac{\text{Percentage Change in Quantity Demanded}}{\text{Percentage Change in Income}}$$

Normal goods
Goods that have positive income elasticities but less than 1. When consumer income grows, quantity demanded rises for normal goods but less than the rise in income.

Luxury goods
Goods that have income elasticities greater than 1. When consumer income grows, quantity demanded rises more than the rise in income for luxury goods.

Inferior goods
Goods that have income elasticities that are negative. When consumer income grows, quantity demanded falls for inferior goods.

Depending on the value of the income elasticity of demand, we can classify goods in three ways. First, a **normal good** is one where income elasticity is positive, but less than 1 ($0 < E_Y < 1$). As income rises, quantity demanded rises as well, but not as fast as the rise in income. Most products are normal goods. If your income doubles, you will probably buy more sporting equipment and restaurant meals, but not twice as many.

A second category, *income superior goods* or **luxury goods**, includes products with an income elasticity greater than 1 ($E_Y > 1$). As income rises, quantity demanded grows faster than income. Goods and services such as Mercedes automobiles, caviar, fine wine, and visits to European spas are luxury or income superior goods.

Finally, **inferior goods** are those goods for which income elasticity is negative ($E_Y < 0$). When income rises, the quantity demanded for these goods falls. Inferior goods include potatoes, beans, compact cars, and public transportation. Get yourself a nice raise, and you will probably be taking the bus a lot less. Note that this is an instance where a minus sign conveys important information.

Understanding how product sales are affected by changing incomes and economic conditions can help firms to diversify their product lines so sales and employment can be stabilized to some extent over the course of the business cycle. For example, firms that produce all three types of goods can try to switch production more toward the good that current economic conditions favor: In boom times, production is shifted more toward the making of luxury goods. Ford will produce more Lincoln Continentals in boom times, and more compact cars during economic slowdowns.

Cross Elasticity of Demand

Cross elasticity of demand (E_{ab}) measures how responsive the quantity demanded of one good (product a) is to changes in the price of another (product b):

$$E_{ab} = \frac{\text{Percentage Change in Quantity Demanded of product a}}{\text{Percentage Change in Price of product b}}$$

Using cross elasticity of demand, we can classify goods in two ways. Products a and b are **substitutes** if their cross elasticity of demand is positive ($E_{ab} > 0$). Common sense tells us that chicken and beef are substitutes. Therefore, if the price of beef rises, people will substitute away from beef and toward chicken, so the quantity demanded for chicken will grow. This illustrates a positive cross elasticity. Similar relationships exist between Toyota and Honda cars, cell phone services provided by AT&T and Sprint, and film and digital cameras.

Second, products a and b are **complements** if their cross elasticity of demand is negative ($E_{ab} < 0$). Complementary products are those goods and services that are consumed together, such as gasoline and large SUVs. When the price of gasoline rises, the result is that the quantity demanded for SUVs declines. Other complementary goods include coffee and cream, hamburgers and french fries, and suntan lotion and flip-flops. Finally, two goods are *not related* if a cross elasticity of demand is zero, or near zero.

This is a good place to stop and reflect on what we have discovered so far. We have seen that elasticity measures the responsiveness of one variable to changes in another. Elasticity measures changes in percentage terms so that products of different magnitudes—a bottle of Coca-Cola and an airplane—can be compared. Products that have a price elasticity of demand greater than 1 have elastic demand; products with price elasticity of demand less than 1 have inelastic demand; and products with a price elasticity of demand equal to 1 have unitary elastic demand. We saw that a straight line demand curve has elastic and inelastic ranges, and we also saw that total revenue changes with elastic or inelastic demand. Finally, we saw that as well as price elasticity of demand, we can also look at income elasticity of demand and cross elasticity of demand. We covered a lot in this first section.

Cross elasticity of demand
Measures how responsive the quantity demanded of one good is to changes in the price of another. Substitute goods have positive cross elasticities: An increase in the price of one goods leads consumers to substitute (buy more) of the other good whose price has not changed. Complementary goods have negative cross elasticities: An increase in the price of a complement leads to a reduction in sales of the other good whose price has not changed.

Substitutes
Goods consumers will substitute for one another depending on their relative prices such as chicken and beef, cable TV and satellite service, and coffee and tea. Substitutes have a positive cross elasticity of demand.

Complements
Goods that are typically consumed together such as coffee and sugar, automobiles and tires, and iPods and iTunes. Complements have a negative cross elasticity of demand.

Checkpoint

Elasticity and Total Revenue

REVIEW

- When demand is inelastic and prices rise, total revenue rises. When demand is inelastic and prices fall, total revenue falls.
- When demand is elastic and prices rise, total revenue falls. When demand is elastic and prices fall, total revenue rises.

- Straight line demand curves have elastic (at higher prices) and inelastic (at lower prices) ranges.
- Income elasticity of demand is a measure of how responsive quantity demanded is to changes in income. This determines whether a good is a luxury, normal, or inferior good.
- Cross elasticity of demand measures how responsive the quantity demanded of one product is to price changes of another. Substitutes have positive cross elasticities while complements have negative ones.

QUESTION

In the 1990s, the government charged Microsoft with being a monopolist (the only seller of operating systems for PCs) with its Windows operating system. Could estimates of cross elasticity of demand help Microsoft defend itself against the charges?

Answers to the Checkpoint question can be found at the end of this chapter.

Elasticity of Supply

So far, we have looked at the consumer when we looked at the elasticity of demand. Now let us turn our attention to the producer, and look at elasticity of supply.

Price elasticity of supply
Measures the responsiveness of quantity supplied to changes in price. An elastic supply curve has elasticity greater than 1, whereas inelastic supplies have elasticities less than 1. Time is the most important determinant of the elasticity of supply.

Price elasticity of supply (E_s) measures the responsiveness of quantity supplied to changes in the price of the product. Price elasticity of supply is defined as

$$E_s = \frac{\text{Percentage Change in Quantity Supplied}}{\text{Percentage Change in Price}}$$

Note that since the slope of the supply curve is positive, the price elasticity of supply will always be a positive number. Economists classify price elasticity of supply in the same way they classify price elasticity of demand. Classification is based on whether the percentage change in quantity supplied is greater than, less than, or equal to the percentage change in price. When price rises just a little and quantity increases by much more, supply is elastic, and vice versa. The output of many commodities such as gold and seasonal vegetables can not be quickly increased if their price increases. In summary:

Elastic supply
Price elasticity of supply is greater than 1. The percentage change in quantity supplied is greater than the percentage change in price.

Inelastic supply
Price elasticity of supply is less than 1. The percentage change in quantity supplied is less than the percentage change in price.

Unitary elastic supply
Price elasticity of supply is equal to 1. The percentage change in quantity supplied is equal to the percentage change in price.

Elastic supply: $E_s > 1$
Inelastic supply: $E_s < 1$
Unitary elastic supply: $E_s = 1$

Looking at the three supply curves in Figure 5, we can easily determine which curve is inelastic, which is elastic, and which is unitary elastic. First, note that all three curves go through point *a*. As we increase the price from P_0 to P_1, we see that the response in quantity supplied is different for all three curves. Consider supply curve S_1 first. When price changes to P_1 (point *b*), the change in output (Q_0 to Q_1) is the smallest for the three curves. Most important, the percentage change in quantity supplied is smaller than the percentage change in price, so S_1 is an inelastic supply curve.

Contrast this with S_3. In this case, when price rises to P_1 (point *d*), output climbs from Q_0 all the way to Q_3. Because the percentage change in output is larger than the percentage change in price, S_3 is elastic. And finally, curve S_2 is a unitary elastic curve because the percentage change in output is the same as the percentage change in price.

Here is a simple rule of thumb. When the supply curve is linear, like those shown in Figure 5, you can always determine if the supply curve is elastic, inelastic, or unitary elastic by extending the curve to the axis and applying the following rules:

FIGURE 5

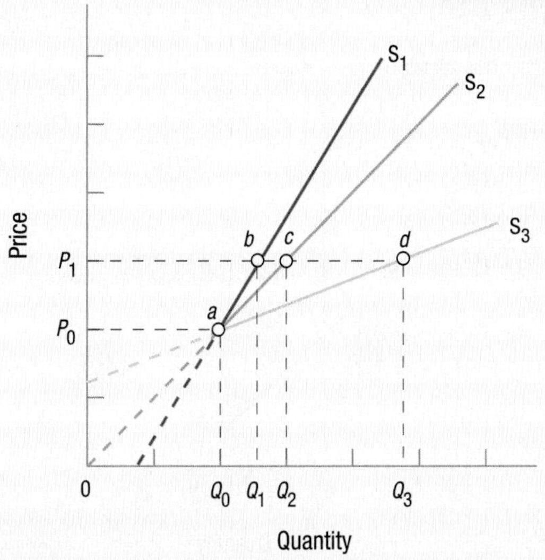

Price Elasticity of Supply

All three supply curves in this figure run through point *a*, but they respond differently when price changes from P_0 to P_1. Considering supply curve S_1 first, when price changes, the percentage change in quantity supplied is smaller than the percentage change in price, so S_1 is an inelastic supply curve. Curve S_2 is a unitary elastic supply curve, since the percentage change in output is the same as the percentage change in price. For supply curve S_3, the percentage change in output is greater than the percentage change in price, so S_3 is elastic. Elastic linear supply curves cross the price axis, inelastic linear curves cross the quantity axis, and unitary elastic linear curves go through the origin.

- Elastic supply curves will always cross the price axis, as does curve S_3
- Inelastic supply curves will always cross the quantity axis, as does curve S_1
- Unitary elastic supply curves will always cross through the origin, as does curve S_2

Time and Price Elasticity of Supply

The primary determinant of price elasticity of supply is time. To adjust output in response to changes in market prices, firms require time. Firms have both variable inputs, such as labor, and fixed inputs, such as plant capacity. To hire more labor, firms must recruit, interview, and hire more workers. This can take as little time as a few hours—a call to a temporary agency—or as long as a few months. On the other hand, building another plant to increase output involves considerably more time and resources. In some industries, such as building a new oil refinery or a computer chip plant, it can take as long as a decade, with environmental permits alone often requiring years of study and costing millions of dollars. Economists typically distinguish among three types of time periods: the market period, the short run, and the long run.

The Market Period

The **market period** is so short that the output and the number of firms in an industry are fixed; firms simply have no time to change their production levels in response to changes in product price. Consider a raspberry market in the summer. Even if consumers flock to the market, their tastes having shifted in favor of fresh raspberries, farmers can do little to increase the supply of raspberries until the next year. Figure 6 on the next page shows a market period supply curve (S_{MP}) for agricultural products like raspberries. During the market period, the quantity of product available to the market is fixed at Q_0. If demand changes (shifting D_0 to D_1), the only impact is on the price of the product. In Figure 6, price moves from P_0 (point *e*) to P_1 (point *a*). In summary, if demand grows over the market period, price will rise, and vice versa.

Market period
Time period so short that the output and the number of firms are fixed. Agricultural products at harvest time face market periods. Products that unexpectedly become instant hits face market periods (there is a lag between when the firm realizes it has a hit on its hand and when inventory can be replaced).

FIGURE 6

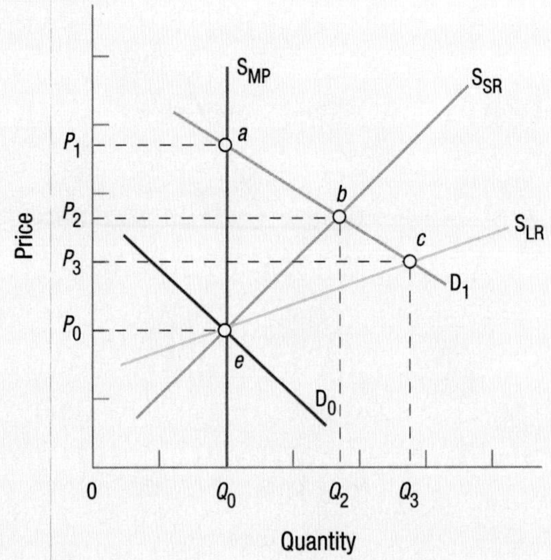

Time and Price Elasticity of Supply

During the market period, the quantity of output available to the market is fixed. Supply curve S_{MP} is therefore vertical, which means that if demand shifts from D_0 to D_1, the only impact will be on the price of the product, which will rise from P_0 to P_1. Over the short run, firms can change the amount of inputs they employ to adjust their output to market changes. Thus, the short-run supply curve (S_{SR}) is more elastic than the market period curve; when demand grows from D_0 to D_1, output expands from Q_0 to Q_2, and price increases to P_2. In the long run, firms can change their plant capacity and enter or exit an industry. Long-run supply curve S_{LR} is elastic with a rise in demand from D_0 to D_1 giving rise to only a small increase in price, while generating a major increase in output, from Q_0 to Q_3.

Changes in demand over the market period can be devastating for firms selling perishable goods. If demand falls, cantaloupes cannot be kept until demand grows; they must either be sold at a discount or trashed.

The Short Run

Short run
A period of time when plant capacity and the number of firms in the industry cannot change. Firms can employ more people, use overtime with existing employees, or hire part-time employees to produce more, but this is done in an existing plant.

The **short run** is defined as a period of time when plant capacity and the number of firms in the industry cannot change. Firms can, however, change the amount of labor, raw materials, and other variable inputs they employ in the short run to adjust their output to changes in the market. Note that the short run does not imply a specific number of weeks, months, or years. It simply means a period short enough that firms cannot adjust their plant capacity, but long enough for them to hire more labor to increase their production. A restaurant with an outdoor seating area can hire additional staff and open this area in a relatively short time frame when the weather gets warm, but manufacturing firms usually need more time to hire and train new people for their production lines. Clearly, the time associated with the short run will differ depending on the industry.

This also is illustrated in Figure 6. The short run supply curve, S_{SR}, is more elastic than the market period curve. If demand grows from D_0 to D_1, output expands from Q_0 to Q_2 and price increases to P_2 as equilibrium moves from point *e* to point *b*. Because output can expand in the short run in response to rising demand, the price increase is not as drastic as it was in the market period (from P_0 to P_1).

Long run
A period of time long enough for firms to alter their plant capacities and for the number of firms in the industry to change. Existing firms can expand or build new plants, or firms can enter or exit the industry.

The Long Run

Economists define the **long run** as a period of time long enough for firms to alter their plant capacity and for the number of firms in the industry to change. In the long run, some firms may decide to leave the industry if they think the market will be unfavorable. Alternatively, new firms may enter the market, or existing firms can alter their production capacity. Because all these conceivable changes are possible in the long run, the long-run supply curve is more elastic, as illustrated in Figure 6 by supply curve S_{LR}. In this case, a rise in demand from D_0 to D_1 gives rise to a small increase in the price of the product, while generating a major increase in output, from Q_0 to Q_3 (point *c*).

In giving long-run supply curve S_{LR} a small but positive slope, we are assuming an industry's costs will increase slightly as it increases its output. Firms must compete with other industries to expand production. Wages and other input prices rise in the industry as firms attempt to draw resources away from their immediate competitors and other industries.

Some industries may not face added costs as they expand. Fast-food chains, copy centers, and coffee shops seem to be able to reproduce at will without incurring increasing costs. Therefore, their long-run supply curves may be nearly horizontal.

At this point, we have seen how elasticity measures the responsiveness of demand to a change in price and how total revenue is affected by different demand elasticities. We have also seen that supply elasticities are mainly a function of the time needed to adjust to price change signals. Now, let's apply our findings about elasticity to a subject that concerns all of us: taxes.

Checkpoint

Elasticity of Supply

REVIEW

- Elasticity of supply measures the responsiveness of quantity supplied to changes in price.
- Elastic supplies are very responsive to price changes. With inelastic supply, quantity supplied is not responsive to changing prices.
- Supplies are highly inelastic in the market period, but can expand (become more elastic) in the short run because firms can hire additional resources to raise output levels.
- In the long run, supplies are relatively elastic since firms can enter or exit the industry, and existing firms can expand their plant capacity.

QUESTION

Rank the following industries and businesses in how elastic you think supply is in the long run, from most elastic to least elastic: (a) fast food, (b) nuclear power, (c) crude oil production, (d) Hollywood (movies), (e) computer microchips, (f) grocery stores, (g) airlines, (h) Starbucks.

Answers to the Checkpoint question can be found at the end of this chapter.

Taxes and Elasticity

On average, families pay more than 40% of their income in taxes. These taxes include income, property, estate, sales, and excise taxes. (An excise tax is a sales tax applied to a specific product, such as gasoline or tobacco.) It often seems the government taxes everything! We saw in the last chapter that supply and demand analysis is helpful in analyzing the impact of taxes on markets. In this section we use elasticity to help policymakers determine the impact of these various taxes on individuals, families, and businesses. Again, to simplify the analysis, we will continue to focus on excise taxes.

Incidence of taxation Refers to who bears the economic burden of a tax. The economic entity bearing the burden of a particular tax will depend on the price elasticities of demand and supply.

Economists studying taxes are interested in the **incidence of taxation** and in *shifts* in the tax burden. The incidence of a tax simply refers to who bears its economic burden. Statutes determine what is taxed, who must pay various taxes, and what agencies are responsible for collecting taxes and remitting the revenue collected. Even so, the individuals, firms, or groups who pay a tax may not be the ones bearing its economic burden. As we will see, this burden, or the incidence of a tax, can be shifted onto others. Considering the elasticities of demand and supply will help us determine the incidence of various taxes—who really bears the tax burden—and thus the ultimate impact of various tax policies.

Elasticity of Demand and Tax Burdens

Let us consider what happens when an excise tax is levied on a product such as strawberries with elastic demand. This is shown in Figure 7. The initial supply curve (S_0) is supply before the tax. Originally, the market is in equilibrium at point *e*, where 5,000 baskets are sold for 65 cents each. We now add a per unit tax—say, $0.25 a basket—paid by the grower. This, in effect, adds 25 cents to the cost for each basket and adds a wedge between what consumers pay and what growers receive. Supply curve S_0 therefore shifts upward by this amount, to $S_{0+\text{Tax}}$. The new supply curve runs parallel to S_0, with the distance the curve has shifted (*ac*) equaling the 25 cent tax per basket.

Assuming demand remains constant at D_0, the new equilibrium will be at point *a,* with 3,000 baskets sold for a price of 75 cents each. The firm receives 75 cents per basket, of which it must send 25 cents to the government, keeping 50 cents for itself. Keep in mind that, because this demand is elastic, many consumers are not really willing to pay a higher price for the product; this is why output declines so much.

Before the tax, both consumer and producer surplus (discussed in Chapter 4) was substantial, equal to area *ghe* and *fge,* respectively. After the tax, the government collects revenue equal to the tax (25 cents) times the number of baskets sold (3,000), or $750 (the cross-hatched area), consumer surplus now equals the area above the crosshatched section, and producer surplus equals the area below it. Note that consumers and producers lose surplus equal to not only the revenue gained by the government but also area *cae.* Economists refer to this area as a *deadweight loss* because this area is lost to society—the government, consumers, and business lose this—because of the tax.

FIGURE 7

Tax Burden with a Relatively Elastic Demand

S_0 is the initial supply curve for a product with elastic demand. When a 25 cent excise tax is placed on the product, the supply curve shifts upward by the amount of the tax, $S_{0+\text{Tax}}$. With demand remaining constant at D_0, equilibrium moves to point *a* (3,000 units). In this case, output falls substantially when the tax is imposed because elastic demand means extreme price sensitivity. As a result, sellers end up bearing most of the burden of this tax, and the deadweight loss is relatively large (area *cae*).

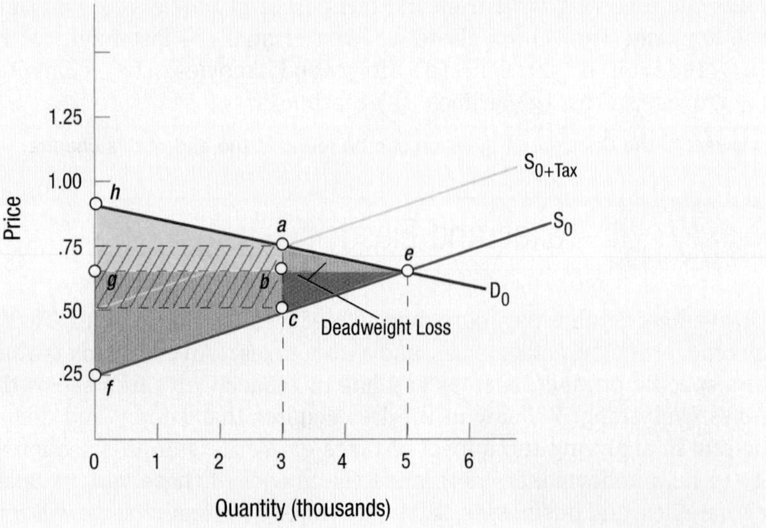

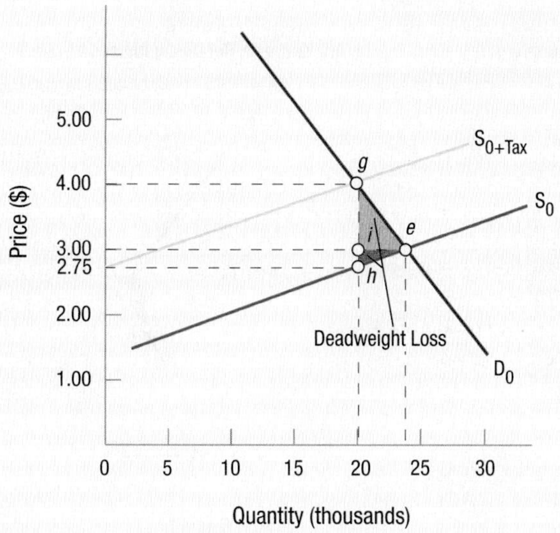

FIGURE 8

Tax Burden with Relatively Inelastic Demand

S_0 is the initial supply curve for a product with inelastic demand. When a $1.25 excise tax is placed on the product, the supply curve shifts upward by the amount of the tax, to S_{0+Tax}. Assuming demand remains constant at D_0, the new equilibrium will be at point *g*. Because this demand curve is inelastic, consumers are willing to pay a higher price for the product, and bear nearly all the burden of the tax. The deadweight loss (area *hge*) will be relatively small when demand is inelastic.

Contrast this situation with the impact of the excise tax when the demand is inelastic (e.g., cigarettes), as in Figure 8. Initially, 23,000 packages are sold at $3.00 a package. With a $1.25 tax, supply shifts to S_{0+Tax}, market equilibrium moves to point *g*, and price increases from $3.00 to $4.00 a pack and output declines from 23,000 to 20,000. Inelastic demands are price insensitive, so output hardly declines when this tax is imposed. The $1.25 tax in this case is *gh*, with consumers paying *gi* (a dollar), sellers paying *ih* (a quarter), and a deadweight loss equal to area *hge*. In general, deadweight losses will be small when demand is inelastic. Small quantity reduction given a higher price means that nearly all the excise tax is shifted forward to consumers. In this case, consumers pay an additional $1.00 for each unit, but firms end up bearing only a small burden (25 cents).

We can generalize about the effects of elasticity of demand on the tax burden. For a given supply of some product, the greater the price elasticity of demand, the lower the share of the total tax burden shifted to consumers and the greater the share borne by sellers, and vice versa.

This simple analysis shows why proposals to raise excise taxes usually focus on such inelastically demanded commodities such as luxury cars, jewelry, tobacco, gasoline, and alcohol. For products with inelastic demands, the reduction in output is lower when prices rise because of the tax—most smokers keep smoking even when the tobacco tax goes up, and the rich will still buy fancy cars even if they must pay a bit more for them. Therefore, these taxes generate more revenue than would excise taxes on elastically demanded products because the quantity demanded will drop considerably when prices rise on elastically demanded products. Proposals to raise excise taxes are often cloaked in public health and welfare rhetoric, politicians finding it easier to sell the idea of taxes that punish sins or soak the rich. But, if the products in question did not have inelastic demands, the tax revenues generated by such taxes would be small. Because consumers substantially reduce their purchases when demand is elastic, many workers in the industries with such elastically demanded products would become unemployed. As a result, such taxes are rarely ever enacted.

Elasticity of Supply and Tax Burdens

In a similar way, the elasticity of supply is an important determinant of who bears the ultimate burden of taxation. In Panel A of Figure 9 on the next page, demand is

FIGURE 9

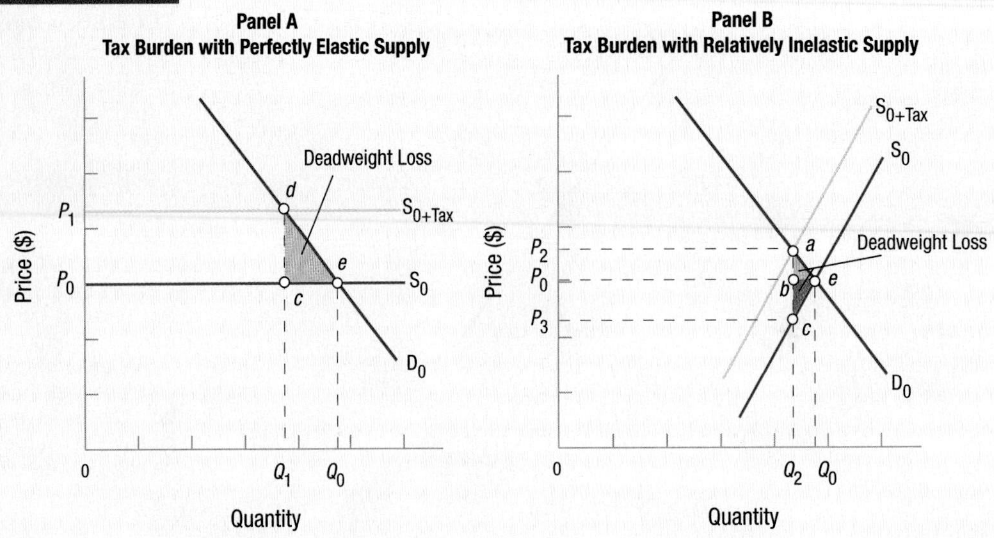

Tax Burden and Supply Elasticities

When supply curve S_0 is perfectly elastic as shown in Panel A, a per unit excise tax added to the product shifts supply vertically to S_{0+Tax}. Demand remaining constant at D_0, market equilibrium moves from point *e* to point *d*, where Q_1 units are sold at price P_1. In this limiting case of perfectly elastic supply, the full burden of the tax ($P_1 - P_0$) is borne by consumers through higher prices. The deadweight loss is relatively large with elastic supply curves and equal to area *cde*. When supply curve S_0 is inelastic as in Panel B, the same excise tax (*ac* in Panel B = *cd* in Panel A) shifts supply to S_{0+Tax}, and market equilibrium moves to point *a*. Price increases less than in Panel A, and the reduction in output is also less than before. Consumers pay only part of the tax, *ab*, while sellers must absorb *bc*. The deadweight loss to society is equal to area *cae*, which is less than with the elastic supply shown in Panel A.

held constant at D_0 and equilibrium is initially at point *e*. Supply curve S_0 is perfectly elastic, or horizontal. When a per unit tax is added to the product, supply shifts vertically to S_{0+Tax} and the new market equilibrium moves to point *d*, with Q_1 units sold at price P_1. Notice that in this limiting situation of perfectly elastic supply, the full monetary burden of the tax ($P_1 - P_0$) is borne by consumers in the form of higher prices, though industry bears an indirect burden of reduced output and employment. The deadweight loss, area *cde*, is relatively large with elastically supplied products.

Now consider the case when the supply curve is inelastic, as with S_0 in Panel B of Figure 9. When we add the same tax as before to this supply curve, market equilibrium moves to point *a*. Price increases less than before (P_2 in Panel B is lower than P_1 in Panel A) and the reduction in output is also less than before ($Q_0 - Q_2$ in Panel B is less than $Q_0 - Q_1$ in Panel A). Consumers pay only part of the tax, *ab*, while sellers must absorb *bc*, and the deadweight loss *cae* is relatively small.

Note what happens in all of these tax cases. Figures 7 to 9 show that whenever a tax is added, the tax moves the market away from its equilibrium point, regardless of whether the tax is borne by consumers, producers, or both. All taxes generate a tax wedge, resulting in a deadweight loss to society (triangle *cae* in Panel B of Figure 9). The more elastic the demand or supply, the greater is this deadweight loss. Table 4 summarizes these general results.

These last three chapters have given us the powerful tools of supply and demand analysis. Elasticity is important because it encapsulates the complex relationships among prices, quantity demanded, and total revenues in just two words: elastic and

Table 4 **Summary of Elasticity and Taxes**

Elasticity		Tax Burdens			
Demand	Supply	On Consumers	On Business	Deadweight Loss	Figure Where Shown
Elastic	No change	Lower	Higher	Large	7
Inelastic	No change	Higher	Lower	Small	8
No change	Elastic	Higher	Lower	Large	9A
No change	Inelastic	Lower	Higher	Small	9B

inelastic. When demands are inelastic and some incident marginally reduces supply, policymakers (and now you) know that price will go up substantially, though consumers will continue to purchase the product. Again, this is what happens when gasoline prices rise—consumers continue to purchase roughly the same amount as before, so oil industry revenue and profits rise substantially in the short run.

If, however, demand is elastic and the same incident reduces supply, prices will rise, but by a smaller amount, and output and employment will fall a lot more. If weather conditions in California and Florida ruin the orange crop, reducing the supply and increasing the price of orange juice, consumers will readily substitute other juices. As a result, output, employment, revenues, and profits will decline in the orange industry.

Checkpoint

Taxes and Elasticity

REVIEW

- Holding supply constant, when the price elasticity of demand is elastic, the lower the share of the total tax burden shifted to consumers, and the greater the share borne by sellers. When demands are inelastic, holding supply constant, the higher the share of the total tax burden shifted to consumers, and the lower the share borne by sellers.
- For a given demand, when the price elasticity of supply is elastic, the greater the share of the tax burden buyers will bear, the lower the share paid by sellers, and the larger the deadweight loss. For a given demand, when supply is inelastic, the lower the share of the tax burden buyers will bear, the higher the share paid by sellers, and the lower the deadweight loss.

QUESTION

Excise taxes were the principal taxes levied for the first hundred years or so after the Revolutionary War. Today, excise taxes fall mainly on cigarettes, liquor, luxury cars and boats, telephones, gasoline, diesel fuel, aviation fuel, bows and arrows, gas-guzzling vehicles, and vaccines. What do all of these products seem to have in common?

Answers to the Checkpoint question can be found at the end of this chapter.

Elnur Amikishiyev

Hubbert's Peak: Are We Running Out of Oil?

Is the world running out of oil? Ever since the early 1970s, that has been a popular refrain by pundits, environmentalists, and some academics. The United States government estimates that there are nearly 3 trillion barrels of oil in the ground worldwide, but some of these oil reserves may require higher prices before they are commercially feasible to pump. In this section, we take a closer look at this issue using the tools of supply, demand, and elasticity.

In the mid 1950s, Marion King Hubbert created a model of known reserves of U.S. oil and predicted that production in the United States would peak in the early 1970s. Production did peak in 1970, and his model now suggests that world oil production will peak within the next decade. Hubbert's model marks the point where half of the recoverable oil has been pumped out and half remains, so production has peaked. If world economic growth continues, world oil demand will continue to grow, oil production will slow, and the gap between supply and demand will grow, with oil prices correspondingly rising. Several authors suggest that production declines and rapid increases in oil prices will lead to a worldwide recession or even a depression.[2]

There are many reasons to believe that oil prices will continue to be high in the future, but our analysis of markets and elasticity suggests that we are unlikely to run out of oil for a long time, if ever.

First, there is a measurement issue. There is controversy surrounding the measurement of world oil reserves. Many experts argue that current estimates understate "proven reserves," and as Daniel Yergin has noted, the reporting system is based on 3-decade-old technology and is "roughly analogous to a doctor restricted to making a diagnosis only on the basis of invasive surgery rather than with a CAT scan."[3] The world may have considerably more oil underground than is currently estimated.

Second, there is a substitution issue. We saw earlier in this chapter that price elasticity of demand is dependent in part on the ability to substitute from a higher-priced good to a lower-priced good. What are the substitutes to oil-based gasoline? We might be running out of cheap \$20–\$30 a barrel oil, but as the price of oil rises to, say, \$40, Canadian tar sands, Brazilian cane-based and switch-grass ethanol, and natural gas and coal converted to liquid become economical. When oil prices reach \$60 a barrel, shale and corn-based ethanol become competitive. If prices go higher, biodiesel and other forms of alternative energy become attractive. These are substitutes for oil-based gasoline.

Third, there is an adjustment issue based on time. Over time, the higher price of oil should lead to an increase in supply as newer, more costly technologies such as steam injection permit the recovery of oil still in the ground that earlier technologies couldn't recover.[4] Also over time, consumers will adjust their demands for oil. The short-term elasticity of gasoline is roughly 0.2, making short-term price changes quite responsive to small changes in supplies. The price of crude oil is particularly sensitive in the short run to the political stability of exporting nations (particularly in the Middle East and Africa), natural disasters (hurricanes along the Gulf coast), and accidents (ruptures in pipelines). In the longer term, the elasticity of

---

[2]See Kenneth S. Deffeyes, *Hubbert's Peak: The Impending World Oil Shortage* (Princeton: Princeton University Press), 2001. Two other books suggest that Saudi Arabia's major oil fields are hitting their peak; see Paul Roberts, *The End of Oil: On the Edge of a Perilous New World* (New York: Houghton Mifflin), 2004, and Matthew R. Simmons, *Twilight in the Desert: The Coming Saudi Oil Shock and the World Economy* (Hoboken, NJ: John Wiley & Sons), 2005.

[3]Daniel Yergin, "How Much Oil Is Really Down There?" *The Wall Street Journal,* April 27, 2006, p. A18.

[4]See "Steady as She Goes: Why the World Is Not About to Run Out of Oil," *The Economist,* April 22, 2006, pp. 65–67.

demand is 0.7 to 0.9, and consumers will adjust to rising prices through conservation in its various forms.

Thus, even if we reach Hubbert's peak in the next decade, it will not be like falling off a precipice where prices skyrocket. Prices will rise gradually especially in the futures markets that reach out 5–7 years. This will give us plenty of time to begin adjusting to higher prices and using the alternatives described earlier.

Long before we run out of oil, the world will begin substituting alternative energy sources, and petroleum will be used only for high-valued uses such as manufacturing. The problems of global warming may force this sooner rather than later. Modern oil companies are becoming less exploration oriented and are focusing more on manufactured oil products. Pure fossil-based fuels will, in the future, need to be blended with other products to reduce their greenhouse emissions. Given all the substitutes for oil, we will never run out. Just what constitutes "oil" will change.

Key Concepts

Chapter Summary

Elasticity of Demand

Price elasticity of demand measures how sensitive the quantity demanded of a product is to price changes. Price elasticity of demand typically is expressed as an absolute value. It is determined by dividing the percentage change in quantity demanded by the percentage change in price. Elasticity measures permit comparisons among diverse products because they are based on percentages.

When the absolute value of the price elasticity of demand is greater than 1, that product is said to have an *elastic* demand. Elastically demanded products have many substitutes and their demand is quite sensitive to price changes. When elasticity is less than 1, demand is *inelastic.* Quantity demanded is not very sensitive to price changes. Necessities such as gasoline, prescription drugs, and tobacco have relatively inelastic demands.

There are four major determinants of elasticity. Elasticity is influenced by the availability of substitute products, the percentage of income spent on the product, the length of time consumers have to adjust, and the difference between luxuries and necessities.

Total revenue is affected by price elasticity of demand. An inelastically demanded product may, for example, have more brand loyalty, and consequently quantity demanded is less sensitive to price changes. When prices rise, total revenue rises since quantity demanded falls off less than price increases. When price declines, total revenue falls since quantity sold increases less than price declines.

If a product is elastically demanded, a small price change can lead to large shifts in quantity demanded. Thus, when prices fall for an elastically demanded good, sales surge and total revenue rises. However, when price rises, consumers quickly find substitutes and sales plunge, resulting in lower total revenues.

Income elasticity of demand measures how quantity demanded varies with consumer income. Normal goods have a positive income elasticity of demand, but less than 1. Luxury goods have income elasticities greater than 1. Inferior goods have negative income elasticities. As income rises, spending on luxury goods grows faster than income, while spending on inferior goods falls. When income rises, spending on normal goods rises, but at a pace that is less than the increase in income.

Cross elasticity of demand measures how responsive quantity demanded of one good is to changes in the price of another good. If cross elasticity of demand is positive, the two goods are substitutes. If negative, the two goods are complements.

Elasticity of Supply

The price elasticity of supply measures how sensitive the quantity of a product supplied is to changes in price for that product. It is found by taking the percentage change in quantity supplied and dividing it by the percentage change in price (essentially the same formula as that for the price elasticity of demand). The slope of the supply curve is positive, so price elasticity of supply is always positive. An elastic supply curve has a price elasticity of supply greater than 1. Price elasticity is less than 1 for inelastic supply curves, and equal to 1 for unitary elastic supply curves.

The market period, short run, and long run are the three basic time periods economists use to study elasticity. The market period is so short that the output of firms is fixed, or perfectly inelastic. In the short run, companies can change the amount of labor and other variable factors to alter output, but the physical plant and the number of firms in the industry are assumed to be fixed. In the long run, companies have time to build new production facilities, and to enter or exit the industry.

Taxes and Elasticity

Elasticity affects the burden and incidence of taxes. The more elastic the demand, the less a company can shift part of a sales or excise tax to consumers in the form of price increases. This is because consumers can readily substitute for elastically demanded products that rise in price. Elastic demand and supplies generate relatively large deadweight losses for society. An inelastically demanded product, however, can absorb the price increase due to a tax without much impact on quantity demanded. Producers can therefore pass most of the burden for such taxes on to consumers, and the deadweight loss is relatively small. When supply is elastic, the tax burden is higher on consumers, and the deadweight loss is larger. With inelastic supplies, the burden on consumers is less, and the deadweight loss is less.

Questions and Problems

1. When the demand curve is relatively inelastic and the price falls, what happens to revenue? If the demand is relatively elastic and price rises, what happens to revenue?

2. Why is the demand for gasoline relatively inelastic, while the demand for Exxon's gasoline relatively elastic?

3. Describe cross elasticity of demand. Why do substitutes have positive cross elasticities? Describe income elasticity of demand. What is the difference between normal and inferior goods?

4. Describe the impact of time on price elasticity of supply.

5. Betty's Bakery estimates that they can sell 400 cookies at 60¢ a cookie and will be able to sell 500 if the price drops to 50¢. Using the midpoint formula, what is the elasticity of demand for Betty's cookies? Will total revenue rise or fall if the price of cookies is lowered?

6. Used music CDs rise in price from $7 to $8, and total revenue falls from $700 to $640.
   a. Is the demand curve over this range elastic or inelastic? Why?
   b. Using the midpoint formula, what is the value of the elasticity of demand over this range?

7. Rising world wholesale fair-trade prices force the local Dunkin' Donuts franchise to raise its price of coffee from 89 cents to 99 cents a cup. As a result, management notices that donut sales fall from 950 to 850 a day. Shortly after the coffee price spike, the local Cinnabon franchise reduced its price on cinnamon rolls from $1.89 to $1.69. This resulted in a further decline in Dunkin' Donuts donut sales to 750 a day.
   a. What is the cross elasticity of demand for coffee and donuts? Are these two products complements or substitutes?
   b. What is the cross elasticity of demand for Dunkin' Donuts donuts and Cinnabon cinnamon rolls? Are these two products complements or substitutes?

8. One major rationale for farm price supports is that demand is inelastic and that rapidly improving technology, better crop strains, improved fertilizer, and better farming methods increased supply so significantly that farm incomes were severely depressed. Explain why this rationale would seem to be correct.

9. If the price of chicken rises by 15% and the sales of turkey breasts expand by 10%, what is the cross elasticity of demand for these two products? Are they complements or substitutes?

10. For which of the following pairs of goods and services would the cross elasticity of demand be negative: (a) iPods and songs downloaded from iTunes, (b) digital satellite service and digital video recorders, (c) recreational vehicles and camping tents, (d) bowling and co-ed softball, (e) textbooks and study guides.

11. Why would the demand for business airline travel be less elastic than the demand for vacation airline travel by retirees?

12. In 2003, London instituted a £5 congestion charge for cars or trucks entering the central city. The levy is said to have reduced congestion by 30% and raised nearly £80 million its first year. London increased the levy to £8 a day, and London's mayor had this to say: "Congestion charging has achieved its key objective of reducing congestion and has also provided an additional stream of revenue to help the funding of other transport measures within my transport strategy. The charge increase will maintain the benefits currently witnessed in the zone and build upon its success, cutting congestion even further and raising more revenue to be invested in London's transport system." Given what the

mayor had to say about the increase in congestion charges and the change in revenue, what must he believe about the elasticity of demand for driving into central London?

13. Many health plans pay for dental care. If the elasticity of demand for dental care is 0.8, and the health plan increases the price for dental care by 10%, what will be the impact?

14. Alan Greenspan, the former Chairman of the Federal Reserve, speaking before the National Petrochemical and Refiners Association in April 2005, made reference to rising oil prices by noting that "higher prices have only brought a modest slowdown in demand for crude oil reflecting a low short-term elasticity of demand. However, the response on the demand side should be more pronounced in the longer term." Is Alan Greenspan correct? Why or why not?

15. Your boss, who is the general manager of the Pontiac Rangers, an adequate AA baseball team, has heard that you are taking a principles of economics course, and has asked you to research the demand for summer night games. She has surveyed a sample of 10 people whom she feels accurately represent the potential market. We will assume that they do as well. The results of the survey are presented below:

Number of Night Games Willing to Attend at Various Prices

Name	$5.00	$4.50	$4.00	$3.50	$3.00	$2.50	$2.00
Arvilla	1	2	2	3	3	4	5
Quintha	3	4	5	6	7	7	8
Mary	0	0	1	2	3	5	5
Ray	5	5	5	5	5	6	7
Vern	0	0	0	1	3	3	3
Fran	5	5	5	5	5	5	5
Jerry	2	2	2	2	3	3	3
Richard	5	5	6	6	6	7	8
Whitey	3	6	8	8	8	8	8
Windy	6	6	6	7	7	7	8

a. What ticket price will maximize total revenue for the team?
b. Using the midpoint formula, what is the price elasticity of demand between $2.50 and $2.00?
c. The local bowling alley has extended league play on Wednesday night. Is the cross elasticity of demand positive or negative between night baseball and bowling? If the manager schedules night games on Wednesday will that affect attendance at the game?

16. J. Crew sells sweaters, pants, and other clothes to college students, among other groups. Many like its clothing, but the company has had financial problems in the past few years. In the belief that these problems stemmed from simple merchandising issues—styles, colors, price—J. Crew started to reposition itself in

2003. While some current and potential customers urged the company to lower prices and thereby expand its appeal, in fact prices were raised on many products. For example, a sweater selling for $48 in 2002 sold for $88 at the end of 2003.

a. By raising prices so much, what did J. Crew's management conclude about the price elasticity of demand of its customers?
b. Assume J. Crew sold 100,000 sweaters at the $48.00 price. How many sweaters would they have to sell at the new $88.00 to have the same total revenue? Assume they sold 80,000 sweaters at the $88.00 price. Using the midpoint formula, what is the price elasticity of demand?

17. Consider chip plants: potato and computer. Assume there is a large rise in the demand for computer chips and potato chips.
    a. How responsive to demand is each in the market period?
    b. Describe what a manufacturer of each product might do in the short run to increase production.
    c. How does the long run differ for these products?

18. Coca-Cola in dispensers located on a golf course sells for $1.25 a can, and golfers buy 1,000 cans. Assume the course raises the price to $1.26 (assume a penny raise is possible) and sales fall to 992 cans.
    a. Using the midpoint formula, what is the price elasticity of demand for Coke at these prices?
    b. Assume the demand for Coke is a linear line. Would the elasticity of demand be elastic or inelastic at 75 cents a can?
    c. At $2.00 a can?

19. If one automobile brand has an income elasticity of demand of 1.5 and another has an income elasticity equal to −0.3, what would account for the difference? Give an example of a specific brand for each type of car.

20. Suppose you estimated the cross elasticities of demand for three pairs of products and came up with the following three values: 2.3, 0.1, −1.7. What could you conclude about these three pairs of products? If you wanted to know if two products from two different firms competed with each other in the marketplace, what would you look for?

Answers to Checkpoint Questions

CHECKPOINT: ELASTICITY OF DEMAND

If prices in Phoenix rose by 40% and sales fell by 8%, then elasticity is $|-.2| = -.08/.40$. Now, if supplies fell by 30% and elasticity is 0.2, then prices could have risen by roughly 150% ($.30/.2 = 1.5$) to clear the market.

CHECKPOINT: ELASTICITY AND TOTAL REVENUE

If Microsoft leaders had shown that there were many or even a few close substitutes with positive cross elasticities of demand, they would have been able to argue it was not a monopoly. Unfortunately, at the time, the Apple Mac was the only real substitute, and it had a small (<5%) share of the market. Today, Linux and Mac

OSX are a growing share of the PC and server markets, although Microsoft still has a commanding share of the market.

CHECKPOINT: ELASTICITY OF SUPPLY

There are some close calls in this list, but here is our answer from most to least elastic: Starbucks, fast food, grocery, Hollywood, airlines, microchips, crude oil, nuclear power.

CHECKPOINT: TAXES AND ELASTICITY

They all appear to have relatively inelastic demands. This reduces the impact on the industries and leads to higher tax revenues.

6 Consumer Choice and Demand

Demand analysis rests on an important assumption: People are rational decision makers. Do people always act rationally? Of course not. A number of economists, called behavioralists, have been studying areas where people make conspicuously irrational decisions. For example, what explains the fact that people often hold on to common stocks long after they rationally recognize that the stocks are dogs and they probably will never make back their losses? It seems that people just do not want to admit—to themselves and others—they have made a stock-picking mistake, and so hold on for years in the vain hope that prices will eventually right themselves.

Important though this work on the irrational is, it does not invalidate the assumption that people choose rationally. If there were a preponderance of irrationality, society would come to a halt because we could not predict anything. In a trivial example, what pedestrian would cross the street even if the light said "walk" if there was a modicum of fear that some driver would act irrationally and ignore a red light? People *do* miss or ignore red lights, but not often.

So we are left with an underlying assumption of rational decision making that is not bedrock, but is reasonable and powerful nonetheless. We can use it to delve into demand analysis a little more. We know that people determine what price they will pay for various products. How do they make this determination?

We have to choose. We all have a finite quantity of resources at our command. The kinds of products we can purchase are determined, to an extent, by the resources we possess or our income level. For most of us, buying an exotic sports car, a luxury yacht, or a large mansion is simply out of the question—we lack the resources to make such purchases. Making consumer choices, therefore, comes down to buying and enjoying those products that we can, given the fact that we are not Bill Gates or part of his immediate family.

In this chapter, we are going to see what lies behind demand curves by looking at how consumers choose. In the next chapter, we will examine what lies behind supply curves by looking at how producers choose to produce what they do.

There are two major ways to approach consumer choice. We will cover both in this chapter.

The first theory that explains what people choose to buy, given their limited incomes, is known as *utility theory* or *utilitarianism.* This theory holds that rational consumers will allocate their limited incomes so as to maximize their happiness or satisfaction. The clear implication of this theory is that higher incomes should lead to more choices and greater happiness.

Consumer decision making has fascinated economists and philosophers for centuries. Jeremy Bentham (1748–1832), an extraordinary eccentric, argued that every human action is submitted to a "Felicific Calculus"—before acting, we ask ourselves which action would bring the most happiness. That calculus, wrote economic historian Robert Heilbroner,[1] treated "humanity as so many living profit-and-loss calculators, each busily arranging his life to maximize the pleasure of his psychic adding machine."

Bentham's writings were so voluminous that a current collection of his works contains 40 volumes. Still, though Bentham wrote massive draft manuscripts and carried out a correspondence with countless contemporaries, he published little. His influence depended not on publications, but on his personal contacts. Bentham's ideas were so far ahead of their time, moreover, that most of them were not fully developed until well after his death. Forty years after Bentham died, his ideas were rediscovered, refined, and published in *The Theory of Political Economy* by William Stanley Jevons (1835–1882). This work of 1871 marked the beginning of the "marginal revolution."

The second approach, *indifference curve analysis,* is covered in the Appendix to this chapter. Developed by Francis Ysidro Edgeworth, a mathematician who wrote for economists (1845–1926), it added analytical rigor to utility analysis by developing *indifference curves,* which portray combinations of two goods of equal total utility. Edgeworth was a shy man, studying in public libraries because he saw material possessions as a burden. Nevertheless, he brought the precision of mathematics to bear on utility theory and international trade and contributed to statistical analysis by developing the correlation coefficient, which numerically shows the relationship between two variables.

After studying this chapter you should be able to

- Use a budget line to determine the constraints on consumer choices.
- Describe the difference between total and marginal utility.
- Describe the law of diminishing marginal utility.
- Understand consumer surplus.
- Use marginal utility analysis to derive demand curves.

Marginal Utility Analysis

Marginal utility analysis A theoretical framework underlying consumer decision making. This approach assumes that satisfaction.

The work of Bentham and Jevons solved the riddles of consumer behavior by developing **marginal utility analysis**. To begin, let us consider more carefully how a limited income puts constraints on our choices.

[1]Robert Heilbroner, *The Worldly Philosophers: The Lives, Times, and Ideas of the Great Economic Thinkers,* 6e (New York: Simon & Schuster), 1986, p. 174.

Jeremy Bentham (1748–1832)

Jeremy Bentham was a social philosopher, legal reformer, and writer who founded the philosophy known as utilitarianism. As an economic theorist, his most valuable contribution was the idea of *utility,* which explained consumer choices in terms of maximizing pleasure and minimizing pain.

Born in 1748, Bentham was the son of a wealthy lawyer. At age 12 he entered Oxford University, then studied for the bar. After hearing Blackstone's famous lectures on English common law, however, Bentham decided not to practice. In 1792, his father died, leaving him a considerable fortune, which allowed him to spend his time writing and thinking. Derided by Karl Marx as the ultimate British eccentric, Bentham dreamed up reform proposals that were both imaginative and remarkably detailed. One of his best-known inventions was the design of a model prison, known as a "Panoptican," which he described as a "mill for grinding rogues honest."

But his primary contribution was analyzing the notion of utility as a driving force in social and economic behavior. Bentham disapproved of notions such as *natural law,* believing that the aim of society and government should be to maximize utility or to promote the "greatest happiness for the greatest number," a phrase Bentham borrowed from a book by Joseph Priestly. In 1789, he published his most famous work, *Introduction to the Principles of Morals,* which laid out his utilitarian philosophy. Bentham believed it was possible to derive a "Felicific Calculus" to compare the various pleasures or pains.

Although modern economists have cast doubt on the notion that utility could be measured or calculated, Bentham had many ideas that were ahead of his time, including the notion of cost-benefit analysis, which logically followed from his utilitarian views on government policies. Bentham also formulated the contemporary notion of marginal utility, noting that the more wealth a person had, the less benefit would be derived from an extra increment of that wealth.

The Budget Line

As a student, you came to college to improve your life not only intellectually but also financially. As a college graduate, you can expect your lifetime earnings to be triple those of someone with only a high school education. Even once you have achieved these higher earnings, there will be limits on what you can buy. But first, let us return to the present. Assume you have $50 a week to spend on pizza and wall climbing. This is a proxy for a more general choice between food and entertainment. We could use different goods or more goods, but the principle would still be the same. In our specific example, if pizzas cost $10 each and an hour of wall climbing costs $20, you can climb walls for 2.5 hours or consume 5 pizzas each week, or do some combination of these two. Your options are plotted in Figure 1.

FIGURE 1

The Budget Constraint or Line

When pizzas cost $10 each, wall climbing costs $20 per hour, and you have $50 a week to spend, you could buy 5 pizzas per week, 2.5 hours of wall climbing, or some combination of the two. The budget line makes clear all of the possible purchasing combinations of two products on a particular budget. Just as with the production possibilities frontier (PPF), you can attain any combination on the budget line, but you cannot attain combinations to the right of the line.

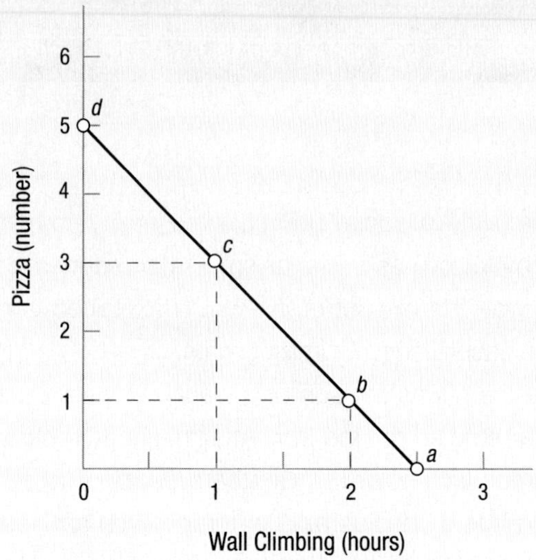

Budget line
Graphically illustrates the possible combinations of two goods that can be purchased with a given income, given the prices of both products.

This **budget line** (constraint) is a lot like the production possibilities frontier (PPF) discussed in Chapter 2. Though you might prefer to have more of both goods, you are limited to consumption choices lying on the budget line, or inside the budget line if you want to save any part of your $50 weekly budget. As with the PPF curve, however, any points to the right of the line are unattainable for you—they exceed your available income.

In this example, the budget line makes clear that many different combinations of wall climbing and pizzas will exhaust your $50 budget. But which of these possible combinations will you select? That depends on your personal preferences. If you love pizza, you will probably make different choices than if you are a fitness fanatic who rarely consumes fatty foods. Your own preferences determine how much pleasure you can expect to get from the various possible options. Economists call this pleasure the *utility* of an item.

Preferences and Utility

Utility
A hypothetical measure of consumer satisfaction.

Utility is a hypothetical measure of consumer satisfaction. It was introduced by early economists attempting to explain how consumers make decisions. The utilitarian theory of consumer behavior assumes, first of all, that utility is something that *can* be measured. It assumes, in other words, that we can quantifiably determine how much utility (satisfaction) you derive from consuming one or more pizzas, and how much utility you derive from spending one or more hours on the climbing wall. Table 1 provides estimates of the utility you derive from both pizzas and wall climbing, measured in *utils,* hypothetical units of satisfaction or utility. Compare columns 1 and 2 with columns 4 and 5.

At first glance, it might seem that if you wanted to maximize your utility, you would simply go wall climbing for 2.5 hours, thereby maximizing your total utility at 270 utils. If you spent a little time with the table, you would notice that combinations give you more total utility. If you went wall climbing for 2 hours and had 1

Table 1 Total and Marginal Utility from Pizzas and Wall Climbing

Pizza			Wall Climbing		
(1) Quantity	(2) Total Utility	(3) Marginal Utility	(4) Quantity	(5) Total Utility	(6) Marginal Utility
0	0	0	0.0	0	0
1	70	70	0.5	90	90
2	130	60	1.0	170	80
3	180	50	1.5	230	60
4	220	40	2.0	260	30
5	250	30	2.5	270	10

pizza, your total utility would be 330 utils (260 + 70 = 330), much more than concentrating on one item alone.

Other than trial and error, how do we determine the best combination? Before we can see just which combination of these two goods would actually bring you the most happiness, we need to distinguish between *total utility* and *marginal utility.*

Total and Marginal Utility

Total utility is the total satisfaction that a person receives from consuming a given quantity of goods and services. In Table 1, for example, the total utility received from consuming 3 pizzas is 180 utils, whereas the total utility from 4 pizzas is 220 utils. Marginal utility is something different.

Total utility
The total satisfaction that a person receives from consuming a given amount of goods and services.

Marginal utility is the satisfaction derived from consuming an *additional* unit of a given product or service. It is determined by taking the difference between the total utility derived from, say, consuming 4 pizzas and consuming 3 pizzas. The total utility derived from 4 pizzas was 220 utils, and that from 3 pizzas was 180 utils. Hence, consuming the fourth pizza yields only an additional 40 utils of satisfaction (220 − 180 = 40 utils).

Marginal utility
The satisfaction received from consuming an additional unit of a given product or service.

The marginal utility for both pizza eating and wall climbing is listed in Table 1. Notice that as we move from one quantity of pizza to the next, total utility rises by an amount exactly equal to marginal utility. This is no coincidence. Marginal utility is nothing but the change in total utility obtained from consuming one more pizza (the marginal pizza), so as pizza eating increases by one pizza, total utility will rise by the amount of additional satisfaction derived from consuming that additional pizza. Also note that, for both pizzas and wall climbing, marginal utility declines the more a particular product or activity is consumed.

The Law of Diminishing Marginal Utility

Why does marginal utility decline as the consumption of one product or activity increases? No matter our personal tastes and preferences, we eventually become sated once we have consumed a certain amount of any given commodity. Most of us love ice cream. As youngsters, some of us imagined a world in which meals consisted of nothing but ice cream—no casseroles, no vegetables, just ice cream. To children this might sound heavenly, but as adults, we recognize we would quickly grow sick of ice cream. Human beings simply crave diversity; we quickly tire of the same product or service if we consume it day after day.

Law of diminishing marginal utility
As we consume more of a given product, the added satisfaction we get from consuming an additional unit declines.

This fact of human nature led early economists to formulate the **law of diminishing marginal utility**. This law states that as we consume more of a product, the rate at which our total satisfaction increases with the consumption of each additional unit will decline. And if we continue to consume still more of the product after that, our total satisfaction will eventually begin to decline.

This principle is illustrated by Figure 2, which graphs the total utility and marginal utility for pizza eating, as listed in Table 1. Notice that total utility, charted in Panel A, rises continually as we move from 1 pizza per week to 5 pizzas. Nevertheless, the rate of this increase declines as more pizzas are consumed. Accordingly, Panel B shows that marginal utility declines with more pizzas eaten. On your student budget, you could not afford any more than 5 pizzas a week, but we can imagine that if you were to keep eating pizzas—50 pizzas in a week—your total utility would actually start to drop with each additional pizza. At some point, it simply hurts to stuff any more pizzas down your throat.

FIGURE 2

Total and Marginal Utility for Pizza

Total utility, charted in Panel A, rises continually as we move from 1 pizza per week to 5 pizzas. Nevertheless, the rate of this increase declines as more pizzas are consumed. Accordingly, Panel B shows that marginal utility declines with more pizzas eaten.

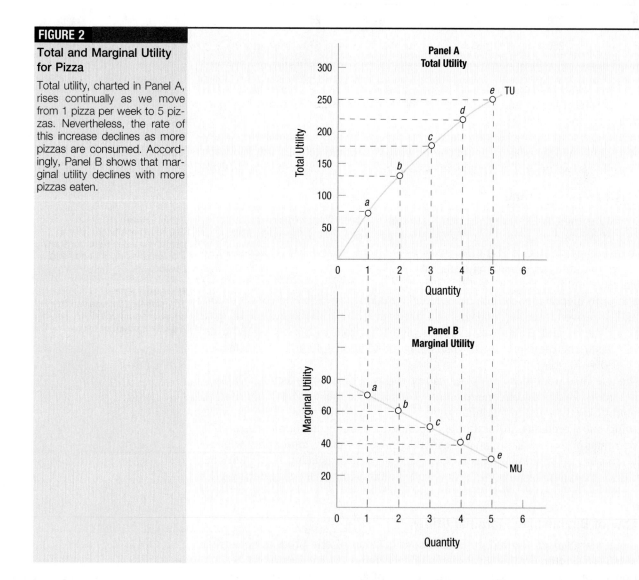

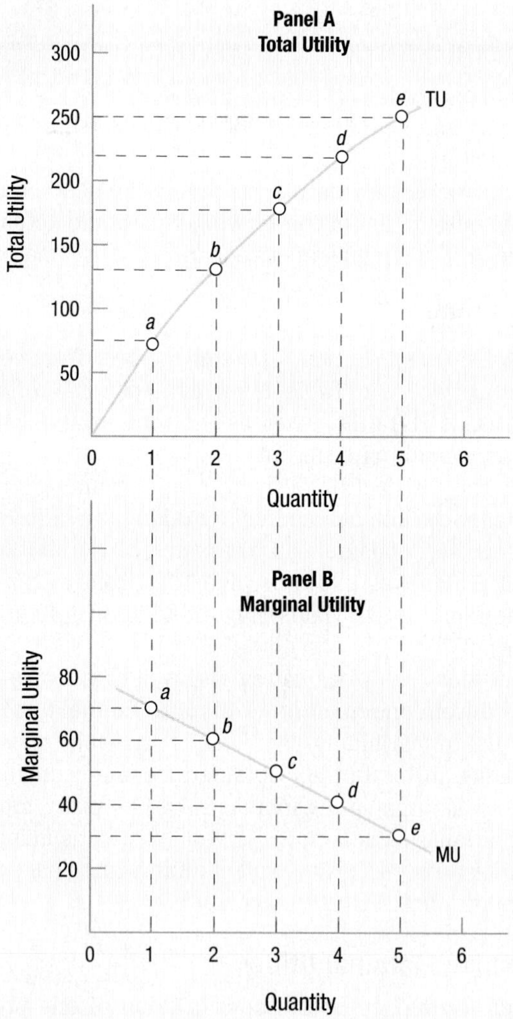

It is one thing to grasp the obvious fact that consumers have limited budgets, and that the products they can choose among provide them increasing satisfaction but are subject to diminishing marginal utility. It is another thing to figure out exactly how consumers allocate their limited funds so as to maximize their total level of satisfaction or utility. We now turn our attention to how early economists solved the problem of maximizing utility and the analytic methods that flowed out of their work.

Maximizing Utility

Let's take a moment to review everything we need to know to plot the budget line in Figure 1: your total income and the prices of all the products you could purchase. In our example, the weekly budget was $50, pizzas cost $10 apiece, and wall climbing was $20 per hour or $10 per half hour. This was enough information to plot all of the options open to you.

Now, we need to consider the utility we receive from our various levels of consumption of these two products. Take a look at columns (4) and (8) of Table 2. These two columns express the marginal utilities of pizzas and wall climbing, respectively, in terms of marginal utility per dollar; these amounts are computed by dividing the marginal utility of each product by the product's price.

Table 2 Total and Marginal Utility per Dollar from Pizzas and Wall Climbing

Pizza				Wall Climbing			
(1) Quantity (units of pizza)	(2) Total Utility	(3) Marginal Utility	(4) Marginal Utility per Dollar (price = $10)	(5) Quantity (units of wall climbing)	(6) Total Utility	(7) Marginal Utility	(8) Marginal Utility per Dollar (price = $10 per half hour)
0	0	0	0	0.0	0	0	0
1	70	70	7	0.5	90	90	9
2	130	60	6	1.0	170	80	8
3	180	50	5	1.5	230	60	6
4	220	40	4	2.0	260	30	3
5	250	30	3	2.5	270	10	1

To see the importance of computing marginal utility per dollar, consider the following. Given the figures in columns (4) and (8), and assuming you want to get the most for your money, on which activity would you spend the first $10 of your weekly budget? You can spend the first $10 on a pizza or a half-hour of wall climbing. A pizza returns 70 utils of satisfaction, whereas a half-hour of wall climbing yields 90 utils. Since 90 is greater than 70, clearly the first $10 would be better spent on wall climbing.

Now, for the sake of simplicity, let us keep your spending increments constant. On what will you spend your next $10—pizza or climbing? Look again at the table. Your first pizza still gives you 70 utils, while the second half-hour of wall climbing returns 80 utils. Wall climbing again is the obvious choice. If your total budget had only been $20 per week, you would have been inclined to give up pizzas completely.

Proceeding in the same way, using your third $10 to buy your first pizza will yield an additional 70 utils of satisfaction, whereas using this money to purchase a third half-hour of wall climbing will bring only 60 utils. (Wall climbing is starting to get a bit boring.) Thus, because 70 is greater than 60, with your third $10 you buy your first pizza.

Finally, using the remaining \$20 of your budget to buy either additional pizzas or additional half-hours of wall climbing would yield an additional 120 utils of satisfaction. Thus, you split the remaining \$20 evenly between these two activities. When the consumption of additional units of two products provides equal satisfaction, economists say consumers are *indifferent* to which product they consume first.

By following this incremental process, therefore, we have determined that you will spend your \$50 on 2 pizzas (\$20) and 1.5 hours of wall climbing (\$30). This results in a total utility of 360 utils (130 for pizza and 230 for wall climbing). *No other combination of pizzas and wall climbing will result in total satisfaction this high,* as you can prove to yourself by trying to spend the \$50 differently.

Note also for the last two units of each product consumed, the marginal utilities per dollar were equal at 6. This result is to be expected. Simple logic tells us that if one activity yields more satisfaction per dollar than some other, you will continue to pursue the activity with the higher satisfaction per dollar until some other activity starts yielding more satisfaction. This observation leads to a simple rule for maximizing utility: You should allocate your budget so that the marginal utilities per dollar are equal for the last units of the products consumed. This **utility maximizing rule**, in turn, leads to the following equation, where MU = marginal utility and P = price.

Utility maximizing rule
Utility is maximized where the marginal utility per dollar is equal for all products, or $MU_a/P_a = MU_b/P_b = \ldots = MU_n/P_n$.

$$\frac{MU_{\text{Pizza}}}{P_{\text{Pizza}}} = \frac{MU_{\text{Wall Climbing}}}{P_{\text{Wall Climbing}}}$$

This equation and the analyses described earlier can be generalized to cover numerous goods and services. For all goods and services $a, b, \ldots n$:

$$\frac{MU_a}{P_a} = \frac{MU_b}{P_b} = \cdots = \frac{MU_n}{P_n}$$

The important point to remember is that, according to this theory of consumer behavior, consumers approach every purchase by asking themselves which of all possible additional acts of consumption would bring them the most satisfaction per dollar.

Checkpoint

Marginal Utility Analysis

REVIEW

- The budget constraint graphically illustrates the limits on purchases for a given income (budget).
- Utility is a hypothetical measure of consumer satisfaction.
- Total utility is the total satisfaction a person gets from consuming a certain amount of goods.
- Marginal utility is the additional satisfaction a consumer gets from consuming one more unit of the good or service.
- The law of diminishing marginal utility states that as consumption of a specific good increases, the increase in total satisfaction will decline.
- Consumers maximize satisfaction by purchasing goods up to the point where the marginal utility per dollar is equal for all goods.

QUESTIONS

Let's apply the theory of diminishing marginal utility to an all-you-can-eat restaurant meal. First, do you think you will eat more than at a normal restaurant? Why? Second, consider the quality of the food offered at an all-you-can-eat restaurant. Recalling what you answered to the first question, what can you predict about the quality of food offered?

Answers to the Checkpoint questions can be found at the end of this chapter.

Using Marginal Utility Analysis

You have seen how the marginal utility analysis of consumer behavior works when we assume that satisfaction or well-being can be measured directly (in utils). We can now use this theory of consumer behavior to derive the demand curve for wall climbing and to examine consumer surplus in a little more depth than when we first introduced this concept in Chapter 4.

Deriving Demand Curves

We know consumers will maximize their utility by spending each dollar of their limited budgets on the goods and services yielding the highest marginal utility per dollar. In our previous example, with pizzas costing $10 each and an hour of wall climbing costing $20, this meant you bought 2 pizzas and 1.5 hours of wall climbing. Would your consumption choices change if these prices changed? Let us consider what happens when the cost of wall climbing rises to $30 per hour.

Now that wall climbing costs $30 per hour or $15 per half hour, column (8) of Table 3 has been altered to reflect this new rate for wall climbing. The first half hour of climbing yields 90 utils and now costs $15, so each dollar yields 6 utils. Now

Table 3 Total and Marginal Utility per Dollar from Pizzas and Wall Climbing (price of wall climbing increases to $30 per hour or $15 per half hour)

Pizza				Wall Climbing			
(1) Quantity (units of pizza)	(2) Total Utility	(3) Marginal Utility	(4) Marginal Utility per Dollar (price = $10)	(5) Quantity (units of wall climbing)	(6) Total Utility	(7) Marginal Utility	(8) Marginal Utility per Dollar (price = $15 per half hour)
0	0	0	0	0.0	0	0	0.00
1	70	70	7	0.5	90	90	6.00
2	130	60	6	1.0	170	80	5.33
3	180	50	5	1.5	230	60	4.00
4	220	40	4	2.0	260	30	2.00
5	250	30	3	2.5	270	10	0.67

your first $10 will be spent on a pizza ($MU/P = 7$ for pizza versus $MU/P = 6$ for wall climbing).

The next $25 is split between another pizza and a half-hour of wall climbing since $MU/P = 6$ for both. Your final $15 is spent on wall climbing since its marginal utility per dollar (5.33) is higher than for a third pizza (5).

Thus, your final allocation is 2 pizzas and 1 hour of wall climbing. Clearly, consumer choices respond to changes in product prices. With wall climbing at $20 per hour, you consumed 1.5 hours of climbing and 2 pizzas. When the price of wall climbing rose to $30 per hour you altered your consumption. Now, instead of 1.5 hours and 2 pizzas, you consume 1 hour and 2 pizzas. This new level is shown in the shaded area of Table 3.

Figure 3 plots both your budget constraint and your demand for wall climbing based on the results of Tables 2 and 3. Panel A shows the effect of increasing the price of wall climbing from $20 to $30 per hour. At the increased price of wall climbing, if you were to spend your entire budget on this activity, you could only climb for 1.66 hours ($50/$30 = 1.66). This price increase shifts the entire budget line leftward, reducing your consumption opportunities, as the figure illustrates.

When the price of wall climbing was $20 per hour, you climbed for 1.5 hours (points *b* in both panels of Figure 3). When the price was increased to $30 per hour,

FIGURE 3

Deriving the Demand for Wall Climbing Using Marginal Utility Analysis

With the price of wall climbing at $20 per hour, you climb for 1.5 hours (point *b* in both panels). When the price increases to $30 per hour, you reduce your consumption of wall climbing to 1 hour (point *a* in both panels). Connecting these points in Panel B yields the demand curve for wall climbing.

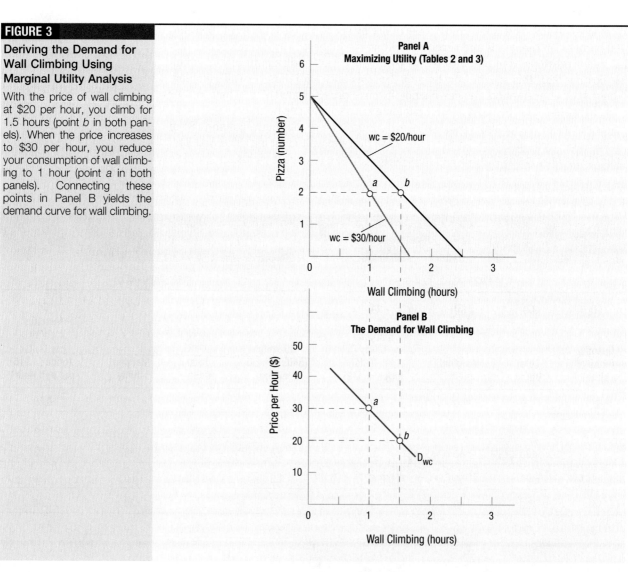

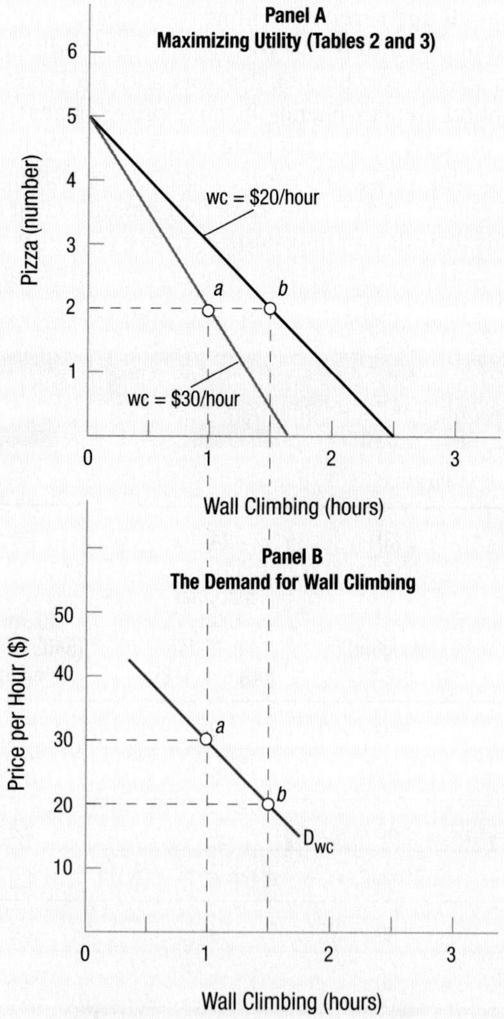

marginal utility analysis led you to reduce your consumption of wall climbing to 1 hour (point *a* in both panels). Connecting these points in Panel B of Figure 3 yields the demand curve for wall climbing.

Thus, the marginal utility theory of consumer behavior helps explain both how consumers allocate their income according to their personal preferences and the law of demand. Remember that the law of demand posited an inverse (negative) relationship between price and quantity demanded. This negative relationship is shown in Panel B. In addition, this analysis shows why consumers almost always get more than they pay for in terms of the goods and services they buy. This surprising phenomenon that we have seen before is known as *consumer surplus.*

Consumer Surplus

Consumer surplus is another example of the gains that accrue from markets, which we discussed in Chapter 4. Remember, it is the difference between what consumers would be willing to pay for a product and what they must actually pay for the product in the market. Typically, when you purchase something, you can buy all you want of it (within your budget) at the market price. In our initial example, we assumed that the market price of wall climbing was $20 per hour and concluded that you would climb for 1.5 hours per week. When the cost rose to $30 per hour, you reduced your climbing to 1 hour per week. Figure 4 reproduces Panel B from Figure 3, highlighting your demand curve for wall climbing for all prices above $20 per hour. Additionally, a supply curve has been superimposed that provides a market equilibrium price of $20 per hour.

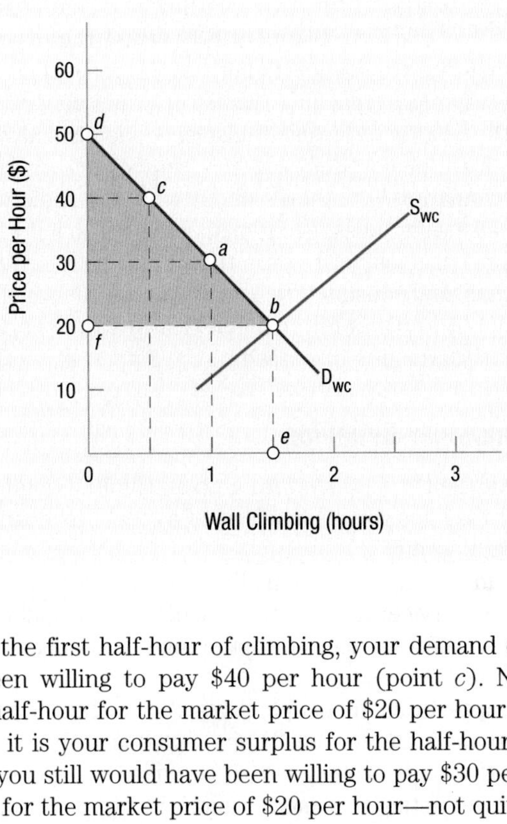

FIGURE 4

Consumer Surplus

For the first half-hour of climbing, you would have been willing to pay $40 per hour (point c), but you received it for the market price of $20 per hour. Only by the time you are purchasing your third half-hour of climbing must you pay exactly what you would have been willing to pay for this activity (point b). Hence, the shaded area marked out by triangle *fdb* represents your total *consumer surplus*.

Notice that for the first half-hour of climbing, your demand curve shows that you would have been willing to pay $40 per hour (point *c*). Nevertheless, you received that first half-hour for the market price of $20 per hour. That represents a nice gain for you; it is your consumer surplus for the half-hour of climbing. For the next half-hour, you still would have been willing to pay $30 per hour (point *a*), but again you got it for the market price of $20 per hour—not quite as good a deal, but still a nice bargain. Only by the time you are purchasing your third half-hour of climbing must you pay exactly what you would have been willing to pay for this activity, $20 per hour, thus marking the end of your consumer surplus. The shaded area marked out by triangle *fdb* in Figure 4 represents your total consumer surplus.

Consumer surplus
The difference between what consumers would be willing to pay and what they actually pay for a product in the market.

The total amount you spend on climbing in Figure 4 is \$30 (\$20 per hour times 1.5 hours = \$30). This is equal to area *0fbe.* Your total satisfaction from climbing is area *0dbe.* Consequently, your **consumer surplus** is equal to shaded area *fdb,* that is, area *0dbe* minus area *0fbe.* Consumer surplus is a nice "bonus" for you.

Marginal Utility Analysis: A Critique

Marginal utility analysis explains not only how consumers purchase goods and services but also how all household choices are made. We can analyze the decision of whether or not to get a job, for example, by comparing the marginal utility of work versus the marginal utility of leisure. As a college student, you are familiar with having many demands made on your time. More work means more money but less time for leisure, and vice versa. Marginal utility theory helps us to identify that point where work and leisure (and hopefully study) balance out.

Though marginal utility theory is an elegant and logically consistent theory that helps us understand how consumers behave, it has faced some important criticisms. First and foremost, it assumes that consumers are able to measure the utility they derive from various sorts of consumption. Yet, this is virtually impossible in everyday life—how many utils do you get out of eating a bowl of ice cream? This is not to suggest that marginal utility theory is invalid. It simply requires one very restrictive assumption, namely, that people are able to measure their satisfaction for every purchase. Clearly, this is an assumption that finds little empirical confirmation in everyday life.

Others have argued that it is absurd to think that we could carry out the mental calculus required to compare the ratios of marginal utility to price for all possible goods and services. This is no doubt true, but even if we do not compare all possible goods and services in this way, we do draw some comparisons. After all, we somehow need to be able to distinguish between the desirability of going to a movie or a concert, since we cannot do both at the same time. Marginal utility theory is still a good way of approaching this choice, in a general way.

Recognizing the validity of these criticisms, economists have tried to limit themselves to working with the sorts of data they can collect, in this case purchases by individuals. By formulating hypotheses about what consumers purchase and what this says about their preferences, economists have managed to develop a theory of consumer behavior that does not require that utility be measured. This more modern approach to analyzing consumer behavior reaches the same conclusions as marginal utility theory but requires fewer theoretical restrictions; it is known as *indifference curve analysis* and is discussed in the Appendix to this chapter.

Tipping and Consumer Behavior

Banana Stock/Jupiter Images

If consumers maximize their utility with a given (limited) budget, why would they ever tip? Consider that tips come at the end of a meal. How can tips affect the quality of service already given?

Many reasons might explain tipping. First, if it is a restaurant you frequent, tips might assure better service in the future. Second, you might consider tips to be rewards for higher-quality service. Third, tipping is custom and is part of the wages for several dozen occupations.

What would happen if many people refused or neglected to tip? Would various occupations seek to make tipping legally binding? It is likely this would be the result, if a recent case in New York is any guide. If you have ever gone to a restaurant with a large party, you will notice that menus and bills often state that a set tip will be added for large parties. One large party gave a very small tip after what they considered to be inadequate service. The restaurant sued, claiming that the 18% tip was mandatory. The court's decision for the tipper turned on the phrasing in the menu. This could be viewed as a first shot: If too many people refuse to tip or tip poorly, we can expect legal redress.

We can establish, then, that tipping is a custom that leads to better service, and so is followed even though the tip comes after the service is performed. In this way, it seems to run counter to the idea of people tipping based on a calculation of marginal utility. And how much we tip raises questions about how we calculate marginal utility.

Economists have found only a weak statistical link between quality of service and size of the tip.[2] Tipping also appears to be unrelated to the number of courses in the meal, and whether or not people intend to return to the restaurant. Table 4 shows some of the things that do affect the size of the tip.

Table 4 Percentage Increase in Tips from Specific Behavior by Wait Staff

Tip Enhancing Action	Change in Tip
Wearing a flower in hair	17%
Introducing yourself by name	53%
Squatting down next to the table	20–25%
Repeat order back to customers	100%
Suggestive selling	23%
Touching customer	22–42%
Using tip trays with credit card insignia	22–25%
Waitress drawing a smiley face on check	18%
Writing "thank you" on the check	13%

See Michael Lynn, *Mega Tips: Scientifically Tested Techniques to Increase Your Tips,* 2004, p. 25. This publication is available free (in PDF format) on the Internet. The author suggests a tip if you find the study helpful.

Obviously, a waiter or waitress cannot do all of these things and expect to see their tips increase by the sum of all the percentages, but we all have experienced many of these techniques in restaurants. Interestingly, if a waitress draws a smiley face on the bill, her tips go up, but if a waiter does the same, his tips go down. Suggestive selling raises the tip because people tend to tip based on the size of the bill. After having read about this study, you probably will find yourself being a little cynical when some of these techniques are used the next time you dine out.

Irrational Consumers: Investing, Gambling, and Saving

P. J. Cook/The Bridgeman Art Library

We end this chapter with the modern challenge to the idea of people as rational utility maximizers. As mentioned at the beginning of this chapter, the challenge comes from a group of economists called behavioralists. Chief among them are Daniel Kahneman and Richard Thaler.[3]

Much of behavioral economics research has focused on investors. For example, take investing in the stock market. The utility maximizing theory would have us believe that investors rationally weigh the prospects of a stock, purchase the stock,

[2]Based on Raj Persaud, "What's the tipping point?" *Financial Times,* April 9, 2005, p. w3.

[3]See the article by Al Lewis, "Stock Market Mind Games: Investors More Lucky than Clever and Rational Thinking Doesn't Rule, Economics Professors Say," *Rocky Mountain News,* September 26, 1999, p. 1G. See also Roger Lowenstein, "Exuberance is Rational," *New York Times Magazine,* February 11, 2001, p. 68.

then rationally weigh its future prospects over time, selling when prospects change dramatically for the worse. Is this what really happens? The answer is a resounding "no." People hold on to stocks that have fallen sharply, even when future prospects are poor. Why such irrational conduct? The behavioralists postulate that people simply do not want to admit they made a mistake, which they would have to do if they sold the stock. So they hold on to their losers long beyond the time that any rational person would do so. There is a corresponding urge—though not as strong—to sell stock when the price rises, out of fear that gains might evaporate, and with the need to tell other people about how successful one has been. This tendency to sell winners too soon and hold on to losers too long has been described by famed investor Warren Buffett as cutting down the flowers and watering the weeds.

Another way people act irrationally is with what Thaler calls the "house money effect." Gamblers often divide their winnings from their own original stake money, calling these winnings "house money." Thaler noted that gamblers behave as if these were two types of money: "If you want to see someone who is ready to gamble, go see someone who has just won $3,000. Because it is a lot easier to lose the casino's money than your own."[4] To a rational utility maximizer, money is money: There should be no such thing as "house money." Yet people act as if this is not the case.

These are interesting, even curious, examples of irrationality. Do they have broader effects? Harvard professor David Laibson examined retirement savings.[5] If we were all rational utility maximizers, Laibson claims that the vast majority of U.S. households would save more for retirement. What causes this poor savings behavior? Limited rationality, limited self-control, and unbounded optimism.

Irrational lack of savings can have policy effects in the near future when the baby boomer generation retires. In this way, behavioral economics has something to say to an economic theory that rests on rational utility maximizing. The behavioralists have not replaced the utility maximizers by any means. They have raised a challenge, however, and will continue to do so as they undertake more research into the irrational behaviors that all of us are prone to at one time or another.

Checkpoint

Using Marginal Utility Analysis

REVIEW

- Demand curves for products can be derived from marginal utility analysis simply by changing the price of one good and plotting the resulting changes in consumption.
- Consumer surplus is the difference between what you would have been willing to pay for a good and what you actually have to pay.
- Even though marginal utility analysis requires us to measure utility explicitly, it still offers significant insight into how consumers make decisions between products, how consumers react when one product's price changes, and when income drops.

QUESTIONS

Even though convenience stores have significantly higher prices than normal grocery stores such as Safeway, they seem to do well, judging by the numbers operat-

[4]Ibid.
[5]Ibid.

ing. Why are people willing to pay these higher prices? If a Safeway began to operate 24/7, would this affect the sales of a nearby convenience store?

Answers to the Checkpoint questions can be found at the end of this chapter.

Key Concepts

Marginal utility analysis, p. 140
Budget line, p. 142
Utility, p. 142
Total utility, p. 143
Marginal utility, p. 143
Law of diminishing marginal utility, p. 144
Utility maximizing rule, p. 146
Consumer surplus, p. 150

Chapter Summary

Marginal Utility Analysis

The budget line shows the different combinations of goods that can be purchased at a given level of income. Because consumer budgets are limited, consumption decisions often require making tradeoffs—more of one good can be purchased only if less of another is bought. The budget line graphically represents both this outer limit on consumption decisions and the various combinations of goods that can be purchased with this given level of income.

The utility of a product is a hypothetical measure of how much satisfaction a consumer derives from the product. Though not something that can be measured directly like weight or length, economists estimate the utility of various products at different levels of consumption to understand consumer preference and predict consumer behavior. The standard unit of utility is the *util.*

Total utility is the entire amount of satisfaction a consumer derives from consuming some product; it is equal to the sum of the utility derived from the consumption of each individual unit of this product.

Marginal utility is the amount of utility derived from consuming one more unit of a given product. Note that as a person consumes more units of a product, marginal utility will change—consuming the ninth unit of a product may lead to a different increase in total utility than did consuming the third unit.

The law of diminishing marginal utility states that as more units of any product are consumed, marginal utility will decline.

Marginal utility analysis provides a theoretical framework that helps economists understand how consumers make their consumption decisions among different products at varying price levels. It assumes that consumers try to maximize the utility they receive on their limited budgets, by adjusting their spending to the point where the utility derived from the last dollar spent on any product is equal to the utility from the last dollar spent on other products.

Using Marginal Utility Analysis

Consumer surplus is the difference between what consumers would be willing to pay for a product and what they must actually pay for the product in the market.

The applicability of marginal utility analysis to the real world is restricted by the fact that it assumes consumers can measure utility accurately and perform complex calculations regarding utility in their heads—both of which are difficult to measure empirically.

Questions and Problems

1. Describe the utility maximizing condition in words. Explain why it makes sense.

2. Assume a consumer has $20 to spend and for both products the marginal utilities are shown in the table below:

Quantity	MU_A	MU_B
1	20	30
2	10	10
3	5	2

   Assume that each product sells for $5 a unit.
   a. How many units of each product will the consumer purchase?
   b. Assume the price of product B rises to $10 a unit. How will this consumer allocate her budget now?
   c. If the prices of both products rise to $10 a unit, what will be the budget allocation?

3. Describe the conditions necessary for total utility to be positive but marginal utility is negative. Give an example of such a situation.

4. Answer the questions following the table below:

First-Run Movie			Wine (bottle)		
Quantity	Total Utility	Marginal Utility	Quantity	Total Utility	Marginal Utility
0	0	____	0	0	____
1	140	____	1	180	____
2	260	____	2	340	____
3	360	____	3	460	____
4	440	____	4	510	____
5	500	____	5	540	____

   a. Complete the table.
   b. Assume that you have $50 a month to devote to entertainment (column labeled First-Run Movies) and wine with dinner (column labeled Wine [bottle]). What will be your equilibrium allocation if the price to see a movie is $10 and a bottle of wine cost $10 as well?
   c. A grape glut in California results in Napa Valley wine dropping in price to $5 a bottle, and you view this wine as a perfect substitute for what you were drinking earlier. Now what will be your equilibrium allocation between movies and wine?
   d. Given this data, calculate your elasticity of demand for wine over these two prices (see the midpoint equation in Chapter 5).

5. A new field called neuroeconomics studies brain activity as people make decisions while trading stocks, gambling, and playing games designed for experiments. Researchers have found that people are particularly afraid of ambiguous risk with unknown odds.[6] Could this simple insight go a long way toward showing why terrorism seems so effective?

---

[6] "Why Do Investors Do What They Do?" *New York Times,* April 20, 2006, p. C3.

6. Harvard economist David Laibson has found that "people tend much to prefer, say $100 now to $115 next week, but they are indifferent between $100 a year from now and $115 in a year and a week"[7] Does this seem rational? Using brain scans, he and colleagues found that short-term decisions are governed by the emotional (limbic system) side of the brain, whereas longer-term decisions are governed by the prefrontal cortex, which is associated with reason and calculation. Why might longer-term decisions be more consistent with the consumer choice theories we discussed earlier in this chapter?

7. One luxury goods manufacturer noted that "Our customers do not want to pay less. If we halved the price of all our products, we would double our sales for six months, and then we would sell nothing." Is there something about luxury goods that suggests consumers are irrational? Do luxury goods not follow the law of demand?

8. Richard Layard, in his book *Happiness: Lessons from a New Science,* found that once a country's income exceeds $20,000 per capita, there is little relationship between happiness and income. But if you are poor, more money does make you happy. Does this fact suggest that the marginal utility from more income above $20,000 per capita is small?

9. Advertisements on television both inform consumers and persuade them to purchase products in differing proportion depending on the ad. But today, digital video recorders can be found in 20 to 30 million households, and much of what these households watch is recorded, and the vast bulk of the ads are skipped. If this trend continues, where will consumers find out about new products?

10. Critics of marginal utility analysis argue that it is unrealistic to assume that people make the mental calculus of marginal utility per dollar for large numbers of products. But when you are making a decision to either go to a first-run movie or buy a used DVD of last summer's blockbuster, does this analysis seem so complex? Is it a reasonable representation of your thought process?

Answers to Checkpoint Questions

CHECKPOINT: MARGINAL UTILITY ANALYSIS

As a general rule, you will eat more because the price for any additional item is zero, so theoretically you eat until the marginal utility is zero. The quality of food, in general, will be lower.

CHECKPOINT: USING MARGINAL UTILITY ANALYSIS

Convenience stores offer a small set of products at high prices nearer to home and have extended hours of operation. They also provide quicker service in that customers are in and out of the store quickly with what they need. The marginal utility of convenience overcomes the higher prices, so people shop because time is money. A 24/7 Safeway would have an impact on convenience store sales. At off-hours, supermarkets might be as fast as convenience stores, but cheaper.

[7]"Economic Focus: Mind Games," *Economist,* January 15, 2005, p.71.

Appendix: Indifference Curve Analysis

Marginal utility analysis provides a good theoretical glimpse into the consumer decision-making process, yet it requires that utility be measured and that marginal utility per dollar be computed for innumerable possible consumption choices. In reality, measuring utility is impossible, as is mentally computing the marginal utility of thousands of products. To get around these difficulties, economists have developed a modern explanation of consumer decisions that does not require measuring utility. The foundation of this analysis is the indifference curve.

Indifference Curves and Consumer Preferences

If consumers cannot precisely measure the exact satisfaction they receive from specific products, economists reason that people can distinguish between different bundles of goods and decide whether they prefer one bundle to another. This analysis entirely eliminates the idea of consumer satisfaction. It instead assumes that consumers will either be able to choose between any two bundles, or else be *indifferent* to which bundle is chosen. An **indifference curve** shows all points at which consumers' choices are indifferent—points at which consumers express no preference between two products.

Indifference curve
Shows all the combinations of two goods where the consumer is indifferent (gets the same level of satisfaction).

To illustrate how an indifference curve works, let us return to our original example of pizzas and wall climbing, now graphed in Figure APX-1 on the next page. Compare the combination represented by point b (2 pizzas and 1.5 hours of climbing) and the combination at point e (2 pizzas and 0.5 hour of wall climbing). Which would you prefer, assuming you enjoy both of these activities? Clearly, the combination at point b is preferable to the combination at point e since you get the same amount of pizza but more wall climbing. By the same logic, bundle f is preferable to bundle b because you get the same amount of climbing, but 3 more pizzas.

These choices have all been easy enough to make. But now assume you are offered bundles d and b. Bundle d contains more pizzas than bundle b, but bundle b has more climbing time. Given this choice, you may well conclude that you do not care which bundle you get—you are indifferent. In fact, all of the different possible combinations lying on the indifference curve I_0 represent bundles for which you are indifferent, such that you would just as soon have any one of these combinations as any other. And this tells us what an indifference curve is: It identifies all possible combinations of two products that offer consumers the same level of satisfaction or utility. Notice that this mode of analysis does not require us to consider

FIGURE APX-1

An Indifference Curve

All of the different possible combinations lying on the indifference curve I_0 represent bundles of goods for which you are indifferent—you would just as soon have any one of these combinations as any other. But compare the combination represented by point *b* and the combination at point *e*. Which would you prefer? Point *b*, of course, because you get more. All points upward and to the right are preferred to all points on indifference curve I_0.

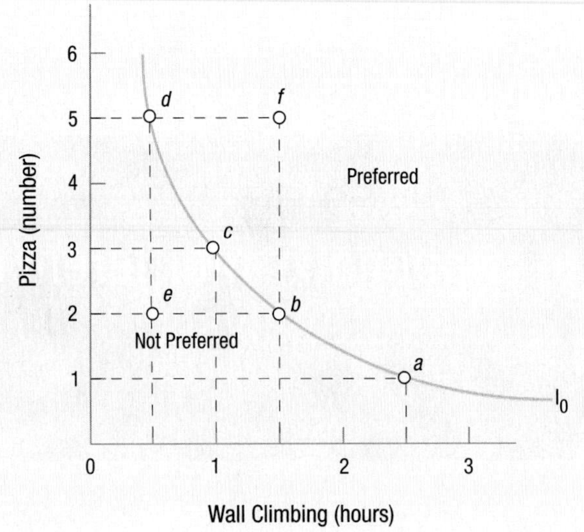

the precise quantity of utility that various bundles yield, but only whether one bundle would be preferable to another.

Properties of Indifference Curves

Indifference curves have negative slopes and are convex to the origin; they bow inward, that is. They have negative slopes because we assume consumers will generally prefer to have more, rather than less, of each product. Yet, to obtain more of one product and maintain the same level of satisfaction, consumers must give up some quantity of the other product. Hence, the negative slope.

Indifference curves are bowed inward toward the origin because of the law of diminishing marginal utility discussed earlier. When you have a lot of pizzas (point *d*), you are willing to give up 2 pizzas to obtain another half-hour of climbing (moving from point *d* to point *c*). But once you have plenty of wall time, yet few pizzas (point *b*), you are unwilling to give up as many pizzas to get more climbing time. This is the law of diminishing marginal utility at work: As we consume more of any particular product, the satisfaction we derive from consuming additional units of this product declines.

Indifference (or Preference) Maps

Indifference map
An infinite set of indifference curves where each curve represents a different level of utility or satisfaction.

An indifference curve is a curve that represents a set of product bundles to which a consumer is indifferent. An **indifference map,** or *preference map,* is an infinite set of indifference curves, each representing a different level of satisfaction. Three possible indifference curves, forming part of a preference map, are shown in Figure APX-2.

Indifference curve I_0 is the same curve shown in Figure APX-1. Indifference curve I_1 provides consumers with greater satisfaction than I_0 since it is located farther from the origin. In general, utility rises as curves move outward from the origin, since these curves represent larger quantities of both goods. Conversely, indifference curve I_2 offers consumers less total satisfaction since it is located closer to the origin and represents smaller amounts of both products than I_0.

To confirm the observations just made, compare point *a* on indifference curve I_2 with point *b* on indifference curve I_0. Points *a* and *b* contain the same amount of pizza, but point *b* contains greater climbing time. Hence, point *b* on indifference curve I_0 offers a higher level of satisfaction than point *a*. An analysis of points *a*

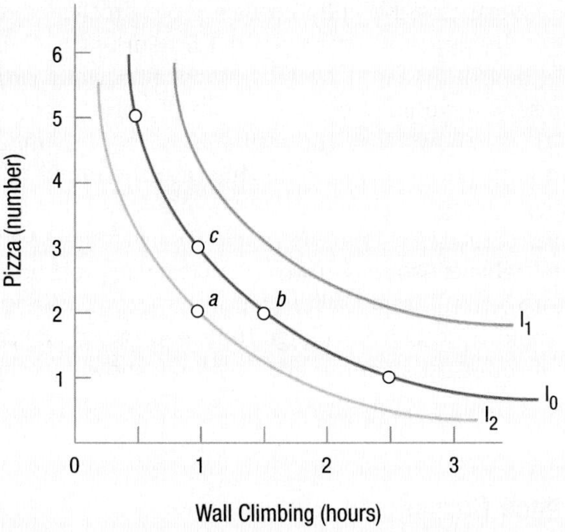

FIGURE APX-2

Three Indifference Curves for Pizza and Wall Climbing (An Indifference Map)

An indifference map or preference map contains an infinite set of indifference curves, each representing a different level of satisfaction. Three possible indifference curves for pizzas and wall climbing, forming part of a preference map, are shown here.

and *c* will yield a similar conclusion. Since both points *c* and *b* on indifference curve I_0 are preferred to point *a* on I_2, indifference curve I_0 must generally offer higher levels of satisfaction than the points on indifference curve I_2.

This result leads us to one final property of indifference curves: They do not intersect. Since all of the points on any indifference curve represent bundles of goods to which consumers are indifferent, if two indifference curves were to cross, this would mean some of the bundles they represent offered the same level of satisfaction (where the curves meet), but others did not (where the curves do not touch). Yet, this is a logical impossibility, since each indifference curve is defined as a set of bundles offering exactly the same level of satisfaction.

We now turn now to the question of how consumers use such preference maps to optimize their satisfaction within their budget constraints.

Optimal Consumer Choice

Figure APX-3 superimposes a budget line of $50 per week onto a preference map that assumes pizzas cost $10 each and wall climbing costs $20 per hour. Maximizing

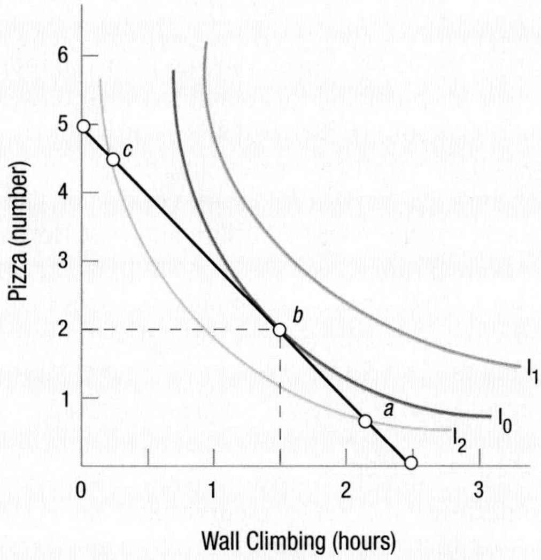

FIGURE APX-3

Optimal Consumer Choice

Maximizing your satisfaction on your limited income requires purchasing some bundle of goods on the highest possible indifference curve. The best you can do in this situation is indicated by point *b:* 2 pizzas and 1.5 hours of wall climbing. Indifference curve I_0 is the highest indifference curve that can be reached with the budget line shown.

your satisfaction on your limited income requires that you purchase some bundle of goods on the highest possible indifference curve. In this example, the best you can do is indicated by point *b:* 2 pizzas and 1.5 hours of wall climbing. Clearly, if you were to pick any other point on the budget line, your satisfaction would be diminished because you would end up on a lower indifference curve (points *a* or *c* in Figure APX-3). It follows that the indifference curve running tangent to the budget line identifies your best option, in this case the indifference curve that just touches the budget line at point *b*.

Of course, this is the same result we reached earlier using marginal utility analysis, specifically in Table 2. Notice, however, that using indifference curve analysis, we did not have to assume that utility can be measured. We were able to understand how you would allocate your budget between two goods so as to achieve the highest possible level of satisfaction, even without knowing exactly how high that level might be.

Using Indifference Curves

Indifference curves are a useful device to help us understand consumer demand. Economists use indifference curves, for instance, to shed light on the impact of changes in consumer income and product substitution resulting from a change in product price. Indifference curve analysis, moreover, provides some insight into how households determine their supply of labor (this analysis, however, is left to a later chapter). Before we move on to applications of indifference curve analysis, however, we first need to derive a demand curve from an indifference map.

Deriving Demand Curves

We derive the demand curve using indifference curve analysis in much the same way we did using marginal utility analysis. Panel A of Figure APX-4 restates the results of Figure APX-3: When you have a budget of $50 per week, the price of pizza is $10, and climbing is $20 per hour, your optimal choice is found at point *b*. In Panel B, we want to plot the demand curve for wall climbing. We know that when wall climbing costs $20 per hour, you will climb for 1.5 hours, so let us indicate this on Panel B by marking point *b*.

To fill out the demand curve, let us now increase the price of wall climbing to $30 per hour. This produces a new budget line, *cd.* (Point *d* is located at 1.66 hours because $50/$30 = 1.66 hours of possible wall climbing.) This shift in the budget line yields a new optimal choice at point *a* on indifference curve I_2, now indicating the highest level of satisfaction you can attain. As Panel A shows, the ultimate result of this hike in the price of wall climbing to $30 an hour is a reduction in your climbing to 1 hour per week. Transferring this result to Panel B, we mark point *a* where price = $30 and climbing hours = 1. Now connecting points *a* and *b* in Panel B, we are left with the demand curve for wall climbing.

Once again, therefore, we arrive at the same conclusion using indifference curve analysis as we did earlier using marginal utility analysis. Both approaches are logical and elegant, and both approaches tell us something about the thought processes consumers must use as they make their spending decisions. Indifference curve analysis, however, arrives at its conclusion without requiring that utility be measurable or that consumers perform complex arithmetic computations.

Income and Substitution Effects

Another way economists use indifference curves is to separate income and substitution effects when product prices change. First we need to distinguish between these two effects.

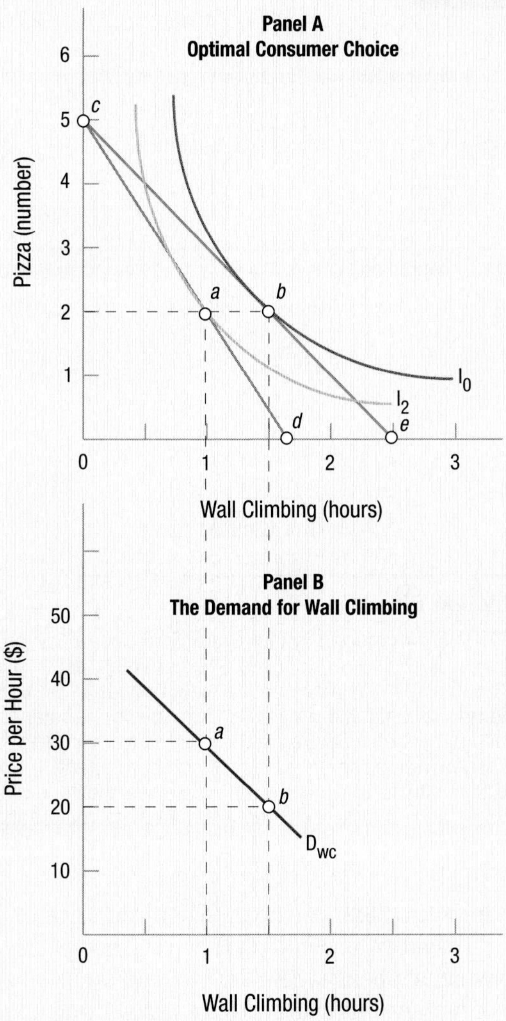

FIGURE APX-4

Deriving the Demand for Wall Climbing Using Indifference Curve Analysis

In Panel A, when wall climbing costs $20 per hour, your optimal choice is found at point *b*. When the price of wall climbing rises to $30 per hour, this produces a new budget line, *cd*, shifting the optimal choice to point *a*. Transferring points *a* and *b* down to Panel B and connecting the points generates the demand curve for wall climbing.

When the price of some product you regularly purchase goes up, your spendable income is thereby essentially reduced. If you always buy a latte a day, for instance, and you continue to do so even when the price of lattes goes up, you must then reduce your consumption of other goods. This essentially amounts to a reduction in your income. And we know that when income falls, the consumption of normal goods likewise declines. Hence, when higher prices essentially reduce consumer incomes, the quantity demanded for normal goods generally falls. Economists call this the **income effect**.

Income effect
When higher prices essentially reduce consumer income, the quantity demanded for normal goods falls.

When the price of a particular good rises, meanwhile, the quantity demanded of that good will fall simply because consumers substitute lower priced goods for it. This is called the **substitution effect**. Thus, when the price of wall climbing rises from $20 to $30, you cut back on your climbing, in part, because you decide to dedicate more of your money to pizza eating. The challenge for us now is to determine just how much of this reduction in your climbing is due to the substitution effect (more pizzas mean less climbing) and how much is due to the income effect (the rise in price effectively leaves you with less money to spend).

Substitution effect
When the price of one good rises, consumers will substitute other goods for that good, so the quantity demanded for the higher-priced good falls.

Figure APX-5 on the next page reproduces Panel A of Figure APX-4, adding one line (*gh*) to divide the total change in purchases into the income and substitution effects. To see how this line is derived, let us begin by reviewing what has happened thus far. At point *b* you split your $50 budget into 2 pizzas at $10 each and

FIGURE APX-5

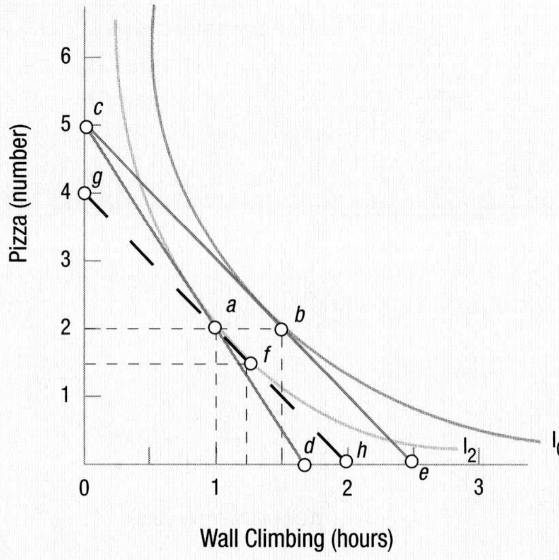

Income and Substitution Effects

Panel A of Figure APX-4 is reproduced in this figure. The price of climbing having risen to $30 per hour, this effectively reduces your budget to $40 per week, assuming you continue climbing as much as you did before. Line *gh* represents a new budget of $40, though reflecting the old price of climbing. This new budget line *gh* allows us to divide the total change in purchases into the income and substitution effects. Increasing the price of wall climbing from $20 to $30 an hour would mean a reduction in wall climbing (holding income constant at $40) from point *f* to point *a*. This is the substitution effect. The income effect is thus the reduction in consumption from point *b* to point *f*. Adding both effects together yields the total reduction.

1.5 hours of wall climbing at $20 per hour. When the price of wall climbing rose to $30 per hour, you reduced your climbing time to 1 hour.

Consider now what happens when we evaluate what you are getting for your *current* allocation of money, but using the *old* price of wall climbing ($20 per hour). You are now getting 2 pizzas, worth $10 piece, plus 1 hour of wall climbing, formerly valued at $20. This means your budget has effectively been cut to $40. The ultimate effect of the rise in the price of climbing, in other words, has been to reduce your income by $10. In Figure APX-5, the hypothetical budget line *gh* represents this new budget of $40, though again reflecting the old price of climbing.

Compare the original equilibrium point *b* on budget line *ce* with the new equilibrium point *f* on budget line *gh*. This new budget line *gh* reflects a budget of $40 with the old price of climbing ($20 per hour). Had your income previously been $40, you would have reduced your climbing by 15 minutes (to point *f*). This is the *income effect* associated with the rise in the price of wall climbing from $20 to $30 per hour. The rising price essentially reduced your income, and your reduction in wall climbing due to this income reduction alone is 15 minutes.

The change in price is the only thing that differentiates equilibrium point *a* from point *f*, income having been held constant. This difference of 15 minutes between point *f* and point *a* therefore represents a *substitution effect.* It is the effect that comes from changing the price of climbing, while holding income constant.

Combined, the substitution and income effects constitute the entire change in quantity demanded when the price of wall climbing rises by $10 per hour. The income effect (movement from point *b* to point *f*) is a movement from one budget line to another. The substitution effect (movement from point *f* to point *a*) is a movement along the new budget line. Together, they represent the total change in quantity demanded. In this case the income and substitution effects were the same, 15 minutes, but this will not always be the case.

This chapter examined how consumers and households make decisions. Households attempt to maximize their well-being or satisfaction within the constraints of limited incomes. We have seen that the analysis of consumer decisions can be approached in two different ways, using marginal utility analysis or indifference curve analysis.

Marginal utility analysis assumes that consumers can readily measure utility and make complex calculations regarding the utility of various possible consumption choices. Both of these assumptions are empirically rather dubious. This does not, however, invalidate marginal utility analysis; it just makes it difficult to use and test in an empirical context. Indifference curve analysis gives us a more powerful set of analytical tools without these restrictive assumptions.

Checkpoint

Indifference Curve Analysis

REVIEW

- Indifference curve analysis does not require utility measurement. All it requires is that consumers can choose between different bundles of goods.
- An indifference curve shows all the combinations of two goods where the consumer has the same level of satisfaction.
- Indifference curves have negative slopes, are convex to the origin due to the law of diminishing marginal utility, and indifference curves do not intersect.
- An indifference map is an infinite set of indifference curves.
- Consumer equilibrium occurs where the budget line is tangent to the highest indifference curve.
- When the price of one product rises, not only will your consumption of that product fall (the substitution effect), but also your income will be reduced as well, and for normal goods you will consume less (the income effect). The opposite occurs when price falls.

QUESTION

Consumers face a set of goods called "credence goods." These are goods where customers must "take it on faith that the supplier has given them what they need and no more."[8] Examples include surgeons, auto mechanics, and taxis. These experts tell us what medical procedures, repairs, and routes we require to satisfy our needs, and very often we don't know the price until the work is done. If we do not know the price and cannot establish whether we actually need some of these goods, how does this square with our indifference curve analysis?

Answers to the Checkpoint question can be found at the end of this chapter.

Rubberball/Jupiter Images

Using Indifference Curves: Economic Analysis of Terrorism

Since the attack on the World Trade Center on September 11, 2001, combating terrorism has taken center stage in national politics and was an important factor in the change of leadership in the 2006 congressional elections. Combating terrorism is a complicated, difficult problem that will confront the country for several generations to come. In this brief section, the household indifference curve model outlined in this appendix is applied to this problem. This discussion is based on work

[8] "Economic Focus: Sawbones, Cowboys and Cheats," *The Economist,* April 15, 2006.

by Professors Enders and Sandler.[9] Using the household model, terrorists are treated as rational actors who maximize a set of goals subject to constrained resources.

Terrorist campaigns are not new and extend back to the French Revolution, Russian Revolutions, the IRA campaign in Northern Ireland, and the Palestinian (PLO) struggle against Israel. In essence, as Enders and Sandler note, "Terrorists want to circumvent the normal political channels/procedures and create political change through threats and violence."[10] Terrorism tactics include bombings, assassinations, threats, suicide attacks, and kidnappings all designed to garner support for their cause through extensive media coverage.

Let's apply our household indifference curve model to terrorist activities. Every terrorist organization can achieve its goals using violent terrorist activities V and nonviolent political means N. The violent means were just described; the nonviolent means include running candidates for political election and acts of civil disobedience. These activities can be modeled using the indifference curves shown in Figure APX-6. Violent activities can be substituted for nonviolent activities along the indifference curves shown. As long as the goal of more support is reached, terrorists would be indifferent between violent terrorist activity and nonviolent political activity. The level of the group's utility (or support for their cause) increases for indifference curves moving away from the origin ($I_2 < I_1 < I_0$). From the perspective of terrorist groups, being able to engage in more of both activities is preferable.

FIGURE APX-6

Optimal Terror-Political Choice

This figure uses the household indifference curve model to show the optimal terrorism-political choices made by terrorist groups given a budget constraint equal to *ab*. The level of a terrorist group's utility (or support for their cause) increases with indifference curves moving away from the origin. The resulting level of terrorism is V_0 combined with N_0 level of nonviolent political activity.

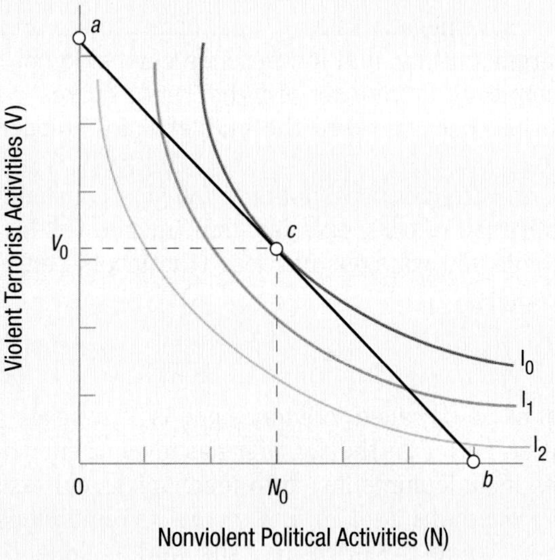

Similar to the households we described earlier, terrorist groups do not have unlimited resources (terrorist activities require funding) and face a budget constraint similar to line *ab* shown in Figure APX-6. Given the groups' limited resources, if all of their activities are devoted to nonviolent activity, they can engage in 0*b* nonviolent acts, and if all their energies are devoted to terrorism, they can complete 0*a* levels of terrorism. Terrorists maximize their "utility" by engaging in V_0 violent terrorist acts and undertaking N_0 political activities (point *c*). This is the best they can do with their limited resources; any other combination will put them on a lower indifference curve. If terrorists can shift their budget constraint out, they will find themselves on a higher indifference curve, with greater opportunities for both violent and nonviolent activities.

[9]Walter Enders and Todd Sandler, *The Political Economy of Terrorism* (New York: Cambridge University Press), 2006.
[10]Enders and Sandler, *The Political Economy of Terrorism*, p. 4.

Policy Implications

What can this simple model tell policymakers about how to fight terrorism? Simply, just as terrorist groups want to shift their budget constraint out, governments want to shift the terrorists' budget (or resource) constraints in.

Governments have two general approaches to fighting terrorism, defensive and offensive (proactive). Defensive policies include elaborate airport screening procedures, inspection activities at ports for cargo, and sophisticated protections or barriers at likely targets. Proactive policies include military campaigns against terrorist strongholds, intelligence activities intended to infiltrate terrorist cells, and cooperation with other governments to freeze financial resources and block transfers of funds to potential terrorist cells.

First, let's look at defensive antiterrorist policies. For example, heightening security measures at airports raises the cost of using airplanes to perpetrate violent terrorist actions. Terrorists have to engage in more elaborate planning, or they might shift resources from targets harder to attack before but now easier because of the relative shift in what is now a hard target or a soft target. If defensive antiterror measures increase the cost (price) of violent acts, the resource constraint rotates from *ab* to *db* in Figure APX-7. There is a rotation of the resource constraint because the cost of violent terrorist activities rises, but there is no change in the cost of nonviolent political activities. The increase in the price of violent activities establishes a new equilibrium at point *e* with a reduction in violence to V_1 and an increase of political activities to N_1.

Alternatively, proactive antiterror measures affect the terrorist resource (or budget) constraint, but in a different way. Proactive intelligence and infiltration of

FIGURE APX-7

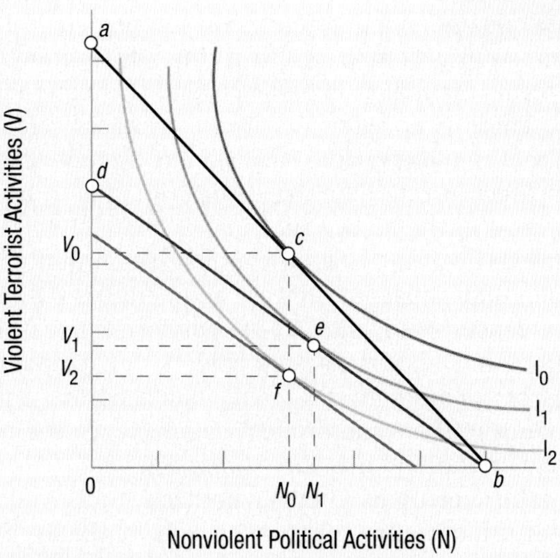

Effectiveness of Preventive (defensive) and Proactive (offensive) Antiterror Policies

Defensive policies against terrorism include airport and seaport screening and erecting barriers around important targets. These policies increase the cost (price) of terrorism, resulting in a rotation of the original terrorist resource constraint from line *ab* to line *db*. This results in a lower level of terrorist activities (V_1), and in this case a small increase in nonviolent activity.

Proactive or offensive antiterror polices include military campaigns, intelligence and infiltration of terrorist cells, and freezing of financial assets along with making transfers of terrorist funds more difficult. These activities mostly have the effect of reducing (shifting) the budget constraint without changing the price or costs of terrorist activities. Intelligence and infiltration activities may increase the costs of maintaining a terrorist cell, and this can be treated as a rotation in the budget constraint from line *ab* to line *db*. But clearly, freezing assets and military action reduces the resources available for terrorist activities and the groups now face a lower budget constraint, with a new level of terrorism at V_2 (point *f*).

terrorist cells will increase the costs of maintaining a terrorist cell and so rotate the terrorist resource constraint as we saw with defensive antiterrorist measures, but other proactive measures have a different effect. Military campaigns, freezing of financial assets, and making transfers of purported terrorist funds more difficult reduce the resources available for terrorist activities and nonviolent political activities. This shifts the entire budget constraint in, and a new equilibrium is established as shown in Figure APX-7 at point *f.* Now, compared to the previous equilibrium at point *e,* terrorism declines to V_2 and in this case nonviolent political activities also decline to N_0.

What comes from this analysis is confirmation of the common sense notion that both defensive and proactive antiterrorist measures reduce terrorism. What we see a little clearer is the different effects of each type of measure. Using the basic household model to describe terrorist activities, we can conclude that a successful antiterrorist campaign will most likely include both defensive and proactive elements that work in tandem to make terrorist activities more costly and reduce the resources available to terrorist groups.

Auto Advertisements: Utility Versus Indifference Curves

Before going on to the next chapter and looking at how producers make their decisions, let's try to apply in an intuitive way these two approaches to consumer decision making by looking at automobile ads.

Contrast ads for luxury autos with ads for more prosaic autos such as minivans (denigrated by the trendsetters as the vehicle for "soccer moms"). Why do ads for luxury autos often have few words but instead have images of fancy houses and deserted beaches, while ads for minivans show a passenger door behind the driver's seat, or cup holders, or ways to fold up seats? We can use our consumer choice models to make a broad hypothesis.

The luxury auto ads use an indifference curve approach. For this higher-priced item that often has a status component to it, the ads in effect ask consumers to compare in broad terms the luxury experience with the experience they have with their current auto. There is no intent to have consumers calculate utility for the various components of the luxury auto—consumers are not asked to calculate the utils received from their current auto's seat with the utils to be received from the high-priced leather seat of the luxury auto.

The less-expensive minivan's ads, in contrast, seem more in line with a marginal utility approach. Individual features are enumerated. Potential customers are pushed into doing at least some mental calculation for each feature. How many utils does one receive from an auto that has cup holders that handle juice boxes as well as cups, since juice boxes are part of a young child's normal equipment? So, for a less expensive product in the same product category, we see more of a marginal utility approach than an indifference curve approach.

We should be a little cautious in our hypothesis. Soft drinks are inexpensive, yet their ads use an indifference curve approach, probably because the differences between competitors are so small that a marginal utility approach does not make sense. Can you enumerate specific differences between Coca-Cola and Pepsi? Nevertheless, it is useful to look at advertisements for products and use the approaches discussed in this chapter to better understand what advertisers are trying to do.

Appendix Key Concepts

Indifference curve, p. 157
Indifference map, p. 158
Income effect, p. 161
Substitution effect, p. 161

Appendix Summary

Indifference Curve Analysis

An indifference curve graphically represents all of the combinations of two products that represent the same level of satisfaction to consumers. An indifference curve, in other words, identifies a set of possible consumption combinations that leaves the consumer indifferent.

Like marginal utility analysis, indifference curve analysis helps economists understand how consumers allocate their limited budgets among diverse goods. In fact, indifference curve analysis leads to the same theoretical conclusions as marginal utility analysis. It is subject to less restrictive assumptions, however, in that it does not require that consumers actually measure utility or calculate marginal utility per dollar; instead, consumers can decide which bundles of goods they would prefer to consume under varying circumstances.

The income effect is a change in quantity demanded that comes about as a result of a change in income due to a change in price. When the price of some regularly purchased good rises, this leaves consumers with less money to spend buying goods of all sorts. The rise in price, therefore, effectively reduces consumer income, resulting in a drop in demand for most normal goods, often including the good whose price has risen.

When the price of some good rises, quantity demanded for the good will typically fall as consumers begin purchasing cheaper substitute products; this is the substitution effect. Note that when the price of a product rises, quantity demanded for it will typically fall, partially due to the income effect, and partially due to the substitution effect; indifference curve analysis helps us determine how much of this drop in quantity demanded is due to each effect.

Appendix Questions and Problems

1. Answer the following questions using the figure below:
   a. Assume that you have \$50 a month to devote to entertainment (First-Run Movies) and wine with dinner (Bottles of Wine). What will be your equilibrium allocation if the price to see a movie or buy a bottle of wine is \$10? Graph the equilibrium on the figure and label it point *a*.

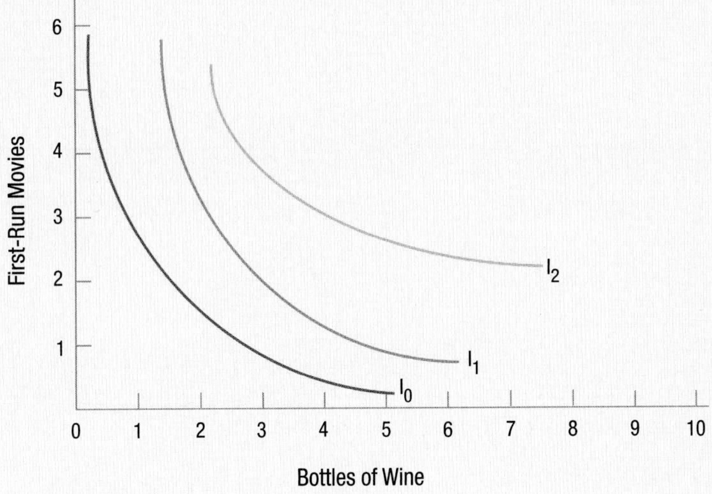

b. A grape glut in California results in Napa Valley wine dropping in price to $5 a bottle, and you view this wine as a perfect substitute for what you were drinking earlier. Now what will be your equilibrium allocation between movies and wine? Graph that on the figure and label the new equilibrium as point *b*.

2. Indifference curves cannot intersect. Why not?

3. Explain why the following bundles of Apples (A) and Bananas (B) cannot be on the same indifference curve: (4A, 2B); (1A, 5B); (4A, 3B).

Answers to Appendix Checkpoint Question

CHECKPOINT: INDIFFERENCE CURVE ANALYSIS

Not very well. They are largely a problem of incomplete information and a challenging problem for consumers. If doctors make more money on complex operations, they will be inclined to prescribe them more often. A recent study found that doctors elect surgery for themselves less often than nondoctors. As long as consumers are aware of the incentive structure of these transactions, they can build this into the decision calculus, but ultimately, information asymmetries are not adequately represented in this model.

7 Production and Cost

twenty years ago, coffee was a commodity product. In the United States, coffee obtained in corporate settings was often dispensed in horrid vending machines: You put your 50 cents in, pressed the button, hoped the paper cup that dropped on the grill would not tip too much the wrong way or even fall out, and waited for the usually tasteless liquid to pour into the paper cup. Coffee brands such as Maxwell House ("good to the last drop") and Folger's advertised on television, but the difference between each was minimal. Not very satisfying, but no great pressure for change, either: How could a new company make any money in such a commodity market?

As you sip your latte or frappuccino now, it may be hard to imagine a world without Starbucks. Howard Schultz, the key person in the development and growth of Starbucks, was touring the coffee houses in Rome when he wondered why coffee in the United States did not come up to European standards. He thought people would appreciate a superior product that brought with it the coffee-house experience. The number of Starbucks establishments in major cities in the United States shows he was right. So does the almost inconceivable notion of a world without double-shot espressos and lattes.

With entrepreneurs such as Howard Schultz, the idea comes first. They see what they think is a market need. The next thing that probably goes through their minds is: Can I make a profit out of it? To gauge profits, entrepreneurs have to estimate revenues and costs.

In this chapter, we look at what motivates firms to do what they do—profits. We then look at the production and cost part of the profit equation. In further chapters, we add the revenue part to the production part. In this way, we begin to examine what lies behind supply curves.

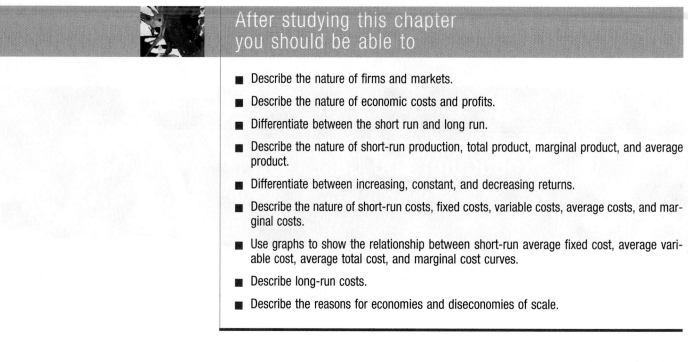

After studying this chapter you should be able to

- Describe the nature of firms and markets.
- Describe the nature of economic costs and profits.
- Differentiate between the short run and long run.
- Describe the nature of short-run production, total product, marginal product, and average product.
- Differentiate between increasing, constant, and decreasing returns.
- Describe the nature of short-run costs, fixed costs, variable costs, average costs, and marginal costs.
- Use graphs to show the relationship between short-run average fixed cost, average variable cost, average total cost, and marginal cost curves.
- Describe long-run costs.
- Describe the reasons for economies and diseconomies of scale.

Firms, Profits, and Economic Costs

Firms produce the products and services that you purchase. Most of the business news you see or read concerns giant corporations, but consumers deal most often with small family-owned firms in their neighborhoods. These small firms run the gamut from pizza parlors and used record and CD shops to barber and beauty shops, small garages, and locally owned McDonald's franchises.

As consumers, we take for granted many of the things producers *voluntarily* provide in the market. We all expect businesses to provide us with our morning lattes, fuel for our cars, and up-to-date books for us to read. In fact, it is entrepreneurs in the pursuit of profits who meet all of our needs as consumers.

Firms

Firm
An economic institution that transforms resources (factors of production) into outputs for consumers.

A **firm** is an economic institution that transforms inputs, or factors of production, into outputs, or products for consumers. Most firms begin as family enterprises or small partnerships. When successful, these firms can evolve into corporations of considerable size.

In the process of producing goods for consumers, firms must make numerous decisions. First, they have to determine a market need. Then, most broadly, firms must decide what quantity of output to produce, how to produce it, and what inputs to employ. The latter two decisions depend on the production technology the firm selects.

Any given product can typically be produced in a wide variety of ways. Some businesses, like McDonald's franchises and Krispy Kreme donut shops, use considerable amounts of capital equipment, whereas others, such as T-shirt shops and wok eateries, require very little. Even among similar firms, the quality and quantity of resources available will often determine what technologies are used. Firms located in areas with an abundance of low-cost labor will tend to use low-technology, labor-intensive production methods. In areas where high-skill, high-wage labor is the norm, production is more often done by high-technology, capital-intensive processes.

Entrepreneurs

If a product or service is to be provided to the market, someone must first assume the risk of raising the required capital, assembling workers and raw materials, producing the product, and, finally, offering it for sale. Markets provide incentives and signals, but it is entrepreneurs who provide products and services by taking risks in the hopes of earning profits.

In the United States, 12% of people ages 18–64 classify themselves as entrepreneurs. This means they are running start-up businesses or businesses less than 42 months old. Entrepreneurial rates in Europe are only half the American rate, and Japanese entrepreneurship is less than 2%.[1]

Entrepreneurs can be divided into three basic business structures: sole proprietorships (one owner), partnerships (two or more owners), and corporations (many stockholders). The United States has over 25 million businesses, over 70% of them sole proprietorships or small businesses. Only 20% of American businesses are corporations. Nevertheless, corporations sell nearly 90% of all products and services in the United States. Likewise, around the world, the corporate form of business has become the dominant form. To see why, we must first take a brief look at the advantages and disadvantages of each business structure.

Sole Proprietors

The **sole proprietor** represents the most basic form of business organization. A proprietorship is composed of one owner, who usually supervises the business operation. Local restaurants, dry cleaning businesses, and auto repair shops are often sole proprietorships. A sole proprietorship is easy to establish and manage, having much less paperwork associated with it than other forms of business organization. But the proprietorship has disadvantages. Single owners are often limited in their ability to raise capital. In many instances, all management responsibilities fall on this single individual. And most importantly, the personal assets of the owner are subject to unlimited liability. If you as a sole proprietor own a pizza shop, and someone slips on your floor, he or she can sue you and take away your house and your life savings if you do not have sufficient insurance.

Sole proprietor
A type of business structure composed of a single owner who supervises and manages the business and is subject to unlimited liability.

Partnerships

Partnerships are similar to sole proprietorships except that they have more than one owner. Establishing a partnership usually requires signing a legal partnership document. Partnerships find it easier to raise capital and spread around the management responsibilities. Like sole proprietors, however, partners are subject to unlimited liability, not only for their share of the business, but for the entire business. If your partner takes off for Bermuda, you are left to pay all the bills, even those your partner incurred. The death of one partner dissolves a partnership, unless other arrangements have been concluded ahead of time. In any case, the death of a partner often creates problems for the continuity of the business.

Partnership
Similar to a sole proprietorship, but involves more than one owner who shares the managing of the business. Partnerships are also subject to unlimited liability.

Corporations

The **corporation** is today the premier form of business organization in most of the world. Roughly 5,000 American corporations sell nearly $20 trillion worth of goods and services every year. This is an amazing statistic when you consider that the country's nearly 20 million sole proprietorships have sales totaling just over $1 trillion. Clearly, corporations are structured in a way that enhances growth and efficiency.

Corporation
A business structure that has most of the legal rights of individuals, and in addition, the corporation can issue stock to raise capital. Stockholders' liability is limited to the value of their stock.

Corporations possess most of the legal rights of individuals; in addition, they are able to issue stock to raise capital, and most significantly, the liability of indi-

[1] *The Economist*, "Enterprising Rising," January 8, 2004, p. 55.

vidual owners (i.e., stockholders) is limited to the amount they have invested in the stock. This is what distinguishes corporations from the other forms of business organization: the ability to raise large amounts of capital because of limited liability.

Some scholars argue that corporations are the greatest engines of economic prosperity ever known.[2] Daniel Akst wrote, "When I worked for a big company, there was a miracle in the office every couple of weeks, just like clockwork. It happened every payday, when sizable checks were distributed to a small army of employees who also enjoyed health and retirement benefits. Few of us could have made as much on our own, and somehow there was always money left over for the shareholders as well."[3] Without the corporate umbrella, most of the jobs we hold would not exist; most of the products we use would not have been invented; and our standard of living would be a fraction of what it is today.

Business owners of all types are people who react to the profit incentives of the market.

Profits

Profit
Equal to the difference between total revenue and total cost.

Revenue
Equal to price per unit times quantity sold.

Entrepreneurs and firms employ resources and turn out products with the goal of making profits. **Profit** is simply the difference between total revenue and total cost.

Total **revenue** is the amount of money a firm receives from the sales of its products. It is equal to the number of units sold times the price per unit ($TR = p \times q$). *Total cost* includes both out-of-pocket expenses and opportunity costs; we will discuss this concept shortly.

Economists explicitly assume that firms proceed rationally and have the maximization of profits as their primary objective. Alternative behavioral assumptions for firms have been tested, including sales maximization, "satisfactory" profits, and various goals for market share. The biography of Nobel Prize winner Herbert Simon discusses these. Although these more complex assumptions for firm behavior often predict different outcomes, economists have not been persuaded that any of them yield results superior to those of the profit maximization approach. Profit maximization has stood the test of time, and thus we will assume it is the primary economic goal of firms.

Economic Costs

Economic costs
The sum of explicit (out-of-pocket) and implicit (opportunity) costs.

Explicit costs
Those expenses paid directly to another economic entity including wages, lease payments, taxes, and utilities.

Implicit costs
The opportunity costs of using resources that belong to the firm including depreciation, depletion of business assets, and the opportunity cost of the firm's capital employed in the business.

Economists approach business costs and profits from the opportunity cost perspective discussed in Chapter 2. They separate costs into explicit costs, or out-of-pocket expenses, and implicit costs, or opportunity costs. **Economic costs** are the sum of explicit and implicit costs.

Explicit costs are those expenses paid directly to some other economic entity. These include wages, lease payments, expenditures for raw materials, taxes, utilities, and so on. A company can easily determine its explicit costs by summing all of the checks it has written during the normal course of doing business.

Implicit costs refer to all of the opportunity costs of using resources that belong to the firm. These include depreciation, the depletion of business assets, and the opportunity cost of a firm's capital. In any business, some assets are depleted over time. Machines, cars, and office equipment depreciate with use and time. Finite oil or mineral deposits are depleted as they are mined or pumped. Even though firms do not actually pay any cash as these assets are worn down or used up, these costs nonetheless represent real expenses to the firm.

Another major component of implicit costs is the capital firms have invested. Even small firms incur large implicit costs from their capital investment. Small entre-

---

[2]John Micklethwait and Adrian Wooldridge, *The Company: A Short History of a Revolutionary Idea* (New York: The Modern Library), 2003.
[3]Daniel Akst, "Where Those Paychecks Come From," *Wall Street Journal,* February 3, 2004.

Nobel Prize Herbert Simon

When he was awarded the Nobel Prize for Economics in 1978, Herbert Simon (1916–2001) was an unusual choice on two fronts. First, he wasn't an economist by trade; he was a professor of computer science and psychology at the time of his award. Second, Simon's major contribution to economics was a direct challenge to one of the basic tenets of neoclassical economics: firms, in fact, do not always act to maximize profits.

In his book *Administrative Behavior,* Simon approached economics and the behavior of firms from his outsider's perspective. Simon thought real-world experience showed that firms are not always perfectly rational, in possession of perfect information, or striving to maximize profits.

Rather, he proposed, as firms grow larger and larger, the access to perfect information becomes a fiction. As a rule, firms always have to make do with less than perfect information. Furthermore, since firms are run by individuals with both personal and social ties, these individuals' decisions are further altered by their inability to remain perfectly and completely rational in their decision making.

To Simon, the reality is not that firms tilt at the mythical windmill of maximizing profits, but that, as he said in his Nobel Prize acceptance speech, they recognize their limitations and instead try to come up with an "acceptable solution to acute problems." In short, each decision maker in each firm tries to come up with the best solution for his or her problems. By recognizing this approach to decision making, firms can then set realistic goals and make reasonable assessments of their successes or failures.

To neoclassical economists, Simon's views attack the basic presumption that drives many of their models and theories. Simon brought data, theories, and knowledge from other disciplines into economics, broadening its scope and applying more realistic conditions actually found in the marketplace.

preneurs, for example, must invest both their own capital and labor into their businesses. Such people could normally be working for someone else, so their "lost salary" must be treated as an implicit cost when determining the true profitability of their businesses. Similarly, any capital invested in a business enterprise could just as well be earning interest in a bank account or returning dividends and capital gains through the purchase of stock in other enterprises. Though not directly paid out as expenses, these foregone earnings nonetheless represent implicit costs for the firm.

Sunk Costs

Sunk costs
Those costs that have been incurred and cannot be recovered including, for example, funds spent on existing technology that have become obsolete and past advertising that has run in the media.

Sunk costs are costs that have already been incurred and *cannot* be recovered. Examples include previous bets in a poker hand, the tuition you paid this semester, and expenditures on advertising that have run in the media. For example, beyond some point in the term, tuition is a sunk cost. If you drop a course near the beginning of the term and pay by credit hour, you might get a refund for some of the cost of this course. After several weeks in the term, however, most colleges do not provide any refund for dropped courses. Should you *not* drop a course you are doing poorly in and likely will not get better in simply because you paid tuition you cannot get back? Of course not—the tuition is a sunk cost and should be irrelevant to your decision to drop the course or not.

Sunk costs are costs that have been incurred in the past, and you are unable to get them back. These expenses are gone, and future decisions should ignore them. The future benefits from the decision either exceed the future costs or the project is not undertaken, no matter how much has already been spent. The decision to advertise a product in a new magazine depends on the benefits and costs of that advertising, not how much has been spent on television ads in the past. You will hear the phrase that "sunk costs are sunk," meaning ignore them; they are gone.

Economic and Normal Profits

Economists define a *normal rate of return* on the capital invested in a firm as the return just sufficient to keep investors satisfied, and thus just sufficient to keep capital in the business over the long run. The normal rate of return therefore represents the opportunity cost of capital. If a firm's rate of return on capital falls below this rate, investors will put their capital to use elsewhere, and the firm will likely perish; at a minimum, the firm will find it virtually impossible to raise any additional capital. For example, if you could obtain 5% interest in a bank's passbook savings account, why would you invest in a firm that pays less than this rate of return?

Economic profits
Profits in excess of normal profits. These are profits in excess of both explicit and implicit costs.

Normal profits
The return necessary on capital to keep investors satisfied and keep capital in the business over the long run.

Economists include both explicit and implicit costs in their analysis of business profits. They say a firm is earning **economic profits** if it is generating profits in excess of zero once implicit costs are factored in. Economic profits of zero therefore mean a firm is earning just the normal rate of return on its capital, or just enough to cover the opportunity cost of this capital. *Zero economic profits* and **normal profits** thus being equated, anything above zero economic profits represents a true economic profit, and anything below an economic loss. Note that a firm may be earning *accounting profits* as defined by the Internal Revenue Service for tax purposes, yet still be suffering economic losses, since taxable income does not reflect all implicit costs. Table 1 lists some examples of both explicit and implicit costs.

Table 1 Examples of Explicit and Implicit Costs

Explicit	Implicit
• Salaries	• Earnings that an owner could have made in an alternative job
• Lease payments	• Interest on capital invested in business that could have been made by putting the capital in a bank account
• Cost of goods sold	
• Utilities	
• Insurance	
• Office supplies	

For example, an entrepreneur who opens a small restaurant and earns a $30,000 accounting profit after deducting her out-of-pocket (explicit) costs may or may not have really earned an economic profit. If she could have earned $35,000 a year working elsewhere, she has suffered a $5,000 economic loss, and we haven't even considered the implicit cost of her capital yet.

Hence, economists designate normal profits as economic profits equal to zero. Normal profits are the profits necessary to keep a firm in business over an extended period of time, or over the long run. This brings us to an important economic distinction, between the short run and the long run.

Short Run Versus Long Run

Although the short and the long run generally differ in their temporal spans, they are *not* defined in terms of time. Rather, economists define these periods by the ability of firms to adjust the quantities of various resources they are employing.

The **short run** is a period of time over which at least one factor of production is fixed, or cannot be changed. For the sake of simplicity, economists typically assume that plant capacity is fixed in the short run. Output from a fixed plant can still vary depending on how much labor the firm employs. Firms can, for instance, hire more people, have existing employees work overtime, or run additional shifts. For discussion purposes, we will here focus on labor as the variable factor, but changes in the raw materials employed can also result in output changes.

Short run
A period of time over which at least one factor of production (resource) is fixed, or cannot be changed.

The **long run**, conversely, is a period of time sufficient for a firm to adjust all factors of production, including plant capacity. Since all factors can be altered in the long run, existing firms can even close and leave the industry, and new firms can build new plants and enter the market.

Long run
A period of time sufficient for firms to adjust all factors of production including plant capacity.

In the short run, therefore, with plant capacity and the number of firms in an industry being fixed, output will vary only as a result of changes in employment. In the long run, as plant capacity and other factors are made variable, the industry may grow or shrink as firms enter or leave the business, or some firms alter their plant capacity.

Because all industries are unique, the time required for long-run adjustment varies by industry. Family-owned restaurants, lawn-mowing services, and roofing firms can come and go fairly rapidly. High-capital industries, on the other hand, such as the chemical, petroleum, and semiconductor industries all face obstacles to change that require a long time to overcome, whether these be strenuous environmental regulation, immense research and development requirements, or huge capital costs for plant construction. Adding plant capacity in one of these industries can take a decade or more and cost billions of dollars.

The important point to note is that firms seek economic profits and determine profits by first calculating their costs. These costs may differ over the short run versus the long run. Therefore, we will first look at production and costs in the short run, then consider costs in the long run.

Checkpoint

Firms, Profits, and Economic Costs

REVIEW

- Firms are economic institutions that convert inputs (factors of production) into products and services.
- Entrepreneurs provide goods and services to markets. Entrepreneurs can be organized into three basic business structures: sole proprietorships, partnerships, and corporations.
- Corporations are the premier form of business organization because they give owners (shareholders) limited liability, unlike sole proprietorships and partnerships.

- Profit is the difference between total revenues and costs.
- Total revenue is price per unit times the number of units sold (TR $= p \times q$).
- Total cost includes both out-of-pocket and opportunity costs.
- Explicit costs are those expenses paid directly to some other economic entity such as taxes, utilities, and the cost of raw materials. Explicit costs can be determined by adding up the checks paid out by a firm.
- Implicit costs represent the opportunity costs of doing business, including depreciation, depletion, and the firm's capital costs.
- Economic profits are those in *excess* of a normal rate of return (that return required to keep capital in the firm over a long term).
- Normal profits are equal to zero economic profits. The firm is earning just enough to keep capital in the firm over the long run.
- The short run is a period of time where one factor of production (usually plant capacity) is fixed. In the long run all factors can vary and the firm can enter or exit the industry.

QUESTION

Assume for a moment you want to go into business for yourself and you have a good idea. What are the pros and cons of buying an existing business versus starting your own from scratch?

Answers to the Checkpoint question can be found at the end of this chapter.

Production in the Short Run

Production
The process of turning inputs into outputs.

Production is the process of turning inputs into outputs. Most products can be produced using a variety of different technologies. As discussed earlier, these can be either capital-intensive or labor-intensive. Which technology a firm chooses will depend on many things, including ease of implementation and the relative cost of each input into the process.

Again, in the simplified model we are working with, firms can vary their output in the short run only by altering the amount of labor they employ, because plant capacity is fixed in the short run. An individual firm's production possibilities follow the same general pattern as the production function for the entire economy introduced in Chapter 2. Hence, in the short run, output for an existing plant will vary by the amount of labor employed. This output is referred to as *total product.*

Total Product

Imagine you decide to begin manufacturing windsurfing rigs in the unused barn of the farmhouse you rent. (You do not farm the acreage, you just rent the buildings.) Your physical plant is constrained in the short run by the size of the barn. Table 2 lists your firm's total output as you hire more workers.

Panel A of Figure 1 displays your total product curve for windsurfing equipment, based on the data in columns 1 and 2 of Table 2. Output of rigs varies with the number of people you employ. Output rises from 0 to 40 when four people are working (point *a* in Panel A) to a maximum of 100 when 12 people are employed (point *c*). As you continue to hire employees beyond 12, you encounter *negative returns.* Total output actually begins to fall, that is, possibly, because your barn has become overly crowded, confusing, hazardous, or noisy. Clearly, hiring any more than 12 employees would be counterproductive, since output falls but costs rise.

Table 2 Production Data for Windsurfing Sail Firm

(1) L labor	(2) Q (total product)	(3) MP (marginal product)	(4) AP (average product)
0	0	0	—
1	7	7	7.00
2	15	8	7.50
3	25	10	8.33
4	40	15	10.00
5	54	14	10.80
6	65	11	10.83
7	75	10	10.71
8	84	9	10.50
9	90	6	10.00
10	95	5	9.50
11	98	3	8.91
12	100	2	8.33
13	98	−2	7.54
14	95	−3	6.79
15	85	−10	5.67

Marginal and Average Product

Marginal product (column 3 in Table 2) is the change in output that results from a change in labor input. Marginal product is computed by dividing the change in output (ΔQ) by the change in labor (ΔL). Thus, marginal product (MP) is equal to $\Delta Q/\Delta L$; it is the change in output that results from adding additional workers.

Marginal product
The change in output that results from a change in labor ($\Delta Q/\Delta L$).

Notice that when employment rises from three to four workers, output grows from 25 to 40 rigs. Marginal product is therefore 15 rigs at this point (point *a* in Panel B of Figure 1). Contrast this with a change in employment when 12 people are already employed. Adding the 13th employee actually reduces the total output of windsurfing rigs from 100 to 98 so marginal product is −2.

Average product (AP) or output per worker is found by dividing total output by the number of workers employed to produce that output (Q/L). Average product is shown in Panel B of Figure 1. When employment is four people and output is 40, for instance, average product is 10 (point *d*).

Average product
Output per worker, found by dividing total output by the number of workers employed to produce that output (Q/L).

Increasing and Diminishing Returns

As Panel B of Figure 1 shows, when four people are employed, marginal product is 15 (point *a*), exceeding the average product of 10 (point *d*). This portion of the total product curve, where average and marginal products are both rising, is called

FIGURE 1

Total Product Curve, Marginal Product, and Average Product

These two panels show the relationship between additional labor and productivity. The top panel shows how increasing labor increases productivity, up to a point. The bottom panel shows marginal and average product. Once you add more than four workers, marginal product starts decreasing. Total product keeps increasing, however, until you hit 12 employees. At that point, marginal product is negative, meaning that each additional employee actually reduces production.

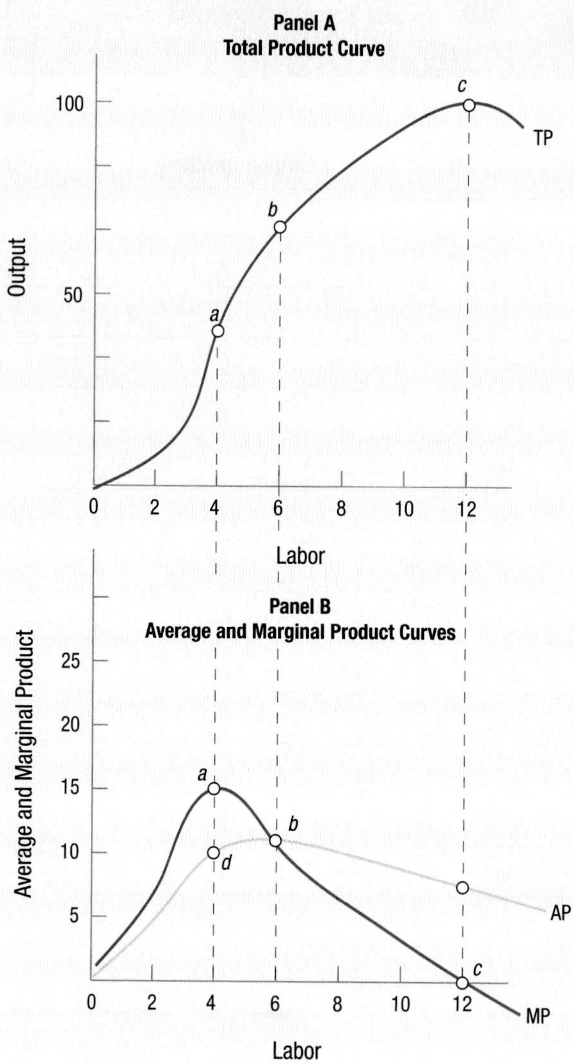

Increasing marginal returns A new worker hired adds more to total output than the previous worker hired so that both average and marginal products are rising.

Diminishing marginal returns An additional worker adds to total output, but at a diminishing rate.

the **increasing marginal returns** portion of the curve. Each of your first four employees adds more to output than the previous worker hired; thus, in this range, output grows faster as you employ additional labor.

Now note that as you hire your first six employees, average product continues to rise, and the marginal product remains higher than average product. When marginal product exceeds average product—when a new worker adds more to output than the average of the previous workers—hiring an additional worker will increase average productivity. This might be because hiring more people allows you to establish more of a production line, say, thus heightening specialization and thereby raising productivity.

Note, however, that after you have employed four people, *marginal productivity* begins to trail off. Between 4 and 12 workers (points *a* to *c*), you face **diminishing marginal returns** since each additional worker adds to total output, but at a diminishing rate. Note that at point *b* (six employees), both marginal and average product are roughly equal and average product is at its maximum (nearly 11 rigs).

Finally, note that once you have hired 12 employees, if you hire any more, this will result in negative marginal returns. Hiring additional people will actually reduce output, so rational firms never operate in this range.

The typical production curves shown in Figure 1 embody the *law of diminishing returns.* Given that your barn size is fixed in the short run, adding more labor will eventually—in this case, once four people have been hired—result in diminishing marginal returns, each additional worker adding to total production by a smaller and smaller amount.

Checkpoint

Production in the Short Run

REVIEW

- Production is the process of turning inputs into outputs.
- Total product is the total output produced by the production process.
- Marginal product (MP) is the change in output that results from a change in labor input and is equal to $\Delta Q/\Delta L$.
- Average product (AP) is output per worker and is equal to Q/L.
- Increasing marginal returns occur when adding a worker adds *more* to output than the previous worker hired.
- Diminishing marginal returns occur when adding a worker adds *less* to output than the previous worker hired.
- Negative marginal returns occur when adding a worker actually leads to less total output than with the previous worker hired.

QUESTIONS

Microsoft has developed and sold Microsoft Office 97, 2000, XP, 2003, and now 2007. Most users have barely scratched the surface on this product, probably using no more than 10% of the program's features. The new version, 2007, which was released with Vista, the new Windows operating system, includes speech recognition that will require a fair amount of operator training. Has Microsoft reached diminishing returns with this product? Are the free Web-based word processors (e.g., www.writely.com or Google Docs and Spreadsheets) with most of the features we use a threat to the Microsoft Office empire?

Answers to the Checkpoint questions can be found at the end of this chapter.

Costs of Production

Production tells only part of the story. We have to calculate how much it costs to produce this output. Let's now bring resource prices, including labor costs, into our analysis to develop the typical cost curves for the firm.

Short-Run Costs

In a very straightforward way, production costs are determined by the productivity of workers. Ignoring all costs except wages, if you, by yourself, were to produce 10 pizzas an hour and you were paid $8 an hour, then each pizza would cost an average of 80 cents to produce—the cost of your labor. Yet, to ignore any other costs would be to neglect a significant portion of business expenses known as *overhead.*

To begin developing the concept of overhead specifically, and production costs more generally, remember that production periods are split into the short run and the long run. In the short run, at least one factor is fixed, whereas in the long run, all factors are variable. This has led economists to define costs as fixed and variable.

Fixed and Variable Costs

Fixed costs
Costs that do not change as a firm's output expands or contracts, often called overhead. These include items such as lease payments, administrative expenses, property taxes, and insurance.

Variable costs
Costs that vary with output fluctuations including expenses such as labor and material costs.

Fixed costs, or overhead, are those costs that do not change as a firm's output expands or contracts. Lease or rental payments, administrative overhead, and insurance are examples of fixed costs—they do not rise or fall as a firm alters production to meet market demands. **Variable costs**, on the other hand, do fluctuate as output changes. Labor and material costs are examples of variable costs, since making more products requires hiring more workers and purchasing more raw materials. To keep things simple, let us assume all costs fit into one of these two categories, such that total cost (TC) is equal to total fixed cost (TFC) plus total variable cost (TVC), or

$$TC = TFC + TVC$$

Note that, in the long run, all costs are variable (TFC = 0), since given enough time, a firm can expand or close its plant, and enter or leave an industry.

Average Costs

When a firm produces a product or service, it will typically want a breakdown of how much labor, raw material, plant overhead, and sales costs are imbedded in each unit of the product. Modern accounting systems permit a detailed breakdown of costs for each unit of production. For our purposes, however, that level of detail is not necessary. For us, cost per unit of output (or *average cost*), average fixed cost, and average variable cost will be sufficient.

If we divide the previous equation determining TC by total output Q, we get

$$TC/Q = TFC/Q + TVC/Q$$

Average fixed cost
Equal to total fixed cost divided by output (TFC/Q).

Average variable cost
Equal to total variable cost divided by output (TVC/Q).

Average total cost
Equal to total cost divided by output (TC/Q). Average total cost is also equal to AFC + AVC.

Economists refer to total fixed costs divided by output TFC/Q as **average fixed cost** (AFC). This represents the average amount of overhead for each unit of output. Total variable costs divided by output is known as **average variable cost** (AVC). It represents the labor and raw materials expenses that go into each unit of output. Adding AFC and AVC together results in **average total cost** (ATC), and thus the equation above can be rewritten as

$$ATC = AFC + AVC$$

Hence, average cost per unit (ATC) is the sum of average fixed cost (AFC) and average variable cost (AVC).

Table 3 provides us with more complete production and cost data for your windsurfing business. Note that we have assumed you pay $1,000 per month for rent of the barn, so total fixed costs equal $1,000 (column 5). Wages per worker are assumed to be $11 per hour, or $88 per day, for 20 days a month, and thus $1,760 per month per employee. Note also that, for the sake of simplicity, we have included all material and other variable costs under your labor costs.

Let's go through one row so you will be sure how we arrived at the numbers in columns 3 to 11. Let's take the row where four workers are hired and therefore 40 windsurfing rigs are produced. Moving right through the table, we see the following. The marginal product of the additional worker as we move from three workers to four is 15 windsurfing rigs because the quantity produced has grown from 25 to

Table 3 Production and Cost Data for Windsurfing Sail Firm

(1) L	(2) Q	(3) MP	(4) AP	(5) TFC	(6) TVC	(7) TC	(8) ATC	(9) AVC	(10) AFC	(11) MC
0	0	0		1000	0	1000	—	—	—	—
1	7	7	7	1000	1760	2760	394.29	251.43	142.86	251.43
2	15	8	7.50	1000	3520	4520	301.33	234.67	66.67	220.00
3	25	10	8.33	1000	5280	6280	251.20	211.20	40.00	176.00
4	40	15	10.00	1000	7040	8040	201.00	176.00	25.00	117.33
5	54	14	10.80	1000	8800	9800	181.48	162.96	18.52	125.71
6	65	11	10.83	1000	10560	11560	177.85	162.46	15.38	160.00
7	75	10	10.71	1000	12320	13320	177.60	164.27	13.33	176.00
8	84	9	10.50	1000	14080	15080	179.52	167.62	11.90	195.56
9	90	6	10.00	1000	15840	16840	187.11	176.00	11.11	293.33
10	95	5	9.50	1000	17600	18600	195.79	185.26	10.53	352.00
11	98	3	8.91	1000	19360	20360	207.76	197.55	10.20	586.67
12	100	2	8.33	1000	21120	22120	221.20	211.20	10.00	880.00
13	98	−2	7.54	1000	22880	23880	243.67	233.47	10.20	−880.00
14	95	−3	6.79	1000	24640	25640	269.89	259.37	10.53	−586.70

40. Note that this marginal product is more than the third worker produced, but also note that the marginal product peaks with this worker. Since average product is Q/L, average product for four workers is 10.

We now move to columns 5–7. As noted above, you pay $1,000 per month for the barn, and this is your total fixed cost—it does not change with the addition of more workers. Total variable cost does change, rising by $1,760 for each additional worker because this is the wage you need to pay for each worker. For four workers, you pay $1,760 × 4 = $7,040. Total cost is simply total fixed cost plus total variable cost, so when the fourth worker is added, total cost is $1,000 + $7,040 = $8,040.

Now let's move to columns 8–10. Average total cost is total cost divided by quantity produced, so when four workers are hired, $8,040 in total cost is divided by 40 windsurfing rigs produced to equal $201 in ATC. Average variable cost takes the total variable cost of $7,040 for four workers and divides it by 40 windsurfing rigs to equal $176 in AVC. We can calculate average fixed costs in two ways. First, we can take total fixed costs of $1,000 and divide it by 40 windsurfing rigs to equal $25 in AFC. Second, we know that ATC = AVC + AFC, so if we know that $201 = $176 + AFC, we can solve for AFC and obtain $25 in AFC. Thus, we see that we can calculate average total cost and its components.

Average total cost is an important piece of information for business firms. ATC does not, however, tell us how much costs will rise or fall if output changes. For this, we need to look at marginal cost.

Marginal Cost

Because of increasing and decreasing returns associated with typical production processes, average costs will vary with the level of output. Assume for a moment that your firm has orders for, and is producing, 98 windsurfing rigs per month. Now assume you get an order for one more rig. Just how much does this additional windsurfing rig cost to produce? Or, in the language of economics, what is the *marginal cost* of the next rig produced?

Marginal cost
The change in total costs arising from the production of additional units of output ($\Delta TC/\Delta Q$). Since fixed costs do not change with output, marginal costs are the change in variable costs associated with additional production ($\Delta TVC/\Delta Q$).

Marginal cost is the change in total cost arising from the production of additional units of output. The delta (Δ) symbol is used to denote "change in." Marginal cost (MC) is equal to the change in total cost (ΔTC) divided by the change in output (ΔQ), or

$$MC = \Delta TC/\Delta Q = \Delta TFC/\Delta Q + \Delta TVC/\Delta Q$$

Note that, for simplicity, we have been discussing changes of one unit of output, but we can calculate MC for a change in output of any amount by plugging in the appropriate value for ΔQ. Note that because fixed costs do not vary with changes in output, $\Delta TFC/\Delta Q = 0$, and thus the equation above can be rewritten as

$$MC = \Delta TVC/\Delta Q$$

Let us now examine Table 3 to determine approximately what the marginal cost would be for producing one more rig if you are currently producing 98 rigs.

As Table 3 suggests, at 98 rigs, you are employing 11 people, but producing an additional rig will require hiring a 12th worker. This will actually raise your output by two rigs, to 100, that is, one rig for the new customer and one additional rig for inventory. Paying this new employee's wages increase your costs by \$1,760 per month. And since you produce two additional windsurfing rigs, each rig effectively costs you \$880 (\$1,760 ÷ 2 = \$880). Consequently, the marginal cost to produce these additional rigs is \$880 per rig, as shown in column 11 in Table 3. Marginal cost again is the change in variable cost associated with producing one more unit of a product.

Short-Run Cost Curves

Table 3 provides the numerical values for costs. Let us now translate these costs into figures to make their analysis simpler.

Average Fixed Cost (AFC)

The average fixed cost (AFC) for your business is shown in Figure 2. Note that AFC falls continuously as more output is produced; this is because your overhead expenses are getting spread out over more and more units of output. At point *a*, for instance, when only 25 rigs are produced, AFC is \$40, and TFC is equal to area $0fad$ = \$1,000. When output grows to 100, however, TFC remains equal to area $0ebc$ = \$1,000, but AFC drops to \$10, since the TFC is being spread over 100 units. (Keep in mind that because AFC = TFC/Q, then TFC = AFC × Q. This will be helpful when we only have graphical analysis to work with.)

Average Variable Cost (AVC)

Borrowing the data from Table 3, Figure 3 shows the AVC, ATC, and AFC for your hypothetical windsurfing firm. Notice that both the AVC and ATC curves are bowl-shaped. At relatively low levels of output, the curves slope downward, reflecting an increase in returns as average costs drop. As production levels rise, however, diminishing returns set in, and average costs start to climb back up. We get some sense of this examining Table 3, but the figure makes it far easier to notice this.

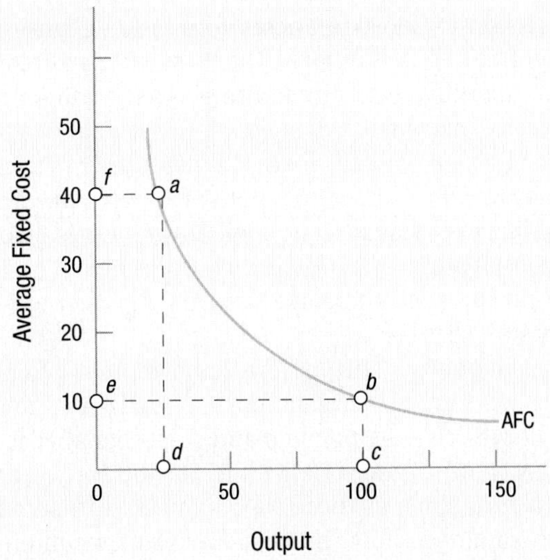

FIGURE 2

The Average Fixed Cost Curve

The average fixed cost (AFC) curve always decreases as production increases. This is because, in the short run, total fixed costs do not change, so that increasing production spreads the fixed costs over more units of output.

In Figure 3, the average variable cost curve reaches its minimum where 65 rigs are produced (point *c*). Since AVC = TVC/Q, then TVC = AVC × Q. Thus, at point *c*, TVC are equal to the rectangular area 0*ace*, or \$10,560 (\$162.46 × 65).

Average Total Cost (ATC)

Average total cost equals average fixed costs plus average variable cost (ATC = AFC + AVC). At an output of 65 rigs in Figure 3, ATC(*de*) = AFC(*ef*) + AVC(*ec*). (Note that *cd* = *ef*, since we are adding AFC to AVC to yield ATC.) We know that ATC = TC/Q, so TC = ATC × Q. Hence, when output is 65, ATC = \$177.85 and TC = \$11,560 (\$177.85 × 65), or the rectangular area 0*bde* in Figure 3.

It is important to note that TC, TFC, and TVC can be found for *any point* on their respective curves by multiplying the average cost at that point by the output produced.

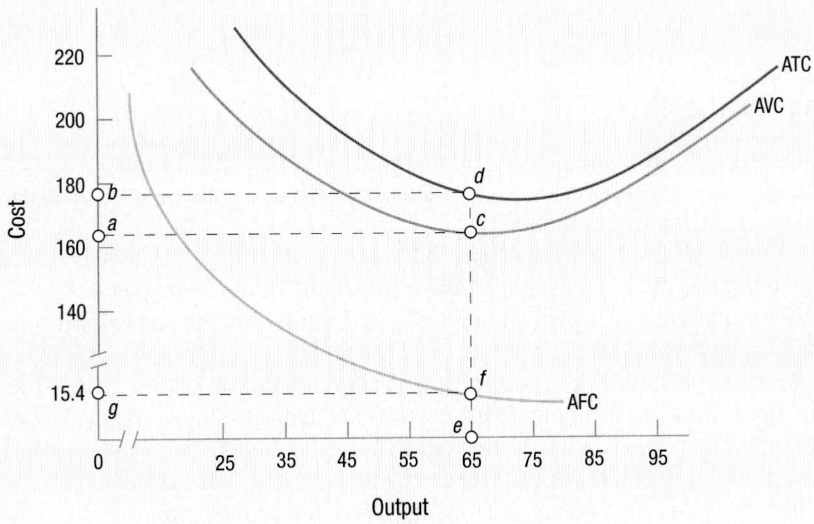

FIGURE 3

Average Total Cost, Average Variable Cost, and Average Fixed Cost

Curves for average total cost and average variable cost have been added to average fixed cost. The bowl shape of these curves demonstrates the law of diminishing returns: Beyond a certain level of output (65 units in this case) average variable costs increase. Total costs are equal to average total costs times output.

Marginal Cost (MC)

Drawing our discussion of short-run costs to a close, Figure 4 plots the marginal cost curve, adding it to the AVC and ATC curves we have plotted already.

Notice that the marginal cost curve intersects the minimum points of both the AVC and ATC curves. This is not a coincidence. Marginal cost is the cost necessary to produce another unit of a given product. When the cost to produce another unit is *less* than the average of the previous units produced, average costs will *fall*. For the AVC curve in Figure 4, this happens at all output levels below point *c* (65 units); for the ATC curve, it happens at all output levels below point *d* (75 units). But when the cost to produce another unit *exceeds* the average cost for all previous output, average costs will *rise*.

In Figure 4, this happens at output levels above point *c* for AVC and above point *d* for ATC. Over these ranges, marginal cost exceeds AVC and ATC, respectively, and thus the two curves rise. At points *c* and *d*, marginal cost is precisely equal to average variable cost and average total cost, respectively, and thus the AVC and ATC curves have a zero slope at these points, when intersecting the MC curve.

We have now examined short-run costs for firms when one factor, in this case plant size, is fixed. Let us now turn to costs in the long run, when all factors, including plant size, are variable.

FIGURE 4

Average Total Cost, Average Variable Cost, and Marginal Cost

Marginal costs represent the added cost of producing one more unit of output. Note that the marginal cost curve passes through the minimum points on both the AVC and ATC curves.

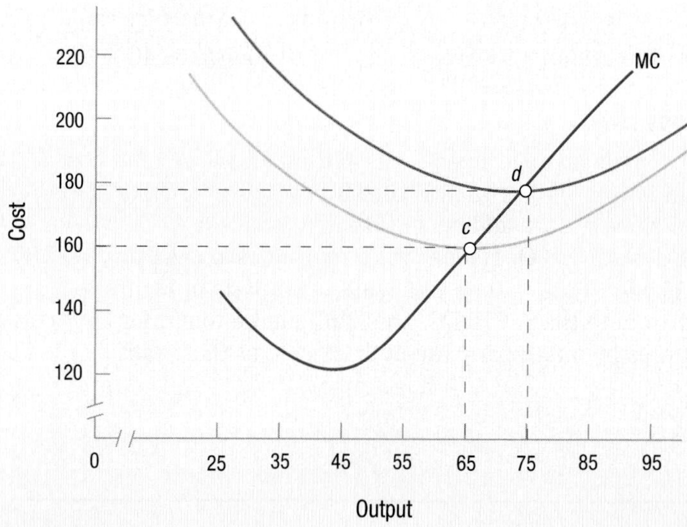

Long-Run Costs

In the long run, firms can adjust all factor inputs to meet the needs of the market. Here we will focus on variations in plant size, while recognizing that all other factors can vary, including technology.

Panel A of Figure 5 shows three different production functions for three different plant sizes. Plant 1 (TP_1) has fewer machines than either plants 2 or 3. As the number of machines rises, economies of scale come into play, as we will see, though only at higher levels of production.

At lower levels of production, the average costs for plants 2 and 3 are quite high, since they have higher fixed costs than plant 1—more expensive machines and more square feet of space to house these machines. This is shown in Panel B of Figure 5. For a small output, say Q_0, plant 1 produces for an average cost of AC_0 (point *b* in Panel B). Plant 2, with its additional overhead, can produce Q_0 output, but only for an average cost of AC_2 (point *a* in Panel B).

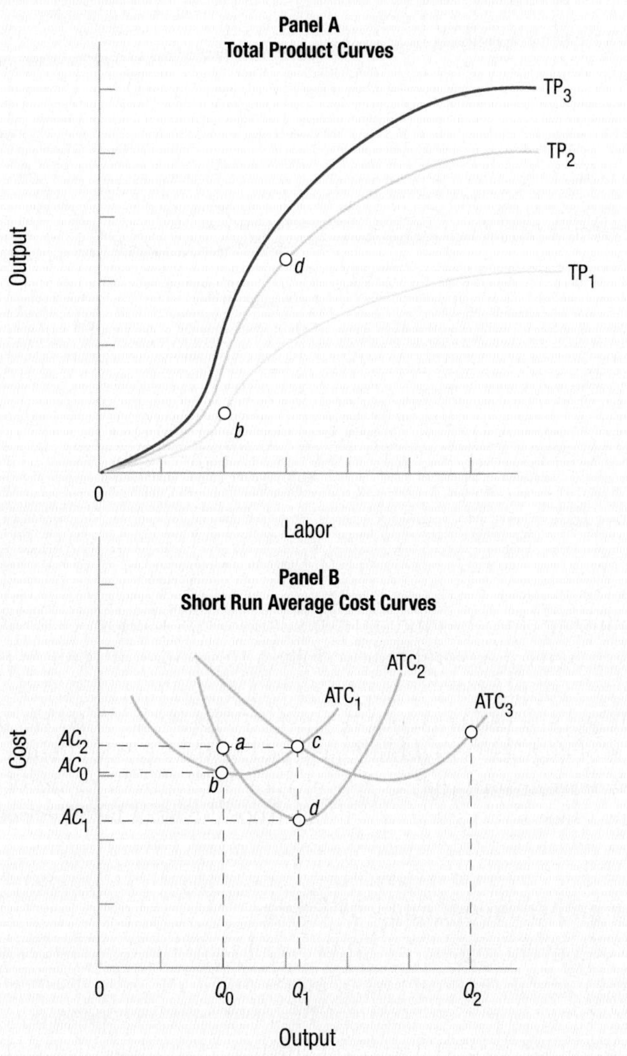

FIGURE 5

Total Product Curve and Various Short-Run Average Cost Curves

This figure shows the relationship between average total cost and plant size. In Panel A, Plant 1 (TP_1) has the fewest machines and the least output capacity; Plant 3 (TP_3) has the most equipment, or capital, and hence the most capacity. Panel B shows the average total cost curve for each of the three plants. The larger plants have relatively high average total costs at lower levels of output, but much lower average total costs at higher output levels.

Once output rises to Q_1, however, plant 2 begins to enjoy the benefits of economies of scale. The additional machines mean that plant 2 can produce Q_1 for AC_1 (point *d*), whereas the machines in plant 1 get overwhelmed at this level of output, resulting in an average cost of AC_2 (point *c*). Similarly, if a firm expects market demand eventually to reach Q_2, it would want to build plant 3 because plants 1 and 2 are too small to efficiently accommodate that level of production.

Long-Run Average Total Cost

The **long-run average total cost (LRATC)** curve represents the lowest unit cost at which any specific output can be produced in the long run, when a firm is able to adjust the size of its plant. Figure 6 on the next page is equivalent to Panel B of Figure 5. In this figure, the LRATC curve is indicated by the darkened segments of the various short-run cost curves; these are the segments of each curve where output can be produced at the lowest per unit cost. In short, the concept of LRATC assumes that, in the long run, firms will build plants of the size best fitting the levels of output they wish to produce.

Long-run average total cost (LRATC)
In the long run, firms can adjust their plant sizes so LRATC is the lowest unit cost at which any particular output can be produced in the long run.

While the LRATC curve in Figure 6 is relatively bumpy, it will tend to smooth out as more plant size options are considered. In some industries, such as agriculture and food service, the options for plant size and production methods are

FIGURE 6

The Long-Run Average Total Cost Curve

This figure shows the long-run average total cost (LRATC) for three plants. Firms are free to adjust plant size in the long run, so they can switch from one plant type to the next to minimize their costs at each production level. The heavy envelope curve represents the LRATC.

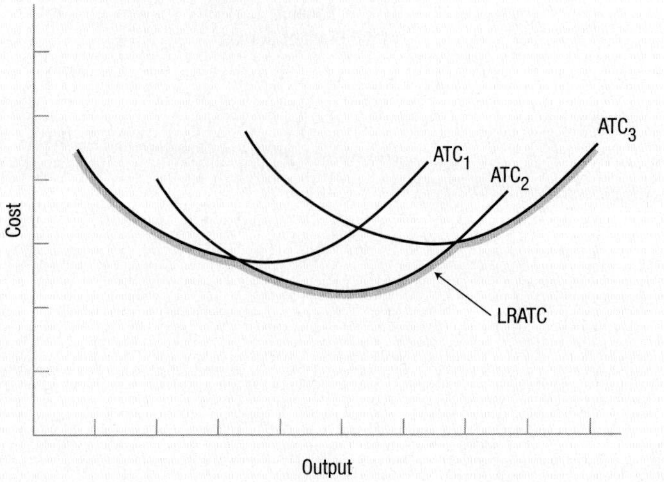

virtually unlimited. In other industries, such as semiconductors, however, sophisticated plants may cost several billion dollars to build and require being run at near capacity to be cost effective.

These huge, sophisticated plants are so complex that Intel Corporation has dedicated teams of engineers that build new plants and operate them exactly as all others. These teams ensure that any new plant is a virtual clone of the firm's other operating facilities. Even small deviations from this standard have proven disastrous in the past.

Economies and Diseconomies of Scale

Economies of scale
As a firm's output increases, its LRATC tends to decline. This results from specialization of labor and management, and potentially a better use of capital and complementary production techniques.

As a firm's output increases, its LRATC will tend to decrease. This is because, as the firm grows in size, **economies of scale** result from such items as specialization of labor and management, better use of capital, and increased possibilities for making several products that utilize complementary production techniques.

A larger firm's ability to have workers specialize on particular tasks reduces the costs associated with shifting workers from one task or another. Similarly, management in larger operations can use technologies not available to smaller firms, for instance, computers to remotely supervise workers. It is true that today's powerful personal computer networks have begun to narrow the gap in this arena. Larger firms, though, can still afford to purchase larger, more specialized capital equipment, whereas smaller firms must often rely on more labor-intensive methods. This equipment typically requires large production runs to be efficient, and only larger firms with correspondingly large marketing efforts can generate the sales necessary to satisfy these production volume requirements. Finally, larger firms are better able to engage in complementary production and use by-products more effectively.

The area for *economies of scale* is shown in Figure 7 as levels of output below Q_0 (average costs are falling).

Constant returns to scale
A range of output where average total costs are relatively constant. Fast-food restaurants and movie theatres are examples.

In many industries, there is a wide range of output where average total costs are relatively constant. Examples include fast-food restaurants, upscale restaurants such as Outback Steakhouse, and automotive service operations such as Jiffy Lube. Such businesses tend to have steady average costs because the cost to replicate their business in any community is relatively constant. Constructing and running a Dairy Queen franchise, for example, costs roughly the same no matter where it is operated. In Figure 7, this area of **constant returns to scale** is represented by output levels between Q_0 and Q_1.

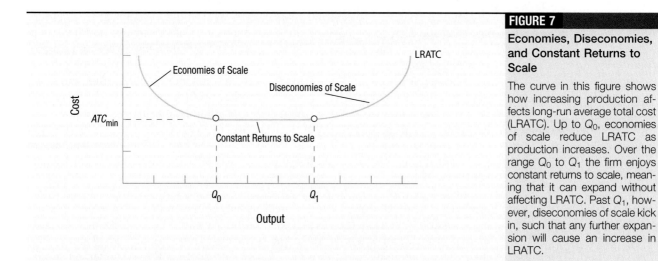

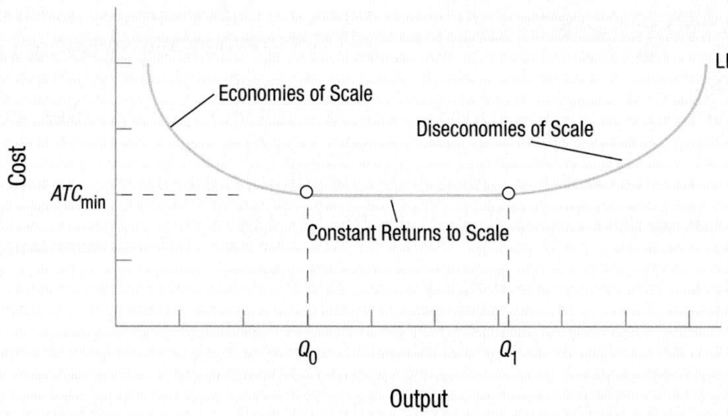

FIGURE 7

Economies, Diseconomies, and Constant Returns to Scale

The curve in this figure shows how increasing production affects long-run average total cost (LRATC). Up to Q_0, economies of scale reduce LRATC as production increases. Over the range Q_0 to Q_1 the firm enjoys constant returns to scale, meaning that it can expand without affecting LRATC. Past Q_1, however, diseconomies of scale kick in, such that any further expansion will cause an increase in LRATC.

As firms continue to grow, they eventually encounter **diseconomies of scale**. At some point, the firm gets so big that management is unable to efficiently control its operations. Some firms become so big that they get bogged down in bureaucracy and cannot make decisions quickly. In the 1980s, IBM fell into this trap—slow to react to changing market conditions for mainframe, mini, and microcomputers, the company was left behind by smaller, sleeker competition. Only through downsizing, reorganizing, refocusing, and a management change did IBM get back on track in the 1990s. Diseconomies of scale—the area where increased output increases costs disproportionately—are shown at outputs above Q_1 in Figure 7.

Diseconomies of scale
A range of output where average total costs tend to increase. Firms often become so big that management becomes bureaucratic and unable to efficiently control its operations.

Economies of Scope

When firms produce a number of products, it is often cheaper for them to produce another product when the production processes are interdependent. These economies are called **economies of scope**. For example, once a company has established a marketing department, it can take on the campaign of a new product at lower costs. It has developed the expertise and contacts necessary to sell the product. Book publishers can introduce a new book into the market more quickly and cheaply, and with more success than can a new firm starting in the business.

Economies of scope
By producing a number of products that are interdependent, firms are able to produce and market these goods at lower costs.

Some firms generate ideas for products, then send the production overseas. After they have been through this process, they become more efficient. Economists refer to this as *learning by doing.* Economies of scope often play a role in mergers as firms look for other firms with complementary products and skills.

Role of Technology

We know that technology creates products that were the domain of science fiction writers of the past. Dick Tracy's wrist radio, first introduced in the comics of 1940s, has now morphed into the many wireless products we see today.

But we should mention in passing the role technology plays in altering the shape of the LRATC curve. The output level where diseconomies of scale are reached has significantly and continuously expanded since the beginning of the industrial revolution.

Enhanced production techniques, instantaneous global communication, and the use of computers in accounting and cost control are just a few recent examples of ways in which technology has permitted firms to increase their scale beyond what anyone had imagined possible 50 years earlier. Who would have imagined a century ago that one firm could have hundreds of thousands of employees and billions of dollars in annual sales? Today, IBM has more than 300,000 employees and sales of over $80 billion.

What spurs firms and entrepreneurs to develop new technologies and bring new products to market? Three words: profits, profits, and profits. In this chapter, we took a large step in analyzing where profits come from by looking at what firms do, how they measure profits, and how they determine the production and cost side of the profit equation. In the next chapter, we will look at revenues, as well as examine how firms can maximize their profits by adjusting output to market demand.

Before we leave this chapter, it would not be amiss to dwell on the role of entrepreneurs. The dynamism in all economies usually comes from entrepreneurs searching for market needs so they can make a profit. We saw a little of this at the beginning of this chapter when we looked at Starbucks. There are individuals known for their entrepreneurial spirit; there are businesses such as those connected to Silicon Valley in California that encourage entrepreneurial activities; and there are businesses that stifle this spirit. Let us close this chapter by looking at Apple's iPod and iTunes network.

Radius/Jupiter Images

Innovation and the Development of the iPod

Your grandmother may have one of those big, heavy radios that were so popular in the 1950s. If you removed the back, you would see a bunch of vacuum tubes. Manufacturers sought to increase the power of each vacuum tube, or get more tubes into the back of each radio. In the early 1960s, Akio Morita of Sony developed the transistor radio, a flimsy-looking yet portable handheld radio that could be taken with you wherever you went. The old-style radio manufacturers pooh-poohed the Sony transistor radio, saying that it was cheap and looked cheap. Maybe more importantly, the manufacturers were bothered aesthetically by the transistor radio: It just was not as elegant as the radio box. Consumers thought otherwise, and the transistor radio was a big hit. And the transistor radio begat the Sony Discman. And the Discman probably had a role in inspiring the creation of the iPod.

The iPod moved consumers away from albums to individual songs. As the iPod, iPhone and Microsoft's Zune develop, these devices' capabilities are being expanded to carry music, video, cell service, email, PDA functionality, and so on. So when you are walking along listening to your iPod, or using your iPhone consider for a moment how entrepreneurs searching for market needs in the hope of generating profits create these new products for you.

Checkpoint

Costs of Production

REVIEW

- Fixed costs (overhead) are those costs that do not vary with output, including lease payments and insurance. Fixed costs occur in the short run—in the long run, firms can change plant and even exit an industry.
- Variable costs rise and fall as a firm produces more or less output. These include raw materials, labor, and utilities.
- Total cost equals total fixed cost plus total variable cost (TC = TFC + TVC).

- Average total cost equals total cost divided by output (ATC = TC/Q).
- Average fixed cost is total fixed cost divided by output (AFC = TFC/Q).
- Average variable cost is total variable cost divided by output (AVC = TVC/Q).
- Marginal cost is the change in total cost divided by the change in output (MC = ΔTC/ΔQ).
- Because total fixed cost does not change with output in the short run, then marginal cost is just the change in total variable cost divided by the change in output (MC = ΔTVC/ΔQ).
- The long-run average total cost curve (LRATC) represents the lowest unit cost at which specific output can be produced in the long run. Remember, firms can vary plant size in the long run, so this curve incorporates different plants to achieve the lowest average cost for a given level of output.
- As a firm grows in size, economies of scale result from specialization of labor, better use of capital, and the potential to produce many different products using complementary techniques.
- Diseconomies of scale occur because a firm gets so big that management loses control of its operations, and the firm becomes bogged down in bureaucracy.
- Economics of scope result when firms produce a number of interdependent products, so it is cheaper for them to add another product to the line.
- Modern communications and computers have permitted firms to become huge before diseconomies are reached.

QUESTION

In the late 1990s, Boeing reported that it takes roughly 12 years and $15 billion to bring a new aircraft from the design stage to a test flight. Boeing signed a 20-year exclusive agreement to supply aircraft to Delta, American, and Continental Airlines. The rationale for the agreement was that every time production of the plane doubled, a fifth was cut off the cost of the plane to the commercial airlines.[4] Why would doubling production cut costs by 20%?

Answers to the Checkpoint question can be found at the end of this chapter.

Key Concepts

[4]"Peace in our Time," *The Economist,* July 26,1997.

Chapter Summary

Firms, Profits, and Economic Costs

Firms produce the products and services we consume. *Firms* are economic institutions that transform inputs (factors of production) into outputs (products and services).

It is entrepreneurs who provide goods and services to the market. Entrepreneurs are organized into three basic business structures: sole proprietorships, partnerships, and corporations.

A *sole proprietorship* is composed of one owner who usually supervises the business's operation. Sole proprietorships are easily established and managed, but proprietors are limited in their ability to raise capital and their personal assets are subject to unlimited liability.

A *partnership* is similar to a sole proprietorship, except that it has more than one owner. Partnerships can raise capital easier and spread around the management responsibilities, but as with sole proprietors, partners are subject to unlimited liability for the entire partnership.

Corporations are the premier form of business organization in most of the world. Corporations possess most of the legal rights of individuals, and in addition, they are able to issue stock to raise capital. Most significantly, the liability of individual owners (stockholders) is limited to the amount they have invested in the stock.

Profits comprise the difference between total revenue and total costs. Firms are assumed to seek to maximize their profits. Although other assumptions about the goals of firms are possible, profit maximization is the typical assumption that economists use.

Economic costs are separated into *explicit* (out-of-pocket) and *implicit* (opportunity) costs. Explicit costs are those costs paid to some other entity. They include wages, lease expenses, taxes, and so on. Implicit costs include those items where the firm does not directly pay others, but still incurs a cost. These costs include the depreciation and depletion of company assets, as well as the cost of the capital the firm employs. Sunk costs are expenses that have been incurred and are not recoverable.

Economists define a *normal return* as that return on capital that keeps investors willing to invest their capital in an industry over the long run. Firms earning just this level of profit are said to be earning normal profits. Firms earning more than this are earning *economic profits,* and firms earning less are taking *economic losses.*

The *short run* is a period of time during which at least one factor of production is fixed, usually plant capacity. Firms can vary output in the short run by hiring more labor or changing other variable factors. In the *long run,* firms are able to vary all factors, including plant size. Moreover, existing firms can leave the industry and new firms can enter.

Production in the Short Run

In the short run, firms can vary the output they produce by varying their labor inputs. The *total product curve* relates labor inputs to outputs. *Marginal product* is the change in output resulting from a change in labor input ($\Delta Q/\Delta L$). Marginal product is thus the change in output associated with hiring one additional worker. *Average product* or output per worker is equal to total output divided by labor input (Q/L).

Typical production functions exhibit both increasing and decreasing returns. When *increasing returns* are present, each additional worker adds more to total output than previous workers. This can occur because of specialization, for instance. All production is eventually subject to the *law of diminishing returns,* whereby additional workers add less and less to total output.

Costs of Production

In the short run, firms have fixed and variable costs. *Fixed costs,* or overhead, are those costs the firm incurs whether it produces anything or not. These costs include administrative overhead, lease payments, and insurance. *Variable costs* are those costs that vary with output, such as wages, utilities, and raw materials costs. Total cost is equal to total fixed cost plus total variable cost (TC = TFC + TVC).

Average total cost (ATC) represents cost per unit of total production, or TC/Q. *Average fixed cost* (AFC) is equal to TFC/Q, and *average variable cost* (AVC) is equal to TVC/Q. Consequently, ATC = AFC + AVC. *Marginal cost* (MC) is the change in total cost associated with producing one additional unit. Since fixed cost does not change in the short run (ΔTFC = 0), marginal cost is equal to the change in variable costs when one additional unit is produced; hence, MC = ΔTVC/ΔQ.

In the long run, all factors of production are variable, and firms can enter or leave the industry. The *long-run average total cost* curve (LRATC) represents the lowest unit costs for any specific output level in the long run. *Economies of scale* associated with larger firm size result from such factors as specialization in labor and management. As a firm grows, the average cost of production falls. Eventually, however, a firm will encounter *diseconomies of scale* when its size becomes so large that efficient management becomes impossible. At this point, average costs begin to rise. Today, advanced computer and communications technologies have radically increased the size of firms that can be efficiently managed. Economies of scope result from the ability of firms producing many interdependent products to add another at substantially lower costs.

Questions and Problems

1. What is the difference between explicit and implicit costs? What is the difference between economic and accounting profits? Are these four concepts related? How?

2. Using the table below, answer the following questions.

Labor	Output	Marginal Product	Average Product
0	0	______	______
1	7	______	______
2	15	______	______
3	25	______	______
4	33	______	______
5	40	______	______
6	45	______	______

a. Complete the table, filling in the answers for marginal and average products.
b. Over how many workers is the firm enjoying increasing returns?
c. At what number of workers do diminishing returns set in?
d. Are negative returns shown in the table?

3. How does the short run differ from the long run? Is the long run the same for all industries? Why or why not?

4. Use the table below to answer the following questions. Assume that fixed costs are $100 and labor is paid $80 per unit (employee).

L	Q	MP	AP	TFC	TVC	TC	ATC	AVC	AFC	MC
0	0	___	___	___	___	___	___	___	___	___
1	7	___	___	___	___	___	___	___	___	___
2	15	___	___	___	___	___	___	___	___	___
3	25	___	___	___	___	___	___	___	___	___
4	40	___	___	___	___	___	___	___	___	___
5	45	___	___	___	___	___	___	___	___	___
6	48	___	___	___	___	___	___	___	___	___
7	50	___	___	___	___	___	___	___	___	___

a. Complete the table.
b. Graph ATC, AVC, AFC, and MC on a piece of graph paper.

5. Skype, the Internet phone company, uses peer-to-peer network principles to enable people to make free phone calls over the Internet anywhere in the world. Skype forwards calls through users' computers without having any central infrastructure. Users agree to let their computer's excess capacity be used as transfer nodes. In this way, Skype does not have to invest in more infrastructure as it adds users, and the system is highly robust and scalable. What is the marginal cost to Skype to add another user to its system?

6. List some of the reasons why the long-run average total cost curve has sort of a flat bowl shape. It declines early on, then is rather flat over a portion, and finally slopes upward.

7. The Finger Lakes region in New York State produces wine. The climate favors white wines, but reds have been produced successfully in the past 15 years. Categorize the following costs incurred by one winery as either fixed or variable:
a. the capital used to buy 60 acres of land on Lake Seneca
b. the machine used to pick some varieties of grapes at the end of August and the beginning of September
c. the salary of the chief vintner, who is employed year-round
d. the wages paid to workers who bind the grape plants, usually in April, and usually over a period of 3 to 4 days
e. the wages paid to the same workers who pick the grapes at the end of August or early September
f. the costs of the chemicals sprayed on the grapes in July
g. the wages of the wine expert who blends the wine in August and September, after the grapes have been picked
h. the cost of the building where wine tastings take place from April to October
i. the cost of the wine used in the wine tasting

8. How do accounting profits and economic profits differ?

9. Why should sunk costs be ignored for decision making?

10. Why is the average fixed cost curve not bowl-shaped, so it eventually turns up like the average variable and average total cost curves?

11. What is the difference between average total cost and average variable cost?

12. If marginal cost is less than average total cost, are average total costs rising or falling? Alternatively, if marginal cost is more than average total cost, are average total costs rising or falling? Give an example outside of economics to explain your answer.

13. Describe how marginal cost is related to marginal product.

14. Economies of scope occur in big organizations with diversified product lines where innovation in one area feeds into others. In his book, *An Army of Davids,* Glen Reynolds argued that "The balance of advantage—in nearly every aspect of society—is shifting from big organizations to small ones. Economies of scale and scope matter much less in the information age than in the industrial one" (published by Nelson Current, 2006).[5] Does this statement seem a little over the top? Why or why not?

15. After the Enron and other business scandals in the early 2000s, the United States passed the Sarbanes-Oxley Act, adding a number of rules and reporting requirements for U.S. corporations. The business community argues that these reporting requirements are extremely costly and cumbersome with only minimal benefit. Most companies, they argue, were not engaged in illegal or unethical behavior, and they are being punished because of a few. One apparent impact of this law is that in 2005, "of the top 25 global initial public offerings (when companies first offer their stock to the general market for purchase), only one was in the United States."[6] This is business lost to the New York Stock Exchange (NYSE) and NASDAQ. Are these kinds of compliance costs established by Sarbanes-Oxley fixed or variable costs? Why would firms care so much about these regulations? Can we expect to see the NYSE and NASDAQ try to buy or merge with other foreign stock exchanges in the near future?

Answers to Checkpoint Questions

CHECKPOINT: FIRMS, PROFITS, AND ECONOMIC COSTS

Buying an existing business has several benefits, including that the business has existing customers and a location. In addition, it will generate cash and profits immediately. One downside is that determining a fair price may be difficult and potentially more than you can afford. Starting your own firm will be cheaper in the beginning, but it involves doing everything from scratch. It typically takes 3 to 4 years for a firm to get a good foothold into the market.

CHECKPOINT: PRODUCTION IN THE SHORT RUN

Microsoft may well have reached diminishing returns with the Office product. Many firms with a large number of users have been reluctant to upgrade, given the licensing costs and the added training required. The bigger and more complex Office becomes, the more it is best suited for specialized professional jobs, not for the majority of the market. Some have suggested that Microsoft's focus on future

[5]Quote is from Adrian Wooldridge, "Small is Powerful," *Wall Street Journal,* March 26, 2006, p. D7.
[6]Jane Sasseen and Joseph Weber, "Taking Their Business Elsewhere," *Business Week,* May 22, 2006, pp. 33–34.

products may need to concentrate on ease of use, although its word processor is relatively easy to use even though it has a lot of power. Yes, the Web-based word processors and other open office programs are a threat to the domination of this market by Microsoft.

CHECKPOINT: COSTS OF PRODUCTION

This immense $15 billion development cost is spread over more planes, and rising volume creates economies. Producing commercial aircraft has huge economies of scale and scope.

8 Competition

In his classic economic treatise, *The Wealth of Nations,* Adam Smith wrote of a "hidden hand" that guides businesses in their pursuit of self-interest, or profits, allowing only the efficient to survive. Some observers have noted similarities between Smith's work, written in 1776, and Charles Darwin's *Origin of Species,* published in 1872. The late biologist and zoologist Stephen Jay Gould wrote that "the theory of natural selection is, in essence, Adam Smith's economics transferred to nature," and that Darwin's account of the struggle for existence and reproductive success is the same "causal scheme applied to nature" as Smith's account of the competitive market.[1] Clearly, the notions of competition and the competitive market have played a prominent role in the history of ideas. In this chapter, we will explore some of the implications competition has for markets and consider why the competitive market structure is so central to the thinking of economists. What you learn in this chapter will give you a benchmark to use when we consider other market structures in the following chapters.

Being engaged in stiff competition is the norm for lawn care companies, retail stores, Internet service providers, and restaurants. Large firms such as General Electric or Berkshire Hathaway compete in many different markets, but some smaller firms, for example, the local newspaper or an oral surgeon, have only a few competitors. Firms specializing in standard products such as lumber, fertilizer, and cement tend to face stiff competition, while those focusing on unique services such as stained glass restoration, Web design, or organ transplants tend to have fewer competitors.

To economists, *competition* means more than just competing against one or two other firms. The model of competition in this chapter focuses on an idealized market structure containing so many small businesses that any one firm's behavior

[1]Stephen Jay Gould, *The Structure of Evolutionary Theory* (Cambridge, MA: Belknap Press of Harvard University Press), 2002, pp. 121–125.

is irrelevant to its competitors. Firms in this competitive climate lack discretion over pricing and must perform efficiently merely to survive.

In this and the next two chapters, keep in mind the profitability equation developed in the previous chapter. Profits equal total revenues minus total costs. Total revenues equal price times quantity sold. So keep in mind the three items that determine profitability: price, quantity, and cost. In the next three chapters, we will see how firms try to control each one of these.

After studying this chapter you should be able to

- Name the primary market structures and describe their characteristics.
- Define a competitive market and the assumptions that underlie it.
- Distinguish the differences between competitive markets in the short run and the long run.
- Analyze the conditions for profit maximization, loss minimization, and plant shutdown for a firm.
- Derive the firm's short-run supply curve.
- Use the short-run competitive model to determine long-run equilibrium.
- Describe why competition is in the public interest.

Market Structure Analysis

Market structure analysis By observing a few industry characteristics, such as number of firms in the industry, the level of barriers to entry, and so on, economists can use this information to predict pricing and output behavior of the firm in the industry.

To appreciate intensely competitive markets, we need to look at competition within the full range of possible market structures. Economists use **market structure analysis** to categorize industries based on a few key characteristics. By simply knowing simple industry facts, economists can predict the behavior of firms in that industry in such areas as pricing and sales.

Below are the four factors defining the intensity of competition in an industry and a few questions to give you some sense of the issues behind each one of these factors:

- **Number of firms in the industry:** Is the industry composed of many firms, each with limited or no ability to set the market price, such as local pizza places, or is it dominated by a large firm such as Wal-Mart that can influence price regardless of the number of other firms?
- **Nature of the industry's product:** Are we talking about a homogeneous product such as salt for which no consumer will pay a premium, or are we considering leather handbags (Coach, Gucci) where consumers may think that some firms produce better goods than other firms?
- **Barriers to entry:** Does the industry require low start-up and maintenance costs such as found in a roadside fruit and vegetable stand, or is it a computer-chip business that may require a billion dollars to build a new chip plant?
- **Extent to which individual firms can control prices:** For example, pharmaceutical companies can set prices for new medicines, at least for a set period of time, because of patent protection. Farmers and copper producers have virtually no control and get their prices from world markets.

Possible market structures range from competition, characterized by many firms, to monopoly, where an industry contains only one firm. These market structures will make more sense to you as we consider each one in the chapters ahead. Right now, use the list on the previous page and the descriptions below as reference points. You can always come back to this point and put the discussion in context.

Primary Market Structures

The primary market structures economists have identified, along with their key characteristics, are as follows:

Competition

- Many buyers and sellers
- Homogeneous (standardized) products
- No barriers to market entry or exit
- No long-run economic profits
- No control over price

Monopolistic Competition

- Many buyers and sellers
- Differentiated products
- No barriers to market entry or exit
- No long-run economic profits
- Some control over price

Oligopoly

- Fewer firms (such as the auto industry)
- Mutually interdependent decisions
- Substantial barriers to market entry
- Potential for long-run economic profits
- Shared market power and considerable control over price

Monopoly

- One firm
- No close substitutes for product
- Nearly insuperable barriers to entry
- Potential for long-run economic profit
- Substantial market power and control over price

Putting off discussion of the other market structures for later chapters, we turn to an extended examination of the requirements for a competitive market. In the remainder of this chapter, we explore short-run pricing and output decisions, and also the importance of entry and exit in the long run. Moreover, we will use the conditions of competition to establish a benchmark for efficiency as we turn to evaluate other market structures in the following chapters.

Defining Competitive Markets

Competition
Exists when there are many relatively small buyers and sellers, a standardized product, with good information to both buyers and sellers, and no barriers to entry or exit.

The theory of **competition** rests on the following assumptions:

1. Competitive markets have many buyers and sellers, each of them so small that none can individually influence product price.

2. Firms in the industry produce a homogeneous or standardized product.
3. Buyers and sellers have all the information about prices and product quality they need to make informed decisions.
4. Barriers to entry or exit are insignificant in the long run; new firms are free to enter the industry if so doing appears profitable, while firms are free to exit if they anticipate losses.

Price taker
Individual firms in competitive markets get their prices from the market since they are so small they cannot influence market price. For this reason, competitive firms are price takers and can produce and sell all the output they produce at market determined prices.

One implication of these assumptions is that competitive firms are **price takers**. Market prices are determined by market forces beyond the control of individual firms. That is, firms must simply take what they can get for their products. Paper for copy machines, most agricultural products, DRAMs (dynamic random access memory chips), and many other goods are produced in highly competitive markets. The buyers or sellers in these markets are so small that their ability to influence market price is nil. These firms must simply accept whatever price the market determines, leaving them to decide only how much of the product to produce or buy.

Panel A of Figure 1 portrays the supply and demand for wind surfing sails in a competitive market; the market is in equilibrium at price $200 and industry output Q_e. Remember that this product is a standardized sail (similar to two-by-four lumber, crude oil, and DRAMs) and that the market contains many buyers and sellers, who collectively set the product price at $200.

Panel B shows the demand for a seller's products in this market. The firm can sell all it wants at $200 or below. Yet, what firm would set its price below $200 when it can sell everything it produces at $200? Were the firm to set its price above $200, however, it would sell nothing. What consumer, after all, would purchase a standardized sail at a higher price when it can be obtained elsewhere for $200? The individual firm's demand curve is horizontal at $200. The firm can still determine how much of its product to produce and sell, but this is the only choice it has. The firm cannot set its own price, therefore it is a *price taker.*

Recall the profitability equation. Profits equal total revenues minus total costs. Total revenues equal price times quantity sold. In competitive markets, a firm's profitability is based on a given market price, quantity sold, and its costs. So how does it determine how much to sell?

FIGURE 1

The Market for Competitive Products with an Equilibrium Price of $200

Panel A shows a market for standardized wind surfing sails in equilibrium at price $200 and industry output Q_e. This price is determined by the market's many buyers and sellers. Panel B illustrates product demand for an individual seller. The individual firm can sell all it wants to at $200 and has no reason to set its price below that. If it tries to sell at prices higher than $200, it sells nothing. The demand curve for the individual firm is horizontal at $200.

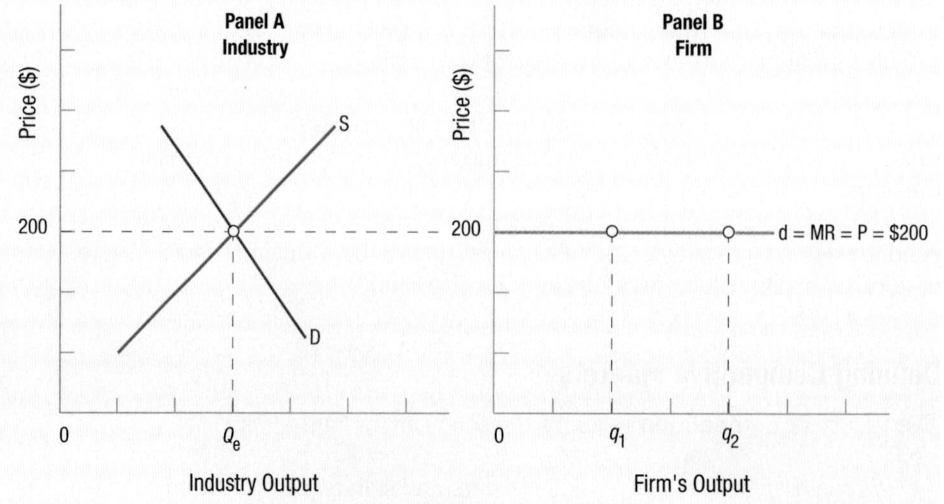

The Short Run and the Long Run (A Reminder)

Before turning to a more detailed examination of how firms decide how much output to produce in a competitive market, we need to recall a distinction introduced in the last chapter between the *short run* and the *long run.*

Again, in the *short run,* one factor of production is fixed, usually the firm's plant size, and firms cannot enter or leave an industry. Thus, in the short run, the number of firms in a market is fixed. Firms may earn economic profits, break even, or suffer losses, but still they cannot exit the industry, nor can new firms enter.

In the *long run,* all factors are variable, and thus the level of profits will induce entry or exit. When losses prevail, some firms will leave the industry and invest their capital elsewhere. When economic profits are positive, new firms will enter the industry. The long run is far more dynamic than the short run.

Checkpoint

Market Structure Analysis

REVIEW

- Market structure analysis allows economists to categorize industries based on a few characteristics and use this analysis to predict pricing behavior.
- The intensity of competition is defined by the number of firms in the industry, the nature of the industry's product, the level of barriers to entry, and how much firms can control prices.
- Market structures range from competition (many buyers and sellers), to monopolistic competition (differentiated product), to oligopoly (only a few firms that are interdependent), to monopoly (a one-firm industry).
- Competition is defined by four attributes: Many buyers and sellers who are so small that none individually can influence price, firms that produce and sell a homogeneous (standardized) product, buyers and sellers who have all the information necessary to make informed decisions, and barriers to entry and exit that are insignificant.
- Firms in competitive markets get the product price from national or global markets. Therefore, competitive firms are price takers.
- In the short run, one factor (usually plant size) is fixed. In the long run, all factors are variable, and firms can enter or leave the industry.

QUESTIONS

Wal-Mart is a huge international firm with over 1,500,000 employees worldwide with sales of many billions of dollars. Where does Wal-Mart fit in our market structure approach? Microsoft? Starbucks? Toyota?

Answers to the Checkpoint questions can be found at the end of this chapter.

Competition: Short-Run Decisions

Figure 1 represents a competitive market with an equilibrium price of $200. This translates into a demand curve for individual firms shown in Panel B. Individual firms are price takers in this competitive situation: They can sell as many units of their product as they wish at $200 each.

Marginal Revenue

Marginal revenue
The change in total revenue from selling an additional unit of output. Since competitive firms are price takers, P = MR for competitive firms.

Economists define **marginal revenue** as the change in total revenue that results from the sale of one added unit of a product. Marginal revenue (MR) is equal to the change in total revenue (ΔTR) over the change in quantity sold (Δq); thus,

$$\text{MR} = \Delta\text{TR}/\Delta q$$

Total revenue (TR), meanwhile, is equal to price per unit (p) times quantity sold (q); thus:

$$\text{TR} = p \times q$$

In a competitive market, we know that price will not change. And since marginal revenue is defined as the change in revenue that comes from selling one more unit, in a competitive market, marginal revenue is simply equal to price. The added revenue a competitive firm receives from selling another unit is product price, or \$200 in Figure 1. So determining marginal revenue in a competitive market is easy. As we will see in later chapters, this gets more complicated in market structures where firms have some control over price.

Profit Maximizing Output

Figure 2 shows the price and marginal cost curve for a firm seeking to maximize its profits. As the price and cost curve show, the firm can sell all it wants at \$200 a sail. Our first instinct might be to conclude that the firm will produce all it can, but this is not the case. Given the marginal cost curve shown in Figure 2, if the firm produces 85 units, profit will be less than the maximum possible. This is because revenue from the sale is \$200, but the 85th sail costs \$210 to produce (point *b*). This means producing this last sail reduces profits by \$10.

Assume the firm produces 84 sails. The revenue from selling the 84th unit (MR) is \$200. This is precisely equal to the added cost (MC) of producing this unit, \$200 (point *e*). Therefore, the firm earns zero economic profits by producing and selling the 84th sail. Zero economic profits or normal profits mean that the firm is earning a normal return on its capital by selling this 84th sail. If the firm starts producing

FIGURE 2

Profit Maximization in the Short Run in Competitive Markets

If the firm produces 85 standardized wind surfing sails, the marginal cost to produce the last sail exceeds the revenue from its sale, thus reducing the firm's profits. For the 84th unit produced, marginal cost and price are both equal to \$200, so the firm earns a normal return from producing this unit. Producing only 83 units means relinquishing the profit that could have been earned from the 84th sail. Hence, the firm will maximize profits at an output of 84 (point *e*) where MC = MR = P = \$200.

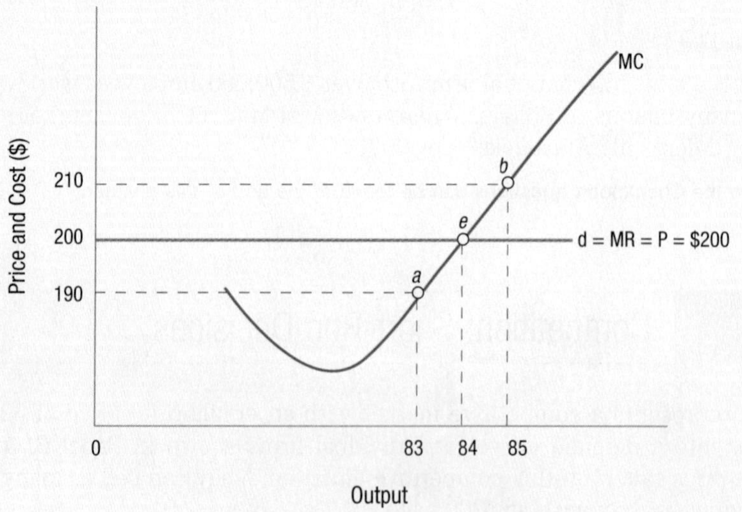

only 83 sails, however, the additional cost (point *a*) will be less than the price, and the firm will have to relinquish the normal return associated with the 84th sail. Profits from selling 83 sails will therefore be lower than if 84 sails are sold because the normal return on the 84th sail is lost.

These observations lead us to a **profit maximizing rule**: *A firm maximizes profit by continuing to produce and sell output until marginal revenue equals marginal cost (MR = MC).* As we will see in subsequent chapters, this rule applies to all firms, regardless of market structure.

Profit maximizing rule
Firms maximize profit by producing output where MR = MC. No other level of output produces higher profits.

Economic Profits

Let us return to our example from the previous chapter of your windsurfing sail manufacturing firm. We will assume the market has established a price of $200 for each sail. Your marginal revenue and cost curves are shown in Figure 3. (Incidentally, the MR and MC curves are the same as those shown in Figure 2.) Complete price, production, and cost data are shown in Table 1 on the next page.

Earlier, we found that profits are maximized when the firm is producing output such that MR = MC, in this case, 84 sails. As Table 1 shows, profit is $1,720 when 84 windsurfing sails are produced and sold at $200 a sail.

Looking at Figure 3, we see that profits are maximized at point *a*, because this is where MR = MC. (This also can be seen in Table 1, where marginal costs of $195.56 closely approximates marginal revenue of $200.00.) We can also compute the profit in this scenario by multiplying average profit (profit per unit) by output. Average profit equals price minus average total costs (P − ATC). Thus, when 84 sails are produced, average profit is the distance *ab* in Figure 3, or $200 − $179.52 = $20.48. Total profit, or average profit times output, is $20.48 × 84 = $1,720; this is represented in Figure 3 by area *cfab*.

Note that there *is* a profit maximizing point. The competitive firm cannot produce and produce—it has to take into consideration its costs. So for the price-taking competitive firm, its cost structure is crucial.

FIGURE 3

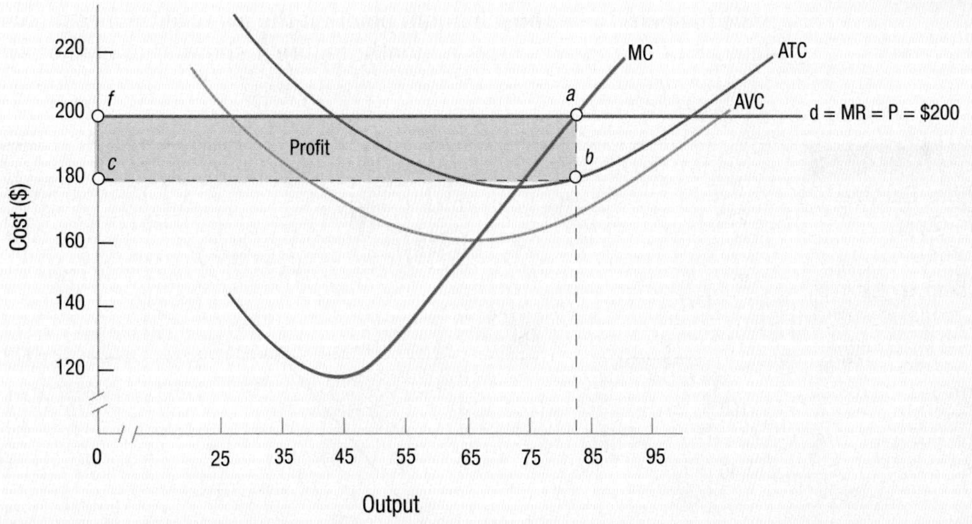

Competitive Firm Earning Economic Profits

The marginal revenue and cost curves derived from the data in Table 1 are shown here. As we can see, profits are maximized where MR = MC, or at an output of 84 and a price of $200. Price minus average total cost equals average profit per unit, represented by the distance *ab*. Average profit per unit times the number of units produced equals total profit; this is represented by area *cfab*.

Table 1 Production, Cost, and Price for Windsurfing Sail Firm

L	Q	MP	AP	TFC	TVC	TC	ATC	AVC	MC	AFC	P	TR	Profit
0	0	0		1000	0	1000					200.00	0	−1000
1	7	7	7.00	1000	1760	2760	394.29	251.43	251.43	142.86	200.00	1400	−1360
2	15	8	7.50	1000	3520	4520	301.33	234.67	220.00	66.67	200.00	3000	−1520
3	25	10	8.33	1000	5280	6280	251.20	211.20	176.00	40.00	200.00	5000	−1280
4	40	15	10.00	1000	7040	8040	201.00	176.00	117.33	25.00	200.00	8000	−40
5	54	14	10.80	1000	8800	9800	181.48	162.96	125.71	18.52	200.00	10800	1000
6	65	11	10.83	1000	10560	11560	177.85	162.46	160.00	15.38	200.00	13000	1440
7	75	10	10.71	1000	12320	13320	177.60	164.27	176.00	13.33	200.00	15000	1680
8	84	9	10.50	1000	14080	15080	179.52	167.62	195.56	11.90	200.00	16800	1720
9	90	6	10.00	1000	15840	16840	187.11	176.00	293.33	11.11	200.00	18000	1160
10	95	5	9.50	1000	17600	18600	195.79	185.26	352.00	10.53	200.00	19000	400
11	98	3	8.91	1000	19360	20360	207.76	197.55	586.67	10.20	200.00	19600	−760
12	100	2	8.33	1000	21120	22120	221.20	211.20	880.00	10.00	200.00	20000	−2120
13	98	−2	7.54	1000	22880	23880	243.67	233.47	−880.00	10.20	200.00	19600	−4280

Normal Profits

When the price of windsurfing sails is \$200, your firm earns economic profits. Consider what happens, however, when the market price falls to \$177.60 a sail. This price happens to be the minimum point on the average total cost curve, corresponding to an output of 75 rigs a month. Figure 4 shows that at the price of \$177.60,

FIGURE 4

Competitive Firm Earning Normal Profits (Zero Economic Profits)

If the market sets a price of \$177.60, the firm's demand curve is tangent to the minimum point on the ATC curve (point *e*). The best the firm can do under these circumstances is to earn normal profits on the sale of 75 windsurfing rigs.

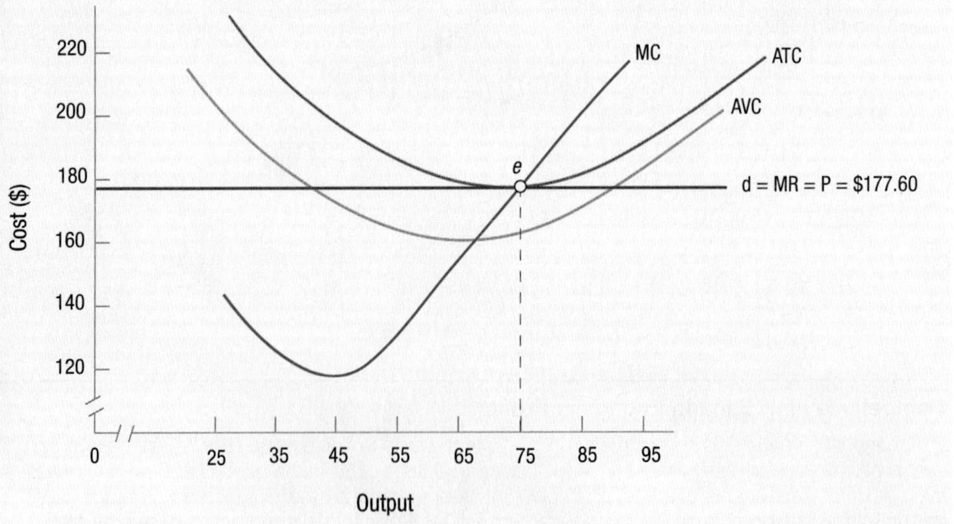

the firm's demand curve is just tangent to the minimum point on the ATC curve (point *e*), which means the distance between points *a* and *b* in Figure 3 has shrunk to zero. By producing 75 sails a month, your firm earns a normal profit, or zero economic profits.

Remember that when a firm earns zero economic profits, it is generating just enough income to keep investor capital in the business. When the typical firm in an industry is earning **normal profits**, there are no pressures for firms to enter or leave the industry. As we will see in a later section, this is an important factor in the long run.

Normal profits
Equal to zero economic profits and where P = ATC.

Loss Minimization and Plant Shutdown

Assume for a moment that an especially calm summer with few winds leads to a decline in the demand for windsurfing equipment. Assume also that, as a consequence, the price of windsurfing sails falls to $170. Figure 5 illustrates the impact on your firm. Market price has fallen below your average total costs of production, but remains above your average variable costs. Profit maximization—or, in this case, *loss minimization*—requires that you produce output at the level where MR = MC. That occurs at point *e,* where output falls somewhere between 65 and 75 units.

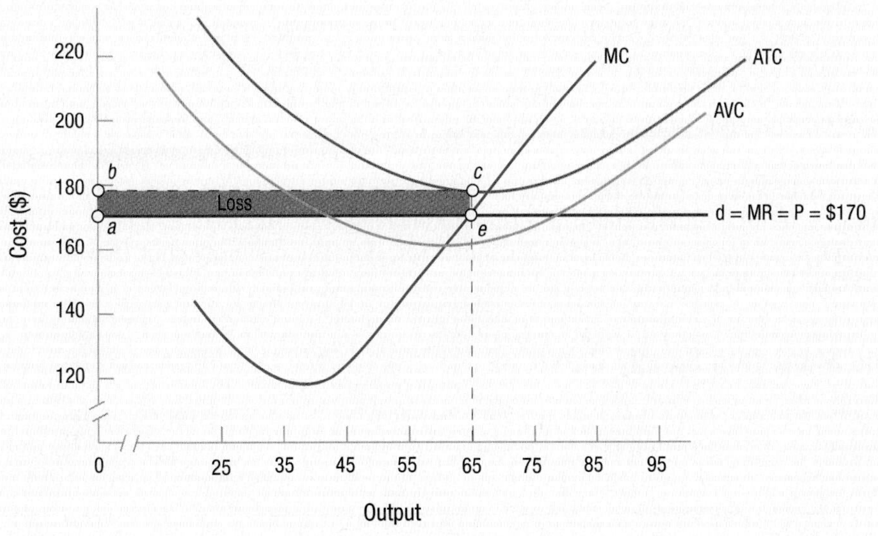

FIGURE 5

Competitive Firm Minimizing Losses

Assume that the price of windsurfing sails falls to $170 a sail. Loss minimization requires an output where MR = MC, in this case at 65 units (point *e*). Average total cost is $177.85 (point *c*) so loss per unit is equal to $7.85. Total loss is equal to $7.85 × 65 = $510.25. Notice that this is less than the fixed costs ($1,000) that would have to be paid even if the plant was closed.

For the sake of simplicity, we will assume you cannot hire a partial employee (ignoring the possibility of part-time workers). From Table 1, we know that producing 65 rigs requires 6 employees. Again referring to Table 1, average total cost at this production level is $177.85, so with a market price of $170, loss per unit is $7.85. The total loss on 65 units is $7.85 × 65 = $510.25, corresponding to area *abce* in Figure 5.

These results may look grim, but consider your alternatives. If you were to produce more or less sails, your losses would just mount. You could, for instance, furlough your employees. But you will still have to pay your fixed costs of $1,000, and without revenue, your losses would be $1,000. Therefore, it is better to produce and sell 65 rigs, taking a loss of $510.25, thereby cutting your losses nearly in half.

But what happens if the price of windsurfing sails falls to $162.50? Such a scenario is shown in Figure 6 on the next page. Your revenue from the sale of sails has fallen to a level just equal to variable costs. If you produce and sell 65 units of output (where MR = MC), you will be able to pay your employees their wages, but

FIGURE 6

Plant Shutdown in a Competitive Industry

When prices fall below $162.50, or below the minimum point of the AVC curve, losses begin to exceed fixed costs. The firm will shut its door if price falls below this minimum point (point *e*); this is the firm's shutdown point.

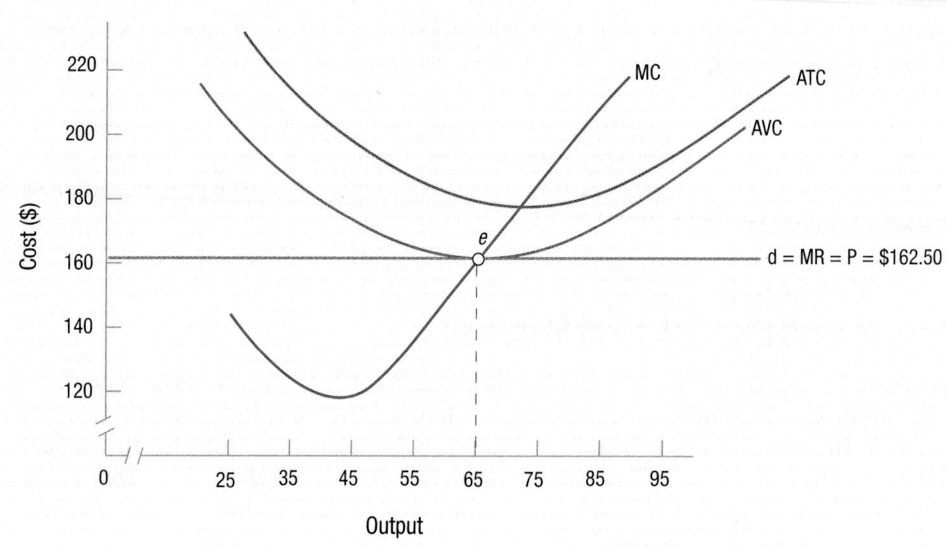

Shutdown point
When price in the short run falls below the minimum point on the AVC curve, the firm will minimize losses by closing its doors and stopping production. Since P < AVC, the firm's variable costs are not covered, so by shutting the plant, losses are reduced to fixed costs.

have nothing left over to pay your overhead; thus your loss will be $1,000. Point *e* in Figure 6 represents a **shutdown point**, since your firm will here be indifferent to whether it operates or shuts down—you lose $1,000 either way.

If prices continue to fall below $162.50 a sail, your losses will grow still further, because revenue will not even cover wages. Once prices drop below the minimum point on the AVC curve (point *e* in Figure 6), losses will exceed total fixed costs and your loss minimizing strategy must be to close the plant. It follows that the greatest loss a firm will be willing to suffer in the short term is equal to its total fixed costs. Remember that the firm cannot leave the industry at this point, since market participation is fixed in the short run, but it can simply shut down its plant and stop production.

The Short-Run Supply Curve

A glance at Figure 7 will help to summarize what we have learned so far. As we have seen, when a competitive firm is presented with a market price of P_0, corre-

FIGURE 7

The Short-Run Supply Curve for a Competitive Firm

If prices fall below P_0, the firm will shut its doors and produce nothing. For prices between P_0 and P_1, the firm will incur losses, but these losses will be less than fixed costs, so the firm will remain in operation and produce where MR = MC. At a price of P_1, the firm earns a normal return. If price should rise above P_1 (e.g., to P_2), the firm will earn economic profits by selling an output of q_2. The portion of the MC curve above the minimum point on the AVC curve, here darkened, is the firm's short-run supply curve.

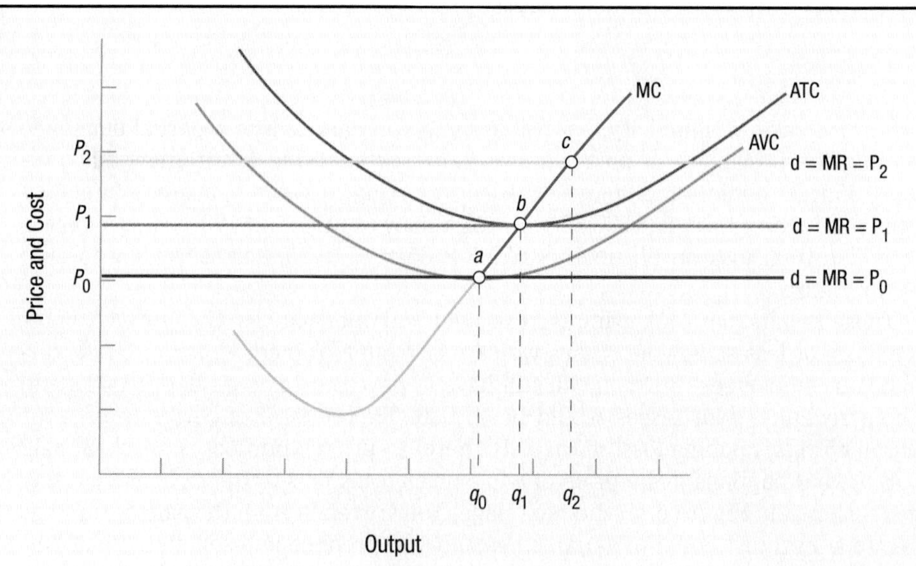

sponding to the minimum point on the AVC curve, the firm will produce output of q_0. If prices should fall below P_0, the firm will shut its doors and produce nothing. If, on the other hand, prices should rise to P_1, the firm will sell q_1 and earn normal profits (zero economic profits). And if prices continue climbing above P_1, say, to P_2, the firm will earn economic profits by selling q_2. In each instance, the firm produces and sells output where MR = MC.

From this quick summary, we can see that a firm's **short-run supply curve** is equivalent to the MC curve above the minimum point on the AVC curve. This curve, shown as the darkened part of the MC curve in Figure 7, shows how much the firm will supply to the market at various prices, keeping in mind that it will supply no output at prices below the shutdown point.

Short-run supply curve The marginal cost curve above the minimum point on the average variable cost curve.

Keep in mind also that the short-run supply curve for an industry is simply the horizontal summation of the supply curves of the industry's individual firms. To obtain industry supply, in other words, we simply add together the output of every firm at various price levels.

Checkpoint
Competition: Short-Run Decisions

REVIEW

- Marginal revenue is the change in total revenue from selling an additional unit of a product.
- Competitive firms are price takers, getting their price from markets, so they can sell all they want at the going market price. As a result, their marginal revenue is equal to product price and the demand curve facing the competitive firm is a straight-line demand at market price.
- Competitive firms will maximize profit by producing that output where marginal revenue equals marginal cost (MR = MC).
- When price is greater than the minimum point of the average total cost curve, firms earn economic profits.
- When price is just equal to the minimum point of the average total cost curve, firms earn normal profits.
- When price is below the minimum point of the average total cost curve, but above the minimum point of the average variable cost curve, the firm continues to operate, but earns an economic loss.
- When price falls below the minimum point on the average variable cost curve, the firm will shut down and incur a loss equal to total fixed costs.
- The short-run supply curve of the firm is the marginal cost curve above the minimum point on the average variable cost curve.

QUESTION

Describe why profit maximizing output occurs where MR = MC. Does this explain why competitive firms do not sell "all they can produce"?

Answers to the Checkpoint question can be found at the end of this chapter.

Competition: Long-Run Adjustments

We have seen that competitive firms can earn economic profits, normal profits, or losses in the short run because their plant size is fixed, and they cannot exit the industry. We now turn our attention to the long run. In the long run, firms can adjust all factors, even to the point of leaving an industry. And, if the industry looks attractive, other firms can enter it in the long run.

Adjusting to Profits and Losses in the Short Run

If firms in the industry are earning short-run economic profits, new firms can be expected to enter the industry in the long run, or existing firms may increase the scale of their operations. Figure 8 illustrates one such possible adjustment path when the firms in an industry are earning short-run economic profits. To simplify the discussion, we will assume there are no economies of scale in the long run.

FIGURE 8

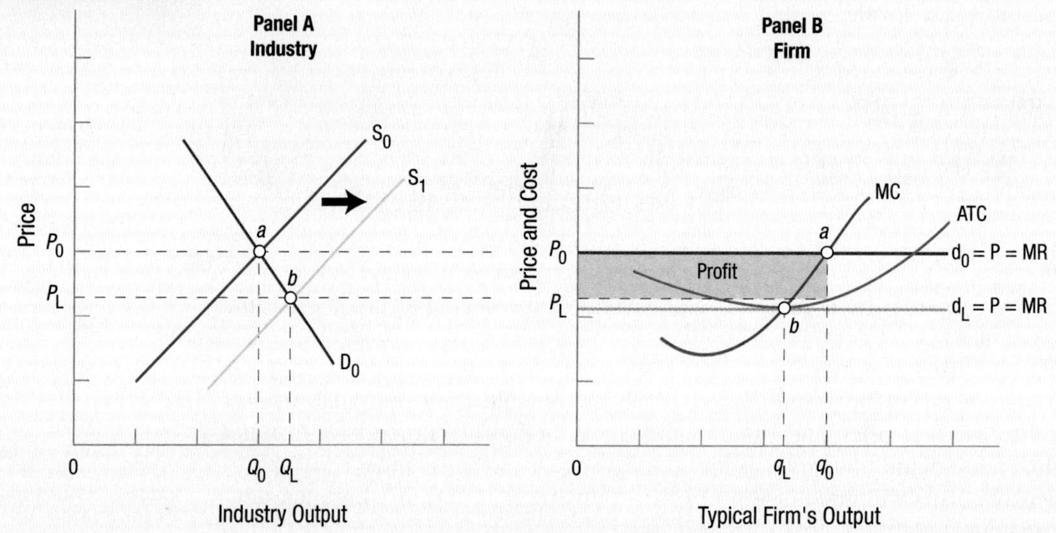

Long-Run Adjustment With Short-Run Economic Profits

Panel A shows a market initially in equilibrium at point *a*. Industry supply and demand equal S_0 and D_0, and equilibrium price is P_0. This equilibrium leads to the short-run economic profits shown in the shaded area in Panel B. Short-run economic profits lead other firms to enter the industry, thus raising industry output to Q_L in Panel A, while forcing prices down to P_L. The output for individual firms declines as the industry moves to long-run equilibrium at point *b* in both panels. In the long run, firms in competitive markets can earn only normal profits, as shown by point *b* in Panel B.

In Panel A, the market is initially in equilibrium at point *a*, with industry supply and demand equal to S_0 and D_0, and equilibrium price equal to P_0. For the typical firm shown in Panel B, this translates into a short-run equilibrium at point *a*. Notice that, at this price, the firm produces output exceeding the minimum point of the ATC curve. The shaded area represents economic profits.

These economic profits (sometimes called supernormal profits) will attract other firms into the industry. Remember that in a competitive market, entry and exit are easy in the long run; so, many firms decide to get in on the action when they see these profits. As a result, industry supply will shift to the right, to S_1, where equilibrium is at point *b*, resulting in a new long-run industry price of P_L. For each firm in the industry, output declines to q_L and is just tangent to the minimum point on the ATC curve. Thus, all firms are now earning normal profits and keeping their investors satisfied. There are no pressures at this point for more firms to enter or exit the industry.

Consider the opposite situation, that is, firms in an industry that are incurring economic losses. Figure 9 depicts such a scenario. In Panel A, market supply and demand are S_0 and D_0, with equilibrium price at P_0. In Panel B, firms suffer economic losses equal to the shaded area. These losses cause some firms to reevaluate their situations and some decide to leave the industry, thus shifting the industry supply curve to S_1 in Panel A, generating a new equilibrium price of P_L. This new price is just tangent to the minimum point of the ATC curve in Panel B. Firms in the industry are now earning normal profits, so the pressures to leave the industry dissipate.

FIGURE 9

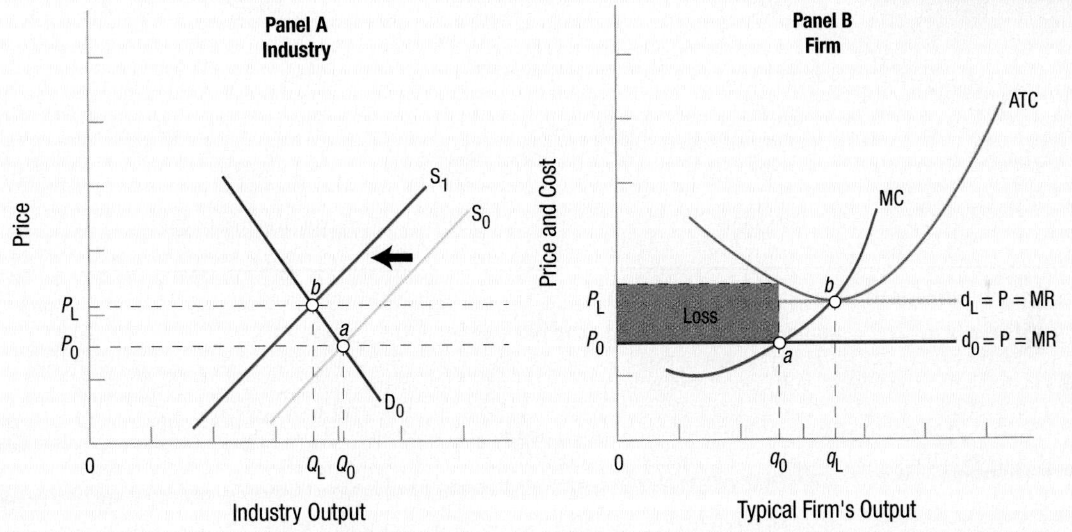

Long-Run Adjustment With Short-Run Losses

Panel A shows a market initially in equilibrium at point *a*. Industry supply and demand equal S_0 and D_0, and equilibrium price is P_0. This equilibrium leads to the short-run economic losses shown in the shaded area in Panel B, thus inducing some firms to exit the industry. Industry output contracts to Q_L in Panel A, raising prices to P_L and expanding output for the individual firms remaining in the industry, as the industry as a whole moves to long-run equilibrium at points *b* in both panels. Again, in the long run, firms in competitive markets will earn normal profits, as shown by point *b* in Panel B.

Notice that in Figures 8 and 9, the final equilibrium in the long run is the point at which industry price is just tangent to the minimum point on the ATC curve. At this point, there are no net incentives for firms to enter or leave the industry. If industry price rises above this point, the economic profits being earned will induce other firms to enter the industry; the opposite is true if price falls below this point. We will now evaluate this long-run equilibrium.

Competition and the Public Interest

Competitive processes dominate modern life. You and your friends compete for grades, concert tickets, spouses, jobs, and many other benefits. Competitive markets are simply an extension of the competition inherent in our daily lives. Figure 10 on the next page illustrates the long-run equilibrium for a firm in a competitive market. Market price in the long run is P_{LR}; it is equal to the minimum point on both the short-run average total cost (SRATC) curve and the long-run average total cost (LRATC) curve. At point *e*, the following is true:

$$P = MR = MC = SRATC_{min} = LRATC_{min}$$

FIGURE 10

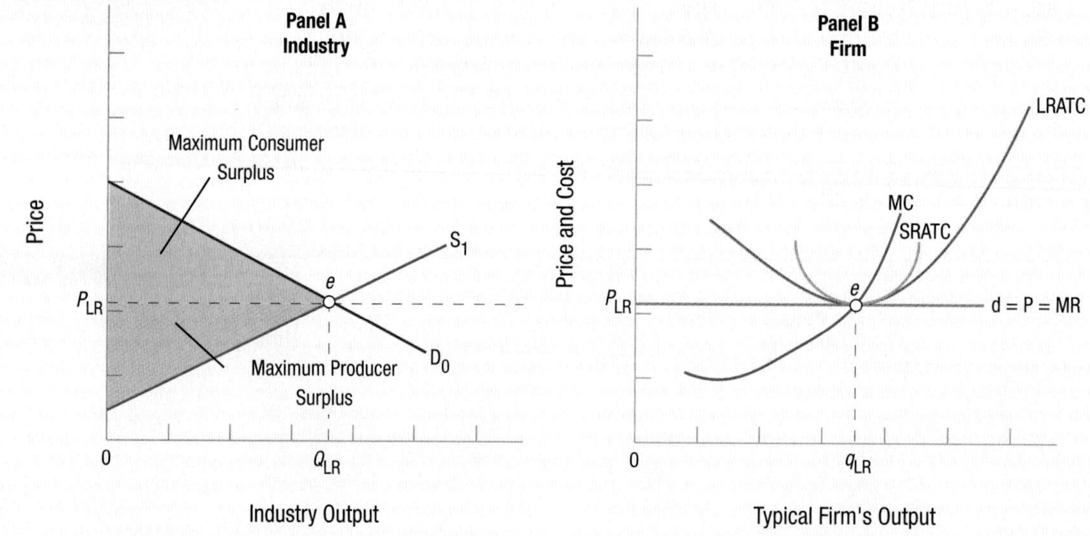

Long-Run Equilibrium for the Competitive Firm

Market price in the long run is P_{LR}, corresponding to the minimum point on the SRATC and LRATC curves. At point *e*, P = MR = MC = $SRATC_{min}$ = $LRATC_{min}$. This is why economists use competitive markets as the benchmark when comparing the performance of other market structures. With competition, consumers get just what they want since price reflects their desires, and they get these products at the lowest possible price ($LRATC_{min}$). Further, as Panel A illustrates, consumer and producer surplus is maximized. Any reduction in output reduces both consumer and producer surplus.

Productive efficiency Goods and services are produced and sold to consumers at their lowest resource (opportunity) cost.

Allocative efficiency The mix of goods and services produced are just what society desires. The price that consumers pay is equal to marginal cost and is also equal to the least average total cost.

This equation illustrates why competitive markets are the standard (benchmark) by which all other market structures are evaluated. First, competitive markets exhibit **productive efficiency**. Products are produced and sold to consumers at their lowest possible opportunity cost, the minimum SRATC and LRATC. Given the existing technology, firms cannot produce these products more cheaply. For consumers, this is an excellent situation: They pay no more than minimum production costs plus a profit sufficient to keep producers in business, and consumer surplus shown in Panel A is maximized. When we look at monopoly firms in the next chapter, consumers will not get such a good deal.

Second, competitive markets demonstrate **allocative efficiency**. The price consumers pay for a given product is equal, not only to the minimum average total cost, but also to marginal cost. As Panel A illustrates, consumer and producer surplus are maximized. Thus, the last unit purchased in the market is sold for a price equal to the opportunity costs required to produce that unit. Because price represents the value consumers place on a product, and marginal cost represents the opportunity cost to society to produce that product, when these two values are equal, the market is allocatively efficient. This means that the market is allocating the production of various goods according to consumer wants.

The flip side of these observations is that if a market falls out of equilibrium, the public interest will suffer. If, for instance, output falls below equilibrium, marginal cost will be less than price. Therefore, consumers place a higher value on that product than it is costing firms to produce. Society would be better off if more of the product were put on the market. Conversely, if output rises above the equilibrium level, marginal cost will exceed price. This excess output costs firms more to produce than the value placed on it by consumers. We would be better off if those resources were used to produce another commodity more highly valued by society.

Long-Run Industry Supply

Economies or diseconomies of scale determine the shape of the long-run average total cost (LRATC) curve for individual firms. A firm that enjoys significant economies of scale will see its LRATC curve slope down for a wide range of output. Firms facing diseconomies of scale will see their average costs rise as output rises. The nature of these economies and diseconomies of scale determines the size of the competitive firm.

Long-run industry supply is related to the degree to which increases and decreases in *industry* output influence the prices firms must pay for resources. For example, when all firms in an industry expand or new firms enter the market, this new demand for raw materials and labor may push up the price of some inputs. When this happens, it gives rise to an **increasing cost industry** in the long run.

Increasing cost industry In the long run, as industry output expands, prices and costs will be higher. Industry expansion puts upward pressure on resources (inputs), causing higher costs in the long run.

To illustrate, Panel A of Figure 11 shows two sets of short-run supply and demand curves. Initially, demand and supply are D_0 and S_0, and equilibrium is at point *a*. Assume demand increases, shifting to D_1. In the short run, price and output will rise to point *b*. As we have seen earlier, economic profits will result and existing firms will expand or new firms will enter the industry, causing product supply to shift to S_1 in the long run. Note that at the new equilibrium (point *c*), prices are higher than at the initial equilibrium (point *a*). This is caused by the upward pressure on the prices of industry inputs, notably raw materials and labor that resulted from industry expansion. Industry output has expanded, but prices and costs are higher. This is an *increasing cost industry.*

Alternatively, an industry might enjoy economies of scale as it expands, as suggested by Panel C of Figure 11. In this case, price and output initially rise as the short-run equilibrium moves to point *b*. Eventually, however, this industry expansion leads to lower prices; perhaps raw materials suppliers enjoy economies of scale as this industry's demand for their product increases. The semiconductor industry seems to fit this profile: As the demand for semiconductors has risen over the past few decades, their price has fallen dramatically. In the long run, therefore, a new

FIGURE 11

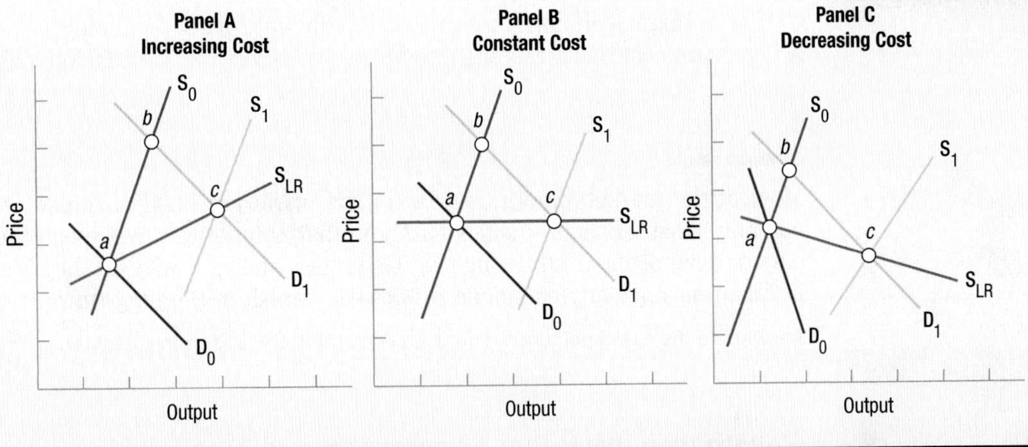

Long-Run Industry Supply Curves

Panel A shows an increasing cost industry. Demand and supply are initially D_0 and S_0, with equilibrium at point *a*. When demand increases, price and output rise in the short run to point *b*. As new firms enter the industry, they drive up the cost of resources. Supply increases in the long run to S_1 and the new equilibrium point c reflects these higher resource costs. In constant cost industries (Panel B), firms can expand in the long run without economies or diseconomies, so costs remain constant in the long run. In decreasing cost industries (Panel C), expansion leads to external economies and thus to a long-run equilibrium at point *c*, with lower prices and a higher output than before.

equilibrium is established at point *c*, where prices are lower and output is higher than was initially the case. This illustrates what happens in a **decreasing cost industry**.

Decreasing cost industry In the long run, as industry output expands, prices and costs will be lower. Some industries enjoy economies of scale as they expand in the long run, typically the result of technological advances.

Finally, some industries seem to expand in the long run without significant change in average cost. These are known as **constant cost industries**, and are shown in Panel B in Figure 11. Some fast-food restaurants and retail stores like Wal-Mart seem to be able to clone their operations from market to market without a noticeable rise in costs.

Constant cost industry In the long run, as industry output expands, prices and costs will be roughly the same. Some industries can virtually clone their operations in other areas without putting undue pressure on resource prices, resulting in constant operating costs as they expand in the long run.

Checkpoint

Competition: Long-Run Adjustments

REVIEW

- When competitive firms are earning short-run economic profits, these profits attract firms into the industry. Supply increases and market price falls until firms are just earning normal profits, and no firms are attracted into the industry.
- The opposite occurs when firms are making losses in the short run. Losses mean some firms will leave the industry. This reduces supply, thus increasing prices until profits return to normal.
- Competitive markets are efficient because $P = MR = MC = SRATC_{min} = LRATC_{min}$.
- Competitive markets are productively efficient because products are produced at their lowest possible opportunity cost.
- Competitive markets are allocatively efficient because $P = MC$, and consumer and producer surplus are at a maximum.
- An industry where prices rise as the industry grows is an increasing cost industry, and increased costs may be caused by rising prices of raw materials or labor as the industry expands.
- Decreasing cost industries see their prices fall as the industry expands, possibly due to huge economies of scale or rapidly improving technology.
- Constant cost industries seem to be able to expand without facing higher or lower prices.

QUESTION

Most of the markets and industries in the world are highly competitive, and presumably most CEOs of businesses know that competition will mean they will only earn normal profits in the long run. Given this analysis, why do they bother to stay in business since any economic profits will vanish in the long run?

Answers to the Checkpoint question can be found at the end of this chapter.

Youssouf Cader

Globalization, Long-Run Adjustments, and "The Box"[2]

When we think of disruptive technologies that radically changed an entire market, we typically think of computers, the Internet, and cellular phones. Competitors must adapt to the change or wither away. One disruptive technology we take for granted

[2]Based on Tim Ferguson, "The Real Shipping News," *Wall Street Journal*, April 12, 2006, pp. D12, and on Mark Levinson, *The Box* (Princeton: Princeton University Press), 2006.

today, but one that changed our world, is "the box"—the standardized shipping container. As Dirk Steenken reported, "Today 60% of the world's deep-sea general cargo is transported in containers, whereas some routes, especially between economically strong and stable countries, are containerized up to 100%."[3]

Before containers, shipping costs added about 25% to the cost of some goods and represented over 10% of U.S. exports. The process was cumbersome; hundreds of longshoremen would remove boxes of all sizes, dimensions, and weight from a ship and load them individually onto trucks (or from trucks to a ship if they were going the other way). This process took a lot of time, was subject to pilferage and theft, and was costly and inconvenient for business.

In 1955 Malcom McLean, a North Carolina trucking entrepreneur, got the idea to standardize shipping containers. He originally thought he would drive a truck right onto a ship, drop a trailer, and drive off. Realizing that the wheels would consume a lot of space, he soon settled on a standard container that would stack together, but would also load directly onto a truck trailer. Containers are 20 or 40 feet long, 8 feet wide, and 8 or 8½ feet tall. This standardization greatly reduced the costs of handling cargo. McLean bought a small shipping company, called it Sealand, and converted some ships to handle the containers. In 1956 he converted an oil tanker and shipped 58 containers from Newark, New Jersey, to Houston, Texas. It took roughly a decade of union bargaining and capital investment by firms for containers to catch on, but the rest is history.

Longshoremen and other port operators thought he was nuts, but as the idea took hold, the West Coast longshoremen went on strike to prevent the introduction of containers. They received some concessions, but containerization was inevitable. Containerization was so cost effective that it could not be stopped. It set in motion the long-run adjustments we see in competitive markets. Ports that didn't adjust went out of business, and trucking firms that failed to add containers couldn't compete. The same was true for ocean shipping companies.

Much of what we call globalization today can be traced to "the box." Firms producing products in foreign countries can fill a container, deliver it to a port, and send it directly to the customer or wholesaler in the United States. The efficiency, originally seen by McLean, was that the manufacturer and the ultimate customer would be the only ones to load and unload the container, keeping the product safer, more secure, and cutting huge chunks off the cost of shipping. Before containers, freight often represented as much as 25% of a product's price. Today, a 40-foot container with 32 tons of cargo shipped from China to the United States costs roughly $2,000, or 3 cents a pound![4] This efficient, disruptive technology has facilitated the expansion of trade worldwide and increased the competitiveness of many industries.

Summing Up

This chapter has focused on markets in which there is competition, that is, in which industries contain many sellers and buyers, each so small that they ignore the others' behavior and sell a homogeneous product. Sellers are assumed to maximize the profits they earn through sale of their products, and buyers are assumed to maximize the satisfaction they receive from the products they buy. Further, we assume that buyers and sellers have all the information necessary for informed transactions, and that sellers can sell as much of their products as they want at market equilibrium prices.

---

[3]Dirk Steenken, et al., "Container Terminal Operation and Operations Research," in Hans-Otto Gunther and Kap Hwan Kim, *Container Terminals and Automated Transport Systems* (New York: Springer), 2005. p. 4.
[4]Christian Caryl, "The Box is King," *Newsweek International,* April 10–17, 2006.

These assumptions allow us to reach some clear conclusions about how firms operate in competitive markets. In the long run, firms will produce output where P = MR = MC = $LRATC_{min}$, and profits are enough to keep capital in the industry. This output level is efficient because it gives consumers just the goods they want and provides these goods at the lowest possible opportunity costs ($LRATC_{min}$ = MC = P). Competitive market efficiency represents the benchmark for comparing other market structures.

Competitive markets as we have described them have what must seem to you like such restrictive assumptions that this model only applies to a few industries such as agriculture, standardized lumber products, minerals, and so on. Businesses you deal with don't look like the assumptions of these competitive markets. This is true, but most businesses you encounter, such as barber shops, salons, bars, restaurants, coffee houses, gas stations, fast food franchises, cleaners, grocery stores, and shoe and clothing stores, all operate like competitive firms. Although their products (and locations) are slightly different, they basically take their prices from the market and earn normal profits over the long term. In the chapter after next, we examine those markets where consumers see products as branded and different and see how that industry's behavior is different from competitive markets.

Because the competitive market model is so clearly in the public interest and is the benchmark for comparing other market structures, we can ponder the answer to the following question: Do firms seek the competitive market structure? The answer is: Generally, no. Why? Recall the profit equation. In competitive markets, firms are price takers. They can achieve economic profits in the short run but find it almost impossible to have long-run economic profits. And crucially, the only way competitive firms can be profitable at all is to be efficient productively and continually so. There are some firms, such as Intel, that seem to thrive on competitive pressures. But most firms want long-run economic profits without facing such continual pressures to minimize costs. They want some ability to control price. In the next chapter, we will see what firms do to mitigate these competitive pressures.

Key Concepts

Market structure analysis, p. 196
Competition, p. 197
Price taker, p. 198
Marginal revenue, p. 200
Profit maximizing rule, p. 201
Normal profits, p. 203
Shutdown point, p. 204
Short-run supply curve, p. 205
Productive efficiency, p. 208
Allocative efficiency, p. 208
Increasing cost industry, p. 209
Decreasing cost industry, p. 210
Constant cost industry, p. 210

Chapter Summary

Market Structure Analysis

Market structure analysis enables economists to quickly categorize industries by looking at a few key characteristics. Once an industry has been properly categorized, its behavior in such areas as pricing and output can be predicted.

Economists have identified four basic market structures: competition, monopolistic competition, oligopoly, and monopoly. They are defined by the following factors: the number of firms in the industry, the nature of the product produced, the scope of barriers to entry and exit, and the extent to which individual firms can control prices.

The competitive market structure assumes, first, that the market has many buyers and sellers, each so small that they cannot influence product prices. Second, a competitive industry is assumed to produce a homogeneous or standardized product. Third, all buyers and sellers have all relevant information about prices and product quality. Fourth, barriers to entry and exit are assumed to be insignificant.

Competitive firms are price takers; they cannot significantly alter the sales price of their products. Product prices are determined in broad markets.

In the short run, at least one factor of production, usually plant capacity, is fixed. Also, in the short run, firms cannot exit an industry, nor can new firms enter. In the long run, all factors of production are variable, with short-run profit levels inducing entry or exit.

Competition: Short-Run Decisions

Total revenue equals price per unit times quantity sold ($TR = p \times q$). Marginal revenue is equal to the change in total revenue that comes from producing an added unit of the product ($MR = \Delta TR/\Delta q$). Since, in a competitive market, a firm can sell all it wants at the market price, marginal revenue is equal to market price for the competitive firm.

Firms will maximize their profits by selling that level of output at which marginal revenue is just equal to marginal cost (MR = MC). For the competitive firm this translates into MC = MR = P. In the short run, a firm can earn economic profits, normal profits, or economic losses, depending on its product's market price.

If price is above the minimum point on the ATC curve, a firm will earn economic profits in the short run. If price is just equal to the minimum point on the ATC curve, the firm will earn normal profits. If price should fall below the minimum ATC, the firm will earn economic losses. Finally, if the price falls below the minimum point on the AVC curve, the firm will shut down and incur a loss equal to its fixed costs, since firms will not operate if they cannot cover their variable costs.

The short-run supply curve for the competitive firm is the marginal cost curve above the minimum point on the AVC curve.

Competition: Long-Run Adjustments

In the long run, all factors of production are variable, including the ability to exit or enter an industry. When the firms in an industry earn economic profits in the short run, this attracts new firms to the industry, thus reducing product price until firms are earning just normal profits. A corresponding adjustment occurs when the firms in an industry suffer short-term economic losses: Some firms leave the industry, thus raising prices until the remaining firms are again earning normal returns.

Competitive markets serve the public interest by ensuring that firms price their products at their marginal cost, which also equals $LRATC_{min}$. Therefore, just the quantity of products that consumers want is provided at the lowest possible opportunity cost ($LRATC_{min}$). In addition, competitive market equilibrium maximizes consumer and producer surplus. A deviation from this output yields reduced benefits for society and consumers.

An industry may be an increasing cost industry, a decreasing cost industry, or a constant cost industry depending on the industry's precise structure, the current state of technology, and the degree of economies and diseconomies of scale.

Questions and Problems

1. Use the table below to answer the following questions. Assume that fixed costs are $100, and labor is paid $80 per unit (per employee).

L	Q	MP	AP	TFC	TVC	TC	ATC	AVC	AFC	MC
0	0	___	___	___	___	___	___	___	___	___
1	7	___	___	___	___	___	___	___	___	___
2	15	___	___	___	___	___	___	___	___	___
3	25	___	___	___	___	___	___	___	___	___
4	40	___	___	___	___	___	___	___	___	___
5	45	___	___	___	___	___	___	___	___	___
6	48	___	___	___	___	___	___	___	___	___
7	50	___	___	___	___	___	___	___	___	___

a. Complete the table.
b. Graph ATC, AVC, AFC, and MC in the blank grid below.

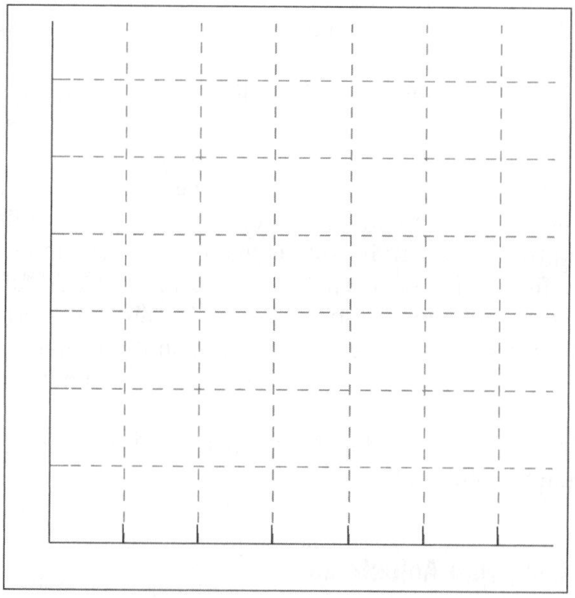

c. Assume the market sets the price at $16 a unit. How much will the firm produce, and what will its profit equal?
d. Assume now that price falls to $10.50. How much will the firm produce, and what will be its profits?
e. Now assume that the price falls to $7.50. Again, how much will the firm produce, and what will be its profits?

2. The media reports each quarter on industry profits and losses. Some firms (most notably the airlines) seem to post losses quarter after quarter. Why do they keep operating?

3. Why must price cover average variable costs if the firm is to continue operating?

4. Describe the role that easy entry and exit play in competitive markets over the long run.

5. Use the figure on the next page to answer the following true/false questions:
a. If market price is $25 the firm earns economic profits.

b. If market price is $20, the firm earns economic profit equal to roughly $100.
c. If market price is $9, the firm will produce roughly 55 units.
d. If market price is $12.50, the firm will produce roughly 70 units and make an economic loss equal to roughly $175.
e. Total fixed costs for this firm are roughly $100.
f. If market price is $15, the firm sells 80 units and makes a normal profit.

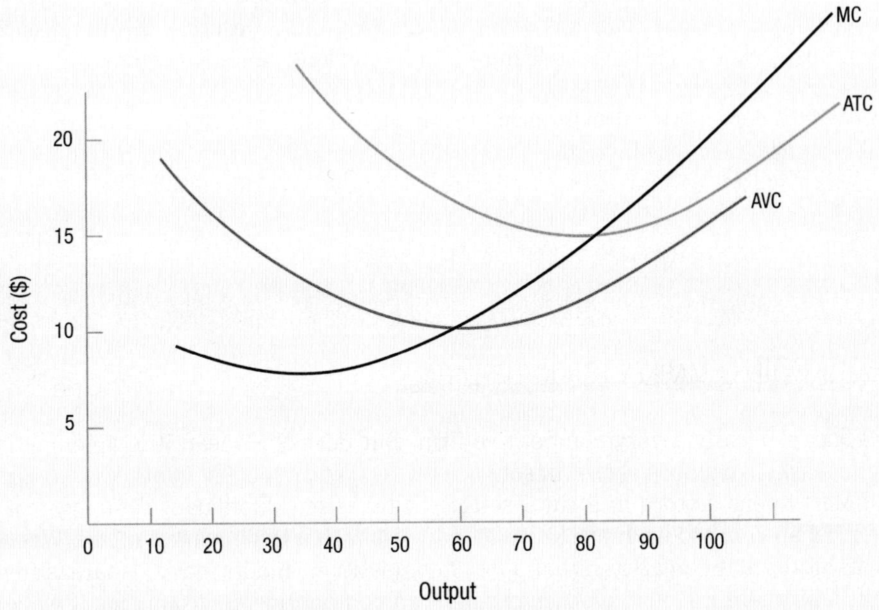

6. Why do competitive firms sell their products only at market price? Why not try to raise prices to make more profit or lower them to garner market share (more sales)?

7. Why are marginal revenue and price equal for the competitive firm?

8. How is the short-run supply curve for the competitive firm determined?

9. Why, if competitive firms are earning economic profits in the short run, are they unable to earn them in the long run?

10. How has the development of the Internet affected small competitive businesses such as used bookstores and antique shops?

11. Michelle Slatalla (*New York Times,* February 3, 2005) stated, "The conventional wisdom a few years back was that the Internet would erase price differences among retailers by giving customers instant access to the best deals. Merchants who charged more would be driven out of business." She further quoted Professor Michael Baye, who noted, "The prediction was price-comparison sites would create perfectly competitive environments in which all firms would have to charge the same price." These forecasts for the Internet creating "perfectly competitive" markets were based on the competitive model we have presented in this chapter. Do you think the Internet has helped create more competitive markets or less? Why?

12. Of the characteristics that are used to define the four market structures discussed at the beginning of the chapter, which two characteristics intuitively seem to be the most important?

13. Describe the reasons why an industry's costs might increase in the long run. Why might they decrease over the long run?

14. Assume a competitive industry is in long-run equilibrium and firms in the industry are earning normal profits. Now assume that production technology improves such that average total costs decline by $5 a unit. Describe the process this industry will go through as it moves to a new long-run equilibrium.

15. When a competitive firm is earning economic profits, is it also maximizing profit per unit? Why or why not?

Answers to Checkpoint Questions

CHECKPOINT: MARKET STRUCTURE ANALYSIS

Wal-Mart is clearly a very competitive firm. But does this mean it is a competitor in the market structure sense: In some cases, yes, and probably in others, no. When Wal-Mart opens a store in a rural setting, it takes on a dominant retailing role in the local area and looks more like a monopolist with a large market share. When it opens stores in urban areas, it has a lot of competition, and its market share is small, so it looks more like just another retailer in a competitive environment. If we look at the market internationally, Wal-Mart is just one of many large retailers around the world, so it looks like it fits the competitive market structure in the international market. Microsoft is more toward the monopoly end of the spectrum. Who are its competitors? Starbucks has many competitors but its products are considered somewhat unique by consumers so it is a monopolistic competitor. Toyota and the automobile industry are more oligopolistic, with only a few auto manufacturers of importance in the market.

CHECKPOINT: COMPETITION: SHORT-RUN DECISIONS

Keep in mind that marginal cost is the additional cost to produce another unit of output, and price equals marginal revenue and is the additional revenue from selling one more unit of the product. If MR is greater than MC, the firm earns more revenue than cost by selling that next unit, so the firm will sell up to where MR = MC. At that last unit where MR = MC, the firm is earning a normal profit on that unit (a positive accounting profit). When MC > MR, the firm is spending more to produce that unit than it receives in revenue and is losing money on that last unit, lowering overall profits. Thus, firms will not produce and sell all they can produce: They will produce and sell up to the point where MR = MC.

CHECKPOINT: COMPETITION: LONG-RUN ADJUSTMENTS

All businesses are looking for the "next new thing" that will generate economic profits and propel them to monopoly status. Even normal profits are not trivial. Remember, normal profits are sufficient to keep investors happy in the long run. When firms do find the right innovation like the iPod, Windows operating system, or a blockbuster breakthrough drug, the short-run returns are huge.

9

Monopoly

In the previous chapter, we constructed a model of competitive markets in which many sellers compete against one another for the business of many buyers. This model assumed that different firms sell almost identical products and that they face no significant barriers to entry, entering, or exiting industries easily.

In this chapter, we turn to the theory of monopoly. Most of us have some sense of what a monopoly is because we have played the game *Monopoly* at one time or other. In the game, having one property does not help much, but having a monopoly of a color immediately doubles the rent of any one property of that color, and further building on the property (houses and hotels) drives the rent up even more. From the game, then, we know that being a monopolist helps us to win: tough luck to the poor player who lands on a monopoly. If we think of consumers in the place of players who land on the monopoly, and the business monopolist as the player who holds the monopoly, we get a visceral sense of what we will discover in this chapter.

Monopoly is at the other extreme from the competitive model. Whereas the competitive model is in the public interest, we can guess at the outset that monopolies are not. We will see why monopolies exist and how they act. Then we will see what it means to have monopoly power. After that, we will see what can be done to mitigate the powers of monopolies that must exist, and how the United States tries to prevent monopolies from arising. Throughout this chapter, remember what it is like to hold a monopoly of Boardwalk and Park Place—and what it is like to land on them if you are not the monopolist.

After studying this chapter you should be able to

- Describe the characteristics of a monopoly and monopoly power.
- Describe the ways in which monopoly power is maintained.
- Use monopoly markets analysis to determine the equilibrium level of output and price for a monopoly.
- Describe the differences between monopoly and competition.
- Describe the different forms of price discrimination.
- Describe the different approaches to regulating a natural monopoly.
- Relate the history and purpose of antitrust legislation to monopoly analysis.
- Apply concentration ratios and Herfindahl-Hirshman indexes to analyze the likelihood of regulation in a given market.
- Describe the conditions of a contestable market and its significance.

Monopoly Markets

Monopoly
A one-firm industry with no close product substitutes and with substantial barriers to entry.

The very word *monopoly* almost defines the subject matter: a market in which there is only one seller. Here again, however, economists have attached a more extensive meaning to the word by specifying the types of products sold and the barriers to entry and exit. For economists, a **monopoly** is defined as follows:

- The market has just one seller—one firm *is* the industry. This contrasts sharply with the competitive market, where many sellers comprise the industry.
- No close substitutes exist for the monopolist's product. Consequently, buyers cannot easily substitute other products for that sold by the monopolist. If you want anything like the product in question, you must purchase it from the monopolist.
- A monopolistic industry has significant barriers to entry. Though competitive firms can enter or leave industries in the long run, monopoly markets are considered nearly impossible to enter. So monopolists face no competition, even in the long run.

This gives pure monopolists what economists call monopoly power. Unlike competitive firms, which are price takers, monopolists are *price makers.* Their monopoly power, in other words, allows monopolists to adjust their output in ways that give them significant control over product price.

As we will see, nearly every firm has some monopoly power, or some control over price. Your neighborhood dry cleaner, for instance, has some control over price since it is found close to you, and you are probably not going to want to drive 5 miles just to save a few cents. This control over price becomes minor, however, as markets approach more competitive conditions.

Sources of Monopoly Power

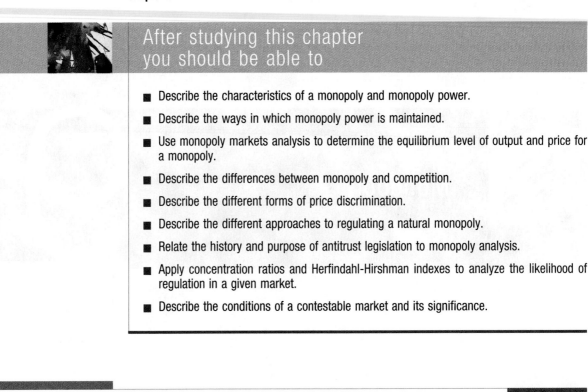

Monopoly and monopoly power do not mean the same thing. *Monopoly* is defined as one firm serving a market in which there are no close substitutes and entry is nearly impossible. *Monopoly power* (often referred to as market power) implies that a firm has some control over price. As a market structure approaches monopoly, one firm gains the maximum monopoly power possible for that industry. The key to monopoly power is significant barriers to entry. These barriers can be of several forms.

Economies of Scale

The **economies of scale** in an industry can be so large that demand will support only one firm. Figure 1 illustrates this case. Here the long-run average total cost curve (LRATC) shows extremely large economies of scale. With industry demand at D_0, one firm can earn economic profits by producing between Q_0 and Q_1. If the industry were to contain two firms, however, demand for each would be D_2, and neither firm could remain in business without suffering losses. Economists refer to such cases as *natural monopolies*.

Economies of scale
As the firm expands in size, average total costs decline.

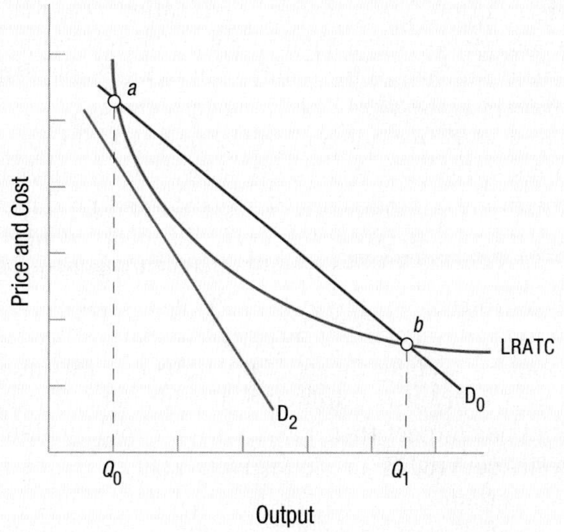

FIGURE 1
Economies of Scale Leading to Monopoly
The economies of scale in an industry can be so large that demand will support only one firm. In the industry portrayed here, one firm could earn economic profits (by producing output between Q_0 and Q_1 when faced with demand curve D_0). If the industry were to contain two firms, however, demand for each would be D_2, and neither firm could remain in business without suffering losses.

Some contemporary natural monopolies include microprocessors, electric utilities, and local newspapers. Though Intel is not a pure monopolist, it sells most of the world's microprocessors. Opening a production plant for its Pentium processors costs Intel around a billion dollars, not to mention the billions of dollars the company must spend each year on research, development, and marketing. The market for microprocessors is huge, but so are the development, production, and marketing scales a firm must attain to be successful. Still, the microprocessor market is so large that Intel does face some competition from a large firm (Advanced Micro Devices, AMD, has annual revenues about one sixth of Intel's) and from smaller niche firms.

Utilities have traditionally been considered natural monopolists because of the high fixed costs associated with power plants and the inefficiency of several different electric companies stringing their wires throughout a city. Recent technology, however, is slowly changing the utilities industry, as smaller plants, solar units, and wind generators permit a smaller yet efficient scale of operations. Smaller plants can be quickly turned on and off, and the energy from the sun and wind can be stored and transported to where it is needed in the system.

Another market where economies of scale can lead to dominance by one firm is the local newspaper market. Profitably producing and distributing a newspaper requires high output. Often local markets are too small to support more than one newspaper. Consequently, many seemingly large local areas can support only one daily newspaper.

Control over a Significant Factor of Production

If a firm owns or has control over an important input into the production process, that firm can keep potential rivals out of the market. This was the case with Alcoa Aluminum 50 years ago. The company owned nearly all the world's bauxite ore, one of the key ingredients for aluminum production. In the end, the Justice Department moved against Alcoa to end this monopoly. We will discuss policies to combat monopolies later in this chapter.

Government Franchises, Patents, and Copyrights

Some barriers to market entry extend from legal government mandates. A government franchise grants a firm permission to provide specific goods or services, while prohibiting others from doing so, thereby eliminating potential competition. The United States Postal Service, for instance, has an exclusive franchise in the delivery of first-class mail. Similarly, some public utilities and cable companies have been granted special franchises by state or local governments.

Patents are extended to firms and individuals who invent new products and processes. For a limited period, usually 20 years, the patent holder is legally protected from competition in production of the patented product. The basic reason behind the patent system is to give firms and individuals the incentive to invent and innovate. If entrepreneurs had to worry about their ideas being stolen by competitors as soon as they brought new products to the market, fewer new products would be developed. Patents are immensely important to many industries, including pharmaceuticals, computers, and chemicals. Many firms in these industries spend huge sums of money each year on research and development—money they would not spend if they could not protect their investments through patenting.

In a similar vein, copyrights give individuals or firms the exclusive right to produce or reproduce certain types of intellectual property for an extended period. A book, a piece of art, or a piece of software code can all be copyrighted. Copyright protection lay at the heart of the Microsoft legal case of the late 1990s. If Microsoft's Windows operating system had not been protected by copyright, Microsoft would not have enjoyed the monopoly power that sparked the government's lawsuit against it. Some firms guard trade secrets to protect their assets for even longer periods than the limited times provided by patents and copyrights. Only a handful of the top executives at Coca-Cola, for instance, know the secret to blending Coke.

Monopoly Pricing and Output Decisions

We have seen how monopoly power is first attained; shortly we will discuss some of the ways it is maintained. First, however, let us consider monopoly pricing and output decisions. In the previous chapter, we saw that competitive firms maximize profits by producing at a level of output where MR = MC, selling this output at the established market price. The monopolist, however, *is* the market. Consequently, we can predict that the quantity of output the monopolist decides to produce will affect market price—that is, the monopolist's price.

MR < P for Monopoly

For the monopolist, marginal revenue is less than price (MR < P). To see why, look at Figure 2. Panel A shows the demand curve for a competitive firm. At a price of

FIGURE 2

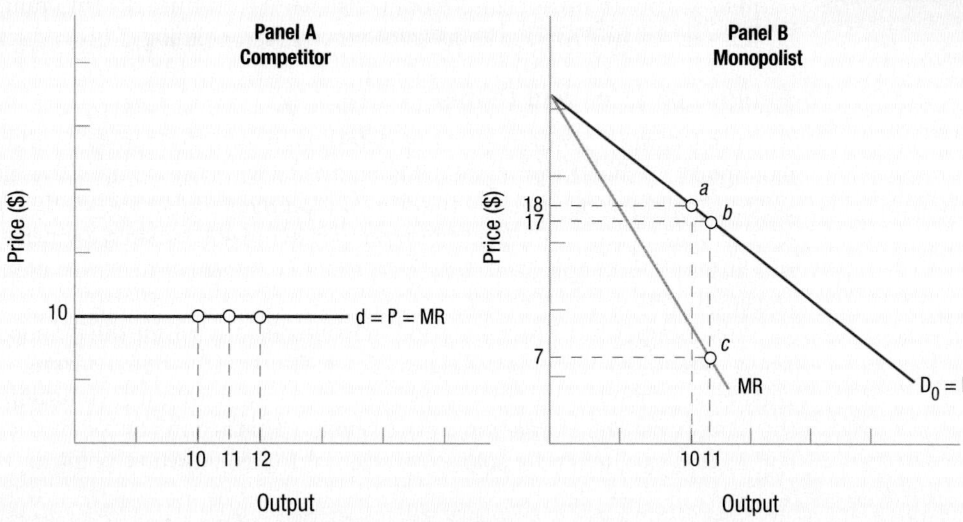

Marginal Revenue for Monopolies and Competitive Firms

Panel A shows the demand curve for a competitive firm. At a price of $10, the competitive firm can sell all it wants. For each unit sold, revenue rises by $10; hence, marginal revenue is $10. Panel B shows the demand curve for a monopolist. Because the monopolist constitutes the entire industry, it faces a downward sloping demand curve (D_0). If the monopolist decides to sell 10 units at $18 each (point *a*), total revenue is $180. Alternately, if the monopolist wants to sell 11 units, price must be dropped to $17 (point *b*). This raises total revenue to $187 (11 × $17), but marginal revenue falls to $7 ($187–$180, point *c*). Gaining the added $17 in revenue from the sale of the 11th unit requires the monopolist to give up $10 in additional revenue that would have come from selling the previous 10 units for $18 each.

$10, the competitive firm can sell all it wants. For each unit sold, total revenue rises by $10. Recalling that marginal revenue is equal to the change in total revenue from selling an added unit of the product, marginal revenue is also $10.

Contrast this with the situation of the monopolist in Panel B. Because the monopolist constitutes the entire industry, it faces the downward sloping demand curve (D_0) shown in Panel B. If the monopolist decides to produce and sell 10 units, they can be sold in the market for $18 each (point *a*), generating total revenue of $180. Alternately, if the monopolist wants to sell 11 units, their price must be dropped to $17 (point *b*). This raises total revenue to $187 (11 × $17). Notice, however, that marginal revenue, or the revenue gained from selling this added unit, falls to $7 ($187–$180). Gaining the additional $17 in revenue from the sale of the 11th unit requires that the monopolist give up $10 in revenue that would have come from selling the previous 10 units for $18 each. Marginal revenue for the 11th unit is shown as $7 (point *c*) in Panel B.

Notice that we are assuming the monopolist cannot sell the 10th unit for $18 and then sell the 11th unit for $17; rather, the monopolist must offer to sell a given quantity to the market for a standard price. We are assuming, in other words, that there is no way for the monopolist to separate the market by specific individuals who are willing to pay different prices for the product. In the next section, we will relax this assumption and discuss *price discrimination.*

In summary, we can see from Panel B of Figure 2 that MR < P, and the marginal revenue curve is always plotted below the demand curve for the monopolist. This contrasts with the situation of the competitive firm, for which price and marginal revenue are always the same. We should also note that marginal revenue can be negative. In such an instance, total revenue falls as the monopolist tries to sell more output. No profit maximizing monopolist would produce in this range, however, because costs are rising even as total revenue is declining, thus reducing profits.

Equilibrium Price and Output

As noted earlier, product price is determined in a monopoly by how much the monopolist wishes to produce. This contrasts with the competitive firm that can sell all it wishes, but only at the *market-determined price.* Both types of firms wish to make profits. Finding the monopolist's profit maximizing price and output is a little more complicated, however, since competitive firms have only output to consider.

Like competitive firms, the profit maximizing output for the monopolist is found where MR = MC. Turning to Figure 3, we find that marginal revenue equals marginal cost at point *e,* where output is Q_M units. Now we must determine how much the monopolist will charge for these Q_M units. This is done by looking to the demand curve. Output Q_M can be sold for a price of P_M as shown at point *a.*

FIGURE 3

Monopolist Earning Economic Profits

Profit maximizing output is found for monopolists, as for competitive firms, at the point where MR = MC. In this figure, marginal revenue equals marginal cost at point *e,* where output is Q_M units. These Q_M units are sold for price P_M (point *a*). Profit is equal to average profits per unit times units sold [Profit = (P – ATC) × Q]. Profit is represented by the shaded area C_MP_Mab.

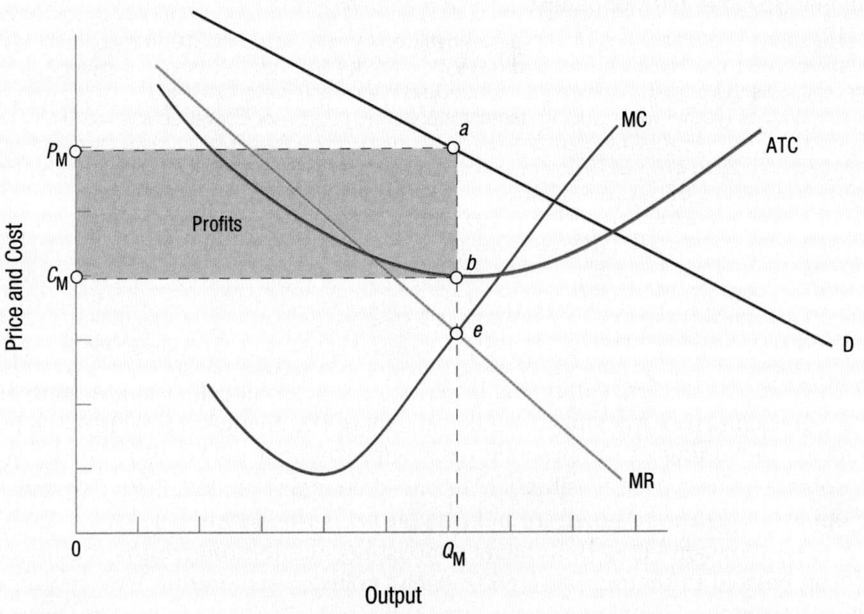

Profit for each unit is equal to *a–b,* the difference between price and average total costs at output Q_M. Output times profit per unit equals total profit and is shown as the shaded area C_MP_Mab in Figure 3 [Profit = (P – ATC) × Q]. Following the MR = MC rule, profits are maximized by selling Q_M units of the product at price P_M.

In summary, to find the equilibrium level of output and price, first find the point where MR = MC. This point determines the profit maximizing output on the horizontal axis, and by extending a vertical line through the point to the demand curve, it determines price on the vertical axis. The difference between this price and average total costs, multiplied by the number of units sold, equals total profit.

Monopoly Does Not Guarantee Economic Profits

We have seen that competitive firms may or may not be profitable in the short run, but in the long run, they must earn at least normal profits to remain in business. Is the same true for monopolists? Yes. Consider the monopolist in Figure 4. Again the firm maximizes profits by producing where MR = MC (point *e*) and selling output Q_M for price P_M.

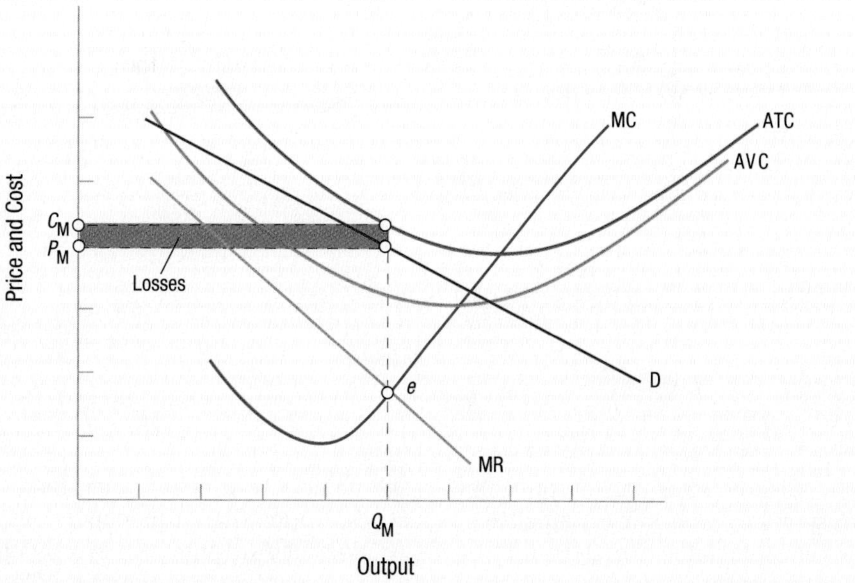

FIGURE 4

Monopolist Firm Making Economic Losses

Like competitive firms, monopolists may or may not be profitable in the short run, but in the long run, they must at least earn normal profits to remain in business. The monopolist shown here maximizes profits by producing where MR = MC (point e), and thus by selling output Q_M at price P_M. Price is lower than average total costs, so the monopolist suffers the loss indicated by the shaded area. Because price still exceeds average variable cost (AVC), in the short run the monopolist will minimize its losses by continuing to produce.

In this case, however, price is lower than average total costs, and thus the monopolist suffers the loss indicated by the shaded area. Because price nonetheless exceeds average variable costs, the monopolist will minimize its losses in the short run by continuing to produce. But if price should fall below AVC, the monopolist, just like any competitive firm, will minimize its losses at its fixed costs by shutting down its plant. If these losses persist, the monopolist will exit the industry in the long run.

This is an important point to remember. Being a monopolist does not automatically mean there will be monopoly profits to haul in. Even monopolies face *some* cost and price pressures.

Comparing Monopoly and Competition

Would our economy be better off with more or fewer monopolies? This question almost answers itself. Who would want more monopolies—except the few lucky monopolists? The answer is, we want fewer monopolies and more competition. The reasons for this have to do with the losses associated with monopoly markets and monopoly power. Monopoly losses include reduced output at higher prices, deadweight losses, rent seeking behavior of monopolists, and x-inefficiency losses. We will discuss each of these.

Higher Prices and Lower Output from Monopoly

Imagine for a moment that a competitive industry is monopolized, and the monopolist's marginal cost curve happens to be the same as the competitive industry's supply curve. Figure 5 on the next page illustrates such a scenario. The competitive industry produces where MC = P, and thus where price and output are P_C and Q_C (point *b*). Monopoly price and output, however, as determined as before, are P_M and Q_M (point *a*).

FIGURE 5

Monopoly Inefficiency

This figure shows what would happen if a competitive industry were monopolized and the new monopolist's marginal cost curve was the same as the competitive industry's supply curve. When the industry was competitive, it produced where MC = P, and thus where price and output are P_C and Q_C (point *b*). Monopoly price and output, however, are P_M and Q_M (point *a*); output is lower and price is higher than the corresponding values for competitive firms. Shaded area *cab* represents the deadweight loss suffered from monopoly.

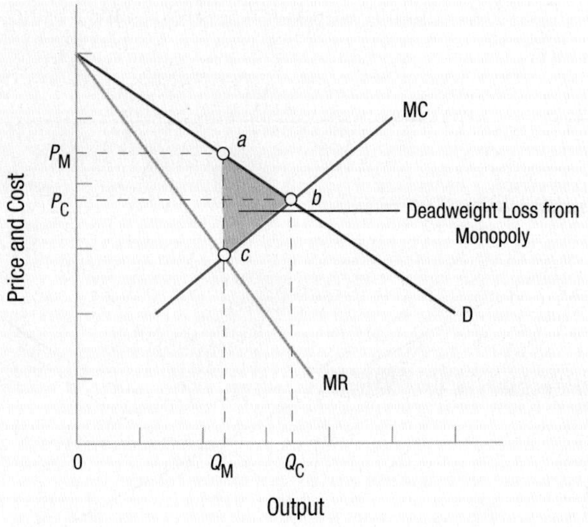

Clearly, monopoly output is lower, and monopoly price is higher, than the corresponding values for competitive industries. Notice that at monopoly output Q_M, consumers value the Q_Mth unit of the product at P_M (point a), even though the cost to produce this last unit of output is considerably less (point c). The *deadweight loss,* otherwise known as the *welfare loss,* from monopoly is shown as the shaded area *cab.* A summation of all the vertical lines connecting D and MC between Q_M and Q_C, this area represents the deadweight loss to society from a monopoly market.

Rent Seeking and X-Inefficiency

Monopolies earn economic profits by charging more and producing less than competitive firms. This inefficiency results in a loss of consumer surplus. Figure 6 resembles Figure 5, except that we are assuming constant-cost conditions. As a result,

FIGURE 6

Rent Seeking and Deadweight Loss in Monopoly

Economic profits are here equal to $P_C P_M ac$. To protect these lucrative profits, the typical monopolist will engage in a variety of rent-seeking behaviors—hiring lawyers and other professionals to lobby the government, for instance, or obtaining patents. Some economists argue that monopolistic firms may engage in so much rent-seeking behavior that all monopoly profits are eliminated.

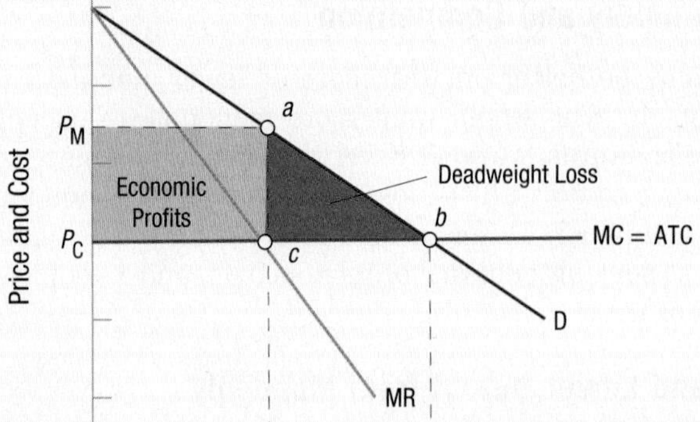

MC is equal to ATC. Again, the monopolist produces Q_M and sells this output for P_M, while the competitive firm sells Q_C at price P_C. This results in a welfare loss equal to area *cab*.

Economic profits in Figure 6 are equal to P_CP_Mac. Clearly, this is something monopolists will wish to protect. If entry to the market were eased, this economic profit would soon evaporate, just as it does in competitive markets. How, then, can a monopolist protect itself from potential competition? One way is to spend resources that could have been used to expand its production on efforts to protect its monopoly position.

Economists call this behavior **rent seeking**—behavior directed toward avoiding competition. Firms hire lawyers and other professionals to lobby governments, extend patents, and engage in a host of other activities intended solely to protect their monopoly position. Taxies in New York City, for instance, require licenses; restricting the number of licenses drives up their price and gives license holders a further incentive to restrict the number of new licenses, by lobbying and other means. Many industries spend significant resources lobbying Congress for tariff protection to reduce foreign competition. All these activities are inefficient, in that they use resources and shift income from one group to another without producing a useful good or service. Rent seeking thus represents an added loss to society from monopoly.

Rent seeking
Resources expended to protect a monopoly position. These include such activities as lobbying, extending patents, and restricting the number of licenses permitted.

To what extent will monopolistic firms engage in rent seeking behavior? Gordon Tullock has suggested that they may go as far as represented by area P_CP_Mac in Figure 6. Since eliminating the entire area of economic profits will still leave firms with a normal return, they may be willing to spend up to this total amount on rent seeking.

Another area where society might lose from monopolies is called **x-inefficiency**. Some economists suggest that because monopolies are protected from competitive pressures, they do not have to operate efficiently. Management can offer itself perks, for instance, without worrying about whether costs are kept at efficient levels. Executive travel in corporate jets, even for private vacations, has been recently criticized "as a symbol of excess," even though the trip is treated as income for tax purposes (but some companies even pay the taxes for the executives).[1] Deregulation over the last several decades, particularly in the airline and trucking industries, has provided ample evidence of inefficiencies arising when firms are protected from competition by government regulations. Many firms in these industries found it tough sledding when competitive pressures were reintroduced into their industries.

X-inefficiency
Protected from competitive pressures, monopolies do not have to act efficiently. Spending on corporate jets, travel, and other perks of business represent x-inefficiency.

Are there any benefits to monopolies? The answer to this question is, "Possibly yes, though generally no." One possible advantage to monopolies is shown in Figure 7 on the next page. The economies associated with this industry are so large that many small competitors would face substantially higher marginal costs than the monopolist. The monopolist produces and sells output Q_M at price P_M, which is more output at a lower price than the competitive firms could offer. Larger firms, moreover, can allocate more resources to research and development than smaller firms, and the possibility of economic profits may be the incentive monopolists require to invest.

Still, economists tend to doubt that monopolies are beneficial enough to outweigh their disadvantages.

In actuality, pure monopolies are rare, in part because of public policy and antitrust laws—more about this later in this chapter—and in part because rapidly changing technologies limit most monopolies to short-run economic profits—

[1]See Geraldine Fabrikant, "Executives Take Company Planes as if Their Own," *New York Times,* May 10, 2006, p. C1.

FIGURE 7

Monopolies and Economies of Scale

One possible advantage of monopolies is shown here. The economies associated with this industry are so large that many small competitors would face substantially higher marginal costs than the monopolist. The monopolist produces and sells output Q_M at price P_M, which is more output at a lower price than competitive firms could offer.

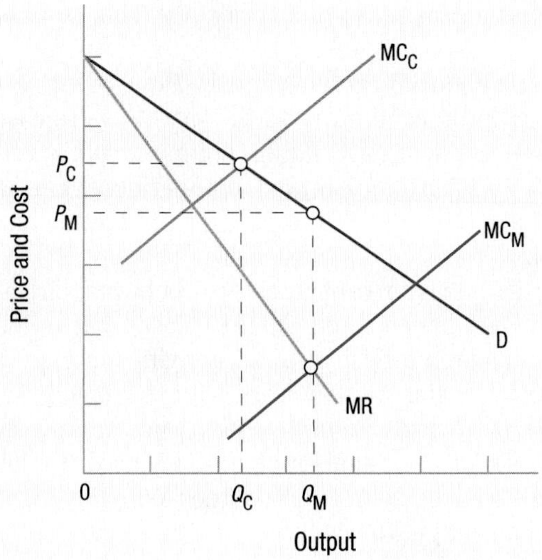

witness the battle among Google, Yahoo, and Microsoft for domination of search services. Even so, all firms seek to increase their market or monopoly power and gain some ability to influence price.

We have seen what monopolies are and how they arise. We also saw why a monopolist produces less than the socially optimal quantity at a higher than socially necessary price, and witnessed how monopoly compares unfavorably to the competitive model. Furthermore, we looked at an expensive drawback of monopolies: the amount of resources wasted in maintaining a monopolist's position. In the next section, we look at what monopolists especially would like to do, and how a society might regulate a natural monopoly.

Checkpoint

Monopoly Markets

REVIEW

- Monopoly is a market with no close substitutes, high barriers to entry, with just one seller; the firm is the industry. Hence, monopolists are *price makers.*
- Monopoly power can result from economies of scale, control over an important input, or from government franchises, patents, and copyrights.
- For the monopolist, MR < P because the industry's demand is the monopolist's demand.
- Profit is maximized by producing that output where MR = MC and setting the price off the demand curve.
- Being a monopolist does not guarantee economic profits if demand is insufficient to cover costs.
- Monopoly output is lower and price is higher when compared to competition, resulting in a deadweight loss from monopoly.
- Monopolies are subject to rent seeking—behavior directed toward avoiding competition (lobbying and other activities to extend the monopoly).

- Because monopolies are protected from competitive pressures, they often engage in x-inefficiency behavior—extending perks to management and other inefficient activities.

QUESTIONS

Google has 85% of the search business on the Internet and generates a lot of advertising revenue. Microsoft has 90% of the operating system business and 80% or so of the Internet browsers in use. In early 2006, Google, the search monopolist, asked the government to rein in Microsoft's new browser, which has a search box in the upper right hand corner, similar to Firefox and Apple's Safari. The default, of course, is that when you type a search term, you go through Microsoft's search engine. Changing the default is, however, quite easy; Google has the instructions on its Web site. Does Google's effort feel a little like monopolistic rent seeking? Should the government step in, or is this just competition between giants?

Answers to the Checkpoint questions can be found at the end of this chapter.

Monopoly Market Issues

Monopolies seek to price discriminate. And when monopolies must exist, there are policies that can be enacted to mitigate their power. We look at these issues in this section.

Price Discrimination

When firms with monopoly power *price discriminate,* they charge different consumers different prices for the same product. For example, senior citizens might pay less for a movie ticket than you do. Remember, competitors cannot price discriminate because they get their prices from the market (they are price takers). Several conditions are required for successful price discrimination.

- Sellers must have some monopoly (or market) power, or some control over price.
- Sellers must be able to separate the market into different consumer groups based on their elasticities of demand.
- Sellers must be able to prevent arbitrage; that is, it must be impossible or prohibitively expensive for low-price buyers to resell to higher-price buyers.

Price discrimination Charging different consumer groups different prices for the same product. The conditions necessary for successful price discrimination include some monopoly power (the firm needs some control over price), different consumer groups with different elasticities of demand, and the ability of the firm to prevent arbitrage (keeping low-price buyers from reselling to high-price buyers).

There are three major types of **price discrimination**. The first is known as perfect, or first-degree, price discrimination. It involves charging each customer the *maximum price* each is willing to pay. Second-degree price discrimination involves charging different customers different prices based on the *quantities* of the product they purchase. Firms may charge a high price for initial purchases, for instance, and then reduce the price after customers have bought a certain quantity.

The final and most common form of price discrimination is third-degree price discrimination. This occurs when firms *charge different groups of people different prices.* This is an everyday occurrence with airline, bus, and theatre tickets.

Perfect Price Discrimination

When perfect price discrimination can be employed, a firm will charge each customer a different price, the maximum price each is willing to pay. This type of price

FIGURE 8

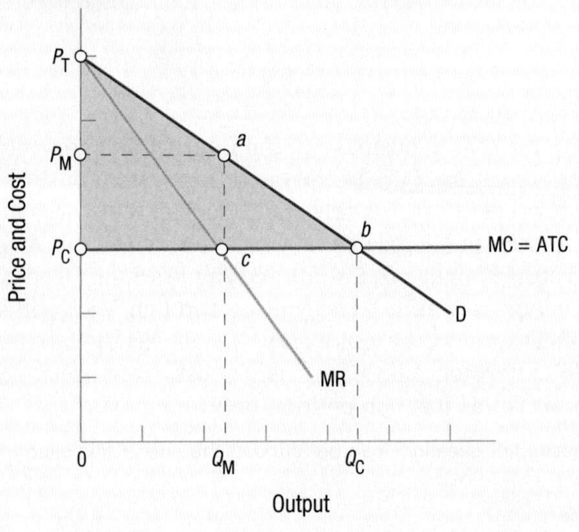

Perfect Price Discrimination

With perfect price discrimination, firms charge each customer the maximum price each is willing to pay. Thus, every point on the demand curve in this figure represents a price. The first few customers—those who value the product most—are charged a high price. The next customers are charged a slightly lower price, the Q_Mth customer is charged P_M (point *a*), and so on, until the last unit is sold to the Q_cth customer for P_C (point *b*). As a result, a perfectly discriminating monopolist earns profits represented by the shaded area P_CP_Tb. This is considerably more profit than the monopolist would earn by selling Q_M units at price P_M, represented by area P_CP_Mac.

discrimination is perhaps best exemplified by the flea market, where sellers and buyers haggle over the price of each product. Figure 8 portrays such a scenario. Every point on the demand curve represents a price. The first few customers—those who value the product most—are charged a high price. The next customers are charged slightly lower prices, the Q_Mth customer is charged P_M (point *a*), and so on, until the last unit is sold to the Q_cth customer for P_C (point *b*). As a result, a perfectly discriminating monopolist earns profits equal to the shaded area P_CP_Tb.

Figure 8 shows why firms would want to price discriminate. Typical monopoly profits in this case, assuming the monopolist sells Q_M units at price P_M, would be the rectangle area P_CP_Mac. This area is considerably smaller than profit triangle P_CP_Tb, earned by the perfectly price discriminating monopolist. That is why price discrimination exists—it is profitable. Note also that the *last* unit of the product sold by this monopolist is priced at P_C, the competitive price. In this limited sense, then, the monopolist who can perfectly price discriminate is as efficient as a competitive firm. Notice that perfect price discriminating monopolists manage to expropriate the entire consumer surplus.

Second-Degree Price Discrimination

Second-degree price discrimination involves charging consumers for different blocks of consumption. Producers of electric, gas, and water utilities often incorporate block pricing. You pay one rate for the first so many kilowatt-hours of electricity and a lower rate for more, and so on. This block pricing scheme is shown in Figure 9.

For the first Q_0 units of the product, consumers are charged P_0; between Q_0 and Q_1, the price falls to P_1; and after that, price is reduced to P_C. This results in profit to the firm equal to the shaded area. The shaded profit area for the discrim-

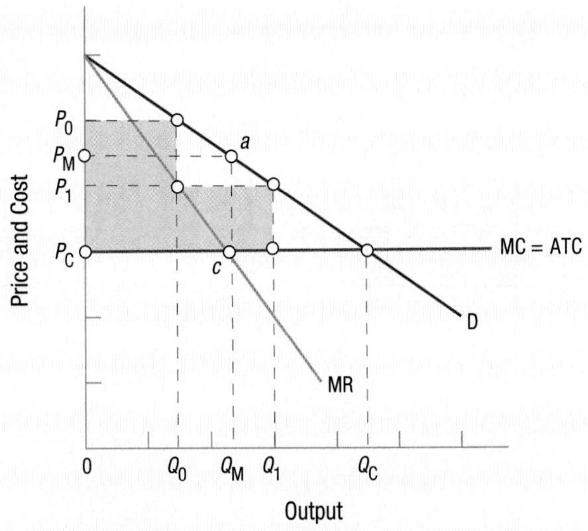

FIGURE 9

Second-Degree Price Discrimination

Second-degree price discrimination involves charging different customers different prices based on the quantities of the product they purchase. By charging these different prices, profits for the monopolist will rise. A nondiscriminating monopolist shown in the figure earns economic profits equal to P_CP_Mac. By charging three different prices—P_0, P_1, and P_C—profits increase, as shown by comparing the shaded area with the hatched area.

inating monopolist is greater than that of the monopolist charging just one price P_M (area P_CP_Mac): Compare the shaded profit area that does not overlap with this area. The most common price discrimination scheme, however, is third-degree, in which groups of consumers are charged different prices.

Third-Degree Price Discrimination

Third-degree, or imperfect, price discrimination involves charging different groups of people different prices. An obvious example would be the various fares charged for airline flights. Business people have much lower elasticities of demand for flights than do vacationers, so airlines place all sorts of restrictions on their tickets to separate people into distinct categories. Purchasing a ticket several weeks in advance, for instance—which vacationers can usually do, but businesspeople may not be able to—often results in a significantly lower fare. Arbitrage (preventing low-cost buyers from selling to higher-price buyers) is prevented, meanwhile, by rules stipulating that passengers can only travel on tickets purchased in their name. Other examples of third-degree price discrimination include different ticket prices for children, adults, and seniors at movies, student discounts for many services, and even ladies night at a bar.

Third-degree price discrimination is illustrated in Figure 10 on the next page. The two demand curves, D_0 and D_1, represent two segments of a market with different demand elasticities. The less elastic market, D_1, is offered price P_1. This is higher than price P_0, offered to the more elastic market, D_0. Profits are maximized for both markets. For market D_0, profits are P_CP_0bc, and for less elastic market D_1, they are P_CP_1ad. Like the perfectly discriminating monopolist, the third-degree price discriminating monopolist earns profits that exceed those which would come from a normal one-price policy.

We can look at price discrimination in an intuitive way by focusing on a restaurant. Regular dinner customers frequent the restaurant probably after 6:30 P.M. However, the restaurant is still open from 4:30 to 6:30 P.M. and incurs fixed costs and variable costs (if workers start their shifts before the 6:30 rush). It is in the restaurant's interest to offer early bird specials, discounting dinners purchased before 6:30, as long as this policy attracts new customers and does not pull in too many of its later-appearing regular diners. In this way, the restaurant generates profits

FIGURE 10

Third-Degree Price Discrimination

This figure illustrates third-degree price discrimination. The two demand curves, D_0 and D_1, represent two segments of a market with different demand elasticities. The less elastic market, D_1, is offered price P_1, which is higher than price P_0, offered to the more elastic market, D_0, thus maximizing the profits for both markets. For market D_0, profits are P_CP_0bc, and for less elastic market D_1, they are P_CP_1ad. These profits exceed what the monopolist could earn from charging one price.

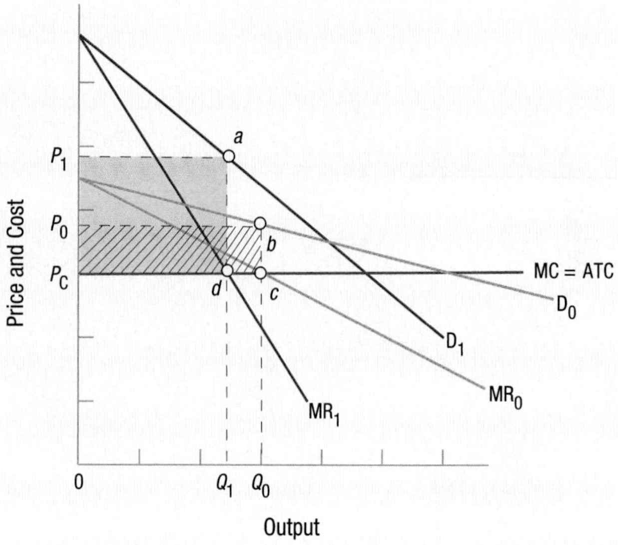

from two separate groups, while charging two separate prices. As long as the restaurant has some monopoly power—it can offer these two prices without driving its regular customers from higher-priced meals to lower-priced meals—it makes sense for it to act this way. Therefore, we can conclude that firms with some monopoly power will always try to price discriminate.

Regulating the Natural Monopolist

Natural monopoly
Large economies of scale mean that the minimum efficient scale of operations is roughly equal to market demand.

A **natural monopoly** exists when economies of scale are so large that the minimum efficient scale of operation is roughly equal to market demand. In this case, efficient production can only be accomplished if the industry lies in the hands of one firm—a monopolist. How can policymakers prevent natural monopolists from abusing their positions of market dominance? There are various approaches to dealing with natural monopolies:

> *First the firm can be publicly owned . . . , the expectation being that the mechanics of political direction and accountability will be sufficient to meet public interest goals. Secondly, the firm may remain in, or be transferred to, private ownership but be subjected to external constraints in the form of price and quantity regulation . . . thirdly, firms desiring to obtain a monopoly right may be forced to compete for it. . . . As part of their competitive bid, they are required to stipulate proposed conditions of supply, relating especially to prices and quality; and those conditions then become terms of the license or franchise under which they exercise the monopoly right.*[2]

A market representing a natural monopoly is shown in Figure 11. Notice that the average cost and marginal cost curves decline continually because of large economies of scale.

If the monopolist were a purely private firm, it would produce only output Q_M and sell this for price P_M (point a). Accordingly, the monopolist would earn eco-

[2]A. I. Ogus, *Regulation: Legal Form and Economic Theory* (Oxford: Oxford University Press), 1996, p. 5, cited in J. Lipczynski and J. Wilson, *Industrial Organization: An Analysis of Competitive Markets* (New York: Prentice Hall—Financial Times), 2001.

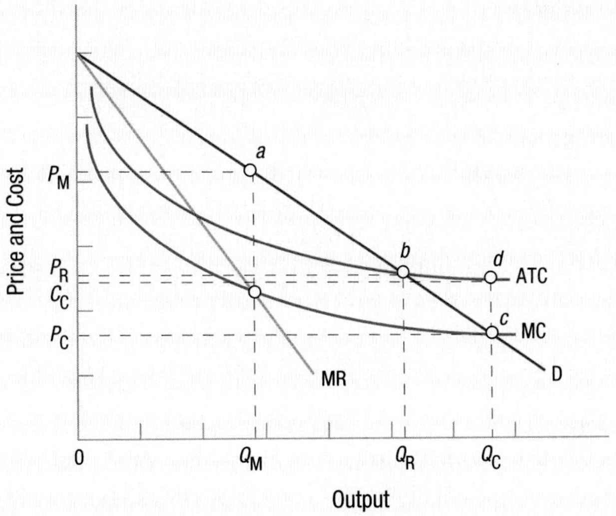

FIGURE 11

Regulating a Natural Monopoly

A natural monopoly exists when economies of scale are so large that the minimum efficient scale of operation is roughly equal to market demand. In this case, efficient production can only be accomplished if the industry lies in the hands of one firm—a monopolist. Yet, if the monopolist is a purely private firm, it will produce only output Q_M, selling it for price P_M (point *a*). This is the principal rationale for regulating natural monopolies to produce output Q_R for a price of P_R (point *b*).

nomic or monopoly profits, and consumers would be harmed, receiving a lower output at a higher price. This is the major argument for regulation.

Marginal Cost Pricing Rule

Ideally, regulators would like to invoke the P = MC rule of competitive markets and force the firm to sell Q_C units for a price of P_C. This is the **marginal cost pricing rule** and would be the optimal resource allocation solution. Yet, because price P_C is below the average cost of production for output Q_C, this would force the firm to sustain losses of *cd* per unit, ultimately driving it out of business. The public sector could subsidize the firm by an amount equal to area $P_C C_C dc$; this subsidy allows the firm to supply the socially optimal output at the socially optimal price, while earning a normal return. This approach has not been used often in the United States. However, Amtrak, with its history of heavy subsidies for maintaining rail service, may be the one major exception.

Marginal cost pricing rule Regulators would prefer to have natural monopolists price where P = MC, but this would result in losses (long term) because ATC > MC. Thus, regulators often must use an average cost pricing rule.

Average Cost Pricing Rule

The more common approach to regulation in the United States has been to insist on an **average cost pricing rule**. Such a rule requires that the monopolist produce and sell output where price equals average total costs. This is illustrated by point *b* in Figure 11, where the demand curve intersects the ATC curve and the firm produces output Q_R and sells it for price P_R. The result is that the firm earns a normal return. Consumers do lose something, in that they must pay a higher price for less output than they would under idealized competitive conditions. Still, the normal profits keep the firm in business, and the losses to consumers are significantly less than if the firm were left unregulated.

Average cost pricing rule Requires a regulated monopolist to produce and sell output where price equals average total costs. This permits the regulated monopolist to earn a normal return on investment over the long term and so remain in business.

Regulation in Practice

America has a long history of public utility regulation. For most of this history, regulation has been accepted as a lesser of two evils. Monopolists have long been viewed with distrust, but regulators have just as often been portrayed as incompetent and ineffectual, if not lapdogs of the industries they regulate.[3] This is

[3]See G. Stigler, "The Theory of Economic Regulation," *Bell Journal of Economics,* 1971, pp. 3–21.

probably a bum rap: Regulating a large enterprise always presents immense difficulties and tradeoffs.

For one thing, finding a point like *b* in Figure 11 is difficult in practice, given that estimating demand and cost curves is an inexact science, at best, and markets are always changing. In practice, regulators must often turn to *rate of return* or *price cap* regulation.

Rate of return regulation Permits product pricing that allows the firm to earn a normal return on capital invested in the firm.

Rate of return regulation allows a firm to price its product in such a way that it can earn a normal return on capital invested. This leads to added regulations about the acceptable items that can be included in costs and capital expenditures. Can the country club memberships of top executives be counted as capital investments? Predictably, firms always want to include more expenses as legitimate business expenses, and regulators want to include fewer. Regulatory commissions and regulated firms often have large staffs to deal with such issues, and protracted court battles are not uncommon.

Price caps Maximum price at which a regulated firm can sell its product. They are often flexible enough to allow for changing cost conditions.

Alternatively, regulators can impose **price caps** on regulated firms, which place maximum limits on the prices firms can charge for products. These caps can be adjusted in response to changing cost conditions, including changes in labor costs, productivity, technology, and raw material prices. When a large part of a regulated firm's output is not self-produced but purchased on the open market, price caps can have disastrous results. This was seen in the California energy market, when wholesale prices for energy went through the roof, but price caps prevented private utilities from raising the retail price of electricity; several firms had to file for bankruptcy.

In sum, though regulation imposes costs on the market, these costs are less than the costs of private monopolies. Today, however, the pace of technological change is so rapid that regulation has lost some of its earlier luster and is not used as often. Rather than regulate the few natural monopolies that do arise, government has sought to prevent monopolies and monopolistic practices from arising at all—a topic we will cover in the next section.

Checkpoint

Monopoly Market Issues

REVIEW

- Firms with monopoly power price discriminate to increase profits.
- To price discriminate, firms must have some control over price and must be able to separate the market into different consumer groups based on their elasticity of demand, and sellers must be able to prevent arbitrage.
- With perfect price discrimination the firm can charge each customer a different price and expropriate the entire consumer surplus for itself.
- Second-degree price discrimination involves charging customers different prices for different quantities of the product.
- Third-degree price discrimination (the most common) involves charging different groups of people different prices.
- Regulating monopolies may involve a marginal cost pricing rule (have the monopolist to set price equal to marginal cost) or an average cost rule (have the monopolist set price equal to average total cost).
- In practice, regulation often involves setting an acceptable rate of return on capital or setting price caps on charges.

QUESTIONS

Researchers at Yale University and the University of California at Berkeley found that minorities and women pay about $500 more on average for a car than white men when bargaining directly with car dealers. However, when minorities and women used Internet services such as Autobytel.com to purchase a car, the price discrimination disappeared. Is this price discrimination the same as that discussed in this section? Why or why not?

Answers to the Checkpoint questions can be found at the end of this chapter.

Antitrust Policy

Like all antitrust cases, this one must make economic sense.

—United States v. Syufy Enterprises

Competition is the market structure that offers consumers the greatest product selection at the lowest prices. Monopolies and firms with substantial monopoly power have the potential to restrict output and increase prices, resulting in significant allocative inefficiencies. The economic model of monopoly forms the basis for the bulk of **antitrust law**, the goal of which is to preserve competition and prevent monopolies and monopoly power from arising.

Antitrust law
Laws designed to maintain competition and prevent monopolies from developing.

Antitrust cases can be filed by the Antitrust Division of the Department of Justice, the Federal Trade Commission (FTC), states' attorneys general, or lawyers for private plaintiffs. Currently, there is debate about the extent of efficiency losses that stem from monopoly power, and how often antitrust action is needed.[4] Even so, Americans have a visceral sense that monopolies are bad, and historically, antitrust policy has targeted monopolies as threats to economic efficiency.

Brief History of Antitrust Policy

The American economy began to change dramatically after the Civil War. Many people left the farm to seek factory jobs in the cities, and the western territories were opened up as rail lines joined them to the rest of the country. Communications expanded along with transportation, the telephone replacing the telegraph. Markets grew from local to regional in size, and many firms dramatically expanded their size. Unfettered competition led many large firms to engage in brutal practices meant to drive competitors from the market. The largest firms established trusts, which brought many firms under one organizational structure that could set price and output levels, extract concessions from railroads, and act as we would expect monopolies to act. By the end of the century, trusts had become so powerful—and so hated—that Congress passed the first antitrust act, the Sherman Act, in 1890. Antitrust laws and policies, thus, had their origins in trust-busting activity.

Most of the legislators who voted for antitrust laws in the late 1800s and early 1900s were more concerned with equitably distributing income and wealth, and the health of small businesses, than with competition and allocative efficiency. The massive accumulations of wealth by such "robber barons" as John D. Rockefeller (Standard Oil) and Jay Gould (railroads and stock manipulation) sparked resentment and fear. Nobel Prize laureate George Stigler has argued, however, that the economists of the day had little enthusiasm for antitrust policy, viewing all limits placed on

[4]See Richard A. Posner, *Antitrust Law,* 2nd ed. (Chicago: University of Chicago Press), 2001.

Nobel Prize George Stigler

Few modern economists have broken ground in so many different areas as George Stigler, described by some admirers as the "ultimate empirical economist." His 1982 Nobel Prize cited seminal work in industrial structure, the functioning of markets, and the causes and effects of public regulation.

Born in 1911 in the Seattle suburb of Renton, Washington, Stigler attended graduate school at the University of Chicago, a center of great intellectual ferment during the late 1930s, with fellow students and Nobel Prize winners Milton Friedman and Paul Samuelson. Professors like Frank Knight and Henry Simons encouraged what he would later describe as "an irreverence toward prevailing ideas bordering on congenital skepticism." Stigler was a professor at the University of Chicago from 1958 until his death in 1991.

Exploring the relationship between size and efficiency led him to the "Darwinian" conclusion that by observing competition in an industry, he could determine the most efficient sizes for firms, a method he called "the survivor technique." In the 1960s, Stigler studied the impacts of government regulation on the economy, arriving at negative conclusions about its potential value to consumers. He later turned to the causes of regulation, observing that government interventions were often designed to optimize market conditions for producers instead of protecting the public interest. This work opened up a new field known as "regulation economics" and kindled greater interest in the relationship between law and economics.

Stigler considered his work on information theory his greatest contribution to economics. Conventional wisdom suggested that prices for homogeneous industries should be uniform, but in the real-world prices often varied. His research suggested that the variation could be explained by the costs of gathering and diffusing information about goods and prices.

business as stifling free enterprise. Today, most economists agree that some antitrust legislation is needed, but that its primary role should be to prevent the allocative inefficiency associated with monopoly behavior.

The Major Antitrust Laws

Several major statutes form the core of the country's antitrust laws. The most important provisions of these laws (as amended) are described in the following sections.

The Sherman Act (1890)

Section 1: *Every contract, combination in the form of trust or otherwise, or conspiracy, in restraint of trade or commerce among the several states, or with foreign nations, is hereby declared to be illegal.*
Section 2: *Every person who shall monopolize, or attempt to monopolize, or combine or conspire with any other person or persons, to monopolize any part of the trade or commerce among the several states, or with foreign nations, shall be deemed guilty of a felony.*

Conviction in either section is a felony and carries a fine of up to $10,000,000 for corporations and $350,000 for individuals, and/or a prison sentence of up to 3 years. Section 1 focuses on the "restraint of trade," whereas Section 2 targets "monopolization" and the "attempt to monopolize." Congress purposefully left these terms undefined, thus requiring the courts to flesh them out.

The Clayton Act (1914)

Section 2: *It shall be unlawful for any person engaged in commerce . . . to discriminate in price between different purchasers of commodities of like grade and quality . . . where the effect of such discrimination may be substantially to lessen competition or tend to create a monopoly in any line of commerce, or to injure, destroy, or prevent competition.*
Section 3: *It shall be unlawful for any person engaged in commerce [to] make a sale or contract for sale of goods . . . or other commodities . . . on the condition . . . that the lessee or purchaser thereof shall not use or deal in the goods . . . or other commodities of a competitor or competitors of the seller, where the effect of such lease, sale or contract . . . may be to substantially lessen competition or tend to create a monopoly in any line of commerce.*
Section 7: *That no corporation engaged in commerce shall acquire, directly or indirectly, the whole or any part of the stock or other share capital and no corporation subject to the jurisdiction of the Federal Trade Commission shall acquire the whole or any part of the assets of another corporation engaged also in commerce, where in any line of commerce in any section of the country, the effect of such acquisition may be substantially to lessen competition, or tend to create a monopoly.*

The act goes on to forbid "tying contracts," agreements whereby the sale of one product is contingent upon the purchase of another product. The act further makes it illegal to acquire a competing company's stock and have interlocking directorates, the directors of one company sitting on the boards of competing companies. These practices are deemed illegal if they substantially lessen competition or tend to create a monopoly.

The Federal Trade Commission Act (1914)

Section 5.(a)(1): *Unfair methods of competition in or affecting commerce, and unfair or deceptive acts or practices in or affecting commerce, are hereby declared unlawful.*

This act established an independent regulatory body, the Federal Trade Commission (FTC), and gave it the power to enforce the Clayton Act and the Robinson-Patman Act. Amended in 1938 by the Wheeler-Lea Amendments to add "unfair or deceptive acts or practices," this act is the centerpiece of federal consumer protection. The Supreme Court has given the FTC the power to enforce antitrust laws, except the Sherman Act.

Other Antitrust Acts

The Robinson-Patman Act amended the Clayton Act in 1936 to prohibit price discrimination. Passed in the middle of the Depression, this act was designed to protect mom and pop stores from the growing menace of chain stores and supermarkets. Chain stores have tremendous buying and bargaining power with manufacturers. This bargaining power translates into price discounts that chains can pass on to their customers, putting small businesses at a disadvantage. This same logic is often used today to prevent a Wal-Mart from opening stores in some towns. Today, the federal government rarely enforces these provisions, viewing them as outdated.

The 1950 Celler-Kefauver Antimerger Act closed a merger loophole in the Clayton Act. The original Clayton Act intended to forbid holding companies, and thus it outlawed one company from holding the stock of its competitors. But the Clayton Act did not prohibit anticompetitive mergers through asset acquisition. The Celler-Kefauver Act closed this loophole, and set up elaborate premerger notification requirements for mergers exceeding a certain size.

The intensity of antitrust enforcement has varied with presidential administrations and courts over the past century. There is general agreement among economists and judges that the reason for antitrust enforcement is to prevent the inefficiencies associated with significant monopoly power. Merger policy through premerger notification for approval or challenge is designed to prevent mergers that have a reasonable likelihood of creating monopoly power. The first problem facing the enforcement community involves defining monopoly power. This entails defining the relevant product market and then agreeing on a proper measuring device.

Defining the Relevant Market and Monopoly Power

We have seen that, as an industry moves from competition to monopoly, pricing power rises from zero to total. One of the challenges economists have faced is developing one measure that accurately reflects market power or concentration for all these market structures.

Industries that become more concentrated increase the losses to society. Therefore, any measure of concentration should accurately reflect the ability of firms to increase prices above that point which would prevail under competitive conditions. Such an index would help the Justice Department, for instance, determine when to bring a Sherman Act case against a firm for monopolizing or attempting to monopolize. It could further be used to determine whether two firms should be permitted to merge. Coming up with such a number requires, first, that we define the relevant market, and then that we compute an index number for this market.

Defining the Market

To measure market power and the concentration of a market, we need to determine the limits of the market, geographically and as defined by the product itself.

Some markets can be severely limited geographically, such as cement, with its extremely high transport costs, and dry cleaning, limited by the unwillingness of consumers to travel far for this service. Other markets are national in scope, like airlines, breakfast cereals, and electronics. Still others extend beyond the borders of a country, with the forces of global competition increasingly reducing domestic market power.

Economists have been unable to reduce the empirical definition of a relevant market to a simple rule. Nearly 50 years ago, George Stigler suggested that "all products or enterprises with large long-run cross-elasticities of supply or demand should be combined into a single industry."[5] This would mean that an industry or market should be regarded as containing those products that are ready substitutes for the main product in the long run. Stigler's suggestion by no means makes delineating a relevant market neat and easy, but at least it gives economists something to work with.

Concentration Ratios

The most widely used measure of industry concentration is the **concentration ratio**. The n-firm concentration ratio is the share of industry sales accounted for by the industry's n largest firms. Typically, 4- and 8-firm concentration ratios (CR-4 and CR-8) are reported.

Concentration ratios
The share of industry shipments or sales accounted for by the top four or eight firms.

Though useful in giving a quick snapshot of an industry, concentration ratios express only one piece of the market power distribution picture: the market share enjoyed by the industry's four or eight largest firms. Yet, consider the following two 4-firm concentration ratios. In the first industry, the four largest firms have market shares equal to 65, 10, 5, and 5. This means the concentration ratio is 85; that is, the top four firms control 85% of industry sales. The second industry has market shares equal to 25, 20, 20, 20. This industry's concentration ratio also equals 85. But do the two industries exhibit the same level of monopoly power? Hardly! The second industry, whose top four firms are roughly equal in size, would be expected to be more competitive than the first, where 65% of the market is controlled by one firm.

Without more information about each industry, concentration ratios are not overly informative, except to point out extreme contrasts. If one industry's 4-firm concentration ratio is 85, for instance, and another's is 15, the first industry has considerably more monopoly power than the second.

Economists and antitrust enforcers, however, need finer distinctions than concentration ratios permit. For this reason, the profession has developed the Herfindahl-Hirshman index.

Herfindahl-Hirshman Index (HHI)

The **Herfindahl-Hirshman index (HHI)** is the principal measure of concentration used by the Justice Department to evaluate mergers and judge monopoly power. The HHI is defined by the equation:

Herfindahl-Hirshman index (HHI)
A way of measuring industry concentration, equal to the sum of the squares of market shares for all firms in the industry.

$$\text{HHI} = (S_1)^2 + (S_2)^2 + (S_3)^2 + \ldots + (S_n)^2,$$

where $S_1, S_2, \ldots S_n$ are the percentage market shares of each firm in the industry. Thus, the HHI is the sum of the squares of each market share. In a five-firm industry, for instance, in which each firm enjoys a 20% market share, the HHI is

$$\begin{aligned}\text{HHI} &= 20^2 + 20^2 + 20^2 + 20^2 + 20^2 \\ &= 400 + 400 + 400 + 400 + 400 \\ &= 2000\end{aligned}$$

The HHI ranges from roughly zero (a huge number of small firms) to 10,000 (a one firm monopoly: $100^2 = 10{,}000$). By squaring market shares, the HHI gives

[5] George J. Stigler, "Introduction," in National Bureau of Economic Research, *Business Concentration and Price Policy* (Princeton, NJ: Princeton University Press), 1955, p. 4.

greater weight to those firms with large market shares. Thus, a 5-firm industry with market shares equal to 65, 15, 10, 5, 5 would have an HHI equal to

$$\begin{aligned} \text{HHI} &= 65^2 + 15^2 + 10^2 + 5^2 + 5^2 \\ &= 4225 + 225 + 100 + 25 + 25 \\ &= 4600 \end{aligned}$$

The HHI is consistent with our intuitive notion of market power. It seems clear that an industry with several competitors of roughly equal size will be more competitive than an industry in which one firm controls a substantial share of the market.

Applying the HHI

In 1976, Congress passed the Hart-Scott-Rodino Act. This act requires prenotification of large proposed mergers to the FTC and the antitrust division of the Justice Department. Prenotification gives federal agencies a chance to review proposed mergers for anticompetitive impacts. This approach prevents some mergers from taking place that would ultimately have to be challenged by Sherman Act litigation, a far more costly alternative for the government and for the firms involved.

During the prenotification review, the Justice Department or FTC can approve the proposed merger or else negotiate a settlement that introduces restrictions designed to reduce anticompetitive outcomes. Sometimes these agreements involve complex rules and reporting requirements that amount to government regulation. If no agreement is reached, the agencies can challenge the merger in court. When agreements cannot be reached, the merger is usually called off.

The Justice Department and FTC in 1992 issued merger guidelines based on the HHI. These guidelines classify industries as follows:

- HHI $<$ 1,000: Industry is unconcentrated.
- 1,000 $<$ HHI $<$ 1,800: Industry is moderately concentrated.
- HHI $>$ 1,800: Industry is highly concentrated.

Mergers where the resulting HHI is below 1,000 will often be approved. Mergers with postmerger HHIs between 1,000 and 1,800 will be closely evaluated; they are often challenged if the proposed merger raises the HHI by 100 points or more. When the HHI for the industry exceeds 1,800, a postmerger rise in the HHI of 50 points is enough to spark a challenge.

These guidelines have worked well, giving businesses a good idea of when the government will challenge mergers. These days, roughly 70% of all mergers are rapidly approved; the remainder often require only minor adjustments or more information to satisfy government agencies. In the end, less than 2% of proposed mergers are seriously challenged.[6] Clearly, most firms that want to merge will ensure their companies and industries fit in the specified guidelines.

Contestable markets
Markets that look monopolistic but where entry costs are so low that the sheer threat of entry keeps prices low. Computer software and Internet Web sites (search, music downloads, and social networking sites) are examples.

Contestable Markets

Sometimes what looks like a monopolist does not act like a monopolist. Markets that are contestable fit this description. **Contestable markets** are those markets with entry costs so low that the sheer threat of entry keeps prices in contestable markets low. Potential competition constrains firm behavior. Microsoft might charge more for its latest version of Windows if Linux was not nipping at its heels.

[6] W. K. Viscusi, J. M. Vernon, and J. E. Harrington, *Economics of Regulation and Antitrust,* 3rd ed. (Cambridge, MA: MIT Press), 2000, pp. 208–209.

Many software firms argue, however, that new software innovations are stifled because once a new product has been released, Microsoft can simply clone the product and package it with Windows for free, thus rendering investment in new products unprofitable for smaller companies. It is far easier and cheaper to copy and enhance a software product than to conceive of the idea and bring it to market in the first place. A significant part of the arguments in the Microsoft legal case revolved around just this issue. Still, the relative ease with which new operating systems can be developed to challenge Windows—witness Linux, Macintosh OS X, Unix—probably keeps Microsoft from significantly overcharging for Windows.

The Future of Antitrust Policy

American antitrust legislation grew out of economic concentration and the resulting predatory behavior over a century ago. The laws passed to nullify these abuses have resulted in some fascinating legal cases, but in the end, antitrust legislation is rooted in the basic economics and market structure analysis discussed in the last two chapters.

As the United States transitioned from an agrarian to an industrial economy, public policy changed. As our economy today moves from its domestic manufacturing roots to more of a global information and service base, public policy again must adapt.

The Microsoft case was the first real attempt to apply the old antitrust rules to the newly emerging circumstances of the "new economy." The government met with some success in this case, but mostly failure.

The new economy differs from the old economy in many ways. The old economy was grounded in manufacturing and distributing physical goods such as steel, automobiles, appliances, and shoes. These old economy industries enjoyed economies of scale in production, often requiring huge capital requirements and modest rates of innovation.

New economy industries turn these requirements on their heads. Such industries as software, telecommunications infrastructure, and e-commerce operate with modest capital, extremely high rates of innovation, easy entry and exit, and economies of scale in consumption known as **network externalities**.

Network externalities Markets in which as more people use (or are connected to) the network, the network becomes more valuable.

One phone or Internet connection is worthless; it cannot be used to communicate with anyone. As more people become connected to the network, however, the network becomes more valuable—hence, the term "network externalities." Every firm therefore has a tremendous interest in seeing its innovation adopted as the industry standard, providing the firm with a monopoly in that technology.

Consumers and the society as a whole may benefit from monopoly standards—how could we exchange computer files if we all used different word-processing programs? But what, then, will keep temporary monopolists from charging excessive prices? To some degree, the answer lies in the contestability of the industry (low capital requirements, easy entry and exit, and rapid innovation). The Linux challenge to Microsoft Windows came from a university student who wrote this operating system as a school project. Often, it is low prices (free, in the case of Linux) that extend markets and create standards. Low prices mean more users, and more users lead to the creation of standards.

Much of what new economy firms produce is intellectual property. In large measure, it is computer code of one form or another. Most of the costs to produce the programs are fixed, already sunk once the product is completed. To produce and distribute the product costs only a fraction of the product's value; if the Internet is used, distribution costs can approach zero. This means markups and profits are high, which creates a strong incentive to clone successful products. Monopolies, therefore, tend to be transitory in the new economy. The travails of Lotus 123, WordPerfect, Borland, and Netscape all testify to the vulnerability of temporary monopolists in the software industry. All were industry leaders at one point, only to be displaced by some new kid on the block (Microsoft).

Antitrust laws and policy need to be adjusted to new market realities. In our global information and service economy, many of the old rules are irrelevant. One federal judge and economist, Richard Posner, argues that we should repeal all the old antitrust laws, chiefly because of the "gross redundancy of their manifold provisions." He suggests these laws be replaced with a simple statute that prohibits "unreasonably anti-competitive practices."[7]

When a firm's market share approaches monopoly levels, turning to antitrust laws is the obvious response.

Checkpoint

Antitrust Policy

REVIEW

- The Sherman Act (1890) prohibited monopolization and attempts to monopolize.
- The Clayton Act (1914) prohibited price discrimination that lessened competition, prohibited tie-in sales, and prohibited corporate directors from serving on competing boards if this would lessen competition.
- The Federal Trade Commission Act (1914) prohibited unfair or deceptive business practices and established the Federal Trade Commission.
- Defining the relevant market is often difficult, but a focus on cross elasticity of demand is useful.
- Concentration ratios measure market concentration by looking at the share of industry sales accounted for by the top n firms.
- The Herfindahl-Hirshman index (HHI) measures concentration by computing the sum of the squares of market shares for all firms in the industry.
- The Justice Department uses the HHI to set premerger guidelines.
- Contestable markets are markets with low entry costs so that the potential threat of entry keeps prices low.

QUESTIONS

Assume the following table represents the sales figures in billions of dollars for the eight largest firms in the auto industry (ignore the other firms) in the United States:

Daimler Chrysler	200.4
General Motors	199.1
Toyota	183.3
Ford	173.0
Honda	90.0
BMW	78.2
Hyundai	22.3
Kia	12.7

[7]Richard A. Posner, *Antitrust Law,* 2nd ed. (Chicago: University of Chicago Press), 2001, p. 260.

a. Compute the 4-firm concentration ratio for the industry.
b. Compute the HHI for the industry.
c. If Toyota and Ford wanted to merge, and you were head of the Justice Department, would you permit the merger? Why or why not? How about if Hyundai and Kia wanted to merge?

Answers to the Checkpoint questions can be found at the end of this chapter.

California Power Shortages and Deregulation

Tivadar Bote/Getty Images

As a final item for this chapter, let us leave antitrust and again examine regulating a monopolist. To apply this chapter's concepts, let us take a closer look at the California power crisis of 2000–01, the one that made "rolling blackouts" a staple of everyday conversation. What happened was clear: Power companies could not meet energy demand, so they rationed available energy supplies by cutting off electricity to a specific area for an hour at a time. After the hour, the lights and computers came back on, while another area became victim to a blackout.

Contrast these rolling blackouts with a systemwide blackout that hit the Northeast on August 14, 2003. With that systemwide blackout, power usage surged because of the hot weather and overwhelmed the power grid. It was a onetime occurrence—or so inhabitants in the Northeast hope. The California rolling blackouts, in contrast, happened over a length of time. It was not caused by a onetime surge in usage.

What happened, then, in California? The simple answer is that deregulation of the power monopoly was done poorly, leading to incentives for energy traders (Enron and others) to use various trading strategies to extract higher prices from California power companies. First, let's get one minor aspect out of the way. Power deliverance depends on economies of scale. Think of the infrastructure required in laying down electric wires. This leads to a natural monopoly. So this delivery aspect of energy supply always needs to be regulated. There can never be total deregulation of power supply, at least not at the current time with current technologies.[8] The good news is that delivery infrastructure is a small part of the cost of energy.

To bring competition into previous monopoly markets and to mitigate the sometimes pernicious influence of monopolies on the decisions of regulators, 24 states have tried to deregulate power companies.[9] Unfortunately, California deregulated the wrong way.

California utilities were prevented from entering into long-term contracts to ensure adequate supply. California regulators thought that long-term prices were higher than short-term prices, and so felt that consumers might be taken advantage of in years to come. They forced utilities always to buy at market prices. This led to fluctuating prices—with a potential political backlash if prices rose too much, too quickly. Recognizing this possibility, California put on price caps, which are limits to the price increase that California utilities could pass on to their customers.[10]

When energy prices to the utilities were stable or falling, all was well because utilities could charge their customers the full cost plus a profit for themselves. When energy prices rose, however, once the price increase went above the cap, utilities

---

[8]David Buchan, "Move Towards Deregulation Comes Slowly," *Financial Times,* April 11, 2002, p. 1.
[9]Buchan, "Move Towards Deregulation."
[10]"A Gloomy End for a Half-Hearted Undertaking: The Lesson of California's Energy Crisis Is Not That Deregulation Is a Bad Idea, but That It Must Be Done Properly," *Financial Times,* January 23, 2001, p. 25.

could not pass this price increase along and so would lose money. Firms will continue in business in the short run even if they are facing losses, as long as variable costs are covered, and there is some contribution to fixed costs. When variable costs cannot be covered, firms have no choice but to shut down.

A supply shock sent market prices climbing in California. The increases were so great that the price exceeded the mandated price caps. Utilities could not pass on the entire increases to their customers. They had no long-term contracts to fall back on for at least some part of their energy supply, so they were completely at the mercy of the short-term price. And with price caps at the retail level, consumers had no incentive to conserve.

California could have eliminated the price caps and solved the energy crisis at the cost to consumers of much higher temporary energy prices. It chose not to: California's then-governor Gray Davis railed against utility "profiteers."[11] Using economic analysis, we can see that if the price caps are not removed, only two things will solve the energy crisis: Either provide incentives for utilities so that they can better bear the loss, or wait for the supply shock to dissipate. Political threats provided some incentive: Utilities had to consider the long-term consequences of not meeting energy demand, even if it meant short-term losses.

The California power crisis showed that there are wrong ways to deregulate. Other states, such as Texas, where intervention is less common than in California, suggest that deregulation can work.

Key Concepts

Monopoly, p. 218
Economies of scale, p. 219
Rent seeking, p. 225
X-inefficiency, p. 225
Price discrimination, p. 227
Natural monopoly, p. 230
Marginal cost pricing rule, p. 231
Average cost pricing rule, p. 231
Rate of return regulation, p. 232
Price caps, p. 232
Antitrust law, p. 233
Concentration ratios, p. 237
Herfindahl-Hirshman index (HHI), p. 237
Contestable markets, p. 238
Network externalities, p. 239

Chapter Summary

Monopoly Markets

A firm can *be* a monopoly; it can *have* monopoly power. For economists, a monopoly is defined by three key characteristics. First, the market has just one seller, thus the monopolistic firm *is* the industry. Second, no close substitutes exist for the monopolist's product, so consumers cannot easily substitute other products for the product sold by the monopolist. Third, significant barriers to entry keep other firms from entering the industry. This means the monopolist faces no competition, even in the long run.

Monopoly power is the degree to which a firm can control the price of its product by adjusting output. Competitive firms are price takers, meaning that they have no monopoly power; the prices for their products are determined by competitive markets. Monopolists, in contrast, are price makers. They enjoy considerable monop-

[11]"A Gloomy End for a Half-Hearted Undertaking."

oly power and much freedom in deciding what to charge for their products. This monopoly power is caused by significant barriers to entry.

The key to monopoly power is significant barriers to entry, which can take several forms. The economies of scale in an industry can be so large that demand will support only one firm. Economists refer to such cases as natural monopolies. Utilities have traditionally been considered natural monopolists because of the high fixed costs associated with power plants.

If a firm owns or has control over an important input into the production process, that firm can keep potential rivals out of the market.

Some barriers to market entry extend from the power of government. A government franchise grants a firm permission to provide specific goods or services while prohibiting others from doing so. Patents are extended to firms and individuals that invent new products and processes. For a limited period, the patent holder is legally protected from competition in the production of the patented product. Copyrights give firms or individuals the exclusive right to intellectual products for a long period of time.

Because the monopolist constitutes the entire industry, it faces a downward sloping demand curve. Product price is determined in a monopoly by how much the monopolist wishes to produce. This contrasts with the competitive firm, which can sell all it wishes, but only at the market determined price.

Like the competitive firm, the monopolist maximizes its profit at output where MR = MC. Because of the monopolist's downward sloping demand curve, however, marginal revenue does not equal price at this point; rather, MR < P. To determine the monopolist's profit maximizing price, extend a vertical line through the point where MR = MC to the demand curve; where this line intersects the demand curve determines the price to be found on the vertical axis. The monopolist's profit equals the difference between this price and average total costs, multiplied by the number of units sold.

Being a monopoly does not guarantee economic profits. If a monopolist's profit maximizing price is lower than average total costs, it will suffer a loss. As long as price exceeds average variable costs, the monopolist will minimize its losses in the short run by continuing to produce. But if price should fall below average variable costs, the monopolist will minimize its losses (equal to its fixed costs) by shutting down. If these losses persist, the monopolist will exit the industry in the long run.

Monopoly output is lower and monopoly price is higher, compared to competitive markets. As a result, monopolies earn economic profits at the expense of consumers: monopoly reduces consumer surplus. The loss to society from monopoly output and pricing is known as deadweight loss, or welfare loss.

To maintain their advantageous position, monopolists often engage in rent-seeking behavior. They undertake a variety of activities to avoid competition, such as hiring lawyers and lobbyists, getting patents and copyrights, and demanding tariff protection from Congress. All these activities are inefficient, in that they shift resources from one group to another without producing a useful good or service, and so rent seeking represents an added loss to society from monopoly.

Some economists argue that monopolies do not have to operate efficiently because they are protected from competitive pressures; this is known as x-inefficiency. Management can offer itself perks without worrying about whether costs are kept at efficient levels.

Monopoly Market Issues

When firms with monopoly power price discriminate, they charge different consumers different prices for the same product. The goal is to maximize profits by charging each customer as much as each is willing to pay. Several conditions are required for successful price discrimination. First, sellers must have some monopoly power, or some control over price. Second, sellers must be able to separate the market into different consumer groups based on their elasticities of demand. Third, sellers must be able to prevent arbitrage; that is, it must be impossible or prohibitively expensive for low-price buyers to resell to higher-price buyers.

There are three major types of price discrimination. First-degree price discrimination involves charging each customer the maximum price each is willing to pay. This is exemplified by the flea market, where sellers and buyers haggle and barter for each product. Second-degree price discrimination involves charging different customers different prices based on the quantities of the product they purchase. Many firms charge a high price for the first units of a product sold to a customer, but then offer a bulk discount on the sale of added units. The most common form of price discrimination is third-degree price discrimination. This involves charging different groups of people different prices, as when airlines set different ticket prices for business travelers and vacationers.

A natural monopoly exists when economies of scale are so large that the minimum efficient scale of operation is roughly equal to market demand. In such cases, policymakers employ a variety of measures to prevent natural monopolists from abusing their positions of market dominance.

A marginal cost pricing rule requires the monopolist to set its price where P = MC, the profit maximizing rule in competitive markets. But because this price is often below the monopolist's average total costs, losses result. For the monopoly to remain in business, it must be heavily subsidized by the government. For this reason, this approach is seldom used.

An average cost pricing rule requires the monopolist to produce and sell at the level where demand equals average total costs. The result is that the firm earns a normal return. Consumers do lose something, in that they must pay a higher price for a lower output than they would if competitive conditions were possible. Still, the normal profits keep the firm in business, and the losses to consumers are significantly less than if the firm were left unregulated.

In practice, estimating demand and cost curves is extremely difficult, so regulators often abandon the regulatory strategies above and turn to rate of return or price cap regulation. Rate of return regulation allows the monopolist to price its product in such a way that it can earn a normal return on capital invested. Price caps place maximum limits on the prices firms can charge for products.

Antitrust Policy

Since 1890, the United States Congress has passed a series of major statutes that form the core of the country's antitrust laws. These include the Sherman Act (1890), the Clayton Act (1914), the Federal Trade Commission Act (1914), the Robinson-Patman Act (1936), and the Celler-Kefauver Antimerger Act (1950).

The early antitrust laws were passed with the intention of promoting an equitable distribution of wealth and protecting small businesses against predatory monopolies. The intensity of antitrust enforcement has varied with presidential administrations and courts over the past century. There is general agreement among economists and judges, however, that some antitrust regulation is needed, and that its basic purpose is to prevent the inefficiencies associated with significant monopoly power.

Economists have developed several means of measuring market concentration. The n-firm concentration ratio reports the share of industry sales accounted for by the n largest firms. Typically, the 4- and 8-firm concentration ratios are reported.

The Herfindahl-Hirshman index (HHI) is the principal measure of concentration used by the Justice Department to evaluate mergers and judge monopoly power. The HHI is defined by the equation:

$$\text{HHI} = (S_1)^2 + (S_2)^2 + (S_3)^2 + \ldots + (S_n)^2$$

where $S_1, S_2, \ldots S_n$ are the percentage market shares of each firm in the industry. By squaring market shares, the HHI gives greater weight to those firms with large market shares.

Contestable markets are those with entry costs so low that firms can enter or leave the industry rapidly. If a firm is earning economic profits, new firms will enter the market until returns have been driven back down to normal levels. The sheer threat of entry, therefore, keeps prices in contestable markets low, even if the market is now a monopoly.

Questions and Problems

1. Are McDonald's and Starbucks monopolies? Why or why not?

2. Synthetic diamonds are getting better, and starting to give De Beers a lot of competition in the diamond market. What will be De Beers' response?

3. How important is the existence of a significant barrier to entry to maintaining a monopoly? What would be the result if a monopoly market could be easily entered? Why might a monopoly in a high-tech field such as computers, Internet, and consumer electronics be rather short-lived?

4. Explain why MR < P for the monopolist, but MR = P for competitive firms.

5. What do they mean when economists call monopolies inefficient? What is the deadweight loss of monopoly?

6. Using the figure for a monopoly firm below, answer the following questions.
   a. What will be the monopoly price, output, and profit for this firm?
   b. If this monopolist could perfectly price discriminate, what would profit equal?
   c. If this industry was competitive, what would be the price, output, and profit?
   d. How large (in dollars) is the deadweight loss from this monopolist?

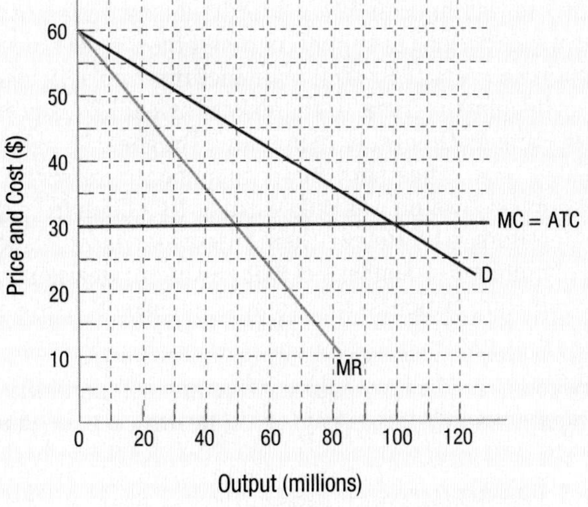

7. Using the figure for a natural monopoly firm below, answer the following questions.
   a. Roughly what would be the monopoly price, output, and profit for this unregulated natural monopolist?
   b. Assume that regulators use the competitive P = MC for regulation. Roughly how high would the total subsidy have to be to keep this firm in the industry over the long run?
   c. Using P = ATC as the regulatory approach, approximately what would be the price, output, and profits for this monopolist?

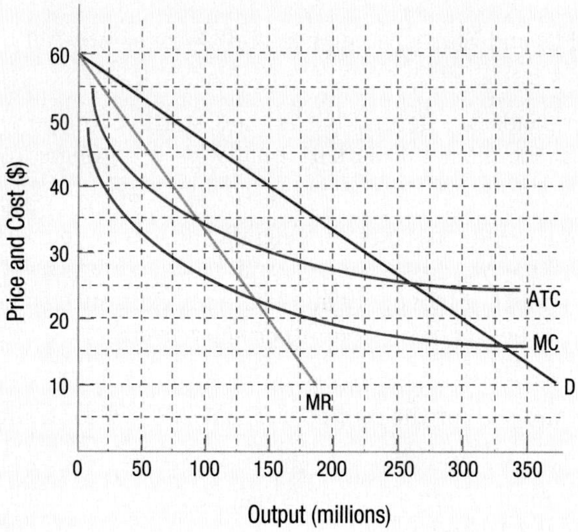

8. The monopoly model we discussed in this chapter suggests that monopolies have little incentive to innovate. In contrast, firms in competitive markets need to keep innovating to continue to exist. Some economists have suggested that if barriers to entry are not large, this is sufficient to keep a monopolist innovating to maintain its monopoly. Does the Internet-tech-software industry seem to fit this argument?

9. Swatch, the Swiss watchmaker famous for its inexpensive watches, announced recently that it will no longer supply high-end mechanical movements or parts to upscale manufacturers.[12] Swatch manufactures and sells roughly 75% of the mechanical movements to such watchmakers as Lacroix, Nardin, and Breitling and has its own brands Omega, Longines, and Breguet. The change will not take place until 2010, but it has sent many manufacturers scrambling to replace Swatch as a supplier. Swatch was only earning $3 million from the sale of movements to competitors, who turned them into watches worth several billions of dollars. One manufacturer suggested that "Swatch's decision was driven by its desire to reduce competition." Does this seem correct? Why or why not?

10. In 2006, Maryland passed a law requiring that any company with 10,000 or more employees must spend 8% of its payroll on health care, or must remit the dif-

[12]For more details, see Peter Marsh, "Swatch Decision Throws a Spanner in Swiss Watch Industry's Works," *Financial Times,* August 10, 2005, p. 6.

ference to the state. Wal-Mart, the only employer approaching that employment level, was the target of the legislation. George Will,[13] writing about this development says, "Maryland's grasping for Wal-Mart's revenues opens a new chapter in the degeneracy of state governments that are eager to spend more money than they have the nerve to collect straightforwardly in taxes. Fortunately, as labor unions and allied rent-seekers in 30 or so other states contemplate mimicking Maryland, Wal-Mart can contemplate an advantage of federalism." What does he mean by "labor unions and allied rent-seekers"? What do they have to gain?

11. Economists Robert Crandall and Clifford Winston[14] ask, "Would consumer welfare seriously be threatened if Ford and General Motors merged?" In 1960, together they would have had almost 75% of the automobile-truck market, but today have only a third of the market. How would you answer their question if this was 1960? Today?

12. Being number one in any business attracts a lot of attention. As *The Economist* has noted,

    As soon as a firm climbs above the sharp elbows of its rivals, it starts getting pelted with the eggs of anti-business activities. People who hate big business aim high. So while big, bad Wal-Mart is pilloried, Target has in the past couple of years blithely cut the benefits of its non-union workers. And when was the last time you saw an anti-globalization mob destroy a Burger King outlet?[15]

    Describe some of the benefits of being number two in a large industry. In terms of total revenues (sales), name the number one and two firms in the following industries: major auto manufacturers, semiconductors, major drug manufacturers, banks, and major integrated oil and gas.

13. If cable television services were deregulated today, what would happen to the monthly charges?

14. We often think that government enforced patents and copyrights are the most used public policies to create (or assist) monopolies. But economist Edward Glaeser argues that zoning laws and other regulatory hurdles have been a major force in escalating housing prices in many cities. He suggests that zoning and other restrictions on development have made "boutique" cities out of Manhattan, Boston, and San Francisco, where only the skilled and privileged can afford to live. As he notes, "Homeowners have a strong incentive to stop new development, both because it can be an inconvenience and also because, like any monopolist, stopping supply drives up the price of their own homes. Lack of affordable housing isn't a problem to homeowners; that's exactly what they want. The thing you want most is to make sure that your home is not affordable if you own it."[16] Is Professor Glaeser right in that homeowners are not monopolists, but often act like them to enhance the value of their houses? Would elimination of zoning laws and building codes result in a greater supply of affordable housing?

---

[13]George Will, "Maryland's Wal-Mart Raid 'a Legislative Mugging'," *Rocky Mountain News,* January 22, 2006, p. 7E.
[14]Robert Crandall and Clifford Winston, "The Breakdown of 'Breakup'," *Wall Street Journal,* March 9, 2006, p. A14.
[15]"Runner-Up, Up and Away," *The Economist,* December 17, 2005, p. 14.
[16]Jon Gertner, "Home Economics," *New York Times,* March 5, 2006, p. 8.

The table below shows data for selected industries for 2002 (the latest data available). Use this table to answer questions 15–17.

Industry	Number of Companies	CR-4	CR-8	HHI-50 Largest
Dental labs	6923	12.7	17.8	54.2
Office furniture, mfg.	4129	24.2	32.4	178.7
Lead pencil and art goods, mfg.	138	58.3	73.1	1276.1
Aircraft engine and parts, mfg.	296	76.9	82.4	2527.7
Electric lamp bulb and parts, mfg.	57	88.5	94.1	2757.6
Household appliance, mfg.	251	62.2	70.8	1131.9
Household vacuum cleaners, mfg.	29	77.9	96.1	2096.3
Electronic computer, mfg.	465	75.5	89.2	2662.4
Pharmaceutical and medicine, mfg.	1444	34.0	49.1	506.0
Petroleum refineries	88	41.2	63.5	639.7

15. If two firms, one in the CR-4 category and another in the CR-8 category, decided to merge, which of the industries in the table would the Justice Department almost automatically permit?

16. Why do you think that there are so many dental labs and that the concentration is so small?

17. What industries in the table would the Justice Department probably reject if any proposed mergers of two firms in the top eight? In these industries, would the Justice Department be likely to permit two small firms to merge?

Answers to Checkpoint Questions

CHECKPOINT: MONOPOLY MARKETS

Yes, this is rent seeking. Google has a huge capital base, cash flow, and could compete with Microsoft in the browser market if it really saw the search box as a threat. The Justice Department announced in May 2006 that it did not feel the search box was a threat to competition.

CHECKPOINT: MONOPOLY MARKET ISSUES

No, this is not the same type of price discrimination discussed in this section. This type of discrimination occurs because of information problems, racism, or other factors. The authors conclude that a large part of the price differences in Internet buying and bargaining in the showroom comes from the fact that Internet purchasers have better information. Price discrimination in this section of the chapter is based on consumers with different elasticities of demand, not information problems or racism. Examples include student, senior, and adult pricing in movie theaters.

CHECKPOINT: ANTITRUST POLICY

Company	Sales	Share	Shares Squared
Daimler Chrysler	200.4	20.89	436.67
General Motors	199.1	20.76	431.02
Toyota	183.3	19.11	365.33
Ford	173.0	18.03	325.42
Honda	90.0	9.38	88.07
BMW	78.2	8.15	66.49
Hyundai	22.3	2.32	5.40
Kia	12.7	1.32	1.75
Totals	**959.0**		**HHI = 1720.19**

4-Firm Concentration Ratio = 0.788

a. The 4-firm concentration ratio is 78.8.
b. The HHI for this industry is 1720.2.
c. You probably would not permit Ford and Toyota to merge, since that would change the upper mix so significantly. Hyundai and Kia would not be a problem since combined they would only be 3.6% of the market.

10 Monopolistic Competition, Oligopoly, and Game Theory

Pure competition and pure monopoly rarely exist in actual practice. Both models provide the two extremes of market structure and provide direction for public policy when markets approach one or the other. However, the vast majority of markets are somewhere in between the extremes. In this chapter, we focus on the market structures between these polar opposites: monopolistic competition and oligopoly. We look at some of the classic models used to determine imperfectly competitive pricing and output decisions, then turn to the more modern analysis of game theory.

Competitive markets are defined by homogeneous products. This restricted our analysis to products that essentially are commodities: microchips and agricultural products such as wheat, for example. But most of the products we purchase are clearly not homogeneous. Hamburgers from Burger King, McDonald's, Wendy's, and Hardee's are similar, but for many consumers they are quite distinct. The same is true for computers, mobile phones, and cars.

Monopoly analysis required only one firm, and competition required a standardized product, but most of the markets that we encounter have only a few firms offering different products. We are now going to relax these monopoly and competition assumptions and look at markets where many firms offer products that are different (monopolistic competition) and at markets where only a few firms operate (oligopoly). Then we are going to look at game theory as an additional way to understand the behavior of oligopolists.

It is worth taking a moment to remember that most firms begin small in highly competitive environments. Some bring unique products to the market like Crocs shoes, while others add something special to existing markets as is the norm in the restaurant business. Unique products are often exciting at their launch, but they eventually mature, and the firm grows by developing newer versions of older products or introducing new products to begin the cycle anew.

Over time, some firms grow through further internal investment, franchising individual operations, or merger with other firms. Only the rare firm begins as a monopolist or even as an oligopolist (typically through a government franchise like local cable TV companies). They emerge as huge, dominant firms in many different ways.

After studying this chapter you should be able to

- Describe product differentiation and its impact on the firm's demand curve.
- Describe short-run pricing and output decisions for monopolistically competitive firms.
- Describe the reasons why in the long run monopolistically competitive firms only earn normal profits.
- Compare the efficiency of monopolistic competition to competition.
- Describe and recognize oligopolistic industries.
- Describe cartels and the reasons for their instability.
- Describe the kinked demand curve model and why some economists feel prices are relatively stable in oligopoly industries.
- Describe the Prisoner's Dilemma and determine the outcome of other games using the approach of minimizing your maximum loss.
- Understand the nature of Nash equilibria and their importance to economists.

Monopolistic Competition

Until the 1920s, competition and monopoly were the only models of market structure that economists had in their tool box. During the 1920s, economists began debating the effects of economies of scale on the competitive model. If economies were large relative to the market, one or a few firms would expand and eventually take over the market. Competition could not survive large economies of scale. Firms would then become large enough to affect prices in the market by their supply decisions.

Edward Chamberlin (1899–1967), as a graduate student at Harvard in 1922, decided to write a dissertation on the problems of the competitive model. Chamberlin was a tireless and tenacious person who wanted to alter the way economists thought about market structure. His 1933 book *The Theory of Monopolistic Competition* was not immediately warmly received, but all recognized the originality of his effort. Six months after the publication of Chamberlin's work, a British economist, Joan Robinson (1903–1983), published her *Economics of Imperfect Competition* and stole some of Chamberlin's thunder.

While Chamberlin was famous for this one contribution to economics, Joan Robinson is remembered for a huge variety of work and its radical nature. She was one of the economists who worked alongside John Maynard Keynes during the 1930s when he was developing *The General Theory.* She was responsible for the analysis of price discrimination discussed in the previous chapter, and she was the first woman to be a finalist for the Nobel Prize in Economics. Today, both Chamberlin and Robinson are generally given equal credit for discovering "imperfect" markets.

Monopolistic competition
Involves a large number of small firms and is similar to competition, with easy entry and exit, but unlike the competitive model, the firms have differentiated their products. This differentiation is either real or imagined by consumers and involves innovations, advertising, location, or other ways of making one firm's product different from that of their competitors.

Monopolistic competition is nearer to the competitive end of the spectrum and is defined by the following:

- A large number of small firms. Like competition, these firms have an insignificantly small market share. They and their competitors cannot appreciably affect the market and, therefore, ignore the reactions of their rivals. They are thus independent of a competitor's reactions.
- Entry and exit is easy.

- Unlike competition, products are different. Each firm produces a product that is different from its competitors or is perceived to be different by consumers. What distinguishes monopolistic competition from competitive markets is product differentiation.

Product Differentiation and the Firm's Demand Curve

Most firms sell products that are differentiated from their competitors. This differentiation can simply take the form of a superior location. Your local dry cleaner, restaurant, grocery, and gas station can have slightly higher prices, and you will not abandon them altogether. Other companies have branded products that give them some ability to increase price without losing all of their customers, as would happen under competition.

Product differentiation gives the firm some (however modest) control over prices. This is illustrated in Figure 1. Demand curve d_c is the competitive demand curve, and d_{mc} is the demand faced by a monopolistic competitor. This is similar to the monopolist's demand, but the demand curve is considerably more elastic. Because a monopolistic competitor is small relative to the market, there are still a lot of substitutes. Thus, any increase in price is accompanied by a substantial decrease in output demanded.

Like a monopolist, the monopolistically competitive firm faces a downward sloping marginal revenue curve shown in Figure 1 as MR_{mc}.

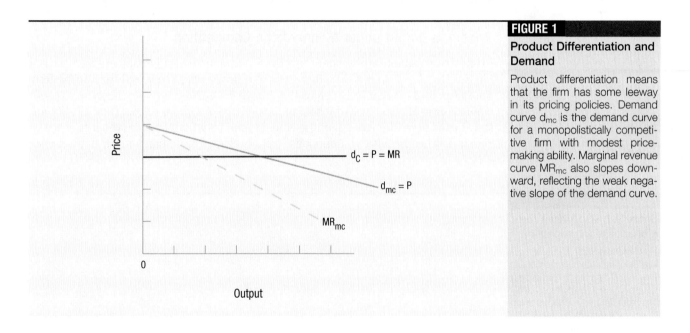

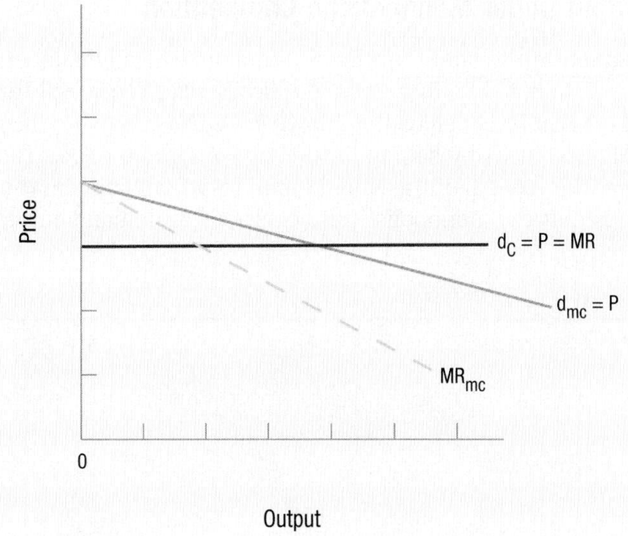

FIGURE 1

Product Differentiation and Demand

Product differentiation means that the firm has some leeway in its pricing policies. Demand curve d_{mc} is the demand curve for a monopolistically competitive firm with modest price-making ability. Marginal revenue curve MR_{mc} also slopes downward, reflecting the weak negative slope of the demand curve.

Product differentiation One firm's product is distinct from another's through advertising, innovation, location, and so on.

Product differentiation can be the result of a superior product, a better location, superior service, clever packaging, or advertising. All of these factors are intended to increase demand or reduce the elasticity of demand and generate loyalty to the product or service.

For some products packaging is paramount; bulk, bagged, and bottled teas seem to fit this mold with their ornate packages and names to fit any mood or occasion. Olive oil—virgin and extra virgin—are sold in bottles and tins covered with pictorial farms, landscapes, animals, and other European scenes. Even wines have succumbed to pictorial animal packaging. The current star, Yellow Tail, a good inexpensive Australian wine, has a very attractive label featuring a yellow-tailed rock wallaby that looks like Australian aboriginal art. In 5 years, Yellow Tail sales in the United States have gone from nothing to nearly 100 million bottles annually. At least a large chunk of Yellow Tail's success has been due to the unique label, and other vintners have begun adding animals to their bottle labels.

Another important way to differentiate products is through advertising. Economists generally classify advertising in two ways: informational and persuasive. The informational aspects of advertising let consumers know about products and reduce search costs. Advertising is a relatively inexpensive way to let customers know about quality and price of a company's products. It can also enhance competition by making consumers aware of substitute or competitive products. Advertising also has the potential to reduce costs by increasing sales, bringing about economies of scale.

But advertising does have a negative side as well. Because so much of advertising is persuasive, designed to shift buyers among competitors of similar products, the result is that the cost of advertising simply drives up the price of many products. Persuasive ads often have little informational content and may result in consumers purchasing inferior products. With all the advertising we see, a significant portion probably cancels each other out.

Advertising is another area where technology has transformed the medium: digital video recorders permit ad-skipping and have significantly reduced the impact of TV ads. A lot of advertising dollars are shifting away from conventional media (newspapers, magazines, and television) and moving to the Internet, where consumers can be targeted more inexpensively and efficiently.

All of these ways to differentiate their products gives monopolistically competitive firms some control over price. This means that their profit-maximizing decisions will be a little different from competitive firms.

Price and Output under Monopolistic Competition

Profit maximization in the short run for the monopolistically competitive firm is a lot like that for a monopolist, but given the firm's size, profit will tend to be less. Short-run profit maximizing behavior is shown in Figure 2. The firm maximizes profit where MR = MC (point *c*) by selling output q_0 for a price of P_0. Total profits are the shaded area C_0P_0ab. All of this should look very familiar from the last chapter. The difference is that the monopolistically competitive demand curve is quite elas-

FIGURE 2

Short-Run Equilibrium for Monopolistic Competition

This monopolistically competitive firm will maximize profits in the short run by producing where MR = MC (point *c*). Profits are equal to the shaded area. The profits for a monopolistically competitive firm are lower than for a monopoly because demand for the monopolistically competitive product is quite elastic, whereas the demand for the monopoly product is less elastic (the industry demand).

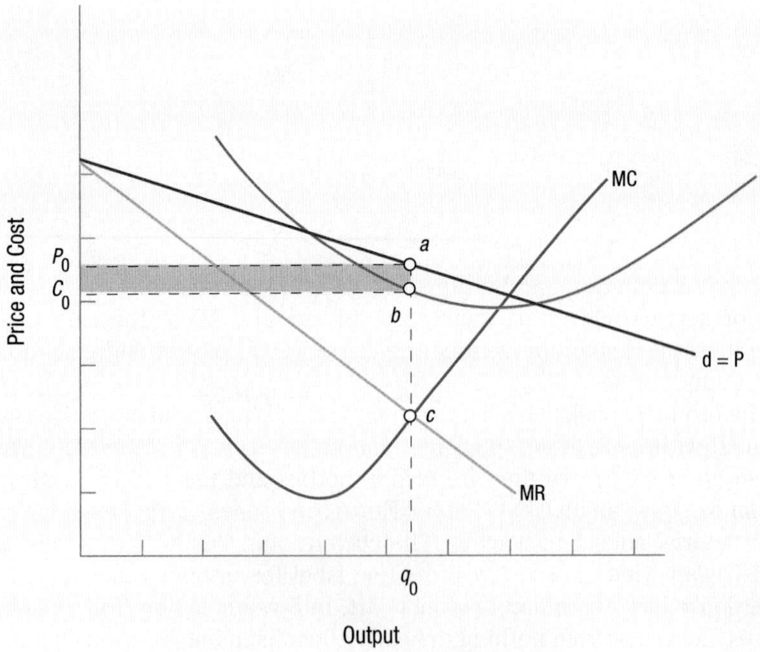

tic, and economic profits are diminished. The level of profits is dependent on the strength of demand, but in any event will be considerably lower than that of a monopolist.

This does not mean that profits are trivial. Many huge global firms sell their products in even larger global markets, and their profits are significant. They are large firms, but do not have significant monopoly power. Many companies such as Armani, Nike, and Sony are all quite large but relative to their markets face daunting competition.

If firms in the industry are earning economic profits like the firm shown in Figure 2, new firms will want to enter. Since there are no restrictions on entry or exit, new firms will enter, soaking up some industry demand and reducing the demand to each firm in the market. Demand will continue to decline as long as economic profits exist. At equilibrium in the long run, the typical firm in the industry will look like the one shown in Figure 3.

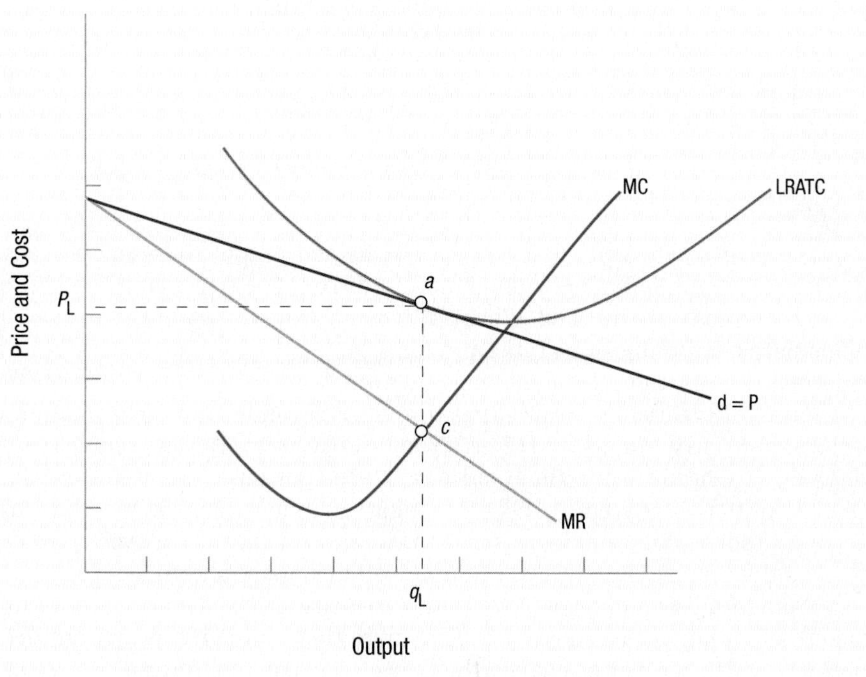

FIGURE 3

Long-Run Equilibrium for Monopolistic Competition

In the long run, easy entry and exit will adjust the demand for each firm so that the demand curve will be tangent (at point *a* in this case) to the long-run average total cost curve. This is long-run equilibrium because existing firms are earning normal profits and there is no incentive for further entry or exit.

Notice that the demand curve is just tangent to the long-run average total cost (LRATC) curve, resulting in the firm earning normal profits in the long run. The firm produces and sells q_L output at a price of P_L (point *a*). Once the typical firm reaches this point, there is no longer any incentive for other firms to enter the industry. Just as the competitive firm does, monopolistically competitive firms earn normal profits in the long run.

Comparing Monopolistic Competition to Competition

How does allocative efficiency compare for the two market structures? Since firms in both earn normal profits, you might think that both market structures are equally efficient. Unfortunately, this is not the case. Look at Figure 4 on the next page. The competitive demand curve has been added to Figure 3. Notice that the long-run competitive output is higher ($q_c > q_{mc}$), and the competitive output is sold at a lower price ($P_c < P_{mc}$). All of this sounds familiar, just as with monopoly. The difference is that the reduction in output is relatively small because firms are small relative to the market whereas a monopoly is the industry.

FIGURE 4

Comparing the Long Run for Monopolistically Competitive and Competitive Firms

Long-run equilibrium is at point *b* for competitive firms and at point *a* for monopolistically competitive firms. Equilibrium price is a little higher, and output is a little lower for the monopolistically competitive firm when compared to the competitive firm. These represent the modest costs we, as consumers, pay for product differentiation.

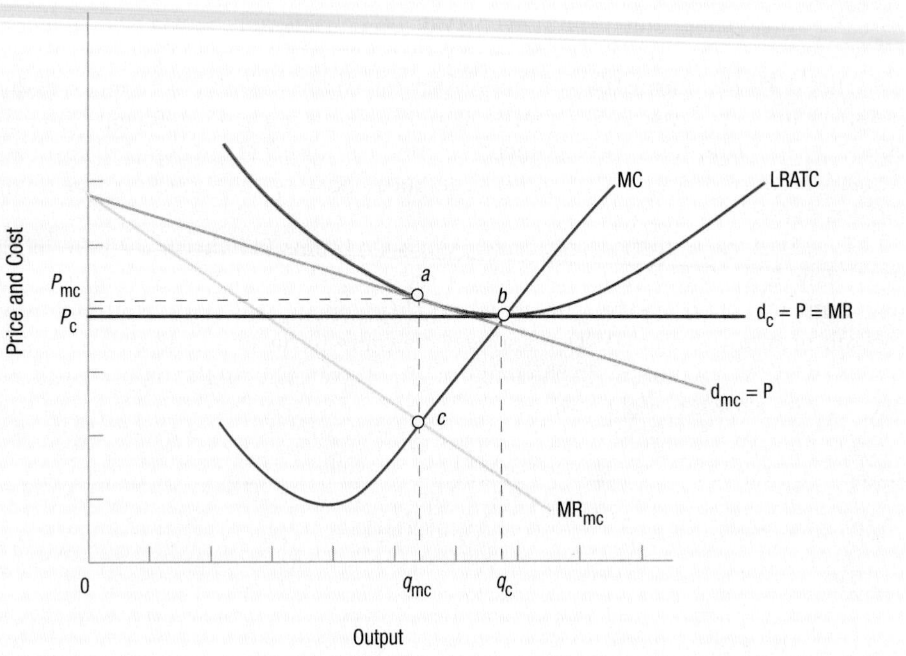

These relatively small differences in price and output represent the costs we pay for product differentiation and innovation. To the extent that these differences are real, the costs are justified. When advertising provides accurate information that helps us select products, or if the products are sufficiently distinct that they provide real choices, then the additional costs are worth it.

Firms differentiate their products through style and features that matter. Coca-Cola offers Cherry, Vanilla, and Cherry Vanilla Coke, as well as diet versions. Watches offer everything from the time and date to temperature, stopwatch capabilities, Global Positioning System (GPS) positioning, altitude, and, most recently, Internet access. Product differentiation is important and for most of us valuable, but not free, as this comparison with the competitive model has shown.

From this discussion, you might get some sense of the dynamic pressures firms face to differentiate their products. The more they can move away from the competitive model, the better chance they have of making more profit. The key is to differentiate the product to obtain a higher price. But since the price advantage evaporates over the long run for monopolistically competitive firms, these firms have to try to sustain the value in the differentiated product. This is hard to do. The price premium charged by Abercrombie and Fitch will not be paid when Abercrombie becomes less fashionable, or more like everyone else. Yet, it is in the firm's interest to product differentiate as long as it can. When you see firms trying to differentiate their products, ask yourself if the products really are so different after all. Then pour yourself a Cherry Coke—or do I mean a Cherry Pepsi?

Checkpoint

Monopolistic Competition

REVIEW

- Monopolistically competitive firms look like competitive firms (large number of small firms in a market where entry and exit is unrestricted) with differentiated products.

- Monopolistically competitive firms have very elastic demands.
- Short-run equilibrium output for the monopolistic competitor (like the monopolist) is at an output where MR = MC, but economic profits will be relatively small compared to an industry monopolist because demand is very elastic for the monopolistic competitor.
- In the long run, easy entry and exit result in monopolistically competitive firms earning only normal profits.
- Output is lower and price is higher for monopolistically competitive firms when compared to price and output for competitive firms.

QUESTION

Kelly Crow reports in the *Wall Street Journal* (August 12, 2005) that many of the 40 or so traveling circuses in America have celebrity clowns as their headline acts. These clowns earn high six-figure salaries plus royalties from souvenir sales. Why would circuses emphasize clowns over animal and trapeze acts?

Answers to the Checkpoint question can be found at the end of this chapter.

Oligopoly

Oligopoly markets are those where a large market share is controlled by just a few firms. What constitutes a few firms controlling a large market share is not rigidly defined. Further, these firms can sell either a homogeneous product (e.g., gasoline, sugar) or a differentiated product (e.g., automobiles and pharmaceuticals).

Oligopoly
A market with just a few firms dominating the industry where (1) each firm recognizes that it must consider its competitors' reactions when making its own decisions (mutual interdependence), and (2) there are significant barriers to entry into the market.

Industries can be composed of a dominant firm with a few smaller firms making up the rest of the industry (e.g., microcomputer operating systems and cell phones), or the industry can be composed of a few similarly sized firms (e.g., automobiles and tobacco). The point of this discussion is that oligopoly models are numerous and varied, and we will explore only a few. Oligopoly models do, however, have several common characteristics.

Defining Oligopoly

All oligopoly models share several common assumptions:

- There are only a few dominant firms in the industry.
- Each firm recognizes that it must take into account the behavior of its competitors when it makes decisions. Economists refer to this as **mutual interdependence**.
- There are significant barriers to entry into the market.

Mutual interdependence
When only a few firms constitute an industry, each firm must consider the reactions of its competitors to its decisions.

Since there are only a few firms, the actions of one will affect the ability of the others to successfully sell or price their output. If one firm changes the specifications of its product or increases its advertising budget, this will have an impact on its rivals, and they can be expected to respond in kind. Thus, one firm cannot forecast its change in sales for a new promotion without first making some assumption about the reaction of its rivals. For example, if Cadillac adds a GPS and advertises this feature, it has to consider whether a competitor such as Lexus will immediately offer this feature as well.

In an industry composed of just a few firms, entry scale is often huge. Plus, with just a few firms, typically brand preferences are quite strong on the part of consumers, and a new firm may need a substantial marketing program just to get a foot in the door. For example, the investment in plant for a new automaker is huge, and the marketing effort also must be large to get people to even consider a new auto brand. New car manufacturers like Kia often must resort to long warranties (10 year, 100,000 miles) to entice customers to try its products.

Cartels: Joint Profit Maximization

Cartel
An agreement between firms in an industry (or countries) to formally collude on price and output, then agree on the distribution of production.

The first oligopoly model we examine is *collusive* joint profit maximization or a **cartel** model. Here we assume a few firms collude (combine secretly) to operate like a monopolistic industry, setting the monopoly price and output and sharing the monopoly profits. Cartels are illegal in the United States, though international laws do not ban them. However, this situation may change with the advent of the European Union.

As *The Economist* noted, "Just a few years ago, America seemed uniquely obsessed with price-fixing. Today, new measures against cartel behavior (which includes bid-rigging and deals to carve up market share, as well as price-fixing) are being taken from Sweden to South Korea, where the competition body levied its first fine against a foreign firm earlier this year [2002]."[1] Europe, in 2006, fined seven firms for running a cartel in bleaching chemicals.[2]

The most famous cartel operating today is OPEC, the Organization of Petroleum Exporting Countries. OPEC countries meet and establish a price that members will charge and an output level that each individual member will produce, thus carving up shares of the profits. OPEC, formed principally of Middle Eastern countries in the early 1960s, really didn't become effective until 1973. Since then, it has had many successes and some failures. When prices were increased in 1973 and again in 1979, a mad search was underway for alternative supplies worldwide.

By the early 1980s, this worldwide search for additional supplies was successful. Additional supplies came online, and prices of crude oil, adjusted for inflation, declined. In 2006, the real (adjusted for inflation) price of oil was approaching the peak in 1980 (see Figure 5). OPEC, while having the bulk of world oil reserves, is not able to totally control entry. Large Russian oil fields are expected to begin producing in the next decade, though higher demands by India and China are expected to soak up this new output.

FIGURE 5

Crude Oil Prices (adjusted for inflation—1982 = 100)

The real (adjusted for inflation) price of oil is currently approaching its high in 1980.

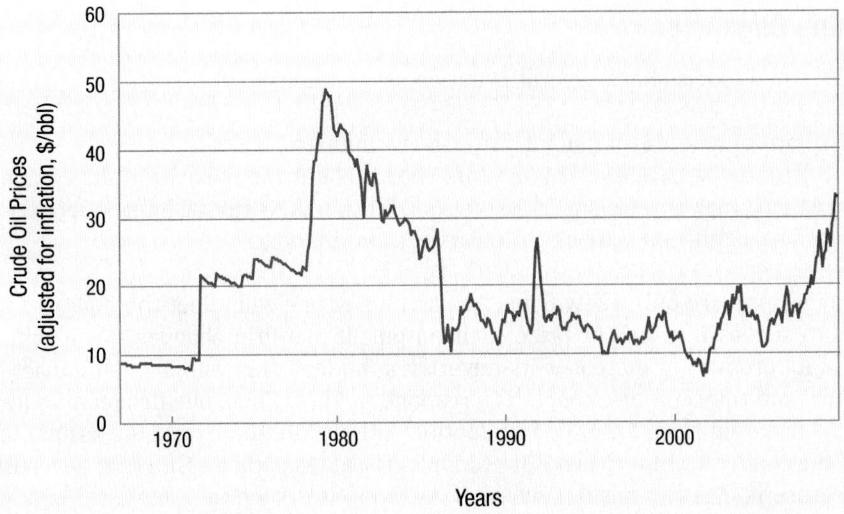

[1] See "Cartels: Fixing for a Fight," *The Economist,* April 20, 2002, p. 63.
[2] William Echikson, "Europe Fines 7 Chemical Firms $489.8 Million for Bleach Cartel," *Wall Street Journal,* May 4, 2006, p. A2.

Cartels are inherently unstable because of the incentive to cheat by individual members. Even though each firm and the cartel jointly are earning economic profits, they are not being maximized. If all other members of the cartel continue to sell their authorized output, any one firm that can sell additional output for a price above marginal cost can earn additional profits. Each firm in the cartel faces these incentives, and if many attempt to sell additional output, the cartel agreement will break down. This analysis has led some economists to lose interest in cartels since cartels are likely to fail in the long run.

Cartel stability will be enhanced with fewer members with similar goals. Further, stability is improved if the cartel is maintained with legal provisions (government protection) and if nonprice competition is not possible. If the firm can give nonprice discounts (enhanced service or some other product as an inducement to purchase), the likelihood of stability is reduced. If their products and cost structures are similar and they are not secretive with each other, stability is enhanced. Finally, if there are significant barriers to entry, the cartel need not worry about new entrants, and the chances improve for the cartel to survive.

1990s Aluminum Cartel: Government-Sponsored Oligopoly[3]

What can a CEO of a major American corporation do when foreign firms sell so much aluminum on the world market that the price decline threatens the corporation? Ask the government for help, of course. In the early 1990s, Russia sold more aluminum in world markets. This increase in supply was matched by a fall in demand brought about by slower worldwide economic growth and Russia's reduced production of aircraft. Prices fell by *half.*

Alcoa's CEO, Paul O'Neill, went to the Clinton administration for help. With its approval and the help of government antitrust lawyers, the Overseas Private Investment Corporation (OPIC), and the State Department, an agreement was made limiting aluminum production. In other words, a cartel was formed.[4] With a $250 million equity investment from OPIC, Russian companies were persuaded to reduce their output. Prices rose from roughly 50 cents a pound to nearly 90 cents, and Alcoa's profits rose.

By 1995 worldwide demand for aluminum increased, and problems enforcing the agreement arose; shortly thereafter, the cartel fell apart. Because cartels are normally illegal in the United States, this "aluminum product–overseas investment agreement" was challenged, but dismissed by the courts. Export cartels are permitted in the United States as long as they do not adversely impact competition in domestic markets.

The Kinked Demand Curve Model

One early oligopoly model that considered the reactions of other firms is the kinked demand curve model jointly developed by Sweezy, Hall, and Hitch in the late 1930s. These authors noticed that prices tended to be stable for extended periods in oligopolistic industries. It was in an effort to model this price stability that they settled on the idea of a kinked demand curve.

Demand curve d in Figure 6 on the next page represents the demand for one firm when all other firms in the industry *do not follow* its price changes. Demand curve D represents demand when all other firms raise or lower prices *in concert.* Demand curve d is relatively more elastic than demand curve D because when the firm raises prices and others do not follow, quantity demanded declines rapidly as customers substitute to the now lower-priced products from competitors. Similarly,

---

[3]Based on Joseph E. Stiglitz, *Globalization and Its Discontents* (New York: WW Norton), 2003, pp. 173–176.

[4]Stiglitz, *Globalization*, p. 268.

FIGURE 6

The Kinked Demand Curve Model of Oligopoly

The kinked demand curve model of oligopoly shows why oligopoly prices appear stable. The model assumes that if the firm raised its price, competitors will not react and raise their prices, but if the firm lowers prices, other firms will lower theirs in response. These reactions create a "kink" in the firm's demand curve at point e, and a discontinuity in the MR curve equal to the distance between points *a* and *b*. This discontinuity permits marginal costs to vary from MC_0 to MC_1 before the firm will change its price.

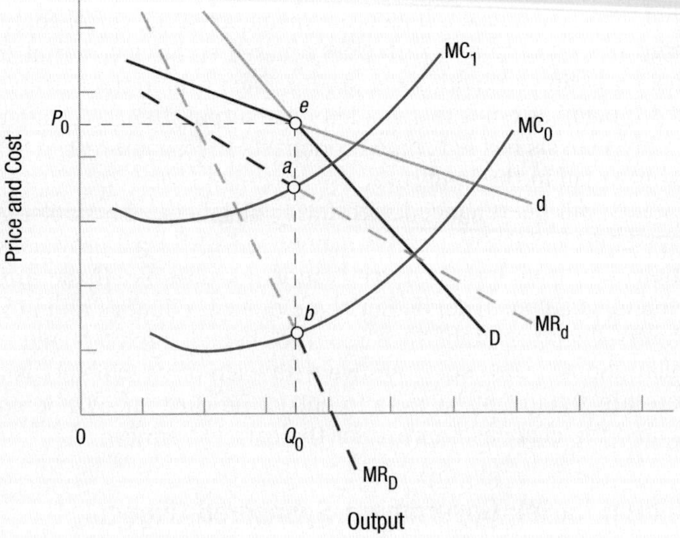

when one firm's prices fall and the others ignore this change, demand for the lower-priced products grows rapidly. Hence, demand curve d is relatively elastic.

Demand curve D, on the other hand, is more like the industry demand. When all firms raise and lower their prices together, demand will be less elastic than demand curve d.

Kinked demand curve
An oligopoly model that assumes that if a firm raises its price, competitors will not raise theirs; but if the firm lowers its price, all of its competitors will lower their price to match the reduction. This leads to a kink in the demand curve and relatively stable market prices.

The **kinked demand curve** model assumes the following:

- If the firm raises prices for its products, its competitors will not react by raising prices, expecting to see their market share rise.
- If the firm lowers its prices, its competitors will meet the new prices with lower ones of their own to make sure that they do not lose market share.

As a result, the relevant demand curve facing the firm is the darkened portion of demand curves d and D that is kinked at point *e*. The relevant portion of the marginal revenue curve is the darkened dashed curve MR_D with the discontinuity between points *a* and *b*. Notice, we are just using the relevant portions of MR_d and MR_D. As shown, marginal cost crosses through the discontinuity, resulting in an equilibrium price and output of P_0 and Q_0.

It is, of course, the discontinuity in the MR curve that gives this model its price stability. The marginal cost curve can vary anywhere between points *a* and *b* before the firm will have any incentive to change prices to maximize profits.

Critics of this model suggest that price stability can be explained by other factors, and that the model doesn't explain how prices were initially determined. It explains the existence of the kink but not how it was determined in an oligopoly context. George Stigler argued that the evidence of price stability was weak at best. However, more recent empirical investigations of retailing and others found price declines were more readily followed than price increases in oligopolistic industries.[5]

One clear result of the search for realistic oligopoly models was the realization by economists that the mutual interdependence of firms and their reactions to each

[5]See A. Kashyap, "Sticky Prices: New Evidence from Retail Catalogs," *Quarterly Journal of Economics,* pp. 245–274, 1995; and S. Domberger, and D. Fiebig, "The Distribution of Price Changes in Oligopoly," *Journal of Industrial Economics,* 1993, pp. 295–313.

other's policies were important. How one firm reacts to a competitor's market strategy determined the nature of competition in the industry. These ideas led to game theory.

Checkpoint

Oligopoly

REVIEW

- Oligopolies are markets (a) with only a few firms, (b) where each firm takes into account the reaction of rivals to its policies or firms recognize their mutual interdependence, and (c) where there are significant barriers to entry.
- Cartels result when several firms collude to set market price and output. Cartels typically act like monopolists and share the economic profits that result.
- Cartels are inherently unstable because individual firms can earn higher profits by selling more than their allotted quota. As more firms in the cartel cheat, prices fall, defeating the agreement.
- The observation that prices were stable in oligopolistic industries gave rise to the kinked demand curve model. The model assumes that competitors will follow price reductions but not price increases. This leads to a discontinuity in MR permitting cost to vary substantially before prices are changed.

QUESTION

Alec Guinness, in the 1951 film *The Man in the White Suit,* invents cloth that shrugs off dirt and doesn't wear out. Rather than treated as a hero, Guinness is attacked by the textile oligopoly and labor unions because "if the cloth is indestructible, how will the industry survive?" Name a recent invention that has had a large disruptive influence on oligopolies.

Answers to the Checkpoint question can be found at the end of this chapter.

Game Theory

> **If you say why not bomb them tomorrow, I say why not today? If you say today at 5 o'clock, I say why not one o'clock?**
>
> *—John von Neumann*

Game theory developed from analysis of imperfect competition. The earliest analysis was done by French economist Augustin Cournot (pronounced core-no), in which he examined pricing principles for a duopolist (two firms). He analyzed how one firm would react to output changes from its rival. He assumed that two profit-maximizing firms produce the same product and that each firm simultaneously determines its output level based on its estimate of the level of output from the other firm. Further, he assumed that each firm assumes that its own output (strategy) will not affect the decision of the other firm. His analysis led to reaction curves (or functions) for each firm representing the best strategy that each firm could adopt given the behavior of the other firm. This model of mutual interdependence of output decisions was the precursor to game theory.

Game theory
An approach to analyzing oligopoly behavior using mathematics and simulation by using different assumptions about the players, time involved, level of information, strategies, and other aspects of the game.

Modern game theory owes its origins to John von Neumann (1903–1957), who published a paper titled "Theory of Parlor Games" in 1928 and subsequently

Antoine Augustin Cournot (1801–1877)

Antoine Cournot is one of the great unsung heroes of microeconomics. He was the first economist to derive a demand curve. He pioneered the use of mathematics in analyzing market structures, prices, and equilibrium. Throughout his career, however, Cournot was bitterly disappointed by the lack of appreciation of his work. It was only near the end of his life that other economists began to notice the importance of what he had written.

Born in 1801 in Gray, a small town in central France, Cournot was a clerk in an attorney's office. After studying at a math preparatory school in a nearby town, he entered the Ecole Normale Superieure in Paris in 1821. He transferred to the Sorbonne and completed his math degree there in 1823. Cournot spent the next 10 years assisting a French official prepare his memoirs. In his free time, he earned a doctorate in science and began publishing articles on mathematics. His work brought him to the attention of the mathematician Simeon-Denis Poisson. With the help of Poisson, he obtained an appointment as a professor at Lyon and later an administrative position at the Academy of Grenoble. In 1838, he was appointed Inspector General of Education in Paris.

That same year he published his most important work, *Researches Into the Mathematical Principles of the Theory of Wealth,* which introduced differential calculus to economic analysis. He was the first to describe the downward slope of a demand curve, suggesting that the quantity demanded of a good such as wine depended on the price of that good. In other words, increasing the price of wine would reduce the quantity demanded. Cournot demonstrated that the equilibrium price was reached at the point where demand and supply were equal.

Cournot made other surprising discoveries, which he described in his book. He explained how, under conditions of monopoly, sellers could maximize profits by producing output where marginal costs equaled marginal revenue. The economist Alfred Marshall later adapted this notion in his *Principles of Economics* in 1890. Cournot also explored the dynamics of duopolies, and his ideas were later used by John Nash in his Nobel Prize-winning work on game theory.

John von Neumann (1903–1957)

The economist Nicholas Kaldor once described fellow Hungarian John von Neumann as "the nearest thing to a genius" he had ever encountered. In addition to being one of the leading mathematicians of his day, von Neumann made important contributions to quantum physics and helped develop the first computer. Von Neumann is best known, however, as the originator of game theory, which has many important uses in economics.

Born in Budapest in 1903, von Neumann was a math prodigy with a photographic memory. He entertained his parents' dinner guests by reciting pages from the phone book by memory. By the age of 8, he had learned calculus. During his final year in high school, he was publishing professional mathematical papers.

According to Tim Harford, von Neumann was "asked to assist with the design of a new supercomputer, required to solve a new and important mathematical problem, which was beyond the capabilities of existing supercomputers. He asked to have the problem explained to him, solved it in moments with pen and paper, and turned down the request."[6]

In 1944, von Neumann and Oskar Morganstern published the *Theory of Games and Economic Behavior,* a seminal work that has inspired a generation of mathematicians and economists, including Kenneth Arrow, Gerard Debreu, and John Nash.

In game theory, individuals compete with one another without knowing what strategies the other will employ. Many economic interactions involve similar dynamics between groups and individuals. For example, von Neumann and Morganstern wrote about situations in which players would form coalitions to gain advantage over players, which is comparable to markets in which two firms in an oligopolistic industry combine to overcome other competitors. Other analogies might be the decision for individuals to form a union or for industry groups to form lobbying organizations to push for favorable legislation from government.

During World War II, von Neumann helped the U.S. military develop the first computer and later worked on the Manhattan Project with Robert Oppenheimer. A strong supporter of the nuclear weapons program, he served as an advisor to President Truman and was appointed to the Atomic Energy Commission by President Eisenhower. Von Neumann died in 1957.

[6]Tim Harford, *The Undercover Economist* (Oxford: Oxford University Press), 2006, p. 156.

published (in 1944) the *Theory of Games and Economic Behavior* with Oskar Morganstern. Born in Hungary at the turn of the century, von Neumann was a brilliant mathematician who was able to divide two 8-digit numbers in his head and by his senior year in high school was considered a professional mathematician.[7] Von Neumann worked on the Manhattan Project during the Second World War, and it has been suggested that he probably was the model for Dr. Strangelove in Stanley Kubrick's 1963 film *Dr. Strangelove, Or How I Learned to Stop Worrying and Love the Bomb.*[8]

Modern game theory has developed into a sophisticated mathematical and simulation science. Five people have been awarded the Nobel Prize in Economics for their work in game theory. To get a feel for the potential richness that game theory offers, let's look at some of the types of games economists use to model oligopolistic market behavior.

Types of Games

Games can be simple or complicated depending on the various characteristics of the market they represent. As you will see by the following breakdown, we can have nearly as many games as we have different markets. Game theory characteristics include the following:

- **Cooperation:** *Cooperative* games permit players to collude on prices, output, or other variables, much as OPEC does in setting output quotas for each producer. *Noncooperative* games are the opposite in that they prevent player communication and collusion.
- **Players:** Simple games involve only two players, but many modern simulation games involve multiplayer environments.
- **Time:** In *static* games, all players choose their strategies at the same time. *Dynamic* games involve sequential decision making; for example, one firm sets a price, and the other responds to this price.
- **Information:** Players could have *complete (perfect)* information about the game or they could have *incomplete (imperfect)* information. Exact payoffs may be unknown or subject to uncertainty. Firms often have good information about their own costs but may not have equal information about their competitor's costs. *Asymmetric* information is also possible (in the case of used cars—sellers usually have better information than buyers).
- **Strategies:** Many games have *discrete* strategies where players choose from a few choices such as "advertise or do not advertise," "confess or do not confess," "enter the industry or not." *Continuous* strategies typify business-constant-pricing decisions where firms often have a large number of prices and products that are subjected to various (and sometimes random) events.
- **Repetition:** Whether the game is a *one-off* decision or will be *repeated* introduces another level of complexity. In a one-off game (as in the Prisoner's Dilemma, described later) players only have to consider the payoffs (impacts) on that one decision. In repeated games, players can react to the other player's past strategies. In one round where one player makes a choice that harms the other player, that harmed player can be expected to change strategies in the future.
- **Profit-Loss:** In a *zero-sum* game (poker, duels, and most sporting events), each winner is essentially paired with a loser. If the game is a *non-zero-sum* game, both players can stand to benefit.

---

[7]Steven Pressman, *Fifty Major Economists* (New York: Routledge), 1999, pp. 124–128.
[8]See William Poundstone, *Prisoner's Dilemma* (New York: Doubleday), 1992, p. 5.

These characteristics permit simple and complex games covering nearly all economic situations and reflect the importance of game theory's analytic method in modern economics. In the remainder of this chapter, we focus on several simple games and apply the general analysis to price discounting and advertising, then take a brief look at the strategies introduced with repeated games. The Prisoner's Dilemma is our first, but widely applicable, game.

The Prisoner's Dilemma

In *noncooperative* games, each player imagines how his opponent intends to play the game, then uses this information to help formulate his own strategy. However, it is impossible for players to communicate or collaborate in making their decisions or strategies. The classic static, noncooperative game is the **Prisoner's Dilemma**.

Prisoner's Dilemma
A noncooperative game where players cannot communicate or collaborate in making their decisions about whether to confess or not and thus results in inferior outcomes for both players. Many oligopoly decisions can be framed as a Prisoner's Dilemma.

Two criminal suspects (Chris and Matthew) are apprehended for robbery. Both are separated, put in solitary confinement, and are unable to speak to each other. Each prisoner is offered the same bargain: Testify against your partner and you will go free while your partner will go to prison for 3 years. If neither confesses, the state likely will convict them both on lesser charges resulting in a 1-year sentence. Finally, if both confess, they each will go to prison for 2 years.

The dilemma facing each prisoner is shown in Table 1. The payoff table is arranged so that Matthew's payoff (time in prison) is the first number, and Chris's payoff is the second number. Thus, a payoff of 3,0 represents 3 years in prison for Matthew while Chris goes free.

Table 1 The Prisoner's Dilemma

	Chris	
Matthew	Do not confess	Confess
Do not confess	1,1	3,0
Confess	0,3	2,2

The prisoners must make a decision, but each cannot find out what the other has done, and both decisions are irrevocable. Each prisoner is only concerned with his own welfare—minimizing his time in prison. Is there a unique solution?

Consider Matthew's situation, shown as the *first* payoff in each cell. Suppose Chris *confesses.* Matthew is better off confessing since 2 years in prison is better than 3. This is read vertically in the "Confess" column of the payoff table. Now suppose that Chris *does not confess.* Matthew is still better off confessing since going free is preferred to 1 year in prison. Thus, from Matthew's perspective, no matter which strategy Chris selects, Matthew is better off confessing because his sentence is reduced by a year in both cases.

Similarly, no matter what Matthew does, Chris is better off confessing. The logical result is that both will confess despite the fact that both would be better off if neither did: 1 year served in prison versus 2.

Von Neumann referred to this strategy and its outcome as a *minimax* solution; both prisoners are minimizing their maximum prison sentences. They are minimizing their worst outcome in this instance. Notice that this is not the best outcome for both prisoners. They would be better off not confessing, but neither could trust the other to not confess given the structure of the payoffs. It is important to note that this result (confess, confess) is due to the structure of the payoffs, not the absolute levels.

The Prisoner's Dilemma is not simply an idle game dreamed up by mathematicians and economists. Robert Harris[9] noted that

> *In robberies where murders occur, for example, there is often more than one criminal involved and thus more than one person who may be eligible for the death penalty. But for a prosecutor, "what's important is that you score one touchdown," in the form of a death sentence, said Franklin R. Zimring, University of California, Berkeley, law professor and a capital punishment expert.*
>
> *Frequently, a race ensues in which the robbers try to be the first to point the finger at an accomplice and make a deal with the prosecutor to testify in return for leniency.*
>
> *Sometimes, Zimring said, it never becomes clear whether the person who got leniency or the person on trial for his life actually pulled the trigger.*

Nash Equilibrium

John von Neumann's focus was on two-person zero-sum games and was the initial building blocks for game theory. In a zero-sum game, the amount won equals the amount lost, as in a poker game where one person's winnings have to come at the expense of another person, or other people. While zero-sum games are realistic for poker, they are not as fruitful for strategic business interactions. It is not always the case that where one firm gains, another must lose. Other possibilities include mutually beneficial or mutually destructive strategies. Sometimes the most interesting economic games are complex multiperson, non-zero-sum games.

In the 28 lines shown in Figure 7, John Nash (of *A Beautiful Mind* fame) was able to prove that an n-person game where each player chooses his optimal strategy, given that all other players have done the same, has a solution. Nash assumed that each player would imagine what all other players would select as their best strategy. Then each player would select a strategy that represented his best strategy given the other players' intended strategies. Nash was able to show that given these conditions, equilibrium (a **Nash equilibrium**) would always exist for any n-person non-zero-sum game.

Nash equilibrium
An important proof that an n-person game where each player chooses his optimal strategy, given that all other players have done the same, has a solution. This was an important proof, because economists now knew that even complex models (or games) had an equilibrium or solution.

This is a very important result. Economists could now develop realistic (and often complex) games or models of market interactions and know that a solution for the game existed.

One-Off Games: Applying Game Theory

In this section, we will examine some examples of how game theory can be used to model oligopoly decisions. First we look at static games where the decisions are made simultaneously, then we take a brief look at dynamic games where decisions are make sequentially.

Static Games

Static games involve simultaneous decisions, and we will focus on those with perfect information and certain payoffs. In addition, these games are one-off and are not repeated.

Static games
One-off games (not repeated) where decisions by the players are made simultaneously and are irreversible.

Price Discounting: Dairy Queen and Foster's Freeze. The game shown in Table 2 is a straightforward extension of the Prisoner's Dilemma applied to business. This example could

[9] R. A. Harris, *Los Angeles Times,* January 29, 1990, cited in William Poundstone, *Prisoner's Dilemma* (New York: Doubleday), 1992, p. 119.

FIGURE 7

The Nash Equilibrium

This one-page paper establishes the basis for the Nash equilibrium. This is an important result that allowed economists to develop realistic but complex games of market interactions knowing that a solution existed. (Reprinted by permission of the author.)

[2]

EQUILIBRIUM POINTS IN N-PERSON GAMES

By John F. Nash, Jr.*

Princeton University

Communicated by S. Lefschetz, November 16, 1949

One may define a concept of an n-person game in which each player has a finite set of pure strategies and in which a definite set of payments to the n players corresponds to each n-tuple of pure strategies, one strategy being taken for each player. For mixed strategies, which are probability [48]
distributions over the pure strategies, the pay-off functions are the expectations of the players, thus becoming polylinear forms in the probabilities with which the various players play their various pure strategies.

Any n-tuple of strategies, one for each player, may be regarded as a point in the product space obtained by multiplying the n strategy spaces of the players. One such n-tuple counters another if the strategy of each player in the countering n-tuple yields the highest obtainable expectation for its player against the $n - 1$ strategies of the other players in the countered n-tuple. A self-countering n-tuple is called an equilibrium point.

The correspondence of each n-tuple with its set of countering n-tuples gives a one-to-many mapping of the product space into itself. From the definition of countering we see that the set of countering points of a point is convex. By using the continuity of the pay-off functions we see that the graph of the mapping is closed. The closedness is equivalent to saying: if $P_1, P_2, \ldots$ and $Q_1, Q_2, \ldots, Q_n, \ldots$ are sequences of points in the product space where $Q_n \to Q$, $P_n \to P$ and Q_n counters P_n then Q counters P.

Since the graph is closed and since the image of each point under the mapping is convex, we infer from Kakutani's theorem[1] that the mapping has a fixed point (i.e., point contained in its image). Hence there is an equilibrium point.

In the two-person zero-sum case the "main theorem"[2] and the existence of an equilibrium point are equivalent. In this case any two equilibrium points lead to the same expectations for the players, but this need not occur in general.

* The author is indebted to Dr. David Gale for suggesting the use of Kakutani's theorem to simplify the proof and to the A. E. C. for financial support.

1 Kakutani, S., *Duke Math. J.*, 8, 457–459 (1941).

2 Von Neumann, J., and Morgenstern, O., *The Theory of Games and Economic Behaviour*, Chap. 3, Princeton University Press, Princeton, 1947.

Table 2 Payoff Matrix for Price Change Game

	Foster's Freeze's Price	
Dairy Queen's Price	$3	$2
$3	$100,000,$100,000	$60,000,$150,000
$2	$150,000,$60,000	$75,000,$75,000

represent dueling advertising campaigns, decisions about research and development expenditures, or price changes. The game in Table 2 represents the decision to lower price facing two oligopolists.

We assume that the two firms Dairy Queen and Foster's Freeze are currently charging $3 for banana splits and face roughly the same costs and demand curves. Now assume that both are thinking about reducing price to gain market share.

Notice that both are currently making $100,000 profit on this product. If only one firm lowers its price, that firm will earn $150,000 in added profit because sales rise. Some of this increase in sales comes from those of the other firm and some comes from the added quantity demanded at the lower price. Both firms, of course, can see that each firm can gain by lowering price. But if both firms lower their price, each will see its profits fall (to $75,000). What is the new equilibrium point? Both firms will lower price, anticipating that the other will lower the price as well. This strategy maximizes their minimum profit (they each make at least $75,000). If their competitor lowers price, they cannot do better.

Advertising: Lowe's and Home Depot. Firms, politicians, special interest groups, and, it often seems, *everyone* advertises. The decision to advertise or not can be put in the Prisoner's Dilemma game theory framework as well.

Advertising costs money, but firms hope to garner market share and greater profits. However, if their competitors advertise as well, little is gained unless the impact of all the advertising is to grow the entire market sufficiently to compensate for the higher costs. Two home improvement big-box operations—Lowe's and Home Depot—face this dilemma.

Table 3 presents hypothetical numbers for the advertising decisions that Lowe's and Home Depot must make. If neither firm advertises, both will earn $100,000 in profit. If either Lowe's or Home Depot decides to spend the $30,000 required to advertise, it will take $50,000 in business away from the other, and its net profit will be $120,000, leaving $50,000 for the other. If both advertise, the market grows a little, but each firm's costs have risen, and profits drop to $80,000 for both firms. If the decision must be made simultaneously without either firm having information about the decision of the other, the equilibrium is that both will advertise, and both will earn $80,000 in profits.

Table 3 Payoff Matrix for Advertising by Lowe's and Home Depot

	Home Depot	
Lowe's	Don't advertise	Advertise
Don't advertise	$100,000,$100,000	$50,000,$120,000
Advertise	$120,000,$50,000	$80,000,$80,000

Dynamic Games

Dynamic games
Sequential or repeated games where the players can adjust their actions based on the decisions of other players in the past.

The static analysis above inherently assumes that pricing and advertising decisions are irreversible, occur simultaneously, and occur before the other knows what has happened. But most markets are dynamic, and firms are constantly trying new prices and other sales techniques to increase profits. This reality has led to the development of **dynamic games**.

Nobel Prize John Nash, John C. Harsanyi, and Reinhard Selten

John Nash

John C. Harsanyi

Reinhard Selten

Like many gifted mathematicians, John Nash completed his most valuable work early in his career, as a 22-year-old doctoral candidate at Princeton University. His original contributions to game theory, as refined by John Harsanyi and Reinhard Selten, have numerous applications in economics. The Nobel Prize in Economic Sciences was awarded to all three men in 1994.

Born in 1928 in Bluefield, West Virginia, a remote rail center for the coal industry, Nash was the child of an electrical engineer and a schoolteacher. He attended Carnegie University, where, after switching majors from electrical engineering to chemistry and then to mathematics, he accomplished so much that he was awarded an M.S. in mathematics when he graduated. Nash then accepted a fellowship to study at Princeton, where he developed an interest in game theory after reading the *Theory of Games and Economic Behavior,* the seminal study by John von Neumann and Oskar Morganstern. In his 1950 dissertation, "Non-Cooperative Games," Nash drew a distinction between cooperative games in which parties could make binding agreements and those in which they could not make such agreements. Nash developed a concept for understanding noncooperative games that later came to be known as the Nash Equilibrium. He demonstrated that even in highly complex interactions with many parties, there was one predictable outcome—no player could improve his or her chances by seeking a different strategy when all parties had accurate ideas about the others' strategies. His solution for cooperative games came to be known as "Nash's Bargaining Solution."

After Princeton, Nash served on the math faculty at MIT, where he solved a classical problem in differential geometry. In 1959, he began his long struggle with mental illness, a struggle that was the subject of a best-selling book and Hollywood film, *A Beautiful Mind.*

Born in Budapest, Hungary, in 1920, John Harsanyi had an eventful early life, being forced to serve in a military labor unit during occupied Hungary in 1944, escaping from a railway station just before being shipped to a concentration camp in Austria, receiving a Ph.D. in philosophy from the University of Budapest after the war, and then emigrating to Australia to escape the repressive climate of the postwar communist regime. He later taught at the University of California in Berkeley. Interested in Nash's work on game theory, Harsanyi analyzed games with incomplete information. This work provided a framework for the "economics of information" in which different agents do not know the objectives of others.

Reinhard Selten was born in the German city of Breslau in 1930. After receiving his Ph.D. in mathematics from the University of Frankfurt in 1961, he refined the Nash Equilibrium by introducing the idea of subgame perfection. By eliminating noncredible equilibria from consideration, Selten found new ways of analyzing strategic interactions between game players. He applied these concepts to the analysis of conditions with small numbers of sellers. His ideas were useful in analyzing conditions of oligopoly and the economics of information. Harsanyi and Selten have actively collaborated with one another on game theory research.

Price Discounting Reconsidered. Another way to look at the pricing outcome in Table 2 is to assume that each firm knows these payoffs and will respond as soon as the other firm lowers its price. This makes the decision process a sequential process. Each firm waits for the other firm to alter price, then it follows suit. Since each firm has perfect knowledge and knows what each payoff is, a new equilibrium is reached; neither firm lowers prices for its banana splits, and profits remain at \$100,000. Neither firm would be inclined to lower price since profits would drop for both firms. This outcome is similar to the kinked demand curve model discussed earlier.

Advertising: Another Look. Once the game becomes dynamic and sequential, the outcome between Lowe's and Home Depot shown in Table 3 will be that neither firm advertises, and profits for each firm remain at \$100,000. You have probably noticed that Lowe's and Home Depot tend to locate near each other, and neither firm advertises except in Welcome Wagon literature and inexpensive local ads. Both tend to focus on competing on the basis of service and somewhat on price. Both have come to the conclusion that spending huge amounts on advertising does not pay, given the nature of the competition.

Predatory Pricing: American Airlines Versus Low-Cost Carriers

Predatory pricing
Selling below cost to consumers in the short run hoping to eliminate competitors so that prices can be raised in the longer run to earn economic profits.

Predatory pricing involves offering sufficiently low prices to consumers in the short run to eliminate competitors, so that eventually prices can be increased in the longer run once the competitors are gone. Firms with monopoly power in a market can use price wars or threaten their use to keep firms from entering the market. Such was the case involving American Airlines and several low-cost carriers at Dallas-Fort Worth Airport (DFW) in the mid-1990s.[10]

American Airlines is the dominant air carrier at DFW and several low-cost carriers (Vanguard, Western Pacific, and SunJet) entered the market. As the court noted:

> *During this period, these low-cost carriers created a new market dynamic, charging markedly lower fares on certain routes. For a certain period (of differing length in each market) consumers of air travel on these routes enjoyed lower prices. The number of passengers also substantially increased. American responded to the low-cost carriers by reducing some of its own fares and*

[10]*U.S. v. AMR et al.*, 140 F. Supp. 2d (2001).

increasing the number of flights serving the routes. In each instance, the low-fare carrier failed to establish itself as a durable market presence, and so eventually moved its operations or ceased its separate existence entirely. After the low-fare carrier ceased operations, American generally resumed its prior marketing strategy, and in certain markets reduced the number of flights and raised its prices, roughly to levels comparable to those prior to the period of low-fare competition.[11]

Table 4 captures the essence of the case using hypothetical data.

Table 4 Payoff Matrix for American Airlines and Low-Cost Carriers

Low Cost Carriers (potential entrants)	American Airlines (incumbent)	
	Normal	Price war
Enter	\$100,000,\$100,000	−\$100,000,−\$100,000
Do not enter	\$0,\$400,000	\$0,\$400,000

Without the entry of the low-cost carriers, American earns \$400,000 in profit. When they enter, American has a choice: continue to operate as normal and not slash prices (Normal column), or compete vigorously by lowering prices and offering more flights (Price War column). Normal activity results in profits to both parties of \$100,000, whereas engaging in a price war brings losses of \$100,000 to both, which ultimately the newly formed, lower-capitalized carriers probably can not sustain. Once the low-cost carriers are gone, prices and routes can return to their original states.

This case raises an interesting issue: Was American just dropping fares to meet competition, or was it actually engaging in predatory behavior? Standard economic theory suggests that predatory behavior is unprofitable and unlikely. The argument goes like this: Suffering large losses to remove competition and then making it up through monopoly pricing is not likely to be profitable in the long run. Once the competitors are removed and high prices return, these same high prices provide a strong incentive for new firms to enter, and the monopoly is stuck continually lowering prices to maintain its monopoly. Modern game theory has challenged this view.

Table 4 and the American Airlines episode illustrate the new thinking by game theorists on predatory pricing. One possibility is that the profits from the monopoly are sufficient to offset the bouts of price wars required to maintain the monopoly. Second, this is a potentially repeatable game, and American (at least at DFW) has effectively shown that it stands ready to defend its turf. This *commitment* to lower prices (Price Wars) is a warning to other airlines that are considering whether to enter the market. Repeated games permit firms to demonstrate their strategic decisions, thereby creating a *reputation* for fierce competitive behavior, thus influencing the decisions of others. Ultimately, American won this case and also won on further appeal in 2003. The courts were not convinced that American did anything except match the prices of its competitors: In the words of the court, American engaged "only in bare, but not brass knuckle competition."

This case makes it clear that when the game is repeatable, the strategic matrix expands substantially. We now turn to some of the strategies that game theorists look at for repeated games.

---

[11]*U.S. v. AMR*, p. 1141.

Repeated Games

Games can be endlessly (infinitely) repeated or repeated for a specific number of rounds. In either case, repeating opens the game to different types of strategies that are unavailable for the one-off game. These strategies can take into account the past behavior of rivals and can be more nuanced than one-off or limited sequential decisions. This section briefly explores these new strategies and some of their implications for understanding oligopoly behavior.

Trigger strategies
Action is taken contingent on your opponent's past decisions. For example, a grim trigger strategy is defined as any unfavorable decision by your opponent is then met by a permanent retaliatory decision forever.

One possibility is simply to cooperate or defect from the beginning. These simple strategies, however, leave you at the mercy of your opponent, or lead to unfavorable outcomes where both firms earn less or suffer losses. A more robust set of strategies are **trigger strategies**: action is taken contingent on your opponent's past decisions. These strategies are described in the following sections.

Grim Trigger

Let's start by looking at the auto industry. GM, Ford, and Chrysler are earning oligopoly profits. Suppose that all of a sudden, GM lowers its price, maybe because it is in financial trouble and wants to increase sales right away. Under the grim trigger rule, Ford and Chrysler lower their prices to match GM—but they do not stop there. Ford and Chrysler permanently lower their prices, making GM's predicament even more dire.

The grim trigger rule, thus, is this: Any decision by your opponent to defect (choose an unfavorable outcome) is met by a permanent retaliatory decision forever. This is a harsh decision rule. Its negative aspect is that it is subject to misreading. For example, has your competition lowered price in an attempt to gain market share at your expense, or has the market softened for the product in general? This strategy can quickly lead to the unfavorable Prisoner's Dilemma result. To avoid this problem, researchers have developed the trembling hand trigger strategy.

Trembling Hand Trigger

This strategy simply allows for one mistake by your opponent before you retaliate forever. This gives your opponent a chance to make a mistake and reduces misreads that are a problem for the grim trigger strategy. In the context of our auto industry example, a price decrease by GM will not be met right away, and it will not occasion numerous additional price decreases. This approach can be extended to accept two nonsequential defects, and so on, but they can be exploited by clever opponents who figure out they can get away with a few "mistakes" before their opponent retaliates.

Tit-for-Tat

This is a simple strategy that repeats the prior move of competitors. If GM lowers its price, Ford and Chrysler follow suit one time. If GM offers rebates or special offers, Ford and Chrysler do exactly the same in the next time period. This strategy has the efficient qualities that it rewards cooperation and punishes defection. It also offers forgiveness for defectors, so it avoids the misreading problems of the grim and trembling hand triggers. **Tit-for-tat strategies** also have been extended to include forgiveness of a single defection on a random basis.

Tit-for-tat strategies
A simple strategy that repeats the prior move of competitors. If your opponent lowers price, you do the same. This approach has the efficient quality that it rewards cooperation and punishes unfavorable strategies (defections).

This short list of strategies illustrates the richness of repeated games. Strategies tend to be more successful if they are relatively simple and easy to understand by competitors, tend to foster cooperation, have some credible punishment to reduce defections, and provide for forgiveness to avoid the costly mistakes associated with misreading opponents.[12]

---

[12]Nick Wilkinson, *Managerial Economics: A Problem Solving Approach* (Cambridge: Cambridge University Press), 2005, p. 373.

Hold Em Poker and Game Theory

Today, game theory is being applied to everything from auctions on eBay, to auctions for U.S. Treasury bonds, to animal conflicts (biology), to bankruptcy law, to OPEC, to poker, to the war on terrorism. The analytics have become extremely complex mathematically but nonetheless are opening up insights into economic and other behavior overlooked in the past. The original focus of John von Neumann's book *A Theory of Games and Economic Behavior*—poker—is back in the spotlight.

Texas Hold Em Poker has recently become a favorite with gamblers. Tournaments are held on a regular basis around the world. The championships have high TV ratings and have created celebrity players who then write books on how to play, and thousands (probably millions) of people play poker on the Internet. Many amateurs earn sizable livings playing online poker. But game theorists and computer scientists are moving in. They have developed PokerBots, software that uses game-theoretic analysis to help amateurs play against others on the net. Today, these artificial intelligence robots can sometimes be beaten by professionals, but as their sophistication grows, some predict the PokerBots will drive the human players from the Net and only Bots will remain.[13]

Game theory took a long time to enter the profession, but it is now firmly entrenched. Its usefulness is in bringing forth insights for not only human behavior, but for oligopolistic market behavior, that is mutually interdependent.

Summary of Market Structures

In this and the previous two chapters, we have studied the four major market structures: competition, monopolistic competition, oligopoly, and monopoly. As we move through this list, market power becomes greater, and the ability of the firm to earn economic profits in the long run grows.

Table 5 summarizes the important distinctions between these four market structures. Keep in mind that market structure analysis allows you to look at the overall

Table 5 Summary of Market Structures

	Competition	Monopolistic Competition	Oligopoly	Monopoly
Number of Firms	Many	Many	Few	One
Product	Homogeneous	Differentiated	Homogeneous or differentiated	Unique
Barriers to Entry or Exit?	No	No	Yes	Yes
Strategic Interdependence?	No	No	Yes	Not applicable
Long-Run Price Decision?	P = ATC	P = ATC	P > ATC	P > ATC
Long-Run Profits?	Zero	Zero	Usually economic	Economic
Key Summary Characteristic	Price taker	Product differentiation	Mutual interdependence	One-firm industry

[13]Tim Harford, "The Poker Machine," *Financial Times,* May 6, 2006, p. W21.

characteristics of the market and predict the pricing and profit behavior of the firms. The outcomes for competition and monopolistic competition are particularly attractive for consumers because firms price their products equal to average total costs and earn just enough to keep them in the business over the long haul.

In contrast, the outcomes for oligopolistic and monopolistic industries are not as favorable to consumers. Concentrated markets have considerable market power, which shows up in pricing and output decisions. However, keep in mind that markets with market power (oligopolies) often involve giants competing with giants. Even though there is a mutual interdependence in their decisions, and they may not always compete vigorously over prices, they often are innovative because of some competitive pressures. We see this today especially in the electronics and automobile markets.

Only the Paranoid Survive is the title of a book by the president of Intel Corporation, Andy Grove. His point is that you must keep ahead of the competition in innovation and technology if you want to remain in business. The last couple of years saw many large firms (Enron, WorldCom, Kmart, and the Italian company Parmalat) fail or go bankrupt, costing their stockholders billions. Bigness does not make firms immune to market pressures.

Checkpoint

Game Theory

REVIEW

- Game theory uses sophisticated mathematical analysis to model oligopolistic mutual interdependence.
- Game theory characteristics include (a) degrees of cooperation, (b) number of players, (c) simultaneous or sequential decision making, (d) information completeness, (e) discrete or continuous strategies, (f) one-off or repeated games, and (g) zero-sum or non-zero-sum games.
- The Prisoner's Dilemma is a static noncooperative game where players minimize their maximum prison time by both confessing.
- Nash equilibrium analysis showed that a solution exists for n-person games if each player chooses his optimal strategy, given that all other players have done the same.
- Games that are repeated lead to more nuanced trigger strategies including grim trigger, trembling hand trigger, and tit-for-tat.

QUESTION

Game theory and sophisticated mathematical modeling can be used to develop PokerBots and chess software such as that suggested by Tim Harford that consistently beat chess champions and will eventually probably beat poker champions. What might keep this same analysis from being used to beat the stock market?

Answers to the Checkpoint question can be found at the end of this chapter.

Merging Brands and Monopoly Power

As a last point, let us look at branding. We saw that firms seek to differentiate their products so they can exercise some market power. In other words, they charge a

Jupiter Images

price premium for their products. One of the key ways of differentiating products is to establish a brand. As said the saying goes: Companies produce products, but customers buy brands.

What is a brand? All of us know brands through their names and logos. Nike has the swoosh; Intel has a logo and the four-note jingle you hear whenever its Pentium processors are advertised (da–da–da–*da*); Coca-Cola has a distinctive way of spelling its name. Names and logos are communication devices. Brands are more than this.[14] They are a promise of performance. A branded product or service raises expectations in a consumer's mind. If these expectations are met, consumers pay the price premium. If expectations are not met, the value of the brand falls as consumers seek alternatives.

Brand names start with the company that makes the product or provides the service.[15] In the past, this meant that brand names came from a limited number of sources. Some companies were named after their founders, such as Walt Disney, and the Disney brand now extends over amusement parks (Disneyland and Disney World), movies, and products such as clothing found in branded Disney stores. Some companies were named after what they supplied, such as IBM (International Business Machines), and the IBM brand has carried over from adding machines to typewriters to computers and servers. Companies have also been named by their main product, such as the Coca-Cola Company, taking on the name of its brand. Sometimes, the company name combines the founder's name with the product, such as the Ford Motor Company. Sometimes, the company name has a tenuous link with the product but is strong nevertheless, such as the Starbucks name for coffee products: Master Starbuck was first mate to Captain Ahab in *Moby-Dick* and did drink coffee in the book, but who remembers that?

Whatever their origins, these brands have recognizable brand names. They are strong brands. They command price premiums. This is just what companies want.

So far, so good. Now we turn to a curious thing about brands in the past decade. Many companies merged. What do you name the new company? Do you keep one of the old names, keep both names and combine them, or come up with a new name? How do these actions affect the brand? It is true that product performance is the ultimate guarantor of price premiums, but people become attached to their brands through its name.

The past 10 years have witnessed a strange time for brands. Merged companies or deregulated companies sought to rebrand themselves. In Britain, the post office went from the Royal Mail to Consignia, and Scottish Telecom became Thus. How can you feel good about Consignia and Thus? How can you willingly pay a price premium for a product or service with such a brand name? And these names are just the most egregious. How do you feel about Aventis, Arriva, Altria, Diageo?

Maybe it was thought that globalization necessitated rebranding. So when Guinness and Grand Metropolitan merged, the new company became Diageo. How long will it be before individual brands take on the rebranded name of the company? Want a pint of Diageo beer?

Branding leads to price premiums, but branding is a tricky business. People get attached to their brands, which is exactly what companies want. However, companies have not helped this attachment with their rebrandings over the past 10 years. Maybe there is still hope. Consignia—what product are we talking about, again?—changed back to a more familiar Royal Mail Group.

---

[14]Sean F. O'Donnell, "Make It a Brand New Year," Life Insurance Marketing and Research Association: *MarketFacts* (Hartford), January/February 1999, 18(1), p. 18.

[15]See Richard Tomkins, "Branding Consultants Get a Chance to Tell It Like It Is," *Financial Times*, January 30, 2004, p. 14.

Key Concepts

Chapter Summary

Monopolistic Competition

Monopolistic competition assumes nearly the same characteristics as the competitive model, including the following:

- There are a large number of small firms with insignificant market share.
- There are no barriers to entry and exit.
- Unlike competition, the products sold by monopolistically competitive firms are different. They are similar, but consumers think them different because of brand preference, physical location, inherent product differences, or many other factors. Product differentiation is the key to this market structure.

Although product differences are often modest, each firm nonetheless faces a downward sloping demand curve with an associated marginal revenue curve. This demand curve is, however, highly elastic.

Pricing and output behavior in the short run for the monopolistically competitive firm looks a lot like that for a weak monopolist. Profit is maximized by selling an output where MR = MC.

In the long run, entry and exit of other firms will eliminate short-run profits or losses. If short-run profits exist, entry will reduce individual demand curves until the demand curve is just tangent to the average total cost curve. If short-run losses are the rule, exit will expand the demand curve of remaining firms until, again, the demand curve is tangent to the long-run average total cost (LRATC) curve.

At long-run equilibrium, P = ATC, and the firm earns normal profits. This output level is not, however, equal to the minimum point on the LRATC curve—it is lower than output needed to minimize costs. This is the cost to consumers from product differentiation. The immense selection of goods to purchase does not come without costs. Costs of advertising, rapid innovation, and "me too" copying are all included in the price of the products we purchase.

Oligopoly

Oligopoly industries are those in which the market is controlled by just a few firms. What constitutes a few firms is not precisely defined. Oligopoly products can be the same or differentiated, and barriers to entry are usually substantial.

Because there are only a few firms, decisions by one firm are dependent on what other firms in the industry decide to do. Economists refer to this as mutual interdependence. This is the key characteristic of oligopolies.

Cartels are illegal in the United States, but they are permitted in other parts of the world. Firms in cartels collude and agree to set monopoly prices and share the market according to some formula. Cartels are inherently unstable because cheating is profitable.

The kinked demand curve model of oligopoly answers the question of why oligopoly prices appear stable. The model assumes that if the firm raised its price, competitors will not react and raise their prices, but if the firm lowers prices, other firms will lower theirs in response. These reactions by competitors create a "kink" in the firm's demand curve and a discontinuity in the MR curve. This discontinuity permits marginal costs to vary considerably before the firm will change its pricing structure.

Game Theory

Modern game theory owes its origins to the mathematician John von Neumann.

The Prisoner's Dilemma is a static, noncooperative game in which each player must anticipate whether the other is going to confess or not. Both players would be better off not confessing, but each will confess in the end. Both players end up minimizing their worst outcome (minimax solution). The Prisoner's Dilemma is applicable to many other areas, including business pricing, advertising, war, and research and development decisions.

John Nash, in a very short paper, showed that there is a solution in an n-person game if each player chooses his optimal strategy given that all other players have done the same. This was an important result that allowed economists to develop realistic but complex games of market interactions, because they knew a solution existed.

Dynamic games allow for sequential decision making. This often changes the equilibrium outcome. When games are repeated, a host of new (more complex) strategies are introduced. They include trigger strategies such as grim trigger, trembling hand trigger, and tit-for-tat.

Questions and Problems

1. How do monopolistic competitive markets differ from competitive markets? If monopolistically competitive firms are making economic profits in the short run, what happens in the long run?

2. Describe the assumption underlying the kinked demand curve model. Describe why marginal cost can vary, but price remains constant.

3. How many firms constitute an oligopoly? What else characterizes oligopoly markets?

4. Google currently has more than 85% of the search activity on the Internet, as well as the online advertising revenue it generates. Microsoft had roughly the same percentage for operating system sales on microcomputers when the government filed its antitrust suit. Why hasn't the government filed a similar suit against Google today?

5. Holding the industry constant, why does a monopolist earn more profits than a firm in an oligopolistic setting? Why does the oligopolist earn more than a monopolistic competitor?

6. "Monopolistic competition has a little of monopoly and a little of competition, hence its name." Do you agree? Why or why not?

7. When economists speak of "mutual interdependence" in oligopoly markets, what do they mean? Why is mutual interdependence such an important element of oligopoly markets?

8. We saw in the last chapter that the HHI (Herfindahl-Hirshman index) is used by the Department of Justice to measure industry concentration. Since domestically we have virtually no monopolies, some would argue that the HHI is really used to measure the degree of oligopoly. However, the HHI represents domestic concentration, and many of the products we purchase are made globally and sold in the United States by foreign firms. Has global competition made these HHI estimates less meaningful? Are old-line American oligopolies (autos, steel, and airlines) more like monopolistic competitors today? Why or why not?

9. In both competitive and monopolistically competitive markets, firms earn normal profits in the long run. What enables oligopoly firms to have the opportunity to earn economic profits in the long run?

10. What makes the strategies so different for repeated games than one-off games?

11. As new firms enter a monopolistically competitive market, what happens to the average total cost curve for existing firms? What happens to the individual firm demand curve? What happens to individual firm profits?

12. Why is it difficult for cartels to effectively maintain high prices over the longer term?

13. Without admitting wrongdoing, Proctor & Gamble (P&G) in 1998 paid a fine and settled antitrust charges brought by the New York Attorney General because P&G eliminated its coupon program. The Attorney General concluded the firms in the industry were colluding and argued that eliminating coupons was only possible (or profitable) "if everybody goes along with it." Is this a clever use of game theory by the New York Attorney General? Construct a Prisoner's Dilemma game that supports his contention.

14. The 1982 Export Trading Company Act and the 1918 Webb-Pomerene Act permit export cartels in the United States. Export cartels are groups of firms that can legally collude, set prices, and share marketing and distribution of their products in foreign countries. These cartels must register with the government, and their activities cannot affect domestic competition. Economic theory suggests that cartels are entities that exist to maximize monopoly profits for members. Given this, why would the United States permit these cartels to exist?

15. When trying to get tickets to the Lion King recently, my wife may have had a chance to see game theory in action. Tickets for shows 6 months away went on sale online at 6:00 in the morning and she was there at 6:02. Every time she requested seats in a good area, she was informed they were unavailable, but others in much worse locations were available. No matter what day or which show, less attractive alternatives were suggested. Can you think of a game theory explanation that might suggest why this was happening?

Answers to Checkpoint Questions

CHECKPOINT: MONOPOLISTIC COMPETITION

Clowns are unique; their acts are copyrighted and protected, and this is one way to differentiate your circus from others. Celebrity clowns draw crowds, especially youngsters, and are cheaper than buying, keeping, training, and insuring animals (not to mention the hassles from animal rights groups).

CHECKPOINT: OLIGOPOLY

The most recent example is the Internet. Barriers to entry in a large number of well-established industries (big and small) are affected. It is clearly changing the software, music, and entertainment industries. In a similar way, sequencing of DNA is another innovation that is rapidly changing the pharmaceutical industry.

CHECKPOINT: GAME THEORY

Game theory is best used with a relatively small number of decision makers. Chess has a finite (but huge) number of moves, and computers can search for the optimal play, and poker involves a limited number of opponents. Games give insights into human behavior that can be used as inputs into stock market decisions. But when the number of participants, stocks, and economic variables are considered, the computing power required to solve the stock market problem probably prevents its use in real time.

11 Theory of Input Markets

Hardly a day goes by without media reference to some celebrity's income or some CEO's astronomical salary laden with stock options. Rock stars and professional athletes command seven-figure salaries (that's millions of dollars), while your economics instructor labors away for a five-figure pittance that barely covers the costs of living. Meanwhile, shortages in nursing and elementary education seem to persist year after year, and we see numerous wage discrimination cases going to litigation. How are all these developments to be explained? Labor markets are complex institutions, and as usual, understanding the issues connected with them will require some simplification.

Input markets, also called factor markets, are extremely important to our economy. To this point in the book, we have focused on product markets, mentioning input markets only incidentally. Lying behind the production of goods and services, however, are workers, machinery, and plants. Few firms can operate without employees or capital. Similarly, few households could survive without the income that work provides.

The analysis of input markets in this chapter will focus on the labor and capital markets, while briefly touching on land rents and entrepreneurial profits. The first two sections will look at competitive labor markets where the participants—firms and employees—are price takers. We will then introduce some imperfections into the labor market and look for differences in outcomes. We then turn to the role that capital markets play in the economy. The chapter closes with a brief examination of land and entrepreneurship, the source of rents and profits. In the following chapter, we will return to the labor market and take a closer look at several labor issues, including human capital, economic discrimination, and the economics of labor unions.

Competitive labor markets are similar to competitive product markets. First, we assume that firms operate in competitive industries with many buyers and sellers, a homogeneous product, and easy entry and exit to the industry. As you will recall, moreover, the firms in competitive industries are price takers. Each firm is so small that it has no perceptible impact on industry price; all firms can do is adjust their output in response to changes in industry price.

A second assumption of competitive labor markets, inhumane as it may sound, is that workers are considered homogeneous, and labor is treated as a homogeneous commodity. One unit of labor is a perfect substitute for another in the competitive market, and no potential employees are "special." More precisely, all employees are regarded as equally productive, such that firms have no preference for one employee over another.

Third, a competitive labor market assumes that information in the industry is widely available and accurate. Everyone knows what the going wage rate is, so well-informed decisions about how much labor to supply are made by workers, and firms can wisely decide how many workers to hire.

A firm's demand for labor is a derived demand; it is derived from consumer demand for the firm's product and the productivity of labor. The labor supply, on the other hand, is determined by the individual preferences of potential workers for work or leisure. Like all competitive markets, supply and demand interact to determine equilibrium wages and employment. Much of this analysis you have seen before, but we now apply these analytical techniques to labor markets. We begin by looking at how the decisions by individuals to participate in labor markets generate the supply of labor.

After studying this chapter you should be able to

- **Define and describe competitive labor markets.**
- **Derive a supply curve for labor.**
- **Describe the factors that can change labor supply.**
- **Describe the factors that can change labor demand.**
- **Determine the elasticity of demand for labor.**
- **Derive the market demand for labor.**
- **Describe monopoly and monopsony power and their impact on imperfect labor markets.**
- **Determine the present value of an investment.**
- **Compute the rate of return of an investment.**
- **Describe the impact of the supply of land on markets.**
- **Describe the impact of economic profits on entrepreneurs and markets.**

Competitive Labor Supply

When you decide to work, you are giving up leisure, understood broadly as non-work activity, in exchange for the income that work brings. Economists assume people prefer leisure activities to work. This may not be entirely true, since work can be a source of personal satisfaction and a network of social connections, as well as provide many other benefits. For our discussion, however, we will follow the practice of economists in simply dividing individual or household time into work and

Karl Marx (1818–1883)

“Working men of all countries unite!” With this exhortation, Karl Marx ended his seminal *Communist Manifesto,* neatly summing up both his philosophy and his view of the world. To Marx, history was the story of class struggle. The solution was revolution by the proletariat—the working class that was the hero of all Marx believed and proposed.

Karl Marx was born in Germany in 1818. He spent much of his adult life, however, in England, where he died in 1883. By the time of his death, Marx and Friedrich Engels had crafted the essence of Communism—the last ideology to seriously challenge capitalism in the 20th century. In their two major works, *The Communist Manifesto* (1848) and *Das Kapital* (1867), Marx and Engels offered a severe critique of capitalism and extolled the virtues of proletariat rebellion and the utopia of a stateless world order.

To Marx, all world history was the history of class struggle. To preserve their privileges, the ruling class had always striven to oppress the underclasses. Marx saw a struggle between the bourgeoisie (or property owners) and the proletariat (or workers). Modern states were merely a way to repress workers for the benefit of the bourgeoisie.

This exploitation—the essence of capitalism—not only kept the bourgeoisie in power, but it also alienated the proletariat from its own labor, which to Marx was the true essence of all economic value. The only prescription to cure the monopolistic and monopsonistic exploitation of labor was proletariat revolution.

leisure. Note that the term *leisure* encompasses all activities that do not involve paid work, including caring for children, doing household chores, and activities that are truly leisurely.

Individual Labor Supply

The **supply of labor** represents the time an individual is willing to work—the labor the individual is willing to supply—at various wage rates. On a given day, the most a person can work is 24 hours, though clearly such a schedule could not be sustained for long, given that we all need rest and sleep. For high wages, you would probably be willing to work horrendous hours for a short time, whereas if wages were low enough, you might not be willing to work at all. Between these two extremes lies the normal supply of labor curve for most of us.

Supply of labor
The amount of time an individual is willing to work at various wage rates.

Panel A of Figure 1 shows a typical labor supply curve for individuals. This individual is willing to supply l_1 hours of work a day when the wage is W_1. What happens if the wage rate increases? Assume that wages increase to W_2: Individuals now will be willing to increase hours spent working from l_1 to l_2 (point b), reducing their hours of leisure.

FIGURE 1

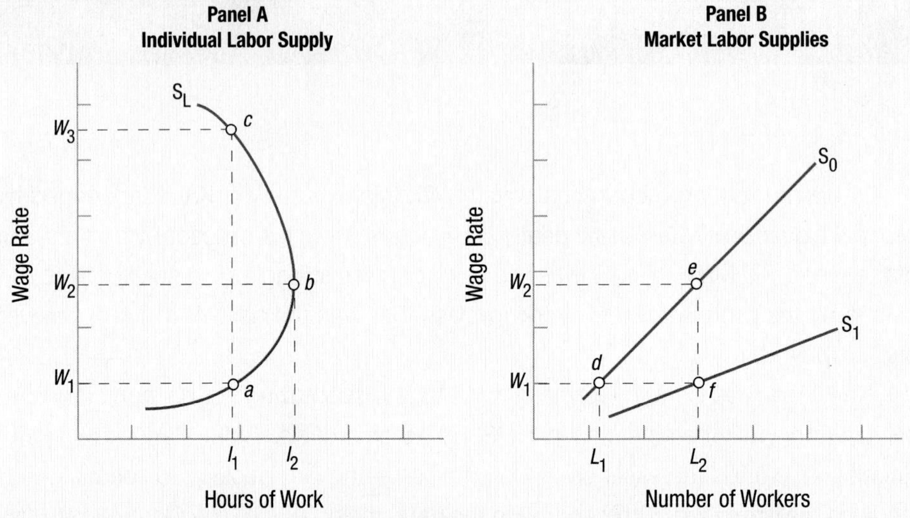

Individual and Market Supply of Labor

Panel A shows a typical individual's supply of labor. When wages are W_1, this individual will work l_1 hours, but when the wage rate rises to W_2, her willingness to work rises to l_2. Over these two wage rates she is substituting work for leisure. Once the wage rises above W_2, the income effect begins to dominate, since she now has sufficient income that leisure is now more important (the income effect dominates) and her labor supply curve is backward bending. Market labor supplies are shown in Panel B and are positively related to the wage rate. Increasing wages in one industry attract labor from other industries (a movement from point d to point e as the wage rises from W_1 to W_2). In contrast, market labor supply curves *shift* in response to demographic changes, changes in the nonwage benefits of jobs, wages paid in other occupations, and nonwage income.

Substitution Effect

When wages rise, people tend to substitute work for leisure since the opportunity cost of leisure grows. This is known as the **substitution effect**. The substitution effect for labor supply is always positive; it leads to more hours of work when the wage rate increases.

Substitution effect
Higher wages mean that the value of work has increased, and the opportunity costs of leisure are higher, so work is substituted for leisure.

Note that this effect is similar to the substitution effect consumers experience when the price of a product declines. When the price of one product falls, consumers substitute that product for others. The substitution effect for consumer products, however, is negative (price falls and consumption rises), while it is always positive for labor (wages rise and the supply of labor increases).

Income Effect

When wages rise, if you continue to work the same hours as before, your income will rise. When wage rates are very high, however, the income from working a few hours may be enough to support the lifestyle you wish. Higher wages may permit you to work fewer hours, but also enjoy a higher standard of living. This **income effect** on labor supply is normally negative—higher wages and income lead to fewer hours worked. As a result, the supply curve for *individuals* in Panel A is *backward bending:* At wages above W_2, workers increasingly elect to substitute leisure for the income that comes from additional work.

Income effect
Higher wages mean you can maintain the same standard of living by working fewer hours. The impact on labor supply is generally negative.

Once again, this is similar to the income effect consumers experience when the price of a common product drops. The falling price of this product permits consumers to purchase the same quantity as before and still have some added income leftover to spend on other products. Higher wages mean a higher income and with a higher income leisure looks more attractive.

The labor supply curve for individuals shows that, at wages below W_2, people will substitute work for leisure; income is more important than leisure at these wage levels. When wages are above W_2, workers will do the opposite, substituting leisure for work; they have enough income so leisure is more important.

When the labor supply curve is positively sloped, as it is below W_2 in Panel A, the substitution effect is stronger than the income effect; thus, higher wages lead to more hours worked. Conversely, when the supply of labor curve bends backward, as it does above W_2, the income effect overpowers the substitution effect. In this case, higher wages mean fewer hours worked.

Backward bending labor supply curves have been observed empirically in developed and developing countries. Still, it takes rather high income levels before the income effect begins to overpower the substitution effect. People like to have incomes well beyond what is required to satisfy their basic needs before they will select more leisure over work as wages rise.

Market Labor Supply Curves

The labor supply for any occupation or industry will be upward sloping; higher wages for a job mean more inquiries and job applications. Thus, although an individual's labor supply curve may be backward bending, market labor supply curves are normally positively sloped as shown in Panel B of Figure 1. Note that this is true for all other inputs to the production process such as raw materials such as copper, steel, and silicon as well as for capital and land: Higher prices mean higher quantities supplied.

Changes in wage rates change the quantity of labor supplied. For example, increasing wages in one industry attracts labor from other industries. This is a movement along the market labor supply curve and is shown in Panel B as a movement along S_0 from points d to e as wages (input prices) rise from W_1 to W_2.

Factors That Change Labor Supply

But what factors will cause the entire market labor supply curve to shift from, say, S_0 to S_1 in Panel B so that L_2 workers are willing to work for a wage of W_1 (point f)? These include demographic changes, nonwage benefits of jobs, wages paid in other occupations, and nonwage income.

Demographic Changes

Changes in population, immigration patterns, and labor force participation rates (the percentage of individuals in a group who enter the labor force) all change labor supplies by altering the number of qualified people available for work. Over the past three decades, labor force participation rates among women have steadily risen, continually adding workers to the expanding American labor force; dual-earner households are increasingly the norm. Today, both parents work in two thirds of all married-couple households with children. Other demographic changes have shifted the labor supply curve by modifying the labor–leisure preferences among workers. Health improvements, for example, have lengthened the typical working life.

Nonmoney Aspects of Jobs

Changes in the nonwage benefits of an occupation will similarly shift the supply of labor in that market. If employers can manage to increase the pleasantness, safety, or status of a job, labor supply will increase. Other nonmoney perks also help. The airline industry, for example, has greatly increased the number of people willing to work in mundane positions by allowing employees (and in some instances their immediate families) to fly anywhere for free on a standby basis.

Wages in Alternative Jobs

When worker skills in one industry are readily transferable to other jobs or industries, the wages paid in those other markets will affect wage rates and the labor supply in the first industry. For example, Web and computer programming skills are useful in all industries, and their wages in one industry affect all industries. And because at least some of the skills that all workers possess will benefit other employers, all labor markets have some influence over each other. Rising wages in growth industries will shrink the supply of labor available to firms in other industries.

Nonwage Income

Changes in income from sources other than working will change the supply of labor. As nonwage income rises, hours of work supplied declines. If you have enough income from nonwork sources, after all, the retirement urge will set in no matter what your age. Maybe this is where the term "idle rich" came from.

The key thing to remember here is that market labor supply curves are normally positively sloped, even though an individual's labor supply curve may be backward bending. We will now go on to put this together with the other blade in the scissors: the demand for labor in competitive labor markets.

Checkpoint

Competitive Labor Supply

REVIEW

- Competitive labor markets assume that firms operate in competitive product markets and purchase homogeneous labor from competitive labor markets, and information is widely available and accurate.
- The supply of labor represents the time an individual is willing to work.
- The substitution effect occurs when wages rise, as people tend to substitute work for leisure because the opportunity cost of leisure is higher or vice versa when wages fall.
- When wages rise and you continue to work the same number of hours, your income rises. When wages rise high enough, an income effect occurs in which leisure is traded for income, and the supply of labor curve for individuals is backward bending.
- Industry or occupation labor supply curves are upward sloping.
- The labor supply curve will shift with demographic changes, changes in the nonwage aspects of an occupation, changes in the wages in alternative jobs, and changes in nonwage income.

QUESTIONS

Assume that you take a job with flexible hours, but initially your salary is based on a 40-hour week. Your salary begins at $15 an hour or $30,000 a year. Assuming your salary rises, at what salary (hourly wage) would you begin to work fewer than 40 hours a week (remember, the job permits flexible hours)? If your rich aunt dies and leaves you $500,000, would this alter the wage rate where you cut your work hours? Do you think this wage rate will be the same when you are 35 and have two children?

Answers to the Checkpoint questions can be found at the end of this chapter.

Competitive Labor Demand

The competitive firm's **demand for labor** is derived from the demand for the firm's product and the productive capabilities of a unit of labor.

Demand for labor
Demand for labor is derived from the demand for the firm's product and the productivity of labor.

Marginal Revenue Product

Assume a firm wants to hire an additional worker, and that worker is able to produce 15 units of the firm's product. Further, assume that the product sells for \$10 a unit, and labor is the only input cost (such as blackberry picking in Oregon), with this cost including a normal return on the investment. The last worker hired is therefore worth \$150 to the firm (15 × \$10 = \$150). If the cost of hiring this worker is \$150 or less (remember, a normal profit is included in the wage), then the firm will hire this person. If the wage rate for labor exceeds \$150, a competitive firm will not hire this marginal worker.

To see how this works in greater detail, look at Table 1. The production function here is similar to the one used earlier in the chapter on production. Column 1 (L) is labor input, Column 2 (Q) is total output, and Column 3 (MPP_L) is the **marginal physical product of labor**. This last value is the additional output a firm receives from employing an added unit of labor ($MPP_L = \Delta Q \div \Delta L$). For example, adding a fourth worker raises output from 25 to 40 units, so the marginal physical product of labor for this additional worker is 15 units.

Marginal physical product of labor
The additional output a firm receives from employing an added unit of labor ($MPP_L = \Delta Q \div \Delta L$).

Table 1 Competitive Labor Market

(1) L	(2) Q	(3) MPP_L	(4) P	(5) $MRP_L = VMP_L$	(6) W
0	0	0	10	0	100
1	7	7	10	70	100
2	15	8	10	80	100
3	25	10	10	100	100
4	40	15	10	150	100
5	54	14	10	140	100
6	65	11	10	110	100
7	75	10	10	100	100
8	84	9	10	90	100
9	90	6	10	60	100
10	95	5	10	50	100
11	98	3	10	30	100
12	100	2	10	20	100
13	98	−2	10	−20	100
14	95	−3	10	−30	100

Marginal revenue product
The value of another worker to the firm is equal to the marginal physical product of labor (MPP_L) times marginal revenue (MR).

In this example, the firm is operating in a competitive market, so it can sell all the output it produces at the prevailing market price of \$10. The value of another worker to the firm, called the **marginal revenue product** (MRP_L), is equal to the marginal physical product of labor times marginal revenue:

$$MRP_L = MPP_L \times MR$$

In our example, adding a fourth worker leads to a marginal revenue product of labor of \$150; we multiply the marginal physical product of 15 units by the marginal revenue—or price in this competitive market—of \$10 per unit.

Column 5 contains the firm's MRP_L. Additional workers add this value to the firm. Thus, the marginal revenue product curve is the firm's demand for labor, which is graphed in Figure 2. Note how the marginal revenue product reaches a maximum for 4 workers, as shown in column 5 of the table and in the figure.

FIGURE 2

The Competitive Firm's Demand for Labor

This figure reflects the data from columns 5 and 6 from Table 1. In this example, the firm is operating in a competitive market, so it can sell all the output it produces at the prevailing market price. The value of the additional worker to the firm, the value of the marginal product (VMP_L), is equal to the marginal physical product of labor times price (or marginal revenue in this case). VMP_L is the firm's demand for labor. If wages are equal to \$100, the firm will hire 7 workers (point *e*).

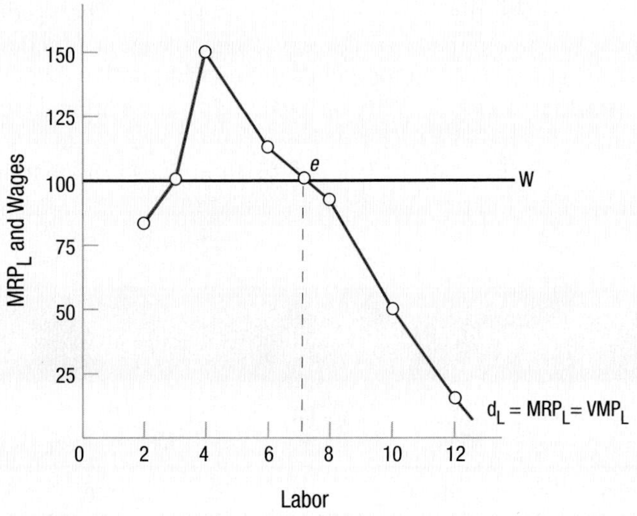

Value of the Marginal Product

Value of the marginal product
The value of the marginal product of labor (VMP_L) is equal to price multiplied by the marginal physical product of labor, or $P \times MPP_L$.

Competitive firms are price takers for whom marginal revenue is equal to the price of the product (MR = P). The **value of the marginal product** is defined as $VMP_L = MPP_L \times P$. For the fourth worker in Table 1, the value of the marginal product of labor is 15 units times \$10, or \$150. This is the same as the marginal revenue product of labor we just calculated. In the competitive case, MR = P, hence $VMP_L = MRP_L$. The distinction between VMP and MRP is of little importance here, but when we look at imperfect labor markets, these two will differ because marginal revenue will not equal price and the difference will have policy implications.

Competitive firms hire labor from competitive labor markets. Because each firm is too small to affect the larger market, it can hire all the labor it wants at the market-determined wage. Remember, we are assuming labor is a homogeneous commodity, and one unit of labor is the same as all others.

Table 1 and Figure 2 assume that the going wage for labor (W) is \$100. For our firm, this results in 7 workers being hired at \$100 (point *e*), since this is the employment level at which $W = VMP_L$. Note that $W = VMP_L$ at 3 workers as well, but since the value of the marginal product is greater than the wage rate for workers 4–6, the firm would hire 7 workers, not 3, to maximize its gains. The value to the firm of hiring the seventh worker is just equal to what the firm must pay this worker. Profits are maximized for the competitive firm when workers are hired out to the point where $VMP_L = W$.

However, if market wages were to fall to $90, the firm would hire an eighth worker to maximize profits, since with 8 employees, VMP_L is also equal to $90.

Factors That Change Labor Demand

The demand for labor is derived from product demand and labor productivity—how much people will pay for the product and how much each unit of labor can produce. It follows that changes in labor demand can arise from changes in either product demand or labor productivity. Because most production also requires other inputs, changes in the price of these other inputs will also change the demand for labor.

Change in Product Demand

A decline in the demand for a firm's product will lead to lower market prices reducing VMP_L, and vice versa. As VMP_L for all workers declines, labor demand will shift to the left. Anything that changes the price of the product in competitive markets will shift the firm's demand for labor.

Changes in Productivity

Changes in worker productivity (usually increases) can come about from improving technology or because a firm uses more capital or land along with its workforce. As MPP_L rises, the demand for the marginal worker rises, and thus the firm is willing to pay higher wages for a workforce of the same size, or else to expand its workforce at the same wage rate. As more capital is employed—say, an excavation company shifts from shovels to back loaders—the demand for labor will rise. To be sure, the number of workers hired for a job may decline with mechanization, but the workers running the digging equipment, since they are more productive, will earn higher wages. This is why capital-intensive industries often employ fewer workers than other industries, but their workers are usually high-skill, high-wage employees.

Changes in the Prices of Other Inputs

An increase in the price of capital will drive up the demand for labor. More expensive capital means that labor will be substituted for capital in new projects, thus increasing the demand for labor.

More labor will be hired when wages fall, but how much more? The answer depends on the elasticity of demand for labor.

Elasticity of Demand for Labor

The **elasticity of demand for labor** (E_L) is the percentage change in the quantity of labor demanded (Q_L) divided by the percentage change in the wage rate (W). This elasticity is found the same way we calculated the price elasticity of demand for products, except that we substitute the wage rate for the price of the product:

Elasticity of demand for labor
Equal to the percentage change in the quantity of labor demanded divided by the percentage change in the wage rate.

$$E_L = \%\Delta Q_L \div \%\Delta W$$

The elasticity of demand for labor measures how responsive the quantity of labor demanded is to changes in wages. An inelastic demand for labor is one where the absolute value of the elasticity is less than 1. Conversely, an elastic curve's computed elasticity is greater than 1.

The time firms have to adjust to changing wages will affect elasticity. In the short run, when labor is the only truly variable factor of production, elasticity of demand for labor will be more inelastic. In the long run, when all production factors can be adjusted, elasticity of demand for labor will tend to be more elastic.

Factors That Affect the Elasticity of Demand for Labor

Although time affects elasticity, three other factors also affect the elasticity of demand for labor: elasticity of product demand, ease of substituting other inputs, and labor's share of the production costs. Let's briefly consider each of these.

Elasticity of Demand for the Product. The more elastic the price elasticity of demand for a product, the greater the elasticity of demand for labor. Higher wages result in higher product prices, and the more easily consumers can substitute away from the firm's product, the greater the number of workers who will become unemployed. An elastic demand for labor means that employment is more responsive to wage rates. The opposite will be true for products with inelastic demands.

Ease of Input Substitutability. The more difficult it is to substitute capital for labor, the more inelastic the demand for labor will be. At this point, computers cannot yet substitute for pilots in commercial airplanes, which results in an inelastic demand for pilots.[1] As a result, pilots have been able to secure high wages from airlines through their union representatives. The easier it is to substitute capital for labor, the less bargaining power workers have, and labor demand will tend to be more elastic.

Labor's Share of Total Production Costs. The share of total costs associated with labor is another factor determining the elasticity of demand for labor. If labor's share of total costs is small, the demand for labor will tend to be rather inelastic. In the example of airline pilots above, the percentage of costs going to pilot wages is small, perhaps 10%. Thus, a 20% increase in pilot wages, though a major raise, would increase ticket prices by only 2%. The resulting change in the demand for air travel would be small, and thus its effect on the demand for pilot labor is small. The opposite is true when labor's share of costs is large.

Competitive Labor Market Equilibrium

Generalized market equilibrium in competitive labor markets requires that we take into account the industry supply and demand for labor. The market supply for labor (S_L) is the horizontal sum of the individual labor supply curves in the market.

The market demand for labor, however, is not simply a summation of the demand for labor by all the firms in the market. When wages fall, for instance, this affects all firms—all want to hire more labor and produce more output. This added production reduces market prices for their output and negatively affects the demand for labor.

Figure 3 shows how the market demand for labor is determined. If wage rates are initially W_0 and the firm is operating on the MRP_0 curve, a given firm will hire L_0 units of labor (point *a*).

Assume the wage rate falls to W_1; the firm will now want to hire L_2 units of labor (point *c*). All the other firms in the industry, however, will also want to hire more workers. The resulting increase in output will drive the price of the industry's product down, thus shifting product demand for all firms down to MRP_1. Equilibrium for each firm is now at point *b*, resulting in an adjusted market demand curve, d_L, which reflects these changes in prices. The industry demand curve is therefore the sum of all the d_L curves for the firms in the industry, not simply the sum of quantities of labor they demand at one point in time.

Turning to Figure 4, we have put both sides of the market together. In Panel A, the competitive labor market determines equilibrium wage (W_e) and employ-

[1]It is worth noting that the military has developed a number of planes that are pilotless. In December 2002, a Northrop Grumman Global Hawk flew from California to South Australia without a pilot. According to the company, the flight only required "two clicks of a mouse." The interesting question is: Will people be willing to fly in pilotless commercial aircraft? See *The Economist* (December 21, 2002), pp. 83–85.

FIGURE 3

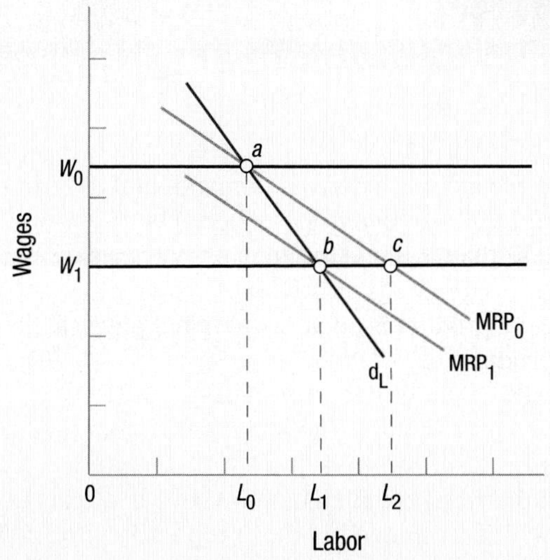

Deriving the Industry Demand for Labor

How are market demands for labor determined? If wage rates are initially W_0, and a given firm is operating on the MRP_0 curve, the firm will hire L_0 units of labor (point *a*). If wages falls to W_1, the firm will want to hire L_2 units of labor (point *c*). But the other firms in the industry will also want to hire more workers. The resulting increase in output will drive down the price of the industry's product, thus shifting product demand for all firms down to MRP_1. Equilibrium for each firm moves to point *b,* resulting in an adjusted market demand curve, d_L, that reflects these changes in prices. The industry demand curve is the sum of the d_L curves for all the firms in the industry.

ment (L_e) based on market supply and demand. Individual firms, in light of their own situation, hire l_e where this equilibrium wage is equal to marginal revenue product (MRP_L), point *e* in Panel B. Much like the product markets we discussed in earlier chapters, the invisible hand of the marketplace sets wages and in the end determines employment.

FIGURE 4

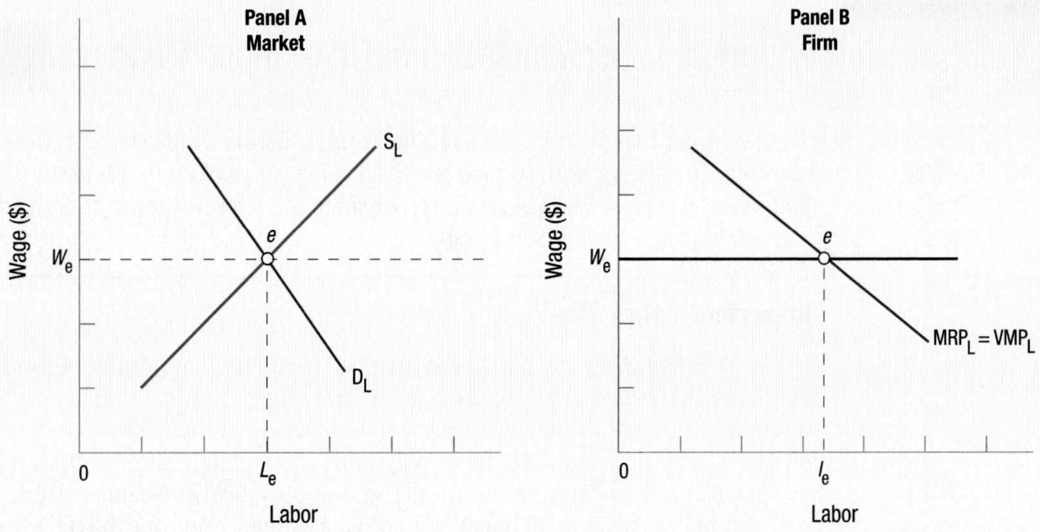

Competitive Labor Markets

In Panel A, the competitive labor market determines equilibrium wages (W_e) and employment (L_e). Individual firms hire l_e where this equilibrium wage is equal to marginal revenue product (MRP_L), point *e* in Panel B.

Checkpoint

Competitive Labor Demand

REVIEW

- The firm's demand for labor is a derived demand–derived from consumer demand for the product and the productivity of labor.
- Marginal revenue product is equal to the marginal physical product of labor times marginal revenue.
- Value of the marginal product is equal to marginal physical product of labor times the price of the product.
- Since MR = P for the competitive firm, $VMP_L = MRP_L$.
- The demand for labor is equal to the value of the marginal product of labor for competitive firms.
- The demand for labor curve will change if there is a change in the demand for the product, if there is a change in labor productivity, or if there is a change in the price of other inputs.
- The elasticity of demand for labor is equal to the percentage change in quantity of labor demanded divided by the percentage change in the wage rate.
- The elasticity of demand for labor will be *more* elastic the greater the elasticity of demand for the product, the easier it is to substitute other factors for labor, and the larger the share of total production costs attributed to labor.
- Market equilibrium occurs where market labor demand and supply intersect.

QUESTIONS

Individuals are different in terms of ability, attitude, and willingness to work. Given this fact, does it make sense to assume labor is homogeneous? Does this model better fit firms such as Wal-Mart that hire 800+ employees at each store at roughly standardized wages than, say, firms such as Google that look for high-skilled computer geeks?

Answers to the Checkpoint questions can be found at the end of this chapter.

Imperfect Labor Markets and Other Input Markets

The previous two sections focused on conditions in competitive product and input markets. In this section, we are going to relax our assumptions and look at imperfect labor markets. We will go on to consider the three other inputs in some depth: capital, land, and entrepreneurship.

Imperfect Labor Markets

In the world as we know it, markets are not perfectly competitive. Product markets and labor markets contain *monopolistic* and *oligopolistic* elements. In many product markets, a few firms control the bulk of market share. They may not be monopolies, but they do have some monopoly power, through brand loyalty if nothing else.

Similarly, in most communities, there is only one government hiring firefighters and police officers. When the market contains only one buyer of a resource, economists refer to this lone buyer as a *monopsonist. Monopsony power,* meanwhile, is the control over input supply the monopsonist enjoys. Before we look at the impact of **monopsony** on the labor market, let us first consider monopoly power in the product market.

Monopsony
A labor market with one employer.

Monopoly Power in Product Markets

As we know, firms that enjoy monopoly power in product markets are price makers, not price takers. Because P > MR, it follows that $VMP_L > MRP_L$. Figure 5 shows why. The firm depicted has monopoly power in the product market, but buys inputs in a competitive environment.

As Figure 5 shows, a competitive firm would equate wage and value of the marginal product (VMP_L), hiring L_C workers and paying the going wage of W_0 (point *c*). The firm with monopoly power, however, will equate wage and marginal revenue product (MRP_L), thus hiring L_0 workers, though again paying the prevailing wage W_0 (point *a*). So, although both firms hire workers at the same wage, the firm with monopoly power hires fewer workers.

FIGURE 5

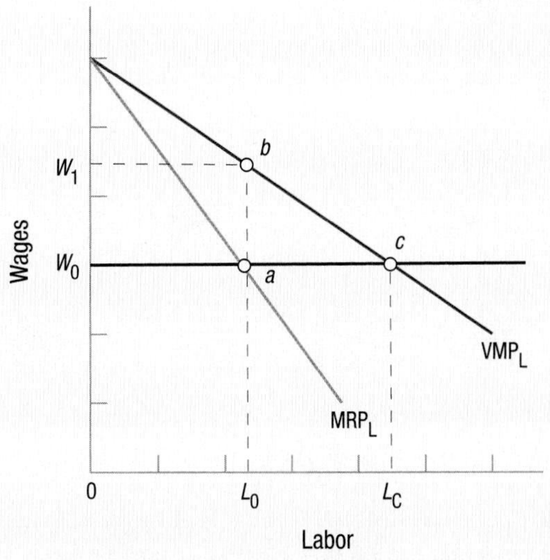

Monopoly Firm in Product Market Employing Labor from a Competitive Market

Firms with monopoly power in product markets are price makers. Because P > MR, it follows that $VMP_L > MRP_L$. A competitive firm would equate wages and value of the marginal product (VMP_L), hiring L_C workers and paying the going wage of W_0 (point *c*). A firm with monopoly power, however, will equate wages and marginal revenue product (MRP_L), thus hiring L_0 workers, though again paying the prevailing wage W_0 (point *a*). Hence, although both firms hire workers at the same wage, the firm with monopoly power hires fewer workers. Also, the value of the marginal product (VMP_L) of workers in the monopolistic firm is much higher than what they are paid; their value to the firm is W_1 (point *b*), though they are only paid W_0 (point *a*). This difference is called monopolistic exploitation.

This means the value of the marginal product (VMP_L) of workers in the monopolistic firm is much higher than what they are paid. Their value to the firm (point *b*) is W_1, though they are only paid W_0. This difference is referred to as **monopolistic exploitation of labor**. The term is loaded, but what economists mean by it is simply that workers get paid less than the value of their marginal product when working for a monopolist. This is, as you might expect, a source of monopoly profits.

Monopolistic exploitation of labor
When a firm has monopoly power in the product market, marginal revenue is less than price (MR < P) and the firm hires labor up to the point where MRP_L = wage. Because MRP_L is less than the VMP_L, workers are paid less than the value of their marginal product, and this difference is called monopolistic exploitation of labor.

Monopsony

A monopsony is a market with one buyer or employer. The Postal Service, for instance, is the sole employer of mail carriers in this country, just as the armed forces are the only employer of military personnel. Single-employer towns used to dot the American landscape, and some occupations still face monopsony power regularly. Nurses and teachers, for example, often face only a few hospitals or local school districts where they can work.

Since a monopsonist is the only buyer of some input, it will face a positively sloped supply curve for that input, such as supply curve S_L in Figure 6. This firm could hire 14 workers for $10 (point *a*), or it could increase wages to $11 and hire 15 workers (point *b*). Since the supply of labor is no longer flat, however, as it was in the competitive market, adding one more worker will cost the firm more than simply the new worker's higher wage. But just how much more?

FIGURE 6

Marginal Factor Cost

This monopsonistic firm faces a positively sloped supply curve, S_L. The firm could hire 14 workers for $10 an hour (point *a*), or it could increase wages to $11 an hour and hire 15 workers (point *b*). Since the supply curve is positively sloped, however, adding one more worker will cost the firm more than simply the cost of a new worker. To hire an added worker requires a higher wage and all current employees also must be paid the higher wage. Therefore, the total wage bill rises by more than just the added wages of the last worker hired. The marginal factor cost curve reflects these rising costs.

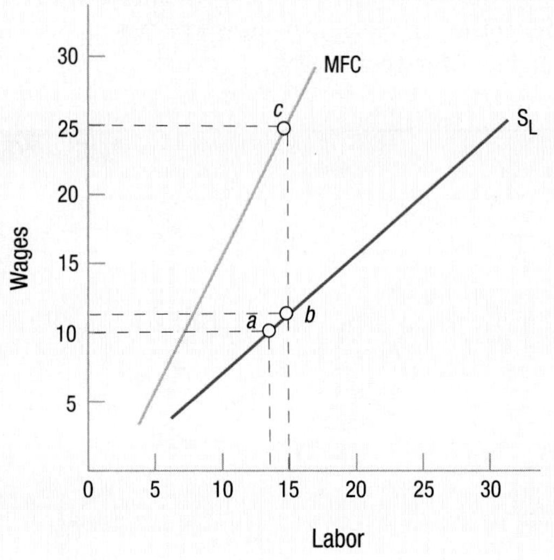

Marginal factor cost (MFC) The added cost associated with hiring one more unit of labor. For competitive firms, it is equal to the wage; but for monopsonists, it is higher than the new wage (W) because all existing workers must be paid this higher new wage, making MFC > W.

Marginal factor cost (MFC) is the added cost associated with hiring one more unit of labor. In Figure 6, assume that 14 workers earn $10 an hour (point *a*), and hiring the 15th worker requires paying $11 an hour (point *b*). Assume that you decide to go ahead and hire a 15th worker. When you employed 14 workers, total hourly wages were $140 ($10 × 14). But when 15 workers are employed at $11 an hour, all workers must be paid the higher hourly wage, and thus the total wage bill rises to $165 ($11 × 15). The total wage bill has risen by $25 an hour, not just the $11 hourly wage the 15th worker demanded. The marginal factor cost of hiring the 15th worker, in other words, is $25. This is shown as point *c*. Because the supply of labor curve is positively sloped, the MFC curve will always lie above the S_L curve.

How does being a monopsonist in the labor market affect the hiring of a firm that is competitive in the product market? The monopsonist shown in Figure 7 is a competitor in the product market and has a demand for labor equal to its VMP_L. This firm faces the supply of labor, S_L. It will hire at the level where MFC = VMP_L (point *a*), thus hiring L_0 workers at wage W_1 (point *b*). Note that these L_0 workers, though paid W_1, are actually worth W_0. Economists refer to this disparity as the **monopsonistic exploitation of labor**. Again, the term is loaded, but to economists it simply describes a situation in which labor is paid less than the value of its marginal product.

Monopsonistic exploitation of labor Because monopsonists hire less labor than competitive firms, and workers are paid less than the value of their marginal products, this difference is referred to as monopsonistic exploitation of labor.

Note that the wages paid in the monopsony situation (W_1) are less than those paid under competitive conditions (W_C), and that monopsony employment (L_0) is similarly lower than competitive hiring (L_C). As was the case with monopoly power, monopsony power leads to results that are less than ideal when compared to competitive markets.

To draw together what we have just discussed, Figure 8 portrays a firm with both monopoly and monopsony power. The firm's equilibrium hiring will be at the point where MFC = MRP_L (point *a*), and thus the firm will hire L_0 workers, though at wage W_0. Note that this is the lowest wage and employment level shown in the

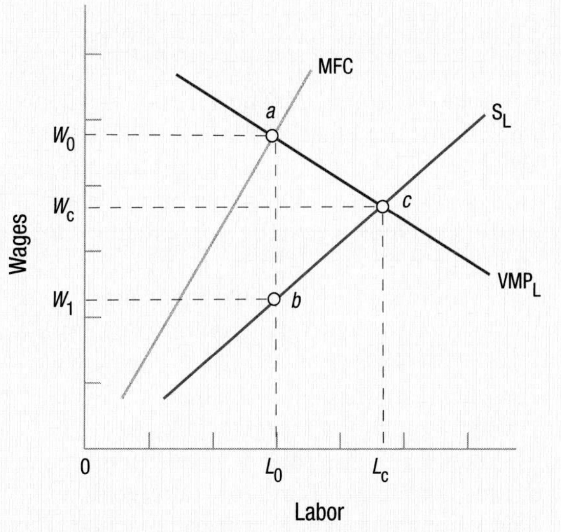

FIGURE 7

Competitive Firm in the Product Market That Is a Monopsonist in the Input Market

The monopsonist in this figure is a competitor in the product market and has a demand for labor equal to its VMP_L, while facing supply of labor, S_L. The firm will hire at the level where $MFC = VMP_L$ (point *a*), hiring L_0 workers at wage W_1 (point *b*). Note that these L_0 workers, though paid W_1, are worth W_0. This is called the monopsonistic exploitation of labor. Note also that the wages paid in this monopsony situation (W_1) are less than those paid under competitive conditions (W_C), and that monopsony employment (L_0) is lower than competitive employment (L_C).

graph. If the firm only had monopsony power, it would hire L_1 workers (point *b*) at a wage of W_1, which is higher than W_0. If the firm only had monopoly power, it would also hire L_1 workers for wage W_1 (point *c*). Both of these employment levels and wage rates are less than the competitive outcome of L_C and W_C (point *d*).

The key lesson to remember here is that competitive input (factor) markets are the most efficient, since inputs in these markets are paid precisely the value of their marginal products, and the highest employment results. This translates into the lowest prices for consumers at the highest output, assuming efficient production. Thus, just as competition is good for product markets, so too is it good for labor and other input markets.

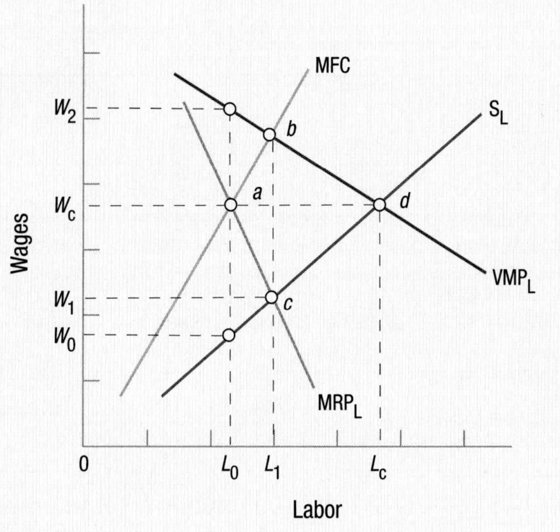

FIGURE 8

A Firm that is a Monopolist in the Product Market and a Monopsonist in the Input Market

This firm has both monopoly and monopsony power. The firm's equilibrium hiring will be at the point where $MFC = MRP_L$ (point *a*), and thus the firm will hire L_0 workers, though at wage W_0. Note that this is the lowest wage and employment level shown in the graph. If the firm only had monopsony power, it would hire L_1 workers (point *b*) at a wage of W_1. If the firm only had monopoly power, it would also hire L_1 workers for wage W_1 (point *c*). Both of these employment levels and wage rates are less than the competitive outcome of L_C and W_C (point *d*).

Capital Markets

Capital
All manufactured products that are used to produce goods and services.

Capital includes all manufactured products that are used to produce goods and services. *Capital markets* are those markets in which firms obtain financial resources to purchase capital goods. Financial resources come from the savings of households and other firms. Suppliers of funds and the demanders of these funds interact through what is called the *loanable funds market.* As with competitive labor markets, in which the market determines wages, each individual firm determines how many workers to employ, and the loanable funds market determines interest rates, leaving individual firms to calculate how much they should borrow.

Through their interactions in the loanable funds market, suppliers and demanders determine the interest rates to be charged for funds. Individual firms then evaluate their investment opportunities to determine their own investment levels. Figure 9 shows how this process works. The demand and supply of loanable funds is shown in Panel A, where equilibrium interest rates equal i_0. Note that the demand for loanable funds looks just like a normal demand curve. Its downward slope shows that, as the price of funds declines—as interest rates go down—the quantity of funds demanded rises. The supply of funds is positively sloped since individuals will be willing to supply more funds to the market when their price (interest rate) is higher.

FIGURE 9

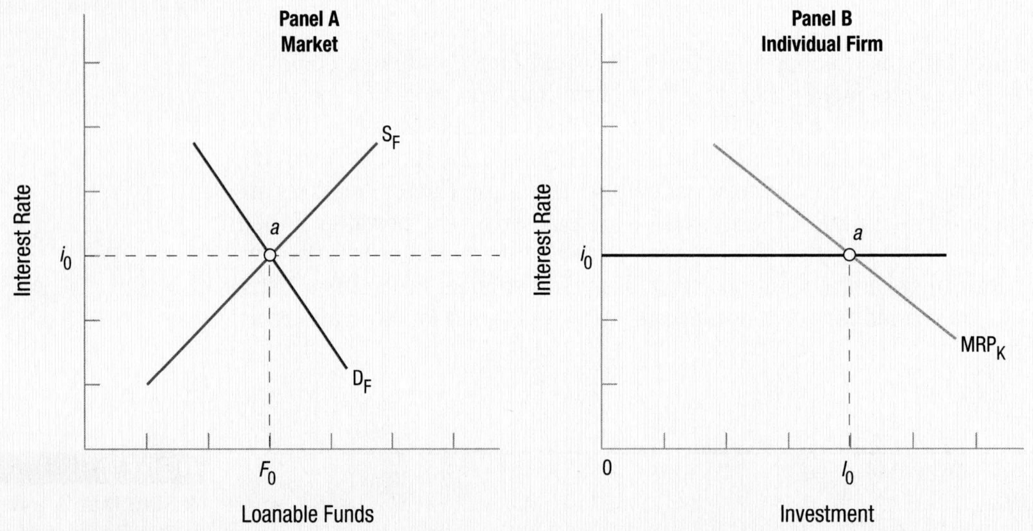

Loanable Funds Market and Individual Firm Investment

Panel A shows the market demand and supply of loanable funds, with equilibrium interest rates equal to i_0. The demand for loanable funds slopes downward; as the price of funds declines, the quantity of funds demanded rises as more investment projects look more favorable. The supply of funds is positively sloped since individuals will be willing to supply more funds to the market when interest rates are higher. Individual firms like the one shown in Panel B will take this rate of interest, or cost of capital, and determine how much to invest. The marginal revenue product of capital (MRP_K) is downward sloping, since the returns a firm earns on its investments diminish as more capital is invested. Firms will make their best investments first, and then continue investing (to I_0) until the cost of capital (i_0) is equal to the MRP_K.

Investment

Once the market has determined an equilibrium rate of interest, an individual firm like the one shown in Panel B will take this rate of interest, or cost of capital, and determine how much to invest. The marginal revenue product of capital (MRP_K) is downward sloping, showing that the returns a firm earns on its investments diminish as more capital is invested. Firms make their best investments first, and then continue investing until the cost of capital (i_0) is equal to the MRP_K. This admittedly simplifies the investment process, but it is a good general model of investment decisions. Next, we turn to two more precise ways in which investment is determined, the present value approach and the rate of return approach.

Present Value Approach

When a firm considers upgrading its information system or purchasing a new piece of equipment, a building, or a manufacturing plant, it must evaluate the returns it can expect over time. Firms invest money today, but earn returns over years. To compare investments having different income streams and different levels of required investment, firms look at the *net* **present value** of the investment.

Present value
The value of an investment (future stream of income) today. The higher the discount rate, the lower the present value today, and vice versa.

One hundred dollars a year from now is worth less than one hundred dollars today. This is illustrated by the fact that you could put less than a hundred dollars in the bank today, earn interest on this money over the next year, and still end up with one hundred dollars at year's end. Yet, just how much less than one hundred dollars would you be willing to take for one hundred dollars a year from today? To answer this question, let us begin by looking at the simplest form of financial assets, annuities.

An annuity is a financial instrument that pays the bearer a certain dollar amount forever. Assume that the market rate of interest is 5%, and you are offered an annuity that pays you or the holder of the annuity $1,000 a year indefinitely. How much would you be willing to pay for this annuity? If you want to follow the market in earning 5% a year, then the simple question you must ask is this: On what amount of money does $1,000 a year forever represent a 5% return? The answer is found through the simple formula:

$$\text{PV} = X/i$$

where PV is the present value of the investment (what you are willing to pay for the annuity today), X is the annual income ($1,000 in this case), and i is the market interest rate. In this case, you would be willing to pay $20,000 for this annuity, since $20,000 = $1,000/.05. We have thus reduced an infinite stream of income to the finite amount you would pay today. You would pay $20,000, and the annuity would give you $1,000 a year, for an annual return on your investment of 5%.

What happens to the value of this annuity if the market interest rate should rise to 10%? You will still receive $1,000 a year, but if you want to sell the annuity to someone else, the buyer will only be willing to pay $10,000 for it ($10,000 = $1,000/.10). Interest rates having doubled, the value of your annuity has been halved. Higher interest rates mean that income in future years is not worth as much today.

Valuing future income today by this process is known as *discounting.* This principle applies not only to annuities, but computing for years less than perpetuity requires a more complex formula. For example, assume that someone agrees to pay you $500 in 2 years, and that the going interest rate is 5%. What would you be willing to pay today for this future payment of $500? The answer is found using the following formula:

$$\text{PV} = X/(1 + i)^n$$

Again, PV is the present value of the future payment, X is the future payment of $500, i is the interest rate (5%), and n is the number of years into the future before the payment is made. In this case the calculations are

$$\begin{aligned} \text{PV} &= \$500/(1 + .05)^2 \\ &= \$500/[(1.05)(1.05)] \\ &= \$500/1.1025 \\ &= \$453.51 \end{aligned}$$

Hence, you would be willing to pay only \$453.51 for this \$500 payment coming 2 years into the future. Again, the higher the interest or discount rate, the lower will be your price.

When only one future payment is at stake, computing the present value of that payment is fairly simple. When future streams of income are involved, however, things get more complicated. We must compute the present value of each individual future payment. The general formula looks nearly the same as before:

$$PV = \Sigma X_n/(1 + i)^n$$

Here, the Greek letter Σ (sigma) stands for "sum of," and X_n is the individual payment received at year n. Assume, then, that you are going to receive \$500, \$800, and \$1,200 over the next 3 years, and that the interest rate is still 5%. The present value of this income stream is therefore

$$\begin{aligned} PV &= \$500/(1.05) + \$800/(1.1025) + \$1200/(1.1576) \\ &= \$476.19 + \$725.62 + \$1{,}036.63 \\ &= \$2{,}238.44 \end{aligned}$$

Given the complexity of such computations, economists often use computers to solve for present value, especially when the annual income stream is complicated. When the annual income is constant, tables of discount factors are also available. In any case, the point to note is that payments to be made in the future are worth a lower dollar amount today.

Firms often use present value analysis to determine if potential investments are worthwhile. Assume a machine will yield a stream of income exceeding operating costs over a given period. The present value of this income is then compared to the cost of the machine. The machine's *net present value* (NPV) is equal to the difference between the present value of the income stream and the cost of the machine. If NPV is positive, the firm will invest; if it is negative, the firm will decline to invest.

When interest rates are high, firms will find fewer investment opportunities where NPV is positive since the higher discount rate reduces the value of the income streams for investments. As interest rates fall, more investment is undertaken by firms. This is why the Federal Reserve Board's actions on interest rates are always headline news.

Rate of Return Approach

An alternative approach to determining whether an investment is worthwhile involves computing the investment's rate of return. This rate of return is also known as a firm's *marginal efficiency of capital,* or its *internal* **rate of return**.

Rate of return
Uses the present value formula, but subtracts costs, then finds the interest rate (discount rate) at which this investment would break even.

Computing an investment's rate of return requires using essentially the same present value formula for income streams introduced above with a slight modification: You have to explicitly consider the cost of capital in the calculation. This new formula is

$$PV = [\Sigma X_n/(1 + i)^n] - C$$

where C represents the cost of capital. The question we must ask is: At what rate of interest (i) will the investment just break even? You would compute the present value of the income streams, then subtract the cost of the capital investment, and finally find the rate of interest (i) where the present value equals zero. This discount rate is the rate of return on the investment.

The calculated rate of return can be compared to the firm's required rate of return on investments to determine whether the investment is worthwhile. The firm might require, say, a 20% yield on all projects, in which case investments yielding returns of less than 20% will be deemed not worthwhile. Risk in investment projects is usually managed by adding a risk premium to the required rate of return for risky projects. This risk premium can vary by project type or with the business cycle. Some investments, such as drilling for oil or researching innovative new drugs, are risky and require high rates of return if they are to be undertaken.

Land

For economists, the term *land* includes both land in the usual sense and other natural resources that are inelastically supplied. **Rent**, sometimes called *economic rent*, is any return or income that flows to land as a factor of production. This is a different meaning than when we speak of the rent on an apartment. Land is unique among the factors of production because of its inelasticity of supply.

Rent
The return to land as a factor of production. Sometimes called economic rent.

In some instances, the supply of land is perfectly inelastic. Finding an empty lot on which to build in San Francisco is virtually impossible. The land available to San Franciscans is fixed by the terrain; it cannot be added to nor moved from one place to another.

Figure 10 shows how rent is determined when the available supply of land is fixed. In this example, the number of acres of usable land is fixed at L_0 (or supply S_0). If the demand for land is D_0, the economic rent will be r_0 (point *a*). When demand rises to D_1, rent increases to r_1 (point *b*). Notice that because the supply of land in this example is perfectly inelastic, rent depends entirely on demand. If demand were to fall, rent would fall as well.

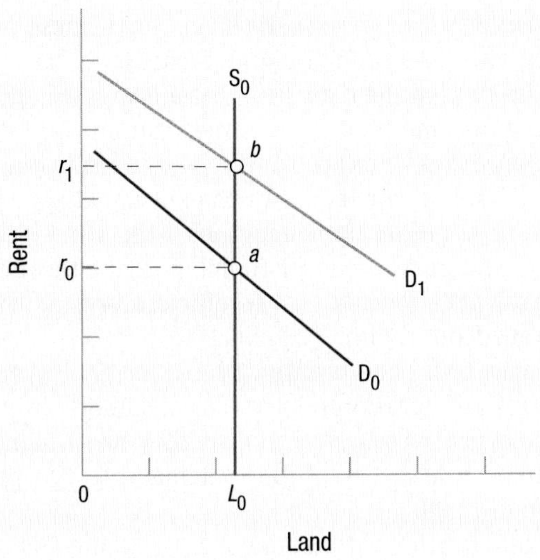

FIGURE 10

Determination of Rent

This figure shows how rent is determined when the available supply of land is fixed. The acres of usable land are fixed at L_0 (supply S_0). If the demand for land is D_0, the economic rent will be r_0 (point *a*). When demand rises to D_1, rent increases to r_1 (point *b*). Notice that because the supply of land in this example is perfectly inelastic, rent depends entirely on demand. If demand were to fall, rent would fall as well.

In a strict sense, land is not perfectly fixed in supply. Land can be improved. Land that is arid, like the deserts of Arizona, can be improved through irrigation. Jungles can be cleared, swamps can be drained, and mountains can be terraced, making land that was once worthless productive. Still, even if the supply of land is not perfectly inelastic, it is quite inelastic when compared to other production inputs.

The supply inflexibility in land led Henry George (1839–1897) to propose a single tax on land to finance government needs. In his 1879 book *Progress and Poverty,* George argued that increases in rents and land values were the result of speculation, population growth, and public improvements in the community's infrastructure (raising demand to D_1 in Figure 10). Since landholders apparently do nothing to earn these rental increases, George thought they could and should be taxed away. His approach became known as the single-tax movement, since he thought all government spending could be financed from the revenue of this tax.

It should be added that George proposed to tax only the pure ground rent of land, not the improvements made on land. Thus, his tax is also sometimes called a "site tax." Although such a tax would probably not cover all government spending today, some economists are sympathetic to the concept. Nobel Prize winner Milton Friedman has noted, "In my opinion, the least bad tax is the property tax on the unimproved value of land, the Henry George argument of many, many years ago."[2]

As a final note, land will theoretically continue to earn rent forever. To quickly approximate the value of a piece of land, we can use our annuity formula ($PV = X/i$). Given a 5% rate of interest, a parcel of land earning \$10,000 a year in rent will be worth \$200,000 (\$200,000 = \$10,000/.05). To apply to the real world, this simple approximation would require a few qualifications. Even so, it gives us a first approximation of how land is valued.

Entrepreneurship

Profits are the rewards entrepreneurs receive for (1) combining land, labor, and capital to produce goods and services and (2) assuming the risks associated with producing these goods and services. Entrepreneurs must combine and manage all the inputs of production; make day-to-day production, finance, and marketing decisions; innovate constantly if they hope to remain in business over the long run; and simultaneously bear the risks of failure and bankruptcy.

As we saw at the turn of the century—just a few years ago in 2000, not 1900—large firms that have become household names can implode within months. Enron and Arthur Anderson come to mind. Even for large firms, business is risky. Bankruptcy or business failure, meanwhile, can be exceedingly painful for business owners, stockholders, employees, and communities. Still, a free economy requires such failures. If firms were guaranteed never to fail, perhaps through government subsidies, they would have little incentive to be efficient or innovate, or to worry about what consumers want from them.

When a firm earns economic profits—profits exceeding normal profits—this is a signal to other firms and entrepreneurs that consumers want more of the good or service the profitable firm provides, and that they are willing to pay for it. Profit signals shift resources from areas of lower demand to the products and services consumers desire more highly.

By far, the largest part of national income—roughly 70%—goes to labor, with the smallest going to rental income with the remainder split between interest and profits. Labor is thus by far the most important factor of production, and labor issues are often paramount for policymakers. The next chapter will look into some specific labor issues, including investment in human capital, economic discrimination, and labor unions.

---

[2]Mark Blaug, *Great Economists Before Keynes: An Introduction to the Lives & Works of One Hundred Great Economists of the Past* (Atlantic Highlands, N.J.: Humanities Press International), 1986, p. 86.

Checkpoint

Imperfect Labor Markets and Other Input Markets

REVIEW

- When a firm is a monopolist in the product market and hires labor from competitive markets, the firm will hire labor where the marginal product of labor is equal to the competitive wage.
- Monopolistic exploitation results because the monopolist pays less than the value of the marginal product of labor.
- Monopsony is a market with one employer. A monopsonist who sells its product in a competitive market hires labor where the value of the marginal product is equal to the marginal factor cost.
- Monopsonistic exploitation occurs when the monopsonist pays labor less than the value of its marginal product.
- Capital markets are markets in which firms get financial resources to purchase capital goods.
- Firms will use either the net present value approach or the rate of return approach to compare investments with different income streams.
- Land includes both land and natural resources and is inelastically supplied. Returns on land are called rents (or economic rent).
- Because land is inelastically supplied, the rent on land is determined by demand.
- Entrepreneurs earn profits for combining other inputs to produce products and for assuming the risks of producing goods and services.

QUESTIONS

Are public schools in rural areas a monopsony? Do they set wages in a way that is different from how wages are set in large urban areas?

Answers to the Checkpoint questions can be found at the end of this chapter.

Estimating the Marginal Value of Professional Baseball Players

Stephanie Carter/Getty Images

Before going on to the next chapter, let us take one last look at the assumption we made earlier about labor being a homogeneous commodity—no one is special. This sounds horrendous. Let us see if it applies to baseball.

Ask people how to field a winning team in baseball, and you will probably get a common reply: Spend money on top free-agent players. In other words, some workers produce much more than others. The recent book *Moneyball* challenges this view.[3] It is based on the experience of the Oakland Athletics, a low-budget ball club that keeps winning its division.

Here is how the analysis goes.[4] In 2003, the least a baseball team could spend on a 25-player team was $5 million (because of fixed minimum salary rates), plus an additional $2 million to cover injured players and other roster slots. Because luck is such a factor in any particular baseball game, and because minimum-wage players do not differ that much in ability from most players (note the "most"—we leave out Albert Pujols and a few others), the fewest wins a minimum-wage team would

[3] Michael Lewis, *Moneyball: The Art of Winning an Unfair Game* (New York: WW Norton), 2003.
[4] Lewis, *Moneyball,* p. xiii (Preface).

likely have in a season is around 49. Okay, the 2003 Detroit Tigers only won 43 games—close. The book was written before the end of the 2003 season. Let us stick with 49 wins as the floor, for the sake of argument. In the book's own words:

> *How many dollars over the minimum $7 million does each team pay for each win over its forty-ninth? How many marginal dollars does a team spend for each marginal win?*[5]

The Oakland A's won 91 games in 2000 with a payroll of $26 million, and 102 games in 2001 with a payroll of $34 million. In 2000–2002, the Oakland A's paid about $500,000 per win. The Baltimore Orioles and Texas Rangers, big losers in the past few years, spent almost $3 million for each win. So marginal analysis tells us that compared to Oakland, Baltimore and Texas are vastly overpaying for each win.

This marginal analysis does not tell a baseball club to stock its roster with minimum-wage players because labor is a homogeneous commodity. However, it does suggest that the current way of evaluating players is faulty: The skills the rich teams are paying a premium for may not be the ones that usually make a difference in a ballgame. The book does reveal these undervalued skills. So, we are better off starting with the assumption that all players are equal, and working from there to analyze the skills that are needed, than accepting the current view that certain players should be compensated so much more than others. The labor commodity assumption is not so far off after all.

Key Concepts

Supply of labor, p. 283
Substitution effect, p. 284
Income effect, p. 284
Demand for labor, p. 287
Marginal physical product of labor, p. 287
Marginal revenue product, p. 288
Value of the marginal product, p. 288
Elasticity of demand for labor, p. 289
Monopsony, p. 292
Monopolistic exploitation of labor, p. 293
Marginal factor cost (MFC), p. 294
Monopsonistic exploitation of labor, p. 294
Capital, p. 296
Present value, p. 297
Rate of return, p. 298
Rent, p. 299

Chapter Summary

Competitive Labor Supply

Competitive labor markets comprise firms that are price takers; these firms compete with other firms in the wider market for labor. Labor is assumed to be a homogeneous input; one unit of labor is just as productive as all others. Information about prices and wages is assumed to be widely available, and supply and demand interact to determine the equilibrium wage for the industry. Each firm then decides how much labor to purchase at the going wage rate.

The supply of labor is the time an individual is willing to work (the labor the person is willing to supply) at various wage rates. The supply of labor is positively sloped, since at higher wages, workers will substitute work for leisure. When wages rise high enough, however, the income effect may swamp the substitution effect. Workers may elect more leisure over greater income, resulting in a backward-bending supply of labor curve.

---

[5]Lewis, *Moneyball,* p. xiii (Preface).

Changes in wage rates will change the quantity of labor supplied, or cause movements along the market supply of labor curve. Demographic changes and changes in the nonmoney aspects of a job, the wages for alternative jobs, and nonwage income will all shift the supply of labor curve. Such a shift might be precipitated, for instance, by a change in the labor force participation rates, a reduction in the riskiness of a job, or a change in nonwage incomes of workers.

Competitive Labor Demand

The demand for labor is a derived demand; it is derived from the productive capabilities of labor and the demand for the good or service produced. The demand for labor is equivalent to the marginal revenue product (MRP_L) curve. Marginal revenue product is equal to marginal physical product of labor times the product's marginal revenue.

Because competitive firms are price takers, marginal revenue is equal to price. So the competitive firm's demand for labor is equal to what economists call the value of the marginal product (VMP_L). The value of the marginal product is equal to marginal physical product times price.

Since the demand for labor is a derived demand, changes in labor demand will come about because of changes in labor productivity or changes in product demand. Anything that changes the price of a firm's product will change its labor demand. If new equipment is added and worker productivity increases, labor demand will rise. An increase in the cost of capital increases the demand for labor because labor-intensive production methods become more attractive to firms.

The elasticity of demand for labor is the percentage change in the quantity of labor demanded divided by the percentage change in the wage rate. An inelastic demand for labor is one where the absolute value of the elasticity is less than 1. An elastic demand, conversely, is greater than 1. Elasticity of demand for labor is determined by the elasticity of demand for the product, the ease of input substitutability, and the size of labor's share in production costs.

Competitive labor markets determine an equilibrium wage, then individual firms must look at their own needs and hire employees up to the point where equilibrium wage is equal to marginal revenue product (or, equivalently for competitive markets, equal to the value of the marginal product of labor).

Imperfect Labor Markets and Other Input Markets

If wages are determined in a competitive market, a firm will hire labor until $MRP_L = W$. But if the firm enjoys some monopoly power in the product market, marginal revenue product will be less than the value of the marginal product because $MR < P$. The difference between the value of the marginal product and marginal revenue product is known as monopolistic exploitation of labor.

A monopsony is a market with a single buyer or employer. Marginal factor cost (MFC) is the added cost associated with hiring one more unit of labor. For the monopsonist, the MFC curve lies above the supply of labor curve because the firm must increase the wages of all workers to attract added labor. If the monopsonist purchases labor from a competitive market, it hires labor up to the point where $MRP = MFC > W$. At this point, the value of labor's marginal product exceeds the wage rate; economists refer to this as monopsonistic exploitation of labor.

Capital includes all manufactured goods that are used to produce other goods and services. Capital markets are those markets where financial resources are available for the purchase of capital goods. The loanable funds market determines equilibrium interest rates for these funds. Firms look at their potential investment projects and borrow money to invest when the rate of return on a project is greater than or equal to the market interest rate.

Two approaches are used to determine whether investments are potentially profitable. The present value approach discounts projected future streams of income to determine their present value. This is then compared to the cost of the investment to determine whether the investment will be profitable. The rate of return approach uses the same present value formula, but looks for the rate of return, or discount rate, where the potential income stream and investment costs will be just equal.

Land, to the economist, means land and other natural resources that are nearly fixed in supply, or inelastically supplied. Because the supply of land is fixed, the rent on land is determined by demand.

Profits are rewards to entrepreneurs for combining the other inputs of production—land, labor, and capital—in ways that produce goods and services and for assuming the risks associated with production. Economic profits are profits that exceed normal levels. They act as signals to other entrepreneurs and firms that consumers want more of the profitable product. These signals produce shifts in resources toward those goods that consumers want.

Questions and Problems

1. *The Economist* magazine recently reported "a woman with middling skills who has a baby at age 24 loses $981,000 in lifetime earning compared with one who remains childless."[6] If the woman waits a few years before having a baby, the figure is lower, but still large. What are the reasons that having children reduces women's earnings so much?

2. As the baby boomer generation—those born between 1946 and 1964—begins retiring in earnest in the near future, wealthy economies like the United States and Europe will need to replace these skilled workers. These workers are an immense storehouse of knowledge and specialized skills that are not easily replaced. This is particularly acute in the engineering fields where college enrollments are falling.[7] Would it make sense for America to "no longer welcome the tired and the huddled; [but] to compete ever more fiercely for the bright and the qualified"[8]? What could companies do to encourage these older workers to remain on the job?

3. Adam Smith, in the *Wealth of Nations,* noted that, "The wages of labour vary with the ease or hardship, the cleanliness or dirtiness, the honourableness or dishonourableness of the employment." He is referring to the nonwage or "amenities" aspect of employment. By making the "job" more enjoyable, cleaner, or more honorable, or adding more amenities, employers should be able to pay lower wages since the positive attributes compensate for higher wages. If so, why don't all employers offer amenities to lower their wage bill?

4. Fifty years ago married women ages 35–44 worked for pay only 10 hours per week; today they work over 26 hours on average. During the same time period, the workweek for married men of the same age has been relatively constant, between 42 and 44 hours. Can you think of reasons why women's working hours has nearly tripled in the last half century?

---

[6]"Women's Pay: The Hand That Rocks the Cradle," *The Economist,* March 4, 2006, p. 51.
[7]See "Turning Boomers Into Boomerangs," *The Economist,* February 18, 2006, pp. 65–67.
[8]From "Economic Focus: Fruit That Falls Far From the Tree," *The Economist,* November 5, 2005, p. 86.

5. Since 1970 the number of dual-earning households as a percent of total U.S. households has grown from 39% to nearly 65% today. Do you think there is a relationship between this growth in dual-earning households and the rapid growth in restaurants?

6. Tightened visa rules since 9/11 have reduced the number of high-skill legal immigrants. Stiffer security rules and insufficient personnel have substantially increased the waiting time (and certainty) of visas. Nobel Prize winner Gary Becker argued, "We benefit enormously from high-skilled immigration . . . we have to try to maintain that." He further suggests that the United States should "give the highest priority to people with high skills and allow large numbers to come in, maybe unlimited numbers."[9] Do you agree with Becker? If so, what might be some of the obstacles to implementing such a policy? If not, why not?

7. How do times of growth in the general economy encourage capital investments? How do recessions discourage capital investments? What happens to the cost of capital in boom times when the economy is growing? What happens in recessionary times?

8. How do the income and substitution effects related to labor supply differ?

9. Why does a monopolist in the product market hire fewer workers than if the industry is competitive?

10. Why do college professors who usually spend 5–7 years in graduate school and play such an important role in shaping our society make so much less than a Hollywood producer such as Jerry Bruckheimer, whom most people don't even know (he has produced over 40 films and a dozen TV shows)?

11. Since all college professors mostly teach classes and do research, why are they not all paid the same wage?

12. "Where labour is scarce and expensive, businesses have an incentive to invest in labour-saving technology, which boosts productivity growth by enabling fewer workers to produce more."[10] Do you agree with this statement? Why or why not? Would bringing in a large number of unskilled workers improve productivity and living standards?

13. We often hear that America needs cheap unskilled foreign workers to do the jobs that Americans will not do. But Professor Barry Chiswick suggested, "If the number of low-skilled foreign workers were to fall, wages would increase. Low-skilled American workers and their families would benefit, and society as a whole would gain from a reduction in income inequality."[11] Is Professor Chiswick's argument consistent with the competitive labor market described in this chapter? Why or why not?

14. If the interest rate is 6% and you are offered a bond that will pay you $2,000 in 2 years, but no interest between now and then, what would you be willing to pay for this bond today?

---

[9]Spencer E. Ante, "Keeping Out the Wrong People," *Business Week,* October 2004, pp. 90–94.
[10]Michael Lind, "A Labour Shortage Can Be a Blessing, Not a Curse" *Financial Times,* June 9, 2006, pp. 13.
[11]Barry R. Chiswick, "The Worker Next Door," *New York Times,* June 3, 2006, p. A23.

15. What factors will increase the demand for labor?

16. The figure below shows the supply of labor, marginal factor costs, and the demand for labor for a firm that is large enough that it is essentially a monopsonist in the community where it operates. Assume that all workers are paid the same wage and that they work 2,000 hours per year (40 hours a week for 50 weeks).

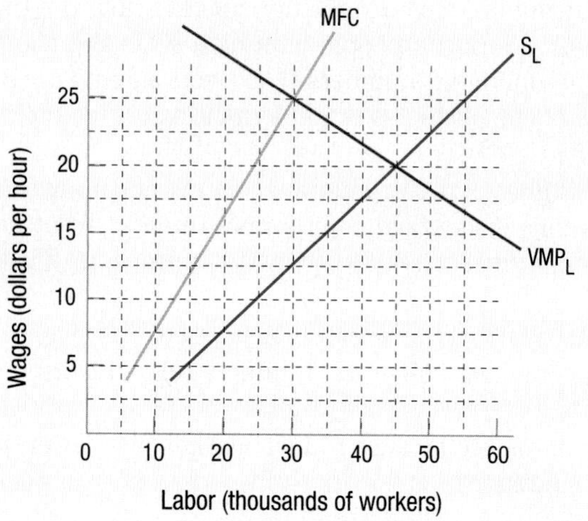

a. What is the total wage bill (total wages paid by the firm) for this monopsonistic firm?
b. If the firm was actually hiring from a competitive labor market, what would be the total wage bill for the firm?
c. What is the total value of the monopsonistic exploitation of labor by this firm?
d. Is the firm a competitor or a monopolist in the product market?

17. Why are individual supply curves of labor potentially backward bending, but market and industry supply curves are always positively sloped?

Answers to Checkpoint Questions

CHECKPOINT: COMPETITIVE LABOR SUPPLY

Each person will have a different wage where their supply of labor curve bends backward. Getting a large inheritance will generate substantial nonwage income and typically leads to fewer hours worked. Having a family will probably raise the income required before you will cut your hours.

CHECKPOINT: COMPETITIVE LABOR DEMAND

For many jobs, firms have standardized procedures that each employee follows. Therefore, the difference in productivity between individuals is relatively narrow. While homogeneous labor is a simplification, taking in everyone's difference would make analysis impractical. The model explains both since markets exist for each broad category of workers.

CHECKPOINT: IMPERFECT LABOR MARKETS AND OTHER INPUT MARKETS

Yes, they are monopsonists when it comes to hiring teachers. Generally, there is only one school district in rural areas. They probably act more like monopsonists when setting wages when compared to their urban counterparts, which have competition for teachers from other districts and private schools.

12

Labor Market Issues

Why are some people paid more than others? Is there a relationship between your earnings and your education? Why does the government pay a substantial part of your college education? Why are there different wages for different occupations? What role will unions play in the 21st century economy?

To get a better sense of what this chapter covers, let us pause for a moment on the last question: What role will unions play in the 21st century? Many of us already have some familiarity with unions, which are legal associations of employees that bargain with employers over terms and conditions of work. Unions use strikes and the threat of strikes to achieve their goals. You may have heard of craft unions such as the Teamsters, which represents truck drivers, or industry unions, such as the UAW (United Auto Workers), which represents auto workers.

One of the fastest growing labor groups is made up of part-time and independent contract workers. They freelance in graphic design, in Web design services and programming, as nannies, and in many other areas. Pay and terms of work are typically set by individual negotiation. This group clearly could use a union, since they are rarely provided benefits beyond the agreed-upon compensation.

But how could a union serve such a diverse group of people in terms of skills, compensation, locations, industries, and working conditions? Sara Horowitz asked herself that question and decided that a union could provide self-employed workers with similar services that full-time employees take for granted. She formed the Freelancers Union in New York and provides her members with health insurance, 401(k)-type retirement plans, redress for employer or client nonpayment, and other benefits.[1] This union does not strike like traditional unions, but the union has grown to 13,000 members and is an advocacy organization for freelance workers.

Labor markets in the 21st century are changing dramatically. Adjustments are being made: flexible hours, job sharing, working at home instead of in a centralized office, and more part-timers and freelancers in the market. In this chapter, we will address these labor market issues, and more.

---

[1]"Face Value: Freelancers of the World Unite," *The Economist*, November 11, 2006, p. 76; and see the Freelancers Union Web site at www.freelancersunion.org.

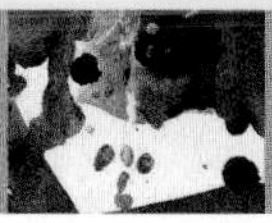

After studying this chapter you should be able to

- Describe the relationship between education and earnings.
- Understand how the rate of return on a college degree is computed.
- Know how market equilibrium levels for human capital are determined.
- Understand the different theories of human capital.
- Describe the difference between general and specific training.
- Describe Becker's theory of economic discrimination.
- Describe the concept of segmented labor markets and how they affect wage levels.
- Describe federal laws and policies regarding discrimination.
- Describe the history, costs, and benefits of trade unions.
- Discuss the evolution of labor markets.

Investment in Human Capital

Let us first consider the role education and on-the-job-training (OJT) play in determining wage levels in labor markets. Workers, students, and firms all invest in themselves or their employees to increase productivity. This is called **investment in human capital**. Workers invest by accepting lower wages while they undertake apprenticeships. Students invest by paying for tuition and books, and by forgoing job opportunities, to learn new skills. Firms invest in their workers through OJT and in-house training programs that involve workers being paid to attend classes. These investments entail costs in the current period that are borne in the interest of raising future productivity. They can be analyzed using the investment analysis we developed in the last chapter.[2]

Investment in human capital Investments such as education and on-the-job training that improve the productivity of human labor.

Education and Earnings

One of the surest ways to advance in the job world and increase your income is by investing in education. The old saying, "To get ahead, get an education," still holds true. Table 1 shows the age/earnings profiles for all Americans between 25 and 64 for 2002. It provides strong evidence that education and earnings are related.

Average earnings for those without a high school education peaked at $24,761 a year, while those completing high school peaked at $31,251, a 26% increase. Getting a college degree bumped peak earnings up to $60,680, nearly a 150% rise. Going on to get a professional degree moved the peak all the way up to $132,372, a whopping 215% increase over a bachelor's degree alone. These figures represent average earnings. It is easy to see that earnings in all age groups were much higher for those with higher levels of education.

Table 1 suggests that education is a good investment. But like any investment, future earnings must be balanced against the cost of obtaining that education. The

[2]Gary S. Becker, *Human Capital,* 2nd ed. (New York: National Bureau of Economic Research), 1975. Becker won the Nobel Prize in 1992 for this and other work in economics.

Table 1 Average Earnings by Highest Degree Earned

Age Grouping	No HS	HS Degree	Some College	College	Professional
25–34	$19,235	$26,278	$28,879	$42,623	$75,247
35–44	22,324	30,253	37,533	58,267	123,811
45–54	21,231	31,251	40,225	60,680	126,230
55–64	24,761	30,893	37,450	55,057	132,372

Source: U.S. Census Bureau, *Statistical Abstract of the United States, 2004–05* (Washington, DC: U.S. Government Printing Office), 2006, Table 215.

costs of education must be borne today, but the earnings benefits do not arrive until later. Evaluating educational decisions therefore requires that we use some of the tools developed in the last chapter when we studied investment in the capital markets.

Education as Investment

To keep our analysis simple, we will focus on the decision to attend college for 4 years. The basic approach outlined in this section will nonetheless apply to other investments in education or training.

Figure 1 presents a stylized graph showing the benefits and costs of a college education. For simplicity, we will assume students go to college at age 18. If an individual chooses not to go to college, the high school earnings path applies: On leaving high school, the person enters the labor market immediately, and earnings begin rising along the path labeled "High School." Note that the increases are positive throughout the individual's working life.

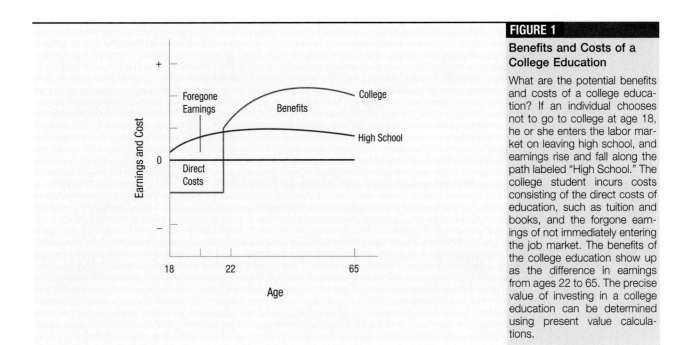

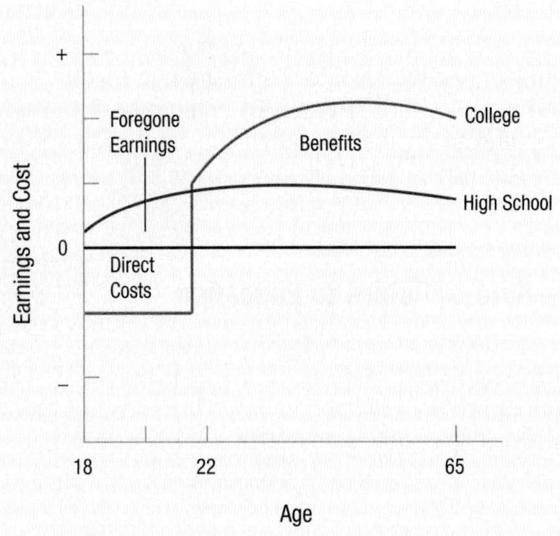

FIGURE 1

Benefits and Costs of a College Education

What are the potential benefits and costs of a college education? If an individual chooses not to go to college at age 18, he or she enters the labor market on leaving high school, and earnings rise and fall along the path labeled "High School." The college student incurs costs consisting of the direct costs of education, such as tuition and books, and the forgone earnings of not immediately entering the job market. The benefits of the college education show up as the difference in earnings from ages 22 to 65. The precise value of investing in a college education can be determined using present value calculations.

A college student immediately incurs costs in two forms. First, tuition, books, and other fees must be paid. These *direct costs* exclude living expenses, such as food and rent, since these must be paid whether you work or go to college. Tuition will vary substantially depending on whether you attend a private or public university.

Second, students give up earnings as they devote full time to their studies (and to the occasional party). These costs can be substantial when compared to the direct costs of an education at a state-supported institution, since the average earnings for high school graduates range between \$15,000 and \$20,000 a year.

The benefits from a college degree show up as the difference in earnings from ages 22 to 65. If the return on a college degree is to be positive, this area must offset the direct costs of college and the forgone earnings. We must also keep in mind that a large part of the income high school and college graduates earn will not come until well into the future. For college graduates, this is especially important, since they will not see income for at least 4 years. How can we tell if this sacrifice is worth it? Using the tools of present value analysis and discounting, we can compare the present value of the future income of high school and college graduates.

If an 18-year-old does not go to college, the present value of that individual's income stream, as shown in Figure 1, is

$$\text{PV} = \Sigma \frac{Y_t}{(1 + i)^{t-18}}$$

where Y_t is the annual income earned each year by the high school graduate from ages 18 to 65, t is the years from age 18 to 65, and i is the interest or discount rate. Discount years $t - 18$ are used so that the first year of discounting, year 19, represents only a 1-year discount. (Earnings begin when the individual is 18 years old, but this is the first year of earnings to be discounted.) This simple formula is essentially the same as the one we used when discounting streams of income for capital investment decisions in the last chapter.

The corresponding present value equation for the student going to college is as follows:

$$\text{PV} = \Sigma \frac{Y_t - C_t}{(1 + i)^{t-18}}$$

Notice that the only difference is that the college student has the costs of education to bear during the first 4 years. Thus, the numerator, or the top half of this equation, is negative for the first 4 years. By comparing the present values of these two streams of income and costs, an individual can decide if a college education is worth the effort. The option with the largest present value would be the one to pursue.

Computing the Rate of Return to Education

An alternate way to decide which of the two career paths is best is by computing the rate of return on a college degree. This yields essentially the same results as the present value approach just presented. To determine the rate of return on college, we compare the two streams of income for the high school and college graduates.

$$\Sigma \frac{Y_t}{(1 + i)^{t-18}} = \Sigma \frac{Y_t - C_t}{(1 + i)^{t-18}}$$

The left-hand side of this equation represents the stream of income to the high school graduate, and the right-hand side is that for the college graduate. To find the rate of return to college, we must solve the equation for *i*. We need not perform that calculation here, but it is not very difficult on a computer.

If $i = .10$ (a 10% return on college), the annual return on a college education over the course of one's working life is 10% a year. Thus, the earnings of the college graduate in middle age will exceed those of the high school graduate by enough to generate a 10% return. A lower return would mean that the difference in earnings is smaller, while a higher return suggests the difference in earnings is greater. Most empirical estimates place the return on a college education between 12% and 20%.[3] That is, college graduates earn on average 12% to 20% more per year over the course of their working lifetime than high school graduates, taking into consideration all of the costs of going to college.

Equilibrium Levels of Human Capital

Each of us must decide how much to invest in ourselves. This decision, like so many in economics, ultimately depends on supply and demand, in this case, the supply of, and demand for, funds to be used for human capital investment. A hypothetical market for human capital is shown in Figure 2. In this scenario, "price" is the percentage rate of return on human capital investments and the interest cost of borrowing funds.

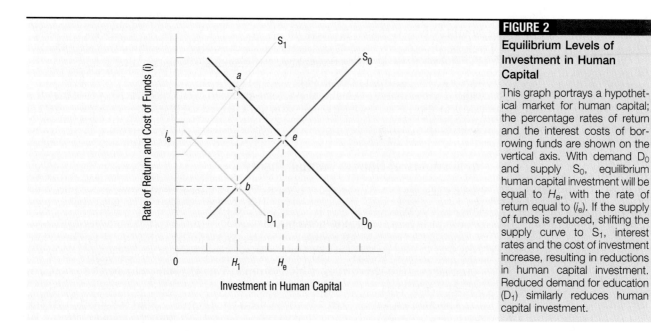

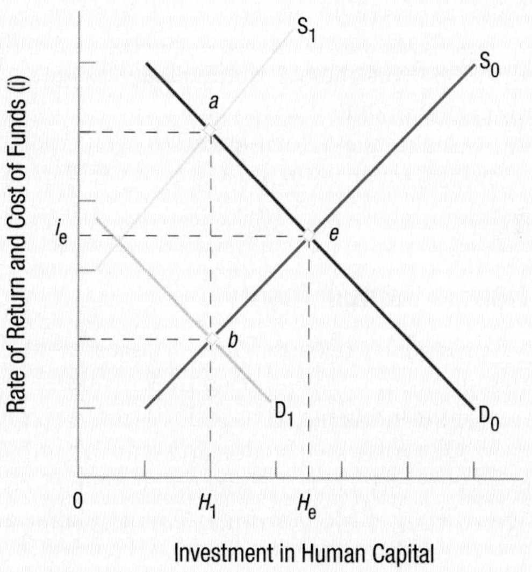

FIGURE 2

Equilibrium Levels of Investment in Human Capital

This graph portrays a hypothetical market for human capital; the percentage rates of return and the interest costs of borrowing funds are shown on the vertical axis. With demand D_0 and supply S_0, equilibrium human capital investment will be equal to H_e, with the rate of return equal to (i_e). If the supply of funds is reduced, shifting the supply curve to S_1, interest rates and the cost of investment increase, resulting in reductions in human capital investment. Reduced demand for education (D_1) similarly reduces human capital investment.

The demand for human capital investment slopes down and to the right, reflecting the diminishing returns of more education and that more time in school leaves you less time to earn back its costs. Students pursuing a Ph.D. or a medical degree are often well into their 30s before they can begin paying back their student loans.

[3]G. Psacharapoulos, "Returns to Investment in Education: A Global Update," *World Development*, September 1994, pp. 1325–1343. These estimates might be too large due possibly to self-selection by those with higher ability. If those with higher abilities are the ones to go to college, then these returns would not reflect the returns we would expect for the population as a whole. However, these returns may be too low if we were to consider the nonincome aspects of a college education. College graduates expect and get better working conditions and more prestigious opportunities, while society gets a better educated citizen, lower crime, and so on.

As a result, they require higher salaries to bring their rates of return up above those of college-educated workers.

The supply of investable funds, meanwhile, is positively sloped, since students will use the lowest-cost funds first—mom and dad paying for college—then turn to government-subsidized funds, and finally use private market funds, if needed.

With demand (D_0) and supply (S_0), equilibrium in this market is at point *e*. Human capital investment is equal to H_e, with the rate of return equaling the interest rate (i_e). Notice that reducing the supply of funds, or shifting the supply curve to S_1, will increase interest rates and the cost of investment. This results in lower investments in education. Similarly, anything reducing the demand for funds, or shifting the demand curve to D_1, will result in reduced human capital investment. Let us briefly consider some of the factors that might cause these curves to shift.

The most important factor determining the supply of investable funds for students consists of family resources. Students from well-off families can draw on a pool of inexpensive funds, but students from poorer families must scratch together funds that are often expensive. At the aggregate level, reductions in federally subsidized low-interest student loans will result in a shift in the supply curve to S_1, meaning lower investments in human capital (H_1). Conversely, the GI Bills enacted after World War II and the Vietnam War greatly increased college enrollments and the stock of human capital in America.

The demand for human capital is influenced by an individual's abilities and learning capacity: the more able the person, the larger the expected benefits of human capital investment.

Discrimination in the labor market also plays an important role in determining whether an investment in education is worthwhile or not, since expected earnings will be affected by wage or occupational discrimination. Assume D_0 represents the demand for human capital investment for individuals facing no discrimination in the labor market. If these same people were to face a reduced wage in the market from wage discrimination, their demand for education would fall to D_1, reflecting the reduced return on investment in human capital. A similar decline in demand will result if the choice of jobs is limited by occupational discrimination.

Implications of Human Capital Theory

Individuals are more productive because of their investment in human capital, and thus they are capable of earning more during their working lives. Because younger people have longer earning horizons, they will be more likely to invest in human capital and education. As workers get older and gain labor market experience and higher wages, their opportunity costs for attending college grow larger, while their potential postcollege earning period shrinks. This explains why most students in college classrooms are young.

The greater the market earnings differential between high school and college graduates, the more people will attend college, since a higher earnings differential raises the return on college educations. Similarly, reductions in the cost of education will lead to greater educational investment.

Last, the more an individual discounts the future—the higher i is in present value formulas—the less investment in human capital we would expect. If your discount rate is high, this means you value the present highly but do not place as much value on future outcomes. People with high discount rates will often not be willing to pursue doctoral or medical degrees because the time between the beginning of the training process and the point when earnings begin is simply too long.

Human Capital as Screening or Signaling

Human capital theorists see investments in human capital as improving the productivity of individuals. This higher productivity then translates into higher wages.

There is another view why higher educational levels lead to higher wages: Higher education acts as a **screening/signaling** device for employers.

Screening/signaling
The argument that higher education simply lets employers know that the prospective employee is intelligent and trainable and has the discipline to potentially be a good employee.

Economists who advocate this view concede that some education will undoubtedly lead to higher productivity. But these economists argue that higher education is largely an indicator to employers that the college graduate is trainable, has discipline, and is intelligent. In their view, the job market is one big competition where entry-level workers compete for on-the-job training. As a result, earning a college degree does little more than give the college graduate a leg up in this competition.

One implication of this view is the controversial suggestion that the social benefits for more public spending on education may be low. If college educations do not enhance productivity but simply trigger competitive pursuits for resume items, then the return to public funds will be low. In the words of *The Economist,*

> *How can more education fail to make a country more prosperous? A first crucial point is that education is a "positional good": that is, getting yourself tagged for high wages is not just about being educated, it is also about being better educated than the next man. To some extent, education is a race: if everybody runs faster, that may be good in itself, but it does not mean that more people can finish in the top 10%. In that sense, much of the extra effort may be wasted. In weighing the social benefits of higher spending on education against the cost, this needs to be borne in mind.*[4]

Still, it is doubtful that screening is the only purpose served by higher education. If it were, the high costs of college education and the higher wages employers must pay college graduates would create tremendous incentives for workers and employers to develop an alternative, less expensive screening device.

On-the-Job Training

On-the-job training (OJT) can take many different forms. Often training amounts to nothing more than receiving instructions from a supervisor on how to help customers, operate a machine, or retrieve items from inventory. Sometimes this training takes place in a more formal setting away from the job, almost like a college course.

On-the-job training
Training typically done by employers, ranging from suggestions at work to sophisticated seminars.

Today, spending on OJT approaches $80 billion a year, including training costs and the wages paid to employees during training. The costs of OJT are usually borne by employers, but workers may bear some of the costs through reduced wages throughout the training period. Firms benefit from OJT by gaining more productive workers, and workers gain by becoming more versatile, and thus more competitive, in labor markets.

General Versus Specific Training

Nobel Prize winner Gary Becker was one of the pioneers of human capital theory. In his book, *Human Capital,* he outlined two distinct forms of OJT: general training and specific training.

General training improves productivity in all firms. Learning to use computers, word processors, and spreadsheets, for example, raises your productivity no matter where you work. The same is true for a college education, as well as for the apprenticeships electricians, plumbers, and carpenters undertake.

General training
Training that improves a worker's productivity in all firms.

Specific training, in contrast, increases a worker's productivity only within the firm. Firm-specific training might cover the way a firm handles such issues as order flow, inventory control and purchasing, or familiarization of workers with the firm's

Specific training
Training that improves a worker's productivity in a specific firm.

[4]"Economic Focus: The Education Shibboleth," *The Economist,* June 8, 2002, p. 73. See A. Wolf, *Does Education Matter? Myths About Education and Economic Growth,* (London: Penguin Books), 2002.

Nobel Prize Gary Becker

The 1992 winner of the Nobel Prize in Economic Sciences, Gary Becker, applied the theory of "rational choice" to areas of human behavior not ordinarily associated with economic analysis and research. Through his academic work and columns in *Business Week* magazine, he has offered provocative insights on a broad array of subjects, including family relations, racial discrimination, and the criminal justice system.

Born in Pottsville, a coal-mining community in eastern Pennsylvania, Becker completed his undergraduate degree in 3 years at Princeton University. He then entered the University of Chicago, where he studied under economist Milton Friedman.

In 1957, he published his dissertation, the *Economics of Discrimination,* an analysis of the effects of racial prejudice on earnings and employment among minorities. The book was favorably reviewed in journals but failed to make an impact on mainstream economics. The support of Friedman and other economists at the University of Chicago, however, encouraged Becker to continue along this line of research. Becker taught for several years at Chicago and then Columbia. In 1970, he rejoined the faculty at Chicago and befriended George Stigler, collaborating with him on two influential papers. His work with Stigler rekindled an interest in the relationship between economics and politics. In the 1980s, he wrote two papers that analyzed the impact of special interest groups on the political process.

In 1981, he published his book, *A Treatise on the Family,* viewing the family as a "small factory." According to his theory, rising wages led to changes in the family, including more women working outside the home instead of "specializing" in child care and housework. He also traced the declining rate of fertility to a rational choice of having fewer children and investing more in education for the individual child.

On questions of crime and punishment, Becker suggested that most criminals react in predictable ways to the costs and benefits of illegal activity. His empirical studies indicated that the probability of being caught and punished was a greater deterrent than the harsh nature of the punishment. On the question of race, Becker viewed discrimination as a "tax wedge" between social and private returns, concluding that prejudice tends to be economically detrimental to all parties concerned.

specific products. Training to use Sun's Solaris operating system, for instance, may not readily transfer to firms using the Windows operating system.

Firms usually will not provide general training. Since productivity is increased equally for all firms, workers must acquire these skills at their own expense. Firms will provide specific training, however, if the returns from this investment compare favorably to other investment alternatives.

Because investing in OJT is just one of many investments a firm can undertake, the rate of return to OJT must equal or exceed those of other investments if it is to be worthwhile. On-the-job investments entail present costs meant to yield future benefits. These investments can be analyzed just like those involving college education that we looked at earlier. Figure 3 shows the benefits and costs of on-the-job training.

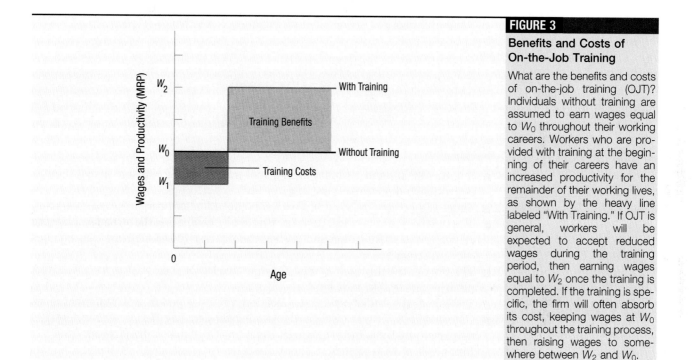

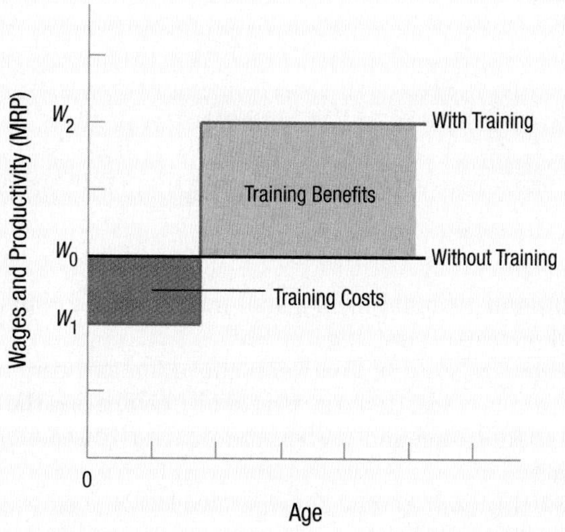

FIGURE 3

Benefits and Costs of On-the-Job Training

What are the benefits and costs of on-the-job training (OJT)? Individuals without training are assumed to earn wages equal to W_0 throughout their working careers. Workers who are provided with training at the beginning of their careers have an increased productivity for the remainder of their working lives, as shown by the heavy line labeled "With Training." If OJT is general, workers will be expected to accept reduced wages during the training period, then earning wages equal to W_2 once the training is completed. If the training is specific, the firm will often absorb its cost, keeping wages at W_0 throughout the training process, then raising wages to somewhere between W_2 and W_0.

Wages and productivity (marginal revenue product, or MRP) are shown on the vertical axis. For simplicity, individuals without training are assumed to have productivity (MRP) and earn wages equal to W_0 throughout their working careers. Further, we will assume that workers are provided training at the beginning of their careers, which improves their productivity in that firm for the remainder of their working lives. The heavy line labeled "With Training" reflects this increased productivity.

If OJT is general training, workers will be expected to accept reduced wages during the training period, and then earn wages equal to W_2 once the training is completed. In Figure 3, the area below W_0 and above W_1 represents the costs workers bear during the training period. Historically, this is how apprenticeship programs in the trades have operated. Today, professional internships provide college students with OJT at reduced wages over the summer. Hiring summer interns is a good way for firms to get an extended look at potential employees. The internships provide students, meanwhile, with a look at several different firms and industries before graduating and entering the job market.

Specific training is usually handled differently. Because this training will increase productivity only within the firm providing the training, the firm will usually absorb the cost of this training, keeping wages at W_0 throughout the training process. Once workers have completed the training, their productivity rises to W_2. The firm will not, however, raise their pay all the way to W_2, since then it would not recoup the training costs. Instead, the firm will share the benefits of specific training with the newly trained workers, raising their pay to somewhere between W_2 and W_0. Paying these workers something more than W_0 will reduce turnover, since the workers could expect to earn only W_0 if they went to another firm, given that specific training only increases productivity in the firm providing the training.

As we have seen, investments in human capital go a long way toward explaining why people are paid different wages. Education and earnings are closely related. Human capital theorists believe that this is because education and productivity are closely related. Other economists question whether more education translates into higher productivity; they view education as little more than a screening device for employers. In any case, the investment in human capital is just one of the reasons for wage differentials; economic discrimination is another.

Checkpoint

Investment in Human Capital

REVIEW

- Investment in human capital includes all investments in human beings such as education and on-the-job training.
- There is a positive relationship between education and earnings.
- The rate of return to education is computed by comparing the streams of income of two levels of education and finding the interest (discount) rate that equates the two streams.
- The greater the wage differential between two levels of education, the more people will pursue that next level of education.
- The higher the rate of return to education, the more people will attain that level.
- Higher education may just be a screening or signaling device telling potential employers that this individual is trainable, has discipline, and is smart.
- Firms will provide specific training (training that enhances productivity in the firm only) but will usually not provide general training (training that enhances productivity in all firms).

QUESTIONS

If the United States decided, as part of an immigration reform package, to restrict immigration only to those with college degrees, and thus decided to allow only 500,000 foreigners a year to enter, what would happen to the rate of return on college education? Alternatively, if, as part of a reform package, 500,000 unskilled people were permitted to enter the United States, what would happen to the rate of return on college education?

Answers to the Checkpoint questions can be found at the end of this chapter.

Economic Discrimination

Growing prosperity gives women more opportunity to become independent and provide for themselves. Experience from Africa and elsewhere shows that women are often lead-

ing entrepreneurs for various kinds of small-scale production and exchange in the informal sector, which suggests that, absent discrimination and regulation by the government, the market is their oyster.

***Johan Norberg*[5]**

Economic discrimination takes place whenever workers of equal ability and productivity are paid different wages or are otherwise discriminated against in the workplace because of their race, color, religion, gender, age, national origin, or disability. This can mean that one group is paid lower wages than another for doing the same job, or that members of different groups are segregated into occupations that pay different wages.

Economic discrimination When workers of equal ability are paid different wages or in any other way discriminated against because of race, color, religion, gender, age, national origin, or disability.

Economic theories of discrimination generally take one of two approaches. The first, developed by Gary Becker, rests on the notion that bias is articulated in the *discriminatory tastes* of employers, workers, and consumers. The second approach, the *segmented markets approach,* maintains that labor markets are divided into segments based on race, gender, or some other category. This approach is often referred to as the *job crowding hypothesis,* or the *dual labor market hypothesis.*

Becker's Theory of Economic Discrimination

Gary Becker's main contribution to economics is that he vastly broadened the issues that economists study. This was no small feat. Before Becker's influence, economists focused almost exclusively on the production and exchange of material goods and services. One early example shows the difficulties Becker faced in broadening this focus.

In 1955, Becker was asked to speak at Harvard about his dissertation on the economics of discrimination. Becker noted that his audience was perplexed. "They thought I would discuss price discrimination," that is, the analysis of why businesses charge different prices for the same goods. "No one conceived that an economist would talk about race discrimination in those days."[6]

Published in 1957, *The Economics of Discrimination* was not warmly received by the profession. Not until the mid-1960s, when the civil rights movement gained momentum, did the book get the recognition it deserved. Surprisingly enough, Becker challenged the conventional view that discrimination benefits the person who discriminates. Let's see why he thought the conventional wisdom was wrong.

We begin with the basic assumption that women are equally productive as men. Becker knew, however, that employers often have a "taste" for discrimination. By this, he meant that employers often perceive less utility in employing a discriminated group, such as women. When this happens, women's wages (W_F) will be less than men's (W_M) by a coefficient of discrimination (d), and thus determined by the equation, $W_F = W_M(1 - d)$. If the discrimination coefficient here were negative ($d < 0$), this would mean the employer favored women, and if d were equal to zero ($d = 0$), no discrimination would exist. If, however, the discrimination coefficient here were positive ($d > 0$), this would mean that discrimination did exist, and women's wages would be lower than men's.

Figure 4 on the next page shows the implications of Becker's model. Demand curve D_0 represents the demand for women's labor absent discrimination. The ratio of women's wages to men's wages (W_F / W_M), shown on the vertical axis, is equal to 1.0 for D_0, meaning that the two wages are equal. The supply of women's labor, meanwhile, is positively sloped, suggesting that higher wages are required to induce more women to work. With no discrimination, L_0 women are employed at the same wages paid to men (point b).

[5]A fellow at the Swedish think tank Timbro.

[6]Peter Passell, "New Nobel Laureate Takes Economics Far Afield," *New York Times*, October 14, 1992, p. D1.

FIGURE 4

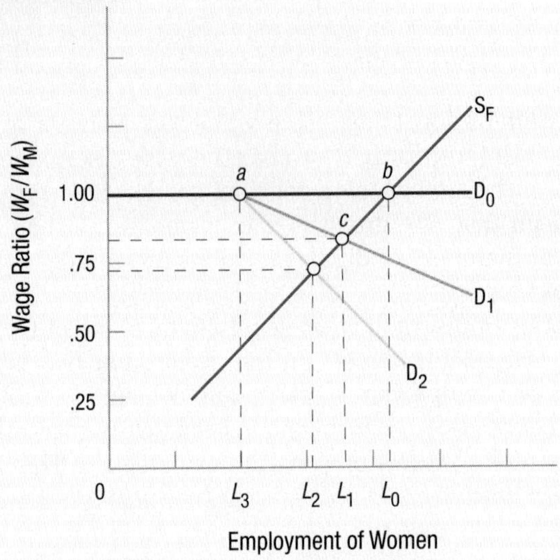

Wage Differentials and Employer Discrimination

This figure illustrates Becker's model of economic discrimination. Demand curve D_0 represents the demand for women's labor absent discrimination. On D_0, the ratio of women's wages to men's wages (W_F/W_M) is equal to 1.0, meaning that wages are equal in this case. But now assume that, although employers do not discriminate out to point *a*, beyond this point some employers start requiring a wage differential associated with a positive discrimination coefficient if they are to hire women workers. The demand for women's labor kinks at point *a*, shifting to D_1. With discrimination, equilibrium employment for women is L_1, at a wage differential of about .80 (point c). If the discrimination is even stronger, demand may shift down to D_2, and the wage differential will be still greater.

Assume that some employers do not discriminate out to point *a*, for instance. In this case, L_3 women can be employed at the same wage as men. Beyond point *a*, however, some employers require a wage differential in line with a discrimination coefficient of *d* if they are to hire women workers. The demand for women's labor kinks at point *a*, and descends along demand curve D_1. With discrimination, equilibrium employment for women is L_1, at a wage differential of roughly .80 (point *c*). If the discrimination is even stronger, demand may shift down to D_2, resulting in a larger wage differential. Note that even employers who do not discriminate will pay women this same lower wage, since firms with and without discriminatory tastes compete and buy labor on the open market, meaning that all will pay their employees roughly the same wages.

Becker argued that employers who discriminate against women will lose market share and profit opportunities, both because they do not hire the best employees available, and because they must pay mostly high-wage male employees. Nondiscriminating firms, in contrast, will have lower labor costs, having more low-wage women on the payroll. Nondiscriminating firms will attract the most productive managers and employees, many of whom will likely be women. Profits for the nondiscriminating firm should therefore be higher. Becker concluded that the cost of wage differentials and the pressures of the marketplace should drive discrimination down to zero in the long run.

In practice, we know that wage discrimination still exists. Why might competition fail to erase wage differentials? For one thing, the adjustment costs of firing unproductive workers, giving them severance pay, then recruiting and training new workers can be extremely high, especially considering the protections unions and the legal system offer workers. Second, women may be less mobile than men when it comes to work. They may be less willing to move to accommodate employer preferences, and thus be forced to accept lower wage positions. Third, if women continue to choose occupations with more flexible career paths that do not heavily penalize extended absences from the labor market, wage differentials between men and women may always exist. Note, however, that such differentials could also be caused by discrimination that precedes labor market entry, as when social norms direct girls toward lower-wage occupations such as elementary education or social work.

Segmented Labor Markets

Economists who advocate **segmented labor market** theories argue that discrimination does not arise due to a lack of competitive labor markets, but rather because these markets, though competitive, are segmented into a variety of constituent parts. And these different parts, while interacting, are noncompeting sectors. Segmented labor market theories have been developed along several different lines.

Segmented labor markets Labor markets split into separate parts. This leads to different wages paid to different sectors even though both markets are highly competitive.

- The *dual labor market hypothesis* splits the labor market into primary and secondary sectors. As Doeringer and Piore wrote, "Jobs in the primary market possess several of the following characteristics: high wages, good working conditions, job stability, chances of advancement, equity and due process in the administration of work rules. Jobs in the secondary market, in contrast, tend to have low wages and fringe benefits, poor working conditions, high labor turnover, little chance of advancement, and often arbitrary and capricious supervision."[7]
- The *job crowding hypothesis* breaks occupations into predominately male and female jobs. In 1922, Edgeworth recognized this problem when he wrote, "The pressure of male trade unions appears to be largely responsible for that crowding of women into a comparatively few occupations, which is universally recognized as a main factor in the depression of their wages. Such crowding is prima facie a flagrant violation of that free competition which results in maximum production in . . . equal pay for equal work."[8]
- The *insider-outsider theory* maintains that workers are segregated into those who belong to unions and those who are unemployed or non-union workers. Alternately, economists have recognized that large firms use internal promotion and job security to inspire loyalty to the firm. Company customs, norms, and policies provide loyal workers with clear advancement paths. The preference given to promotion from within can be a good recruiting vehicle for a firm, but it can also become an indirect method of segregating the labor market.

These hypotheses all predict that separate job markets will emerge for different groups. Figure 5 on the next page shows how segregated markets can lead to significant wage differentials, such as those we see for men and women in Table 2.

In a world without discrimination, equilibrium wages for everyone would be W_e, with total employment at $M_0 + F_0$. If some form of discrimination in male-dominated jobs is present, labor supply to that segment will decline to S_1, wages will rise to W_1, and hiring will fall to M_1 (point a). Those women who are excluded from jobs in this sector will have to move to jobs available in the female-dominated sector, thus increasing the supply of labor there to S_2 and reducing wages to W_2, employment climbing to F_2 (point b). The result is a wage differential equal to $W_1 - W_2$.

Notice that once such a wage differential is established, the firms in competitive markets have no real incentive to eliminate the gap. Men and women are both being paid their marginal revenue products, so no profits are gained by substituting workers.

Wage differentials can arise for a variety of reasons. Some people may simply prefer one occupation to another. If such preferences have their roots in specific social groups, groupwide wage differentials can be expected to arise. Wages

[7]Doeringer P. and Piore, M., *Internal Labour Markets and Manpower Analysis* (1971), p. 165, cited in Stephen Smith, *Labour Economics* (New York: Routledge), 1994, p. 104.

[8]Edgeworth, F. Y., "Equal Pay to Men and Women for Equal Work" (1922), p. 439, cited in Stephen Smith, *Labour Economics* (New York: Routledge), 1994, p. 102.

FIGURE 5

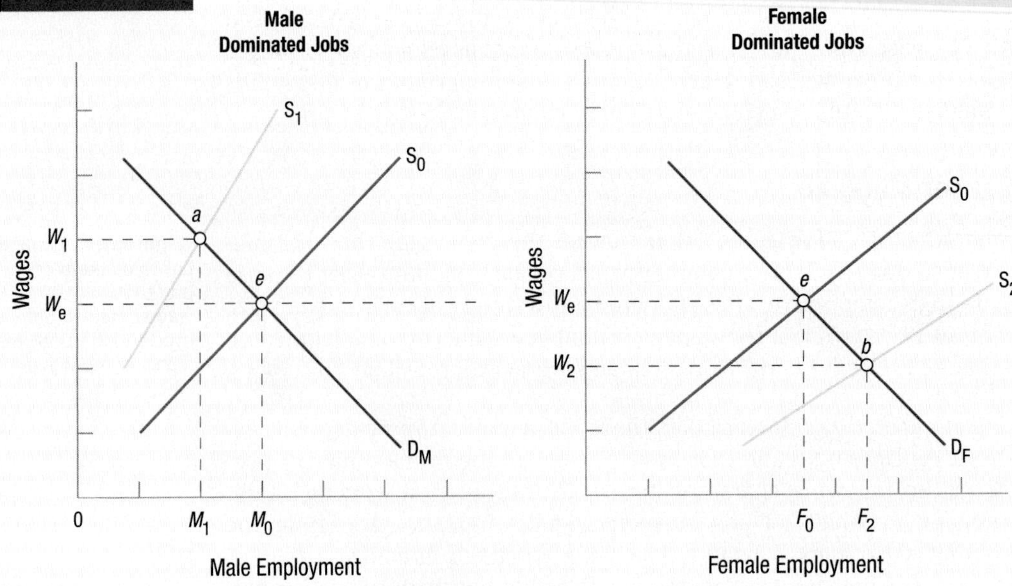

Job Crowding and a Dual Labor Market

Segregated markets can lead to significant wage differentials, such as those we see for men and women in Table 2. Absent discrimination, equilibrium wages will be W_e for everyone, with total employment at $M_0 + F_0$. If, however, there is some form of discrimination in male-dominated jobs, the supply of labor to that segment will decline to S_1, wages will rise to W_1, and employment will fall to M_1 (point *a*). Those women who are excluded from jobs in this sector will have to move to available jobs in the female-dominated sector, thus increasing the labor supplied for these jobs to S_2, raising employment to F_2, but reducing wages to W_2 (point *b*). The result is a wage differential equal to $W_1 - W_2$.

will vary between occupations, moreover, because of differences in their attractiveness, difficulty, riskiness, social status, and the human capital investments required.

Markets may naturally gravitate toward different equilibrium wage levels for different occupations. Two occupations may require the same skills and effort, for instance, but be valued differently by consumers. Finally, government policies that promote or restrict entry into occupations or professions will affect wages. Licensing requirements for everything from hair styling to surgery today create wage differentials in over 700 different occupations.

Occupational segregation may also arise from disparate degrees of labor force attachment. Female labor force participation is often interrupted when women take a break from working to have children. Skills and other forms of human capital depreciate during these interruptions, which influences the occupational choices of women and employer decisions concerning which employees to offer specific training. For women who anticipate spells out of the labor force, jobs that mostly involve general training—nursing, teaching, retail sales, and secretarial or administrative work—may look attractive. These occupations do not require climbing long career ladders, so women can leave their jobs, later returning or finding a new employer, with little loss in salary or benefits. The downside to these occupations, however, is that most of them do not pay high wages.

Some occupational wage differentials are the result of socialization: Our culture stereotypes some occupations as "men's work" and others as "women's work." Some of this may be rational; men, for instance, are better suited to jobs involving heavy lifting. For most occupations today, however, gender differences should be irrelevant. Still, lingering wage differentials today may be the result of past discriminatory practices that barred women from entering some occupations or professional schools. At one time or another, firms, educational institutions, and

Table 2 Median Weekly Earnings for Selected Occupations and Gender, 2006

	Earnings		Percent	
Occupation	Men	Women	% Men	Women's Wage as % of Men
Human resource manager	1,391	967	36.5	69.5
Computer and information systems manager	1,492	1,300	62.1	87.1
Accountant/Auditor	1,160	844	38.8	72.8
Computer programmer	1,229	1,034	74.3	84.1
Social worker	749	728	19.4	97.2
Lawyer	1,891	1,333	63.3	70.5
Teacher (elementary)	920	824	17.9	89.6
Teacher (college)	1,228	915	58.4	74.5
Doctor/Surgeon	1,847	1,329	66.3	72.0
Registered nurse	1,074	971	9.7	91.3
Cook	377	340	60.4	90.2
Cashier	387	327	26.4	84.5

Source: U.S. Census Bureau, Current Population Survey, Weekly Earnings Data (Washington, DC: U.S. Government Printing Office), 2007, Table 39.

unions have all restricted the entry of women into high-paying occupations and professions.

Do wage differentials necessarily mean that discrimination exists in the market? Job crowding and wage differentials could just reflect different levels of human capital investment or different professional choices. Many women, for instance, may truly prefer occupations that are complementary to parenting. These will tend to be jobs without significant career ladders and that do not require considerable specific training, mobility, or travel.

Developments over the past two decades, however, have reduced the explanatory power of these suggestions. Today, women get more bachelors' degrees than men, and the rate of women earning advanced and professional degrees is rapidly closing in on that of men. With today's dual-earner households on the rise and female labor force participation rates approaching that of males, wage differentials are also on the decline.

Public Policy to Combat Discrimination

For the first half of the last century, the inequities associated with various forms of discrimination were simply accepted as a part of life in the United States. Gradually, however, a groundswell developed to end racial segregation and other forms of discrimination, culminating in passage of the Civil Rights Act in 1964. In what follows, we briefly outline the major acts and public policies that have been implemented with the goal of ending discrimination. Because of these policies, discrimination, wage differentials, and segmented labor markets have declined markedly over the past four decades.

Equal Pay Act of 1963

This act amended the Fair Labor Standards Act of 1938; it requires that men and women receive equal pay for equal work. Equal work is defined as work performed under similar circumstances requiring equal effort, skill, and responsibility. Some argue that the Equal Pay Act was a hollow victory because occupational segregation forced women into specific occupations, causing them to earn less than men for essentially comparable work.

Comparable Worth

Comparable worth
An approach to determining wage rates for specific occupations that assumes that every job has essential characteristics that possess an inherent worth independent of market forces.

This has led to a drive to establish **comparable worth** as the standard for wages and salaries. Comparable worth rests on the assumption that every job has essential characteristics that possess an inherent worth, independent of market forces. Unregulated labor markets, it is argued, frequently set wage rates that fail to reflect the true worth of jobs and such wages are therefore inequitable. The solution, advocates of comparable worth theory argue, is to evaluate the characteristics of each job and use this data to fine-tune employer pay structures. This is not an easy task, and the information required is substantial.

> *First, job descriptions are written for the jobs in question. Then a set of relevant job characteristics, called compensable factors, is identified and a weight is assigned to each factor. These factors frequently include the degree of skill, education, and mental effort required to perform the job, the pleasantness of the working conditions, and the responsibility involved. Finally, the job descriptions are evaluated to determine how much of each compensable factor each job entails.*[9]

The comparable worth approach to solving male–female wage differentials has been losing momentum, both because of the complexity of the job evaluation process[10] and because more recent studies have shown that person-specific labor preferences account for much of the observed differentials.[11] As wage differentials have shrunk, moreover, the calls for further reform have abated.

Civil Rights Act of 1964

Title VII of the Civil Rights Act of 1964 makes it unlawful to "refuse to hire or to discharge any individual, or otherwise to discriminate against any individual with respect to his compensation, terms, conditions, or privileges of employment, because of such individual's race, color, religion, sex, or national origin." The act also created the Equal Employment Opportunity Commission (EEOC) to administer the act.

To date, most of the litigation brought under this statute has focused on the meaning of the phrase *to discriminate.* Amendments to the statute and court cases have ruled that, to show discrimination, a plaintiff must show that an employment practice inflicts a "disparate" or unequal impact on members of a minority group, as compared to its impact on others. Once this has been demonstrated, the burden shifts to the defendant (the employer) to show that its employment practices—seniority rules, prehiring examinations or other screening devices, weight or height requirements—are related to employee performance or are otherwise a matter of "business necessity." Plaintiffs may sue for a full range of remedies including back pay, reinstatement, court costs, attorney's fees, and punitive damages.

---

[9]E. Jane Arnault et al., "An Experimental Study of Job Evaluation and Comparable Worth," *Industrial and Labor Relations Review,* July 2001, p. 806.
[10]Arnault et al., "An Experimental Study," p. 806.
[11]David Macpherson and Barry Hirsch, "Wages and Gender Composition: Why Do Women's Jobs Pay Less?" *Journal of Labor Economics,* July 1995, pp. 426–471.

Executive Order 11246—Affirmative Action

In 1965, President Lyndon Johnson issued Executive Order 11246. This order established the Office of Federal Contract Compliance Programs (OFCCP) in the Department of Labor. A key provision of this order required that firms doing at least $50,000 in business with the federal government submit an affirmative action program that includes a detailed analysis of their labor force.

Affirmative action programs have been controversial from the outset. Critics see such programs as "enforced quotas," whereas supporters see them as a way of breaking down discriminatory hiring barriers.

In the summer of 2003, the U.S. Supreme Court ruled in the University of Michigan case (*Gratz v. Bollinger*) that adding a large specific numerical adjustment for minority group status to university admission criteria was unacceptable. The undergraduate admissions program automatically added 20 points (out of a total of 100) to minority candidates for admission. The Law School at Michigan, on the other hand, simply took race into account in a nuanced approach to improving diversity of the class. This approach the Supreme Court found acceptable (*Grutter v. Bollinger*).

Age and Disabilities Acts

Two other acts were designed to reduce discrimination based on age and physical or mental disabilities. The Age Discrimination in Employment Act of 1967 protects workers over age 40 from discrimination based on age. The Americans With Disabilities Act of 1990, prohibits discrimination against people with a physical or mental disability who could still perform a job with reasonable accommodation by an employer. What constitutes a "reasonable accommodation" has been a point of contention in many recent court cases.

Empirical Evidence of Discrimination

Just how pervasive is wage discrimination? Many empirical studies have examined race- and gender-based wage differentials, and most have found some evidence of discrimination. These studies try to account for wage differences by factoring in such variables as education and experience. Researchers estimate the degree to which these variables explain observed differences in wages; what disparity remains unexplained is attributed to discrimination.

One recent study used 1990 U.S. Census data on annual earnings, years of schooling, work experience, union membership, public versus private employment, geographical residence, occupation, industry, and hours of work to determine the extent of discrimination.[12] The results of this study are summarized in Table 3 on the next page.[13]

In this study, the unexplained residual attributed to discrimination ranged from 1% for Hispanic men to 30% for black women. For black men, who average 1 year less of education than white men but are more likely to be represented by a union, identified variables explain 81% of the wage differential, leaving 19% unexplained and potentially caused by discrimination. Even though Hispanic men earn less than black men, their discrimination residual was only 1%, their significantly lower levels of education and experience explaining nearly their entire wage differential.

A recent British study looked at how costly family obligations are for women. Only about a quarter of all working women work full time throughout their careers;

---

[12]Garey Durden and Patricia Gaynor, "More on the Cost of Being Other Than White Male: Measurement of Race, Ethnic, and Gender Effects on Yearly Earnings," *American Journal of Economics and Sociology,* January 1998, pp. 95–103.

[13]This table is based on Table 9.4 in Bruce Kaufman and Julie Hotchkiss, *The Economics of Labor Markets,* 5th ed. (New York: Dryden Press), 2000, p. 497.

Table 3 Average Worker Characteristics and Wage Differentials and Percent of Wage Gap Unexplained

	White Men	Black Men	Hispanic Men	White Women	Black Women	Hispanic Women
Years of education	13.4	12.4	10	13.3	12.7	10.9
Years of experience	19.4	19	17.8	19	18.7	17.6
Employed full-time (%)	76	71	76	61	68	61
Represented by a union (%)	3.9	5	3.6	2.5	3.7	2.3
Annual earnings (1997$)	21,163	15,561	14,810	12,733	12,612	10,875
Wage gap unexplained (%)		19%	1%	28%	30%	22%

Source: Bruce Kaufman and Julie Hotchkiss, *The Economics of Labor Markets* (New York: Dryden Press), 2000, p. 497. Table was adapted from Garey Durden and Patricia Gaynor, "More on the Cost of Being Other Than White Male: Measurement of Race, Ethnic, and Gender Effects on Yearly Earnings," *American Journal of Economics and Sociology,* 57 (January 1998).

the rest drop out for a portion or work part-time at some point in their career. Taking just 1 year off reduces a woman's earnings by 32% over the 15 years the study covered, and dropping out for 2 years cut earnings by nearly a half.[14]

Most evidence points to declining wage ratios and declining occupational segregation over the last four decades. This is attributable to changing attitudes and public policies, and a general recognition that discrimination harms not just the victims of discrimination but its perpetrators as well (recall Becker). Our changing economy, rising labor force participation rates for women, and legal prohibitions of discrimination have all worked to reduce economic discrimination.

Checkpoint

Economic Discrimination

REVIEW

- Economic discrimination occurs whenever workers of equal ability and productivity are paid different wages or otherwise discriminated against because of their race, color, religion, gender, age, national origin, or disability.
- Becker's analysis of discrimination assumed that employers had a taste for discrimination, and he showed that both parties were harmed by discrimination.
- Segmented labor markets assume that separate markets lead to wage differentials that represent discrimination.
- Public policy to eliminate discrimination has included the Equal Pay Act of 1963, Civil Rights Act of 1964, Executive Order 11246 (Affirmative Action), Age Discrimination in Employment Act of 1967, and Americans With Disabilities Act of 1990.

---

[14]Reported in "Women's Pay: The Hand That Rocks the Cradle," *The Economist,* March 4, 2006, pp. 51–52. The original study, "Shaping a Fairer Future," was conducted by the Women and Work Commission, presented to the Prime Minister in February 2006.

- Wage ratios and occupational segregation has declined over the past four decades. However, differences in wage rates that can be attributed to discrimination still exist.

QUESTION

The Civil Rights Act of 1964 made defendants liable for the plaintiffs attorney's fees if they lost the case, but it did not have the same provision for plaintiffs if they lost the case. Why do you think Congress wrote this part of the law this way? (Hint: Who did Congress assume would be plaintiffs and who would be defendants under the Civil Rights Act?)

Answers to the Checkpoint question can be found at the end of this chapter.

Labor Unions and Collective Bargaining

A friend who had been working for a large construction company for 8 years as an engineer and project coordinator recently staged a one-man strike. He had been training new employees on various aspects of cost estimating and job specification, and he noticed that these new people were being hired at salaries approaching his own. He requested a raise several times, but was essentially ignored. Exasperated, he refused to go to work one day, informing his boss that he would not return without a raise. He did not quit; he simply staged a walkout and refused to return until given a raise. He was out for 2 weeks before his supervisor called and asked him how much he wanted. They settled on a raise of over 20%.

This story is unique in that one-person strikes are rarely successful; more often they are career busters. In most instances, individual employees have little control over wages or job conditions, essentially being at the mercy of employers and the market. This is the primary reason that unions exist: Collective action is more powerful than the action of one individual. As individuals, we can easily be replaced (except, apparently, my friend above). To replace an entire workforce, on the other hand, imposes serious costs to an employer. This section looks at the role unions play in our economy, their history, and their effects.

Types of Unions

Labor unions are legal associations of employees that bargain with employers over terms and conditions of work, including wages, benefits, and working conditions. They use strikes and threats of strikes, as well as other tactics, to try to achieve their goals. Elections determine union representatives who negotiate on the workers' behalf, and employers are legally required to "bargain in good faith" with the union.

Unions are usually defined by industry, or by craft or occupation. A *craft* union represents members of a specific craft or occupation, such as air traffic controllers (PATCO), truck drivers (Teamsters), and teachers (AFT). An *industrial* union represents all workers employed in a specific industry. Examples include auto workers (UAW) and public employees (AFSCME).

Benefits and Costs of Union Membership

Without a union, each individual employee would have to bargain with management for his or her own wages, benefits, and working conditions. Unions bring collective power to this bargaining arrangement. The source of this power is ultimately the willingness of the union to strike if no agreement is reached during negotiations. Collective bargaining often leads to a more equitable pay schedule than individual negotiation. It also provides workers with greater job security by protecting them against arbitrary or vindictive decisions by management.

Management's unilateral authority is curbed by the union contract, specifically through restrictions on job assignments and restrictions that severely limit the ability of management to fire employees without good cause and due process. These rules are subject to an elaborate grievance procedure laid out in the union contract's work rules.

Union membership, like everything else, has its price. First, union members must pay monthly dues. Then, if negotiations break down and a strike is called, wages are lost and the possibility exists, however remote, that management will refuse to settle with the union and replace the entire workforce. Finally, union workers must give up some individual flexibility since their work rules are more rigid.

Brief History of American Unionism

Labor unions date from the late 18th century in England. In this country, public attitudes toward unions were highly unfavorable until the Great Depression. In the early part of the 20th century, employers could easily secure legal injunctions against union organization by arguing that unions behaved like monopolies, in violation of antitrust laws. Employers often required employees to sign enforceable *yellow dog contracts,* in which they agreed not to join a union as a condition of employment.

Figure 6 shows union membership as a percentage of total employment since 1930. Going into the 1930s, unions represented just over 11% of workers because of public attitudes and legal restrictions. With the onset of the Depression, attitudes about collective bargaining began to change. In 1932, Congress passed the Norris-LaGuardia Act, which outlawed yellow dog contracts and prohibited injunctions against union organizing. Then, in 1935, Congress passed a sweeping reform by enacting the Wagner Act, or the National Labor Relations Act (NLRA). It prohibited a variety of unfair labor practices by employers, including firing employees for engaging in union activities. The Act also required employers to "bargain in good faith" with those unions that had won recognition through a majority vote of the firm's workers.

FIGURE 6

Union Membership as a Percent of Employment

Union membership grew dramatically from the mid-1930s until after World War II. Following the war, nearly a third of American workers were unionized. Union membership has fallen because benefits obtained by unions for union members spread throughout a wider populace and so made the benefits of joining a union less valuable. Also, the changing economy led to growth in the more difficult-to-unionize service sector, which has become a larger proportion of economic activity.

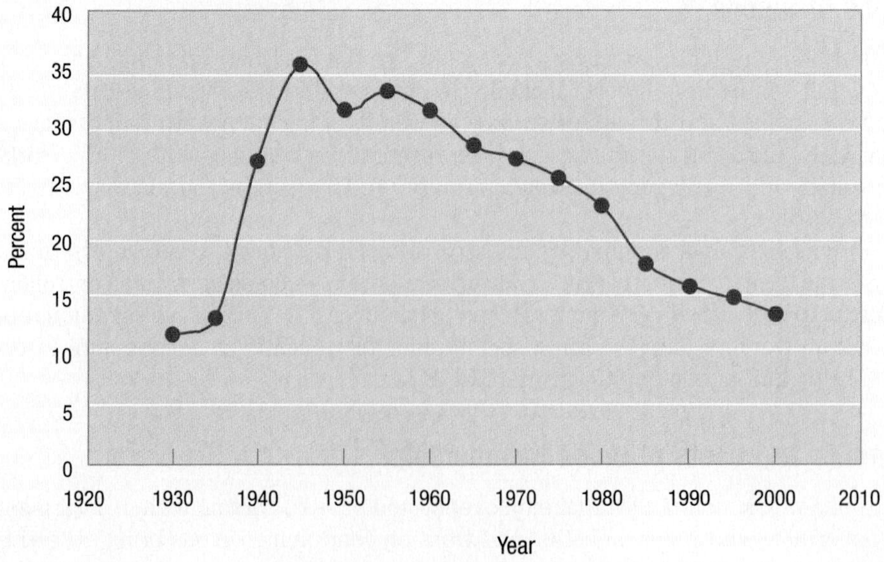

The NLRA also established the National Labor Relations Board (NLRB) to oversee union certification elections. These elections were to be held to determine which union, if any, would represent employees. The NLRB was also given the power to investigate complaints by labor and management about elections and the bargaining process.

As Figure 6 illustrates, union membership grew dramatically from the mid-1930s until after World War II. Following the war, union membership covered nearly a third of American workers. It was concentrated in a few major industries.

Figure 7 shows work stoppages, or strikes, since the late 1940s. In 1946 a rash of strikes turned public opinion against the unions; many people felt unions had become too powerful. Because of this swing in popular opinion, in 1947 Congress passed the Taft-Hartley Act, which prohibits some unfair labor practices by unions. Unions could no longer coerce or discriminate against workers who chose not to join the union, and unions were required to bargain in good faith, just like employers. With the passage of this act, the prolabor aspects of the 1935 Wagner Act were balanced.

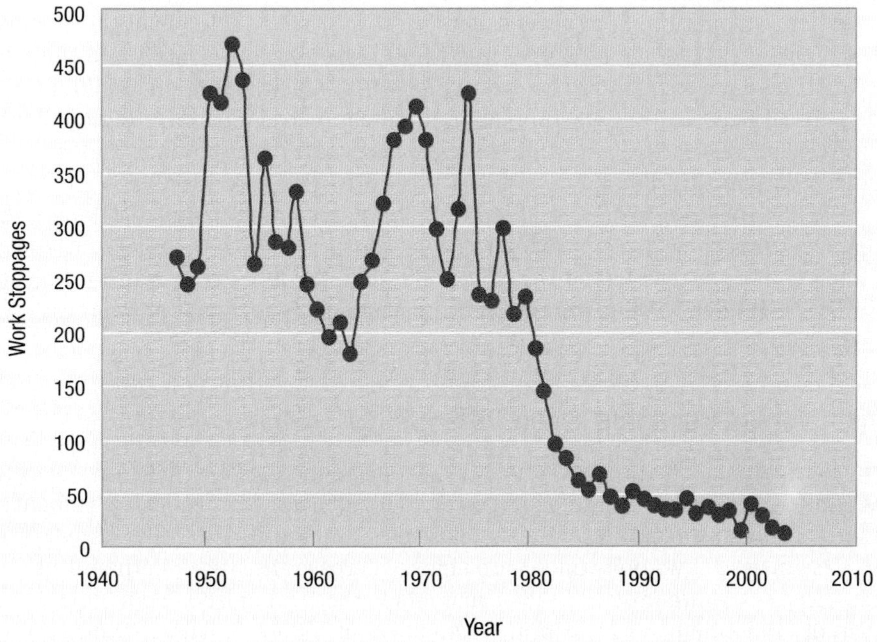

FIGURE 7

Work Stoppages (strikes)

This figure shows work stoppages, or strikes, since the late 1940s. In 1946 a rash of strikes turned public opinion against the unions; many people felt unions had become too powerful. Because of this swing in popular opinion, in 1947 Congress passed the Taft-Hartley Act, seeking a balance between unions and management. After this, the use of work stoppages by unions gradually began to decline.

Taft-Hartley changed the collective bargaining landscape dramatically by ending secondary boycotts and closed shops, and establishing procedures for decertification elections. A **secondary boycott** occurs when unions clash with one firm—the primary firm—but put pressure on neutral secondary firms by getting their union members to refuse to process the products of the primary firm. A **closed shop** is a workplace where workers are required to be union members before they can be hired. A **union shop** is one where nonunion hires must join the union within a specified time period, usually 30 days. In an **agency shop**, employees are not required to join the union, but they must pay union dues to compensate the union for its services. The Taft-Hartley Act outlawed closed shops outright, while permitting states to pass *right-to-work statutes* that prohibit union shops. Today, over 20 states have **right-to-work laws**.

Near the end of the 1950s, union corruption had become a serious issue, as various union leaders were accused of taking kickbacks, committing pension fund fraud, and engaging in a variety of other illegal activities. In response to these problems,

Secondary boycott
Occurs when unions clash with one firm and put pressure on a neutral, second firm to enlist the help of the second firm to obtain the union's objectives with the original firm.

Closed shop
Workers must belong to the union before they can be hired.

Union shop
Nonunion hires must join the union within a specified period of time.

Agency shop
Employees are not required to join the union, but must pay dues to compensate the union for its services.

Right-to-work laws
Laws created by the Taft-Hartley Act that permitted states to outlaw union shops.

Congress in 1959 passed the Labor Management Reporting and Disclosure Act, or the Landrum-Griffin Act. This act protects union members from their leaders by promoting union democracy and requiring financial transparency.

Until 1962, all collective bargaining statutes focused on the private sector; public employees were prohibited from organizing. In 1962, however, President Kennedy signed Executive Order 10988, giving federal workers the right to bargain collectively. Still, public employees are not permitted to strike. Rather, when an impasse is reached, both sides must submit to binding arbitration in which a neutral arbitrator resolves the dispute.

Why has union membership declined as a percentage of wage and salary workers since World War II? The answer lies partly with the changes in labor laws just discussed, the country's changing economy—notably, a larger service sector that is hard to organize—and ironically, the very success of labor at pushing its agenda through Congress and the courts. In addition, management has become more aggressive and sophisticated in defeating certification elections along with the rising labor force participation of women who historically have been difficult to organize.

Before unionization, employees were *hired at will*, which meant they could be fired "for a good reason, a bad reason, or no reason at all." Unions and their supporters pressed Congress and the courts for work safety legislation, minimum wage laws, Social Security, antidiscrimination statutes, restrictions on firing employees, laws that put restrictions on plant closures, and many other statutes and rules that protect workers.

Each of these successes resulted in union membership being a little less valuable. Over this same period, the service sector has become a bigger share of our economy. This sector has always been difficult for labor to organize, and as a result, union membership will probably continue to shrink as a percentage of the workforce.

Union Versus Nonunion Wage Differentials

Why join a union? The primary benefit to unionization should be higher wages, given the union's collective bargaining power. The general theoretical argument for union–nonunion wage differentials is illustrated in Figure 8.

This figure shows how unions are able to increase the wages in their sectors by restricting entry into union jobs. The markets for both unionized and nonunion labor begin at equilibrium, at point e in both panels of Figure 8. Thus, union and nonunion wages are initially equal, at W_0. If the union successfully restricts supply to S_1 in Panel A, union wages will rise to W_1, but employment will fall to L_1 (point a). Those workers who are released have no choice but to move over to the nonunion sector represented in Panel B, thus shifting its supply to S_2. Equilibrium in the nonunion sector moves to point b, where more workers (L_2) are employed at lower wages (W_2). The resulting wage differential, $W_1 - W_2$, is caused by successful collective bargaining in the union sector. Notice that this analysis is substantially the same as that for discrimination in the segmented labor force described in Figure 5 earlier.

Unions also have several ways of negotiating higher wages without losing members to unemployment. They can engage in activities that increase demand for their firm or industry's products, reduce the elasticity of demand for the product, or increase union productivity. One approach, advertisements encouraging consumers to buy the union label, fell flat.

More successful activities have included featherbedding, or forcing companies to hire redundant personnel. Examples include the firemen kept on trains long after diesels had replaced coal-burning steam engines, and the backup orchestras required by union contracts in New York City. This approach works in industries

FIGURE 8

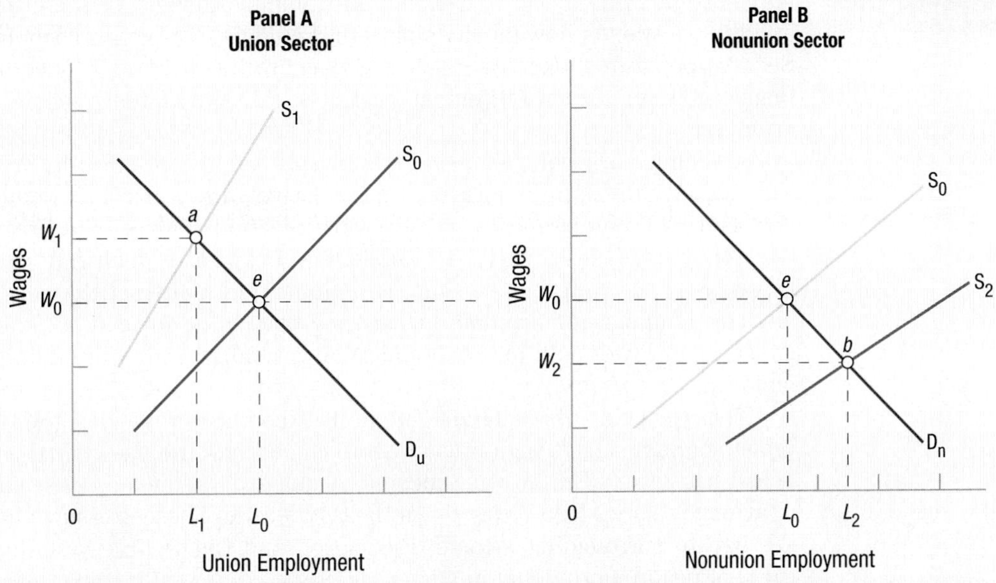

Union Versus Nonunion Wage Differentials

This figure illustrates the theoretical argument for union–nonunion wage differentials. Unions increase wages in their sectors by restricting entry into union jobs. Assuming the markets for unionized and nonunionized jobs begin at equilibrium, at point *e* in both panels, union and nonunion wages are initially W_0. If the union successfully restricts supply to S_1 in Panel A, union wages will rise to W_1, but employment will fall to L_1 (point *a*). Those workers released will have no choice but to move to the nonunion sector represented in Panel B, thus increasing its supply to S_2. Equilibrium in the nonunion sector thus moves to point *b*, where more workers (L_2) are employed at a lower wage (W_2). The result is a wage differential equal to $W_1 - W_2$.

with significant pricing power, and in which labor costs are a small fraction of total costs. Under such conditions, it is simply not worth it for a firm to fight union demands for a few extra positions.

Union–nonunion wage differentials vary by the union, occupation, industry, and historical period. In the 1980s and 1990s, the average union wage was 10% to 20% higher than the average nonunion wage.[15] Union wage effects are most pronounced among blue-collar workers, private sector employees (as opposed to public employees), younger workers, and those with the least education.[16] These results suggest that unionization may tend to reduce the inequities inherent in labor markets.

Evolving Labor Markets and Issues

Labor markets, like all other markets, change with time and the wishes of their participants. Over the last three decades, the entry of women into the labor force has been a major factor spurring economic growth. Over this same period, two-earner families increased so that today over half of all families with small children are two-earner households.

[15]David Blanchflower, "Changes Over Time in Union Relative Wage Effects in Great Britain and the United States," NBER Working Paper 6100, July 1997.

[16]Kaufman and Hotchkiss, *The Economics of Labor Markets,* pp. 632–635.

These demographic changes have shifted the focus of labor politics from union bargaining to issues such as telecommuting, family leave policies, affirmative action, and the question of how much employers should pay for medical benefits. As Social Security begins to look more fragile and the baby boomers begin flooding the retirement ranks, employer retirement packages will undoubtedly receive even more attention.

Immigration, legal and illegal, has caught the attention of labor economists. The United States, unlike Europe, has relatively open borders. Some argue that we need new immigrants to do the work that most Americans are unwilling to do. Other economists suggest that, in the absence of such inflows, salaries in these low-skill occupations would be high enough to attract the needed labor. In any case, immigrants are doing what they have done for centuries: entering the economy at lower-skill levels, hoping that circumstances will be better for their children.

This great tide of immigrants into low-skilled, low-wage jobs, together with the growth of high-skilled, high-wage, high-tech jobs, and the rise in dual-earner households, has resulted in growing income inequality. Executive pay scales compared to average salaries have exploded in the last decade. These pressures have renewed the debate surrounding income distribution and the welfare system. We discuss these issues in more detail in a later chapter.

Checkpoint
Labor Unions and Collective Bargaining

REVIEW

- Unions are typically organized around a craft or an industry.
- Unions and the managers of firms must bargain "in good faith."
- Secondary boycotts occur when unions put pressure on a neutral second firm to not process the products of the intended target. They were outlawed by the Taft-Hartley Act.
- In a closed shop, only union members are hired. In a union shop, nonunion workers can be hired, but they must join the union within a specified time period. An agency shop permits both union and nonunion workers, but the nonunion workers must pay union dues.
- Union wage differentials empirically are between 10% and 20%, depending on the industry.

QUESTION

Union negotiations seem to always run up against a "strike deadline." Are there incentives for both sides to put off a settlement until the very last moment?

Answers to the Checkpoint question can be found at the end of this chapter.

Unions in the 21st Century: Pledge Cards, Neutrality Agreements, and Organizing Success

As if declining membership wasn't enough trouble for labor, in the summer of 2005 several big unions broke away from the AFL-CIO in a disagreement over whether extensive political involvement or a focus on organizing new members was the best long-run strategy for the union movement. The breakaway unions, essentially led by the Service Employees International Union (SEIU), want to emphasize organizing new members and they are fighting with new strategies.

Under the National Labor Relations Act, the union creation process starts with pledge cards. Either employees of a non-union firm contact a union or a union contacts employees of a firm and offers to represent them. Interest in a union is revealed by employees signing pledge cards. Nothing official occurs until employee "interest" in a union is shown by obtaining pledge cards from 30% of employees. A petition is then filed with the NLRB, and a secret ballot is held. This often results in a heavily contested brawl with employers, and unions typically will win well below half of the elections. As a result, unions employ new strategies and tactics that emphasize "pledge card check recognition," neutrality agreements, public relations, and advertising to win new members.

Pledge cards are index size cards that workers sign indicating that they would like to have a union represent them. Before organizing begins, unions approach employers for voluntary recognition if more than 50% of workers sign pledge cards. If employers insist on following NLRB election certification rules, the union tries to get employers to sign neutrality agreements whereby employers are restricted from actively campaigning against union recognition.

Now, why would an employer want to voluntarily recognize a union or agree to remain neutral during the election campaign? Here's where the second half of the union's new tactics, the "corporate campaign," comes into play. Firms who refuse the unions' overtures will face public relations and advertising campaigns to harm their corporate image and grassroots community opposition to new facilities, mergers, or requests for regulatory relief (à la Wal-Mart).[17]

These tactics have proven quite successful. When unions get neutrality agreements signed, the organizational success rate climbs to 45%; when card check agreements are added, the union success rate exceeds 75% of their attempts to organize. In 2006, janitors at the University of Miami staged walkouts, sit-ins, and hunger strikes to get the university service contractor to agree to pledge card recognition if the union got 60% of the workers to sign cards, thus avoiding a secret ballot election. Some students supported the janitors. During the walkout, the service contractor increased wage rates one third at the request of the university. Media attention was directed at university President Donna Shalala, the former Clinton Administration's Secretary of Health and Human Services, who tried to keep neutral. In the end, the service contractor agreed to the union's demands.

These strategies are effective. With labor union membership such a small fraction of the workforce, unions are using these new tactics to increase membership and influence.

Key Concepts

Investment in human capital, p. 310
Screening/signaling, p. 315
On-the-job training, p. 315
General training, p. 315
Specific training, p. 315
Economic discrimination, p. 319
Segmented labor markets, p. 321
Comparable worth, p. 324
Secondary boycott, p. 329
Closed shop, p. 329
Union shop, p. 329
Agency shop, p. 329
Right-to-work laws, p. 329

[17]See "Unions Favor Card Check Recognition in Organizing," *National Law Journal,* January 10, 2005; and Timothy Aeppel, "Not-So-Big Labor Enlists New Methods For Greater Leverage," *Wall Street Journal,* August 29, 2005, p. A2.

Chapter Summary

Investment in Human Capital

Workers invest in themselves by going to school or learning a trade. Firms invest in workers through OJT or in-house training for employees. The value of these activities can be analyzed using investment analysis.

Investments in education involve the direct costs of education and foregone earnings. The benefits of such investments are then spread over the individual's working life. Human capital analysis uses present value calculations to determine the return to human capital investment.

Anything that reduces the availability of funds will reduce investments in human capital. The demand for human capital, meanwhile, is influenced by an individual's abilities and learning capacity. Human capital improves an individual's productivity, thereby resulting in higher lifetime earnings. Productivity thus links education and earnings.

Some economists suggest that investments in human capital do little more than serve as screening or signaling devices for employers. With this view, a college degree is merely a proxy for trainability, discipline, good work habits, and intelligence.

On-the-job training falls into two categories: general and specific training. General training improves productivity at all firms, while specific training improves productivity only at one specific firm. Firms will rarely provide general training; workers must get this training on their own. Firms will, however, provide specific training if the returns are high enough.

Economic Discrimination

Economic discrimination occurs whenever workers of equal ability and productivity are paid different wages or otherwise discriminated against in the workplace because of their race, color, religion, gender, age, national origin, or disability. Lower wages, segregation into different occupations, and restrictions on entry into professions are all examples of economic discrimination.

Gary Becker offered an account of economic discrimination that assumes employers have a taste for discrimination. Becker concluded that employers who discriminate lose profit opportunities, so competitive pressures should end this discrimination. Competitive forces, however, may not be enough to end discrimination because of the significant costs associated with hiring and firing and otherwise restructuring a firm's workforce. Some workers, moreover, are less mobile than others. If this is true of a group of workers, such as women, this could lead to wage differences that are not clearly discriminatory.

Another approach to analyzing economic discrimination in labor markets rests on the existence of segmented markets. Various forces can segment workers from different groups into different, noncompeting sectors of the labor market. The labor market can be split into primary and secondary markets (the dual labor market hypothesis); it can be broken into predominately male and female jobs (the job crowding hypothesis); or it can be split into union or non-union or unemployed workers (insider-outsider theory). All these approaches predict separate job markets and different wages for different groups.

Public policies and laws have been enacted to counter economic discrimination. These include the Equal Pay Act of 1963, Civil Rights Act of 1964, Executive Order 11246 on affirmative action, Age Discrimination in Employment Act of 1967, and Americans With Disabilities Act of 1990.

Labor Unions and Collective Bargaining

Labor unions are legal associations of employees formed to bargain collectively with employers over the terms and conditions of employment.

Collective bargaining provides workers with increased job security, a more structured work environment, and potentially higher wages. The benefits of unionization, however, do not come free. Monthly dues must be paid to the union, flexibility on the job is often restricted, and infrequently strikes are required, resulting in a loss of wages and possible job loss.

A closed shop requires workers to be members of a union before they can be hired. A union shop permits union and nonunion hires, but requires new employees to join the union within a specified time period. In an agency shop, employees are not required to join the union, but they must pay union dues to reimburse the union for its services. The Taft-Hartley Act of 1947 outlawed the closed shop and permitted states to pass right-to-work statutes that prohibit union shops.

Questions and Problems

1. Would unions be more likely to successfully organize firms in highly competitive markets or firms with monopsony power? Why or why not?

2. When a company uses resources to train staff or subsidize tuition for employees, it is clearly investing in human capital. However, this investment is treated as current spending (cost of selling or producing goods) rather than investment. Should these activities be treated as investments and be reflected in the investment statistics of the economy?

3. Why do we all work Monday through Friday? Why not stagger the workweek and reduce highway congestion and pollution?

4. Americans work on average 400 hours more (roughly 10 weeks) each year than German or French workers. What might be some of the reasons for this?

5. Two decades ago, General Motors, Chrysler, and Ford were the top firms in an aging oligopolistic auto industry. Profits seemed secure. During negotiations with the UAW, all three gave their workers wage and benefit packages that cannot be sustained in today's rapidly changing highly competitive auto markets. General Motors agreed to provide full pay for all laid-off workers until they are recalled to work (known as the Job Bank). After seeing its market share fall from 50% to 25% in three decades, General Motors in 2006 offered buyouts to employees that ranged from $35,000 to $140,000 depending on how long they had been with the company. What can the UAW do to help these companies and their employees get through this tough competitive patch and remain as viable competitors?

6. Has globalization made it more difficult for unions to negotiate higher wages? Why or why not?

7. We saw in the previous chapter that wage rates rose when productivity rose. Unions now face serious foreign competition that restricts its ability to simply use its bargaining strength to increase wages. What can unions do to increase the productivity of its members to make it easier to bargain for higher wages?

8. Why are colleges filled with young people rather than middle-aged individuals? If interest rates rose to over 10%, would this have any impact on the number of people attending college or its composition?

9. Does it seem reasonable that a certain portion of the benefits of a college education is essentially a way to show prospective employers that you are reasonably intelligent, trainable, and have a certain degree of discipline?

10. Some politicians during any election campaign offer proposals to make college more affordable by increasing subsidies through higher Pell grants and subsidizing reduced rate loans. If these policies come to pass, and college becomes less expensive, more people will attend college. What will this do to the rate of return on a college education?

11. If unions can raise wages 10%–20%, as suggested by the empirical studies, why doesn't everyone join a union?

12. The airline pilots union has been very successful in negotiating six-figure salaries for pilots. The unions representing flight attendants have not been nearly as successful. What probably accounts for the difference?

13. Why would it be so difficult to unionize part-time and contract employees (independent contractors)?

14. When there is discrimination in the labor market, who loses? Why? Why is it harder to discriminate when both labor and product markets are competitive?

15. Why do we permit price discrimination with different ticket prices at movies based on age, or ladies' nights at bars, when women get in free or get cheaper drinks, or insurance where women sometimes pay more (health) or less (automobile), but we do not permit discrimination in wage rates?

Answers to Checkpoint Questions

CHECKPOINT: INVESTMENT IN HUMAN CAPITAL

Letting in a large number of college-educated immigrants would drive the rate of return on college down as wages of college graduates would not grow very rapidly. The opposite would occur when unskilled immigrants enter, holding down the wages of those without college educations, leading to a growing gap between those with college degrees, increasing the rate of return to a college degree.

CHECKPOINT: ECONOMIC DISCRIMINATION

Congress knew that most people who were discriminated against were poor and could not afford an attorney. This provision encourages lawyers to take on these cases knowing that if they prevail, they will be paid.

CHECKPOINT: LABOR UNIONS AND COLLECTIVE BARGAINING

Both sides work hard to get the best bargain for their constituents. There are incentives to continue negotiations up to the last moment to get the most and to appear to be driving a hard bargain. Strikes involve costs, and both sides use the threat of imposing these costs as a bargaining chip.

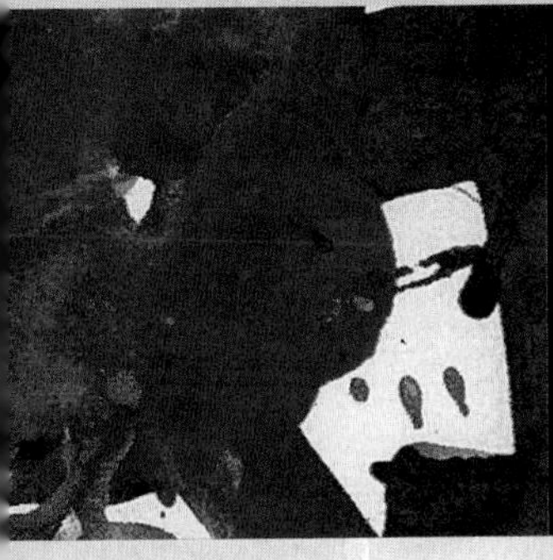

13 Public Goods, Common Resources, and Externalities

We humans are about as subtle as the asteroid that wiped out the dinosaurs. . . . The damage we do is increasing. In the next 20 years, the population will increase by 1.5 billion. These people will need food, water and electricity, but already our soils are vanishing, fisheries are being killed off, wells are drying up, and the burning of fossil fuels is endangering the lives of millions. We are heading for cataclysm.

April 2001 Global Supplement from *New Scientist*

Psychologically, the population explosion first sunk in on a stinking hot night in Delhi. The streets were alive with people. People eating, people washing themselves, people sleeping, people working, arguing and screaming. People reaching their hands in through taxi windows to beg. People sitting, people pissing. People hanging off buses. People driving animals through the streets. People, people, people.

Paul Ehrlich, *The Population Bomb,* 1968

This is my long-run forecast in brief: The material conditions of life will continue to get better for most people, in most countries, most of the time, indefinitely. Within a century or two, all nations and most of humanity will be at or above today's western living standards. I also speculate, however, that many people will continue to think and say that the conditions of life are getting worse.

Julian Simon (1932–98)

At its most basic, all environmental policy involves a rearrangement of property rights.

Charles Pearson

As the quotes on the previous page illustrate, people have radically different ideas about how well we live and what impact human existence is having on the globe. Many environmentalists and others see the Earth as wasting away as human beings exhaust its natural resources, foul its air and water, and decimate animal species. Others optimistically regard advancing technologies, newfound efficiencies, and rising standards of living as signs that people are taking ever better care of the planet.

In 1980, Julian Simon offered the following bet

> *This is a public offer to stake $10,000, in separate transactions of $1,000 or $100 each, on my belief that mineral resources (or food or other commodities) will not rise in price in future years adjusted for inflation. You choose any mineral or other raw material (including grain and fossil fuels) that is not government controlled, and the date of settlement.*

The bet was an open offer, but Simon aimed it at environmental activist Paul Ehrlich, author of *The Population Bomb.* Ehrlich and two other Stanford University colleagues accepted the bet in October 1980, selecting copper, chrome, nickel, tin, and tungsten for a 10-year period. Ehrlich noted that he would "accept Simon's astonishing offer before other greedy people jumped in," since the "lure of easy money can be irresistible."[1]

Ten years later, in October 1990, Ehrlich sent Simon a check for $576.07. The real value (adjusted for inflation) of the basket of minerals had gone down over the decade by $576.07. New sources of supply had been discovered, the tin cartel collapsed during the intervening period, and other minerals had become substitutes for some in the original five. Not only had the value of the five resources declined, the price of each one of the metals had fallen. Simon offered the same bet again, but Ehrlich declined.

Are there lessons to be drawn from this bet? Surely one is that forecasting economic and market conditions far into the future is difficult, at best. Another is that overly pessimistic predictions about growth and the environment almost always turn out to be wrong.[2] It is true that the Earth is finite in size, and the natural resources it contains are limited. Even so, economic growth is often accompanied by increasing efficiencies in resource use. Rising incomes and standards of living, moreover, are typically accompanied by falling population growth rates. Were it not for immigration, population would be declining in the United States today.

Many trends involving living standards and the environment are moving in the right direction, yet that does not mean all is well. Clearly, we still have many environmental problems that must be addressed, including global climate change, species extinction, overharvesting of fisheries, and overcrowding of our highways and parks at the national level.

Environmental economics is a discipline that applies the principles and methods of economics to the study of the environment and natural resources. This marriage of economics and the environment may seem like a stretch to some, but economists must already deal with the environment regularly; environmental and natural resources are frequently inputs into economic production, and at times are economic products or services. Resources such as coal, iron, and oil, for instance, are extracted from the Earth and moved directly into the production process. National parks and the restrictions on their use, meanwhile, show that the natural environment is itself a product that has value to us.

---

[1]Bjorn Lomborg, *The Skeptical Environmentalist: Measuring the Real State of the World* (Cambridge: Cambridge University Press), 2001, p. 137.

[2]Both Simon's book *The Ultimate Resource 2* and Lomborg's book *The Skeptical Environmentalist* provide numerous examples.

After studying this chapter you should be able to

- Describe the market failures that lead to environmental problems.
- Describe the impact of negative and positive externalities on society.
- Describe the Coase theorem on social costs and the role transaction costs play in the optimal allocation of resources.
- Describe government failures in dealing with market failures.
- Recognize the importance of the discount rate in assessing the costs and benefits of environmental policies.
- Use marginal analysis to determine the optimal level of pollution.
- Describe the differences between command and control policies and market-based approaches to environmental regulation.

Market Failure

Market failure occurs when a market does not provide the socially optimal amount of a good at the socially optimal price. Either too much or too little of the good is produced, or it is offered at too high or too low a price. Before we dive into our discussion of how market failures can lead to environmental problems, let us first briefly review the concepts of consumer and producer surplus. These two concepts are often used to measure the impact environmental policies have on social welfare.

A Brief Refresher on Producer and Consumer Surplus

Recall that demand curves represent, in dollar terms, the utility consumers receive from a given product. Supply curves represent the marginal cost to producers of producing goods and services; a supply curve similarly represents the opportunity cost to society of producing and distributing a given product. Figure 1 on the next page depicts a market for a product that has no environmental impacts. The supply curve thus represents the full marginal cost to society of producing this product.

Consumer Surplus

Equilibrium in Figure 1 is found at point e, where Q_e units are sold at price P_e. The area under the demand curve, $0P_1eQ_e$, is the total utility consumers derive from consuming Q_e units of the product. Consumers, however, pay only $0P_eeQ_e$, and thus area P_eP_1e is **consumer surplus**. When we look at changes in environmental policy, monitoring changes in consumer surplus will help us measure the gains or losses to consumers from policy changes.

Consumer surplus
The difference between what consumers (as individuals or the market) would be willing to pay and the market price. It is equal to the area above market price and below the demand curve.

FIGURE 1

Consumer and Producer Surplus

The product in this market has no environmental impacts. The supply curve therefore represents the full marginal costs to society of producing this product. The area under the demand curve, $0P_1eQ_e$, is the total utility consumers derive from consuming Q_e units of the product. Consumers, however, pay only $0P_eeQ_e$, and thus area P_eP_1e is consumer surplus. The total cost for manufacturers to produce Q_e units of output is $0P_0eQ_e$, yet firms receive total revenue equal to $0P_eeQ_e$; thus, area P_0P_ee represents producer surplus. Total social welfare is equal to consumer surplus plus producer surplus; it is represented by area P_0P_1e.

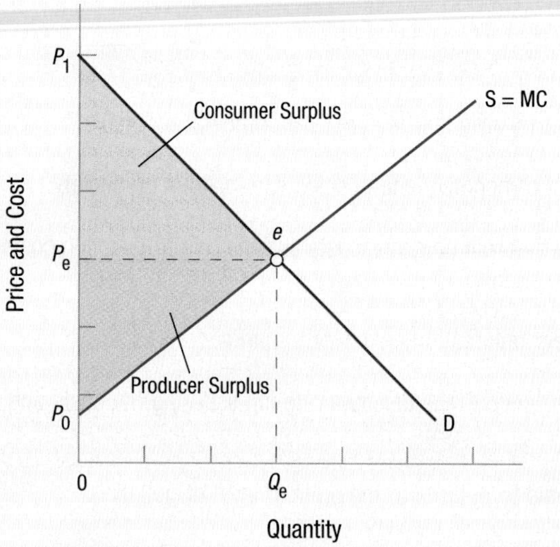

Producer surplus
The difference between market price and the price at which firms would be willing to supply the product. It is equal to the area below market price and above the supply curve.

Social welfare
The sum of consumer and producer surplus.

Market failures
When markets are not competitive or involve public goods, externalities, or common property resources, markets will fail to provide the optimal level of output, and will provide output at too high or low a price.

Public goods
Goods that, once provided, no one person can be excluded from consuming (i.e., nonexclusion), and one person's consumption does not diminish the benefit to others from consuming the good (i.e., nonrivalry).

Nonrivalry
The consumption of a good or service by one person does not reduce the utility of that good or service to others.

Nonexcludability
Once a good or service is provided it is not feasible to exclude others from enjoying that good or service.

Producer Surplus

The total cost for manufacturers to produce Q_e units of output is $0P_0eQ_e$, the area under the marginal cost curve. Yet, firms receive revenue equal to $0P_eeQ_e$; thus, area P_0P_ee represents **producer surplus,** the revenue firms get over the costs they would willingly bear to supply the product.

Social Welfare

Social welfare is equal to consumer surplus plus producer surplus. This is the value produced over what would be required for the product to be brought to market; it is represented by area P_0P_1e. This is often referred to as the net welfare resulting from the production and consumption of this product. An activity or policy that increases net welfare is considered efficient.

Markets provide us with most of the products and services we consume. Under competitive conditions, as we have seen, markets will provide consumers with what they want at the lowest possible opportunity costs. In what follows, we will examine some of the reasons why a competitive market allocation may not always be the best solution for society. These reasons all fall under the heading of **market failures,** and they underpin our environmental laws and regulations.

As noted earlier, market failure occurs when a market does not provide the socially optimal amount of a good at the socially optimal price. Either too much or too little of the good is produced, or it is offered at too high or too low a price. There are three main causes of market failure: The product or service in question is a *public good,* the good is a *common property resource,* or the production or consumption of the product or service creates *externalities.*

Public Goods

Pure **public goods** are nonrival in consumption, and exhibit nonexcludability. **Nonrivalry** means that the consumption of a good or service by one person does not reduce the utility of that good or service to others. **Nonexcludability** means that it is not feasible to exclude some consumers from using the good or service once it has been provided.

By way of contrast, a can of Coke is a rival product. When you drink a can of Coke, no one else can drink that same can. Airline flights exhibit excludability—when a flight is full, no one else is allowed to board the plane. But consider a lighthouse. Once it is built and in operation, all ships can see the lighthouse and use the light to avoid obstacles. One captain's use of the lighthouse does not prevent another from using it, nor can a ship realistically be excluded from using the lighthouse's services. Hence, the lighthouse is a public good. Other examples of public goods include national defense, accumulated knowledge, standards such as a national currency, protection of property rights, vaccinations, mosquito spraying, and clean air. Table 1 provides a taxonomy of private and public goods.

Table 1 **Taxonomy of Private and Public Goods**

	Property Rights	
Characteristics of Goods	**Exclusive**	**Nonexclusive**
Rival	Pure private good • Airline seat • Ice cream bar	Common property resource • Ocean fishery • Highways
Nonrival	Public good with exclusion • Cable TV • National park	Pure public good • National defense • Law enforcement

Since consumers cannot be excluded from a public good once it is provided, they have little incentive to pay for the good in question. Instead, most will essentially be free riders. Think of the lighthouse again. If you have a ship and cannot be excluded from the benefits the lighthouse provides, why should you contribute anything to its upkeep? But if everyone took this position, there would be no support for the lighthouse, and it would go out of business. With free riders, private producers cannot hope to sell many units of a good, and so they have no incentive to produce it. Private markets will therefore fail to provide public goods, even if the goods are things everyone would like to see produced. This is why the government must get involved in the provision of products and services that have significant public good characteristics.

The Demand for Public Goods

Assessing the public's demand for public goods is clearly different from that of private goods where we found market demand by horizontally summing private demands. But the fact that once a public good is supplied, no one can be excluded from consuming, and one person's consumption does not affect another's, plays a crucial role. Figure 2 on the next page provides a solution to finding the demand for public goods.

Figure 2 shows demand for a public good by two different consumers. Individual A wants none when the price is $40 and is willing and able to buy 40 units when the price approaches zero. Individual B wants none when price is $60 and only is willing to buy 30 units when the price nears zero. Because each consumer can consume any given amount of a public good at the same time, the total demand for a public good is found by summing the individual demands *vertically.* To see why, consider when both individuals demand 20 units. This is the point where the two demand curves cross, and both are willing to pay $20 for 20 units. Thus, total demand for 20 units is $40. The total demand for the public good in Figure 2 is shown by

FIGURE 2

Demand for Public Goods: Vertical Summation of Individual Demand Curves

For public goods, exclusion is not possible, individuals can consume the good simultaneously, and market demand is found by summing vertically. Market demand for public goods is really a willingness to pay curve since the government will have to provide the good and levy taxes to pay the cost. Because each consumer can consume any given amount of a public good at the same time. The total demand for the public good is shown by the heavy line labeled $D_{\text{Public Goods}}$ and is the vertical summation of individual demands.

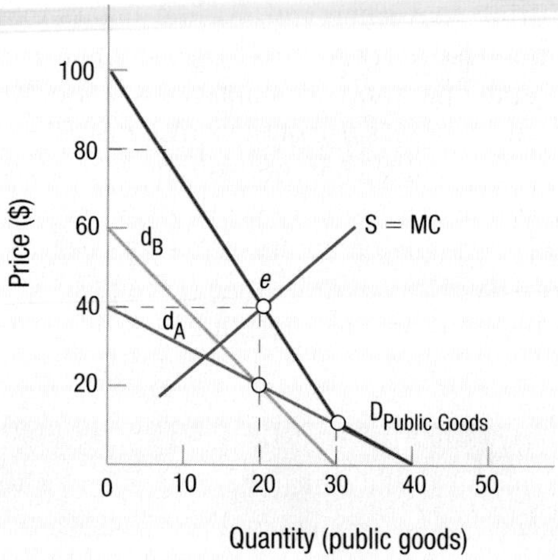

the heavy line labeled $D_{\text{Public Goods}}$ and is the vertical summation of individual demands.

Notice how this differs from our discussion of market demand curves for private goods. There others could be excluded from consuming any good we bought, so demands were horizontally summed. In contrast, with public goods, exclusion is not possible, so we both can consume the good simultaneously, and market demand is found by summing vertically. Market demand for public goods is really a *willingness to pay curve,* because the government will have to provide the good and levy taxes to pay the cost.

Optimal Provision of Public Goods

Providing the optimal amount of public goods is easy in theory and is illustrated in Figure 2. The supply of public goods is equal to the marginal cost curve (S = MC) shown in the figure. Just like the competitive market equilibrium we covered earlier, optimal allocation is where MC = P, and in this instance, it is 20 units of the good at a total price of $40 (point *e*). In this example, the taxes are split equally between individuals A and B. Determining how much tax each person should (or would be willing to) pay is hampered by the fact that once the public good is provided, no one can be excluded, so individuals will be unwilling to reveal their true preferences for the good because it might mean they would have to pay a higher tax.

Cost-benefit analysis A methodology for decision making that looks at the discounted value of the costs and benefits of a given project.

In reality, providing public goods involves the political process. This means that politicians, bureaucrats, special interest groups, and many others generate the decisions on how much of any particular public good to provide. The typical provision process uses some form of **cost-benefit analysis** (CBA). Since the demand for a public good represents the benefits to society and the supply curve represents society's costs, equating marginal benefits and marginal costs yields the optimal amount. But estimating the demand (benefits) from public goods and their costs can be a complex process. Since people cannot be excluded from the good, once provided, people have little incentive to reveal their demand curve. Cost-benefit analysis was developed to help policymakers bridge this gap. The following section is a brief overview of CBA to give you an idea of the issues involved.

Cost-Benefit Analysis

Cost-benefit methodology was introduced into the Flood Control Act of 1936 and eventually grew more sophisticated; by 1960, it became an important element of the decision making process of the Office of Management and Budget (OMB). The OMB's circular A-94 provides a straightforward summary of what CBA is designed to accomplish:

> *The standard criterion for deciding whether a government program can be justified on economic principles is net present value—the discounted monetized value of expected net benefits (i.e., benefits minus costs). Net present value is computed by assigning monetary values to benefits and costs, discounting future benefits and costs using an appropriate discount rate, and subtracting the sum total of discounted costs from the sum total of discounted benefits. Discounting benefits and costs transforms gains and losses occurring in different time periods to a common unit of measurement. Programs with positive net present value increase social resources and are generally preferred. Programs with negative net present value should generally be avoided. Although net present value is not always computable (and it does not usually reflect effects on income distribution), efforts to measure it can produce useful insights even when the monetary values of some benefits or costs cannot be determined.*

Cost-benefit analysis provides a rational model for policy decisions, forces a focus on alternatives—opportunity costs, draws conclusions about the optimal *scale* of projects, makes the intergenerational aspects explicit through discounting, and takes into account the explicit preferences of individuals. The explicit steps of a CBA are:[3]

- Specify the set of alternative projects.
- Decide whose benefits and costs count (the standing question).
- Catalogue the impacts and select measurement indicators.
- Predict the impacts quantitatively over the life of the project.
- Monetize (attach dollar values to) all impacts.
- Discount benefits and costs to obtain present values.
- Compute the net present value of each alternative.
- Perform sensitivity analysis (change some variables to see impacts).

One of the major difficulties with CBA for big public projects and environmental programs is measuring nonmarket or intangible aspects of projects. Economists have developed several different approaches to measuring these intangibles.[4] Some environmental goods have a bundle of characteristics, and some of them resemble market traded goods, so determining values in this way provides an estimate. Another approach looks at the travel costs people incur to recreational sites. The operating assumption is that these costs infer something about the value of parks and other recreational sites. Another approach is to look to the funds and effort people expend to avert harm. If you live by an airport and install double-pane glass to reduce noise, or purchase safety equipment (helmets, car seats, or bigger automobiles) to avoid injury from auto accidents, you are providing some evidence of the value (cost) of the harm.

A more controversial method is contingent valuation. This method uses direct surveys to determine the value of such environmental qualities as species and

[3]Anthony E. Boardman et al., *Cost-Benefit Analysis: Concepts and Practice* (Upper Saddle River, NJ: Pearson-Prentice Hall), 2006, p. 8.

[4]Organisation for Economic Co-operation and Development, *Cost-Benefit Analysis and the Environment* (OECD), 2006.

forest preservation, biodiversity, and water quality projects. Those surveyed are provided an open-ended willingness-to-pay question or an iterative bidding questionnaire. The open-ended approach might ask how much you would pay (in increased taxes) to keep the Preble's meadow jumping mouse from going extinct. The iterative approach provides an initial value: If you agree with that number, then the number is iteratively increased until you say no; if you initially answer no, the number is reduced until you express willingness to pay. The numbers are then aggregated by the population to get total values.

Cost-benefit analysis, then, is a rational approach to valuing some things that are hard to put a price on, because people have no incentive to reveal their willingness to pay. This is what makes the decision to provide public goods so difficult.

Common Property Resources

Common property resources Resources that are owned by the community at large (e.g., parks, ocean fish, and the atmosphere) and therefore tend to be overexploited because individuals have little incentive to use them in a sustainable fashion.

The second main cause of market failure occurs when a good is a **common property resource.** Commonly held resources are subject to nonexclusion but are rival in consumption. The market failure associated with commonly owned properties is often referred to as "the tragedy of the commons."[5] The tragedy here is the tendency for commonly held resources to be overused and overexploited. Because the resource is held in common, individuals will all race to "get theirs" before others can grab it all.

One example of commonly held resources giving rise to problems involves oil fields. Oil reservoirs often span the surface property of many landowners. Because oil reservoirs are regarded as common property, each surface owner has an incentive to drill as many wells as possible and to pump out oil as rapidly as possible. Having too many wells pumping too quickly, however, reduces the oil field's water and gas pressure, thus reducing the total recoverable oil from the reservoir. Each owner's decision to drill a well therefore imposes an external cost on the other owners of land over the reservoir. At one point, this problem grew so severe that it resulted in passage of the 1935 Connolly "Hot Oil" Act. This act restricted drilling, regulated the number and location of oil wells, and capped pumping rates.[6]

Rodez/Getty Images

Tragedy of the Commons: The Perfect Fish

Ocean fisheries are another good example of the problem of common property resources. Fish in the ocean were once in excess supply; there was no need to restrict the use of this resource. As the global demand for fish has risen, improved fishing technologies have allowed fishing boats to increase their hauls. Because many of the world's fisheries are still unregulated, one population after another has been fished out. Each fishing fleet grabbed as much as they could, and there was no incentive to hold back. The situation is clearly unsustainable, and indeed, as fish populations have shrunk, so have fishing fleets.

The Patagonian toothfish, as it is known, lives up to 50 years and can weigh over 200 pounds. This big, ugly, gray-black fish lives in the cold deep waters of the Southern Ocean near Antarctica, and in the 1990s, it became the signature dish of top restaurants in the United States, Japan, and Europe. It became so popular that during the mid-1990s, the annual catch was estimated at 100,000 metric tons.

How did such an ugly fish with such a unappetizing name become so popular? In the late 1970s, Lee Lantz, a Los Angeles fish merchant, visited the docks in Valparaiso, Chile, and spotted a toothfish. He bought a sample and cooked it, but the oily flesh had little taste. Most fish have bladders that they inflate to adjust their buoyancy, reducing the energy it takes to move up and down in the water. Toothfish do not have bladders, but use oil (lighter than water) secreted to create buoyancy. Also, Patagonian toothfish are predators, waiting in ambush for prey. Thus,

[5]Hardin, Garrett, "The Tragedy of the Commons," *Science,* 162: 1243–1248, 1968.
[6]Daniel Yergin, *The Prize* (New York: Simon & Schuster), 1991.

they do not need a lot of blood rushing through their system. As a result, toothfish meat is oily and white like cod. It is this oiliness—along with the fact that it absorbed any spice—that made the toothfish a hit with restaurants. No matter what you do, you can't overcook it, and this made it a hit with busy restaurateurs and chefs.

As the reputation of the toothfish spread, so did the take in the ocean. Because this fish is found in the Southern Ocean, where it is cold and where few venture, it was highly susceptible to poaching. A full hold of toothfish could bring a million dollars wholesale!

Soon it became clear to many that the species was being seriously overharvested, and chefs began to notice that the filets were getting smaller. The tragedy of the commons was playing out again. So the chefs from the best restaurants organized a boycott campaign called "Take a Pass on Chilean Sea Bass." The Patagonian toothfish found fame and near extinction after being renamed Chilean Sea Bass by Lee Lantz in 1977.

Today, limits are set on the catch, and Chilean Sea Bass is coming back from the brink. But as G. Bruce Knecht reported in his book *Hooked,* keeping pirates from poaching the toothfish is a dangerous job for the Australian Customs patrols.[7] The toothfish's problem is that it is the perfect fish.

Highway Congestion

Road congestion provides yet another illustration of the tragedy of the commons. Figure 3 shows a market for usage of a road that is fully used and is right at the tipping point before becoming congested. In Figure 3, demand for driving on this road is D_0, and the marginal cost to use the road—gas, time, and auto expenses—is initially MC_0. Equilibrium is at point *e,* with Q_0 miles per day driven. Consumer surplus is area P_0ae for the typical driver.

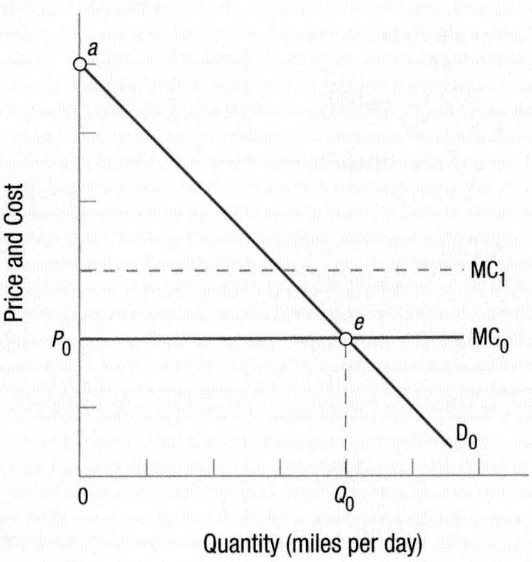

FIGURE 3

Road Congestion

Assume this road is fully used and is right at the tipping point before becoming congested. Demand for driving on this road is D_0, and the marginal cost of using the road—gas, time, and auto expenses—is MC_0. Equilibrium is at point *e,* with Q_0 miles a day being driven. Consumer surplus is area P_0ae for the typical driver. Now assume a new driver begins using the road. This increases the marginal cost of driving to MC_1 for everyone, since the tipping point has been passed, and the road is now congested. Consumer surplus shrinks because of overuse of this common good.

Now assume a new driver begins using the road. This increases the marginal costs of driving to MC_1 for everyone, since the tipping point has been passed, and the road is now congested. Consumer surplus shrinks because of overuse of the commons. Note that the new driver did not take these external costs into consideration; the driver assumed that MC would be equal to MC_0, not MC_1.

[7]G. Bruce Knecht, *Hooked: Pirates, Poaching, and the Perfect Fish* (Emmaus, PA: Rodale), 2006.

Possible solutions to common property resource problems can involve establishing private property rights or using government policy to restrict access to, or reduce the demand for, the common resource. Reduced congestion, for example, could be achieved by raising the tax on gasoline, subsidizing bus or rapid transit travel, or privatizing roads and allowing the owners to charge tolls.

Externalities

Externalities
The impact on third parties of some transaction between others where the third parties are not involved. An external cost (or negative externality) harms the third parties, whereas external benefits (positive externalities) result in gains to them.

Externalities, often called *spillovers,* arise when two parties engage in a transaction, yet some third party uninvolved in the transaction either benefits or is harmed. If the market exchange imposes costs on others, it is called a *negative externality* or an *external cost.* If a third party benefits, this is a *positive externality* or an *external benefit.* Negative externalities include air and water pollution, littering, and chemical runoff that affect fish stocks. Some examples of activities that generate *positive externalities* are education, bee hives next to apple orchards, and quieter lawn equipment.

Both producers and consumers can create externalities and can feel the effects of them. The matrix in Table 2 identifies the origin and impact of some common external effects. The effects are negative unless otherwise noted.

Table 2 Externalities by Origin and Impact

Origin of Externality	Impact: Victims and Beneficiaries of Externality — Consumers	Impact: Victims and Beneficiaries of Externality — Producers
Consumers	• Auto air pollution • Littering • Park congestion • Smoking • Private schools and colleges (beneficial)	• Private auto use that adds to road congestion, slowing down commercial traffic
Producers	• Factory air pollution on wilderness hikers • Clear-cutting of forest trees • Agricultural pesticide runoff affecting trout fishing	• Honey bees and apple orchards (beneficial) • Commercial pollution that harms commercial fishing

Analysis of Negative Externalities

Again, when a market transaction harms people not involved in the transaction, negative externalities exist. Pollution of all sorts is the classic example. Firms and consumers rarely consider the impact their production or consumption will have on others. For simplicity, we focus on the pollution caused by production. Figure 4 shows a typical market.

Supply curve S_P represents the manufacturer's supply curve when only its private costs are considered (the subscript P stands for private). This supply curve ignores the external costs imposed on others from the pollution generated during production. These external costs might include toxic wastes dumped into lakes or streams, smokestack soot, or the clear cutting associated with timber harvests.

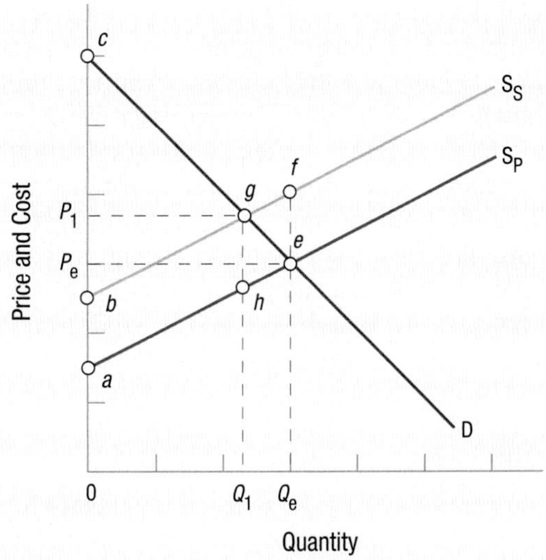

FIGURE 4

The Negative Externality Case

Supply curve S_P represents the manufacturer's supply curve when only its private costs are considered, ignoring the external costs imposed on others through pollution. Market equilibrium is at point *e,* where price is P_e and output is Q_e. If pollution costs equal to *ef* are generated for every unit produced, the true marginal cost to society, including pollution costs, of producing the product is equal to supply curve S_S. This new supply curve shifts supply upward by an amount equal to *ef,* thus moving equilibrium to point *g,* where less of the product is sold (Q_1) at a higher price (P_1). This is socially optimal production for this good, given the pollution it creates.

Ignoring these costs, market equilibrium is at point *e,* where the product is priced at P_e and output Q_e is sold.

Assume that for every unit of the product produced, pollution costs (or effluent) equal to *ef* is generated. This means the true marginal cost of producing the product, including pollution costs, is equal to supply curve S_S (the subscript S stands for social). This new supply curve incorporates both the private and social costs of production, thus shifting supply upward by an amount equal to *ef* (or $ab = gh$). Equilibrium moves to point *g,* where less of the product (Q_1) is sold at a higher price (P_1). This is the socially optimal production for this product, given the pollution it creates.

When output is Q_e, the total external costs from pollution are equal to area *abfe,* or pollution per unit of output (*ef*) times output Q_e. When output drops to Q_1, external costs fall to *abgh.* So why is Q_1 better for society than Q_e?

First, notice that when output is Q_1, the cost of the last unit produced—including the costs of pollution—is P_1 (point *g*). This is just equal to the value society attributes to the product. Hence, consumers get just what they want when all costs are considered.

Second, note that at Q_1, total consumer and producer surplus is equal to area *bcg.* At an output of Q_e, however, total private costs are $0aeQ_e$, and total pollution costs are *abfe,* which means total private and social costs are equal to area $0bfQ_e$. When output climbs to Q_e, consumer and producer surplus minus external costs ($ace - abfe$) is equal to area bcg – area *egf.* So at Q_1, total consumer and producer surplus is area *bcg,* but at Q_e, total consumer and producer surplus is area bcg – area *egf.* Therefore, consumer and producer surplus is greater at the lower output with the higher price.

When production grows from Q_1 to Q_e, social welfare is reduced by area *egf.* Each unit of output produced beyond Q_1 costs more—taking both private and social costs into account—than its value to consumers. For the last unit produced, Q_e, costs (including pollution) exceed benefits to society by an amount equal to *ef.* As a result, the total consumer and producer surplus is less when the costs of pollution are ignored.

Imagine a situation in which area *egf* is larger than area *bcg*. In this case, external costs (*egf*) exceed the consumer and producer surplus from consuming the good (*bcg*). Such an example might arise when an extremely toxic substance is a by-product of production. Society is better off not permitting production of this good.

What has this analysis shown? First, when negative externalities are present, an unregulated market will produce too much of a good at too low a price. Second, optimal pollution levels are not zero, except in the case just mentioned of extremely toxic agents. The socially optimal production is Q_1, with total pollution costs of *abgh,* pollution having been reduced by *hgfe* through a reduction in output from Q_e. Pollution reduction as a good has no price. Even so, we can infer a price, known as a shadow price, equal to the marginal damages—*ef* in this case. As we will later see, prices for "rights to pollute" will provide us with better approximations of the costs of pollution.

The Coase Theorem

Ronald Coase was awarded the Nobel Prize in economics for his seminal paper, "The Problem of Social Cost." Coase has written few articles—less than a dozen—but, as economist Robert Cooter noted, though "most economists maximize the amount they write, Coase maximized the amount others wrote about his work."[8] Indeed, Coase's paper on social cost is one of the most cited works in economics.

Figure 4 shows Coase's argument that reducing output to the optimal level (Q_1) results in gains to "victims" equal to area *hgfe.* Pollution is reduced by that much, in other words. The reduction in output, however, also causes producers and consumers to lose area *hge,* the change in producer and consumer surplus. The presence of losses and gains to two distinct parties, Coase argued, introduces the possibility of bargaining, provided the parties are awarded the property rights necessary for negotiation.

First, let us assume polluters are given the right to pollute. In this case, victims will be willing to pay polluters a sum of up to area *hgfe* to limit their production to Q_1. Polluters, meanwhile, will agree to accept any such payment larger than area *hge.* Clearly, this leaves some room for a bargain to be struck.

If victims are given the right to be free of pollution, producers and consumers will offer victims up to area *acgh*—their combined producer and consumer surpluses—for permission to produce Q_1. Victims, for their part, will accept anything greater than area *abgh,* the harm from pollution when Q_1 is produced. Again, since $acgh > abgh$, a bargain can be reached.

Coase theorem
If transaction costs are minimal (near zero), a bargain struck between beneficiaries and victims of externalities will be efficient from a resource allocation perspective. As a result, the socially optimal level of production will be reached, for example, whether polluters are given the right to pollute, or the victims are given the right to be free of pollution.

The **Coase theorem** states that if transaction costs are minimal (near zero), the resulting bargain or allocation of resources will be efficient—output will decline from Q_e to Q_1—regardless of the initial allocation of property rights. The socially optimal level of production will be reached, that is, no matter whether polluters are given the right to pollute or victims are given the right to be free of pollution.

Even so, the distribution of benefits or income will be different in these two cases. If victims, for example, are assigned the property rights, their income will grow by at least area *abgh,* but if polluters are assigned these rights, the income of victims will decline by at least area *hge.*

As Coase noted, for these efficient results to be achieved, transaction costs must approach zero. This means it must be possible for polluters and victims to accurately determine their collective interests, then negotiate and enforce an agreement. In many situations, however, this is simply not feasible. In cases involving air pollution, for instance, polluters and victims are so widely dispersed that negotiating is impracticable. In other cases, individuals may be both victims and polluters, making it difficult for an agreement to be reached and enforced.

[8] Peter Passell, "Economics Nobel to a Basic Thinker," *New York Times,* October 16, 1991, p. D6.

Nobel Prize Ronald Coase

University of Chicago professor Ronald Coase won the Nobel Prize in Economic Sciences in 1991 for "his discovery and clarification of the significance of transaction costs and property rights" in the institutional structure and functioning of the economy. According to his analysis, traditional microeconomic theory was incomplete because it neglected the costs of executing contracts and managing firms. To Coase, these "transaction costs" were the principal reason that firms existed. Economic actors found it cost efficient to create a more complex organization to minimize transaction costs.

Coase also analyzed the economy in terms of the *rights* to use goods and factors (inputs) of production rather than the actual goods and factors themselves. These "property rights" could be defined in different ways according to contracts and rules within organizations. Coase introduced the concept of property rights as an important element of economic analysis. His work stimulated interest in the intersection between economics and legal theory for which the University of Chicago is well-known.

Born in 1910 in Willesden, England, Coase attended the London School of Economics, where he earned a Bachelor of Commerce degree in 1932 and a Doctor of Science degree in economics in 1951. Coase later cited a seminar with the commerce professor Arnold Plant as a life-changing experience. "What Plant did was to introduce me to Adam Smith's hidden hand," he wrote. "He made me aware of how a competitive economic system could be coordinated by the pricing system."

Coase taught at the Dundee School of Economics, the University of Liverpool, and the London School of Economics before immigrating to the United States in 1951 and teaching at the University of Buffalo. Coase's article on the "Problem of Social Cost" questioned whether governments could efficiently allocate resources for social purposes through taxes and subsidies. Coase suggested that the best way to allocate finite resources such as broadcast frequencies was through the price system.

In 1964, Coase joined the faculty at the University of Chicago and became editor of the *Journal of Law and Economics.* The journal was an important catalyst in developing the economic interpretation of legal issues.

Another problem associated with assigning rights to one party or another might be called *environmental mugging.* Polluters might at first threaten to pollute more than they anticipate, for instance, simply to increase their bargaining leverage and, ultimately, their income. Victims, in like manner, might assert exaggerated environmental concerns, again simply to bid up their compensation. Alternately, if negotiations should prove unfruitful, polluters might start lobbying for legal relief, thus devoting their money to rent-seeking behaviors rather than buying pollution-abatement equipment.

Although the private negotiations Coase proposed have their limitations, his insights proved to be a turning point in environmental policy. Coase challenged the prevailing practice of assuming victims had a right to be pollution free. His analysis stressed that a clear assignment of rights and responsibilities by the law might not be needed. No matter how property rights were assigned, if information was good and transaction costs were low, efficiency would result. Given the costs of pollution, affected parties have an incentive to work out efficient agreements.

This idea was so radical when Coase published "The Problem of Social Cost" in 1960 that another Nobel Prize winner, George Stigler, wondered "how so fine an economist could make such an obvious mistake." Coase was later invited to the University of Chicago to discuss his ideas; Stigler described what transpired:

> *We strongly objected to this heresy. Milton Friedman did most of the talking, as usual. He also did much of the thinking, as usual. In the course of two hours of argument the vote went from twenty against and one for Coase to twenty-one for Coase. What an exhilarating event! I lamented afterward that we had not had the clairvoyance to tape it.*

The Coase theorem has changed the way economists look at many issues, not just environmental problems. In cases where the costs of negotiation are negligible and the number of parties involved is small, economists and jurists have begun to look more closely at legal rules assigning liability.

Monopolies and Negative Externalities

Monopolies are considered bad for consumers because they overcharge for their products and keep output below what competitive firms would have produced. Yet, when we take negative externalities into account, monopolies may not always be so bad. Figure 5 shows why.

Marginal cost curve MC and demand curve D here represent the supply and demand facing a competitive industry without consideration of negative externalities. Competitive equilibrium will be at point e, with output Q_c and price P_c. The monopolist, meanwhile, would equate MR and MC at point f, selling output Q_m at price P_m.

Assume that the product in question produces pollution, with costs to society represented by MC_S. In this case, pollution costs rise with output. Output Q_m is now the socially optimal output—which just happens (in this case) to equal the monopoly output when pollution costs are not considered. By restricting output to maximize profits, this monopolist just happens to produce the socially desirable output. Monopoly price P_m, moreover, reflects the true costs to society of the product, including production and external costs. Note, however, that the monopolist earns economic profits; the larger society does not recoup the costs it bears from pollution. Nevertheless, expanding competition in this instance could be considered socially harmful if this were to raise output above its optimal level.

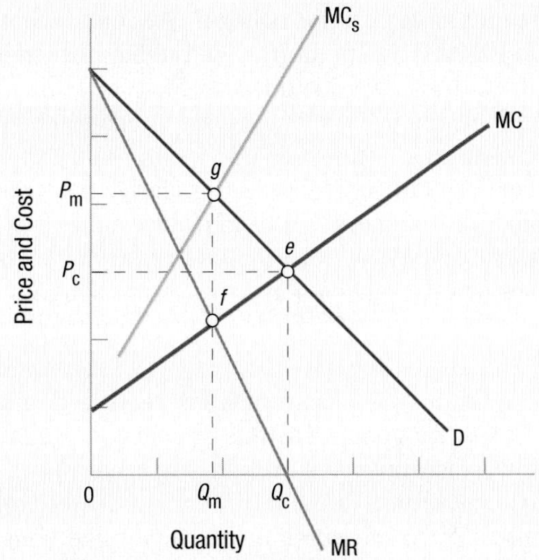

FIGURE 5

Monopoly and Pollution

When we take negative externalities into account, monopolies may not be so bad. Marginal cost curve MC and demand curve D represent the supply and demand facing a competitive industry without considering negative externalities. Competitive equilibrium is at point *e*, with output Q_c and price P_c. Once this industry is monopolized, the monopolist equates MR and MC at point *f*, thus selling output Q_m at price P_m. If this product creates pollution, costs to society are represented by MC_S. Output Q_m is now the socially optimal output, which in this case just happens to equal the monopoly output. Monopoly price P_m, moreover, represents the true costs to society of the product, including production and external costs.

Positive Externalities

When private market transactions generate benefits for others, a situation opposite to that just described results. Figure 6 illustrates a positive externality. Market supply curve S and private demand curve D_P represent the market for private college education. Equilibrium is at point *e*, with Q_e students enrolling. Society would clearly benefit, however, if more people earned college educations: Tax revenues would rise, crime rates would fall, and a better-informed electorate might produce a better-operating democracy.

Taking these considerations into account, social demand curve D_S is the private demand for college education plus the external benefits that flow from it.

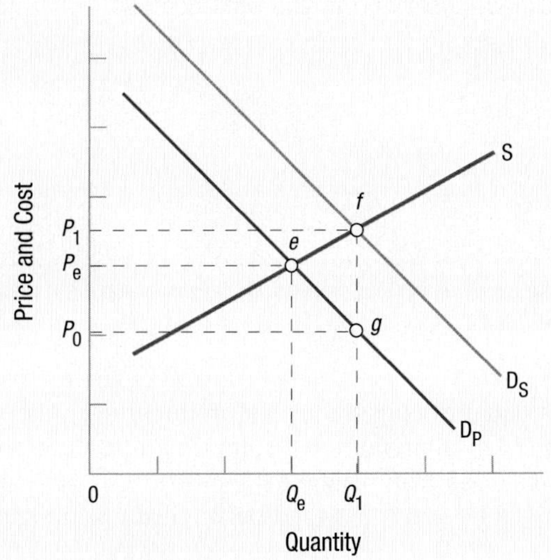

FIGURE 6

The Positive Externality Case

Market supply curve S and private demand curve D_P represent the market for private college education. Equilibrium is at point *e*, and students enrolled are Q_e. Society would benefit, however, if more people would go to college. Social demand curve D_S represents the private demand for college education plus the external benefits that flow from it. Socially optimal enrollment would be Q_1 (point *f*).

Socially optimal enrollment would be Q_1 (point *f*). How can society tweak the market so that more students will attend college? Students will demand Q_1 levels of enrollment only if its price is P_0 (point *g*). The public must therefore subsidize private education by *fg* to draw its price down to P_0.

The U.S. government recognizes that private education benefits society at large when it provides low-interest student loans, grants, and scholarships to students attending private colleges and universities. Similarly, the argument for providing low-income students with vouchers to attend private schools is not merely that this would introduce more competition into the education market, but that it is appropriate to compensate private schools for the external benefits they provide.

Limitations

Some caveats about our analysis of externalities need to be noted. First, producer and consumer surpluses are good measures of society's welfare if all incomes are weighted equally or the distribution of income is optimal. When income is unequally distributed, the gross unfairness created throughout society swamps any improvements from efficiency. Thus, measures of efficiency like consumer and producer surplus can become unconvincing for public policy. Since no one can agree on the correct distribution of income, economists generally ignore this question and focus on efficiency.

Second, the discussion here has focused on the pollution that arises from production, not consumption. The results applied to congestion and littering, however, would be substantially the same.

Third, the examples presented here have assumed, moreover, that pollution has no cumulative effects. And, indeed, smaller amounts of pollution effluence may just flow into the ocean, for instance, with no lasting effects. But the same will not hold true for sustained higher pollution levels.

Fourth, for convenience, we have assumed we can assign specific amounts to the damages resulting from pollution. In practice, this is not always easy to do.

Fifth, we have assumed pollution can be reduced only by reducing output, but in real markets, there are other ways to reduce pollution.

Despite these limitations, the analysis presented here helps us focus our attention on ways of reducing the harm done to society by negative externalities.

In summary, the market failures associated with public goods, externalities, and commonly held resources will all lead to overuse of resources and environmental degradation. To address these problems, collective or government action is required. Solutions range from privatization—assigning property rights—to government regulations or prohibitions, described in the next section.

Checkpoint

Market Failure

REVIEW

- Social welfare is equal to consumer plus producer surplus.
- Pure public goods are nonrival in consumption, and once the good is provided, no one can be excluded from using it.
- The demand for public goods is found by vertically summing individual demand curves.
- Optimal provision of public goods is found where the marginal benefit of public goods (demand) is equal to the marginal cost of provision.

- Determining the optimal provision of public goods is easy in theory, but difficult in practice. Cost-benefit analysis (CBA) helps policymakers allocate scarce public funds to competing projects.
- Common property resources have the characteristics of nonexcludability but are rival. This typically leads to overuse and overexploitation.
- Externalities arise when the production of one good generates benefits (positive externalities) or costs (negative externalities) for others not involved in the transaction.
- When negative externalities exist, overproduction is the result. When positive externalities are generated, underproduction of the good is the norm.
- The Coase theorem states that if transaction costs are minimal (near zero), no matter which party is provided the property rights to pollution (polluter or victim), the resulting bargain will result in the socially optimal level of pollution.
- Since monopolies produce less output and sell at higher prices than competitive markets, if negative externalities exist, then the monopoly will produce output levels closer to the socially optimal level.

QUESTIONS

In the June 1, 2006 issue of the *New York Times,* the Humane Society ran a full page ad with a picture of a baby harp seal and the headline, "Did You Know That Over 300,000 Baby Seals Were Killed in Canada This Year for Their Fur?" Below the picture, it read, "Over 1,000 U.S. Restaurants, Grocers and Seafood Distributors Do and They're Doing Something to End It." The ad then asks you to join them and 256,000 individuals who are boycotting *Canadian Seafood* until commercial seal hunting ends. Is this essentially the equivalent of a secondary boycott that labor unions once used but was subsequently outlawed by the Taft-Hartley Act? Does this boycott seem fair to Canadian fishermen who do not hunt seals? How does this boycott differ from the one by restaurants to save the Chilean Sea Bass?

Answers to the Checkpoint questions can be found at the end of this chapter.

Environmental Policy

We have seen that market failure can lead to excessive amounts of products that pollute or generate other negative externalities. This section looks at the broad approaches to environmental policy available to the government, focusing on emissions. First, we will look briefly at government failure. Government policies can fail to improve such situations if the incentives of politicians and policymakers are not aligned with the public interest. Balanced public policies must take intergenerational effects into account. Then, we will look at the actual policies used by government regulators to reduce pollution, ranging from direct intervention and control to the use of various market instruments to reduce emissions. Policymakers also occasionally use publicity and moral suasion to encourage polluters to voluntarily reduce emissions.

Government Failure

Market failure is one reason unregulated markets may produce inequitable or inefficient results. Government policies, however, do not always make things better. The terrible environmental record the Eastern Bloc countries accumulated during the Soviet era illustrates that, in environmental policy as elsewhere, governments—like markets—can fail.

Government failure
When the incentives of politicians and government bureaucrats are not in line with the public interest.

Government failure occurs when (1) public policies do not bring about an optimal allocation of resources and/or (2) the incentives of politicians and government bureaucrats are not in line with the public interest. As Nobel Prize winner George Stigler has argued, economic regulation often benefits the group being regulated at the expense of the larger public. Government failures will often be more acute in nondemocratic societies. Yet, even in the United States, public policy formation involves a struggle among interest groups, lobbyists, politicians, large corporate interests, and the public at large. The sausage that results from this tug-of-war, calling itself "public policy," is often not pretty.

Government failure may result from the practical inability of policymakers to gather enough information to set good policies. Water pollution, for instance, is well understood, resulting in fairly obvious regulatory policies, but the same is not true for issues like global warming. Even if we all agree that the Earth is getting warmer and humans are partly to blame, controversy remains about the adequacy of public policy to address this problem. Though calls for government action—"there ought to be a law"—are often justified, we do well to maintain a healthy skepticism about the ability of the public sector to solve our problems.

Intergenerational Questions

Should politicians consider the interests of voters whose great grandparents have not yet been born? Environmental issues raise complex questions involving how resources are to be allocated across generations. Some resources, such as sunlight, are continual and renewable. Others, like forests, fisheries, and the soil are exhaustible yet renewable, though they can be exhausted if overexploited. And some resources are nonrenewable, such as oil and coal. These resources are finite and cannot be renewed, but their available stock can be expanded through exploration or the use of new technologies that allow greater extraction or more efficient use.

When we develop environmental policies, we need to consider and evaluate different possible futures. Discounting was discussed earlier, but Figure 7 is a reminder of the effects discount rates have on the present value of a fixed payment that will come due at some date in the future. For environmental policies, the discount rate we choose is crucially important.

FIGURE 7

Present Value of $1,000 to be Paid in 30 Years Discounted at 1%, 5%, and 10%

This figure is a reminder of the effects discount rates have on the present value of a fixed payment that will come due at a future date. A higher discount rate means the value today of a future payoff will be lower. At a 10% discount, for instance, a payment of $1,000 in 30 years is worth only $42 today. Discounting the same $1,000 at 1% yields a present value of $748. The higher the discount rate we choose, the lower the value we place on the environmental damage to be suffered by future generations. The lower our discount rate, the more we are willing to protect the health of the future environment.

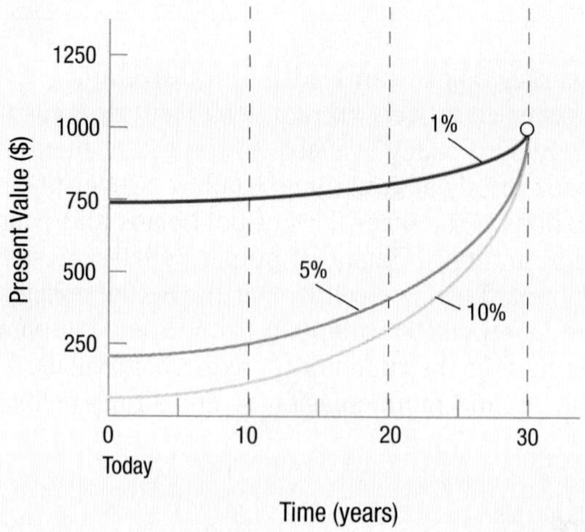

A higher discount rate means the value today of a future payoff will be less. At a 10% discount, a payment of $1,000 in 30 years is worth only $42 today, whereas discounting the same $1,000 at 1% yields a present value of $748. The higher the discount rate we choose, the lower the value we place on the environmental damage to be suffered by future generations. The lower our discount rate, conversely, the more we are willing to protect the health of the future environment. As always, crafting good public policies requires striking a balance between the two.

Socially Efficient Levels of Pollution

We have already seen that some pollution is acceptable to society. To require that no one pollute, period, would bring most economic activity as we know it to a halt. Yet, pollution damages our environment. The harmful effects of pollution range from direct threats to our health coming from air and water pollution to reductions in species from deforestation.

In general terms, the more pollution we create, the greater the harm to the environment. The damages that come from pollution are a cost we incur for living: To be alive is to generate some pollution. Our focus is on marginal damage, which resembles the marginal cost curves we have studied earlier. The marginal damage (MD) curve in Figure 8 shows the change in damages that come from a given change in emission levels. Notice that as emissions levels rise, the added damages rise.

The horizontal axis of Figure 8 measures the tons of pollution emitted into the environment (tons per year). Note that E_0 represents the maximum pollution (no environmental cleanup at all). The vertical axis measures the environmental costs in dollars. These costs represent a dollar value for various environmental losses, including the physical costs of pollution (asthma attacks and other lung diseases), the aesthetic losses (visual impact of clear cutting), and the losses associated with species reduction (we all miss the dodo bird).

Abatement costs are the costs associated with reducing emissions. A utility plant dumping effluent into a river can treat the effluent before discharge, but this costs

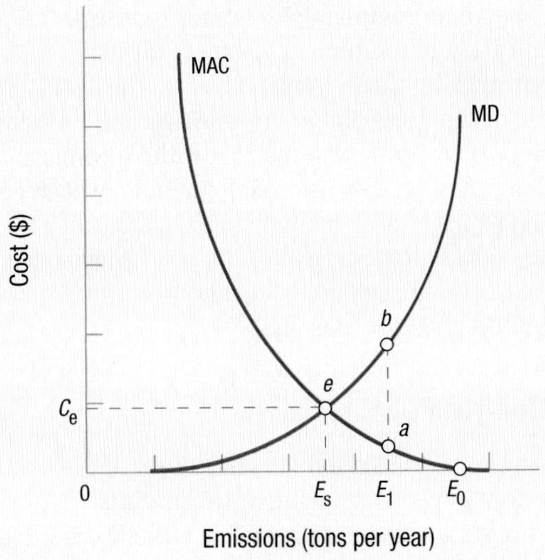

FIGURE 8

Marginal Damages and Marginal Abatement Costs

The marginal damage curve (MD) shows the *change* in damages that come from a given *change* in emission levels. The horizontal axis measures pollution. Note that E_0 is the maximum pollution that can occur without environmental cleanup. The vertical axis measures the environmental costs of this pollution in dollars. Marginal abatement costs curve (MAC) begins at zero at E_0, then rises as emission levels are reduced (moving leftward from E_0). Socially optimal pollution is E_S, at a cost to society of C_e (point *e*). The total damage from pollution is represented by the area beneath the marginal damages curve and to the left of E_S. Total abatement costs are equal to the area beneath the marginal abatement costs curve and to the right of E_S.

money. In Figure 8, marginal abatement costs (MAC) begin at zero at E_0, and then rise as emission levels are reduced (moving leftward from E_0). The MAC curve in Figure 8 is a generalized abatement cost function, but in practice, the costs will vary for different sources of pollution and the technologies available for reducing them. Chemical plants face different problems than utilities that release hot water into rivers. Cooling water before release will clearly require a different technology—and be much easier—than eliminating toxic chemicals from effluent flow.

The socially optimal level of pollution in Figure 8 is E_S, at a cost to society of C_e (point e). To see why this is so, assume we are at pollution level E_1. The cost to reduce another unit of emissions is equal to point a (measuring on the vertical axis), while the damage that would result from this pollution is shown at point b. Since $b > a$, society would be better off if emissions are reduced. Once we begin reducing below E_S, however, abatement costs overtake marginal damages, or the costs of clean up begin to outweigh the benefits.

The total damage from pollution in Figure 8 is represented by the area beneath the marginal damages curve and to the left of E_S. Total abatement costs, meanwhile, are equal to the area beneath the marginal abatement costs curve and to the right of E_S. Combined, these two costs represent the total social costs from emissions. We turn now to consider how environmental policy can ensure that emissions approach this optimal level.

Overview of Environmental Policies

Over the years, many types of environmental policies have been developed in response to different problems, covering the spectrum from centralized control to decentralized economic incentives. To be effective, all environmental policies must be efficient, fair, and enforceable, and they must provide incentives for improvement in the environment.

Command and control policies
Environmental policies where standards are set and regulations are issued, and these are then enforced by the legal and regulatory system.

Market-based policies
Environmental policies that use charges, taxes, subsidies, deposit-refund systems, or tradable emission permits to achieve environmental ends.

As a general rule, the more centralized an environmental policy, the more likely it represents a **command and control** philosophy. This means a centralized agency sets the rules for emissions, including levels of effluents allowed, usable technologies, and enforcement procedures. Command and control policies usually set standards of conduct that are enforced by the legal and regulatory system. Abatement costs at this point become compliance costs of meeting the standards. Standards are popular because they are simple, they treat all firms in an industry the same, and they prevent competing firms from polluting.

At the other end of the spectrum are **market-based policies,** which use charges, taxes, subsidies, deposit-refund systems, or tradable emission permits to achieve the same ends. Examples of this approach include water effluent charges, user charges for water and wastewater management, glass and plastic bottle refund systems, and tradable permits for ozone reduction. We will begin with a brief look at command and control policies, contrasting them with abatement taxes, then look at the case for tradable emission permits.

Command and Control Policies

Policymakers determine the pollution control or abatement that is best, then introduce the most efficient policies to achieve those ends. Figure 9 shows the supply and demand for pollution abatement. Demand curve $D_A = MB_A$ represents society's demand for abatement; it is a reflection of the marginal damage curve we looked at earlier. Note that the demand curve for abatement is negatively sloped because the *marginal benefit* from abatement declines as the environment becomes cleaner. The gains from an ever cleaner environment eventually become smaller and smaller because of the law of diminishing returns.

The marginal costs of abatement are the costs of cleaning up pollution. These costs rise with abatement efforts and become high as zero pollution, A_0, is

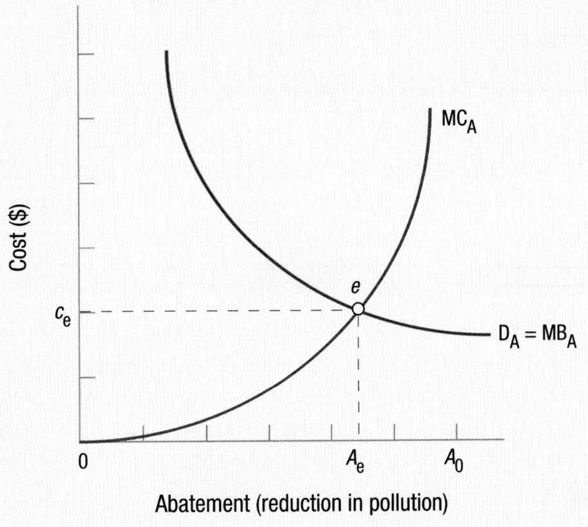

FIGURE 9

Marginal Cost of Abatement and Abatement Demand

Demand curve D_A represents society's demand for abatement. The marginal benefit from abatement (MB_A) declines as the environment becomes cleaner, since the gains from an ever cleaner environment become smaller and smaller (diminishing returns). The marginal costs of abatement are the costs of reducing pollution. These costs rise with abatement efforts and become high as zero pollution A_0 is approached (again, because of the law of diminishing returns or increasing costs). Optimal abatement is A_e, costing c_e. This means optimal pollution, $A_0 - A_e$, is greater than zero.

approached. Optimal abatement comes at A_e, costing c_e. This means optimal pollution, $A_0 - A_e$, is greater than zero. Command and control policies could set A_e as the abatement requirement and then set the right standards to meet this requirement. Aiming for abatement higher than A_e would be inefficient, since marginal costs would exceed benefits.

Setting abatement requirements (or standards) equal to A_e in Figure 9 is a classic example of command and control policies. Alternatively, policymakers could enact an effluent tax equal to c_e per unit of pollution. Firms would adopt pollution controls up to A_e, because the costs to reduce pollution to this point are less than the tax. Firms would emit only $A_0 - A_e$ pollution.

Again, command and control policies that set rigid standards for polluters have long been a favorite of policymakers. Yet, this approach can lead to inefficiencies, since different industries may emit the same (or equivalently dangerous) substances but face different technical problems and costs in reducing their pollution. To minimize the cost of reducing pollution, each source of pollution needs to be reduced to the point where the marginal cost of abatement is equal for all sources.

Market-Based Policies

Economists have increasingly begun to argue that market-oriented, or indirect, approaches to environmental policy are more efficient than command and control policies. One of the most popular and effective of these indirect approaches is marketable or tradable permits.

Marketable or Tradable Permits

Economists first proposed marketable or tradable permits when environmental laws were first being debated and enacted in the 1960s and 1970s. Environmental regulators essentially ignored this suggestion until the 1990s.

Today, tradable permits are used to reduce water effluents in the Fox River in Wisconsin, Tar-Pamlico River in North Carolina, and Dillon Reservoir in Colorado. One of the most successful uses of marketable permits for air pollution has reduced the sulfur dioxide (SO_2) emissions in the Midwest that create acid rain in the East. Originally, the cost of this cleanup was expected to be significant, and the price of permits did start out fairly high. As the cleanup has progressed, however, technical advances have steadily reduced abatement costs, causing the price of the permits to decline sharply. This success with SO_2 has spawned the use of similar permits in Europe, where opposition to marketable permits historically was strong.

Marketable permits require that a regulatory body set a maximum allowable quantity of effluents allowed and issue permits granting the "right" to pollute a certain amount. These permits can be bought and sold, thus creating the property rights that permit transactions of the sort Coase advocated. Sales are normally between two polluters, with one polluter buying a permit from a more efficient operator. Polluters do not have to be the only purchasers: victims or environmental groups could conceivably purchase pollution rights and hold them off the market, thereby reducing pollution below the established cap.

Figure 10 illustrates how such a market works. We assume two firms in the market each producing 10 tons of pollution and that the government wishes to limit pollution to a total of 10 tons. Remember that, without restrictions, firms do zero abatement and total pollution is 20 tons. Setting a goal of 10 tons amounts to cutting pollution in half.

FIGURE 10

Tradable Permits

This figure illustrates how a market for tradable pollution permits works. Again, assume there are only two firms (X and Y) in the market and the government wishes to limit total pollution to 10 tons. Without restrictions, both firms do zero abatement and pollution is 20 tons. Setting a goal of 10 tons therefore amounts to cutting pollution in half. Assume the government gives the permits to firm X. Demand curve D_Y represents firm Y's demand for these permits. Given a competitive market for permits, equilibrium will be at point *e* with a permit price equal to \$300. Firm Y buys 7 permits and pollutes that amount and Firm X emits 3 tons of pollution.

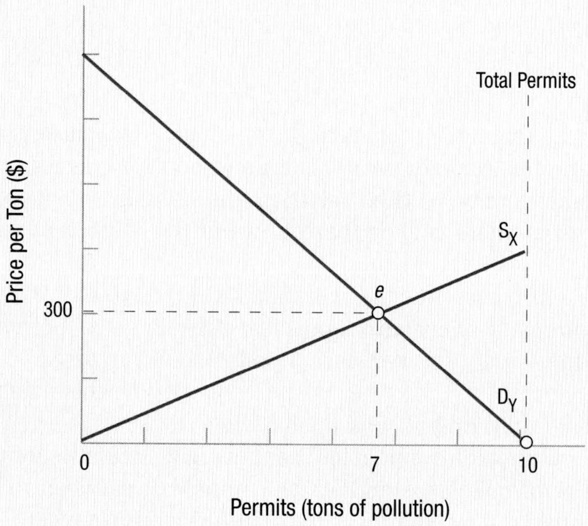

Assume, for simplicity, that the government at first gives the permits to firm X. (Remember that the Coase theorem suggests efficiency is not affected by who owns the rights to pollute.) Demand curve D_Y represents firm Y's demand for these permits. Assume that the market for permits is competitive, thus equilibrium will be at point *e* with a permit price equal to \$300. Firm Y buys 7 permits and pollutes that amount, and Firm X pollutes 3 tons.

Firm X pollutes less and sells 7 permits to firm Y because its marginal costs of abatement are less. Firm X in this example ends up with the revenue from permit sales, while firm Y's income declines by the same amount (\$2,100). Auctioning off the permits produces the same result, but the government gets the revenue.

One advantage of permits over taxes is that no knowledge of marginal abatement costs is needed to ensure that the tax rate is optimal. The market price of permits will adjust to variances in abatement costs; all the regulator must determine is how much to reduce pollution levels. If reducing pollution by a certain amount, regardless of the cost, is the goal, permits are the best way to achieve this goal.

Other Market-Based Policies

We have looked at two of the most frequently used market-based policies, taxes/charges and marketable permits. Emission taxes and charges have been used for water effluents, waste management, pesticide packaging, batteries, tires, and other products and processes. User charges are the most common way to finance wastewater treatment facilities.

Federal subsidies, the flip side of taxes or charges, are used when local communities do not have the resources for pollution control. Marketable permits have been most successful in programs to reduce air pollution, as well as those targeting acid rain and ozone reduction. Deposit-refund systems have been used mainly for recyclable products such as cans, bottles, tires, and batteries.

Over the years, most environmental policies have been of the command and control variety. The 1969 Clean Air Act focused on specific forms of air pollution—particulates, carbon dioxide (CO_2), and so forth—and established air quality standards. Standards were set for vehicles and stationary sources of pollution including power plants and factories.

Today, economic or market-based approaches to environmental policy are considered more efficient than command and control policies. Most environmental agencies, however, in this country and abroad, have not used these tools until recently.

One reason for this is probably that many people in the regulatory and environmental communities resist viewing environmental resources as commodities to be subjected to market forces of supply and demand. It is market failures, after all, that led to environmental decay in the first place; why would we want to put the environment on the market? Many pollutants, moreover, are frequently mixed together and their individual impacts are difficult to determine. Consequently, setting the right tax rate or issuing the right number of allowable permits is difficult. Finally, some policymakers balk at giving corporations the right to pollute, even for a limited amount of pollution.

Public Pressure to Achieve Environmental Goals

We have discussed environmental policy as if government action, whether exercised in command and control policies or setting market-based policies, were the only way to deal with environmental problems. This is not the case.

Those of you who dine at McDonald's may recall that your Big Macs and Quarter-Pounders are served in cardboard boxes to keep them warm, not in the simple wrap used for smaller hamburgers and cheeseburgers. This was not always the case. Big Macs, Quarter-Pounders, and other large sandwiches used to be served in Styrofoam "clamshells," as the boxes were called. From an environmental point of view, these clamshells were a disaster. Though they would biodegrade eventually, this would not happen for decades. They would clutter up landfill. The Styrofoam clamshells were not environmentally friendly at all.

Public pressure—not government action—was put on McDonald's. In 1989, McDonald's worked with the Environmental Defense Fund to rid the world of Styrofoam clamshells. Cardboard containers made their appearance.

The environmental collaboration did not end there. Ten years later, in 1999, McDonald's was still working with the Environmental Defense Fund to become more environmentally friendly. McDonald's claims it has saved 150,000 tons of packaging in the decade after 1989.[9] With a global presence such as McDonald's, cutting one inch off the size of a napkin can have tremendous ramifications. New initiatives, to be phased in over time, include dimming the lights, metering the water used in flushing the toilets, and using more recycled and recyclable products.

---

[9]Frank Swoboda, "McDonald's Leads Way for Efficient Retrofits," *Fresno Bee* (previously in the *Washington Post*), December 27, 1999.

The point is, government action is not always necessary. Sometimes personal action is effective enough. It helped start McDonald's along its environmentally friendly path. An added bonus—McDonald's competitor Burger King is now walking along the same path.

When the environmental problem is more intractable, such as global warming, government action is the obvious way to go. Global warming is controversial, high on the public's radar screen, and paid considerable attention by special interest groups and economists.

Checkpoint

Environmental Policy

REVIEW

- Government failure can occur when politicians and government do not have the right incentives to bring about an optimal allocation of resources.
- The discount rate chosen for environmental policies determines the intergenerational impact of policy.
- The socially optimal level of pollution occurs where the marginal damage is equal to the marginal abatement costs.
- Policymakers determine the optimal pollution levels and then often use command and control policies to set the most efficient regulations or levels of abatement.
- Tradable permits use market forces to bring pollution within limits set by regulators.

QUESTION

In the 1960s, the Environmental Protection Agency (EPA) initially focused on pollution, principally air and water. In a similar way, the Bureau of Land Management initially honed in on multiple-use of public lands with an emphasis on timber harvests. Today both agencies have a much broader focus that looks at maintaining an ecological balance, and their activities extend beyond pollution and timber to species and habitat protection. Is this just another example of bureaucratic mission creep?

Answers to the Checkpoint question can be found at the end of this chapter.

Antar Dayal/Getty Images

The Economics of Climate Change

Global warming may turn out to be the mother of all market failures.[10] There is a growing scientific consensus that "without big changes in emission rates, global warming from the buildup of greenhouse gases is likely to lead to substantial, and largely irreversible, transformations of climate, ecosystems and coastlines later this century."[11] The economics surrounding this issue are complex and require almost all of the tools of microeconomics we have studied, and then some.

[10]Nicholas Stern, *The Economics of Climate Change* (Cambridge: Cambridge University Press), 2007. This section draws heavily from this study, also known as the "Stern Review."

[11]Andrew C. Revkin, "Yelling 'Fire' on a Hot Planet," *New York Times,* April 23, 2006, p. wk1.

There is a sense of urgency surrounding climate change, because the state of climate science has advanced to the point where scientists can now put probability estimates on certain impacts of warming, some of which are catastrophic. Current levels of greenhouse gases are roughly 430 parts per million (ppm). This compares to 280 ppm before the Industrial Revolution. If the annual levels of emissions remain constant at today's levels across the world, levels of greenhouse gases will rise to 550 ppm by 2050. And if emissions increase, the level of greenhouse gases will be greater than 550 ppm.

What will happen as greenhouse gases increase and lead to global warming? Figure 11 estimates these effects. The top panel shows a range of greenhouse gases from 400 ppm to 750 ppm, with its predicted effects on temperature below it. The bottom panel estimates the impacts likely to arise with each increase in temperature. The estimated effects of a difference of just 1 or 2 degrees are harrowing.

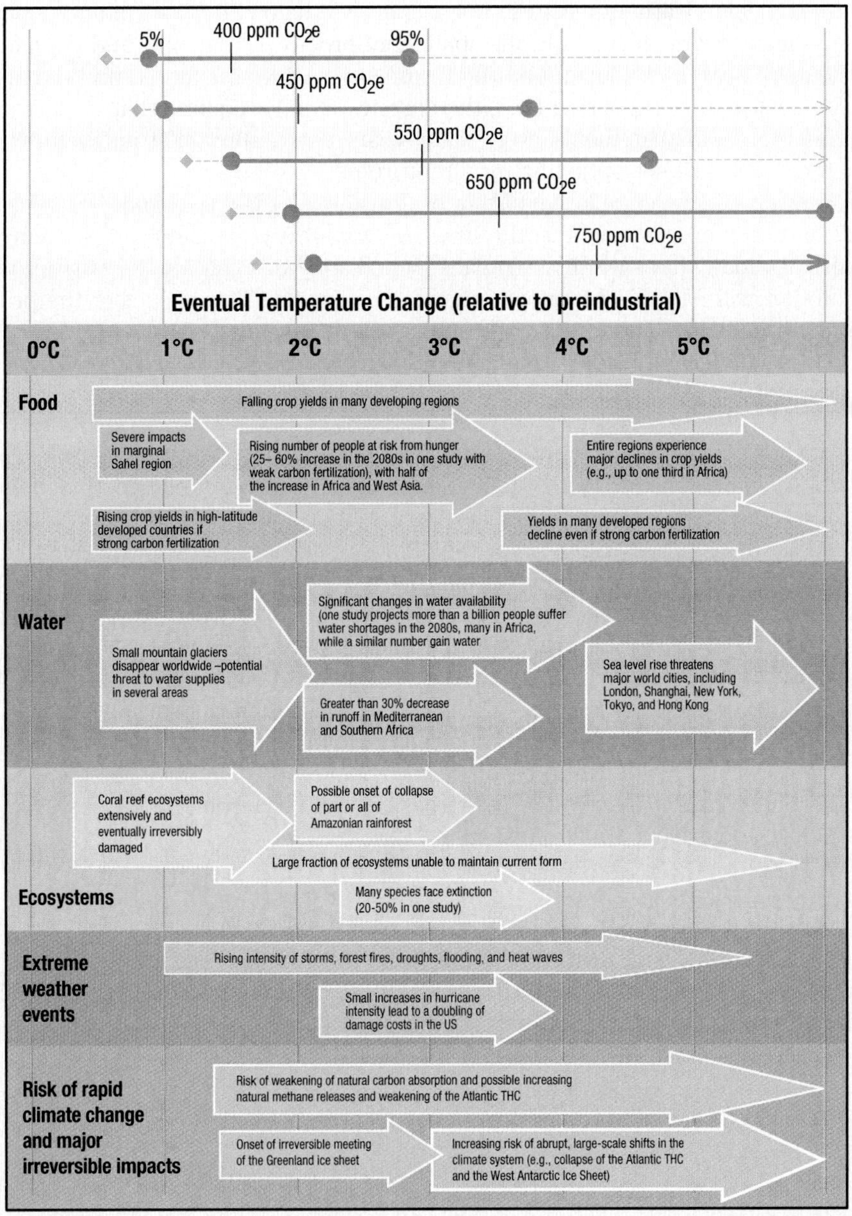

FIGURE 11

Greenhouse Gases, Likely Temperature Changes, and Estimated Impacts

The top panel shows the range of temperatures projected at greenhouse gas levels between 400 and 750 ppm. The solid horizontal lines indicate the 5–95% range based on climate sensitivity estimates. The vertical line indicates the mean of the 50th percentile point. The dashed lines show the 5–95% range based on 11 recent studies. The bottom panel illustrates the range of impacts expected at different levels of warming. This figure shows potential changes based on current scientific literature.

Source: Stern Review.

Unique Timing Aspects

Global warming is essentially a huge global negative externality. But what makes analysis and decision making so difficult is the long time horizon that must be considered. Most cost-benefit studies do not look out 50–100 years and beyond. This extended time horizon adds a host of difficulties and uncertainties.

Air or water pollution is something that we can see on the horizon, can be measured, is typically localized, and can be altered in a short period of time by some of the approaches discussed earlier. Global warming, in contrast, is not something we can generally see; it is cumulative (this year's CO_2 adds to that from the past to raise concentrations in the future); and once it reaches a certain level, it may lead to extreme consequences that cannot be reversed.

Cleaning up pollution problems typically involves finding that level of abatement where the marginal costs of abatement equal the marginal benefits from abatement and either taxing, assigning (or auctioning) marketable permits, or using command and control policies to require the optimal level of abatement. However, reducing global warming gases is not a onetime change, but a cumulative process across many years. As a result, the abatement process is dynamic, and the marginal benefits of abatement depend on the future stock of emissions. To find the optimal abatement in any one period (say, the current period) requires that we look at the optimum path of abatement across many years, and assume that in the future that abatement will be set optimally for all future periods.

Because of the cumulative nature of greenhouse gases, our short-run decisions will have immense impacts in the long run (50–100 years out). Small changes in emissions today have will little impact immediately or even for the current generation, but will have sizable effects many decades out. This aspect of the problem seriously complicates any policymaking and economic analysis.

Public Good Aspects

To further compound the problem, global climate change is a public good. Greenhouse gas emissions "are the purest example of a negative public good; nobody can have less of them because someone else has more; and nobody can be excluded from their malign consequences or the efforts of others to ameliorate them."[12] One of the solutions is technical innovation that reduces our output of CO_2. But knowledge and technology have large public good aspects, so private firms will find it difficult to collect the full returns on their innovation investments that reduce greenhouse gases. Other firms and countries will to some extent be free riders on private innovation, so society (and the world) may get less than the socially optimal level of innovation. This will mean that a substantial amount of climate change research and development will have to be financed by governments. Since the governments of developed nations have more resources than the governments of less-developed nations, the burden will fall on them.

Equity Aspects

Much of what we do today will have little immediate impact on our lives. The impacts will show up in the later half of the century. So any action taken today principally benefits our great grandchildren. This fact makes it more difficult to get a political consensus to act.

Also, rich countries will have to make the biggest sacrifices, yet they will not get the biggest benefits from efforts to reduce the impacts of global warming. Let

[12]Martin Wolf, "Curbs on Emissions Will Take a Change of Political Climate," *Financial Times,* November 8, 2006, p. 15.

us say that the United States reduces its dependence on carbon. What about China and India? They may decide that growth is worth more than a cleaner environment. At that point, the United States would have to be willing to pay China and India large sums to get them to decarbonize their economies. How well will that sell to American voters? Probably not well, but it may be what is ultimately necessary. After all, the developed world is responsible for three quarters or more of all greenhouse gasses emitted since the Industrial Revolution began.

People in developing countries living along bodies of water will face floods if current climate forecasts come to pass. These are some of the world's poorest people, and adapting to flooding will be extremely difficult given their hopelessly limited resources. In addition, developing nations rely heavily on agriculture, one industry that will be hardest hit as the warming of the Earth inevitably leads to famines.

The long time horizon for policymaking and global climate change puts a different light on the discounting process typically used in cost-benefit analysis. When you use any reasonable discount rate (3–5%) on benefits 75–100 years into the future, they become miniscule numbers today. Nicholas Stern argued that "there is no compelling reason to value the welfare of future generations much below our own."[13] As a result, the Stern Review adopts a discount rate near zero.

Finding a Solution

Since climate change is global, it will take a concerted international effort and cooperation. According to the Stern Review, it will take cooperation "in creating price signals and markets for carbon, spurring technology research, development and deployment, and promoting adaptation, particularly in developing countries."[14]

A temperature rise of 3–4°C will likely lead to serious consequences for food and water in developing nations, increasing rate of species extinction, and possibly more extreme weather events (see Figure 11). If the temperature increase is large, the events become catastrophic. Since there is a positive probability that these extreme events will occur, we should invest in ways to reduce the risks of this happening. Consider it a form of insurance.

Many economists, including Nicholas Stern, argue that using smaller levels of resources now will result in lower spending in the future. The Stern Review estimates that the costs of stabilizing greenhouse gases at 550 ppm will cost roughly 1% of world gross domestic product (GDP) if we begin soon.

This will require a transition to a low-carbon economy that will only be accomplished by establishing a worldwide price for carbon that includes its external costs. This can be done using carbon taxes or tradable permits. Permits for acceptable levels of carbon emissions could be auctioned and then traded on open markets on exchanges such at the EU-ETS (Emissions Trading Scheme) and the recently opened US-CCX (Chicago Climate Exchange). Europe's system is a good start, but it has been plagued by national governments issuing too many permits (for free and to specific industries), so the resulting market price for carbon offsets was one fourth what was needed to provide the right incentives to reduce emissions. Firms bought permits at these cheap prices rather than attempting to reduce their emissions.[15] There is the problem of having too many permits: Prices are too low. For carbon markets to operate effectively and provide the right incentives to reduce emissions, "countries need independent agencies to issue the permits, just as there are independent central banks to issue money."[16]

---

[13]Martin Wolf, "After the Arguments, the Figures Still Justify Swift Climate Action," *Financial Times*, November 15, 2006, p. 15.
[14]Stern Review, p. i.
[15]Kevin Morrison, "Carbon Permits Too Cheap to Bite," *Financial Times*, November 28, 2006, p. 26.
[16]"Charlemagne: Soot, Smoke and Mirrors," *The Economist*, November 18, 2006, p. 54.

Robert Socolow of Princeton University has suggested that much of the technology needed to reduce our carbon footprint is available today.[17] He and several colleagues suggest that we could use techniques such as the following to keep our carbon emissions constant over the next 50 years:

- Use more efficient vehicles and reduce use.
- Build more efficient buildings.
- Capture CO_2 at power plants.
- Use nuclear power.
- Exchange biomass fuels for fossil fuels.
- Use wind and solar power.
- Reduce deforestation.

Each of these has the capacity to reduce CO_2 emissions by 1 billion tons per year by 2057. The wedges shown in Figure 12 would prevent our CO_2 emissions from doubling over the next 50 years.

Clearly, undertaking some policies to reduce our carbon footprint as a nation represents an insurance policy on the future. All of the activities suggested in Figure 12 are sufficiently flexible such that as new climate change information becomes available, we can adjust our policies. And making some moves now will reduce the potential costs in the future.

FIGURE 12

Stabilization Wedges

This figure, based on the work of Robert Socolow and colleagues, shows the contribution to reduction in carbon emissions that seven wedges can make. Each approach can reduce our carbon footprint by 1 billion tons per year by 2057. Adopting these changes will stabilize our carbon emissions to roughly 7–8 billion tons per year.

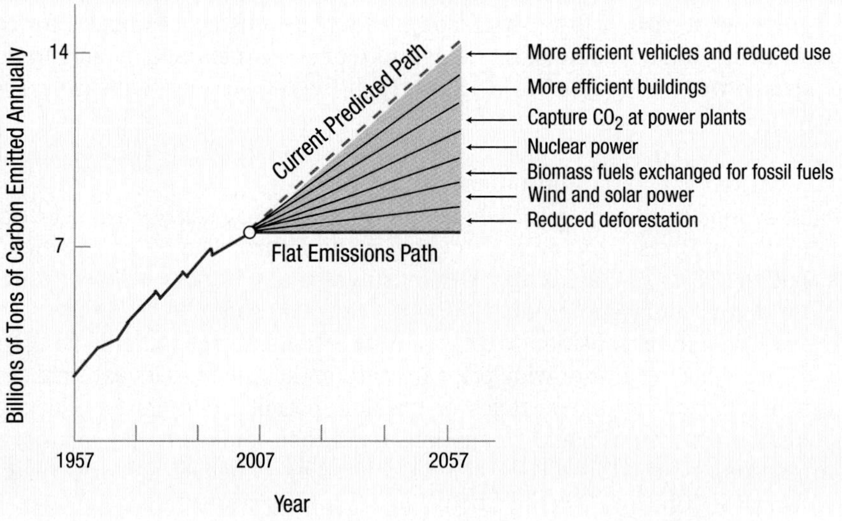

[17] Robert Socolow et al., "Solving the Climate Problem: Technologies Available to Curb CO_2 Emissions," *Environment,* December 2004, p. 8–19.

Key Concepts

Consumer surplus, p. 341
Producer surplus, p. 342
Social welfare, p. 342
Market failures, p. 342
Public goods, p. 342
Nonrivalry, p. 342
Nonexcludability, p. 342
Cost-benefit analysis, p. 344
Common property resources, p. 346
Externalities, p. 348
Coase theorem, p. 350
Government failure, p. 356
Command and control policies, p. 358
Market-based policies, p. 358

Chapter Summary

Market Failure

Consumer surplus is the difference between what people are willing to pay for a product and what they actually pay for it. Producer surplus is the difference between the revenues firms earn from a product and the costs they would be willing to bear to supply it.

Market failure occurs whenever a market does not provide the socially optimal quantity of a product at the socially optimal price. Market failure can occur because of public goods, externalities, or common property resources.

Public goods exhibit both nonrivalry in consumption and nonexcludability. Nonrivalry means that one person's consumption of a good does not reduce the availability of that good to others. Nonexcludability means that once a product has been provided, no consumers can be excluded from consuming the product. Candy bars are a rival and exclusive product; clean air is nonrival and nonexclusive.

Because common property resources are owned by the community, individuals will tend to overuse and overexploit them, as has happened with ocean fishing. Solutions to such problems involve either direct government regulation or establishing private property rights.

Externalities, or spillovers, arise when a transaction benefits or harms parties not involved in the transaction. Pollution and littering are examples of negative externalities, or external costs. Positive externalities, or external benefits, include education and vaccinations.

The Coase theorem suggests that if transaction costs are near zero, how property rights are allocated (to pollute or to be free from pollution) will not affect the efficiency of the ultimate allocation of resources. The resulting bargain between the parties will lead to an optimal allocation of resources. Benefits, however, will be distributed differently, depending on the original assignment of property rights.

Since monopolies restrict output, if their products involve significant negative externalities, pressing for greater competition could produce socially harmful consequences. Still, to reduce pollution, few people would argue for policies permitting monopolies.

Environmental Policy

Sometimes (often, according to some critics) government policies do not make things better. Government failures occur when the incentives of policymakers and bureaucrats do not coincide with the public interest. Government regulators are often captured by the industries they regulate, resulting in regulations that benefit the industry rather than consumers.

When developing environmental policies, policymakers must consider and evaluate different possible futures. This intergenerational aspect of environmental issues requires a balancing of interests and complicates policymaking. The decisions made will depend on the discount rate chosen. The higher the discount rate, the lower the value we place on events farther into the future, which can result in significant burdens being placed on future generations. Conversely, if we select a low discount rate, the current generation may be overburdened in paying for benefits to be enjoyed by future generations.

Some pollution is acceptable to society. Optimal pollution levels are found where marginal abatement costs equal the marginal benefits. These costs and benefits will vary for different types of pollution, industries, and regions of the country.

Environmental policy in the United States has been based on command and control. Command and control policies set standards for polluters—acceptable levels of effluents, for instance—which are systematically enforced through inspections and reports. Another option, however, is to enact effluent taxes that lead to optimal pollution levels.

More recently, market-based policies have been recognized as being more efficient than command and control policies. First, the government determines a permissible pollution level; then firms are allocated permits to pollute, which they may buy, sell, and trade.

Global climate change is a huge global externality accompanied by public goods aspects and extremely long time horizons. These issues complicate the solution, and the fact that the developed countries will have to bear the brunt of containing the impacts from climate change—but will get few of the benefits—introduces equity issues into the policymaking equation. The solution to this problem must include global carbon pricing that is credible and covers the full costs of carbon-based products.

Questions and Problems

1. Environmental regulation is undergoing change as many companies seek to be part of the regulatory process and get ahead of regulation. The *New York Times*[18] reported that

   > *the Environmental Protection Agency has long been concerned about the possible toxicity of perfluorooctanoic acid (usually called PFOA), a chemical in waterproof clothing and nonstick cookware. Regulating the substance could take years, said Susan B. Hazen, acting assistant administrator for the agency's Office of Prevention, Pesticides and Toxic Substances. So last year, the agency called together a group of chemical companies and environmentalists to discuss how to control PFOA's. Each company voluntarily curtailed its use of the substance. "Everyone set aside their parochial interests, and we reached agreement in a few months," Ms. Hazen said.*

   Does knowing that regulations are inevitable make it easier for companies to get on board early? What is the benefit to companies from adapting their production to reduce toxic waste and pollution?

2. As a way to increase the funds for wildlife conservation, why don't we just auction off (say, on eBay) the right to name a new species when it is discovered? Why not do the same for existing species?

[18]Claudia H. Deutsch, "Companies and Critics Try Collaboration." *New York Times,* May 17, 2006, p.10.

3. We can estimate the emissions caused in one year from automobile use. What can you do to offset these emissions? Buy a *green tag*. These voluntary purchases are akin to carbon offsets traded in Europe. For a small fee, individuals can purchase carbon offsets for their cars or SUVs, or companies can use them as a way to purchase wind power for their stores. Organizations selling the green tag (both for-profit and nonprofit) provide a decal; most of the fee collected is provided to alternative energy producers as a subsidy, which then can lower their prices to the market to encourage use. Is this a public good being sold privately? Why would someone or a business buy a tag when they can free ride?

4. Assume that you are convinced that if something isn't done now, global warming is going to create extensive problems and damage at the end of this century. If you were preparing a CBA of the impacts and had a 100-year horizon for your projections, would you use a 3% or an 8% discount rate?

5. What makes public goods so different from private goods?

6. Put the following list of goods and services in order of mostly public goods in nature to mostly private: National Public Radio, a slice of pizza, cable TV, music downloaded from iTunes, your economics class, a seat in a sports bar for Monday Night Football, summer spraying for mosquitoes, the Coast Guard, a ski patrol on Aspen mountain, and an Oklahoma toll road.

7. One's home (or apartment) is typically thought of as one's castle. But not so in the condominiums with homeowners associations (HOAs) in Jefferson County, Colorado. In an older four-unit condo, the HOA voted 3–1 to adopt a no-smoking rule (inside the individual condos) after smokers bought one of the units and smoke permeated the walls of the structure. In 2006, a district judge ruled that the HOA's adoption of no-smoking rules were reasonable restrictions on ownership rights, stating that the rules were designed to prevent the odor of cigarettes from penetrating the walls of neighboring condos.

   Since there are a small number of people involved (3 nonsmoking units, 1 smoking), you would think that transaction costs would be minimal. Why do you think the homeowners could not work out an agreement (à la Coase) and ended up in court? According to the Coase theorem, would it have made any difference if the judge had ruled against the HOA?

8. Some environmentalists suggest that the airline industry is contributing greatly to global warming. This is because aircraft emit greenhouse gases at high altitudes, and these gases have several times the impact of the same gases emitted at ground level. Air travel alone could account for roughly 5% of our total impact on climate change. Aside from restricting air travel, there doesn't appear to be much that can be done about it. Other nonfossil fuels are not technically or safely possible, and the other small fixes (towing aircraft to the runway, filling all seats in the plane, etc.) don't really reduce fuel consumption enough. Could this just be a situation where society is better off with more pollution? In general, when are we better off with more pollution?

9. Internalizing the cost of negative externalities means that we try to set policies that require each product to include the full costs of its negative

spillovers in its price. How do such policies impact product price and industry output and employment? Are these kinds of policies easy to implement in practice? How has globalization of production affected our ability to control pollution?

10. When trying to estimate the external benefits of a college education, what kinds of specific benefits would you include?

11. Garbage dumps are a particular source of a potent global-warming gas, the methane that bubbles up as the garbage decomposes. Does it make sense for companies in the European Union (EU) to help Brazilian garbage dumps reduce their releases of methane as a way of meeting their Kyoto obligations?

12. The Presidio, previously a military base in San Francisco, is now a national park. It sits in the middle of San Francisco on some of the most valuable real estate in the United States. Congress, when it created the park, required that it rehabilitate the aging buildings and be self-sufficient within a decade or so, or the land would be sold off to developers. The park appears to be well on its way to self-sufficiency by leasing the land to private firms—Lucas Films has built a large digital animation studio, and another firm wants to convert an old hospital into upscale apartments with an ocean view, and so on. These projects all must maintain the general character of the park, and they generate rent that will cover the park's expenses in the future. Would this privatization approach work with most of America's other national parks? Why or why not?

13. What is the tragedy of the commons? How can it be solved?

14. How might the government use market forces to encourage recycling?

15. Nobel Prize winner Simon Kuznets once suggested that poor nations tend to pollute more as they grow—until they reach a certain level of income per capita—after which they pollute less. Does this observation by Kuznets seem reasonable? Why or why not?

Answers to Checkpoint Questions

CHECKPOINT: MARKET FAILURE

Yes, it is a secondary boycott, designed to get the Canadian seafood industry to put pressure on the government to eliminate the hunts. No, it does not seem fair. Chilean Sea Bass was one product that chefs focused on. Since most Sea Bass was sold to restaurants, the boycott was successful. Also, the price of Sea Bass rose as supply declined (as the result of overfishing), making it easier for restaurants to substitute other fish.

CHECKPOINT: ENVIRONMENTAL POLICY

In the last 50 or so years, as the United States has become richer, environmental issues and our willingness to pay have grown. Simultaneously, science has developed new insights, changing approaches to managing natural environments. Also, when the EPA was formed, pollution was a high-priority item because many streams and cities were fouled. Yes, the EPA probably has suffered mission creep, but it probably reflects the public's desire for a cleaner environment as the U.S. economy has become more prosperous.

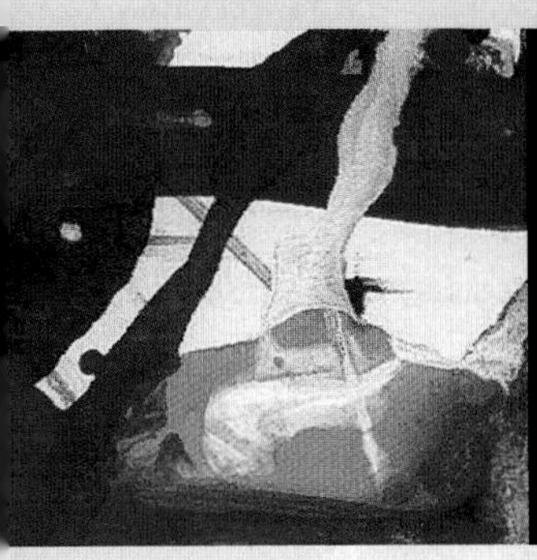

Poverty and Income Distribution

14

Income inequality and poverty are among the most contentious issues facing economists and other social scientists today. Many people have trouble accepting that baseball pitchers earn millions, while teachers earn only thousands, (and just a few at that) and many others eke out wages that just barely permit subsistence.

Is it fair that some people earn so much when others have so little? Questions of fairness are normative questions. They can only be answered through individual value judgments; economics has no right or wrong answers to offer in this area. Still, economists can contribute *something* to our discussions of economic fairness. What might this be?

Earlier, we saw that when input and product markets are competitive, wages are determined by worker productivity and the market value of output produced. The supply of people willing and able to work and the demand for labor sets the prevailing wages. Many of us are willing to play professional baseball, but few are called, and those who do reach "The Show" are so much more skilled than the rest of us that they command huge contracts.

The teaching profession, in contrast, requires far fewer specific skills and less training. Besides, hundreds of thousands of positions are always available. The result is that teacher salaries are much closer to what average folks earn. Clearly, teachers perform a valuable service, arguably more valuable than the service performed by professional baseball players. Still, there is no real shortage of people willing and able to teach at prevailing wages. But there is a real shortage of people able to throw a 95 mph fastball.

It must also be remembered that our economy contains people whose skill levels and discipline are so low that their income-earning possibilities are dismal. High school dropouts, transients, and many other people with all variety of problems are of little economic value in a market economy. Society has various safety net programs designed to provide these people with basic services to help them become more self-sufficient.

Economic analysis gives us some insight into why income inequality exists. We have already seen how monopoly, monopsony, unions, and discrimination can potentially skew income distribution. Even when public policy focuses on reducing these market imperfections, inequalities persist.

This chapter looks at income inequality, its trends, its causes, and how it is measured. We then take a brief historical look at income inequality and the policies designed to reduce it. Next, we turn our attention to poverty, focusing on how poverty is traditionally measured, and the U.S. Census Bureau's new approach to measuring poverty. Finally, we look at current poverty trends and the causes of poverty. Throughout this chapter, we will use economics to provide a framework for analyzing income distribution, poverty, and the public policies used to combat poverty and to change the distribution of income.

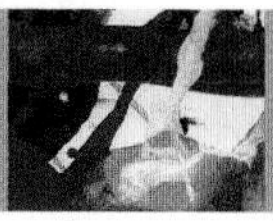

After studying this chapter you should be able to

- Describe the difference between wealth and income.
- Describe the effects of life cycles on income.
- Analyze functional, personal, and family income distributions.
- Use a Lorenz curve and Gini coefficient to graphically depict the distribution of wealth and income.
- Describe the impact of income redistribution efforts.
- Describe the causes of income inequality.
- Describe the means for determining poverty thresholds.
- Describe the two measures for determining depth of poverty for families.
- Describe the prevailing theories on how to deal with poverty and income inequality.

The Distribution of Income and Wealth

Income
A flow measure reflecting the funds received by individuals or households over a period of time, usually a week, month, or a year.

Wealth
A stock measure of an individual's or family's assets net of liabilities at a given point in time.

Income is a *flow,* **wealth** is a *stock.* Income measures the receipts of funds by individuals or households over time, usually a week, month, or year. Income is a *flow of funds* measure. Wealth, in contrast, measures a family's assets and net liabilities at a given point in time. You may earn a certain income in 2008, but your net wealth is measured on a specific day, say, December 31, 2008. Many people were wealthy on January 1, 2000, but after suffering the ravages of a falling stock market, they were considerably less wealthy on July 1, 2003.

You can be wealthy with low income if you do not work and your assets are in low-yielding certificates of deposit. Alternately, you can have little wealth, yet a high income, like a rookie pro ball player who earns a seven-figure salary but has not yet accumulated assets.

Life Cycle Effects

We should also note that family and individual incomes vary significantly over the course of people's lives. Young people who are just starting their careers and their families will often earn only modest incomes. Over their working careers, they become more experienced and their salaries increase, with income peaking roughly between the ages of 45 and 55. At some point between ages 45 and 60, family size will begin to decline as the kids grow up and leave home. Somewhere approaching 60, income also begins declining, though household saving rises as the family prepares for retirement. Incomes decline with retirement, but then again, so do family responsibilities.

One result of this economic life cycle is that a society that is growing older can expect to see changes in income distribution as greater numbers of households fall into lower income brackets. The life cycle also has implications for the economic effects of immigration. Newcomers to the United States are often unskilled, so when the country admits more immigrants, it can expect more low-income households. The children of immigrants, however, move up the income distribution ladder.

The Distribution of Income

Income distribution can be considered from several different perspectives. First, we can look at the **functional distribution of income,** which splits income among the inputs (factors) of production. The functional distribution for the United States between 1929 and 2005 is shown in Table 1.

Functional distribution of income
The distribution of income for resources or factors of production (land, labor, capital, and entrepreneurial ability).

Labor's share of national income has gradually risen since 1929 and has been fairly stable, at around 70% over the last four decades. The share of income going to small businesses, called "proprietor's income," has declined over this period, as has rental income. The share accruing to corporate profits has hovered around 10% but has jumped somewhat by 2005.

As Table 1 illustrates, the biggest fluctuations in income share have been associated with income from interest. It declined into the 1960s, then rose again until

Table 1 Functional Distribution of Income (absolute dollars in billions, numbers in parentheses are percentages)

Year	Wages	Proprietor's Income	Rent	Corporate Profits	Net Interest
1929	51.1 (60.3)	14.9 (17.6)	4.9 (5.8)	9.2 (10.8)	4.7 (5.5)
1940	52.1 (65.4)	12.9 (16.2)	2.7 (3.4)	8.7 (10.9)	3.3 (4.1)
1950	154.8 (65.5)	38.4 (16.3)	7.1 (3.0)	33.7 (14.3)	2.3 (1.0)
1960	296.4 (69.4)	51.9 (12.1)	16.2 (3.8)	52.3 (12.2)	10.7 (2.5)
1970	617.2 (73.7)	79.8 (9.5)	20.3 (2.4)	81.6 (9.7)	38.4 (4.6)
1980	1651.7 (73.6)	177.6 (7.9)	31.3 (1.4)	198.5 (8.8)	183.9 (8.2)
1990	3351.7 (72.2)	381.0 (8.2)	49.1 (1.1)	408.6 (8.8)	452.4 (9.7)
2000	5715.2 (71.6)	715.0 (9.0)	141.6 (1.8)	876.4 (11.0)	532.7 (6.7)
2005	7030.3 (71.1)	970.7 (9.8)	72.8 (0.7)	1330.7 (13.5)	483.4 (4.9)

Source: Economic Report of the President (Washington, DC: U.S. Government Printing Office), 1980 and 2006.

just recently, when the budget surpluses and falling interest rates of the late 1990s again reduced the share of income going to interest. The recession in the early 2000s and the resulting deficits caused interest's share to rise early but recently that growth has slowed.

Personal or Family Distribution of Income

Personal or family distribution of income The distribution of income to individuals or family groups (typically quintiles or fifths of the population).

When most people use the term "the distribution of income," they mean **personal or family distribution of income.** This distributional measure is concerned with how much income, in percentage terms, goes to specific segments of the population.

To analyze personal and family income distribution, the Census Bureau essentially arrays households from the lowest incomes to the highest. It then splits these households into quintiles, or fifths, from the lowest 20% of households to the highest 20%. After totaling and averaging household incomes for each quintile, the Census Bureau computes the percentage of income flowing to each quintile.

Today, the United States contains just over 100 million households. So the 20 million households with the lowest incomes compose the bottom quintile, and the 20 million households with the highest incomes compose the upper quintile.

Table 2 shows the official income distribution estimates for the United States since 1970. These estimates are based "solely on *money income before taxes* and do not include the value of employment based fringe benefits nor of government-provided noncash benefits such as food stamps, Medicaid and public or subsidized housing."[1]

Table 2 Share of Aggregate Income Received by Each Household Quintile (fifth): 1970–2005 and the Gini Coefficient

Year	Lowest	Second	Third	Fourth	Highest	Gini Coefficient
1970	4.1	10.8	17.4	24.5	43.3	0.394
1975	4.4	10.5	17.1	24.8	43.2	0.397
1980	4.3	10.3	16.9	24.9	43.7	0.403
1985	4.0	9.7	16.3	24.6	45.3	0.419
1990	3.9	9.6	15.9	24.0	46.6	0.428
1995	3.7	9.1	15.2	23.3	48.7	0.450
2000	3.6	8.9	14.9	23.0	49.6	0.462
2005	3.4	8.6	14.6	23.0	50.4	0.469

Source: U.S. Census Bureau, Current Population Reports, P60-231, *Income, Poverty, and Health Insurance in the United States: 2005* (Washington, DC: U.S. Government Printing Office), 2006.

Note that if the income distribution were perfectly equal, all quintiles would receive 20% of aggregate income. A quick look at these income distributions over the past three decades suggests that our distribution of income has been growing more unequal: Every income quintile except the highest has declined in percentage of total income. Keep in mind that these numbers ignore taxes and transfers.

[1]U.S. Bureau of the Census, *Money Income in the United States: 2004–05,* p. 2.

Compressing distribution data into quintiles allows us to see how distribution has evolved. Economists have developed two primary measures that allow comparisons to be drawn with ease across time and between countries. These measures are Lorenz curves and the Gini coefficient.

Lorenz Curves

Lorenz curves cumulate families of various income levels on the horizontal axis, relating this to their cumulated share of total income on the vertical axis. Figure 1, for simplicity, shows a two-person economy. Assume that both people earn 50% of the total income, or that income is divided evenly. Point *a* in Figure 1 marks out this point, resulting in equal distribution curve 0*ac*.

The second curve in Figure 1 shows a two-person economy where the low-income person earns 25% of the total income and the upper income person receives 75% (point *b*). This graph is skewed to the right (curve 0*bc*), indicating an unequal distribution. If this two-person income distribution were as unequal as possible (0% and 100%), the Lorenz curve would be equal to curve 0*dc*.

Lorenz curves
A graphical method of showing the income distribution by cumulating families of various income levels on the horizontal axis and relating this to their cumulative share of total income on the vertical axis.

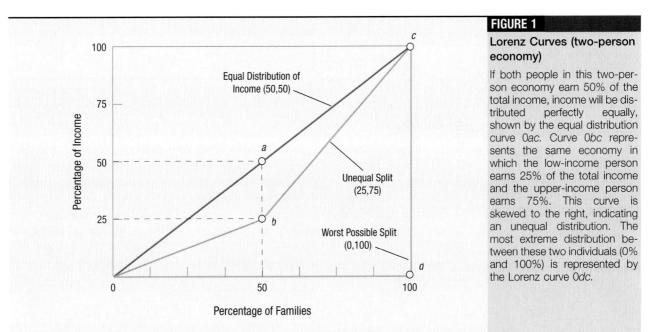

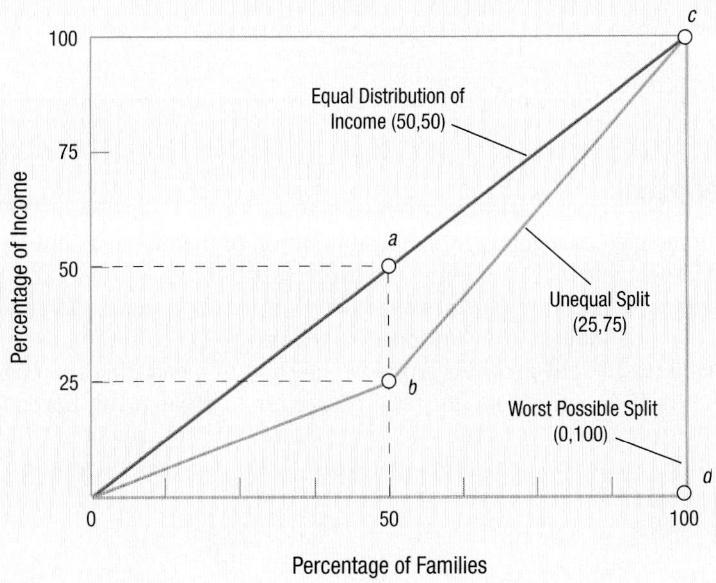

FIGURE 1

Lorenz Curves (two-person economy)

If both people in this two-person economy earn 50% of the total income, income will be distributed perfectly equally, shown by the equal distribution curve 0*ac*. Curve 0*bc* represents the same economy in which the low-income person earns 25% of the total income and the upper-income person earns 75%. This curve is skewed to the right, indicating an unequal distribution. The most extreme distribution between these two individuals (0% and 100%) is represented by the Lorenz curve 0*dc*.

Figure 2 and its accompanying table on the next page offer more realistic Lorenz curves for income and wealth data for the United States in 2001. The quintile income distribution in the second column of the table is cumulated in the third column and plotted in Figure 2. (To *cumulate* a quintile means to add its percentage of income to the percentages earned by all lower quintiles.)

In Figure 2, for instance, the share of income received by the lowest fifth is 3.5%; it is plotted as point *a*. Next, the lowest two quintiles are summed (3.5 + 8.7 = 12.2) and plotted as point *b*. The process continues until all quintiles have been plotted to create the Lorenz curve.

Figure 2 also plots the Lorenz curve for wealth; it shows how wealth is much more unequally distributed than income. The wealthiest 20% of Americans control over 80% of wealth, even though they earn only half of all income.

FIGURE 2

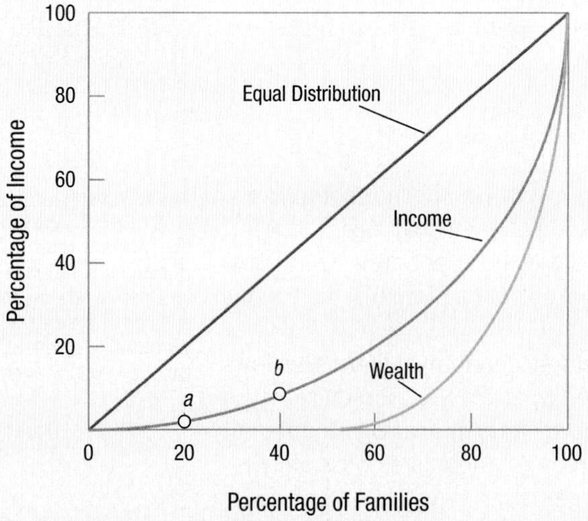

	Income 2001		Wealth 2001	
Quintile	**Income**	**Cum.**	**Wealth**	**Cum.**
Lowest	3.5	3.5	0	0
Second	8.7	12.2	0	0
Third	14.6	26.8	3	3
Fourth	23.0	49.8	11	14
Highest	50.1	100.0	86	100

Lorenz Curves (for the United States: 2001)

The graph shows the Lorenz curves for income and wealth in the United States in 2001. The quintile distribution of income, found in the second column of the accompanying table, is cumulated in the third column and then plotted as a Lorenz curve. Notice how wealth is much more unequally distributed than income.

Gini Coefficient

Lorenz curves give us a good graphical summation of income distributions, but they can be inconvenient to use when comparing distributions between different countries or across time. Economists would like one number that represents an economy's income inequality. The **Gini coefficient** provides such a number.

Gini coefficient
A precise method of measuring the position of the Lorenz curve as the area between the Lorenz curve and the equal distribution line divided by the total area below the equal distribution line.

The Gini coefficient provides a precise method of measuring the position of the Lorenz curve. It is defined as the ratio of the area between the Lorenz curve and the equal distribution line, in the numerator, and the total area below the equal distribution line, in the denominator. In Figure 3, the Gini coefficient is the ratio of area A to area $(A + B)$.

FIGURE 3

The Gini Coefficient

The Gini coefficient is a precise method of measuring the position of the Lorenz curve. It is defined as the ratio of the area between the Lorenz curve and the equal distribution line, and the total area below the equal distribution line. Thus, the Gini coefficient is equal to the ratio between area *A* and area (*A* + *B*). If distribution were equal, area *A* would be zero, and the Gini coefficient would equal zero. If distribution were as unequal as possible, area *B* would disappear, so the Gini coefficient would be 1.

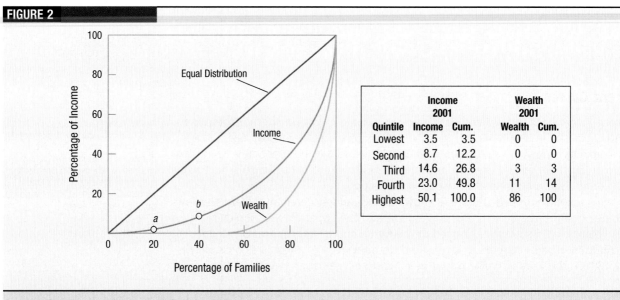

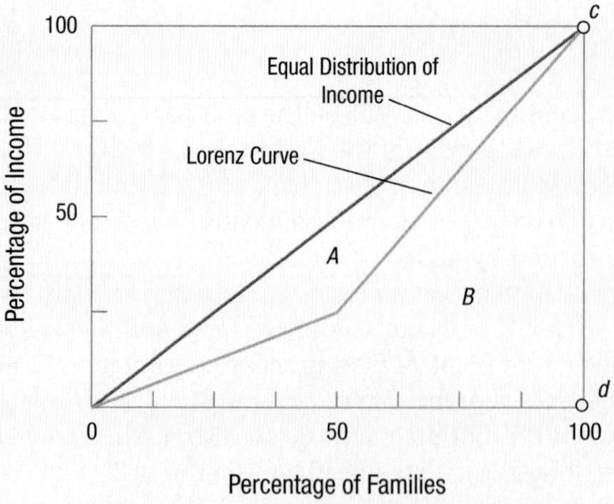

If the distribution were equal, area A would disappear (equal zero), so the Gini coefficient would be zero. If the distribution were as unequal as possible, with one individual or household earning all national income, area B would disappear, so the Gini coefficient would be 1.

As a rule, the lower the coefficient, the more equal the distribution; the higher the coefficient, the more unequal. Looking back at the last column in Table 2, the Gini coefficient confirms that the basic income distribution has become more unequal since 1970. The Gini coefficient has risen from 0.394 in 1970 to 0.462 in 2000 and 0.469 in 2005.

The Impact of Redistribution

In the United States, there is a vast array of income redistribution policies, including the progressive income tax (a tax that taxes higher incomes at a higher rate than lower incomes), housing subsidies, and other transfer payments such as Medicaid and Medicare, Social Security, and traditional welfare programs. Remember that the income distribution data in Table 2 *excluded* such government-provided cash and noncash benefits, and the effects of taxation.

Figure 4 provides an estimate of the impact progressive taxes and transfer payments (cash and in-kind) had on the income distribution for 2001. As we would expect, distribution became more equal: The Gini coefficient declined from 0.466 according to the official measure using gross income to 0.412 after adjusting for taxes and transfer payments.

FIGURE 4

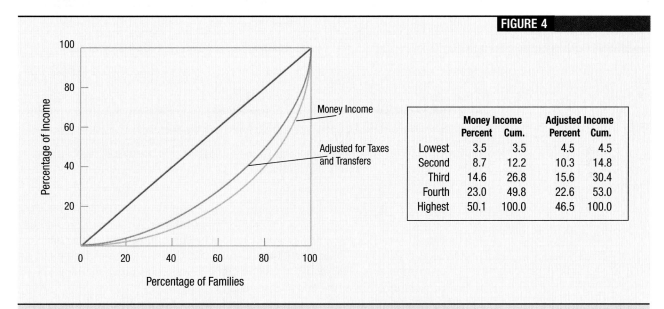

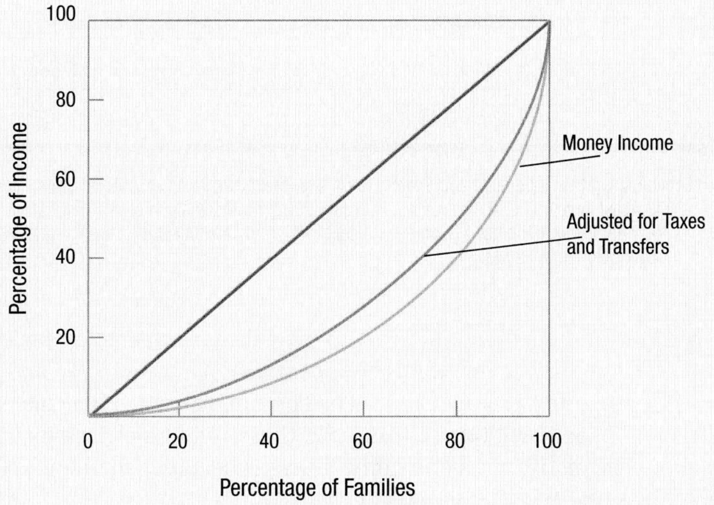

	Money Income Percent	Money Income Cum.	Adjusted Income Percent	Adjusted Income Cum.
Lowest	3.5	3.5	4.5	4.5
Second	8.7	12.2	10.3	14.8
Third	14.6	26.8	15.6	30.4
Fourth	23.0	49.8	22.6	53.0
Highest	50.1	100.0	46.5	100.0

Lorenz Curves for the United States, 2001: Money Income and Income Adjusted for Taxes and Transfer Payments

These Lorenz curves provide an estimate of the impact progressive taxes and transfer payments (cash and in-kind) had on income distribution in 2001. As one would expect, distribution becomes more equal once taxes and transfer payments are taken into account. In this case, the Gini coefficient declined from .466 to .412.

Table 3 on the next page provides some examples of how income distribution varies around the world. Income in European countries is generally more equally distributed than in the United States, while many South American countries have more unequal distributions.

Redistribution policies are the subject of intense debates. Those on the political right argue that differences in income are the natural result of a market system

Table 3 Gini Coefficients for Various Countries and Years

Year	Country	Gini Coefficient
1995	Algeria	.353
1998–2001	Argentina	.502
1985	Australia	.212
1998–2001	Brazil	.567
1987	Canada	.253
1998–2001	Chile	.558
1998	China (urban)	.403
1997	India	.378
1998	Indonesia	.375
1998–2001	Mexico	.525
1996–97	Pakistan	.312
1997	Philippines	.461
1987	Sweden	.190
1998	Thailand	.414
2004	United States	.466
1998–2001	Venezuela	.452

Source: Richard Adams, "Economic Growth, Inequality and Poverty: Findings for a New Data Set," *World Bank Policy Research Working Paper #2972* (Washington, D.C.: World Bank), February 2002; M. Mackintosh et al.., *Economics and Changing Economies* (New York: International Thomson Business Press), 1996; and "Inequality in Latin America: A Stubborn Curse," *The Economist*, November 6, 2003.

in which different individuals possess different personal endowments, schooling, and ambition. They believe, moreover, that the incentives of the marketplace are needed to encourage people to work and produce. The opportunities that markets provide mean that some people will be winners and others will lose. These analysts are unconcerned about the distribution of income unless it becomes so unequal that it discourages incentives and reduces efficiency.

Those on the political left argue that public policy should ultimately be guided by human needs. They see personal wealth as being the product of community effort as much as individual effort, and therefore they favor greater government taxation of income and wealth. By and large, European nations have found this argument more compelling than has the United States. This is reflected in the breadth of European social welfare policies. Because there is no correct answer (except possibly keeping distribution away from the extremes), this debate continues.

Causes of Income Inequality

Many factors contribute to income inequality in our society. First, as just mentioned, people are born into different circumstances with differing natural abilities. Families take varying interest in the well-being of their children, with some kids receiving immense inputs of family time and capital, while others receive little. These family choices largely fall outside the realm of public policy.

Human Capital

The guarantee of a free public education through high school and huge subsidies to public colleges and universities for all Americans are designed to even out some of the economic differences among families. Still, public education will not eliminate the disparities. Some parents plan their children's educations long before they are born, while other parents ignore education altogether.

Table 4 provides evidence of the impact investments in education have on median earnings. Those without high school diplomas earned the least, roughly half of what high school graduates earned. A college degree resulted in median earnings nearly four times higher than what individuals without high school diplomas earned.

Table 4 Impact of Education on Median (real 1998$) Earnings and Median Net Worth: 1989–98

	1998 Median Earnings (dollars)					1998 Median Net Worth (thousands of dollars)				
Education	1989	1992	1995	1998	Change (89–98)	1989	1992	1995	1998	Change (89–98)
No high school	17,300	14,000	15,500	15,500	−10.4	30.7	21.3	24	20.9	−31.9
High school diploma	28,800	27,200	27,700	29,200	1.4	46.9	43.9	54.7	53.8	14.7
Some college	37,200	31,600	32,700	35,500	−5	58.5	65.9	49.7	73.9	26.3
College degree	53,100	51,500	48,700	54,700	3	141.4	112.1	110.9	146.4	3.5

Source: U.S. Department of Commerce, *Statistical Abstract of the United States: 2004–05* (Washington, DC: U.S. Government Printing Office), 2005.

If the amount of education is a major factor accounting for inequalities in earnings, the effects are even more profound when we consider net worth. Note that in 1998, the median net worth of those with college degrees was over *seven times higher* than that of individuals without high school diplomas. Note also that, in real terms (1998 dollars), median income and net wealth declined for those without high school diplomas between 1989 and 1998.

One factor that might help explain this decline in real income and wealth for those at the bottom of the income and wealth ladder is the huge influx of immigrants from Mexico and Central and South America. Many of these individuals lack high school educations, and their numbers have driven real wages down in those occupations requiring few skills.

At the same time, our economy has become more technologically complex. Manufacturing jobs have dwindled, reducing the demand for lower-skilled workers, reducing their real wages. Several decades ago, people with low education levels could find highly productive work in manufacturing, with good wages and benefits. Globalization and increased capital mobility, however, have led many of these jobs to migrate to lower-wage countries. The result: Real wages have declined for Americans in lower-skilled occupations.

Our economy is increasingly oriented toward service industries, making investments in human capital more important than ever. The service industry spans more than just burger flipping, maid service, and landscaping. The United States is still the world leader in the design and development of new products, basic scientific research and development, and other professional services. All these industries and occupations have one thing in common: the need for highly skilled and highly educated employees.

Other Factors

In an earlier chapter, we saw that economic discrimination (dual labor markets or segmented markets) leads to an income distribution skewed against those subject to discrimination. Reduced wages then reduce an individual's incentive to invest in human capital since the returns are lower, perpetuating a vicious circle.

Table 5 outlines some characteristics of households occupying two different income quintiles. By comparing the lowest quintile with the highest, we can see some of the reasons for income inequality. As the Census Bureau summarizes these

Table 5 Distribution of Households by Selected Characteristics within Income Quintiles: 2005

Characteristic	Lowest Quintile	Highest Quintile
Type of Residence		
Inside metropolitan area	78.8	90.8
Inside central city	39.9	29.3
Outside central cities	39.0	61.5
Outside metro area	21.2	9.2
Type of Household		
Family households	41.0	87.5
Married-couple families	17.9	79.0
Nonfamily households	59.0	12.5
Householder living alone	55.5	6.8
Age of Householder		
15 to 34 years	23.5	14.8
35 to 54 years	25.9	57.2
55 to 64 years	13.5	19.7
65 years or older	37.1	8.3
Number of Earners		
No earners	58.7	2.6
One earner	35.9	21.1
Two or more earners	5.5	76.3
Work Experience of Householder		
Worked	35.8	88.7
Worked full-time, year-round	14.0	73.0
Worked part-time or part year	21.9	15.7
Did not work	64.2	11.3

Source: U.S. Census Bureau, Current Population Reports, P60-231, *Income, Poverty, and Health Insurance in the United States: 2005* (Washington, DC: U.S. Government Printing Office), 2006.

differences, "High-income households tended to be family households that included two or more earners, lived in the suburbs of a large city, and had a working householder between 35 and 54 years old. In contrast, low-income households tended to be in a city with an elderly householder who lived alone and did not work."[2]

The rise in two-earner households over the last two decades accounts for a large part of the growing inequality in income. Note in Table 5 that only 5.5% of lowest quintile households had two earners, while 76.3% of the highest quintile did. Also, only 11.3% of top quintile householders did not work, but 64.2% of those in the bottom quintile were not working.

It is hardly surprising that households with two people working should tend to have higher incomes than households with only one person or none working. In most households, whether one or two people work represents a choice. And today, clearly more couples are opting for two incomes. This is significant, given that rising income inequality is often cited as evidence that the United States needs to change its public policies to reduce inequalities. Yet, if the rise in inequality is due largely to changes in household attitudes toward work and income, with more couples choosing dual-career households, changes in public policy may not be needed. Rising inequality may simply be a reflection of the changing personal choices of many households.

This overview of income distribution and inequality provides a broad foundation for the remainder of the chapter, which focuses on poverty, its causes, and possible cures.

Checkpoint
The Distribution of Income and Wealth

REVIEW

- The functional distribution of income splits income among factors of production.
- The family or personal distribution of income typically splits income into quintiles.
- Lorenz curves cumulate families of various income levels on the horizontal axis and their cumulative share of income on the vertical axis.
- The Gini coefficient is the ratio of the area between the Lorenz curve and the equal distribution line to the total area below the equal distribution line. It is used to compare income distribution across time and between countries.
- Income redistribution activities such as progressive taxes, Medicare, Medicaid, and other transfer and welfare programs reduce the Gini coefficient and reduce the inequality in the distribution of income.
- Income inequality is caused by a number of factors including individual investment in human capital, natural abilities, and discrimination.

QUESTIONS

Economist Charles Murray has suggested doing away with all social insurance including Social Security, Medicare, Medicaid, and other welfare programs and instead, simply giving $10,000 a year to every citizen of the United States over 21 years of age. The purpose of the idea is to reduce bureaucracy and the government's role in the decision making of families. Expand his idea slightly by eliminating the age restriction. Would this improve the income distribution in America? Why or why not?

Answers to the Checkpoint questions can be found at the end of this chapter.

---

[2]U.S. Bureau of the Census, *Money Income in the United States: 2001,* p. 9.

Poverty

Thus far, we have examined income distribution in general terms, looking from the top of the spectrum to the bottom. This section focuses on the bottom of the income spectrum; those who live in poverty. First, we will look at poverty thresholds and how they are defined. Then we will turn to the incidence of poverty and its trends. Last, we will take a brief look at some experimental measures of poverty, considering their impact on measured rates of poverty.

Measuring Poverty

Poverty thresholds
Income levels for various household sizes below which these people are considered living in poverty.

Poverty thresholds were developed by Mollie Orshansky in the 1960s. They were based on the Agriculture Department's Economy Food Plan, the least expensive plan by which a family could feed itself. The Agriculture Department first surveyed the food-buying patterns of low-income households, using these data to determine the cost of a nutritionally balanced food plan on a low-income budget. Orshansky then extrapolated these costs to determine the cost of maintaining such a food plan for households of various compositions. Finally, to determine the official poverty threshold, Orshansky multiplied the cost of the food plan, adjusted for family size, by 3. This multiplier was based on an earlier household survey that had shown the average family of three or more spends roughly a third of its income on food.[3]

Since the 1960s, the poverty thresholds have been updated every year for changes in inflation using the consumer price index (CPI). Table 6 shows the poverty thresholds for 2005. If a family's income is less than the threshold, every person in the household is considered poor. Official thresholds do not vary geographically. "Income" includes all money income before taxes, including cash benefits, but not

Table 6 Average Poverty Thresholds: 2005

One person	$9,973
Two people	12,755
Three people	15,577
Four people	19,971
Five people	23,613
Six people	26,683
Seven people	30,249
Eight people	33,610
Nine people or more	40,288

Source: U.S. Census Bureau, Current Population Reports, P60-231, *Income, Poverty, and Health Insurance in the United States: 2005* (Washington, DC: U.S. Government Printing Office), 2006.

[3]See Constance F. Citro and Robert T. Michael, *Measuring Poverty: A New Approach* (Washington DC: National Academy Press), 1995, p. 13 and Chap. 2 for more detail on how thresholds are measured.

capital gains or noncash benefits such as public housing, food stamps, and Medicaid. Later, we will briefly look at some new alternative measures that do adjust for these factors.

The Incidence of Poverty

Poverty rates for the United States since 1959 are shown in Figure 5. Poverty fell rapidly between 1959 and 1975 but has remained roughly stable ever since, fluctuating with the business cycle: rising around recessions (the shaded vertical bars) and falling when times are good.

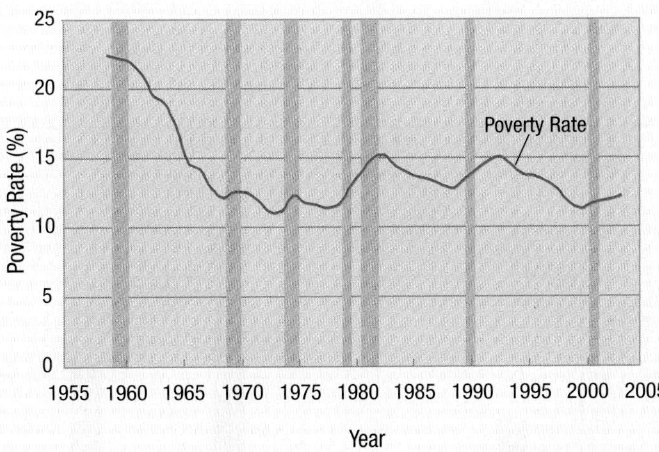

FIGURE 5

Poverty Rates in the United States, 1959–2004

Poverty fell rapidly between 1959 and 1975 but has remained roughly stable ever since, fluctuating with the business cycle: rising around recessions (the shaded vertical bars) and falling when times have improved.

Source: U.S. Census Bureau, Current Population Reports, P60-222, *Poverty in the United States: 2004,* U.S. Government Printing Office, Washington, DC, 2005.

Poverty rates vary considerably along racial and ethnic lines. Figure 6 charts the poverty rate by race over 45 years, from 1959 to 2004. Over most of this time, the poverty rate for blacks and Hispanics was roughly twice the rate for whites.

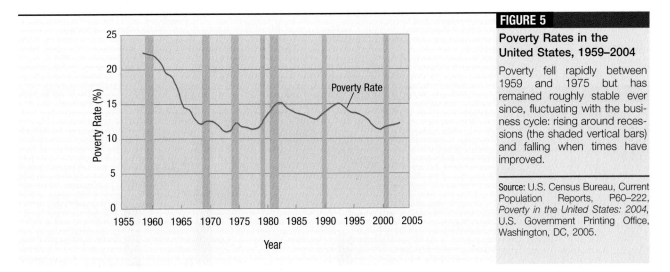

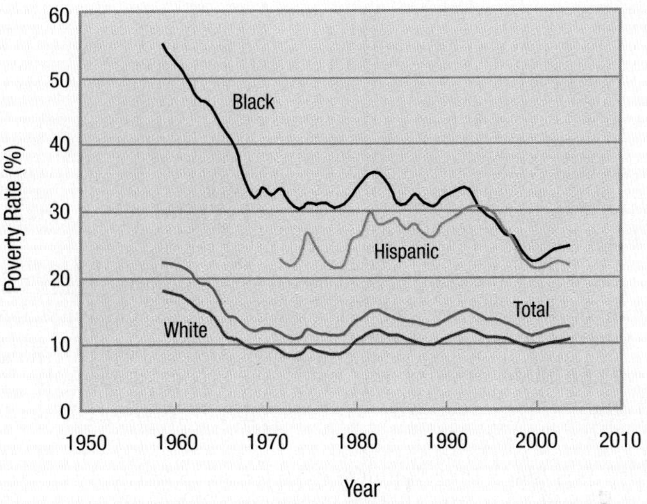

FIGURE 6

Poverty Rates by Race and Ethnic Origin, 1959–2004

Poverty rates vary considerably along racial and ethnic lines. Over most of the 45 years from 1959 to 2004, the poverty rate for blacks and Hispanics was roughly twice the rate for whites. Both of these minority groups benefited, however, from the strong economic growth of the 1990s, their poverty rates dropping from around 30% at the beginning of the decade to below 25% today. White poverty remained fairly steady over the 1990s, fluctuating between 10% and 11%.

Source: U.S. Census Bureau, Current Population Reports, P60-229, *Poverty in the United States: 2004,* U.S. Government Printing Office, Washington, DC, 2005, Table B1.

Both of these minority groups benefited, however, from the strong economic growth of the 1990s, their poverty rates dropping from around 30% at the beginning of the decade to below 25% today. White poverty remained fairly steady over the 1990s, fluctuating between 10% and 11%.

These data suggest that robust economic growth is a major force for reducing poverty. The expression "a rising tide floats all boats" would appear to have something to it.

In families where one person worked at any time during the year, poverty rates tended to be lower. Among the poor, nearly 40% worked, but less than 12% worked full-time year-round. One family member's work status, moreover, affected the poverty status of all family members. Figure 7 charts 2002 poverty rates by the type of family a person lived in and the presence or absence of working family members. As expected, when no family member was employed, poverty rates soared.

FIGURE 7

Poverty Rates of People in Families by Family Type and Presence of Workers, 2002

In families where one person worked at any time during the year, poverty rates tend to be lower. Among the poor, nearly 40% worked, but less than 12% worked full-time year-round. One family member's work status, moreover, affected the poverty status of all family members. The figure charts 2002 poverty rates by the type of family a person lived in and the presence or absence of working family members. When no family member was employed, poverty rates soared.

Source: U.S. Census Bureau, Current Population Reports, P60–222, *Poverty in the United States: 2002*, U.S. Government Printing Office, Washington, DC, 2003, Figure 4, p. 8.

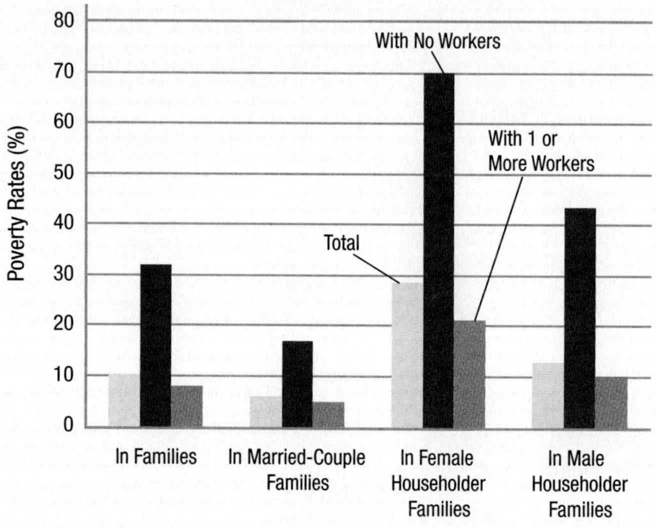

Depth of Poverty

It is one thing to say that a certain percentage of the population is poor. It is another to determine just how poor they are. The poverty threshold for a family of four today is nearly $20,000. If most poor families had incomes approaching this threshold, we could be confident poverty was just a transitory stage—one phase of the life cycle—and that many people who were poor today would have higher incomes tomorrow.

But if, conversely, many poor families have incomes below $10,000, our view of poverty will be different, and our public policies aimed at reducing poverty will need to be considerably more robust.

To gain a view of the broad spectrum of poverty, economists have developed two *depth of poverty* measures that describe the economic well-being of lower-income families. One measure, the **income deficit,** tells us how far below the poverty threshold a family's income lies. In 2002, the income deficit for families living in poverty averaged just over $7,200.

Income deficit
The difference between the poverty threshold and a family's income.

The second measure of poverty, the one we will focus on, is the **ratio of income to poverty.** It compares family income to the poverty threshold and expresses this comparison as a ratio. Thus, the ratio for families with incomes equal to the poverty threshold will equal 1.0; the ratio for those living at half the threshold income will be 0.5. The Census Bureau considers people who live in families with ratios below 0.5 to be "severely or desperately poor." Those with ratios between 0.5 and 1.0 are "poor," and people with ratios above 1.0 but less than 1.25 (less than 25% above the poverty threshold) are considered to be "near poor."

Ratio of income to poverty
The ratio of family income to the poverty threshold. Families with ratios below 0.5 are considered severely poor, families with ratios between 0.5 and 1.0 are considered poor, and those families with ratios between 1.0 and 1.25 are considered near poor.

Table 7 lists the 2005 data for these categories of poverty. Nearly 5% of Americans, or over 15 million people, lived in families that were severely poor, having incomes of less than half the poverty threshold.

Table 7 **Ratios of Family Income to Poverty Threshold by Race: 2005**

	Severely Poor Under 0.5		Poor 0.5 to 1.0		Near Poor 1.0 to 1.25		Total U.S. Population	
	Number (thousands)	% of Total	Number (thousands)	% of Total	Number (thousands)	% of Total	Number (thousands)	%
White	10,288	64.5	14,584	69.4	8,992	72.7	235,430	80.3
Non-Hispanic white	6,916	43.4	9,311	44.3	6,035	48.8	195,553	66.7
Black	4,302	27.0	4,866	23.1	2,316	18.7	36,802	12.6
Asian and Pacific Islander	647	4.1	755	3.6	507	4.1	12,580	4.3
Hispanic	3,710	23.3	5,667	27.0	3,214	26.0	43,020	14.7
Totals	15,928	100.0	21,022	100.0	12,377	100.0	293,135	100.0

Source: U.S. Census Bureau, Current Population Reports, P60-231, *Income, Poverty, and Health Insurance in the United States: 2005* (Washington, DC: U.S. Government Printing Office), 2006. Note that numbers are in thousands and that totals only include a summation of white, black, and other ethnic categories; Hispanics can be of any race and are included in the prior three categories.

The ethnic breakdown in Table 7 shows that blacks, who represent less that 13% of the U.S. population, nonetheless constituted 23.1% of those living in poverty in 2005, including 27.0% of those considered "severely poor." Non-Hispanic whites are nearly 70% of the population, but represent less than 44% of those who are desperately poor. Hispanics fared marginally better than blacks. At nearly 15% of the population, over a quarter of Hispanics lived in poverty and represent over a fifth of those considered "severely poor." Note that numbers are in thousands and that totals only include a summation of white, black, and other ethnic categories.

Alternative Measures of Poverty

Many researchers have questioned the relevance of the current method for determining poverty thresholds. The National Academy of Science studied the official approach to poverty thresholds and concluded that the measure is flawed because "[it] counts taxes as income, [and] is flawed in the adjustments to the households for different family circumstances."[4]

The panel further concluded that the current poverty measure does not distinguish well among working parents, workers generally, nonworkers, or people with higher versus lower health care needs and costs. Finally, noting that the current threshold is simply the threshold from "1963 updated for price changes," the panel questioned the value of such a simplistic approach, given how much the U.S. standard of living has changed.

Given the Committee's findings, the Census Bureau has recently developed some new ways of measuring poverty. These alternative measures of poverty differ from the old in basing their estimates on after-tax income plus capital gains and counting as income such noncash benefits as food stamps and housing subsidies plus imputed return on home equity.

The Census Bureau derived its new estimates of income thresholds from a survey of expenditures on food, clothing, housing, utilities, and other necessities for the typical family of four (two adults and two kids). These figures were then adjusted to reflect differences in family composition and size, given that children consume less than adults, some household economies are associated with larger families, and the first child in a one-adult family costs more to support than the first child in a two-adult family.

The results of these adjustments are shown in Table 8. Under these measures, poverty rates fell by roughly a quarter.

Eliminating Poverty

Poverty can be a relative or an absolute measure. As we saw in the previous section, the official measure of poverty in the United States is based on an absolute number, the poverty threshold. Some researchers, however, think a relative measure would be more useful, such as labeling the bottom 20% of American households "poor."

If we decide to use such a measure, poverty will never be eliminated, no matter how wealthy our country might become. A relative measure obscures the fact that poverty in the United States means something different than it does in the developing world. The official U.S. poverty threshold for an individual is an income of roughly $25 a day. In the developing world, by contrast, the World Bank and other agencies define poverty as incomes of less than $2, or even $1, a day. By World Bank standards, poverty has already been eradicated in the United States.

Reducing Income Inequality

Regardless of how poverty is defined, the question of how to reduce it is controversial. The political left views income and wealth redistribution as the chief means of reducing poverty. Social justice, they argue, requires that the government provide an extensive safety net for the poor. In their view, services the government already provides, including public education, housing subsidies, Medicaid, and unemployment compensation should be greatly expanded.

They say these policies should be supplemented, moreover, by increasing the progressivity of the tax system. This would reduce the inequalities in wealth and income. By increasing the tax burden on the well-to-do, people of modest incomes could lead more meaningful and just lives.

Increasing Economic Growth

The opposite side of the political spectrum argues that such programs, when allowed to become too expansive, can be disastrous. Welfare significantly reduces

[4]Citro and Michael, *Measuring Poverty*, pp. 97–98.

Table 8 Alternative Poverty Measures by Selected Characteristics: 2003

Characteristic	Poverty Measure: Official	Poverty Measure: Alternative
Total	12.5	9.0
People in Families	10.8	7.4
People in Married-Couple Families	6.2	4.0
People in Families with a Female Householder Present	30.0	21.4
People in Families with a Male Householder, no Wife Present	14.2	10.5
Age		
Under 18 years	17.6	12.0
18–64 years	10.8	8.5
65 years and over	10.2	5.7
Race and Hispanic Origin		
Non-Hispanic white	8.2	6.0
Black	24.4	17.5
Hispanic	22.2	15.8
Region		
Northeast	11.3	7.8
Midwest	10.7	7.8
South	14.1	10.4
West	12.6	9.0

Source: U.S. Census Bureau, Current Population Reports, P60-227, *Alternative Poverty Estimates in the United States: 2003* (Washington, DC: U.S. Government Printing Office), 2005.

the incentive to work and produce, thereby reducing the economy's output. A vibrant market economy accommodates the wishes of those who want full-time, upwardly mobile careers as well as those who only want just enough work to pursue other goals.

Since wages provide 70% of all income, those on the political right note, there inevitably will be some inequality in a market system. Some people, after all, make bad choices and fail to invest enough in their education or job skills. Yet, the possibility of failure itself provides an incentive to work hard and invest, and the political right sees this sort of efficiency in the economy as being more important than equity or fairness. The best way to cure poverty, they argue, is by implementing policies that increase the economic pie shared by all, not just by splitting up the pie more evenly.

This political dispute has fueled a controversy in economics. One group of economists argues that economic growth raises low incomes at a rate similar to that of average incomes, such that the poor benefit from growth just as much as anyone else.[5] Other economists reply that the shift toward freer markets around the world, combined with the resulting economic growth, has widened inequalities, causing the poor to fall further behind.

Who is right? Economist Richard Adams launched a major study to determine whether policies designed to foster growth or policies geared toward reducing income and wealth inequalities do more to reduce poverty in developing countries.[6] His basic conclusions are

> *Economic growth represents an important means for reducing poverty in the developing world. . . . Economic growth reduces poverty because first and foremost growth has little impact on income inequality. . . . Since income distributions are relatively stable over time, economic growth—in the sense of rising incomes—has the general effect of raising income for all members of society, including the poor.*

Adams's study also notes that "for any given rate of economic growth, the more inequality falls, the greater is the reduction in poverty." For income redistribution to reduce poverty, there must be a significant economic pie to redistribute. For most developing nations, the size of the pie is not large enough to measurably reduce poverty.

Rawls and Nozick

Unfortunately, there is no unified theory of income distribution that takes the various issues we have discussed into account. Earlier chapters suggested that income depends on productivity—in competitive markets, each input (factor) is paid the value of its marginal product.

Human capital analysis adds that as people invest in themselves, their productivity and income will rise. Analysis of imperfect input markets, however, shows that income distribution advantages accrue more to those with monopoly or monopsony power.

Our analysis of economic discrimination and dual labor or segmented markets suggested several more reasons why incomes may be skewed in favor of some groups rather than others. The bargaining strength of labor unions is yet another factor that can skew income distribution, in this case in favor of union members.

These analyses have focused, in one way or another, on whether certain patterns of income distribution are economically efficient. Yet, how do we know whether various income distributions are equitable or fair? Is there anywhere to turn for theoretical help in addressing this question? The answer is a qualified "yes." Two philosophers, John Rawls and Robert Nozick, published competing views on this subject in the early 1970s.[7]

John Rawls proposed the "maximin principle," in which he argued that society should maximize the welfare of the least well-off individual. He asks us to conduct a thought experiment: Assume you must decide on the income distribution for your society, without knowing where in the distribution you will end up. Since chance could lead to you being the least well-off individual in the society, Rawls suggests people would favor significant income redistribution under these circumstances.

---

[5]David Dollar and Aart Kraay, "Growth is Good for the Poor," *World Bank Policy Research Working Paper #2587,* (Washington, DC: World Bank), August 2001.

[6]Richard Adams, "Economic Growth, Inequality and Poverty: Findings for a New Data Set," *World Bank Policy Research Working Paper #2972* (Washington, DC: World Bank), February 2002.

[7]John Rawls, *A Theory of Justice* (Oxford: Clarendon), 1972; and Robert Nozick, *Anarchy, State and Utopia* (Oxford: Blackwell), 1974.

Robert Nozick argued that it is "illegitimate to use the coercive power of the state to make some better off at the expense of others." To Nozick, justice requires protecting property rights "legitimately acquired or legitimately transferred."[8] Nozick argued strongly for competitive market equilibriums, suggesting that the state has no role in selecting which equilibrium is best.

This debate highlights the perennial tradeoff in economic policy between equity and efficiency, a tradeoff that serves as a bone of contention in nearly every discussion of economic and public policy. Though microeconomics is sometimes beset by controversy itself, at its best, it provides us with a dispassionate framework in which to analyze and discuss many issues.

Income Mobility and Poverty

Todd Davidson/Getty Images

In 1964, President Lyndon Johnson declared war on poverty in America. As a way of summing up this chapter, let us consider how well the United States has done in this war on poverty more than 40 years later.[9]

In general terms, the United States has made progress. We saw above that poverty rates fell in the first 10 years since Johnson declared war on poverty. After that, poverty rates rose in the 1970s and 1980s, and then fell again during the economic boom of the 1990s. A growing economy helped.

This general decrease in poverty rates in the last 40 years did not translate across all groups. The most dramatic drop came in the percentage of aged people who were poor, dropping from 30% in 1963 to 10.4% in 2002. Programs such as Social Security, Medicare, and Medicaid undoubtedly helped. For blacks, the story has not been so bright: A poverty rate of 40% in 1963 dropped to 24% in 2002. This is progress, but the rate is still too high. Most troubling is the rate for children in poverty, falling from 23.1% in 1963 to 14.4% in 1973, then rising back up to 16.7% recently. New changes in welfare laws are meant to combat this: Children in poor families are now entitled to Medicaid even if the head of the household goes off public assistance, taking away a large disincentive for a parent to seek work.

We saw earlier that two-earner families and married couples with children were highly unlikely to be poor (6.8% in poverty). Contrast to this the fact that approximately one third of the families headed by an unmarried woman were likely to be poor.

Program changes in the 1990s increased the value of work by increasing incentives. The earned income tax credit (EITC) was expanded. Although time limits were placed on welfare use, more benefits were available for those who worked.

Let us look at poverty another way. The poverty rates provide a snapshot in time. How about over time? What is the human side to this? Do people start in poverty or fall into poverty and then stay there, or is there movement out of poverty?

A study tracking over 180,000 workers in California from 1988 to 2000 provides an answer.[10] People in all quintiles moved up the economic ladder, but those workers who started out at the lowest wages had the greatest real wage gains. More than 80% of workers in the bottom bracket moved up to a higher earnings quintile. In particular, those with the lowest wages gained the most when they switched industries, searching for better career and earnings potential. This finding points to the dynamism in the economy, and the recognition of opportunity by all income classes.

---

[8]Kay, John, *The Truth About Markets: Their Genius, Their Limits, Their Follies* (London: Penguin Books), 2003, p. 187.

[9]The following commentary is based in part on the article by Alan B. Krueger, "After 40 Years, What Are Some Results and Lessons of America's War on Poverty?" *New York Times,* January 8, 2004, p. C2.

[10]See Michael Dardia, Elisa Barbour, Akhtar Khan, and Colleen Moore, "Moving Up? Earnings Mobility in California, 1988–2000," *California Policy Review,* vol. 1, num. 4, April 2002; see also the editorial "An Embarrassment of Riches," *Wall Street Journal,* November 12, 2002, p. A20.

Another recent study used data from the University of Michigan's Panel Study of Income Dynamics, which has followed 5,000 families since 1968.[11] It shows how fluid the income distribution really is and the important role played by working wives.

Figure 8 shows the mobility of under-55, married-couple families between 1988 and 1998. Each color represents a different quintile in 1988.

FIGURE 8

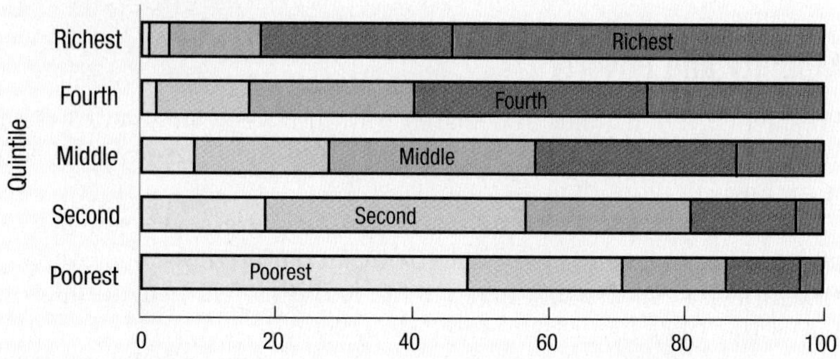

Mobility Patterns for Under-55, Married-Couple Families (1988–98)

This figure illustrates the percentage of families from each quintile in 1988 that remained in that quintile or moved to other quintiles in 1998. For example, the poorest quintile in 1988 is shaded white; follow how some of the poorest quintile families moved into other quintiles by 1998 by seeing where the white bars are in each 1998 quintile. For the lowest quintile, over half moved up the income ladder. Over 45% of the richest quintile moved down. This figure illustrates how quickly (over one decade) families move up and down in the income distribution. Note that the quintile percentages sum to 100%.

Source: Data from Katharine Bradbury and Jane Katz, "Wives' Work and Family Income Mobility," *Public Policy Discussion Papers,* Federal Reserve Bank of Boston, May 12, 2005.

Here is how we read the graph. First, focus on the poorest quintile. The poorest quintile in 1988 is shown as a white bar. Start with the bar on the bottom. Reading across the bar, we see that almost half of the married-couple families in the poorest quintile at the beginning of 1988 remained in this poorest quintile 10 years later. But the other half in this poorest quintile moved up. Following the white bars up, we see that over 20% moved up to the second quintile in 1998. Some in the poorest quintile in 1988 even made it up to the highest quintile in 1998.

Using this same procedure to look at the other quintiles, note that almost 20% of the married-couple families in the second quintile at the beginning of the period dropped down to the poorest quintile by 1998 (follow the beige quintile). The third and fourth quintiles show similar amounts of mobility.

In just one decade, over half of the poorest families moved up the income distribution ladder, but nearly half remained in the poorest quintile. The richest quintile was surprising, roughly a mirror image of the poorest quintile. Slightly less than half dropped out and were replaced by families from the other quintiles. Looking at all quintiles, only one third to one half remained in their original quintile after a decade.

The families that remained in the lowest quintile after a decade are the most worrisome. Research by Richard B. Freeman of Harvard tells us that there is a core

[11] Katharine Bradbury and Jane Katz, "Wives' Work and Family Income Mobility," *Public Policy Discussion Papers,* Federal Reserve Bank of Boston, May 12, 2005.

of poor people who stay poor.[12] This core has physical disabilities, suffers from substance abuse, or is unable to work for a host of other reasons.

This suggests that poverty will never be totally eradicated. It also suggests that policies to deal with core poverty should be different from policies that deal with people who start or who have fallen into poverty but are highly likely to escape.

Checkpoint

Poverty

REVIEW

- Poverty thresholds were developed in the 1960s based on a food budget, adjusted for family size, and then multiplied by 3.
- Economic growth is a major force in reducing poverty.
- The income deficit measures how far below the poverty threshold a family's income lies.
- The other depth of poverty measure is the ratio of income to poverty. If the ratio is below 0.5, the family is considered "desperately or severely poor." A ratio greater than 1.0 but less than 1.25 indicates the family is "near poor."
- The Census Bureau has introduced new measures of poverty that consider health care costs, transportation needs, and child care costs.
- The controversy surrounding reducing poverty centers on whether reducing income inequality or increasing economic growth is the best approach.
- Philosopher John Rawls proposed a "maximin principle" that suggested that society should maximize the welfare of the least well-off individual.
- Robert Nozick argued that the state should not use its coercive power to make some people better off at the expense of others.
- Income mobility is quite robust in the United States, with more than half of all families moving up and down the income distribution ladder in any decade.

QUESTIONS

Return to the suggestion by economist Charles Murray that the United States should eliminate all social insurance including Social Security, Medicare, Medicaid, and other welfare programs and instead give $10,000 each year to each citizen over 21 years of age. Again, expand his idea by eliminating the age restriction. Would this eliminate poverty in America? Would this satisfy those on the left who wish to reduce inequality in income distribution? What do you think will be the response to such an idea by those on the right of the political spectrum?

Answers to the Checkpoint questions can be found at the end of this chapter.

Key Concepts

Income, p. 374
Wealth, p. 374
Functional distribution of income, p. 375
Personal or family distribution of income, p. 376
Lorenz curves, p. 377
Gini coefficient, p. 378
Poverty thresholds, p. 384
Income deficit, p. 387
Ratio of income to poverty, p. 387

[12]Mentioned in the article by Krueger (see note 9).

Chapter Summary

The Distribution of Income and Wealth

Income is a flow; it measures the receipts of funds by individuals or households over time. Wealth is a stock; it measures a family's assets and net liabilities at a given point in time.

Family and individual incomes vary significantly over the course of the life cycle. Young people just starting their careers and their families will usually have modest incomes. As people grow older and gain experience, their incomes usually rise, peaking between the ages of 45 and 55. Incomes then normally decline with retirement, as do family responsibilities.

The functional distribution of income refers to the income distribution among inputs (factors) of production. The share of national income going to labor has gradually risen since 1929; it is now fairly stable at around 70%. The remainder of the national income is divided among proprietor's income (small business profits), rent, corporate profits, and net interest.

Personal or family income distribution refers to the percentage of income flowing to families in specific segments of the population. To analyze family income distribution, the Census Bureau arranges households in quintiles, or fifths, ranging from the 20% of households with the lowest incomes to the 20% with the highest. After totaling and averaging household incomes for each quintile, the Census Bureau computes the percentage of income flowing to each quintile. Since the 1970s, the income distribution in the United States has become more unequal.

Economists have developed two primary methods of measuring inequality. Lorenz curves cumulate and plot the percent of people below various income levels on the horizontal axis, relating this to their share of income on the vertical axis. A perfectly equal distribution results in a Lorenz curve that bisects the axes, and deviations from this equal distribution curve indicate inequality.

The Gini coefficient is another method of measuring income inequality. The Gini coefficient is defined as the ratio of the area between the Lorenz curve and the equal distribution line, and the total area below the equal distribution line. When distribution is perfectly equal, the Gini coefficient is zero; when distribution is as unequal as possible, the coefficient rises to 1.0.

Income distribution is influenced by redistribution policies that include progressive taxes and cash and in-kind transfer payments. Redistribution policies are contentious. Those on the political left tend to push for greater redistribution of income and wealth, while those on the right argue that such policies are harmful.

Income inequality in our society has many causes. Individuals and families invest in human capital to varying degrees, some placing a strong emphasis on education, and others fail to do so. Different education levels are a major factor determining inequalities in income and wealth. Economic discrimination can lead to an income distribution skewed against those suffering the discrimination. The growth of two-earner households over the last three decades is a major reason for rising income inequality.

Poverty

The poverty threshold was first determined by the U.S. Department of Agriculture. Surveying the food-buying patterns of low-income households, the USDA used these data to estimate the cost of financing a nutritionally balanced diet. It then multiplied the cost of this food plan, adjusting for family size, by 3. The resulting dollar amount is the income threshold beneath which families are officially deemed to be living in poverty. When the Census Bureau calculates the official poverty rate, it counts as income all money income before taxes, including cash benefits, but does not include capital gains or noncash benefits such as public housing or food stamps.

The poverty rate in the United States fell rapidly between 1959 and 1975, but it has remained roughly stable since then, fluctuating around 12–15%, following the business cycle. Over most of this period, the poverty rate for blacks and Hispanics was roughly twice the rate for whites.

Economists have developed two depth-of-poverty measures that describe the economic well-being of lower-income families. The first, the income deficit, measures how far below the poverty threshold a family's income lies. In 2002, the average income deficit for families living in poverty was just over $7,200.

The ratio of income to poverty compares family income to the poverty threshold and expresses this comparison as a ratio. The ratio for families with incomes equal to the poverty threshold will equal 1.0; the ratio for those living at half the threshold income will be 0.5. The Census Bureau considers people who live in families with ratios below 0.5 to be "severely or desperately poor," those between 0.5 and 1.0 to be "poor," and those with ratios above 1.0 but less than 1.25 to be "near poor." In 2001, nearly 5% of Americans lived in severely poor families.

Many researchers have criticized the Census Bureau's official method of determining poverty thresholds. In response, it has developed experimental measures that differ from the old in basing their estimates on after-tax income and counting as income such noncash benefits as food stamps and housing subsidies. Work-related expenses, such as transportation and child care, are deducted from income, as are out-of-pocket medical expenses. When these new measures were applied, poverty rates fell by almost one quarter.

Poverty can be a relative or an absolute measure. The official measure of poverty in the United States is based on an absolute number, the poverty threshold. Some researchers, however, think a relative measure would be more useful, for instance, labeling the bottom 20% of American households "poor." Whether poverty can ever be eliminated depends largely on how we choose to define this term.

The question of how to go about reducing poverty is controversial. The political left sees income and wealth redistribution as the main tool for curing poverty. They suggest expanding welfare-related programs and enhancing the progressivity of the tax system. Those on the right argue that such an approach is too expensive, and it significantly reduces the incentives to work and produce, thereby reducing the economy's output. These people maintain that the best way to cure poverty is by implementing policies that increase the economic pie shared by all, not just by splitting the current pie more evenly.

There is no unified theory of income distribution that takes all issues into account, or that tells us which distribution is the fairest. Some contemporary philosophers have weighed in on this issue. John Rawls has argued that low inequality is the fairest, since this is what everyone would choose if he or she did not know where in the income distribution he or she would fall. Robert Nozick has replied that it is unfair to use the coercive power of the state to deprive people of their private property to redistribute it to others.

Studies of income mobility suggest that there is a lot of shifting by individuals and families between quintiles of the income distribution. Roughly half of all families move out of their existing quintile into others over a decade.

Questions and Problems

1. Use the two different distributions of income in the table below to answer the questions that follow.

Quintile	A	B
Poorest	11.2	10.5
Second	12.0	11.6
Middle	21.2	20.3
Fourth	26.0	25.7
Richest	29.6	31.9

a. Use the grid below and graph the two Lorenz curves.
b. Which curve has the least unequal distribution?
c. Are these distributions more or less equal than that for the United States today?

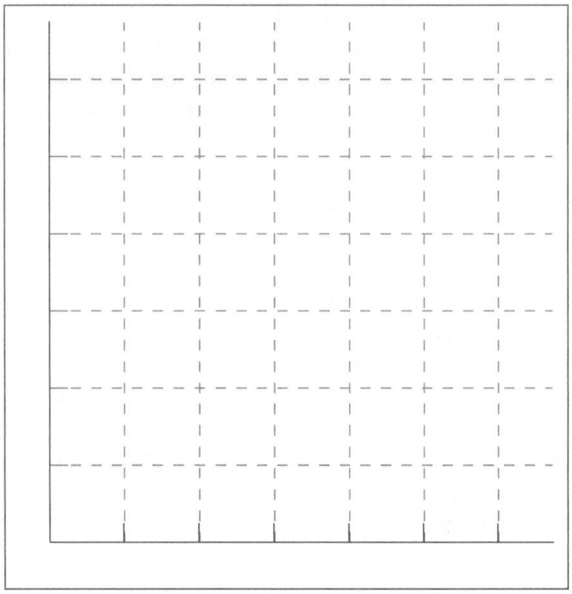

2. If you look at income distribution over the life cycle of a family, would it be more equally distributed than for one specific year?

3. Is there an efficiency-equity tradeoff when income is redistributed from the rich to the poor? Explain.

4. Currently the poverty threshold for a family of four is roughly $20,000 a year. Does this seem about right to you? This family would also probably qualify for food stamps, Medicaid, and subsidized housing. Does the poverty threshold still seem about right?

5. What do you think has been the impact on the distribution of income in the United States from the combined impact of the huge number of unskilled illegal immigrants and the growing number of dual-earner households?

6. List some of the reasons why household incomes differ.

7. It is probably fair to say that when we classify people as rich or poor at any given moment in time, we are simply describing similar people at different stages in life. Does this life cycle of income and wealth make the income distribution concerns a little less relevant? Why or why not?

8. How does the Gini coefficient differ from the Lorenz curve?

9. What would be the change in the distribution of income (Gini coefficient) if the United States decided to permit 10 million new immigrants into the United States who were highly skilled doctors, engineers, executives of large foreign firms, and wealthy foreigners who just want to migrate to the United States? How would the Gini coefficient change if, instead, the United States decided to permit 10 million unskilled foreign workers to enter?

10. If the poverty threshold is roughly $20,000 for a family, why don't we just raise the minimum wage to $12.50 an hour and eliminate poverty?

11. Roughly half of all marriages in the United States end in divorce. What is the impact of this divorce rate on the distribution of income and poverty?

12. According to the U.S. Department of the Treasury, people in the top income quintile (20%) pay roughly 75% of all personal income taxes, with the remaining 80% paying less than 25%. Further, the bottom half of the population pays less than 4% of all personal income taxes. Many politicians often assert that they want to bring tax relief (presumably with the idea of redistributing income) to "middle- and lower-income" families. Given this distribution of income tax payments, what would middle- and lower-income tax relief look like?

13. Are the poor in 2008 just as poor as the poor in 1958? What, if anything, has changed in 50 years to make poverty different today?

14. What are some of the reasons for income inequality? Is income inequality necessarily a bad thing?

15. Poverty rates have declined for blacks and have been relatively stable for everyone else over the last 40 years. But, the poverty rate still hovers around 13%. What makes it so difficult to reduce poverty below 10–15% of the population?

Answers to Checkpoint Questions

CHECKPOINT: THE DISTRIBUTION OF INCOME AND WEALTH

It would clearly improve (make more equal) the before-tax and benefits distribution of income. The impact on the distribution of income after adjusting for current benefits of such a policy would depend on the explicit value of current benefits. Murray suggests that his proposal would cost more for a decade and then begin saving money.

CHECKPOINT: POVERTY

Based on the poverty thresholds, poverty would be eliminated by this proposal. In general, the political left would welcome this redistribution except for the elimination of the social safety net. Some people will make bad decisions and not save for retirement or purchase health care, and the political left will still want these services to exist, defeating the idea of the proposal. The political right will worry that once the redistribution scheme is introduced, enough people will reduce their working hours to harm economic growth. Further, the political right will worry that after the redistribution, the safety net will creep back into existence, eroding the benefits of the original idea.

15 International Trade

The world economy is becoming increasingly intertwined. Capital, labor, goods, and services all flow across borders. Most Americans wear foreign-made clothing, over half of us drive foreign cars, and even American cars contain many foreign components. Australian wines, Swiss watches, Chilean Sea Bass, and Brazilian coffee have become common in the United States; while overseas, Ford Escorts, Nike athletic shoes, and Intel Pentium computers with Microsoft Windows can be found in abundance. Trade is now part of the global landscape.

Worldwide foreign trade has quadrupled over the past 25 years. In the United States today, the combined value of exports and imports approaches $3 trillion a year. Twenty-five years ago, trade represented just over 15% of gross domestic product (GDP); today it accounts for more than a quarter of GDP. Nearly a 10th of American workers owe their jobs to foreign consumers. Figure 1 on the next page shows the current composition of U.S. exports and imports. Note that the United States imports and exports a lot of capital goods, that is, the equipment and machinery used to produce other goods. Also, we export nearly twice as many services as we import. Services include, for example, education and health care. Third, petroleum products represent nearly 12% of imports, totaling over $235 billion a year.

Improved communications and transportation technologies have worked together to promote global economic integration. In addition, most governments around the world have reduced their trade barriers in recent years. But free trade has not always been so popular.

In 1929–30, as the Great Depression was just beginning, many countries attempted to protect their domestic industries by imposing trade restrictions that discouraged imports. In 1930, the United States enacted the Smoot-Hawley tariffs, which imposed an average tax of 60% on imported goods. This move deeply hurt industries around the world, and it has been credited with adding to the severity of the global depression. Since World War II, in the wake of Smoot-Hawley's obvious failure, governments have steadily reduced trade barriers through a series of international agreements.

FIGURE 1

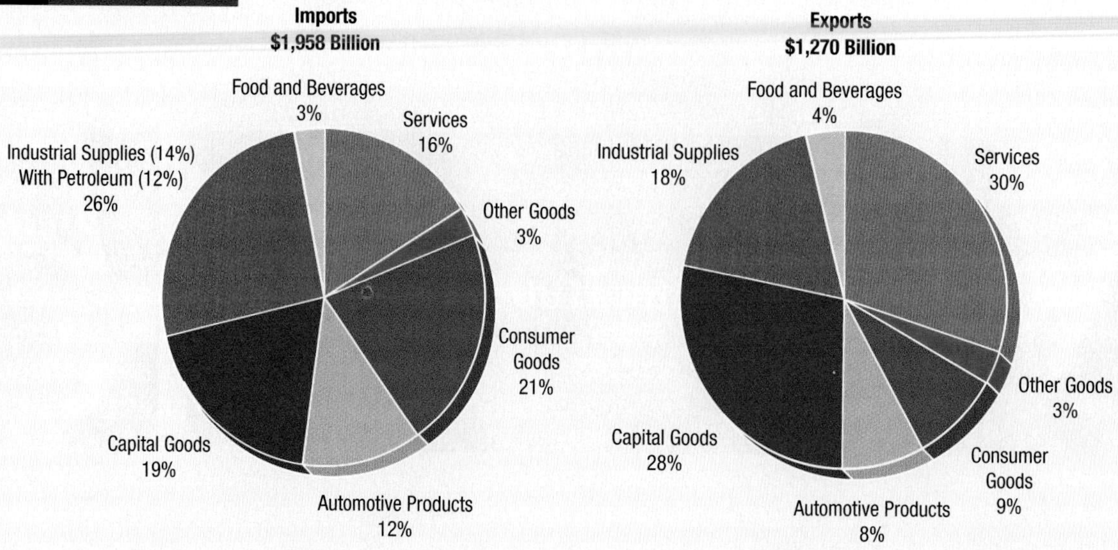

U.S. Trade by Sector (2005)

This figure shows trade by sector. The United States imports and exports large amounts of capital goods, the equipment and machinery used to produce other goods. Also, the United States exports nearly twice as many services as it imports.

Trade must yield significant benefits or it would not exist. After all, there are no laws requiring countries to trade, just agreements permitting trade and reducing impediments to it. This chapter begins with a discussion of why trade is beneficial. We look at the terms of trade between countries. We then look at the tariffs and quotas sometimes used to restrict trade, calculating their costs. Finally, we will consider some arguments critics have advanced against increased trade and globalization.

After studying this chapter you should be able to

- Describe the benefits of free trade.
- Distinguish between absolute and comparative advantage.
- Describe the economic impacts of trade.
- Describe the terms of trade.
- List the ways in which trade is restricted.
- Discuss the various arguments against free trade.
- Describe the issues surrounding increasing global economic integration.

The Gains from Trade

Economics studies voluntary exchange. People and nations do business with one another because they expect to gain through these transactions. Foreign trade is nearly as old as civilization. Centuries ago, European merchants were already sailing to the Far East to ply the spice trades. Today, people in the United States buy cars from Japan and electronics from South Korea, along with millions of other products from countries around the world.

Many people assume that trade between nations is a zero-sum game: a game in which, for one party to gain, the other party must lose. Poker games fit this description; one person's winnings must come from another player's losses. This is not true, however, of voluntary trade. Voluntary exchange and trade is a positive-sum game, meaning that both parties to a transaction can gain.

To understand how this works, and thus, why nations trade, we need to consider the concepts of absolute and comparative advantage. Note that nations per se do not trade; individuals in specific countries do. We will, however, refer to trade between nations, but recognize that individuals, not nations, actually engage in trade. We covered this earlier in Chapter 2, but it is worthwhile to go through it again.

Absolute and Comparative Advantage

Figure 2 shows hypothetical production possibilities curves for the United States and Canada. For simplicity, both countries are assumed to produce only beef and

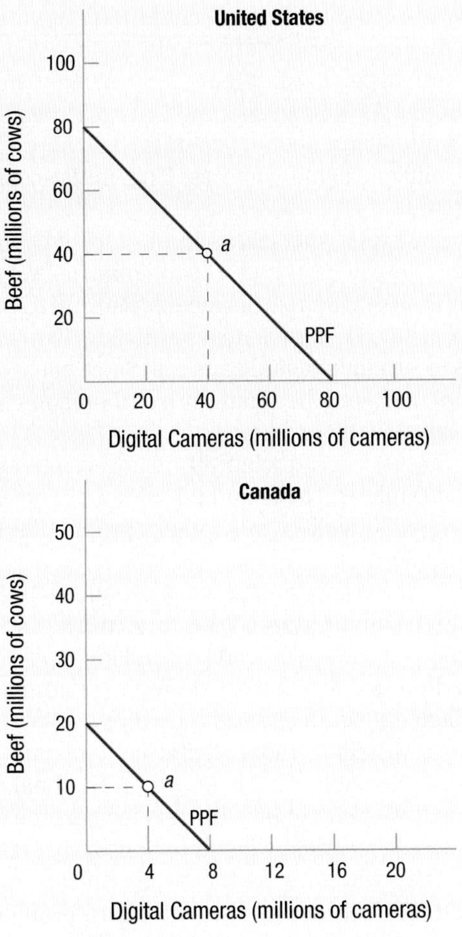

FIGURE 2

Production Possibilities for the United States and Canada

The production possibilities curves shown here assume that the United States and Canada produce only beef and digital cameras. In this example, the United States has an absolute advantage over Canada in producing both products; the United States can produce 4 times as many cattle and 10 times as many cameras as Canada. Canada nonetheless has a comparative advantage over the United States in producing beef.

Absolute advantage
One country can produce more of a good than another country.

Comparative advantage
One country has a lower opportunity cost of producing a good than another country.

digital cameras. Given the production possibility frontiers (PPFs) in Figure 2, the United States has an absolute advantage over Canada in the production of both products. An **absolute advantage** exists when one country can produce more of a good than another country. In this case, the United States can produce 4 times as much beef and 10 times as many cameras as Canada.

At first glance, we may wonder why the United States would be willing to trade with Canada. Because the United States can produce so much more of both commodities, why not just produce its own cattle and cameras? The reason lies in comparative advantage.

One country enjoys a **comparative advantage** in producing some good if its opportunity costs to produce that good are lower than the other country's. In this example, Canada's comparative advantage is in producing cattle. As Figure 2 shows, the opportunity cost for the United States to produce another million cows is 1 million cameras; each added cow essentially costs 1 camera.

Contrast this with the situation in Canada. For every camera Canadian producers forgo producing, they can produce 2.5 more cows. This means cows cost only 0.4 camera in Canada (1/2.5 = 0.4). Canada's comparative advantage is in producing cattle, since a cow costs 0.4 camera in Canada, while the same cow costs an entire camera in the United States.

By the same token, the United States has a comparative advantage in producing cameras: 1 camera in the United States costs 1 cow, but the same camera in Canada costs 2.5 cows. These relative costs suggest that the United States should focus its resources on digital camera production and that Canada should specialize in beef.

Gains From Trade

To see how specialization and trade can benefit both countries even when one has an advantage in producing more of both goods, assume that the United States and Canada at first operate at point *a* in Figure 2, producing and consuming their own beef and digital cameras. As we can see, the United States produces and consumes 40 million cattle and 40 million digital cameras. Canada produces and consumes 10 million cattle and 4 million digital cameras. This initial position is similarly shown as points *a* in Figure 3.

Assume now that Canada specializes in producing cattle, producing all that it can, 20 million cows. We will assume the two countries want to continue consuming 50 million cows between them. This means the United States needs to produce only 30 million cattle, since Canada is now producing 20 million. This frees up some American resources to produce digital cameras. Since each cow in the United States costs a digital camera, reducing beef output by 10 million cattle means that 10 million more cameras can now be produced.

So, the United States is producing 30 million cattle and 50 million cameras. Canada is producing 20 million cattle and no cameras. The combined production of cattle remains the same, 50 million, but camera production has increased by 6 million (from 44 to 50 million).

The two countries can trade their surplus products, and will be better off. This is shown in Table 1. Assuming they agree to share the added 6 million cameras between them equally, Canada will trade 10 million cattle in exchange for 7 million digital cameras. Points *b* in Figure 3 show the resulting consumption patterns for each country. Each consume the same quantity of beef as before trading, but each country now has 3 million more digital cameras: 43 million for the United States and 7 million for Canada. This is shown in the final column of the table.

One important point to remember is that even when one country has an absolute advantage over another, countries will still benefit from trade. The gains are small in our example, but they will grow as the two countries approach one another in size and their comparative advantages become more pronounced.

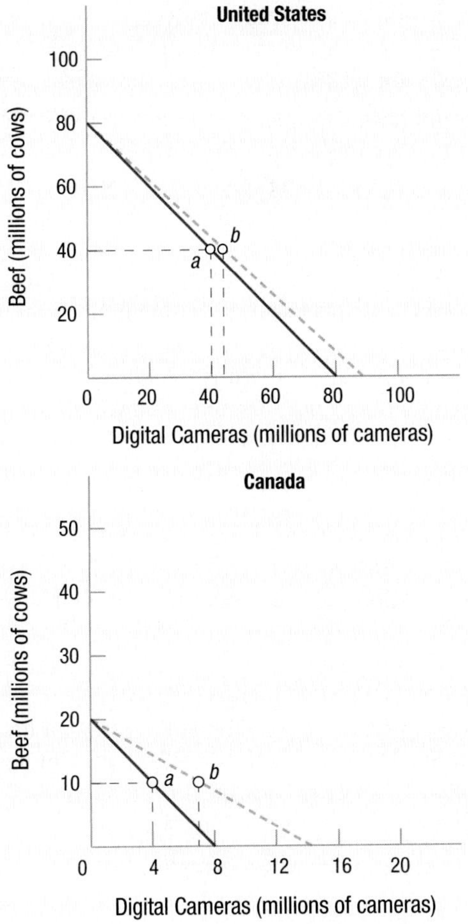

FIGURE 3

The Gains from Specialization and Trade to the United States and Canada

Assume Canada specializes in cattle. If the two countries want to continue consuming 50 million cows between them, the United States needs to produce only 30 million. This frees up resources for the United States to begin producing more digital cameras. Since each cow in the United States costs 1 camera to produce, reducing beef output by 10 million cattle means that 10 million more cameras can be produced. When the two countries trade their surplus products, both are better off than before.

There is one recent theoretical objection to this trade model. Nobel Prize winner Paul Samuelson has shown that under certain conditions outsourcing and trade could, on the whole, be negative for the United States.[1] Other economists have argued that while such an outcome is theoretically possible, empirically the chance

Table 1 **The Gains from Trade**

Country and Product		Before Specialization	After Specialization	After Trade
United States	Cows	40 million	30 million	40 million
	Cameras	40 million	50 million	43 million
Canada	Cows	10 million	20 million	10 million
	Cameras	4 million	0	7 million

[1]Paul Samuelson, "Where Ricardo and Mill Rebut and Confirm Arguments of Mainstream Economists Supporting Globalization," *Journal of Economic Perspectives*, Summer 2004, pp. 135–146. If, for example, trading with the United States improves technology and productivity so much in developing nations that their greater output leads to a reduction in the price of U.S. exports, we might be worse off. This could even be the case despite cheaper consumer goods. The important point is that not just some industries and workers lose, but the economy as a whole could be a loser.

of trade not benefiting the United States in general is remote.[2] Nevertheless, his work adds a nuance to traditional trade analysis.

Practical Constraints on Trade

At this point, we should take a moment to note some practical constraints on trade. First, every transaction involves costs. These include transportation, communications, and the general costs of doing business. Over the last several decades, however, transportation and communication costs have declined all over the world, resulting in growing world trade.

Second, the production possibilities curves for nations are not linear; rather, they are governed by increasing costs and diminishing returns. Countries find it difficult to specialize only in one product. Indeed, specializing in one product is risky since the market for the product can always decline, new technology might replace it, or its production can be disrupted by changing weather patterns. This is a perennial problem for developing countries that often build their exports and trade around one agricultural commodity.

Although it is true that trading partners will benefit from trade, some individuals and groups within each country may lose. Individual workers in those industries at a comparative disadvantage are likely to lose their jobs, and thus may require retraining, relocation, or other help if they are to move smoothly into new occupations.

When the United States signed the North American Free Trade Agreement (NAFTA) with Canada and Mexico, many U.S. workers experienced this sort of dislocation. Some U.S. jobs went south to Mexico because of low wages. Still, by opening up more markets for U.S. products, NAFTA has stimulated the U.S. economy. The goal is that displaced workers, newly retrained, will end up with new and better jobs, although there is no guarantee this will happen.

Checkpoint

The Gains from Trade

REVIEW

- An absolute advantage exists when one country can produce more of a good than another country.
- A comparative advantage exists when one country can produce a good at a lower opportunity cost than another country.
- Both countries gain from trade when each specializes in producing goods in which they have a comparative advantage.
- Transaction costs, diminishing returns, and the risk associated with specialization all place some practical limits on trade.

QUESTIONS

In the 1990s, there was a surge of interest in sports memorabilia. In particular, baseball memorabilia shows witnessed lines of people willing to pay for a baseball player's autograph on a picture, baseball, or baseball card. All of this attention increased the interest of kids in buying baseball cards. A natural corollary of this is the trading of baseball cards. Assume you have a set of baseball cards for the current year but are

---

[2] Jagdish Bhagwati, Arvind Panagariya, and T. N. Srinivasan, "The Muddles Over Outsourcing," *Journal of Economic Perspectives,* Fall 2004, pp. 93–114.

missing some. In particular, you are a Cardinals fan and have all of the Cardinals cards except Albert Pujols. Would you trade for it? What would you want to give up for the Pujols card? What would the Pujols card holder expect in return? Who benefits from this trade?

Answers to the Checkpoint questions can be found at the end of this chapter.

The Terms of Trade

How much can a country charge when it sells its goods to another country? How much must it pay for imported goods? The terms of trade determine the prices of imports and exports.

To keep things simple, assume each country has only one export and one import, priced at P_x and P_m. The ratio of the price of the exported goods to the price of the imported goods, P_x/P_m, is the terms of trade. Thus, if a country exports computers and imports coffee, with two computers trading for a ton of coffee, the price of a computer must be one half the price of a ton of coffee.

When countries trade many commodities, the **terms of trade** are defined as the average price of exports divided by the average price of imports. This can get a bit complicated, given that the price of each import and export will be quoted in its own national currency, while the exchange rate between the two currencies may be constantly changing. We will ignore these complications by translating currencies into dollars, focusing our attention on how the terms of trade are determined and the impact of trade.

Terms of trade
The ratio of the price of exported goods to the price of imported goods (P_x/P_m).

Determining the Terms of Trade

To get a feel for how the terms of trade are determined, let us consider the trade in computers between the United States and Japan. We will assume the United States has a comparative advantage in producing computers; all prices are given in dollars.

Panel A of Figure 4 on the next page shows the demand and supply of computers in the United States. The upward sloping supply curve reflects increasing opportunity costs in computer production. As the United States continues to specialize in computer production, resources less suited to this purpose must be employed. Thus, ever-increasing amounts of other goods must be sacrificed, resulting in rising costs for computer production. Because of this rise in costs as ever more resources are shifted to computers, the United States will eventually lose its comparative advantage in computer production. This represents one limit on specialization and trade.

Let us assume the United States begins in pretrade equilibrium at point *a*, with the price of computers at P_1. Panel B shows Japan initially in equilibrium at point *h*, with a higher computer price of P_2. Since prices for computers from the United States are lower, when trade begins, Japanese consumers will begin buying U.S. computers.

American computer makers will increase production to meet this new demand. Japanese computer firms, conversely, will see the sales of their computers decline in Japan as prices begin to fall. For now, let us ignore transport costs, such that trade continues until prices reach P_e. At this point, U.S. exports ($Q_2 - Q_1$) are just equal to Japanese imports ($Q_4 - Q_3$). Both countries are now in equilibrium, with the price of computers somewhere between two pretrade equilibrium prices.

FIGURE 4

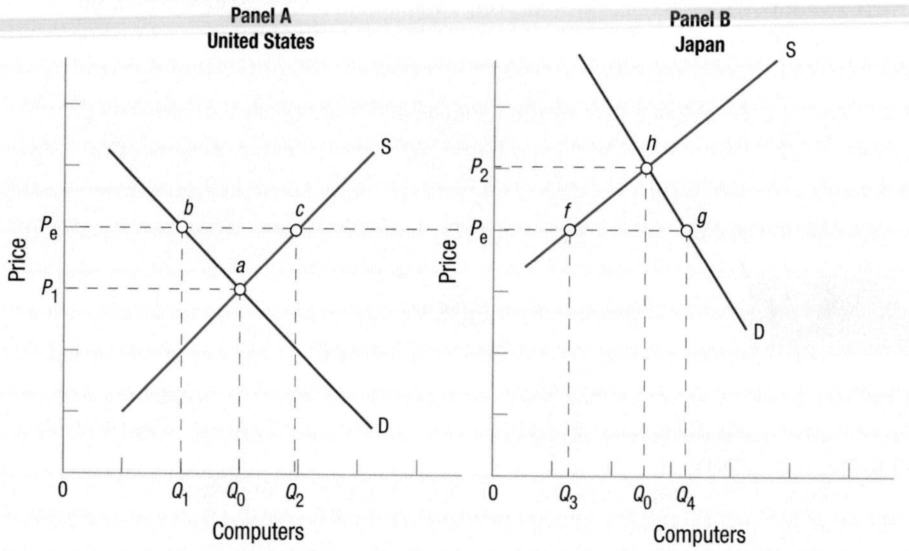

Determining the Terms of Trade

Panel A shows the demand and supply of computers in the United States; the upward slope of the supply curve reflects increasing opportunity costs to produce more computers. The United States begins in pretrade equilibrium at point *a*, with the price of computers at P_1. Panel B shows Japan's initial equilibrium at point *h*, with a higher price of P_2. With trade, Japanese consumers will begin buying American computers because of their lower price. American computer makers will increase production to meet this new demand. Japanese computer firms will see sales of their computers decline as prices begin to fall. Ignoring transport costs, trade will continue until prices reach P_e. At this point, American exports ($Q_2 - Q_1$) are just equal to Japanese imports ($Q_4 - Q_3$). Both countries are in equilibrium, with the price of computers somewhere between two pretrade equilibrium prices.

Imagine this same process simultaneously working itself out with many other goods, including some at which the Japanese have a comparative advantage, such as cameras and electronic components. As each product settles into an equilibrium price like P_e, the terms of trade between these two countries get determined.

The Impact of Trade

Our examination of absolute and comparative advantage has thus far highlighted the blessings of trade. A closer look at Figure 4, however, shows that trade produces winners and losers.

Picking up on the previous example, computer producers in the United States are happy, having watched their sales rise from Q_0 to Q_2. Predictably, management and workers in this industry will favor even more trade with Japan and the rest of the world. Yet, domestic consumers of computers are worse off, since after trade they purchase only Q_1 computers at the higher equilibrium price of P_e. Computer users will likely oppose increased trade, and may even look to Congress to restrict trade.

Contrast this situation in the net exporting country, the United States, with that of the net importer, Japan. Japanese computer producers are worse off than before since the price of computers fell from P_2 to P_e, and their output was reduced to Q_3. Consequently, they must cut jobs, leaving workers and managers in the Japanese computer industry unhappy with its country's trade policies. Japanese consumers, however, are beneficiaries of this expanded trade, since they can purchase Q_4 computers at lower price P_e.

These results are not merely hypothetical. This is the story of free trade, which has been played out time and again: Some sectors of the economy win, and some lose. American consumers have been happy to purchase Japanese cameras such as Minolta and Nikon, given their high quality and low prices. American camera makers such as Kodak and Polaroid have not been so pleased, nor have their employees. These firms, watching their prices, sales, and employment decline, have had to adapt to the competition from abroad.

Similarly, the ranks of American textile workers have been decimated over the past two decades as domestic clothing producers have increasingly become nothing but designers and marketers of clothes, shifting their production overseas to countries where wages are lower. American-made clothing is now essentially a thing of the past.

To be sure, American consumers have enjoyed a substantial drop in the price of clothing, because labor forms a significant part of the cost of clothing production. Still, being able to purchase inexpensive T-shirts made in China is small consolation for the unemployed textile worker in North Carolina.

The undoubted pain suffered by the losers from trade often is translated into pressure put on politicians to restrict trade in one way or another. The pain is often felt more strongly than the "happiness" felt by those who benefit from trade.

How Trade Is Restricted

Trade restrictions can range from subsidies provided to domestic firms to protect them against lower-priced imports to embargoes in which the government bans any trade with a country. Between these two extremes are more intermediate policies, such as exchange controls that limit the amount of foreign currency available to importers or citizens who travel abroad. Regulation, licensing, and government purchasing policies are all frequently used to promote or ensure the purchase of domestic products. The main reason for these trade restrictions is simple: The industry and its employees actually feel the pain and lobby extensively for protection, while the huge benefits of lower prices are diffused among millions of customers whose benefits are each so small that fighting against a trade barrier isn't worth their time.

The most common forms of trade restrictions are tariffs and quotas. Panel A of Figure 5 on the next page shows the average U.S. tariff rates since 1900. Some economists have suggested that the tariff wars that erupted in the 1920s and culminated in the passage of the Smoot-Hawley Act in 1930 were an important factor underlying the severity of the Great Depression. Panel B shows the impact of higher tariffs on worldwide imports. The higher tariffs reduced trade, leading to a reduction in income, output, and employment, and added fuel to the worldwide depression. Since the 1930s, the United States has played a leading role in trade liberalization, with our average tariff rates declining to a current rate of roughly 5%.

Effects of Tariffs and Quotas

What exactly are the effects of tariffs and quotas? **Tariffs** are often ad valorem taxes. This means the product is taxed by a certain percentage of its price as it crosses the border. Other tariffs are unit taxes: A fixed tax per unit of the product is assessed at the border. Tariffs are designed to generate revenues and to drive a wedge between the domestic price of a product and its price on the world market. The effects of a tariff are shown in Figure 6.

Tariff
A tax on imported products. When a country taxes imported products, it drives a wedge between the product's domestic price and its price on the world market.

Domestic supply and demand for the product are shown in Figure 6 as S and D. Assume that the product's world price P_W is lower than its domestic price P_0. Domestic quantity demanded Q_2 will consequently exceed domestic quantity supplied Q_1 at the world price of P_W. Imports to this country will therefore be $Q_2 - Q_1$.

Now assume that the firms and workers in the industry hurt by the lower world price lobby for a tariff and are successful. The country imposes a tariff (T) on this product. The results are clear. The product's price in this country rises to P_{W+T} and imports fall to $Q_4 - Q_3$. Domestic consumers consume less of the product at higher prices. Even so, the domestic industry is happy, since its prices and output have risen. The government, meanwhile, collects revenues equal to the shaded area

FIGURE 5

Average U.S. Tariff Rates (1900–2004) and the Downward Spiral of World Imports, 1930–33

Tariffs and quotas are the most common forms of trade restrictions. Panel A shows that tariff rates in the United States peaked during the Great Depression. For the last several decades, tariffs have stayed at roughly a rate of 5%. When tariffs jumped with the passage of the Smoot-Hawley Act in 1930, world imports spiraled downward as shown in Panel B. As trade between nations declined, incomes, output, and employment also fell worldwide. In Panel B, total monthly imports in millions of U.S. dollars for 75 countries is shown spiraling downward from $2,738 million in January 1930 to $1,057 in March of 1933.

Source: Charles Kindleberger, *The World Depression 1929–1939* (Berkeley: University of California Press), 1986, p. 170.

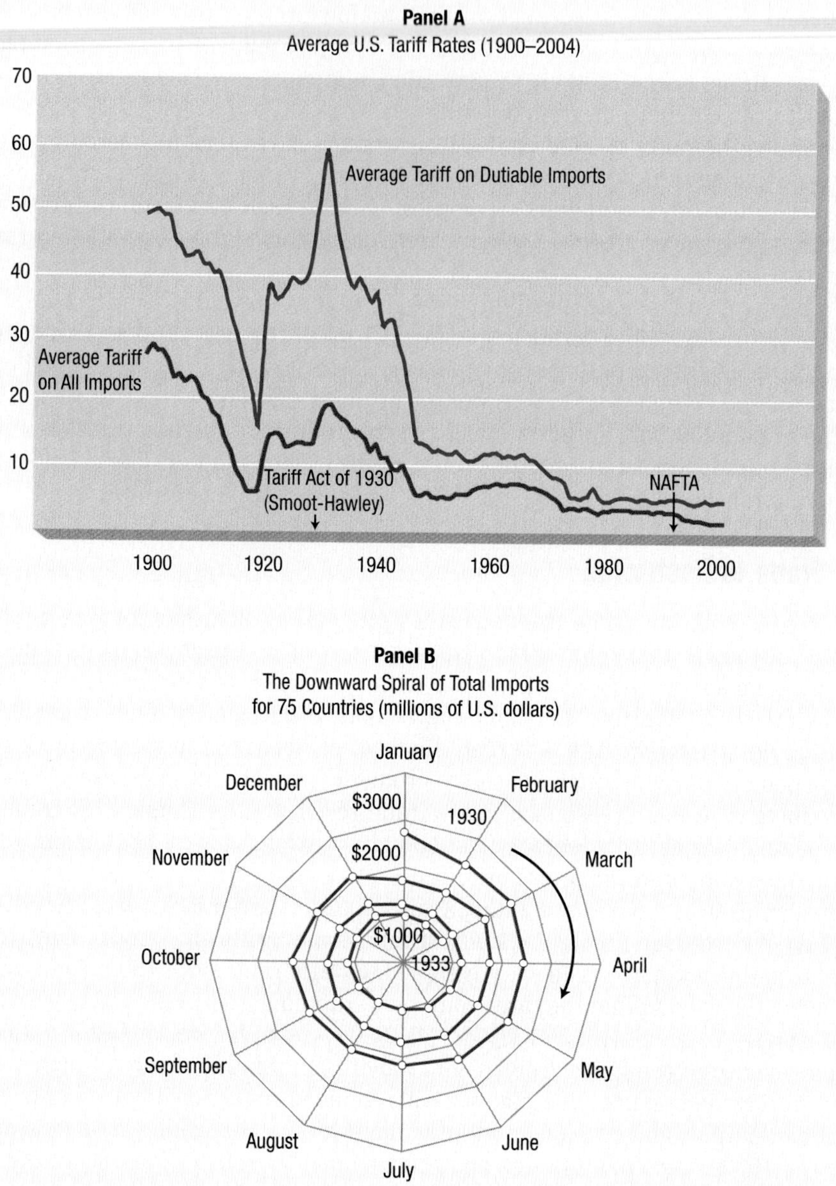

in Figure 6. These revenues can be significant: In the 1800s, tariffs were the federal government's dominant form of revenue. It is only in the last century that the federal government has come to rely more on other sources of revenue, including taxes on income, sales, and property.

Quota
A government-set limit on the quantity of imports into a country.

Figure 7 shows the effects of a **quota.** They are similar to what we saw in Figure 6, except that the government restricts the quantity of imports into the country to $Q_4 - Q_3$. Imports fall to the quota level, and consumers again lose, because they must pay higher prices for less output. Producers and their employees gain as prices and employment in the domestic industry rise. For a quota, however, the government does not collect revenue. Then who gets this revenue? The foreign exporting company will get it, in the form of higher prices for its products. This explains why governments prefer tariffs over quotas.

The United States imposed quotas on Japanese automobiles in the 1980s. The primary effect of these quotas was initially to dramatically raise the minimum standard equipment and price for some Japanese cars and to increase ultimately the

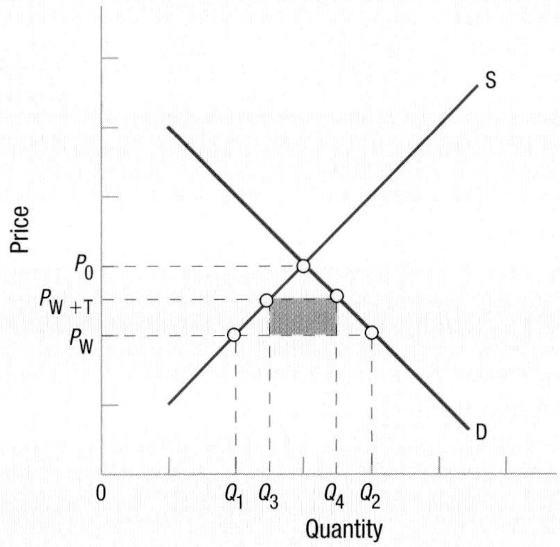

FIGURE 6

Effects of a Tariff

What are the effects of a typical tariff? Supply and demand curves S and D represent domestic supply and demand. Assume the product's world price P_W is lower than its domestic price P_0. Domestic quantity demanded Q_2 will consequently exceed domestic quantity supplied Q_1 at the world price of P_W. Imports will therefore be $Q_2 - Q_1$. If the country imposes a tariff (T) on this product, the domestic price rises to P_{W+T}, and imports fall to $Q_4 - Q_3$. Domestic consumers now consume less of the product at higher prices. However, the domestic industry is happy since its prices and output have risen. Also, the government collects revenues equal to the shaded area.

number of Japanese cars made in American factories. If a firm is limited in the number of vehicles it can sell, why not sell higher-priced ones where the profit margins are higher? The Toyota Land Cruiser, for instance, was originally a bare-bones SUV selling for under $15,000. With quotas, this vehicle became a $60,000 luxury behemoth with all the extras standard.

One problem with tariffs and quotas is that when they are imposed, large numbers of consumers pay just a small amount more for the targeted products. Few consumers are willing to spend time and effort lobbying Congress to end or forestall these trade barriers from being introduced. Producers, however, are often few in number, and they stand to gain tremendously from such trade barriers. It is no wonder that such firms have large lobbying budgets and provide campaign contributions to congressional candidates.

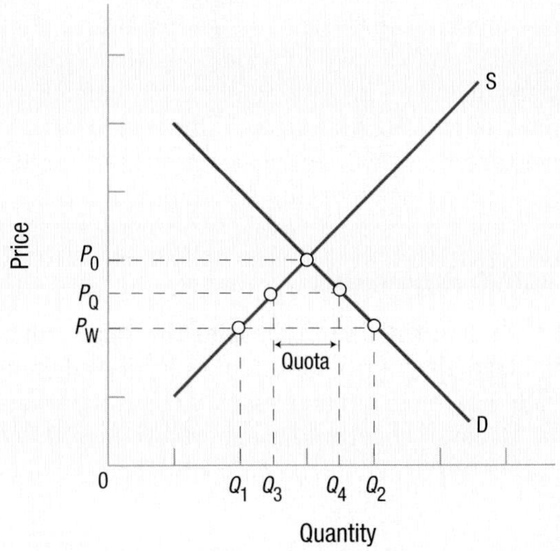

FIGURE 7

Effects of a Quota

What are the effects of a quota? They are similar to the effects of a tariff, except that the government restricts the quantity of imports into the country to $Q_4 - Q_3$. Imports fall to the quota level, and again consumers lose as they must pay higher prices for less output. Producers and their employees gain as prices and employment in the domestic industry rise. With a quota, however, the government does not collect revenues.

Checkpoint
The Terms of Trade

REVIEW

- The terms of trade are determined by the ratio of the price of exported goods to the price of imported goods.
- The terms of trade are set by the markets in each country and by exports and imports that eventually equalize the prices.
- Trade leads to winners and losers in each country and in each market.
- Trade restrictions vary from subsidies to domestic firms to government bans on the import of foreign products.
- Tariffs are taxes on imports that protect domestic producers and generate revenue.
- Quotas represent restrictions on the volume of particular imports that can come into a country. Quotas do not generate revenue for governments and are infrequently used.

QUESTION

When the government imposes a quota on a specific imported product, who benefits and who loses?

Answers to the Checkpoint question can be found at the end of this chapter.

Arguments Against Free Trade

> **"If goods do not cross borders, soldiers will."**
>
> ***Frédéric Bastiat***

We have seen the benefits of trade, and have looked at how trade undoubtedly benefits some and harms others. Those who are harmed by trade often seek to restrict trade, primarily in the form of tariffs and quotas. Because trade leads to some loss, those who are harmed by trade have made arguments against free trade.

The arguments against free trade fall into two camps: traditional economic arguments including protection for infant industries, protection against dumping, low foreign wages, and support for industries judged vital for national defense. Second are globalization (social and economic) concerns that embody political-economy characteristics. These include domestic employment concerns, environmental concerns, and the impact of globalization on working conditions in developing nations. In what follows, we take a critical look at each of these arguments, showing that most of these arguments do not have a solid empirical basis.

Traditional Economic Arguments

Arguments against trade are not new. Despite the huge gains from trade, distortions (subsidies and trade barriers) continue, as Kym Anderson has noted, "largely because further trade liberalization and subsidy cuts redistribute jobs, income, and wealth in ways that those in government fear will reduce their chances of remaining in power."[3] In other words, changing current policies will hurt those dependent

---

[3]Kym Anderson, "Subsidies and Trade Barriers," in Bjorn Lomborg, *Global Crises, Global Solutions* (Cambridge, UK: Cambridge University Press), 2004, p. 542.

on subsidies and trade restrictions, and these firms and workers will show their displeasure at the voting booth. All of these traditional economic arguments against free trade seem reasonable on their face, but on closer examination, they look less attractive.

Infant Industry Argument

An **infant industry,** it is argued, is one that is too underdeveloped to achieve comparative advantage or perhaps even to survive in the global environment. Such an industry may be too small or undercapitalized, or its management and workers may be too inexperienced, to compete. Unless the industry's government provides it with some protection through tariffs, quotas, or subsidies, it might not survive in the face of foreign competition.

Infant industry
An industry so underdeveloped that protection is needed for it to become competitive on the world stage or to ensure its survival.

In theory, once the infant industry has been given this protection, it should be able to grow, acquiring the necessary capital and expertise needed to compete internationally. Germany and the United States used high tariffs to protect their infant manufacturing sectors in the 1800s, and Japan continued to maintain import restrictions up until the 1970s.

Though the infant industry argument sounds reasonable, it has several limitations. First, protecting an industry must be done in a way that makes the industry internationally competitive. Many countries coddle their firms, and these producers never seem to develop into "mature," internationally viable firms. And, once protection is provided (typically a protective tariff), it is difficult to remove after an industry has matured. The industry and its workers continue to convince policymakers of the need for continued protection.

Second, infant industry protection often tends to focus on capital manufacturing. Countries with huge labor supplies, however, would do better to develop their labor-intensive industries first, letting more capital-intensive industries develop over time. Every country, after all, should seek to exploit its comparative advantages, but it is difficult to determine which industries have a chance of developing a comparative advantage in the future and should be temporarily protected.

Third, many industries seem to be able to develop without protections, so countries may be wasting their resources and reducing their incomes by imposing protection measures.

Clearly, the infant industry argument is not valid for advanced economies such as the United States, much of Europe, and Japan. The evidence for developing nations shows some benefits but is mixed for the reasons noted above.

Antidumping

Dumping means that goods are sold at lower prices *below cost* abroad than in their home market. This often is a result of government subsidies.

Dumping
Selling goods abroad at lower prices than in home markets, and often below cost.

In the same way that price discrimination improves profits, firms can price discriminate between their home markets and foreign markets. Let's assume that costs of production are $100 a unit for all firms (domestic and foreign). A state subsidy of $30 a unit, for example, reduces domestic costs to $70 a unit and permits the firm to sell its product in world markets at these lower prices. Since home and foreign markets can be segregated and often have different elasticities of demand, this price discrimination raises profits if the price in the foreign markets is greater than $70 a unit. These state subsidies give these firms a cost advantage in foreign markets.

Firms can use dumping as a form of predatory pricing, using higher prices in their domestic markets to support unrealistically low prices in foreign markets. The goal of predatory pricing is to drive foreign competitors out of business. When this occurs, the firm doing the dumping then comes back and imposes higher prices. In the long run, these higher prices thereby offset the company's short-term losses.

Dumping violates American trade laws. If the federal government determines that a foreign firm is dumping products onto the American market, it can impose antidumping tariffs on the offending products. The government, however, must distinguish among dumping, legitimate price discrimination, and legitimate instances of lower cost production arising from comparative advantage.

Low Foreign Wages

Some advocates of trade barriers maintain that domestic firms and their workers need to be protected from displacement by cheap foreign labor. Without this protection, it is argued, foreign manufacturers that pay their workers pennies an hour will flood the market with low-cost products. As we have already seen, this argument has something to it: Workers in advanced economies can be displaced by low-wage foreign workers. This is what has happened in the American textile industry.

Once a handful of American clothing manufacturers began moving their production facilities overseas, thereby undercutting domestic producers, other manufacturers were forced to follow them. American consumers have benefited from lower clothing prices, but many displaced textile workers are still trying to get retrained and adapt to work in other industries. More recently, many manufacturing jobs have drifted overseas, and high-technology firms today are shifting some help desk facilities and computer programming to foreign shores.

On balance, however, the benefits of lower-priced goods considerably exceed the costs of lost employment. The federal government has resisted imposing protection measures for the sake of protecting jobs, instead funding programs that help displaced workers transition to new lines of work.

National Defense Argument

In times of national crisis or war, the United States must be able to rely on key domestic industries, such as oil, steel, and the defense industry. Some have argued that these industries may require some protection even during peacetime to ensure that they are already well established when crisis strikes and importing key products may be impossible. Within limits, this argument is sound. Still, the United States has the capacity to produce such a wide variety of products that protections for specific industries would seem to be unjustified and unnecessary.

So what are we to make of these traditional arguments? Although they all seem reasonable, they all have deficiencies. Infant industries may be helped in the short run, but protections are often extended well beyond what is necessary, resulting in inefficient firms that are vulnerable on world markets. Dumping is clearly a potential problem, but distinguishing real cases of dumping and comparative advantage has often proven difficult in practice. Low foreign wages are often the only comparative advantage a developing nation has to offer the world economy, and typically, the benefits to consumers vastly outweigh the loss to a particular industry. Maintaining (protecting) industries for national defense has merit and may be appropriate for some countries, but for a country as huge and diversified as the United States, it is probably unnecessary.

Globalization Concerns

Expanded trade and globalization have provided the world's producers and consumers with many benefits. Some observers, however, have voiced concerns about globalization and its effects on domestic employment, the global environment, and working conditions in developing nations. Let's look at each one of these globalization concerns.

Trade and Domestic Employment

Some critics argue that increased trade and globalization spell job losses for domestic workers. We have seen that this can be true. Some firms, unable to compete with imports, will be forced to lay off workers or even close their doors. Even so, increased trade usually allows firms that are exporters to expand their operations and hire new workers. These will be firms in industries with comparative advantages. For the United States, these industries tend to be those that require a highly skilled workforce, resulting in higher wages for American workers.

Clearly, those industries that are adding workers, and those that are losing jobs are different industries. For workers who lose their jobs, switching industries can be difficult and time consuming, and often it requires new investments in human capital. American trade policy recognizes this problem, and the Trade Adjustment Assistance (TAA) program provides workers with job search assistance, job training, and some relocation allowances. In some industries sensitive to trade liberalization, including textiles and agriculture, trade policies are designed to proceed gradually, thus giving these industries and their workers some extra time to adjust.

Possible employment losses in some noncompetitive industries do not seem to provide enough justification for restricting trade. By imposing trade restrictions such as tariffs or quotas in one industry, employment opportunities in many other industries may be reduced. Open, competitive trade encourages producers to focus their production on those areas in which the country stands at a comparative advantage. Free trade puts competitive pressure on domestic firms, forcing them to be more productive and competitive, boosting the flow of information and technology across borders, and widening the availability of inputs for producers. At the end of the day, consumers benefit from these efficiencies, having more goods to choose from and enjoying a higher standard of living.

Trade and the Environment

Concerns about globalization, trade, and the environment usually take one of two forms. Some people are concerned that expanded trade and globalization will lead to increased environmental degradation as companies take advantage of lax environmental laws abroad, particularly in the developing world. Others worry that attempts by the government to strengthen environmental laws will be challenged by trading partners as disguised protectionism.

Domestic environmental regulations usually target a product or process that creates pollution or other environmental problems. One concern in establishing environmental regulations, however, is that they not unfairly discriminate against the products of another country. This is usually not a serious problem. Nearly all trade agreements, including the General Agreement on Tariffs and Trade (GATT) and the NAFTA, have provisions permitting countries to enforce measures "necessary to protect human, animal or plant life or health" or to conserve exhaustible natural resources. Nothing in our trade agreements prevents the United States from implementing environmental regulations as long as they do not unreasonably discriminate against our trading partners.

Will free trade come at the expense of the environment? Every action involves a tradeoff. Clearly, there can be cases where the benefits of trade accruing to large numbers of people result in harm to a more concentrated group. In 1995, however, President Clinton's Council of Economic Advisors concluded:

> *There are also complementarities between good trade policies and good environmental policies. Agricultural protection in industrialized countries is a case in point. The protection of developed-country agriculture leads to more intensive farming, often of lands that are of marginal use, causing unnecessary soil erosion, loss of biological diversity, and the excessive use of pesticides and chemicals. Liberalizing trade in agriculture and lowering agriculture production subsidies can lead to a pattern of world farming that causes less environmental damage.*

Also, high trade barriers to labor-intensive imports, such as clothing, from developing countries lead these countries instead to export products that are intensive in natural resources, causing environmental damage. In addition, high-value-added natural resource-based products such as wood or paper products often face high tariff barriers, whereas the raw natural resource itself does not; this forces developing countries to rely on exports of unprocessed natural resources while denying them the revenue gains from the downstream products.[4]

We have seen that trade raises incomes in developed and developing countries. And environmental protection is an income elastic good: As incomes rise, the demand for environmental protections rises faster. Studies suggest that once a country's per capita income exceeds roughly $5,000, its environmental protection efforts begin to improve.

In poor, developing nations, environmental protection will not at first be a priority. Critics of globalization are concerned that because environmental and labor standards in many developing nations are well below those of the developed countries, there will be pressure to adopt these lower standards in rich nations due to trade and foreign direct investment. But as Bhagwati and Hudec argue, there has been no systematic "race to the bottom" and many corporations often have the highest environmental and labor standards in the developing world.[5] Also, it is worth noting that over time, as incomes rise, environmental protection takes on added importance even in poorer nations. On balance, trade probably benefits the environment over the longer term, as incomes grow in developing nations and environmental protections take on greater importance.

Trade and Its Effect on Working Conditions in Developing Nations

Some antiglobalization activists argue that for the United States to trade with developing countries where wages are low and working conditions are deplorable simply exploits workers in these developing countries. Clearly, such trade does hurt American workers in low-wage, low-skilled occupations who simply cannot compete with the even lower-wage workers overseas. But it is not clear that workers in developing countries would be helped if the United States were to cut off its trade with those countries that refuse to improve their wages or working conditions.

Restricting trade with countries that do not raise their wages to levels we think acceptable or bring working conditions up to our standards would probably do more harm than good. Low wages reflect, among other factors, the low investments in human capital, low productivity, and low living standards characteristic of developing nations. Blocking trade with these nations may deprive them of their key chance to grow and to improve in those areas where we would like to see change.

Liberalized trade policies, economic freedom, and a legal system that respects property rights and foreign capital investment probably provide the best recipe for rapid development, economic growth, environmental protection, and improved wages and working conditions.

In summary, trade does result in job losses in some industries, but the gain to consumers and the competitive pressures that trade puts on domestic companies is beneficial to the economy as a whole. Trade raises incomes in developing nations, resulting in a growing demand for more environmentally friendly production processes. Trade is not the reason for low environmental standards in developing

---

[4]*Economic Report of the President* (Washington, D.C.: U.S. Government Printing Office), 1995, p. 242.
[5]Jagdish Bhagwati and Robert Hudec (eds.), *Fair Trade and Harmonization, Vol. 1: Economic Analysis* (Cambridge, MA: MIT Press), 1996, cited in Anderson (see note 3).

countries; they result from low income, low standards of living, and poor governmental policies. Trade brings about higher levels of income and ultimately better working conditions.

Checkpoint
Arguments Against Free Trade

REVIEW

- The infant industries argument claims that some industries are so underdeveloped that they need protection to survive in a global competitive environment.
- Dumping involves selling products at different prices in domestic and foreign markets, often with the help of subsidies from the government. This is a form of predatory pricing to gain market share in the foreign market.
- Some suggest that domestic workers need to be protected from the low wages in foreign countries. This puts the smaller aggregate loss to small groups ahead of the greater general gains from trade. Also, for many countries, a low wage is their primary comparative advantage.
- Some argue that select industries need protection to ensure they will exist for national defense reasons.
- Clearly, globalization has meant that some U.S. workers have lost jobs to foreign competition, and some advocates would restrict trade on these grounds alone. But, on net, trade has led to higher overall employment. The U.S. government recognizes these issues and has instituted a Trade Adjustment Assistance (TAA) program to help workers who lose their jobs transition to new employment.
- Concern about the environment is often a factor in trade negotiations. Those concerned about globalization want to ensure that firms do not move production to countries with lax environmental laws, while others are concerned that environmental regulation not be used to justify protectionism. Trade ultimately raises income and environmental awareness in developing nations.
- Some antiglobalization activists consider shifting production to countries with low wages as exploitation and demand that wages be increased in other countries. Globalization has typically resulted in higher wages in developing nations, but not up to the standards of developed nations.

QUESTION

"The biggest gains in exports, imports, employment, and wages all occurred during the 1990s which was one of our greatest periods of economic growth. Thus it is clear that trade benefits both consumers and the economy." Evaluate this statement.

Answers to the Checkpoint question can be found at the end of this chapter.

The Dynamics of Trade: Cashmere

Ted Wood/Getty Images

As a way of bringing together many of the concepts discussed in this chapter, let us look at one particular industry for a moment. When we hear the word *cashmere,* most of us conjure up images of soft, classy sweaters and scarves, whether we own any of these expensive items or not. It is the cashmere industry we will look at here.

The modern cashmere industry rests on international trade. It began in the 19th century when British colonialists in India discovered the fancy shawls of the

Indian rulers.[6] The word *cashmere* comes from Kashmir, the home of the goats used to provide the special soft fleece. Since that time, the goat herders moved to Inner Mongolia, part of China. The modern cashmere industry began when British entrepreneurs acquired the cashmere fleece and sent it to Scotland for weaving. Scottish companies became the main producers of finished cashmere products to the world. There were some Italian producers of cashmere as well, though the Scottish firms predominated.

This is changing. Competition had been limited by worldwide regulation of the textile industry. This regulation was undertaken under the guise of the familiar "cheap foreign labor" argument. By the end of 2004, the World Trade Organization (WTO) removed the remaining quotas in the textile industry.

What potential competitor stands to gain from this freer trade? In the cashmere industry, the obvious first choice is the provider of the cashmere fleece (China). And when you hear *China*, what immediately pops into your mind? (plenty of cheap labor). So the question then becomes: Is it worthwhile for Chinese entrepreneurs to develop their own cashmere industry by relying on ready access to the raw materials and cheap labor, or are they better off selling the raw materials to the Scottish cashmere producers?

It turns out that in fact Chinese entrepreneurs have been developing their own cashmere manufacturing industry over the past 10 years. They have been helped in part by the low capital costs of entry, as well as the plentiful labor pool in China. The issue then becomes one of the build up in skills. The natural thing for Chinese firms to do is start on the low end of the cashmere market, building up skills over time. For example, a fledgling firm can start with solid color sweaters and move up to more elaborate patterns once the basic skills are down pat. This is exactly what the Chinese firms have done. A joint venture between a Scottish firm and a Chinese firm in the mid-1990s likely hastened the transfer of manufacturing skills from Scotland to China.

From your study of the concepts in this chapter, you should be able to predict the likely effect on Scottish cashmere producers. In fact, the Scottish cashmere industry was hit on the low end but not on the high end of its market. There has been a loss of Scottish jobs as lower-priced Chinese cashmere sweaters and scarves have driven out the low end of what was once almost an exclusive Scottish market.

Again, based on what you have learned in this chapter, you should be able to predict the Scottish response. If Scottish firms still have an advantage producing more elaborate patterns, we can expect these patterns to become even more intricate. This is one way to justify a higher price. Also, the pressure is on Scottish firms to innovate. A previous innovation, by the Scottish firm Pringle, was the creation of the twin set: matching sweater and cardigan both worn at the same time. Queen Elizabeth wears twin sets. This means two products are sold at once. We can expect further innovations like this one from Scottish firms.

We can ask whether the "Cashmere: Made in Scotland" label will keep its cachet or eventually fade away in the face of continual Chinese advances in the cashmere industry. Only time will tell. This chapter helps us make several predictions. First, as Chinese workers build up skills, Chinese firms will expand up market. As these skills improve, Chinese workers will witness an increase in wages. As Chinese firms produce more cashmere, market demand for cashmere in China is likely to grow. Second, Scottish firms will face continual pressure to cut costs and innovate. The current job loss is likely to increase. New products will come to market, though we cannot predict what the market reaction will be. Third, as the price of cashmere products falls in the lower part of the market, more of us consumers worldwide will be able to afford these soft sweaters and scarves. There may come a time when even at the high end, "Cashmere: Made in China" becomes equivalent to "Cashmere: Made in Scotland." Such is the dynamism of international trade.

---

[6]Alan Cowell, "Cashmere Moves on, and Scotland Feels a Chill," *New York Times*, March 27, 2004, p. C1.

Key Concepts

Absolute advantage, p. 402
Comparative advantage, p. 402
Terms of trade, p. 405
Tariff, p. 407
Quota, p. 408
Infant industry, p. 411
Dumping, p. 411

Chapter Summary

The Gains from Trade

Worldwide foreign trade has quadrupled over the past 25 years. Improved communications and transportation technologies have worked together to promote global economic integration. Most governments around the world have reduced trade barriers in recent years.

Free trade has not always been popular. In 1929–30, many countries attempted to protect their domestic industries by imposing trade restrictions that discouraged imports. In 1930, the United States enacted the Smoot-Hawley tariffs, which imposed an average tax of 60% on imported goods. This hurt industries around the world and has been credited with adding to the depth of the global depression.

In a zero-sum game such as poker, for one party to gain, the other party must lose. Voluntary exchange and trade is a positive-sum game, meaning that both parties to a transaction can gain. These gains arise because of comparative advantage.

One country has an absolute advantage over another if it can produce more of some good than the other country. A country has a comparative advantage over another if its opportunity cost to produce some good is lower than the other country's. Even when one country has an absolute advantage over another, both stand to benefit from trade if each focuses its production on the goods or industries with a comparative advantage.

There are some practical constraints on trade. First, every transaction involves costs; and second, production is governed by increasing costs and diminishing returns. This makes it difficult for countries to specialize in the production of just one product. Indeed, specializing in one product is risky, since the market for a product can always decline or its production can be disrupted. Third, even though countries benefit from engaging in trade, some individuals and groups can be hurt by trade.

The Terms of Trade

The terms of trade determine the prices of imports and exports. If a country exports computers and imports coffee, with two computers trading for a ton of coffee, the price of a computer will be one half the price of a ton of coffee. When countries trade many commodities, the terms of trade are defined as the average price of exports divided by the average price of imports.

When two countries begin trading, the price charged for one good may be different in the two countries. As market forces lead each country to focus its production on the goods and industries at which it has a comparative advantage, that good's price will tend to equalize in the two countries, moving to an equilibrium level somewhere between the two original prices.

Though beneficial to both countries, trade can produce winners and losers. If the United States has a comparative advantage over Japan in the production of computers and it begins exporting more computers to Japan, American manufacturers and workers will benefit from this increased business. American consumers will be hurt, however, as the price of computers rises to meet the Japanese demand. In Japan, where computers had been more expensive, computer manufacturers and workers will be hurt by the competition from American computers, but Japanese consumers will benefit from falling computer prices.

The most common forms of trade restrictions are tariffs and quotas. A tariff is a tax on imports. Most tariffs are ad valorem taxes, meaning that a product is taxed by a certain percentage of its price as it crosses the border. Other tariffs are unit taxes, meaning that a fixed tax per unit of the product is assessed.

Tariffs generate revenues while driving a wedge between a product's domestic price and its price on the world market. When a tariff is imposed on a product, its price will rise. This benefits domestic producers, increasing their sales and the price they can charge, but the resulting price increase hurts domestic consumers. The government collects the tariff revenues.

Quotas restrict the quantity of imports into a country. Quotas have much the same effect as tariffs, except that they do not generate revenues for the government.

Arguments Against Free Trade

Despite the many benefits of free trade, arguments continue for restricting trade. One is that infant industries exist and require some protection to survive. These are industries that are too underdeveloped to achieve a comparative advantage or perhaps even to survive in the global marketplace. The problem is, when do these industries mature?

Some American trade laws target dumping, which occurs when a foreign firm sells its goods below cost in the United States or at a price below what it charges in its domestic market. One goal of such dumping may be to drive American firms out of business, thus allowing the foreign firm to come back and impose higher prices on American consumers in the long run. Another may just be to gain a foothold or market share in a foreign market. Also, dumping may simply be a form of subsidized price discrimination. If the federal government determines that a foreign firm is dumping products onto the American market, it can impose antidumping tariffs on the offending products.

Some advocates of trade barriers maintain that domestic firms and their workers need to be protected from displacement by cheap foreign labor. Without this protection, it is argued, foreign manufacturers that pay their workers low wages will flood the market with low-cost products. This has occurred. On balance, however, most economists estimate that the benefits of lower-priced imported goods exceed the costs of lost employment. The federal government has resisted imposing measures to protect jobs, instead funding programs that help displaced workers transition to new lines of work.

In times of national crisis or war, the United States must be able to rely on key domestic industries such as oil, steel, and the defense industry. Some argue that these industries require some protection even during peacetime to ensure that they exist when a crisis strikes and importing may be difficult.

Some critics argue that increased trade and globalization spells job losses for domestic workers. Firms unable to compete with imports will be forced to lay off workers or even close their doors. Increased trade, however, allows firms that are exporters to expand their operations and hire new workers. For workers who lose their jobs, switching industries can be difficult and time consuming, and often requires new investments in human capital. American trade policy recognizes this problem. The Trade Adjustment Assistance (TAA) program provides workers with job search assistance, job training, and some relocation allowances.

Concerns about globalization, trade, and the environment usually take one of two forms. Some people are concerned that expanded trade and globalization will lead to increased environmental degradation as companies take advantage of lax environmental laws abroad, particularly in the developing world. Others worry that attempts by the government to strengthen environmental laws will be challenged by trading partners as disguised protectionism. Environmental protection is an income elastic good: As incomes rise, the demand for environmental protections rises faster. And since trade increases incomes in developed and developing countries, free trade may further the cause of environmental protection.

Some antiglobalization activists argue that for the United States to trade with developing countries where wages are low and working conditions are deplorable simply exploits workers in these developing countries. But restricting trade with these countries would probably do more harm than good. Low wages reflect low investments in human capital, low productivity, and low living standards characteristic of developing nations. Blocking trade with these nations may deprive them of their only chance to grow and thus improve in these areas.

Questions and Problems

1. Brandeis University professor Stephen Cecchetti has argued that "if people understood the benefits of free trade as well as they do the rules of a favorite sport, there would be solid support for trade liberalization." Do you agree with Professor Cecchetti? Why or why not?

2. South Korean film production companies have been protected for half a century by policies enacted to protect an infant industry. But beginning in July 2006, the days that local films *must* be shown by any movie house was reduced to 73 from 146. South Korean film celebrities and the industry are fighting the changes even though local films command half the box office. Why would a country enact special protection for the local film industry? Who would be the major competitor threatening the South Korean film industry? If films made by the local industry must be shown 146 days a year, does the local industry have much incentive to develop good films and be competitive with the rest of the world?

3. Expanding trade in general benefits both countries, or they would not willingly engage in trade. But we also know that consumers and society often gain while particular industries or workers lose. Since society and consumers gain, why don't the many gainers compensate the few losers for their loss?

4. In a recent study, three economists estimated the benefits of trade to the American economy since 1950.[7] Looking at the benefits from comparative advantage, economies of scale, diffusion of production technology, and many other factors, they estimated that trade accounted for roughly 20% of the gains in GDP per person. With such gains from trade to the average household, why would so many people seem to be against trade and globalization?

5. Some activist groups are calling for "fair trade laws" in which other countries would be required to meet or approach our environmental standards and provide wage and working conditions approaching those of developed nations in order to be able to trade with us. Is this just another form of rent seeking by industries and unions for protection from overseas competition?

6. Is outsourcing another example of the benefits of trade, in this case, trade between two companies? Many of the opponents of outsourcing are fans of the "open source" software movement that farms programming out to "volunteer"

[7]Scott C. Bradford, Paul L. E. Grieco, and Gary Clyde Hufbauer, "The Payoff to America From Global Integration," in C. Fred Bergsten and the Institute for International Economics, *The United States and the World Economy* (Washington, D.C.: Institute for International Economics, 2005), Chap. 2.

programmers or firms around the world. These individuals or firms must give their changes to the software to the open source community (run by a few people) and cannot sell the software, but can charge for services such as a help desk, technical improvements, or other services. Does the open source concept seem like trade between individuals?

7. Why is there free trade between states in the United States but not necessarily between countries?

8. What is the difference between absolute and comparative advantage? Why would Michelle Wie, who is better than you at both golf and laundry, still hire you to do her wash?

9. Automobiles built by General Motors, Chrysler, and Ford have fallen out of favor with American consumers as evidenced by their falling market shares over the last several decades and the acceptance of buyouts in late 2006 and 2007 by over 100,000 current employees of GM and Ford. Several decades ago, at the behest of the United Auto Workers (UAW) union and the big three automakers, quotas were placed on the importation of Japanese cars to protect American auto manufacturers. Why didn't these quotas work? Would additional trade restrictions benefit American auto workers in the UAW? Would they benefit American consumers?

10. Remittances from developed countries are over $200 billion each year. These funds are sent to their home countries by migrants in developed nations. Is this similar to the gains from trade discussed in this chapter, or are these workers just taking jobs that workers in developed countries would be paid more to do in the absence of the migrants?

11. Who are the beneficiaries from a large U.S. tariff on French and German wine? Who are the losers?

12. The figure below shows the production possibilities frontiers (PPFs) for Italy and India for their domestic production of olives and tea. Without trade, assume that each is consuming olives and tea at point *a*.

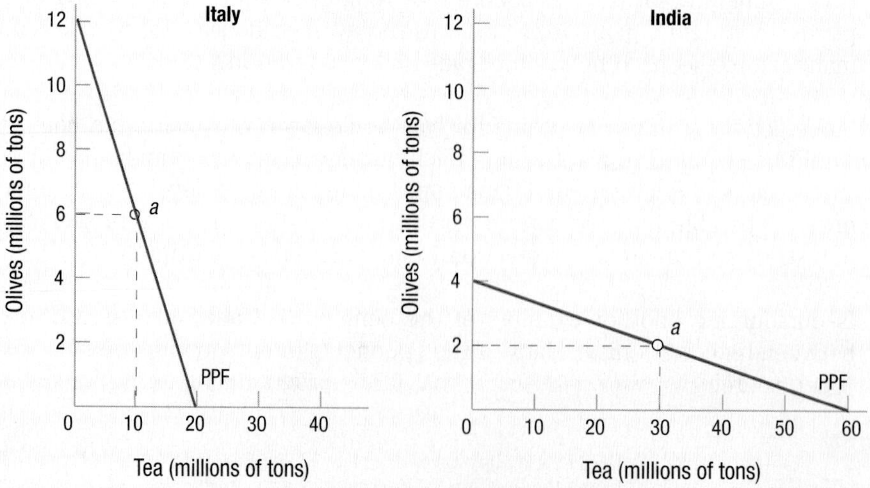

a. If Italy and India were to consider specialization and trade, what commodity would each specialize in? What is India's opportunity cost for tea and olives? What is Italy's opportunity cost for tea and olives?

b. Assume the two countries agree to specialize entirely in one product (Italy in olives and India in tea), and agree to split the total output between them. Complete the table below. Are both countries better off after trade?

Country and Product		Before Specialization	After Specialization	After Trade
Italy	Olives	6 million tons	______	______
	Tea	10 million tons	______	______
India	Olives	4 million tons	______	______
	Tea	30 million tons	______	______

13. The figure below shows the annual domestic demand and supply for 2GB compact flash cards for digital cameras.
    a. Assume the worldwide price of these 2GB cards is $10. What percent of United States sales would be imported?
    b. Assume the U.S. government puts a $5 tariff per card on imports. How many 2GB flash cards will be imported into the United States?
    c. Given the tariff in question *b,* how much revenue will the government collect from this tariff?
    d. Given the tariff in question *b,* how much more sales revenue will domestic companies enjoy as a result of the tariff?

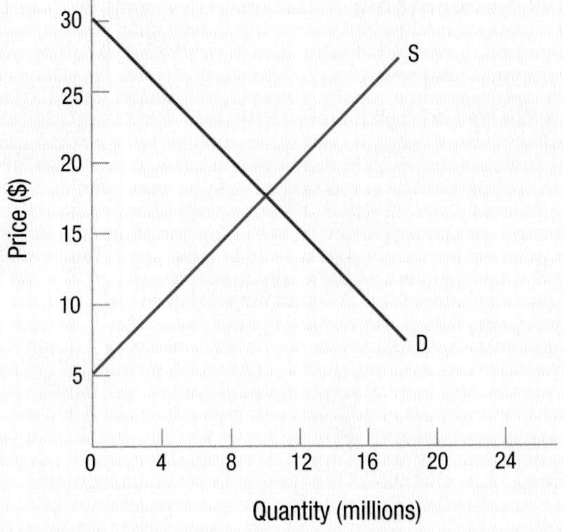

14. Why might protectionist trade barriers not save American jobs or benefit the economy?

15. Suppose Brazil developed a secret process that effectively quadrupled its output of coffee from its coffee plantations. This secret process enabled it to significantly undercut the prices of our domestic producers. Would domestic producers receive a sympathetic ear to calls for protection from Brazil's lower-cost coffee? How is this case different from that of protection against cheap foreign labor?

Answers to Checkpoint Questions

CHECKPOINT: THE GAINS FROM TRADE

Trading baseball cards is as old as the cards themselves. You would trade your extra cards for a Pujols card and others would do the same. Those with extra Pujols cards are your most likely trading partners. Clearly both parties benefit from trading cards in this instance. All *voluntary* exchange results in benefits to both parties or the trade would not take place.

CHECKPOINT: THE TERMS OF TRADE

When a quota is imposed, the first beneficiary is the domestic industry. Competition from foreign competition is limited. If the market is important enough (as we saw with automobiles), the foreign companies build new plants in the United States and compete as if they are domestic firms. A second beneficiary is foreign competition in that they can increase the price or complexity of their products and increase their margins. Losers are consumers and, to some extent, the government because a tariff could have accomplished the same reduction in imports, and the government would have collected some revenue.

CHECKPOINT: ARGUMENTS AGAINST FREE TRADE

Clearly the 1990s were a period of high growth in both trade and employment. The 1990s were also a time of heavy investment by businesses in technology and communications. Some industries and their employees were losers from trade, but the economy and other industries were clearly winners. Production employment has been on a steady decline over the last half century as services have become more important. When the most recent recession led to lost jobs and unemployment rose, more attention was focused on trade and outsourcing as a source of those lost jobs. But as the recession ended and our economy recovered, job gains have tended to quiet these voices.

GLOSSARY

Absolute advantage One country can produce more of a good than another country.

Adverse selection Occurs when products of different qualities are sold at the same price because of asymmetric information. Insurance is a typical example because people know far more about their health and risk levels than the companies insuring them.

Agency shop Employees are not required to join the union, but must pay dues to compensate the union for its services.

Allocative efficiency The mix of goods and services produced are just what society desires. The price that consumers pay is equal to marginal cost and is also equal to the least average total cost.

Antitrust law Laws designed to maintain competition and prevent monopolies from developing.

Asymmetric information Occurs when one party to a transaction has significantly better information than another party.

Average cost pricing rule Requires a regulated monopolist to produce and sell output where price equals average total costs. This permits the regulated monopolist to earn a normal return on investment over the long term and so remain in business.

Average fixed cost Equal to total fixed cost divided by output (TFC/Q).

Average product Output per worker, found by dividing total output by the number of workers employed to produce that output (Q/L).

Average total cost Equal to total cost divided by output (TC/Q). Average total cost is also equal to AFC + AVC.

Average variable cost Equal to total variable cost divided by output (TVC/Q).

Budget line Graphically illustrates the possible combinations of two goods that can be purchased with a given income, given the prices of both products.

Capital Includes manufactured products such as welding machines, computers and cellular phones that are used to produce other goods and services. The payment to capital is referred to as interest.

Cartel An agreement between firms in an industry (or countries) to formally collude on price and output, then agree on the distribution of production.

Ceteris paribus Assumption used in economics (and other disciplines as well), where other relevant factors or variables are held constant.

Change in demand Occurs when one or more of the determinants of demand changes, shown as a shift in the entire demand curve.

Change in quantity demanded Occurs when the price of the product changes, and is shown as a movement along an existing demand curve.

Change in quantity supplied Occurs when the price of the product changes, and is shown as a movement along an existing supply curve.

Change in supply Occurs when one or more of the determinants of supply change, shown as a shift in the entire supply curve.

Closed shop Workers must belong to the union before they can be hired.

Coase theorem If transaction costs are minimal (near zero), a bargain struck between beneficiaries and victims of externalities will be efficient from a resource allocation perspective. As a result, the socially optimal level of production will be reached, for example, whether polluters are given the right to pollute, or the victims are given the right to be free of pollution.

Command and control policies Environmental policies where standards are set and regulations are issued, and these are then enforced by the legal and regulatory system.

Common property resources Resources that are owned by the community at large (parks, ocean fish, and the atmosphere) and therefore tend to be overexploited because individuals have little incentive to use them in a sustainable fashion.

Comparable worth An approach to determining wage rates for specific occupations that assumes that every job has essential characteristics that possess an inherent worth independent of market forces.

Comparative advantage One country has a lower opportunity cost of producing a good than another country.

Competition Exists when there are many relatively small buyers and sellers, a standardized product, with good information to both buyers and sellers, and no barriers to entry or exit.

Complementary goods Goods that are typically consumed together.

Complements Goods that are typically consumed together such as coffee and sugar, automobiles and tires, and iPods and iTunes. Complements have a negative cross elasticity of demand.

Concentration ratios The share of industry shipments or sales accounted for by the top four or eight firms.

Constant cost industry In the long run, as industry output expands, prices and costs will be roughly the same. Some industries can virtually clone their operations in other areas without putting undue pressure on resource prices, resulting in constant operating costs as they expand in the long run.

Constant returns to scale A range of output where average total costs are relatively constant. Fast-food restaurants and movie theatres are examples.

Consumer surplus The difference between market price and what consumers (as individuals or the market) would be willing to pay. It is equal to the area above market price and below the demand curve.

Contestable markets Markets that look monopolistic but where entry costs are so low that the sheer threat of entry keeps prices low. Computer software and Internet Web sites (search, music downloads, and social networking sites) are examples.

Corporation A business structure that has most of the legal rights of individuals, and in addition, the corporation can issue stock to raise capital. Stockholders' liability is limited to the value of their stock.

Cost-benefit analysis A methodology for decision making that looks at the discounted value of the costs and benefits of a given project.

Cross elasticity of demand Measures how responsive the quantity demanded of one good is to changes in the price of another. Substitute goods have positive cross elasticities: An increase in the price of one goods leads consumers to substitute (buy more) of the other good whose price has not changed. Complementary goods have negative cross elasticities: An increase in the price of a complement leads to a reduction in sales of the other good whose price has not changed.

Deadweight loss The loss in consumer and producer surplus due to inefficiency because some transactions cannot be made and therefore their value to society is lost.

Decreasing cost industry In the long run, as industry output expands, prices and costs will be lower. Some industries enjoy economies of scale as they expand in the long run, typically the result of technological advances.

Demand The maximum amount of a product that buyers are willing and able to purchase over some time period at various prices, holding all other relevant factors constant (the *ceteris paribus* condition).

Demand curve Demand schedule information translated to a graph.

Demand for labor Demand for labor is derived from the demand for the firm's product and the productivity of labor.

Determinants of demand Other nonprice factors that affect demand including tastes and preferences, income, prices of related goods, number of buyers, and expectations.

Determinants of supply Other nonprice factors that affect supply including production technology, costs of resources, prices of other commodities, expectations, number of sellers, and taxes and subsidies.

Diminishing marginal returns An additional worker adds to total output, but at a diminishing rate.

Diseconomies of scale A range of output where average total costs tend to increase. Firms often become so big that management becomes bureaucratic and unable to efficiently control its operations.

Dumping Selling goods abroad at lower prices than in home markets, and often below cost.

Dynamic games Sequential or repeated games where the players can adjust their actions based on the decisions of other players in the past.

Economic costs The sum of explicit (out-of-pocket) and implicit (opportunity) costs.

Economic discrimination When workers of equal ability are paid different wages or in any other way discriminated against because of race, color, religion, gender, age, national origin, or disability.

Economic profits Profits in excess of normal profits. These are profits in excess of both explicit and implicit costs.

Economies of scale As a firm's output increases, its LRATC tends to decline. This results from specialization of labor and management, and potentially a better use of capital and complementary production techniques.

Economies of scope By producing a number of products that are interdependent, firms are able to produce and market these goods at lower costs.

Efficiency How well resources are used and allocated. Do people get the goods and services they want at the lowest possible resource cost? This is the chief focus of efficiency.

Elastic demand The absolute value of the price elasticity of demand is greater than 1. Elastic demands are very responsive to changes in price. The percentage change in quantity demand is greater than the percentage change in price.

Elastic supply Price elasticity of supply is greater than 1. The percentage change in quantity supplied is greater than the percentage change in price.

Elasticity of demand for labor Equal to the percentage change in the quantity of labor demanded divided by the percentage change in the wage rate.

Entrepreneurs Entrepreneurs combine land, labor, and capital to produce goods and services. They absorb the risk of being in business, including the risk of bankruptcy and other liabilities associated with doing business.

Entrepreneurs receive profits for this effort.

Equilibrium Market forces are in balance where the quantities demanded by consumers just equal quantities supplied by producers.

Equilibrium price Market equilibrium price is the price that results when quantity demanded is just equal to quantity supplied.

Equilibrium quantity Market equilibrium quantity is the output that results when quantity demanded is just equal to quantity supplied.

Equity The fairness of various issues and policies.

Explicit costs Those expenses paid directly to another economic entity including wages, lease payments, taxes, and utilities.

External benefits Positive externalities (also called spillovers) such as education and vaccinations. Private markets provide too little at too high a price of goods with external benefits.

External cost Occurs when a transaction between two parties has an impact on a third party not involved with the transaction. External costs are negative such as pollution or congestion. The market provides too much of the product with negative externalities at too low a cost.

Externalities The impact on third parties of some transaction between others where the third parties are not involved. An external cost (or negative externality) harms the third parties, whereas external benefits (positive externalities) result in gains to them.

Firm An economic institution that transforms resources (factors of production) into outputs for consumers.

Fixed costs Costs that do not change as a firm's output expands or contracts, often called overhead. These include items such as lease payments, administrative expenses, property taxes, and insurance.

Free rider When a public good is provided, consumers cannot be excluded from enjoying the product, so some consume the product without paying.

Functional distribution of income The distribution of income for resources or factors of production (land, labor, capital, and entrepreneurial ability).

Game theory An approach to analyzing oligopoly behavior using mathematics and simulation by using different assumptions about the players, time involved, level of information, strategies, and other aspects of the game.

General training Training that improves a worker's productivity in all firms.

Gini coefficient A precise method of measuring the position of the Lorenz curve as the area between the Lorenz curve and the equal distribution line divided by the total area below the equal distribution line.

Government failure When the incentives of politicians and government bureaucrats are not in line with the public interest.

Herfindahl-Hirshman index (HHI) A way of measuring industry concentration, equal to the sum of the squares of market shares for all firms in the industry.

Horizontal summation Market demand and supply curves are found by adding together how many units of the product will be purchased or supplied at each price.

Implicit costs The opportunity costs of using resources that belong to the firm including depreciation, depletion of business assets, and the opportunity cost of the firm's capital employed in the business.

Incidence of taxation Refers to who bears the economic burden of a tax. The economic entity bearing the burden of a particular tax will depend on the price elasticities of demand and supply.

Income A flow measure reflecting the funds received by individuals or households over a period of time, usually a week, month, or a year.

Income deficit The difference between the poverty threshold and a family's income.

Income effect When higher prices essentially reduce consumer income, the quantity demanded for normal goods falls.

Income effect, labor Higher wages mean you can maintain the same standard of living by working fewer hours. The impact on labor supply is generally negative.

Income elasticity of demand Measures how responsive quantity demanded is to changes in consumer income.

Increasing cost industry In the long run, as industry output expands, prices and costs will be higher. Industry expansion puts upward pressure on resources (inputs), causing higher costs in the long run.

Increasing marginal returns A new worker hired adds more to total output than the previous worker hired so that both average and marginal products are rising.

Indifference curve Shows all the combinations of two goods where the consumer is indifferent (gets the same level of satisfaction).

Indifference map An infinite set of indifference curves where each curve represents a different level of utility or satisfaction.

Inelastic demand The absolute value of the price elasticity of demand is less than 1. Inelastic demands are not very responsive to changes in price. The percentage change in quantity demand is less than the percentage change in price.

Inelastic supply Price elasticity of supply is less than 1. The percentage change in quantity supplied is less than the percentage change in price.

Infant industry An industry so underdeveloped that protection is needed for it to become competitive on the world stage or to ensure its survival.

Inferior goods Goods that have income elasticities that are negative. When consumer income grows, quantity demanded falls for inferior goods.

Investment in human capital Investments such as education and on-the-job training that improve the productivity of human labor.

Kinked demand curve An oligopoly model that assumes that if a firm raises its price, competitors will not raise theirs; but if the firm lowers its price, all of its competitors will lower their price to match the reduction. This leads to a kink in the demand curve and relatively stable market prices.

Labor Includes the mental and physical talents of individuals that are used to produce products and services. Labor is paid wages.

Land Includes natural resources such as mineral deposits, oil, natural gas, water, and land in the usual sense of the word. The payment to land as a resource is called rents.

Law of demand Holding all other relevant factors constant, as price increases, quantity demanded falls, and as price decreases, quantity demanded rises.

Law of diminishing marginal utility As we consume more of a given product, the added satisfaction we get from consuming an additional unit declines.

Law of supply Holding all other relevant factors constant, as price increases, quantity supplied will rise, and as price declines, quantity supplied will fall.

Long run A period of time long enough for firms to alter their plant capacities and for the number of firms in the industry to change. Existing firms can expand or build new plants, or firms can enter or exit the industry. In other words, a period of time sufficient for firms to adjust all factors of production including plant capacity.

Long-run average total cost (LRATC) In the long run, firms can adjust their plant sizes so LRATC is the lowest unit cost at which any particular output can be produced in the long run.

Lorenz curves A graphical method of showing the income distribution by cumulating families of various income levels on the horizontal axis and relating this to their cumulative share of total income on the vertical axis.

Luxury goods Goods that have income elasticities greater than 1. When consumer income grows, quantity demanded rises more than the rise in income for luxury goods.

Macroeconomics Macroeconomics is concerned about the broader issues in the economy such as inflation, unemployment, and national output of goods and services.

Marginal cost The change in total costs arising from the production of additional units of output ($\Delta TC/\Delta Q$). Since fixed costs do not change with output, marginal costs are the change in variable costs associated with additional production ($\Delta TVC/\Delta Q$).

Marginal cost pricing rule Regulators would prefer to have natural monopolists price where $P = MC$, but this would result in losses (long term) because $ATC > MC$. Thus, regulators often must use an average cost pricing rule.

Marginal factor cost (MFC) The added cost associated with hiring one more unit of labor. For competitive firms, it is equal to the wage; but for monopsonists, it is higher than the new wage (W) because all existing workers must be paid this higher new wage, making $MFC > W$.

Marginal physical product of labor The additional output a firm receives from employing an added unit of labor ($MPP_L = \Delta Q \div \Delta L$).

Marginal product The change in output that results from a change in labor ($\Delta Q/\Delta L$).

Marginal revenue The change in total revenue from selling an additional unit of output. Since competitive firms are price takers, $P = MR$ for competitive firms.

Marginal revenue product The value of another worker to the firm is equal to the marginal physical product of labor (MPP_L) times marginal revenue (MR).

Marginal utility The satisfaction received from consuming an additional unit of a given product or service.

Marginal utility analysis A theoretical framework underlying consumer decision making. This approach assumes that satisfaction.

Market failures When markets are not competitive or involve public goods, externalities, or common property resources, markets will fail to provide the optimal level of output, and will provide output at too high or low a price.

Market period Time period so short that the output and the number of firms are fixed. Agricultural products at harvest time face market periods. Products that unexpectedly become instant hits face market periods (there is a lag between when the firm realizes it has a hit on its hand and when inventory can be replaced).

Market structure analysis By observing a few industry characteristics, such as number of firms in the industry, the level of barriers to entry, and so on, economists can use this information to predict pricing and output behavior of the firm in the industry.

Market-based policies Environmental policies that use charges, taxes, subsidies, deposit-refund systems, or tradable emission permits to achieve environmental ends.

Markets Institutions that bring buyers and sellers together so they can interact and transact with each other.

Microeconomics Microeconomics focuses on decision making by individuals, businesses, industries, and government.

Monopolistic competition Involves a large number of small firms and is similar to competition, with easy entry and exit, but unlike the competitive model, the firms have differentiated their products. This differentiation is either real or imagined by consumers and involves innovations, advertising, location, or other ways of making one firm's product different from that of their competitors.

Monopolistic exploitation of labor When a firm has monopoly power in the product market, marginal revenue is less than price (MR < P) and the firm hires labor up to the point where MRP_L = wage. Because MRP_L is less than the VMP_L, workers are paid less than the value of their marginal product, and this difference is called monopolistic exploitation of labor.

Monopoly A one-firm industry with no close product substitutes and with substantial barriers to entry.

Monopsonistic exploitation of labor Because monopsonists hire less labor than competitive firms, and workers are paid less than the value of their marginal products, this difference is referred to as monopsonistic exploitation of labor.

Monopsony A labor market with one employer.

Moral hazard Asymmetric information problem that occurs when an insurance policy or some other arrangement changes the economic incentives and leads to a change in behavior.

Mutual interdependence When only a few firms constitute an industry, each firm must consider the reactions of its competitors to its decisions.

Nash equilibrium An important proof that an n-person game where each player chooses his optimal strategy, given that all other players have done the same, has a solution. This was an important proof, because economists now knew that even complex models (or games) had an equilibrium or solution.

Natural monopoly Large economies of scale mean that the minimum efficient scale of operations is roughly equal to market demand.

Network externalities Markets in which as more people use (or are connected to) the network, the network becomes more valuable.

Nonexcludability Once a good or service is provided it is not feasible to exclude others from enjoying that good or service.

Nonrivalry The consumption of a good or service by one person does not reduce the utility of that good or service to others.

Normal goods Goods that have positive income elasticities but less than 1. When consumer income grows, quantity demanded rises for normal goods but less than the rise in income.

Normal profits Equal to zero economic profits and where P = ATC. The return necessary on capital to keep investors satisfied and keep capital in the business over the long run.

Oligopoly A market with just a few firms dominating the industry where (1) each firm recognizes that it must consider its competitorsí reactions when making its own decisions (mutual interdependence), and (2) there are significant barriers to entry into the market.

On-the-job training Training typically done by employers, ranging from suggestions at work to sophisticated seminars.

Opportunity cost The cost paid for one product in terms of the output (or consumption) of another product that must be forgone. The next best alternative; what you give up to do something or purchase something.

Partnership Similar to a sole proprietorship, but involves more than one owner who shares the managing of the business. Partnerships are also subject to unlimited liability.

Personal or family distribution of income The distribution of income to individuals or family groups (typically quintiles or fifths of the population).

Poverty thresholds Income levels for various household sizes below which these people are considered living in poverty.

Predatory pricing Selling below cost to consumers in the short run hoping to eliminate competitors so that prices can be raised in the longer run to earn economic profits.

Present value The value of an investment (future stream of income) today. The higher the discount rate, the lower the present value today, and vice versa.

Price caps Maximum price at which a regulated firm can sell its product. They are often flexible enough to allow for changing cost conditions.

Price ceiling A government-set maximum price that can be charged for a product or service. When the price ceiling is set below equilibrium, it leads to shortages. Rent control is an example.

Price discrimination Charging different consumer groups different prices for the same product. The conditions necessary for successful price discrimination include some monopoly power (the firm needs some control over price), different consumer groups with different elasticities of demand, and the ability of the firm to prevent arbitrage (keeping low-price buyers from reselling to high-price buyers).

Price elasticity of demand A measure of the responsiveness of quantity demanded to a change in price, equal to the percentage change in quantity demanded divided by the percentage change in price.

Price elasticity of supply Measures the responsiveness of quantity supplied to changes in price. An elastic supply curve has elasticity greater than 1, whereas inelastic supplies have elasticities less than 1. Time is the most important determinant of the elasticity of supply.

Price floor A government-set minimum price that can be charged for a product or service. If the price floor is set above equilibrium price it leads to surpluses. Minimum wage legislation is an example.

Price system A name given to the market economy because prices provide considerable information to both buyers and sellers.

Price taker Individual firms in competitive markets get their prices from the market since they are so small they cannot influence market price. For this reason, competitive firms are price takers and can produce and sell all the output they produce at market determined prices.

Prisoner's Dilemma A noncooperative game where players cannot communicate or collaborate in making their decisions about whether to confess or not and thus results in inferior outcomes for both players. Many oligopoly decisions can be framed as a Prisoner's Dilemma.

Producer surplus The difference between market price and the price that firms would be willing to supply the product. It is equal to the area below market price and above the supply curve.

Product differentiation One firm's product is distinct from another's through advertising, innovation, location, and so on.

Production The process of converting resources (factors of production)—land, labor, capital, and entrepreneurial ability—into goods and services. Also can be considered the process of turning inputs into outputs.

Production efficiency Goods and services are produced at their lowest resource (opportunity) cost.

Production possibilities frontier (PPF) Shows the combinations of two goods that are possible for a society to produce at full employment. Points on or inside the PPF are feasible, and those outside of the frontier are unattainable.

Productive efficiency Goods and services are produced and sold to consumers at their lowest resource (opportunity) cost.

Profit Equal to the difference between total revenue and total cost.

Profit maximizing rule Firms maximize profit by producing output where MR = MC. No other level of output produces higher profits.

Property rights The clear delineation of ownership of property backed by government enforcement.

Public goods Goods that, once provided, no one person can be excluded from consuming (nonexclusion), and one person's consumption does not diminish the benefit to others from consuming the good (nonrivalry).

Quota A government-set limit on the quantity of imports into a country.

Rate of return Uses the present value formula, but subtracts costs, then finds the interest rate (discount rate) at which this investment would break even.

Rate of return regulation Permits product pricing that allows the firm to earn a normal return on capital invested in the firm.

Ratio of income to poverty The ratio of family income to the poverty threshold. Families with ratios below 0.5 are considered severely poor, families with ratios between 0.5 and 1.0 are considered poor, and those families with ratios between 1.0 and 1.25 are considered near poor.

Rent The return to land as a factor of production. Sometimes called economic rent.

Rent seeking Resources expended to protect a monopoly position. These include such activities as lobbying, extending patents, and restricting the number of licenses permitted.

Resources Productive resources include land (land and natural resources), labor (mental and physical talents of people), capital (manufactured products used to produce other products), and entrepreneurial ability (the combining of the other factors to produce products and assume the risk of the business).

Revenue Equal to price per unit times quantity sold.

Right-to-work laws Laws created by the Taft-Hartley Act that permitted states to outlaw union shops.

Scarcity Our unlimited wants clash with limited resources, leading to scarcity. Everyone faces scarcity (rich and poor) because, at a minimum, our time is limited on earth. Economics focuses on the allocation of scarce resources to satisfy unlimited wants.

Screening/signaling The argument that higher education simply lets employers know that the prospective employee is intelligent and trainable and has the discipline to potentially be a good employee.

Secondary boycott Occurs when unions clash with one firm and put pressure on a neutral, second firm to enlist the help of the second firm to obtain the union's objectives with the original firm.

Segmented labor markets Labor markets split into separate parts. This leads to different wages paid to different sectors even though both markets are highly competitive.

Short run A period of time over which at least one factor of production (resource) is fixed, or cannot be changed.

Shortage Occurs when the price is below market equilibrium, and quantity demanded exceeds quantity supplied.

Short-run supply curve The marginal cost curve above the minimum point on the average variable cost curve.

Shutdown point When price in the short run falls below the minimum point on the AVC curve, the firm will minimize losses by closing its doors and stopping production. Since P < AVC, the firm's variable costs are not covered, so by shutting the plant, losses are reduced to fixed costs.

Social welfare The sum of consumer and producer surplus.

Sole proprietor A type of business structure composed of a single owner who supervises and manages the business and is subject to unlimited liability.

Specific training Training that improves a worker's productivity in a specific firm.

Static games One-off games (not repeated) where decisions by the players are made simultaneously and are irreversible.

Substitute goods Goods consumers will substitute for one another depending on their relative prices. Substitutes have a positive cross elasticity of demand.

Substitution effect When the price of one good rises, consumers will substitute other goods for that good, so the quantity demanded for the higher-priced good falls.

Substitution effect, labor Higher wages mean that the value of work has increased, and the opportunity costs of leisure are higher, so work is substituted for leisure.

Sunk costs Those costs that have been incurred and cannot be recovered including, for example, funds spent on existing technology that have become obsolete and past advertising that has run in the media.

Supply The maximum amount of a product that sellers are willing and able to provide for sale over some time period at various prices, holding all other relevant factors constant (the *ceteris paribus* condition).

Supply curve Supply schedule information translated to a graph.

Supply of labor The amount of time an individual is willing to work at various wage rates.

Surplus Occurs when the price is above market equilibrium, and quantity supplied exceeds quantity demanded.

Tariff A tax on imported products. When a country taxes imported products, it drives a wedge between the product's domestic price and its price on the world market.

Terms of trade The ratio of the price of exported goods to the price of imported goods (P_x/P_m).

Tit-for-tat strategies A simple strategy that repeats the prior move of competitors. If your opponent lowers price, you do the same. This approach has the efficient quality that it rewards cooperation and punishes unfavorable strategies (defections).

Total revenue Price times quantity demanded (sold). If demand is elastic and price rises, quantity demanded falls off significantly and total revenue declines, and vice versa. If demand is inelastic and price rises, quantity demanded does not decline much and total revenue rises, and vice versa.

Total utility The total satisfaction that a person receives from consuming a given amount of goods and services.

Trigger strategies Action is taken contingent on your opponent's past decisions. For example, a grim trigger strategy is defined as any unfavorable decision by your opponent is then met by a permanent retaliatory decision forever.

Union shop Nonunion hires must join the union within a specified period of time.

Unitary elastic supply Price elasticity of supply is equal to 1. The percentage change in quantity supplied is equal to the percentage change in price.

Unitary elasticity of demand The absolute value of the price elasticity of demand is equal to 1. The percentage change in quantity demand is just equal to the percentage change in price.

Utility A hypothetical measure of consumer satisfaction.

Utility maximizing rule Utility is maximized where the marginal utility per dollar is equal for all products, or $MU_a/P_a = MU_b/P_b = \ldots = MU_n/P_n$.

Value of the marginal product The value of the marginal product of labor (VMP_L) is equal to price multiplied by the marginal physical product of labor, or $P \times MPP_L$.

Variable costs Costs that vary with output fluctuations including expenses such as labor and material costs.

Wealth A stock measure of an individual's or family's assets net of liabilities at a given point in time.

X-inefficiency Protected from competitive pressures, monopolies do not have to act efficiently. Spending on corporate jets, travel, and other perks of business represent x-inefficiency.

INDEX

Note: page numbers followed by f indicate figures; those followed by n indicate notes; those followed by t indicate tables.

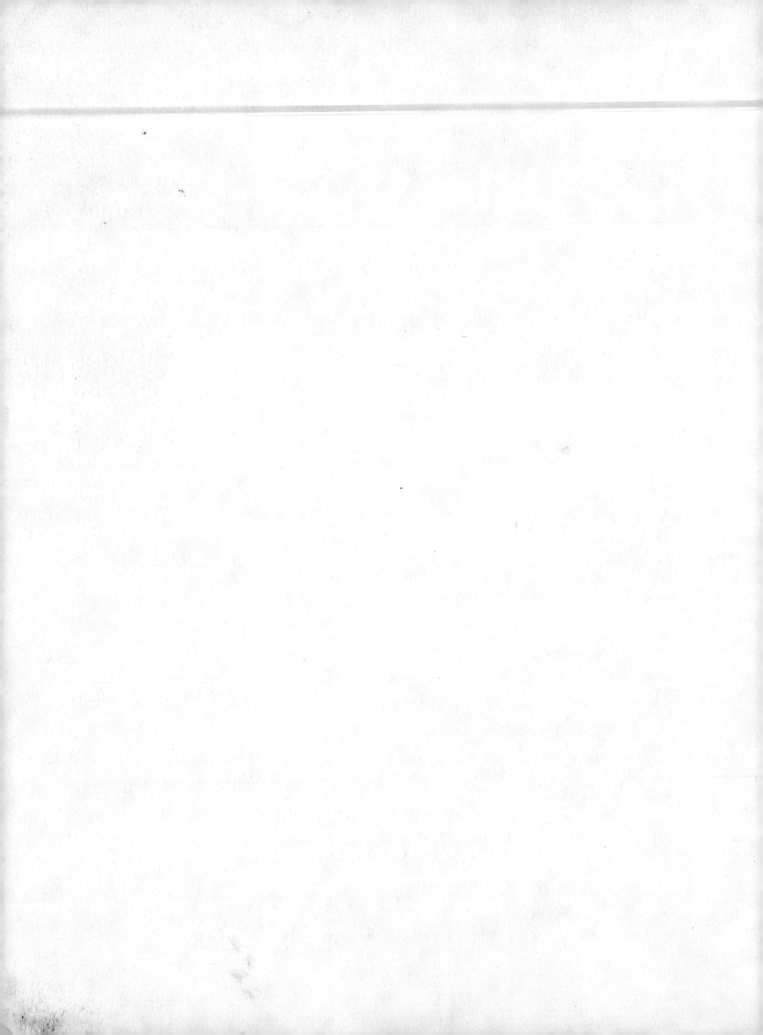